Special Edition
Using
XHTML™

Molly E. Holzschlag

201 W. 103rd Street
Indianapolis, Indiana 46290

CONTENTS AT A GLANCE

SPECIAL EDITION USING XHTML™

Copyright © 2001 by Que

International Standard Book Number: 0-7897-2431-6

Library of Congress Catalog Card Number: 00-108358

Printed in the United States of America

First Printing: December, 2000

02   01   4   3   2

TRADEMARKS

WARNING AND DISCLAIMER

Associate Publisher
Dean Miller

Acquisitions Editor
Todd Green

Development Editor
Sean Dixon

Managing Editor
Thomas Hayes

Project Editor
Heather McNeill

Copy Editor
Sossity Smith

Indexer
Rebecca Salerno

Proofreader
Harvey Stanbrough

Technical Editors
Kynn Bartlett
Andrew H. Watt
David Gulbransen

Team Coordinator
Cindy Teeters

Interior Designer
Ruth Lewis

Cover Designers
Dan Armstrong
Ruth Lewis

Production
Brandon Allen
Darin Crone
Steve Geiselman
Susan Geiselman
Brad Lenser
Liz Patterson

CONTENTS

CONTRIBUTORS

Kynn Bartlett (kynn.com) is an author, a programmer, a Web designer, and a teacher, whose cause is increasing accessibility of the Internet for everyone. He is Director of Accessibility for Edapta, Inc., past president of the HTML Writers Guild, and Chief Technologist for Idyll Mountain Internet.

As the founder and director of the HWG's Accessible Web Authoring Resources and Education Center, Kynn has worked to increase awareness among Web designers of accessible design for people with disabilities. He teaches online courses in web design and web management, and is active in the World Wide Web Consortium's working groups.

Kynn's current interests are in using XML, XSLT, and XHTML to create dynamic user interfaces which adapt to the needs of the users. He lives in Southern California with his wife Liz and their three Tibetan Mastiffs.

Cassandra Greer actually studied Linguistics, but has always been interested in computers and how people work with them. She fed herself in college by working in a computer lab and teaching non-native English speakers how to survive at an American University. After she graduated with a M.A. in Linguistics, she moved to Munich, Germany, where she continued teaching English and computer skills in large companies such as BMW, Siemens, Xerox, and ComputNet, and at two universities in the Physics and Engineering Departments. She also does technical translations which is how she hooked up with Mozquito Technologies, where she now does technical documentation for software and new Internet technologies. Her alter-ego dresses up in 13th century clothes, reads medieval literature and stays as far away from modern technological magic as possible.

Christian Jarolim started his professional career in Web design in 1996. Before that he studied architecture and industrial design in Graz and Linz and worked and lived in Graz, London, New York, Salzburg and Vienna. Christian now works for Mozquito Technologies in Munich as a Web designer, trainer and consultant with an emphasis on XHTML and XHTML-FML. Christian also publishes chapters and articles on how to best use XHTML and its extensions. He really likes mountain biking and jazz. Send him free tickets to the Lausanne Jazz Festival if you want a friend for life.

Lee Anne Phillips, www.leeanne.com/, cut her first networking tooth on ARPANet at UC Berkeley and has worked in networking and telephony since her tender years. She writes on Internet subjects and programming and knows how to punch down cable too. She currently works with Voxeo Corp, which has products touching the voice processing domain space. She is the author of numerous technology books, including Special Edition Using XML.

Derrick Story is the Managing Editor for the O'Reilly Network www.oreillynet.com/ and runs the Northern California photography business, Story Photography, www.storyphoto .com/. He writes and speaks on numerous technology and photography-oriented topics, including digital photography and writing for the Web.

DEDICATION

For my family.

ACKNOWLEDGMENTS

Although it may seem like it at times, no computer book author exists in a complete vacuum. There are many people I'd like to acknowledge for their support during the writing of this book.

From Que: Todd Green, Sean Dixon, Sossity Smith, and Heather McNeill for each personally seeing the book through; Kynn Bartlett and Andrew H. Watt for their diligent technical edits.

My agent, David Fugate, who is simply awesome.

I couldn't have accomplished putting together a book on such a transitional topic without the guidance and contributions of many people in the industry. Their total names certainly extend beyond those acknowledged here, but the following individuals helped me in profound ways directly related to the process of this book, and for their perspectives I thank them so very much: Kynn Bartlett, Cassandra Greer, Christian Jarolim, Jennifer Kettell, Lee Anne Phillips, Sebastian Schnitzenbaumer, Simon St. Laurent, Derrick Story, and Randal S. Schwartz.

To my family and friends, I simply want to say thank you for your blessings of love and kindness.

And last, but most certainly not least: to all the readers of my books. I thank you for your letters, gifts, and ongoing encouragement and support. You make any of the harder days worthwhile.

ABOUT THE AUTHOR

A writer, instructor, and designer, Molly E. Holzschlag brings attitude and enthusiasm to books, magazines, classrooms, and Web sites. Honored by Webgrrls as one of the Top 25 Most Influential Women on the Web, Molly has spent over a decade working in the online world. She has written 15 books on HTML and Web Design and Development topics, including the best-selling *Special Edition Using HTML 4.0* and internationally acclaimed *Web by Design*.

Her popular column, "Integrated Design," appears monthly in *WebTechniques* Magazine. Molly is presently the Executive Editor of *Web Review*, and has contributed features and columns to *Adobe Magazine*, *Builder.Com*, *DesignShops.Com*, *Digital Chicago*, *Digital New York*, *IBM developerWorks*, *MacWorld*, *MSDN*, and *PlanetIT* and other developer publications.

When offline, Molly plays guitar and sings in the original, acoustic duo, "Courage Sisters." For books, giveaways, training, speaking events, and other items of fun and interest, drop by her Web site at, where else? `www.molly.com/`.

TELL US WHAT YOU THINK!

As the reader of this book, *you* are our most important critic and commentator. We value your opinion and want to know what we're doing right, what we could do better, what areas you'd like to see us publish in, and any other words of wisdom you're willing to pass our way.

As an associate publisher for Que, I welcome your comments. You can fax, email, or write me directly to let me know what you did or didn't like about this book—as well as what we can do to make our books stronger.

Please note that I cannot help you with technical problems related to the topic of this book, and that due to the high volume of mail I receive, I might not be able to reply to every message.

When you write, please be sure to include this book's title and author as well as your name and phone or fax number. I will carefully review your comments and share them with the author and editors who worked on the book.

Fax: 317-581-4666

Email: quefeedback@macmillanusa.com

Mail: Dean Miller
          Que
          201 West 103rd Street
          Indianapolis, IN 46290 USA

INTRODUCTION

In this introduction

The big question on everyone's mind is if HTML worked just fine, why did we have to go and reformulate it into an XML application? It's a fair question, one I've asked myself in darker hours too.

But the reality is that the world is changing. With it comes changes in the way people live and work. Wireless technologies are becoming more and more a part of our everyday lives. Broadband is available and affordable to many more people than ever before. Web sites have grown up in profound and detailed ways. These changes not only affect the way we as individuals use technology, but the way we as technologists must accommodate change.

XHTML 1.0 is, for the Web designer and developer, a change that will help shift the limited and often cumbersome HTML methods for the Web browser into a potentially limitless and ideally easier method for many browsers and user agents. XHTML 1.0 is in a sense a bridge, rooted on one side in the territory of standard Web sites, and on the other side, a future of extended and even unknown lands.

XHTML 1.0 helps authors to transition documents that prepare them for the new types of delivery that exist today, as well as those to come. Even more importantly, learning XHTML 1.0 positions you as a Web author to be able to embrace other XML applications with ease, giving you much more power and flexibility than you've ever had before.

Because XHTML 1.0 is new, and because technologies related to it are often even newer, I cannot tell you with absolute confidence that the information in this book is wholly accurate. I, and the team of contributors and technical editors who assisted me in the writing process, have worked hard to ensure that the information provided is the most specific and up-to-date available for the topics included at the time of the writing.

I encourage you to explore the topics and techniques herein, and find out how XHTML 1.0 can work for you. But also, please make use of the many resources I've referred to throughout the text—particularly the recommendations and working group efforts of the World Wide Web Consortium (W3C), www.w3.org/. These resources will help you greatly in answering any errors and ommissions on my part, and help deepen your own knowledge as XML and its applications grow and change.

WHO SHOULD BUY THIS BOOK

Although anyone with an interested in Web site authoring a will be able to use this book to learn to create well-written, great-looking Web sites, the book is most appropriate for the HTML professional interested in transitioning from HTML into XHTML, XML, and beyond. Programmers who have a lot of experience in XML might find it helpful, but also might find it more client-side oriented than is appropriate for their needs. The perfect reader of this book is someone who has been writing HTML for at least a little while, is interested in the future of the Web and related technologies, and wants to learn how to improve his or her markup skills.

Readers of my *Special Edition Using HTML 4.0* Fifth and Sixth Editions might notice that certain portions of this book are familiar. That's because this book would have been a revision had HTML 5.0 come to light instead of XHTML 1.0. So, the topics that I felt were most immediately relevant for client-side Web developers have been kept in the book. They've been updated and refreshed where new software or information has become available. I've balanced that with a slew of new information of immediate and related interest to the contemporary Web author.

How This Book Is Organized

Each chapter in this book is written to stand alone but work in tandem with other chapters within the book. The best way to read the book will be determined by you! You can start at the beginning and work your way through—this is an especially good way for intermediate readers to build and refine skills—or if you want to know about a specific topic, you can jump right to that topic by using the Table of Contents as your guide or checking the Index for topic references. You can go right to that topic to get the information you need. Throughout this book, I've taken every opportunity to include cross-references with related materials, so you can follow your needs and preferences to the next topic of interest.

Special Edition Using XHTML 1.0 includes 39 chapters in 9 separate parts, along with 2 helpful appendixes.

Summary of Parts

Part I: Preparing to Use XHTML

This section gives you a good look at XHTML 1.0. The rationale for XHTML 1.0 is set forth, as well as its foundations. A look at how XHTML 1.0 can be used in the real world is covered, as is a section on the current state of tools available for Web markup.

Part II: XHTML Syntax

Here, readers will find how XHTML 1.0 is structured, what well-formed documents are, and how to manage XHTML documents.

Part III: Using XHTML to Build Web Pages

So you want to format text, add lists, align text, link pages, use images, and lay out your designs using tables? What about frames and forms? This section will teach you how you can use XHTML 1.0 to do all that, and make it work in today's browsers.

Part IV: Adding Style and Scripting

If you want to add style to your pages, this is the section. Topics covered are cascading style sheets, Extensible Style Sheets (XSL), and JavaScript.

Part V: Advanced XHTML Concepts and Applications

XHTML 1.0 is growing and changing, and is related to complementary technologies. In this section, you'll get a look at XHTML modularization (the future of XHTML), DTDs in detail and how they can be used in XHTML, and a look at modularization in action via XHTML Basic, a subset of XHTML 1.1 written especially for wireless and other alternative devices.

Part VI: Visual Design for the Web

Had enough code? It's time to step out of the technology realm for a while and spend some time learning about Web graphics. Whether the concern is designing pages effectively, using color, working with the computer screen, using graphic design tools for the Web, or creating a range of graphics, this section will give you what you need.

Part VII: Multimedia

So you want to add audio, video, or streaming media to your sites? Here's where you can learn to do just that.

Part VIII: Creating Content for Alternative Devices

If wireless excites you and convergent technologies are your thing, this section is sure to help. An overview of alternative devices, languages, and protocols starts the section off. You'll learn about WAP, WML, WebTV, and Web Clippings. Whether you'll be designing for TV or for wireless pagers along with your Web sites, the information to help you is right here.

Part IX: XML and Related Technologies Overview

Are you ready for the future? Moving toward XML concepts is extremely important. What's more, XML's applications are now well within your reach because you have a *much* better understanding of how to use one. So try out SMIL and SVG, too.

Part X: Appendixes

There are two appendixes in *Special Edition Using XHTML 1.0.*

- Appendix A, "XHTML Reference." An exhaustive XHTML 1.0 reference, including tags, attributes, values, and related information.
- Appendix B, "CSS2 Reference." A comprehensive overview of cascading style sheets 1.0 and 2.0.

CONVENTIONS USED IN THIS BOOK

Special conventions are used to help you get the most from this book and from XHTML 1.0.

TEXT CONVENTIONS

Various typefaces in this book identify terms and other special objects. These special typefaces include the following:

Type	Meaning
Italic	New terms or phrases when initially defined. An italic term followed by a page number indicates the page where that term is first defined.
<u>Underline</u>	Menu and dialog box options with letters that appear underlined onscreen indicate shortcut keys (hotkeys).
`Monospace`	Information that you type or onscreen messages.
`Bold Monospace`	Web addresses.
Initial Caps	Menus, dialog box names, dialog box elements, and commands are capitalized.

Key combinations are represented with a plus sign. For example, if the text calls for you to enter Ctrl+S, you would press the Ctrl key and the S key at the same time.

DESIGNING IN THE REAL WORLD

Many chapters in this book contain a project page or case study at the end of the chapter. Use these to enhance your skills with professional applications, examples, tips, and wisdom.

SPECIAL ELEMENTS

Throughout this book, you'll find Tips, Notes, Cautions, Sidebars, Cross References, and Troubleshooting Tips. These elements provide a variety of information, ranging from warnings you shouldn't miss to ancillary information that will enrich your XHTML 1.0 experience.

NOTES

Note

Notes provide extra information on a topic that is related and relevant to the topic, but not specific to the given task at hand.

CAUTIONS

Caution

Watch your step! Avoid pitfalls by keeping an eye on the cautions available in many of this book's lessons.

TROUBLESHOOTING NOTES

 These elements call attention to common issues. When you see a Troubleshooting note, you can flip to the "Troubleshooting" section at or near the end of the chapter to learn how to solve or avoid a problem.

CROSS REFERENCES

Cross-references are designed to point you to other locations in this book (or to other books in the Que family) that will provide supplemental or supporting information. Cross-references appear as follows:

→ To learn more about adding video to your page, **see** Chapter 31, "Audio and Video," **p. 641**.

SIDEBARS

Want to Know More?

Sidebars are designed to provide information that is ancillary to the topic being discussed. Read these if you want to learn more about an application or task.

PREPARING TO USE XHTML

CHAPTER 1

UNDERSTANDING XHTML 1.0

In this chapter

WHAT IS XHTML?

Readers who have been working with HTML are sure to have the question "What is XHTML" foremost in their minds. Why on earth do we need *another* language when we're still struggling to make the one we've got work?

Well, XHTML is an optimistic approach to solving the problems inherent to both the world of Web development as well as giving us tools with which to face the future.

This chapter will help provide you with what precisely XHTML is, why it exists, and how you can put it into a perspective that makes real-world sense.

ADDING EXTENSIBILITY

A visit to the past might well help clarify XHTML's reason for being. As many readers are aware, HTML came from SGML, the *Standard Generalized Markup Language*. SGML has been around for many years. Its role is to provide a standard for technical documentation. It's been used by many large corporations such as IBM to create standards for a variety of internal document management needs.

XML, the *Extensible Markup Language*, also derives from SGML. Unlike its HTML sibling, XML retains structural integrity, whereas for numerous reasons, HTML has run amok. XHTML seeks to draw from XML's integrity with HTML's creativity to create a more refined and logical method of markup.

FROM FORMATTING TO DESIGN

SGML is a highly structured markup language. When HTML was in its infancy, it had very lucid and straightforward rules. Documents were formatted in a simplistic way, using headers, paragraphs, and some limited text formatting. There wasn't a lot to HTML that diverted from the structural concerns of SGML, except that HTML was a whole lot less complex.

With the rapid-fire growth of the Web, HTML quickly became putty in the hands of Web designers and browser developers. To accommodate the sudden demand to make what was once a simple, text-based markup language flex to a graphic environment, an entire generation of imaginative tags and attributes were born.

There is perhaps no clearer example of this than the <center> tag (see Listing 1.1). This tag, offered to the world by Netscape, evolved to center text and images on a page (see Figure 1.1).

LISTING 1.1   AN EARLY EXAMPLE OF HTML, WITH THE <center> TAG IN PLACE

```
<html>
<head>
<title>My Page</title>
</head>
<body>
```

```
<h1>Welcome To My Web Page</h1>
<p>This Web page contains a bit about me, my family, and favorite World Wide Web
links</p>
<center><a href="more.html">Click Here for More</a></center>
<p>Thanks for visiting, and be sure to send an email!</p>
</body>
</html>
```

Figure 1.1
The <center> tag at work. Once a solution, now the tag is deprecated for not conforming to syntactical integrity.

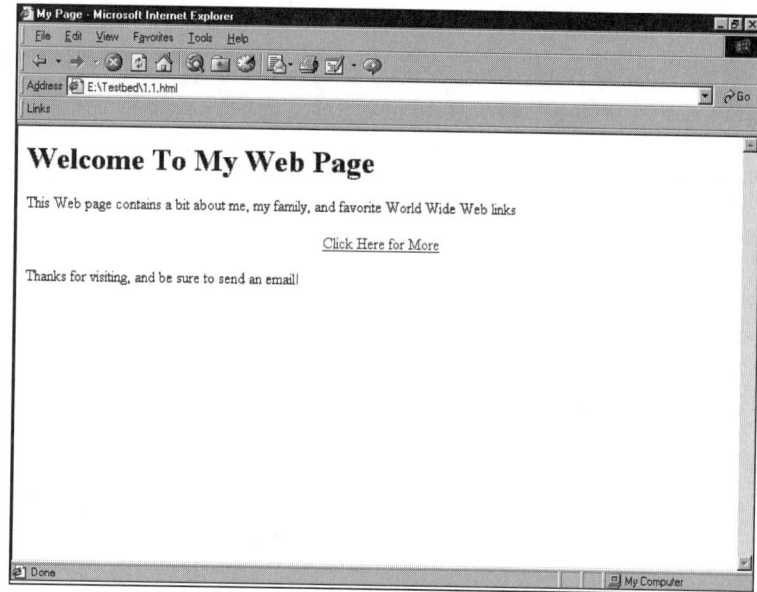

But the <center> tag doesn't follow any particular rule structure. It's an arbitrary tag that says nothing about the structure of a document, but only how to present it. Although it worked, it also signified a break from any formal tradition. HTML—originally used for document formatting—was now becoming a language of design.

Not long after the appearance of the <center> tag, tables emerged to provide us with a neater alternative to creating tabular data without having to resort to the difficult <pre> (preformatted text) tag (see Listing 1.2). The preformatted text tag ensures that anything within it, including spaces and tabs, is kept intact (see Figure 1.2).

LISTING 1.2   USING THE <pre> TAG TO FORMAT TABULAR DATA

```
<html>
<head>
<title>Fruits & Veggies</title>
</head>
<body>
<pre>
```

LISTING 1.2 CONTINUED

```
Fruits              Veggies
Avocado             Asparagus
Coconut             Carrot
Strawberry          String Beans
</pre>
</body>
</html>
```

Figure 1.2
Originally, the preformatted text (<pre>) tag was used to create tabular data. Note the default monospaced font within the text.

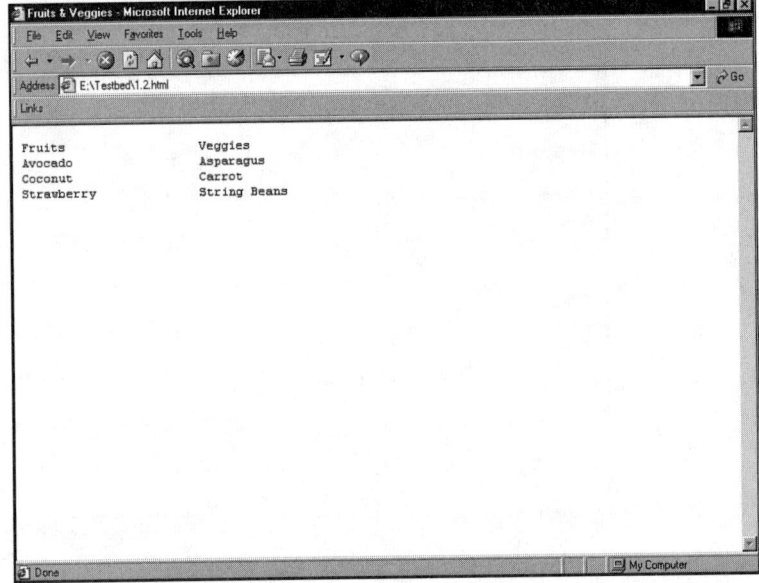

> **Note**
>
> Preformatted text also forces a monospaced font as its default. This is great for showing code snippets, perhaps.

Tables gave us more precise control over data (see Listing 1.3), allowing us to position each bit of table content within an individual cell and row (see Figure 1.3).

LISTING 1.3 GAINING CONTROL OVER DATA WITH TABLES

```
<html>
<head>
<title>Fruits & Veggies</title>
</head>
<body>
<table border="1">
<tr>
<th>Fruits</th>
<th>Veggies</th>
```

LISTING 1.3   CONTINUED

```
    </tr>
    <tr>
    <td>Avocado</td>
    <td>Asparagus</td>
    </tr>
    <tr>
    <td>Coconut</td>
    <td>Carrot</td>
    </tr>
    <tr>
    <td>Strawberry</td>
    <td>String Beans</td>
    </tr>
    </td>
    </table>
    </body>
    </html>
```

Figure 1.3
A table solution to the
same tabular data.
Tables make grids,
which in turn made
the layout system
used by HTML coders
to design Web pages.

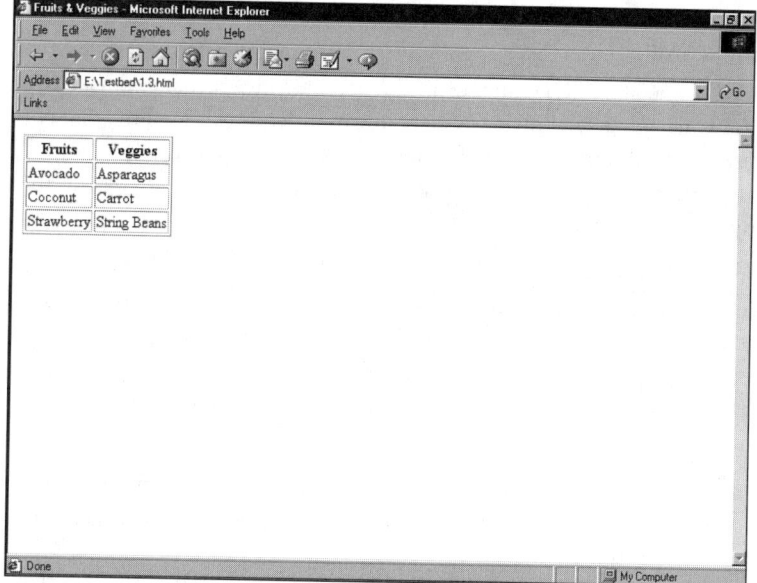

Tables create grids. What happens when you turn off the borders of a table? The grid lines
become invisible and guess what? You've got a system for placing images and text in a more
controlled environment, using tables in a way they were never intended. This is, in simplistic terms, how we got from basic markup to HTML as a language of design.

Quicker than you can say "browser wars," new tags and attributes began to appear along
with entire new technologies such as JavaScript, CSS (cascading style sheets), and DHTML
(Dynamic HTML). And, the way in which these technologies were supported had every-

thing to do with the way the browser manufacturers did or did not incorporate them into a given browser.

HTML was soon in a state of chaos. The World Wide Web Consortium (W3C), an industry association of universities, research organizations, and companies such as IBM, Sun, Microsoft, and Netscape, worked to find some solution to the refinement of HTML. What emerged from the Consortium were formal specifications for HTML and other Web technologies.

Of course, what was agreed upon at the table and what later appeared in browsers has always been inconsistent. So we have standards, but they are poorly supported—and as working coders in the real world, we can't fully apply the standards if we want to meet the needs of our site visitors using those browsers.

Despite that little problem, the Consortium managed to corral many of the renegade aspects of HTML into some refined sense of syntactical integrity. The most mature form of syntactical rigor prior to XHTML 1.0 came about with the HTML 4.0 standard, where a formal and intelligent structure was reintroduced to the language.

ENTER XML

XML came about as an answer to the need for diverse data management. XML's extensibility—which I like to think of as customization features—enables coders to create tags that are seemingly arbitrary. So, if I am interested in creating a memo in XML, I can decide to create a `<memo>` . . . `</memo>` tag set. And it will work, because it's up to me to define what my tags do and how they do it.

But as arbitrary as that seems, XML is really a very logically structured markup language. It draws from its parent, SGML, a syntactical quality referred to as *rigor*. You'll be looking more at this in Chapter 2, "XHTML Foundations," where I'll do a comparison of markup to show you just how things fit together. And, XML is already hard at work on the server-side, helping build effective, extensible documents. But for the client-side developer, the main concern for now is to understand that XML is

- **Flexible**—XML can manage data unique to banking and data unique to medicine. No matter the data type, XML offers a method by which to accommodate that data.

- **Customizable**—XML's flexibility is directly related to the fact that tags are custom rather than formal.

- **Rigorous**—XML retains the syntactical integrity and strict structure that its SGML parent defines.

→ For further information about XML and how it relates to SGML and HTML, **see** "Historical Relationships," **p. 31**.

Looking at XML's features, it becomes immediately evident that XML could conceivably replace HTML as a means of marking up Web sites. This is in fact why it was, when it first hit the press, referred to as the "HTML Killer." And, in a sense, it is becoming that from a standards point of view. XHTML as an XML application conceivably does mean the end of HTML *as a distinct and contemporary* standard. HTML remains important as a vocabulary for XHTML and other related languages. And of course it's in widespread use all over the Web today.

Note

For a comprehensive text on XML, try *Special Edition Using XML* by Lee Anne Phillips, from Que.

Browsers are beginning to incorporate more and more of XML's intelligence, which is very good news. XML will indeed be able to give Web developers on the client side a lot of power. But even given an environment where browsers completely support XML, there are a few problems with XML as a client-side language.

Note

Both Microsoft Internet Explorer 5.0+ and Netscape Navigator 6.0+ contain some support for XML. This support is expected to expand considerably in subsequent browser versions

First, for many, the learning curve is steeper than HTML. While the basic syntax of XML is easy to understand, the deeper an individual delves into related technologies, such as writing Document Type Definitions and Schemas, and studying related issues such as Xlink and transformations, there's a lot of detail that HTML authors don't necessarily need to get their job done.

Second, precious few tools currently exist to generate XML, so its accessibility—and subsequent popularity—on the client side is limited.

Finally—and perhaps most importantly—XML isn't backward compatible. There's close to a decade's worth of HTML files out there that need to be acknowledged. This legacy is one of the most compelling reasons to keep HTML itself alive.

REDEFINING XHTML AS AN XML APPLICATION

So we've got HTML, and we've got XML. Both do different things, and do them with a certain amount of respectability and historical intelligence. As we look to the future of what is needed, and what is necessary, in the way that code works and accommodates all the interesting technologies coming down the pike, it's easy to see that some combined force is necessary.

To deal with this disparity, a working group within the W3C began to discuss ways in which to give HTML XML's structure and extensibility, but still honor HTML as a real-world and legacy methodology.

What resulted is, as you've by now guessed, XHTML. Essentially, HTML is now redefined as an application of XML. No longer a sibling, HTML now is in essence a child of XML, and must conform to its parental rules (see Figure 1.4).

Figure 1.4
The original and current relationship of SGML, HTML, and XHTML.

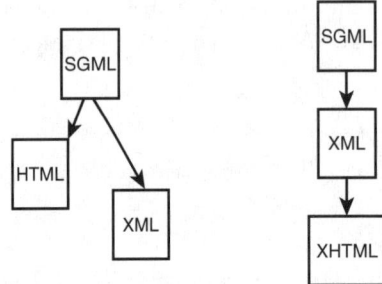

As you move through the subsequent chapters, you'll begin to see just how XML influences HTML to come up with the XHTML markup. Many readers—especially those from a more disciplined programming or markup background—will instantly appreciate why XHTML is a refined and, in essence, superior approach to coding.

XHTML AS A TRANSITIONAL LANGUAGE

This book is dedicated to teaching you about XHTML. But it's important to understand that as much as XHTML will help you—now and in the future—the reality is that XHTML is essentially a language of transition.

This transition is important. It puts professional coders in the position of writing standardized, quality code. It puts browser manufacturers on the hot seat and tells them "get your acts together!" It also moves us toward the extensible intelligence of XML and away from the limitations of HTML. And, it helps us accommodate new Web access methods.

MOVING TOWARD XML

A strong knowledge of HTML, especially in its 4.01 version, is critical. Because of that, I'll be spending plenty of time making sure that the primary concepts that carry over from HTML to XHTML are well covered.

But transition also means that readying yourself for XML is very important. Fortunately, XHTML contains enough of each to help strengthen your HTML skills and to get those of you unfamiliar with XML more comfortable with other XML applications.

I'll take a closer look at this transition in Chapter 2, "XHTML Foundations," and at which qualities of HTML and XML are incorporated into XHTML.

ACCOMMODATING NEW DEVICES

Part of the drive to accommodate XML in the Web development environment has to do with an intriguing phenomenon. If the 1990s were the years of the information explosion and the movement of the PC from the workplace to the home, this decade will be known for the movement away from the desktop.

The Web is increasingly being accessed by alternative devices (see Table 1.1). These include everything from small computers to wireless devices such as Palm Pilots and related devices, cell phones, and pagers.

→ For further information about alternative devices, **see** Part VIII of this book, "Creating Content for Alternative Devices," **p. 681**.

TABLE 1.1   ALTERNATIVE DEVICE USE PROJECTIONS (SOURCE: JESSE BERST'S ANCHOR DESK, NOVEMBER 11, 1999)

Year	Projection
1999	13.9 million handheld devices were sold.
2001	18.5 million Internet appliances will ship in the United States by the end of 2001, compared with only 15.7 million home PCs.
2002	The Internet appliance market will hit $15.3 billion. 55 million handheld devices alone will be sold.

XML has technologies such as XSL (Extensible Stylesheet Language) and XSLT (XSL transformations) related to it that allow, at least theoretically, for the extension of markup to accommodate these devices. Fortunately, XHTML can access these technologies as well.

→ To read about XSL and XSLT, **see** "Extensible Stylesheet Language (XSL)," **p. 419**.

Of course, a lot of how this will all play out is theoretical. I won't tell you that we have the answers and solutions ready to go today. What I will say in terms of new device applications is that they are up and coming, and once the languages and protocols learn how to play nice with each other, it's going to be a whole new World Wide Web.

For that we must all be prepared, which is a fundamental reason that XHTML exists. And why you—the professional developer with concerns about the future—want to know and understand how to put it to work today.

STANDARDS VERSUS CONVENTIONS

Now that we've explored some of the foundational issues of XHTML, let's move toward a deeper understanding of Web markup.

There's a lot of talk about standards, but what does *standardized* really mean? It's evident to any developer that by not following the HTML standard you can still deliver the content to the PC desktop user, provided that you've coded within the limits of common Web browsers.

THE IMPORTANCE OF STANDARDS

We've found then that what is in the rules, and what we do to make things really work, can be two separate things. And the World Wide Web Consortium, unlike a governing body, can only make strong recommendations on how we write markup, and as to how browser developers support that code. There are no laws enforced.

In fact, Web browsers don't even validate HTML. In other words, if you make an error in HTML, the browser won't tell you. It will either display what it can, or stop displaying the content when it reaches something it doesn't understand.

Note　　To validate HTML code, you have to use an external validation application, such as those found online or within your HTML editing programs. One such online validation service is offered by the W3C at `validator.w3.org`.

→ To learn more about HTML validation, **see** Chapter 4, "XHTML Tools," **p. 49**.

XML, on the other hand, is a language that can and should be validated by the user agent (or browser) that accesses it. This means error-checking the code within the reading application. When this is done, many serious problems can be avoided. But it also means that the coder has to do his or her job more effectively!

XHTML embraces the importance of error checking and validation, at least conceptually. With time, it's expected that validation will occur via user agents and not require external processes. This move toward a balance between what occurs in the standard, and the way browser developers (and for that matter, Web authors) carry the standards out, is one of the goals of XHTML.

Standards, in this context, are formal rules that must pass rigorous examination by committee. In the case of HTML, XHTML, and XML, that committee is the W3C.

But despite the fact that the Consortium has no role in ensuring that its recommended practices are upheld, standards are important because we need the guidelines. This need becomes more apparent as we are faced with having to deliver information to such a wide range of user agents.

CONVENTIONAL CODE PRACTICES

Conventions, unlike standards, aren't rules. A *convention* is simply a commonplace way of doing a particular task. Unlike a standard, which formalizes the rules and expected behavior of a community, a convention reflects the real-world practices of that community.

Think about a hobby, profession, or pastime you have, and try to determine if there are standards and conventions applied to that activity. One example would be photography. At the professional level, complex standards exist when working with photographic technologies. Does that mean great pictures can't be taken outside of those standards? Of course not—in fact, even the professionals don't always follow the rules.

I first learned how to cook from my mother and father. Many of the dishes they prepared were derived from Old World Hungarian, Polish, and traditional Jewish recipes. A measuring spoon or cup was never a factor in the process! It was always a pinch of this, a dab of that, to taste. In fact, I doubt there are any true recipes (standardized methods of preparing food) that reflect the kinds of dishes my parents taught me how to make.

When I was in college, I worked for a time in a bakery, assisting the baker. Baking, as I quickly learned, is very standardized. Without those standards, cakes will fall, crumble, or be rendered inedible! Measure by measure, standards were applied to baking to ensure consistent taste from cake to cake.

Working as an HTML author has always required a sense of compromise. You have to know both the conventional trends as well as the standard process to make effective decisions at every turn.

Furthermore, your conventional actions have a direct affect on the adoption of standards. Once again, let's turn to the `<center>` element as an example. The tag worked effectively, but it didn't match any known structural aspect of HTML. What's happened since? Well, although the `<center>` element is still in wide use and highly supported, it's been set to the side in HTML 4.01 in favor of other alignment tags, attributes, and styles because it didn't fit the logical structure of the language.

But the fact that HTML has allowed its authors to work both in a standard and conventional fashion has to change. It's the only way we'll be able to plug in new technologies to our code with ease. XHTML offers the ways and means to do this more effectively, and still respect our HTML past as well as our XML future.

THE WORLD WIDE WEB CONSORTIUM: A CLOSER LOOK

Because the Consortium is so fundamentally involved in the rule-making aspect of what we do, it's a good idea to take a closer look at the role they play in our day-to-day coding choices.

The Consortium was formalized on December 14, 1994. It's an independent, international organization made up of people and organizations from across the Internet and Web development community—from researchers at universities such as MIT to representatives from major corporations such as Microsoft, IBM, Sun Microsystems, and Netscape.

The job of the Consortium is to oversee the standardization of HTML, as well as the various protocols and languages related to the Web, including XML, XHTML, CSS, SMIL, HTTP, URL, FTP, NNTP, and SGML. Its Web site is frequently updated to keep us posted as to what is new in the world of standards.

Figure 1.5
The World Wide Web Consortium Web site provides detailed information on current HTML and related technology standards.

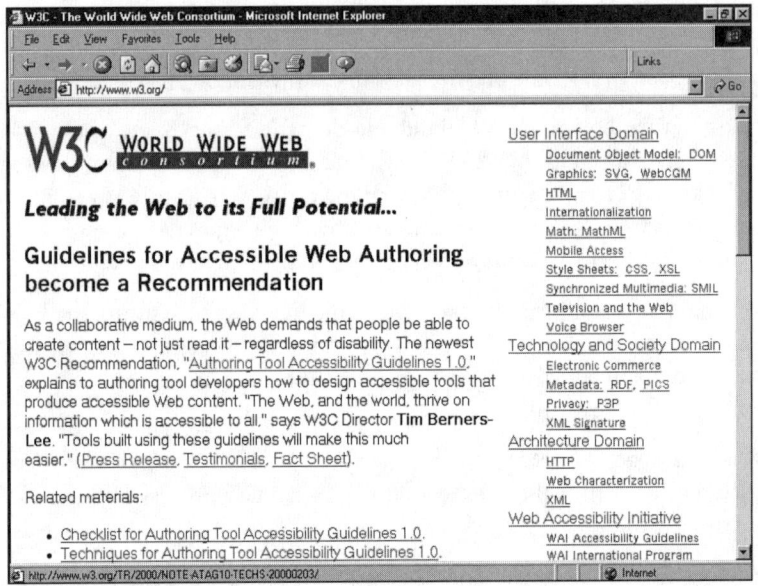

Note

You can access the W3C's Web site by pointing your browser to `www.w3.org`.

Although the W3C has been the leader in providing Internet recommendations, the Web has been overcome, as described earlier, by the popularity of the format and the demands of developers and audiences alike. Some concerns of the Consortium have been set aside to accommodate more pressing needs to appease Web enthusiasts and developers itching for more flexibility.

Some of the proposed changes include protocol enhancements. HTTP, the transport mechanism for HTML, is undergoing major changes. The proposed changes speak to the technologies that will enhance Web-site design and functionality.

Anyone interested in the history, evolution, use, and future of HTML should visit the W3C at regular intervals.

Note

To keep up with what's happening with current standards, visit the W3C at `http://www.w3.org/`.

TROUBLESHOOTING

DECISION-MAKING FOR XHTML AUTHORS

How does an XHTML author effectively apply the standard but embrace conventional or progressive options, too?

Although HTML authors have had to strive to understand and incorporate the important contributions of the Consortium, in reality the organization has no official enforcement status. It exists only as an advisory and consultative organization. It can recommend the adoption of formalized standards to facilitate efficient and effective transfer of information.

Therefore, as HTML authors, the approach to the problem of accessibility versus progress has always been in our hands. It is our responsibility to adopt and administer the standard to the best of our abilities and circumstances. We are personally entrusted with the task of making implementation decisions within the framework and structure of a given site's individual HTML needs.

But XHTML is different in that we are no longer looking at having that flexibility, much less wanting it. We must code to the recommendation, which means getting our HTML authoring in order before framing it within the context of XHTML. Fortunately, Chapter 2 will help you do just that.

DESIGNING FOR THE REAL WORLD

XHTML AND WEB DEVELOPERS: REAL WORLD CONCERNS

At a recent Web Design and Development conference in Chicago, I presented a class on XHTML. I wanted to gain a sense of the general skill level of attendees, so I asked several questions.

The first question was "How many people here know what XHTML is?" Of several hundred attendees, only a handful responded positively.

My next question was "How many people here have been coding HTML for longer than two years?" This time, the response was overwhelming. At least three-fourths of the attendees were seasoned HTML coders.

I asked, "How many people here feel somewhat familiar with the HTML 4.0 specification?" I expected maybe half of the attendees to respond positively. In fact, maybe 10 of the nearly 400 students in that room expressed any confidence that they had a fundamental understanding of the HTML 4.0 specification.

Then, I asked, "How many of you are concerned with what XHTML means to your future as professional Web programmers?" I wasn't surprised to see everyone in the room raise their hands.

Naturally, one of the reasons these individuals were in the class in the first place was to gain a better understanding of XHTML. But for that many skilled, professional developers not to feel confident with the HTML 4.0 specification indicates some concern about the ability for the professional to transition from HTML to XHTML with ease.

The first thing that comes to mind as to this lack of confidence is that HTML coders are a busy lot. They might know where the information is, but getting there means taking time out from the demands of the day. The other issue that comes to mind is that, despite the W3C's excellent work, the material is very detailed and often difficult to decipher. Certainly, many popular columns and books exist to help offset the button-down, white-paper details.

My goal with this book is to offer firm foundations in HTML 4.0, and then transition you— just as XHTML transitions all of us—into a more rigorous language approach.

I believe it is imperative that anyone coding in today's world has some understanding of the current status of the languages with which they work. And I am confident that it's not going to be difficult to get there. It will just take a bit of study.

CHAPTER 2

XHTML FOUNDATIONS

In this chapter

REVISITING THE HTML 4.0 STANDARD

If you're a working Web professional, chances are you fit into one of several categories when it comes to authoring documents. You might be a person who uses a visual editor such as Microsoft FrontPage, Dreamweaver UltraDev, or Adobe GoLive exclusively, letting the editor do the code for you. Or, you might be a hard-core author, pounding out your markup in a text editor such as Emacs, vi, NotePad, or SimpleText. Maybe you like to write your own documents, but prefer a power editor such as HomeSite or BBEdit. As with more and more Web professionals, a hybrid methodology might exist for you: you work between a visual editor and do some hand coding, too.

No matter your method, you probably know something about HTML. And although some readers might not have studied the principles of HTML 4.0 in great detail, most will be aware that it exists.

With the reformulation of HTML as an XML application comes the cleaning up of many of HTML's problems. So why revisit HTML? Well, for those readers who have been working with HTML for some time, understanding the principles of what you already do will most assuredly give you some perspective as to why XHTML is not only going to be useful to you, but how you can transition your documents to it with a deep rather than superficial knowledge of its main ideas, which after all, in part emerged from HTML 4.0.

HTML's most recent version is HTML 4.01, which improved some bugs found in HTML 4.0. It is the last version of HTML we'll see—by all accounts no HTML 5.0 will exist.

Instead, XHTML 1.0 is at this writing the current recommended Web markup standard. XHTML 1.1 is on the plate, being discussed in detail by the working groups involved in making XHTML a reality.

Speaking of reality, despite the fact that XHMTL 1.0 is now a formal standard, it appears that Web developers are either slow to get the news or slow to adopt XHTML 1.0. Whether it's a matter of poor publicity on the part of the W3C combined with disinterest or frustration from the busy professional, the bottom line is that XHTML hasn't been all the rage, despite many reasons that it should be.

For that matter, when we study standard practices, it appears that *most professional Web developers* do not have a deep understanding of what standards are, why they exist, and the benefit of using them.

This is all the more reason to spend some time with HTML before moving on to XHTML.

HTML 4.0: MAIN CONCEPTS

Many of the foundational concepts in HTML 4.0 are the same as those that appear in XHTML. If we pretended that HTML 4.0 is on one side of a bridge, XML the other, and XHTML was the bridge in between, XHTML can then be seen as being anchored in both HTML and XML.

On the HTML side of the gap, XHTML 1.0 shares these goals in common with HTML 4.0:

- to separate document structure and style
- to improve document rendering
- to encourage the authoring of accessible documents
- to encourage authors and developers of user agents (including Web browsers) to adhere to a base standard

XHTML 1.0 embraces all these goals, and then adds XML-inspired goals on top of this. So understanding each side of the relationship is imperative.

SEPARATE DOCUMENT FORMATTING AND PRESENTATION

One of HTML 4.0's prime directives is to separate document formatting from the presentation of that document. But what does this mean in human terms?

Document structure is just that: the skeletal structure of a Web document. This would include the head and body, as well as some structural components like headings, block components such as paragraphs, and select additional elements that flesh it out.

But presentation is anything that changes the appearance of that structure. Whether it's color, text formatting, addition of background, or placement of objects—these things are considered to be ornamental to the actual structure of the document.

HTML recommends leaving the HTML document empty of presentational detail, and putting all that detail into a style sheet.

The problem, of course, is that style sheet support in Web browsers is very inconsistent where it exists at all. So to acknowledge that Web developers need to use more real-world–compliant methods, HTML 4.0 provides a transitional means to get the results necessary. In other words, HTML 4.0 includes a set of rules that enables authors to put presentational elements into a document as long as it is clearly denoted as being a transitional document. XHTML 1.0 shares this goal as well as this transitional means. But at their purest, both HTML 4.0 and XHTML 1.0 separate formatting from presentation.

IMPROVEMENT OF DOCUMENT RENDERING

The rendering of documents in a Web browser can be improved by adhering to common practices. At its most strict, HTML 4.0 suggests that the author leaves tables behind as a means of presenting layout, and use style sheets for the positioning of objects on a page instead.

Because that's hardly realistic for fully interoperable design, once again a transitional option exists for HTML 4.0 document authors. Also, a number of elements, specifically for table rendering, exist to improve the rendering of table-based pages, and tables in general (see Table 2.1).

Element	Description
caption	Creates a caption for the table
summary	Provides a link to a summary of the table's contents
colgroup	Groups columns to streamline structural rendering
col	Groups table cell attributes together
thead	Groups information at the top of the table which describes columnar data
tfoot	Also groups rows that contain information about columnar data, appears at the bottom of the table
tbody	Contains the rows and cells of the body of the table

TABLE 2.1 METHODS OF IMPROVING DOCUMENT RENDERING IN HTML 4

Note

If a browser encounters one of these HTML 4.0 elements and doesn't understand it, it simply ignores it.

ACCESSIBILITY GUIDELINES

A critically important issue under study in terms of present-day and future standards is that of accessibility.

Originally, HTML was designed to be a language that could be easily and readily distributed across platforms and read by anyone, regardless of their software. But browser competition quickly changed that reality. With everyone rushing hither and yon to create the coolest technology on the block, this fundamental aspect of HTML has been disrupted.

One of HTML 4.0's goals is to bring that accessibility back. By using intelligent options, page authors can add a variety of aids that will help individuals understand and negotiate pages no matter their platform—or their physical abilities.

Many people with low or no vision have tremendous difficulty accessing today's World Wide Web, largely due to the fact that screen readers that browse the screen and read the content aloud are significantly more challenged by complex graphical pages. However, with a little forethought, authors can make it much easier. Other individuals with physical limitations are assisted by devices as well—and whether it's a screen reading device or special keyboard, the methodologies that HTML 4 proposes to aid access are extremely helpful.

Note

Of course, browser support is an important issue as well. Netscape has lagged far behind Microsoft in this regard. There's some pressure on browser developers to include support for accessibility guidelines, particularly in the United States, where the Americans with Disabilities Act might eventually enforce accessibility guidelines on everyone's part because of the extensive use of the Web in the workplace and commercial enterprise.

The Web Accessibility Initiative (WAI) of the W3C has an official document describing guidelines that Web developers, software developers, and browser developers are encouraged to follow.

Note

For more information on the activities of WAI, visit www.w3.org/WAI/.

ACCESSIBILITY FOR WEB DEVELOPERS

The following guidelines are recommended for all developers creating HTML 4.0-compliant documents (which of course extends to XHTML 1.0 documents):

- **Provide equivalent alternatives to auditory and visual content**—If you're using sound or graphics, include text descriptions and employ HTML-based aids, such as the `alt` attribute in images, wherever possible.

- **Ensure that text and graphics are understandable when viewed without color**—Many people are color-blind, and many people can't use visual displays with which to see color. Also, contrast is an imperative for all people, even those without vision problems.

- **Use markup and style sheets properly**—This guideline is an important one! It encourages the creation of well-formed documents in accordance with the standards. Of course, you might make decisions that go against the grain, but if you do so, I encourage you to at least do so with *awareness.*

- **Ensure that the pronunciation and interpretation of different languages is facilitated**—By defining the language of a document, and any changes in language (see Internationalization later in this chapter) and using expansive elements such as `acronym`, authors can ensure that language changes within their documents are understood.

- **Be aware of how you use tables**—Use tables for strictly tabular information, not for visual layout, or if you are using tables for visual layout, follow accessibility guidelines for markup.

- **Ensure accessibility even when new technologies are in use**—Documents should be readable without style sheets, dynamically changed content should be made available for its equivalents in text or another form, and pages should be usable if various scripting and programmed objects are turned off.

- **Time-sensitive content changes should have user controls**—Blinking, flickering, movement, content refresh, and auto-direct should all have controls for the user, or alternative methods of accessing the content.

- **Embedded interfaces should have accessible counterparts**—Any embedded user interface elements, such as Java-based drop-down menus and the like, should have accessible features or an accessible alternative.

- **Design for device independent input**—Many users access Web content with special keyboards, mouth or head wands, voice, or other devices. No matter the input device, there should be consistent or at least similar results independent of the device in use.

- **Use interim solutions**—Because many accessibility features are not yet available in all browsers, use options that are as interoperable as possible.

- **Follow the W3C technologies**—Learn and employ technologies recommended by the W3C. These technologies go through rigorous testing for accessibility features.

- **Provide context**—Wherever possible, group, title, describe, and detail page elements. This is especially important when using tables, frames, forms, and multimedia.

- **Provide clear navigation mechanisms**—Clear and consistent navigation is not only an imperative in accessibility, it's an imperative in user interface design. Links should be clearly identified and organized, and graphical options should have appropriate alternatives available.

- **Author documents that are clear and simple**—Consistent layout and design of pages, clarity of language and direction, and clarity of orientation help keep your sites understandable and easy to navigate.

> **Note**
>
> For details and tests for each of these recommended accessibility guidelines, see `www.w3.org/TR/WAI-WEBCONTENT/`.

ACCESSIBILITY FOR AUTHORING TOOLS

The WAI has set up seven important checkpoints for authoring tools. To meet the requirements of accessibility, each Web authoring tool must be able to do the following:

- **Support accessible authoring practices**—Because many editing environments generate the code rather than the person using the tool, the tool itself must generate accessible code.

- **Generate standard markup**—Tools should use the latest W3C recommendations and have ways to inform the author when something that is non-conforming is entered into the markup.

- **Support the creation of accessible content**—The tool should encourage authors to add alternative content where appropriate and help separate document information from presentation.

- **Provide ways of checking and correcting inaccessible content**—The tool should be able to identify inaccessible areas of the markup, and make recommendations so the author might make corrections.

- **Integrate accessibility solutions into the software tool itself**—Accessibility options should be built into the software seamlessly, not set apart in an accessibility section. The idea behind this is to ensure adoption by authors of these accessibility features as common practice.

■ **Promote accessibility in help features and documentation**—The use of accessible markup and methods should be quickly available in help areas of the tool, and plenty of documentation about promoting and using these features should be made available.

■ **Ensure that the tool is accessible to authors with disabilities**—The tool itself should conform to standard interface elements as well as offer options such as methods to enlarge the text so as to be visible during the editing process.

Note

For software conformance details, please see www.w3.org/TR/WAI-AUTOOLS/.

ACCESSIBILITY GUIDELINES FOR USER AGENTS

One of the things many people don't realize about the W3C is that its work is not just about how we as Web professionals are authoring documents. As the last section clearly showed, the W3C is concerned with encouraging software developers to follow standard practices.

Perhaps even more critical is the influence the W3C ideally has with Web browser developers. The WAI provides the following eleven guidelines to encourage browser manufacturers to follow to conform to accessibility guidelines:

■ **Support input and output device independence**—No matter the input and output devices in use, the user agent must include as much broad functionality as possible to allow for access. Input must be facilitated for mice, voice, keyboards, touch screens, wand devices, and so on. Output must include multiple types of cues; auditory, graphical, and textual should all be available to cover the bases.

■ **Ensure user access to all content**—Ensure that content is readily available including such content that is alternative to the referring page, such as a page that is text-only and accessible via a link element.

■ **Allow user to turn off rendering or behavior that might interfere with accessibility**—Users should be able to easily access a method to stop the rendering or behavior of any element that interferes with their ability to get to the content.

■ **Ensure user control of styles**—Users should be able to access or write their own style sheets to override browser defaults, or have options contained within the user agent interface.

■ **Observe system conventions and standard interfaces**—User agents should use conventional systems and interfaces, as well as facilitate the use of assistive device technologies where available.

■ **Implement accessible specifications**—The user agent should support all specifications from the W3C that include accessibility guidelines.

■ **Provide navigation mechanisms**—Employ a variety of navigation methods so that users can get from here to there.

- **Orient the user**—Users should know where they are at all times. Employing methods to show what items are currently selected and include a history mechanism in a user agent are good examples of orientation features.

- **Allow users to customize and configure to their needs**—Users should be able to modify the user agent to their own specifications.

- **Provide accessible documentation**—Plenty of online help should be available that is easily accessed by anyone with any disability.

Note

For more information on user agent conformance for accessibility guidelines, see `www.w3.org/TR/UAAG/`.

FACILITATE INTERNATIONALIZATION

Just as access is important to those with disabilities, it is equally important to ensure that access is worldwide—it is the World Wide Web after all!

To accommodate access for international users, the World Wide Web Consortium makes a concerted effort in HTML 4.0 and beyond to include international issues for authors, agents, and tools.

Current areas of activity include

- Increasing awareness among Web and browser developers regarding international access issues.

- Stressing the importance of Unicode as a mechanism for character encoding.

- Creating study groups within the Consortium to look at details of international concerns.

Note

Internationalization activities can be monitored with a visit to `www.w3.org/International/`.

Much of internationalization involves ensuring that characters are available for languages and scripts including Chinese, Japanese, Hebrew, Arabic, and Cyrillic. There are two primary methods by which to do this, although browser support is varied at this time.

The first method involves using Unicode characters to accomplish the task. The other method uses the lang attribute within any relevant element tag.

A Unicode example would look like this:

```
&#x202B;&#x05F4; &#x05F4;&#x202C;
```

Whereas the `lang` attribute is used as follows:

```
<html lang="es">
```

Interestingly, this is the first time many experienced HTML coders will see an attribute placed in the opening `html` tag. This code sets up the page to be displayed in Spanish.

Spanish mostly uses characters used in English. So how does the language attribute make a difference in how the HTML is coded? Well, with proper support from browsers, instead of having to use Unicode characters to invoke an N with a tilde above it, all the coder has to do is type that character with their keyboard, or with a combination of the tilde and N keys. After the appropriate letter is entered, the browser will know how to interpret that code when the language attribute is in place.

The unfortunate reality is that despite the fascinating work being done in the area of internationalization—and despite the fact that many of the proposed elements, attributes, and special characters necessary to support internationalization are considered part of HTML 4.0—the support in browsers is very limited.

This problem, however, is really changing as we move from the HTML side of things toward XML, which is very concerned with character encoding. So, there's definite hope on the horizon for improvement of internationally supported data in Web documents.

PART
I
CH
2

Note   Unicode information is available via the Unicode Consortium, `www.unicode.org/`.

EXAMINING HTML AS AN XML APPLICATION

With a lot of information about HTML 4.0's goals under your belt, it's time to start walking across that bridge toward XML, where extensible concepts add to the mix to create XHTML.

HISTORICAL RELATIONSHIPS

It is perhaps important to begin with a bit of the history that gets us to XHTML 1.0. It's funny in a way, because the history of XHTML reads like some distorted biblical begetting fest.

Begin with SGML, the Standardized General Markup Language. SGML is what is known as a *meta-language*. SGML is essentially a massive document type definition (DTD) used to create other markup languages.

From SGML came HTML. HTML, as an application of SGML, follows some intrinsic concepts of SGML.

However, the incredibly broad and loose use of HTML created rapid declines in the adherence to the standards SGML set forth.

From SGML also came XML. XML, like its parent SGML, is a meta-language for the sharing of documents and information on the Internet and related networks. XML doesn't necessarily beget other languages. Rather, it begets applications.

XHTML is one such application.

So follow along with this little analogy. HTML is the elder child of SGML. As elder children are often wont to do, HTML ran hither and yon to find its own identity. XML, raised in a more stable environment, is the more thoughtful, younger child.

When concerned relatives began to realize that the wanton ways of HTML were potentially destructive, they called upon the wisdom of the younger child, XML. XML took HTML under its wing and made some firm-but-supportive suggestions about how HTML might get its life back on track. This resulted in XHTML, a more organized, self-protective application (see Figure 2.1).

Figure 2.1
The parenting tree of XHTML.

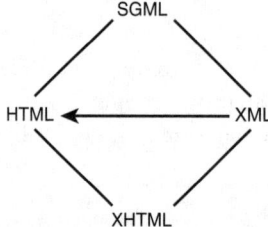

BRIDGING THE GAP

To help authors bridge the gap between the more conventional practices found in HTML, and the more standardized practices found in XML, XHTML offers a great deal of familiar information. However, the deeper we study XHTML, the more obvious it becomes that there are significant steps being taken away from the familiar realm of HTML.

XHTML 1.0

I've heard more than one person say, "They should have just called it HTML 5.0 instead of XHTML 1.0." There's wisdom in this for a number of reasons. First, XHTML 1.0 is close enough to HTML 4.01 in premise and practice so as to still be considered very HTML-like. Next, that XML is involved in any way may be a bit daunting to HTML authors who don't have extensive backgrounds in markup. This might have a lot to do with why people have been somewhat reluctant to transition to its use.

XHTML 1.0, however, should be seen as no more complicated, and perhaps in its own way even less complicated, than HTML. It just embraces a little bit of rigor that some would say should have been part of HTML all along. A few simple rules and you're on your way to creating XHTML 1.0 documents—no muss, no fuss.

XHTML 1.0 AND MODULARIZATION

I recently bought an ultra-light notebook computer. This computer can be so light because most of the components that are ancillary to the the the main functions of the computer itself have been separated. The system can be considered *modular*. There is the central computer, but the floppy, CD, and DVD drives are all separate components. Even the battery is detachable.

This modularization is exactly the next step that is underway for XHTML. Although XHTML 1.0 is, again, more like an HTML 5.0, XHTML 1.1 takes a big jump from XHTML 1.0 in the form of modularization. There's a central core of basic elements, but everything else must be plugged in to provide ancillary support of the language.

→ For a detailed look at modularization, **see** Chapter 21, "XHTML Modularization," **p. 469.**

IS IT TOO COMPLEX AND IS IT HAPPENING TOO FAST?

Although XHTML 1.0 has been the recommendation since January 26, 2000, XHTML modularization became a Formal Candidate Proposal in October 2000.

The problem with this scenario is obvious. It will be extremely difficult for HTML authors—who are often too busy with the demands of creating documents for the realities of today's busy Web world—to embrace a highly modular and somewhat elusive recommendation without first practicing and using XHTML 1.0. So, even if XHTML modularization is a recommendation by the time you're reading this, you'll want to learn how to write XHTML 1.0 documents before diving in. I've made sure to include enough information on the direction of XHTML for the future.

Are the complexities of XHTML and the speed at which it is growing moving too quickly? And, as a result, will many authors find themselves disgusted by the whole thing and just stick to what works for their needs until motivated by necessity to learn a newer technology?

The case study in this section is about you. Your mission is to examine the issues regarding XHTML and how you feel now, before getting too deep into the book. Write your reactions down. Then, I'll ask you to come back *after* you've read the book and put XHTML to use. Compare your notes at that point. It'll be an interesting journey, I have no doubt!

CHAPTER

XHTML IN THE REAL WORLD

In this chapter

A RETURN TO CLEAN CODE

As I discussed in Chapter 1, "Understanding XHTML 1.0," and Chapter 2, "XHTML Foundations," part of the major drive with regards to XHTML is to bring a clean and organized methodology back into the picture of Web development. Years of rapid growth and a demand for bigger, better, faster, cooler Web pages have laid waste to some of the initial integrity of Web markup.

When XML hit the scene, people talked about it being the "HTML Killer." It turned out that they were right, but not necessarily in the sense they originally meant! Although XML has not replaced HTML as a Web markup language at this time, it has significantly changed the way HTML is being viewed in terms of standards.

Assessing Present Concerns

This chapter deals with a lot of complex and historical issues surrounding HTML and how it got the way it got. And, how it can be fixed. Some of my commentary might seem negative, but I want to set in your minds up front that the problems with Web markup today are *not necessarily our fault*. However, these problems do, at many levels, become our responsibility. After all, we're the ones paying attention. We're the ones being challenged to make our documents and designs work in the real world. Our agendas are probably quite different from those of profit-oriented software developers. So when I talk about sloppy code and how we need to clean it up, I mean that not as a criticism of past practices per se, but as an honest assessment of where we as Web authors have been, where we are today, and where we need to go to make our lives and work less frustrating and more progressive.

THE TROUBLE WITH HTML

When we look more closely at what this rapid-fire growth and disregard for rules has done to HTML, we see significant degradation of the initial goal of HTML: to create documents that are readily accessible across browsers, platforms, and user interfaces. In fact, the very reasons HTML came into being were rapidly bastardized in the name of progress.

Is this a bad thing? On the side of innovation's defense, it probably couldn't have happened any other way. That rapid pace was necessary to push the envelope and create the dynamic, wild, and profitable Web we know today.

However, looking around at the amount of HTML out there that is poorly written, it's amazing that Web pages work as well as they do—much less work at all. And although most of the Web does seem to work, the reality is that we are very limited in terms of being able to make progress, to create truly interoperable sites, and to create sites that are both well-designed *and* authored correctly.

POORLY WRITTEN CODE

The first and most upsetting thing about the state of HTML is that there is no consistency among the way documents are developed. Whether a person authors HTML by hand or uses a development tool of some kind, code results tend to be as far from the standards as one can imagine.

Think of it this way: If I have two people apply for a job as an HTML author (and this has really happened), and I provide a table and ask the authors to hand code it (see Figure 3.1), each of the individuals will mark it up in a different way. Part of the reason is that HTML itself is somewhat arbitrary. For example, in Listing 3.1, I show one way to mark up the table in Figure 3.1. Listing 3.2 shows another—both equally correct.

Figure 3.1
A simple HTML table
for code reproduction.

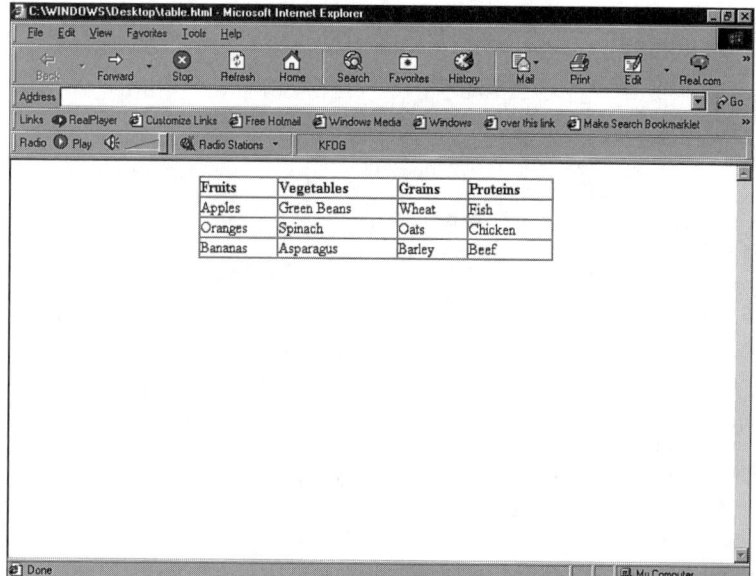

LISTING 3.1   TABLE CODE EXAMPLE OPTION 1

```
<table border="1" cellpadding="0" cellspacing="0" width="50%" align="center">
<tr>
    <th align="left">Fruits</th>
    <th align="left">Vegetables</th>
    <th align="left">Grains</th>
    <th align="left">Proteins</th>
</tr>
<tr>
    <td>Apples</td>
    <td>Green Beans</td>
    <td>Wheat</td>
    <td>Fish</td>
</tr>
<tr>
    <td>Oranges</td>
    <td>Spinach</td>
    <td>Oats</td>
    <td>Chicken</td>
</tr>
```

LISTING 3.1   CONTINUED

```
<tr>
    <td>Bananas</td>
    <td>Asparagus</td>
    <td>Barley</td>
    <td>Beef</td>
</tr>
</table>
```

LISTING 3.2   TABLE CODE EXAMPLE OPTION 2

```
<div align="center">
<table border="1" cellpadding="0" cellspacing="0" width="50%">
<tr>
    <td><b>Fruits</b></td>
    <td><b>Vegetables</b></td>
    <td><b>Grains</b></td>
    <td><b>Proteins</b></td>
</tr>
<tr>
    <td>Apples</td>
    <td>Green Beans</td>
    <td>Wheat</td>
    <td>Fish</td>
</tr>
<tr>
    <td>Oranges</td>
    <td>Spinach</td>
    <td>Oats</td>
    <td>Chicken</td>
</tr>
<tr>
    <td>Bananas</td>
    <td>Asparagus</td>
    <td>Barley</td>
    <td>Beef</td>
</tr>
</table>
</div>
```

And these are clean examples! The sad fact is that most individuals—even those who have been writing or producing HTML documents for several years—will not mark up the document in any consistent or mature way. They'd leave out attributes, put in ones that don't belong (or exist), or run into problems because they've always relied on a visual editor to get the job done for them.

Now to be fair, it's important to point out that this lack of consistency and lack of knowledge has very little to do with the integrity of the individuals in question. It has ever so much more to do with the fact that the way HTML has been learned is by the boot-strap method. Early adopters used View Source and picked up others' mistakes. Later on, when visual editors became pervasive and browsers very forgiving, people relied more on what the programs were producing. As long as the page was readable, that's what mattered. And finally, the more forgiving of poor markup browsers became, the less people had to concern themselves with consistent code practices, much less standardized ones.

My goal here is to impress upon you—readers who are obviously interested in what XHTML 1.0 is offering to Web authors—how grave the situation with HTML has become. XHTML 1.0 seeks, through its rigorous syntax and adherence to standard rules, to improve the quality of code. And that quality, at least at this point in history, rests in the hands of the author.

CODE FOR PRESENTATION, NOT FOR FORMATTING

I'm a designer, interested in color, space, shape, typography, and the impact that a visual display can make on another person. I like things to look good! And, I want them to work properly. But another of the troubles that HTML has had is that it was forced, by default, into being a language of design rather than document structure. I discussed, in brief, the fact that HTML was *never intended* to be anything but a formatting language for documents in Chapter 1, "Understanding XHTML 1.0." I want to take a closer look at these concepts, and provide examples in this chapter so you can see just how this problem—and those related to it—have escalated concerns about HTML's integrity.

The rapid advancements of the visual Web, and the excitement that surrounded its growth, put a lot of weight on HTML to accommodate design as well as structure. This is seen very clearly in two places: the use of tables for layout; and the introduction of presentational tags such as the `font` tag.

Let's revisit the table in Figure 3.1. Its purpose is to take tabular information and present it logically. It fulfills the purpose for which tables were brought into HTML.

But not long after, someone figured out that if you remove the borders from a table, suddenly you have a complex grid that you can use to place graphics, text, even Java applets, Flash objects, or video files. You've got a way to lay out a design. Suddenly, the very foundation of Web pages is relying on HTML elements that were *never intended* to perform the duties that they have performed for years, and will probably perform for some years to come.

Similarly, presentation of type on a page became an issue as more designers came to the Web. You had very few options before the `font` tag. You could rely on the default, or you could use a tag that forced a monospaced font, such as `pre` or `tt`:

```
<pre>This text appears in the user's default monospaced font.</pre>
<p><tt>So does this</tt>
<p>This text is in the default proportional font.
```

Either way, both were limited and not necessarily very elegant (see Figure 3.2).

Figure 3.2
Forcing monospaced fonts in HTML using pre and tt.

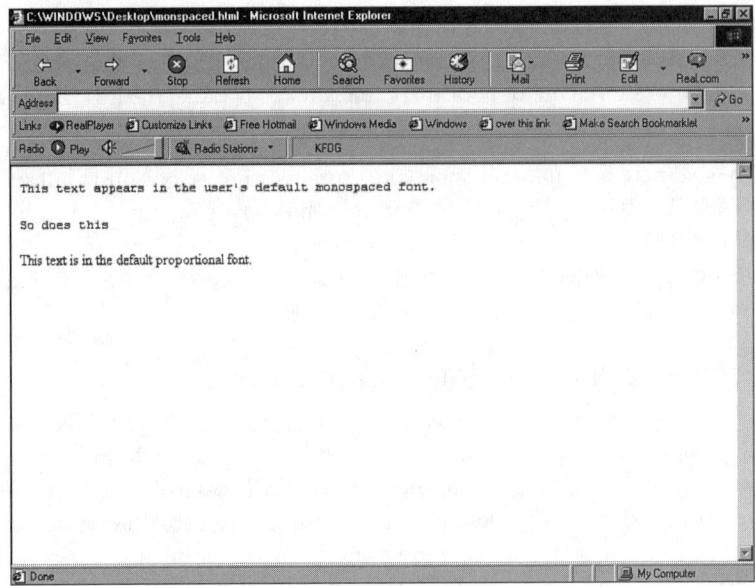

So along comes the font tag, and suddenly we've got ways to add some level of typographic presentation to our pages. Yes, it's imperfect display due to the limitations of Web typography—a visitor's machine must have that font face installed, the browser must support the tag, and so on.

But even more devastating to HTML as a formatting language is the absolute *mess* that font tags create. They work extremely poorly. You can't set a default font on a page with them, you must open and close them every time you want to change some attribute related to them, and you must open and close them within sections of your HTML, such as within each table cell. Begin with a nice, tight document (see Listing 3.3), and by the time you're done adding pretty fonts to a page, you've definitely doubled, possibly tripled—and maybe even quadrupled the weight of your document (see Listing 3.4). Plus, you've made it harder to read, harder to troubleshoot, and simply said, much sloppier.

LISTING 3.3 A SIMPLE HTML PAGE LAYOUT, NO FONTS. WEIGHT: 1KB

```
<html>
<head>
    <title>King Lear: Act 2, Scene 1</title>
</head>

<body>

<h3>Edmund</h3>

<p>The duke be here to-night? The better! best!
This weaves itself perforce into my business.
My father hath set guard to take my brother;
And I have one thing, of a queasy question,
Which I must act: briefness and fortune, work!
Brother, a word; descend: brother, I say!</p>
```

LISTING 3.3 CONTINUED

```
<p>Enter EDGAR</p>

<p>My father watches: O sir, fly this place;
Intelligence is given where you are hid;
You have now the good advantage of the night:
Have you not spoken 'gainst the Duke of Cornwall?
He's coming hither: now, i' the night, i' the haste,
And Regan with him: have you nothing said
Upon his party 'gainst the Duke of Albany?
Advise yourself.</p>

</body>
</html>
```

LISTING 3.4 THE SAME LAYOUT WITH FONTS. WEIGHT: 2KB

```
<html>
<head>
    <title>King Lear: Act 2, Scene 1</title>
</head>

<body bgcolor="#000000">

<h2><font face="arial, helvetica, sans-serif"
➥color="#FFFFCC">Edmund</font></h2>

<p><font face="garamond, times, serif" size="4" color="#CCFFFF">
The duke be here to-night? The better! best!
This weaves itself perforce into my business.
My father hath set guard to take my brother;
And I have one thing, of a queasy question,
Which I must act: briefness and fortune, work!
Brother, a word; descend: brother, I say!</font></p>

<p><font face="arial, helvetica, sans-serif" color="#FFFFCC">
Enter EDGAR</font></p>

<p><font face="garamond, times, serif" size="4" color="#CCFFFF">
My father watches: O sir, fly this place;
Intelligence is given where you are hid;
You have now the good advantage of the night:
Have you not spoken 'gainst the Duke of Cornwall?
He's coming hither: now, i' the night, i' the haste,
And Regan with him: have you nothing said
Upon his party 'gainst the Duke of Albany?
Advise yourself.</font></p>

</body>
</html>
```

Of course, by HTML 4.0, it became very apparent that there was a serious need to remove document presentation from document structure to bring back some rigor to HTML. So, under this concept, your basic HTML document would begin limiting to document formatting elements such as is seen in Listing 3.3. It would then incorporate a stylesheet externally (see Listing 3.5), with a link to that sheet found in the head of the document.

LISTING 3.5   STYLE SHEETS ALLOW FOR THE ADDITION OF STYLE, SEPARATE FROM THE
DOCUMENT'S FORMATTING ELEMENTS

```
H2  {
font-family : arial, helvetica, sans-serif;
    color : #FFFFCC;
}
p.1  {
    font-family : arial, helvetica, sans-serif;
}
p.2  {
    font-family : arial, helvetica, sans-serif;
    font-size : 14pt;
    color : #CCFFFF;
}
```

→ For further information about style sheets, **see** Chapter 18, "Cascading Style Sheets and XHTML," **p. 377** and Chapter 19, "Extensible Stylesheet Language(XSL)," **p. 419**.

However, browser support for style sheets, which are the most lucid and useful answer to presentation and placement concerns, are to this day poorly supported across browsers and platforms, making them at best quite challenging to use in real-world situations.

The irony here is that style sheets are not a new idea. They've been around since the early desktop publishing days, when the same issues came to the forefront in DTP software. Once again, the rapid development of Web design forced HTML into corners it was too willing yet linguistically less than capable of controlling. In many ways, this is why we have the problems we have today when trying to gain consistency with layouts, fonts, and other presentational concerns.

DIFFICULTIES ACROSS PLATFORMS AND BROWSERS

So, the demand for better visual sites altered HTML as a language. And, as a result, the bane of the Web designer's existence has become trying to figure out ways to make HTML work as a tool of design across platforms.

What we create for the Windows environment is always going to be somewhat different from what is created for the Mac environment, or Linux environment, and so on.

Platform-wise, there is little we can control as designers because hardware and software issues influence the way that user agent software—in most instances the Web browser—read our documents.

But to make our sites cross-platform, cross-browser compliant, we have to work extra hard. Imagine if browser developers adhered to certain standards with the way they wrote their software and the way that software in turn displayed our code? Our lives would be made much more simple. But browser developers have had their own agenda, and it's done very little to help us. As a result, Web designers in contemporary times typically have to

- Test their work on numerous platforms.
- Test their work in numerous browser types.
- Use legacy as well as current browsers in testing.
- Rely on authoritative charts and materials to compare and contrast what works and what doesn't work in a given platform/browser environment.
- Learn stress-management techniques to cope with the extra long hours spent trying to make a great design be interoperable.

My bottom line here is that it's simply not enough to make the author completely responsible for code compliance! Browser manufacturers have as much—if not more—responsibility when it comes to both the messes of the past and the fixes of the future.

Note

A coalition of Web developers and Web users make up the Web Standards Project, which exists to call browser developers on the floor and demand they pay attention to standards. You can visit the Web Standards Project at `http://www.webstandards.org/`.

POOR HABITS EXTENDING TO SOFTWARE

One of the most frustrating issues surrounding HTML is how the bad habits and non-standard methods of its evolutionary being have traveled into HTML editors. This is especially disconcerting in today's Web production environment, where many authors and designers are being asked to use specific editors (especially visual editors) to do a job. And, given the wealth of collaborative tools and production environments that exist in visual editors, it makes sense in many cases to do this.

→ To learn more about visual editors and other tools **see** Chapter 4, "XHTML Tools," **p. 49**.

It becomes imperative that people understand the limitations of the software products being used. What's more, knowing the standard methods of code can totally empower you as an individual to troubleshoot problem code, refine code, reduce code overhead, and bring generated code up to standards.

Some of the major concerns in primary visual editors that I'm concerned about are defined in Table 3.1.

TABLE 3.1 GENERAL COMMON MARKUP PROBLEMS ASSOCIATED WITH POPULAR VISUAL EDITING SOFTWARE

Product	Problem
Adobe GoLive	Introduction of proprietary code, extra code, extraneous code, complicated, unnecessary table structures, no support for XHTML 1.0.
Macromedia Dreamweaver	Some extraneous code problems, complex table structures, no current direct support for XHTML 1.0.
Microsoft FrontPage	No accommodation for hands-on coding in versions prior to 2000, introduction of own and often extraneous code, table structure problems, symmetry problems, no direct support for XHTML 1.0

In Figure 3.3, I created a very simple design and then laid it out using each of these programs. Listing 3.6 shows my results in Adobe GoLive; Listing 3.7 in Macromedia Dreamweaver; and 3.8 in Microsoft FrontPage.

Figure 3.3
A prototype of the look I was after.

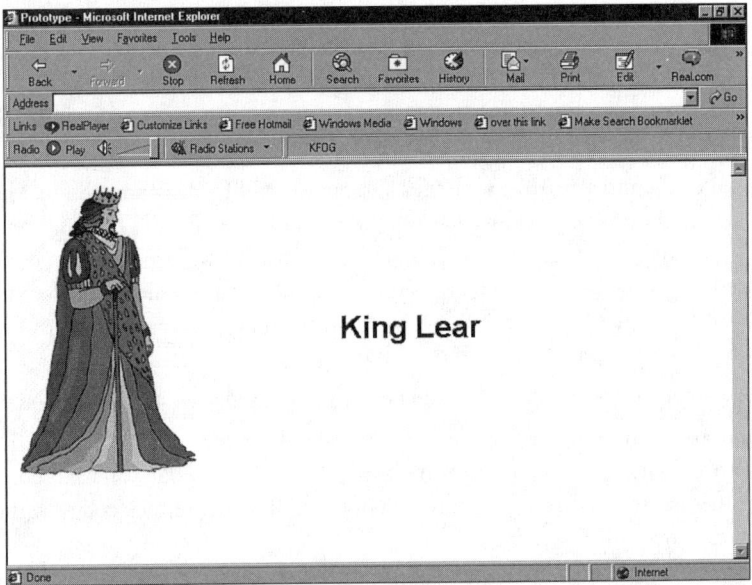

LISTING 3.6 SIMPLE LAYOUT AS CODED IN ADOBE GOLIVE. NOTE PROPRIETARY CODE AND EXTRANEOUS MARKUP (BOLDFACE TYPE).

```
<html>

    <head>
        <meta http-equiv="content-type" content="text/html;charset=iso-8859-1">
```

LISTING 3.6   CONTINUED

```
            <meta name="generator" content="Adobe GoLive 4">
            <title>Welcome to Adobe GoLive 4</title>
        </head>

        <body>
        <table cool width="586" height="317" border="0" cellpadding="0"
        ➥cellspacing="0" gridx="16" showgridx usegridx gridy="16"
        ➥showgridy usegridy>
            <tr height="1" cntrlrow>
                <td width="1" height="1"></td>
                <td width="16" height="1">
                ➥<spacer type="block" width="16" height="1"></td>
                <td width="569" height="1">
                ➥<spacer type="block" width="569" height="1"></td>
            </tr>
            <tr height="16">
                <td width="1" height="16">
                ➥<spacer type="block" width="1" height="16"></td>
                <td width="16" height="16"></td>
                <td width="569" height="16"></td>
            </tr>
            <tr height="300">
                <td width="1" height="300">
                ➥<spacer type="block" width="1" height="300"></td>
                <td width="16" height="300"></td>
                <td width="569" height="300" colspan="1"
                ➥rowspan="1" valign="top" align="left"
pos="16">
                    <table border="0" cellpadding="0" cellspacing="0" width="510">
                        <tr>
                            <td width="195"><img height="300" width="195"
                            ➥src="king.gif" border="0" alt="King Lear"></td>
                            <td width="311">
                                <table cool width="317" height="248" border="0"
                                ➥cellpadding="0" cellspacing="0"
                                ➥gridx="16" showgridx usegridx gridy="16"
showgridy usegridy>
                                    <tr height="1" cntrlrow>
                                        <td width="1" height="1"></td>
                                        <td width="32" height="1">
                                        ➥<spacer type="block"
                                        ➥width="32" height="1"></td>
                                        <td width="256" height="1">
                                        ➥<spacer type="block"
                                        ➥width="256" height="1"></td>
                                        <td width="28" height="1">
                                        ➥<spacer type="block"
                                        ➥width="28" height="1"></td>
                                    </tr>
                                    <tr height="16">
                                        <td width="1" height="16">
                                        ➥<spacer type="block"
                                        ➥width="1" height="16"></td>
                                        <td width="32" height="16"></td>
                                        <td width="256" height="16"></td>
```

LISTING 3.6   CONTINUED

```
                                        <td width="28" height="16"></td>
                        </tr>
                        <tr height="231">
                                <td width="1" height="231">
                        ➥<spacer type="block"
                        ➥width="1" height="231"></td>
                                <td width="32" height="231"></td>
                                <td width="256" height="231" colspan="1"
                        ➥rowspan="1" valign="top"
                        ➥align="left"
                        ➥xpos="32" content csheight="44">
                                        <center>
                                                <font size="6" face="Arial,
                                        ➥Helvetica,Geneva,Swiss,
                                        ➥SunSans-Regular">
                                        ➥<b>King Lear</b></font> </center>
                                </td>
                                <td width="28" height="231"></td>
                        </tr>
                        </table>
                </td>
                <td></td>
            </tr>
            </table>
        </td>
    </tr>
    </table>
</body>
</html>
```

LISTING 3.7   SIMPLE LAYOUT AS CODED IN MACROMEDIA DREAMWEAVER. MUCH CLEANER, BUT STILL SOME CODE PROBLEMS, SUCH AS THE CENTER div WITHIN THE SECOND TABLE CELL.

```
<html>
<head>
<title>Dreamweaver Sample</title>
<meta http-equiv="Content-Type" content="text/html; charset=iso-8859-1">
</head>

<body bgcolor="#FFFFFF">
<table width="75%" border="0" cellspacing="5" cellpadding="0" align="left">
  <tr>
    <td width="50%"><img src="king.gif" width="195" height="300"></td>
    <td width="50%" align="top">
      <div align="center"><font face="Arial, Helvetica, sans-serif" size="6">
    ➥<b>King
        Lear</b></font></div>
    </td>
  </tr>
</table>
</body>
</html>
```

LISTING 3.8   SIMPLE LAYOUT AS CODED IN MICROSOFT FRONTPAGE. ALSO CLEANER THAN ADOBE GOLIVE, BUT LOOK AT THE UNNECESSARY USE OF A PARAGRAPH WITHIN A TABLE CELL.

```
<html>

<head>
<meta http-equiv="Content-Language" content="en-us">
<meta http-equiv="Content-Type" content="text/html; charset=windows-1252">
<meta name="GENERATOR" content="Microsoft FrontPage 4.0">
<meta name="ProgId" content="FrontPage.Editor.Document">
<title>New Page 1</title>
</head>

<body>

<div align="left">
  <table border="0" width="47%" cellpadding="0" cellspacing="0">
    <tr>
      <td width="23%"><img border="0" src="king.gif" width="195" height="300">
      ➡</td>
      <td width="77%">
        <p align="center"><b><font face="Arial" size="6">King Lear</font>
        ➡</b></td>
    </tr>
  </table>
</div>

</body>

</html>
```

Most visual editors have table problems when tables start becoming complex. It's no wonder, since tables are being forced by the software to accommodate the designer's layout. Software is not as sophisticated in its methodology as a human being who has studied the ins-and outs of markup. This is one of the many reasons I advocate learning how to do things by hand, even if you use a visual editor in your work.

TRANSCENDING LIMITATIONS ON PROGRESS

If you take all these issues: poor code education and practices from authors, troublesome concerns with browsers, and code problems inherent to editing tools, the end result is sobering. HTML is in a sad state of disrepair.

Just as you wouldn't want to build a home on a faulty foundation, anyone concerned with the structural integrity of what he or she is building must also be concerned with the faulty foundation in HTML. XHTML exists to fix the foundation so we can build our buildings better, higher, and more creatively. What seems rigorous and strict is actually what will bring us the most freedom. Without that structure beneath us, the chances of problem on top of problem becomes manifold.

RETURNING TO THE WELL-FORMED DOCUMENT

So how does this move from HTML to XHTML translate to the real-world? Here are a few of the primary ways that this can occur:

- Clean up hand coding approaches using standard markup, which at this time is XHTML. Try to separate document formatting and presentation wherever possible. Write documents that also conform to the basic tenets of the last HTML legacy and current XHTML concerns: accessibility, improved rendering, and internationalization methods.

- Make requests of Web development software applications to extend capabilities to the current standards. This can be done via feedback to the company from which you purchase your software.

- Make demands that Web browsers come up to par with the standards. In part, simply writing documents that are standardized will help get the message across. You also might want to become involved with organizations such as the Web Standards Project, mentioned earlier, as well as sending feedback to browser developers requesting their compliance with standard code.

There are perhaps no stronger, more compelling reasons and opportunities to begin looking at XHTML 1.0 as a method by which to empower yourself as an author, and make a statement to browser and editor developers that you want—and demand—better tools with which to do your work.

CHAPTER 4

XHTML Tools

In this chapter

APPROACHES TO CODING

How many times have you tried to use a screwdriver because you couldn't find a hammer, a knife when scissors would have been better, or tried a cheap corkscrew on a stubborn cork? If you're like me, you have suffered sore thumbs, painful nicks and cuts, and ended up drinking cork along with your wine!

Hard-won experience teaches us all that using the right tool for the job is going to make that job easier and will help to avoid painful or unfortunate results. To generate Web markup, using the right tool is imperative. XHTML has few tools as of yet, but there are many HTML production tools on the market. And, depending upon your situation, you might well find that you have to use an HTML tool and *then* convert your document to XHTML. There are so many tools available, it's hard to decide which one is appropriate to your circumstances.

Whether you are a hobbyist, newcomer, or professional, selecting the appropriate tools for XHTML is going to make an enormous difference in the way you work. This chapter will help you understand the tools that are available, the advantages and disadvantages that come with specific types of tools, and how you can maximize your work productivity and minimize risk.

Your first task is to put aside everything you've heard about Web software applications: that coding HTML and XHTML is easy or hard, or that the best coders only code by hand. All these attitudes are just that—attitudes. From experience I can confidently tell you that no one tool is the catchall answer for every situation. Just as you want to choose a hammer when a hammer is required, and a knife when you need a knife, so you must choose the best tool for the circumstance in which you work.

There are several approaches to coding XHTML that are popular. These include text-based, or "hand" coding; using editing environments and coding XHTML within those environments; working with HTML conversion programs and then running through an XHTML conversion process; and employing What-You-See-Is-What-You-Get (WYSI-WYG) applications to develop your markup and converting to XHTML.

HAND CODING USING SIMPLE TEXT EDITORS

Some time ago, I attended a figure drawing class. I found it challenging because I knew precious little about the actual mechanics of drawing. As I became more acquainted with techniques—such as visualizing a grid and breaking down areas into small sections—my skills improved. Without the mechanical knowledge, however, I could be creative and expressive, but I was not accurate, adept, or confident in my approach.

If you want total control over your code and your design, you must know the mechanics of XHTML. This book focuses on giving you the opportunity to control your Web design issues and XHTML documents.

The most powerful and effective way of gaining that control and relying on the underlying mechanics of XHTML is learning the code, and then coding XHTML in a text-based environment.

XHTML information is saved in plain-text format. Many of you are already familiar with this concept—plain text is text that has no formatting codes added by a program such as a word processor. Text is the natural format for XHTML; therefore, coding in text is a natural approach. Historically speaking, it was the first approach.

But coding in a text editor means having to *know the code*. There are no cheat sheets available in this environment. Yes, you'll want to keep a copy of this book around for reference purposes while coding in this fashion, but text editing means relying on your own knowledge with no added power tools.

The advantages? There are many. The most important one is that knowing the code is incredibly empowering—especially for professionals. Text editing forces you to know your XHTML and this in turn frees you from the constraints of a software interface. If something doesn't work, you'll have the skills to troubleshoot, debug, and eventually repair the problem.

Relying on your own skills also allows you to be creative. The better you know the language, the more creatively you can use it. This creativity is the precursor to progress in the industry. By knowing the rules, using them creatively, or even breaking them, new opportunities are born.

As you'll soon read in the WYSIWYG section of this chapter, software applications are limited by software update issues. For example, if a new code standard (and XHTML is a very good example of this) is adopted, a text-coder can begin to use that code immediately. The software application might not support it until the next update, however, and could possibly cause endless frustration as you attempt to work with that new code standard.

Finally, if you know your code and are comfortable coding in a text environment, you can take that anywhere you go, to any company, onto any computer platform. What's more, text editors are native to all operating systems, and that means you'll spend *no money* on Web-authoring software!

Are there disadvantages to hand-coding? You bet. One of the most pervasive is the time it takes to become proficient with XHTML. The language and its supporting technologies have become very sophisticated, and it takes time, not only to learn the individual aspects of the language, but also to integrate that knowledge into your working world.

Along the same lines, even a proficient and fast author will require extra time during the markup process without power tools. To provide you with a down-to-earth example, I've been coding HTML since 1993 and XHTML since its birthday on January 26, 2000, and although I'm knowledgeable and experienced, I still have to rely on reference materials to do more advanced or obscure processes.

This extra time is costing someone precious money. That's a definite disadvantage, and one that you'll want to weigh seriously when analyzing your personal needs and coming up with a good coding approach.

TEXT EDITORS FOR WINDOWS

Most text editors are native or freely available within any given operating system.

In Windows, the choice is Notepad, shown in Figure 4.1, which is an extremely popular tool for writing markup. It is available in the 3.x, 95, 98, and 2000 versions of Windows and 3.51 and 4.0 Windows NT.

Figure 4.1
Windows Notepad requires the coder to enter every tag manually and provides no special features for color-coding or other special helps.

TEXT EDITORS FOR MACINTOSH AND UNIX

In contrast, Macintosh fans can use SimpleText as their editor.

I like SimpleText because it allows you to color-code your text editing, giving you reference points for your tags, as shown in Figure 4.2.

Many coders are working on UNIX or Linux servers and require easy access to line-based HTML editors. Three such editors that are recommended by coders are

- **vi**—This UNIX and Linux text editor is extremely popular among hard-core coders from the "old school" of Web coding.
- **Pico**—This basic, no-frills text editor can be used for generating XHTML.

Figure 4.2
Macintosh's SimpleText provides the color coding capabilities, which can help make coding more efficient and debugging a little quicker.

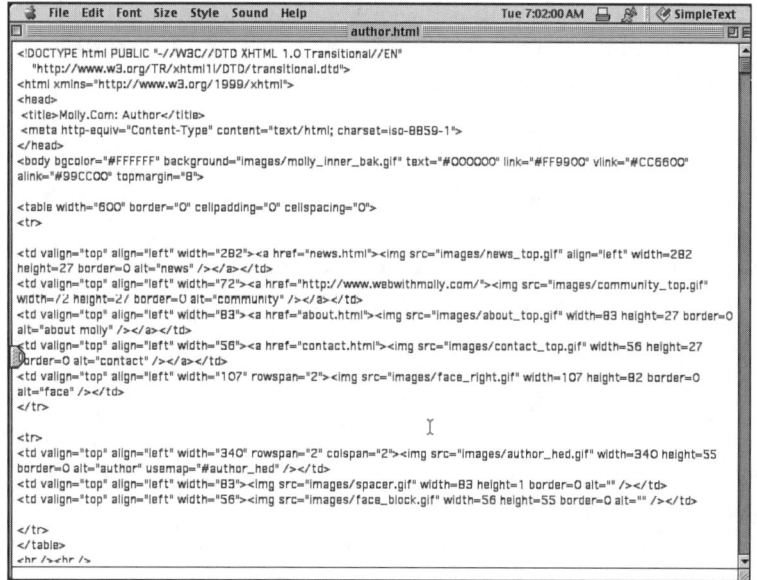

- **Emacs**—Another popular editor used on the UNIX and Linux platforms (it's also prevalent among VMS users). It's more complicated than vi or Pico, so much so that it comes with an online psychologist "Meta-X-Doctor" to help you endure the psychological problems you will face while using it. It is considered very powerful, and many programmers prefer it to other options.

Although you must weigh all the advantages and disadvantages of XHTML coding approaches and make decisions based on your needs, there simply *is* no substitute for knowing XHTML well. If you are running a professional design company, or have sophisticated XHTML requirements, having someone on your staff who is proficient with code—no matter what approach you ultimately select for your needs—is going to be a very valuable resource.

 Looking to improve the spelling of your XHTML documents? See "Spell Checking Documents" in the "Troubleshooting" section near the end of this chapter.

HTML AND XHTML EDITING ENVIRONMENTS

An HTML or XHTML editing environment is the middle ground between the hard-core text editor and the WYSIWYG application. All the advantages that come with text editing are available to those of you who choose editing environments, and the disadvantages are addressed.

Editing environments typically use a graphical user interface (GUI), so there are a lot of intuitive, familiar options available on the toolbar as well as numerous power tools. It's good to think of the editing environment as a text editor with enhancements.

PART

I

CH

4

I personally rely on HTML editing environments when doing the bulk of my code work. It affords me all the control and creativity of a text editor, but speeds up the process by providing tools such as online help, quick tag interfaces, and spell checking.

If your Web-authoring skills are strong, and you're looking for an application that will help you work more effectively, an editing environment might suit you well. To help determine if this is true, consider some of the features of this popular coding approach.

ADVANTAGES OF HTML EDITING ENVIRONMENTS

The HTML environment of my choice, Allaire HomeSite, offers templates, toolbars that automatically insert specific tags, and an image wizard that automatically inserts the size of my images as well as providing me with a full range of alternative text options. This places value-added services right at my fingers—whether by mouse click or keyboard shortcut, I get what I need done, and done fast. Granted, I have to undo a lot of HTML and turn it into XHTML, or use a conversion tool, but I've gotten pretty quick about it with just a little practice—and you will too.

→ For more information on adding images to XHTML documents, **see** Chapter 13, "Using Images in XHTML Documents," **p. 221**.

A common problem on the Web is that people forget that spell checking is a critical part of the site development process. Well-written, properly spelled language is extremely important if you want to maximize site success. Spell checking is available in most HTML editing environments, and I know you'll appreciate this option as much as I do.

Another advantage is that most editing environments come with a syntax checker. This helpful tool examines your code, helping you troubleshoot problems, and fixes any unsightly errors.

Although the SimpleText editor on the Macintosh allows you to color code your work, text options for Windows and UNIX do not. This problem is solved with the editing environment. Tag colorization is very effective in terms of making tags quickly identifiable. You can color all your image tags yellow, for example, and your table tags blue. This will help you find information quickly, particularly within very complex pages of code.

By far, my favorite tool in the HTML editing environment is the multi-file search and replace. This feature allows you to search documents for a specific code string and replace it with a new string. You can update hundreds of pages with this feature. Imagine having to use a text editor to do this task—it could take you days, even weeks! The editing environment addresses this need quickly and efficiently.

In terms of the pocketbook, HTML editing environments are affordable, running between $50.00 and $200.00 each.

Caution

> Because most HTML editing environments have not added full features for XHTML, if you're using them you will have to be aware of problems inherent to that particular environment. For example, Homesite, prior to version 4.5, left many numeric attributes unquoted. Similarly, most of these editors don't add the proper termination syntax to empty elements (a space and a slash, as in br /). You'll need to adjust to your favorite editor and either run your finished code through a converter, or go back and make the changes by hand.

HTML EDITING ENVIRONMENT APPLICATIONS

Users of Windows are in luck—there are several excellent HTML editing environments available in which you can write XHTML documents.

My favorite is Allaire HomeSite. It has all the features I've mentioned, and its interface can be customized to your tastes (see Figures 4.3 and 4.4).

Figure 4.3
Allaire's HomeSite 4.0 standard view offers the hand coder with many useful features, including access to all available toolbars and a powerful file-management system.

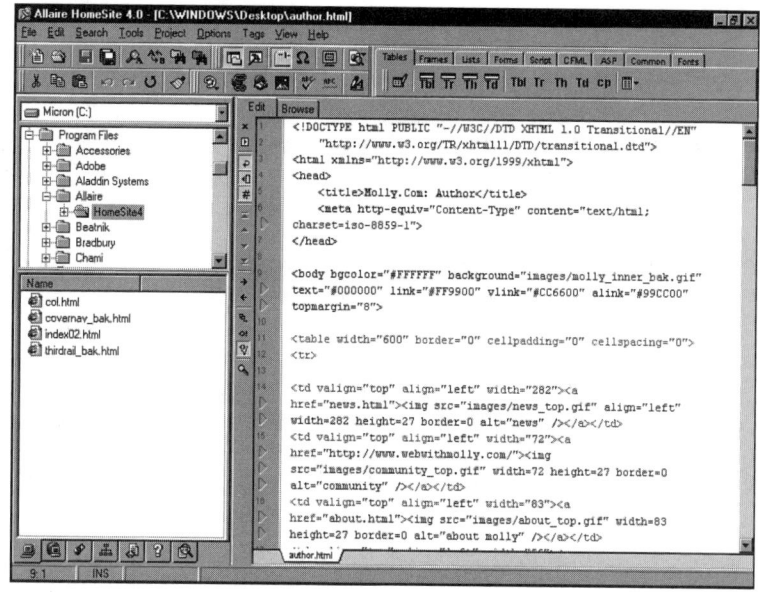

HTML Tidy

It's imperative at this stage of the game to tell you about an awesome tool known as HTML Tidy. Created by David Raggett, this utility is available for almost every conceivable platform and is often written into shareware or other software applications. It converts HTML to XHTML and generally cleans up syntax problems. It's a must-have in every XHTML author's toolkit. You can get HTML Tidy free (it's open-source software) by visiting its home page at **http://www.w3.org/People/Raggett/tidy/**.

Figure 4.4
Allaire's HomeSite 4.0, custom view.

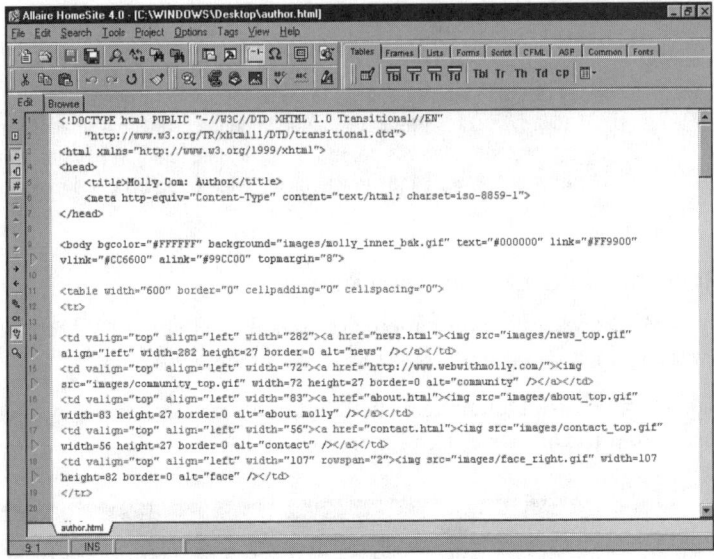

I sometimes use HotDog Pro from Sausage software. The interface isn't as user-friendly as HomeSite's; still, I highly recommend this editor. I encourage you to download it (you'll find the URL in a note later in the chapter) and try it for yourself.

Specific to XHTML is Mozquito Factory, (see Figure 4.5) a very good XHTML editing environment that offers all kinds of specialty features such as XHTML-FML editing options. XHTML is from Stack Overflow, which also provides a lot of enthusiastic information about XHTML and has contributed to portions of this book.

Figure 4.5
Working with Mozquito Factory.

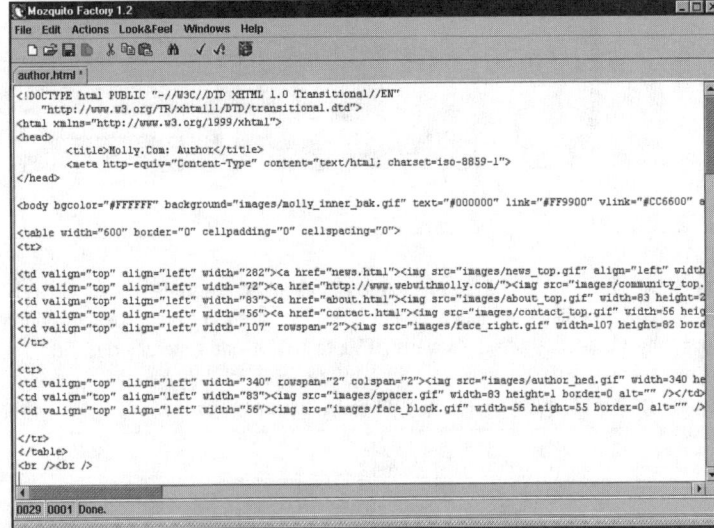

A fantastic shareware tool from Chami is HTML-Kit. This product has HTML-Tidy built right in. Light, fast, and worth its weight in gold, it's available for Windows (see Figure 4.6).

Figure 4.6
HTML-Kit from Chami has conversion utilities for XHTML built right in. Here, you can see an original document in the left frame being checked by HTML Tidy. Warnings appear below, and the converted document appears in the right frame.

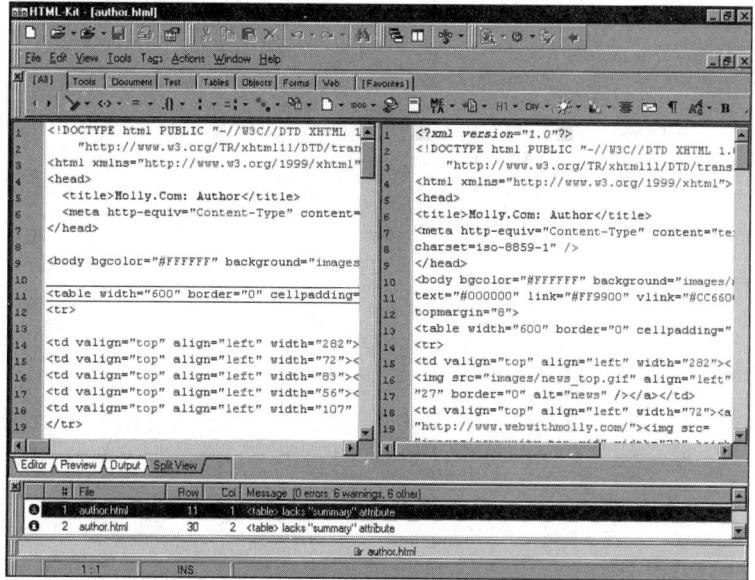

Although there are many Macintosh editing environments, I only have three favorites. BBEdit from Bare Bones Software is probably the more popular of my recommendations. It is really a plain text editor with some extensions added to bump it up into the editing environment class. Web Weaver is a fine editing environment, and I use it as an editing environment example when I teach Web design on the Macintosh platform. Another favorite is PageSpinner, which has quite the cult following.

Where to Find HTML Editing Environments

Download demos of software previously mentioned from these Web sites:

Allaire's HomeSite: `http://www.allaire.com/products/homesite/`

HotDog Pro: `http://www.sausage.com/`

HTML Assistant Pro: `http://www.brooknorth.com/`

HTML-Kit: `http://www.chami.com/html-kit/`

Mozquito Factory: `http://www.mozquito.org/`

BBEdit: `http://www.barebones.com/products/products.html`

PageSpinner: `http://www.optima-system.com/pagespinner/`

Emacs Add-In: `http://www.tnt.uni-hannover.de/~muenkel/software/own/hm--html-menus/overview.html`

PART

I

CH

4

For those of you out there using UNIX or Linux, there is one popular editing environment option available. Emacs, described earlier, has an add-on package that provides an HTML mode to the editor. This emulates an editing environment by providing you with a variety of power tools.

HTML AND XHTML CONVERSION UTILITIES

If you have a lot of documents to process, and aren't highly concerned about the consistency and quality of your code, an HTML conversion utility might be in order. But, to make that code even somewhat compliant with XHTML, you'll have to go in and change the markup, or run it through a conversion utility such as HTML Tidy.

HTML conversion utilities are software applications that stand alone or are integrated within another application. For example, a word processor might offer a Save As option for HTML. When you invoke this option, the document you've created will be converted to and saved as an HTML document.

The advantages to this process are obvious. You don't need to learn HTML to have a document processed as HTML, and it's the utility—not you—that has to take the time to code the page.

Sadly, however, what you trim off the HTML learning curve and coding time issues, you pay for heavily in the type of code that is generated. Typically, conversion utilities create what I call "fat code."

Fat code is filled with unnecessary tags and information. Fat code also tends to be illogical and messy. Let's take a comparative look at a short passage of code generated by an HTML conversion utility, and the same code as I would create it.

Listing 4.1 shows the code from the conversion utility. The one I used is Word 97's integrated application, and I converted a selection from this chapter.

LISTING 4.1   HTML CODE PREPARED BY A CONVERSION UTILITY

```
<HTML>
<HEAD>
<META HTTP-EQUIV="Content-Type" CONTENT="text/html; charset=windows-1252">
<META NAME="Generator" CONTENT="Microsoft Word 97">
<TITLE>Fat Code</TITLE>
</HEAD>
<BODY>

<P>Fat code is filled with unnecessary tags and information. Fat code also tends
to be illogical and messy. Let's take a comparative look at a short passage of
code generated by an HTML conversion utility, and the same code as I would
create it. </P>

<P>Here's the code from the conversion utility. The one I used is Word 8.0's
integrated application:</P>

<B><I><P>***List 4.1***</P>
```

LISTING 4.1 CONTINUED

```
<P>Code Prepared by a Conversion Utility</P>

<P>***End List***</P>
</I>
</B><P>And here's the same code as I would create it by hand. Note the
cleanliness, and take a look at how "slim," or free of extraneous tags,
my code is:</P>

<OL START=4 TYPE="a">

<B><LI>Summary</LI></OL>

</B><P> </P>
<P> </P></FONT></BODY>
</HTML>
```

Listing 4.2 shows the same code as I would create it by hand in XHTML. Note the cleanliness, simplicity, and take a look at how "slim," or free of extraneous tags, my code is.

LISTING 4.2 THE SAME CODE DONE BY HAND

```
<!DOCTYPE html PUBLIC "-//W3C//DTD XHTML 1.0 Transitional//EN"
"http://www.w3.org/TR/xhtml1/DTD/xhtml1-transitional.dtd">
<html xmlns="http://www.w3.org/1999/xhtml">
<head>
<title>Fat Code</title>
</head>
<body>

<p>Fat code is filled with unnecessary tags and information. Fat code also tends
to
be illogical and messy. Let's take a comparative look at a short passage of code
generated by an HTML conversion utility, and the same code as I would create
it.</p>

<p>Here's the code from the conversion utility. The one I used is Word 97's
integrated application:</p>

<p><b><i>***List 4.1***
<p>Code Prepared by a Conversion Utility
<br />
<br />

***End List***</b></i>
<p>And here's the same code as I would create it by hand. Note the cleanliness,
and
take a look at how "slim," or free of extraneous tags, my code is:</p>

<p><b><ol><li>Summary</ol></b>

<body>
</html>
```

PART

I

CH

4

Now, compare the following two screen shots of the output in Figures 4.7 and 4.8. Notice that there *is no visual difference* in the results, but there sure is a difference in the way the code is written.

Figure 4.7
Screen shot of HTML converted from a Word 97 document as seen in Internet Explorer 5.0.

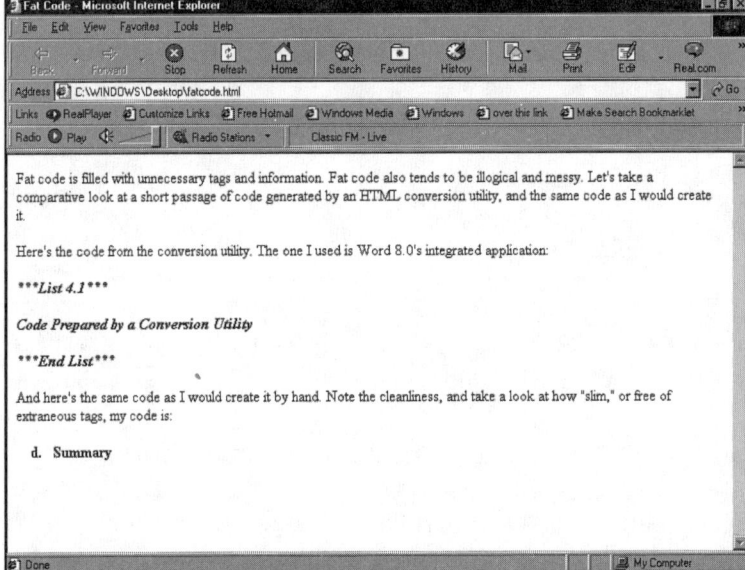

Figure 4.08
Screen shot of hand-coded XHTML.

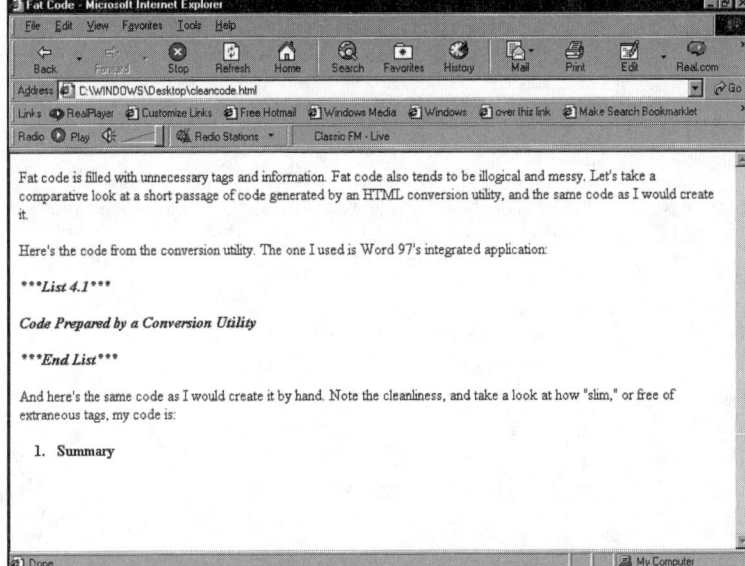

Why Should You Care?

So if the output of HTML looks the same, why should you care about the way the code looks? There are several important reasons, including

- Superfluous code can translate to extra page weight.

- If you want to open the code and add something, or change it, finding your way around might be difficult.

- HTML conversion utilities typically write very poor code, potentially rendering HTML pages useless in certain browsers.

- Professionals should aim to adhere to some conventions, if not the standards themselves. This is an issue of quality control: conversion utilities cannot replace a savvy coder's ability to ensure that the code is compliant, neat, and human-readable.

Another problem with conversion utilities is that they usually cannot properly manage graphics, multimedia applications, or specialty coding such as JavaScript or other programming oriented functions. These utilities are best for text documents or documents created from their primary applications, such as Microsoft Word or Excel.

Because of their speed, conversion utilities are certainly good resources to have on hand. However, if you're working in a professional situation, you're going to have to ask your XHTML expert to sweep up some of the code mess conversion utilities create and add your graphics and code by hand anyway. Otherwise, you risk having your documents be text-based, technically problematic, and unprofessional in appearance.

Note

It's important to point out that some of the editing environments mentioned in this chapter have HTML conversion utilities integrated into the interface. The level of sophistication in some of these utilities is a bit better in less code-specific programs. Check to see if your editing environment offers this option. And, if you like the code it generates, you've found an excellent method of quickly converting text documents to HTML. Then, you can bring *that* information into HTML Tidy, and have compliant XHTML documents.

POPULAR CONVERSION APPLICATIONS

Windows-based conversion was originally available via Microsoft's Internet Assistant. This utility integrated word processing, Web browsing, and Web document creation. Its understanding of HTML was very limited and development stopped in 1995, being replaced in concept by Microsoft's popular WYSIWYG application, FrontPage.

Internet Assistant conversion capabilities, however, are still included within Microsoft applications. The conversion software now exists in all major products within the Microsoft Office 2000 suite. I've known some savvy Web developers who have tapped into the power of macros and created extensive, customized add-ins to the utility, cleaning up code problems and automating conversion processes.

The same conversion utilities are available for Microsoft applications on the Macintosh platform.

A set of HTML conversion utilities for Word documents, called The Ant, is used enthusiastically by some coders. The Ant is available in both Windows and Macintosh flavors. The Ant provides support for tables and a utility for forms, and it can also manage batch processing.

Interleaf is a code-conversion program that supports a variety of word processing and publication applications. Included in that list are Microsoft Word, WordPerfect, and FrameMaker.

> **Tip**
>
> Use these Web addresses to check out some popular conversion utilities:
>
> Microsoft Internet Assistant: `http://support.microsoft.com/support/kb/articles/Q154/8/60.asp`
>
> The Ant: `http://telacommunications.com/ant/`
>
> Interleaf: `http://www.interleaf.com/`

WHAT-YOU-SEE-IS-WHAT-YOU-GET (WYSIWYG) APPLICATIONS

Relying on a graphical interface to effectively relate with users, WYSIWYG is popular not only because of its low learning curve, but because of its easy portability from user to user. This is especially important for companies who have a lot of individuals working on HTML code—a WYSIWYG application will help keep coding styles consistent.

Another advantage is that WYSIWYG applications allow you to design a Web page without *ever* learning Web markup. In the graphical interface, a user will place the graphics and text he or she requires, and then manipulate them until he or she finds the most satisfying look. The software, then, is responsible for generating the code.

Certain WYSIWYGs, such as Microsoft's FrontPage, are very powerful beyond the scope of design: they have extensions that allow for project management and specialty applications, such as search and forms support. These features make the WYSIWYG option attractive for many people.

Although I totally understand the reasons why WYSIWYG software is such a popular choice, I also find most WYSIWYGs to be extremely problematic, for a number of reasons.

The first of those reasons has to do with control. XHTML and HTML were never meant to be languages of design and layout, so the real-world employment of these technologies is still limited. An XHTML author relies on the relationship of XHTML to his or her entire design. It is an integrated process—one that is best determined by experience, which a software application simply cannot match.

Whether it's choosing percentages over pixels in a given instance, or wanting to adjust a selection of code to your own tastes, WYSIWYGs typically do not give you that option, or if they do give you that option, you might be unaware of why you should be making a specific choice.

Many WYSIWYG programs—especially older versions of FrontPage—change or modify code that you write in the interfaces of the program in question.

You've already been introduced to the concept of fat code, and WYSIWYGs are equally a culprit in this problem. Although you have more control over customizing WYSIWYGs to suit your tastes, the application does the coding—not you. This means, ultimately, that the code is going to reflect the style of the application and not the coder. Listing 4.3 shows code generated by the WYSIWYG application, Adobe GoLive, and Listing 4.4 shows my approach.

LISTING 4.3   CODE FROM GOLIVE

```
<HTML>

<HEAD>
<META http-equiv="content-type" content="text/html;charset=iso-8859-1">
<META name="generator" content="Adobe GoLive 4">
<TITLE>Home Page</TITLE>
</HEAD>

<BODY>
          <TABLE cool width="586" height="586" border="0" cellpadding="0"
cellspacing="0" gridx="16" showgridx usegridx gridy="16" showgridy usegridy>
<TR height="1" cntrlrow>
<TD width="1" height="1"></TD>
<TD width="585" height="1"><SPACER type="block" width="585" height="1"></TD>
</TR>
<TR height="585">
<TD width="1" height="585"><SPACER type="block" width="1" height="585"></TD>
<TD width="585" height="585" colspan="1" rowspan="1" valign="top" align="left"
xpos="0" content csheight="176">Whether it's choosing percentages over pixels
in a given instance,
or wanting to adjust a selection of code to your own tastes, WYSIWYGs
typically do not give you that option. sure, you can go in and
change the information and save the file, but open it again and
your code will have been altered by the application!
<P>You've already been introduced to the concept of &quot;Fat Code,&quot; and
WYSIWYGs are equally a culprit in this problem. while you have
more control over customizing WYSIWYGs to suit your tastes, the
application does the coding, not you. this means that ultimately,
the code is going to reflect the style of the application, and
not the coder.</TD>
</TR>
</TABLE>
</BODY>

</HTML>
```

LISTING 4.4   CODE AS I'VE CODED IT IN XHTML

```
<!DOCTYPE html PUBLIC "-//W3C//DTD XHTML 1.0 Strict//EN"
    "http://www.w3.org/TR/xhtml1/DTD/strict.dtd">
<html xmlns="http://www.w3.org/1999/xhtml">
<head>
<title>Home Page</title>
</head>
<body>
<p>Whether it's choosing percentages over pixels in a given
instance, or wanting to adjust a selection of code to your own
tastes, WYSIWYGs typically do not give you that option. sure, you
can go in and change the information and save the file, but open
it again and your code will have been altered by the
application!</p>

<p>You've already been introduced to the concept of "Fat Code,"
and WYSIWYGs are equally a culprit in this problem. while you
have more control over customizing WYSIWYGs to suit your tastes,
the application does the coding, not you. this means that
ultimately, the code is going to reflect the style of the
application, and not the coder.</p>
</body>
</html>
```

You'll note that I used no tables; I just used strict, but straight-forward XHTML. Furthermore, I used no extra graphics, such as a spacer graphic to achieve the end result. This demonstrates how a coder who *knows the code* can make much more sophisticated decisions about how to work with a given page.

In Listing 4.3, you see a lot of extraneous and proprietary code. Certainly, a skilled Web author would fix this problem, but what of the novice who isn't familiar with HTML? He or she is going to have output that lacks professional appeal, much less complies with the XHTML standard.

Note

The code problems demonstrated here reflect my bias toward clean code with maximum control for the Web author and designer. This example should serve to help you understand the issues that arise when working with WYSIWYGs, not to dissuade you from their use. Adobe GoLive, and other similar WYSIWYG products, have tremendous advantages, including great layout environments, a variety of preset styles, built-in graphic optimization, and an array of other power features that make them all worthy of consideration.

Another problem with WYSIWYG applications is that they are limited by release dates. XHTML is a growing, dynamic language. Software applications can logically only produce software updates at certain intervals, usually determined by fiscal concerns rather than customer demand. For this reason, you still have to use WYSIWYG to generate HTML, and *then* convert to XHTML by hand or with another tool to be compliant with contemporary standards.

So, certain tags or updated techniques that you might like to use might not be available until an upcoming software version. Try to add the tag or technique anyway, and your current software version might override code it doesn't recognize, removing it from your work. This makes it difficult to update, alter, or effectively troubleshoot problems in the WYSIWYG environment.

To be fair, many companies accommodate this issue by offering patches and updates via the Web, but the bottom line is that the software package you bought last year is probably not going to have the sophistication you may require today—a serious disadvantage that you need to consider before investing in a software application that might not suit your needs.

POPULAR WYSIWYGS

Despite the problems with WYSIWYGs, the needs of individuals and companies interested in a quick, portable solution for HTML generation are undeniably met by WYSIWYGs.

Some of the more popular WYSIWYG applications include Microsoft's FrontPage, which is available on both the Windows and Macintosh platforms. This prevalent program is used by hobbyists and professionals alike, and, as I've mentioned, there are many extended features that make the product well worth a serious test-drive. Improvements to the software in the 2000 version include the fact that it does not rewrite a coder's HTML to its own specifications, an improved interface greatly facilitates the software's usability, and I can confidently say that many individuals use the product with a great deal of satisfaction.

Adobe fans might lean toward Adobe's WYSIWYG software, GoLive, now available for the Windows 98 and Mac platforms. GoLive has the advantage of being integrated into the Adobe suite of design software, making it a strong contender in the design marketplace.

Macromedia's Dreamweaver, a venerable visual authoring tool, and its new companion program, Dreamweaver UltraDev, which includes application development capabilities (see Figure 4.9), is an especially impressive product. Of all the WYSIWYG programs, Macromedia's code tends to be the cleanest. UltraDev also packs serious application options server-side as well as client. This product was created with the designer in mind—not only is the user interface sensible, the WYSIWYG editor comes packaged with an editing environment so you can make adjustments as you see fit.

Macromedia offers BBEdit as the companion editing environment for the Mac, and for Windows, Allaire's HomeSite is the environment of choice. This approach is extremely considerate because the author is given *options*. Furthermore, after a file that you have altered is reloaded into the WYSIWYG, no alterations to the code are made. And, you can run your code through HTML Tidy after, which results in neat and clean code insofar as a WYSIWYG application can create.

A variety of other WYSIWYG editors, such as NetObjects Fusion and Softquad's HotMetal Pro, also are used across platforms by a portion of dedicated professionals.

PART

I

CH

4

Figure 4.9
Macromedia's
DreamWeaver
UltraDev uses panels
and inspectors to pro-
vide the Web designer
with a wide variety of
tools and options.

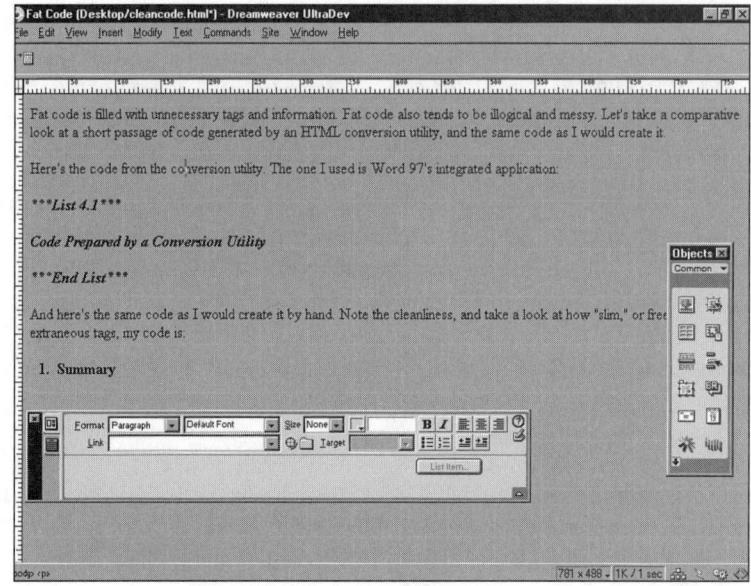

 If you want a fast solution for HTML concerns, see "Need Your Site Yesterday?" in the "Troubleshooting" section near the end of this chapter.

UNIX users have many choices, as quite a few of the previously mentioned applications have been made available for the UNIX platform. Quadralay's WebWorks Publisher is a specific program that you can combine with FrameMaker for a full HTML WYSIWYG package for UNIX.

Available WYSIWYG Software Applications

Microsoft FrontPage: `http://www.microsoft.com/frontpage/`

NetObjects Fusion: `http://www.netobjects.com/`

Softquad HotMetal Pro: `http://www.sq.com/`

Qudralay's WebWorks: `http://www.quadralay.com/`

Adobe GoLive: `http://www.adobe.com/prodindex/golive/main.html`

Macromedia DreamWeaver UltraDev: `http://www.macromedia.com/software/`

One thing that becomes obvious when working with these software applications is that what you see is decidedly *not* always what you get. The ultimate decision is to weigh the pros and cons, test them against your personal needs, and see what pans out. An easy decision? No. But an important one that will help you save time, money, and countless hours of frustration.

TROUBLESHOOTING

SPELL CHECKING DOCUMENTS

I am very happy coding my XHTML in an ASCII or plain-text editor. But, I want to be able to spell check documents. How can I do it?

One way to check the spelling in your documents is to view the page in a browser, and then copy and paste the text into a Word processor that has spell-checking. This is a bit of an awkward and time-consuming process, but it works. You also might consider using an HTML editor with built-in spell checking. This way, you get the best of the ASCII world with the best HTML tools available. And, you can customize most HTML editors so that no extraneous windows or menus are showing—just the tools you want to use as you code.

NEED YOUR SITE YESTERDAY?

I'm just beginning to dig seriously into XHTML and I want to learn to code by hand, but also need to be developing sites today. What's the best way to go?

Any WYSIWYG editor worth its salt has an HTML editing environment available alongside the graphic layout workspace. This is true of major players such as Adobe GoLive, Macromedia Dreamweaver, and Microsoft FrontPage 2000. You can use the HTML editors in any of these programs to work on XHTML yourself, and the graphic interfaces to generate the pages you need right now.

Do be cautious, however. Some older versions of HTML WYSIWYG programs will alter your code to their own methods after you've made a change. This used to be the case in FrontPage, but the 2000 version offers hands-off coding, allowing you to tinker without any tinkering back! Dreamweaver should be applauded for stepping into the fray and ensuring hands-off coding for its users. Adobe GoLive will leave code that you add to a page alone, but you'll notice a lot of odd, proprietary tags that GoLive uses as a mechanism to create its own layout grids. When converting to XHTML, these pesky problems can cause inconsistencies and invalid code.

DESIGNING FOR THE REAL WORLD

CREATING TEMPLATES FOR SPEED AND ACCURACY

An advanced concern for professionals is how to work with the variety of XHTML editors and maximize the speed, accuracy, and consistency between documents. In this section, you'll create a basic template that will help set you up for future XHTML exercises. You also can use this template as a starting point for all your XHTML pages. I'm also including some helpful information in your quest for solid solutions, including creation of company guidelines and the development of proprietary applications where necessary.

To build the template, follow these steps:

1. Begin by opening your text, HTML, or WYSIWYG editor in HTML mode.

2. Type the template code directly into your editor (as shown in Listing 4.5).

LISTING 4.5   SIMPLE PAGE TEMPLATE

```
<?xml version="1.0"?>
<!DOCTYPE html PUBLIC "-//W3C//DTD XHTML 1.0 Strict//EN"
    "http://www.w3.org/TR/xhtml1/DTD/strict.dtd">
<!-- site design by: Molly E. Holzschlag molly@molly.com -->
<!-- http://www.molly.com/ -->
<!-- page last updates: *add date here* -->
<html xmlns="http://www.w3.org/1999/xhtml">
<!-- Begin Head Information -->
<head>
<title>place_title_here</title>
</head>
<!-- Begin Body (add <p> after each individual paragraph -->
<body>
<!-- Begin Footer Information (copyright, mailto, etc) -->
</body>
</html>
```

3. Modify the code to match your own custom needs. For example, add your own name in place of mine, and your URL and contact information.

4. Save the file as `template.html` to a directory or folder where you keep frequently used files.

Templates can be of great assistance to you and your co-workers. Naturally, they will become more complex as your sites evolve. Sometimes I create a template for an individual site, and use it for only that site. Another approach would be to set up templates for different types of sites: framed sites, left-margin table sites, standard pages, and so on. These templates can then act as guidelines for the company standards you want to remain consistent no matter the type of site being constructed.

COMPANY GUIDELINES AND CHECKLISTS

Help new members of your company become accustomed to your style by first defining what that style is and then developing a style guide and companion checklist. Hobbyists or individuals will appreciate such a guide too because it will help keep them on track when a style question arises.

Let's say I want all the XHTML authors in my company to use indented table style, as opposed to a flush left code for tables. I would put this in my guide, along with an example of its use. I also could create a checklist that employees can use to make sure they've followed the guidelines effectively.

PROPRIETARY APPLICATIONS

In many advanced environments, the requirements of the day-to-day management of Web sites becomes very complex. Think about a daily newspaper, for example. That's a lot of content to prepare effectively and continuously if you're working by hand. It becomes obvious that although you'll require knowledge of HTML hand-coding to troubleshoot and solve problems, the task of publishing that much content on a daily basis screams "automate!"

In these cases, it's wise to investigate available software that might exist in your specialty niche. If you're having trouble finding such software, or you are not satisfied with what's available, you might consider working with a qualified analyst and programmer who can help create a proprietary management tool for your needs. This approach is often the best, most professional solution for today's aggressive and varied site needs.

Tip

Looking for a qualified programmer to help you determine your software needs? There are many online databases that can help employers find the qualified individuals they need. Visit `http://www.jobengine.com/` and `http://www.jobs-online.net/`. There are plenty of other databases, so a visit to your favorite search engine for a list of high-tech resumés online will help expand your options.

No matter the toolkit you ultimately end up with, understanding the pros and cons of the available types of tools will help you customize that toolkit to your personal needs. Whether your desire is to use this book to learn XHTML, or to have a comprehensive, desktop reference for available tools and materials, you end up ahead by knowing how to approach the job at hand.

XHTML SYNTAX

CHAPTER **5**

DEFINING XHTML SYNTAX

In this chapter

SYNTAX AND STRUCTURE

To build a strong understanding of XHTML, we look to the structure of the markup language itself. You might remember the painful task of diagramming sentences in grammar school. You might already know that working with XHTML, although similar, isn't quite as painful. However, it does follow certain rules of order.

XHTML is really quite logical, unlike the English language (and many other languages, for that matter). Certainly, there are exceptions to rules, and there are modifications or interpretations of those rules. However, after a sense of the basic structure is intact, it's easy to see that XHTML is simply a set of logical pieces that make up a fairly sensible language.

Although change has been the natural state of XHTML, and HTML before it, these changes usually do *not* affect the basic rules. As aspects of the language become obsolete and new components are added to the language, the *syntax*, or correct structure, rarely, if ever, changes.

→ For more about the nature of XHTML as a changing language, **see** Chapter 1, "Understanding XHTML 1.0," **p. 9**.

To understand the concept of syntax, think of a sentence. You have to have a subject and a verb. Adjectives and adverbs are added to provide color and quality, making that sentence more descriptive.

DOCUMENT CONFORMANCE AND DOCUMENT TYPE DEFINITIONS

In Chapter 2, "XHTML Foundations," I revisited the HTML 4.01 standard, where I reviewed conformance concepts and Document Type Definitions allowed within HTML 4.01. The information in this section will be very familiar to you now, as XHTML 1.0 builds heavily on the concepts in HTML 4.01, but with the influence of XML.

A conforming document is one that adheres to all the rules of the vocabulary as set forth by the standards committee. In the case of XHTML 1.0, there are several rules to which a document must conform. Within conformance rules are specific vocabularies that define the individual language of the document.

For a document to conform to the XHTML 1.0, it must adhere to the following:

- The document must validate against one of the three DTDs—Strict, Transitional, or Frameset
- The root element of an XHTML 1.0 document is `<html>`
- The root element declares an XHTML namespace using the `xmlns` attribute
- A DOCTYPE (document type) definition must appear in the document prior to the root element

Figure 5.1 shows a basic XHTML document broken down to its necessary parts.

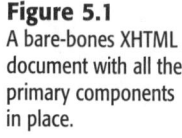

Figure 5.1
A bare-bones XHTML document with all the primary components in place.

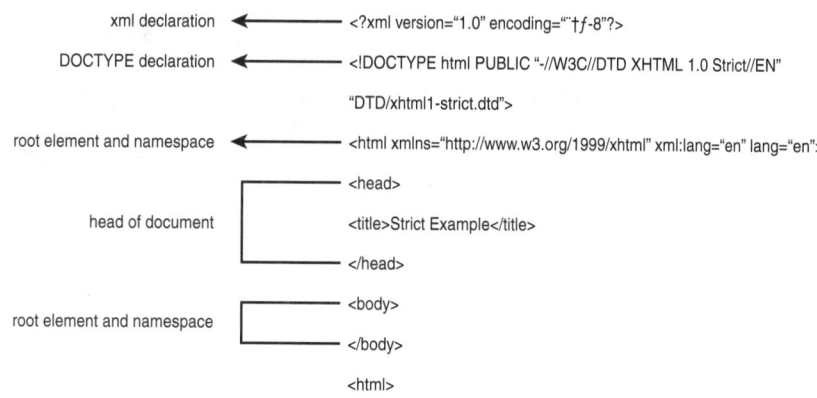

xml declaration ← `<?xml version="1.0" encoding="˝†ƒ-8"?>`

DOCTYPE declaration ← `<!DOCTYPE html PUBLIC "-//W3C//DTD XHTML 1.0 Strict//EN"`

`"DTD/xhtml1-strict.dtd">`

root element and namespace ← `<html xmlns="http://www.w3.org/1999/xhtml" xml:lang="en" lang="en">`

head of document
- `<head>`
- `<title>Strict Example</title>`
- `</head>`

root element and namespace
- `<body>`
- `</body>`

`<html>`

About the XML Declaration in XHTML

A recommended, but not absolutely necessary, component to XHTML 1.0 documents is the XML declaration, `<?xml version="1.0"?>`.

The XML declaration is used to define the document as an XML document and describe the XML version.

Many XHTML authors leave the XML declaration out because it is not understood by many browsers. Using it will cause the code to render improperly or not render at all if used.

There is a problem with leaving the XML declaration out, however. Because the XML declaration allows you to specify the character encoding within a document (this is important for documents that use non-ASCII encoding), leaving it out leaves your pages vulnerable to improper rendering of special characters. As a workaround, you can include a META tag in the head portion of your document that defines the character encoding you're using (this will usually be UTF-8 or UTF-16):

`<meta http-equiv="Content-Type" content="text/html;charset=UTF-8" />`

You will see examples in this book that include the XML declaration, that do not include the declaration, and that do or do not use the META tag workaround. It's important that you determine which approach is best for your unique needs.

For more information on character encoding, please see **www.unicode.org**.

Note

It's interesting to point out that XHTML is the first instance where we see an attribute and value included in the html root.

Again, as I covered in Chapter 2, the vocabulary rule sets used in Web markup are called *document type definitions*, or DTDs. In XHTML 1.0, as with HTML 4.01, there are only three preset dictionaries. How you write your XHTML documents depend on the vocabulary set you choose.

> **Note**
>
> In XML, and for future versions of XHTML, DTDs can be customized. This adds a great deal of power to the developer's toolkit, for he or she can define the rules and the actual tags that a document must use to conform to that common language. So, if a company makes a special product, they can create their own vocabulary to manage that product. Or, DTDs specific to entire industries, such as medical or financial, can share DTDs specific to their unique needs.

→ To learn more about DTDs, **see** Chapter 22, "Document Type Definitions in Detail," **p. 485**.

The three DTDs available for your use in XHTML 1.0 are

- Strict
- Transitional
- Frameset

You should immediately recognize these DTDs, for they are the same DTDs available in HTML 4.01. The actual vocabularies are somewhat different, however, reflecting the rigor and syntactical shifts that occurred in XHTML since HTML became an XML application.

→ Want more information on rigor and syntactical changes between HTML and XHTML 1.0? **See** Chapter 6, "Well-Formed XHTML Documents," **p. 89**.

To implement the DTDs effectively, let's look at the primary concepts inherent to each.

XHTML 1.0 STRICT DTD

XHTML 1.0 that follows the strict document type definition is the most rigorous—and the most pure—of XHTML syntax.

The following general concepts must be followed for a document to be validated as a strict XHTML 1.0 document:

- Only elements, attributes, and values defined in the XTHML 1.0 Recommendation are used
- Nothing deprecated or obsolete is ever used
- Style is removed from document formatting
- Deprecation of style tags in favor of style sheets
- Recommendation to use style positioning over table grids for layout

When writing a strict XHTML 1.0 document, you'll use the strict DOCTYPE declaration, as follows:

```
<!DOCTYPE html PUBLIC "-//W3C//DTD XHTML 1.0 Strict//EN" "DTD/xhtml1-strict.dtd">
```

Listing 5.1 shows a strict and conforming XHTML 1.0 document:

Listing 5.1   A Strict and Conforming XHTML 1.0 Shell

```
<?xml version="1.0"?>
<!DOCTYPE html PUBLIC "-//W3C//DTD XHTML 1.0 Strict//EN"
```

```
"http://www.w3.org/TR/xhtml1/DTD/xhtml1-strict.dtd">
<html xmlns="http://www.w3.org/1999/xhtml">
<head>
<title>Strict Document Sample</title>

</head>
<body>


</body>
</html>
```

XHTML 1.0 TRANSITIONAL DTD

Transitional XHTML 1.0 is the more forgiving vocabulary within the standard. This forgiveness appears in general concepts rather than syntactical adherence. In other words, you must follow XML

syntax rules and rules for well-formed documents. But, you do have leeway with certain elements, attributes, and code approaches.

A transitional XHTML 1.0 document

- Allows tags from HTML 3.2 and HTML 4.01
- Allows use of presentational markup, such as the font element
- Encourages the use of style sheets
- Allows simultaneous use of style sheets and presentational markup

Note

Because of more flexible practices, XHTML 1.0 transitional is the most real-world friendly and accessible document type definition at this point.

Transitional XHTML 1.0 documents use the transitional DOCTYPE declaration:

```
<!DOCTYPE html PUBLIC "-//W3C//DTD XHTML 1.0 Transitional//
EN" "DTD/xhtml1-transitional.dtd">
```

Listing 5.2 provides a look at a transitional XHTML 1.0 document.

LISTING 5.2 A TRANSITIONAL XHTML 1.0 SHELL

```
<?xml version="1.0"?>
<!DOCTYPE html PUBLIC "-//W3C//DTD XHTML 1.0 Transitional//EN"
"http://www.w3.org/TR/xhtml1/DTD/xhtml1-transitional.dtd">
<html xmlns="http://www.w3.org/1999/xhtml">
<head>
<title>Transitional Document Sample</title>

</head>
<body>


</body>
</html>
```

XHTML 1.0 FRAMESET DTD

The Frameset DTD denotes a document as a frameset. Any frameset you create in XHTML 1.0 must be declared as such or it will not validate.

The Frameset DTD

- Exists to create valid framesets in accordance with XHTML 1.0
- Allows the use of transitional and strict XHTML 1.0
- Adopts new HTML 4.01 elements into the standard: `frame`, `frameset`, `noframes`, and `iframe`

The Frameset DTD in XHTML 1.0 requires the following DOCTYPE declaration:

```
<!DOCTYPE html PUBLIC "-//W3C//DTD XHTML 1.0 Frameset//EN" "DTD/xhtml1-frameset.dtd">
```

Listing 5.3 is a conforming frameset in XHTML 1.0.

LISTING 5.3   FRAMESET IN XHTML 1.0

```
<?xml version="1.0"?>
<!DOCTYPE html PUBLIC "-//W3C//DTD XHTML 1.0 Frameset//EN"
"http://www.w3.org/TR/xhtml1/DTD/xhtml1-frameset.dtd">

<html xmlns="http://www.w3.org/1999/xhtml">
<head>
<title>Frameset Document Sample</title>

</head>
<frameset>


</frameset>
</html>
```

ELEMENTS, ATTRIBUTES, AND VALUES

XHTML is at its heart, no different from a simple sentence. In fact, the components of XHTML follow the same concept as subject, verb, and descriptor.

The central pillar of all XHTML documents is the *element*. XHTML elements are made up of a Tags and their content.

A tag is enclosed in two angle brackets, the less than < and greater than > symbols. There are starting tags and end tags. The tag can be seen as the identity of XHTML, it says "do this." But tags become powerful with modification, and that modification begins with an *attribute*. Attributes are made up of Attribute Names and Attribute Values.

Attributes are like verbs in that they promote activity—with them, the XHTML tag can suddenly come to life and not only do something, but do it in a certain way.

Attributes must be modified by an *attribute value*. A value defines the way an attribute will act. Think of an adverb modifying an action—How did John run? John ran quickly! Values add concepts such as "quickly," telling the tag, and the attribute, not only what and how, but to what specific degree.

Metaphorically, the sentence "John ran quickly" equals the basic syntactical structure of XHTML. "John" is the equivalent of an XHTML tag, "ran" is much like an XHTML attribute, and "quickly" is the value ascribed to that attribute and ultimately describes the way in which the tag will act.

ELEMENTS

There are specific as well as general rules and conventions about XHTML tags. The first is that all start tags are contained within a less-than and greater-than symbol, as follows:

```
<link>
```

Note that there are no spaces between the symbols and the tag, and no spaces between the letters that denote the tag.

Other rules and conventions involve non-empty and empty elements.

NON-EMPTY ELEMENTS

A non-empty element is an element that contains information within an opening and closing tag. A good example of this is the `<html>` element, which contains the document's content information within its opening and closing counterparts, `<html>` and `</html>` respectively.

Another non-empty element to study in the context of XHTML is the paragraph element, which requires a tag set of `<p>` and `</p>` surrounding the element's contained data. In this case, that data is text, as in the following code snippet:

```
<p>The text in this paragraph makes up the data that is contained by the XHTML
paragraph element.</p>
```

In HTML, it was perfectly legal to use an opening `<p>` only, despite the fact that there was data contained within the element:

```
<p>The text in this paragraph makes up the data that is contained by the XHTML
paragraph element.
```

However, in XHTML, you *must* close any non-empty element. Those of you who are already quite familiar with HTML will know that there are other instances where HTML allowed for non-empty elements to have no terminating tag, such as the list item, or `li` tag. In XHTML, tags that are not empty *must* terminate.

So, while the following code is valid in HTML

```
<ul>
<li>One tag
<li>Two tags
<li>Three tags
<li>Four
</ul>
```

it is *not* valid in XHTML. Instead, you must close the non-empty element, as follows:

```
<ul>
<li>One tag</li>
<li>Two tags</li>
<li>Three tags</li>
<li>Four</li>
</ul>
```

A little more code to write, but the results are consistent and well-formed XHTML.

EMPTY ELEMENTS

An empty element is a tag that contains no content. For example, the img tag displays an image, but has no closing tag and contains no content outside of the tag and its related attributes and values. The same is true of break tags, horizontal rules, meta tags, and the link tag.

In XML, all empty elements require termination. Similarly, XHTML demands this termination. XHTML borrows a markup convention from XML to solve this concern, which was never addressed in HTML. The termination of an empty element is a forward slash after the element and before the greater-than symbol:

```
<element/>
```

Note

In order for XHTML to be read across HTML browsers, which weren't built in most cases to interpret XML, a space is added to ensure that the markup is read and displayed. So, instead of XML's `<element/>`, in XHTML we use `<element />`.

This means that any empty element will now contain this termination. Here's an example using the img element:

```
<img src="images/molly_logo.gif" width="50" height="50" border="0" alt="molly.com
logo" />
```

ATTRIBUTES

Attributes, as mentioned, modify the action of a tag. Many tags can act perfectly fine alone, but there are a variety of tags that *must* have attributes to function properly.

Many attributes in HTML have historically had to do with modifying the way something on a page looks. In the strict DTDs of HTML 4.01 and XHTMl 1.0, any attribute that defines a style is not allowed; instead, you are to use style sheets. However, you can use these attributes and their companion values freely in transitional HTML 4.01 and XHTML 1.0.

Caution

Attributes, when applied to a tag, *exist only in the opening tag*. Never, ever put an attribute into a closing tag. For example, `<body bgcolor="#ffffff">` is a correct syntactical string, and will be closed simply with `</body>`. I've seen many student coders try to close a tag with the attribute, coding the closing tag as `</body bgcolor="#ffffff">`. This is completely illegal, and you should be vigilant in making sure that you never do it.

Attributes are often whole-words, and sometimes they are partial words. Some whole word attributes include `align`, `color`, `link`, and `face`. Partial-word examples include `src` for "source," and `vlink` for "visited link."

Where do attributes go in a statement? They follow the tag and one space:

```
<body bgcolor ...
```

and are then modified by a value before the tag is closed.

A tag can have more than one attribute, and in fact, some tags take on many attributes at the same time. In this case, the syntax follows the same concept: first the tag, a space, and then an attribute. The attribute will receive a value, and then a space is once again introduced *before* the next attribute:

```
<body bgcolor="#ffffff" text="#000000">
```
and so forth, until all the attributes and companion values are included.

→ For more information on the `body` element and its attributes, **see** Chapter 7, "Structuring XHTML Documents," **p. 103**.

VALUES

Values are the defining aspect of attributes and ultimately modify the tag.

Their responsibility is to determine the way a particular activity is to take place by quantifying or qualifying it in some way.

Attribute values, like attributes, can be made up of a whole word. If I'm using the `<div>`, or division, tag, and I want to align all the information in that division in a transitional XHTML document, I can select from several values that will modify the `align` attribute. Such values include `left`, `right`, `center`, and `justify`.

A resulting string would be

```
<div align="right">
```

and, because I know that the `<div>` tag does in fact require a closing tag, I would be sure to end my division with

```
</div>
```

Now, all the information in that division will be aligned to the right, because I've first used the `<div>` tag to identify the start of the division, modified that tag with the `align` attribute, and further modified the attribute with the *value* of `right`. This action will continue until I've appropriately closed the division, `</div>`.

Some values are numeric, referring to pixels or percentages, browser-defined sizes, or hexadecimal numbers to define color. A pixel value example is well described by the `width` attribute. If I'm coding a table, I might define that table's width as being 585 pixels wide. The syntax for this would be

```
<table width="585">
```

and, of course, the table would be closed using the `</table>` tag in the appropriate place.

Similarly, I can use a percentage value in the same instance. The code would then be

```
<table width="100%">
```

and in this case, the table would flex to 100 percent of the available space.

➜ For more information on the `<table>` tag, including its attributes and values, **see** Chapter 14, "Laying Out Tables Within XHTML Documents," **p. 243**.

Browser-defined sizes are those sizes that the browser selects. In other words, you cannot predetermine the exact size, such as with pixels, but you can approximate the size. The best example of this is with the deprecated `<font>` tag attribute `size`. The `size` attribute can opt to take a value ranging from 1–7, 1 being the smallest, 7 the largest:

```
<font size="5">
```

Any text between this and the closing `</font>` tag takes on the browser's interpretation of a size 5. Figure 5.2 shows a paragraph of size 5 text as viewed through Netscape Navigator for Windows. The same page is shown in Figure 5.3, but in Internet Explorer. On close examination, you'll see that there is a visual difference in the respective interpretation of the numeric value.

Figure 5.2
Text sizing in Netscape. I've set the size to 5.

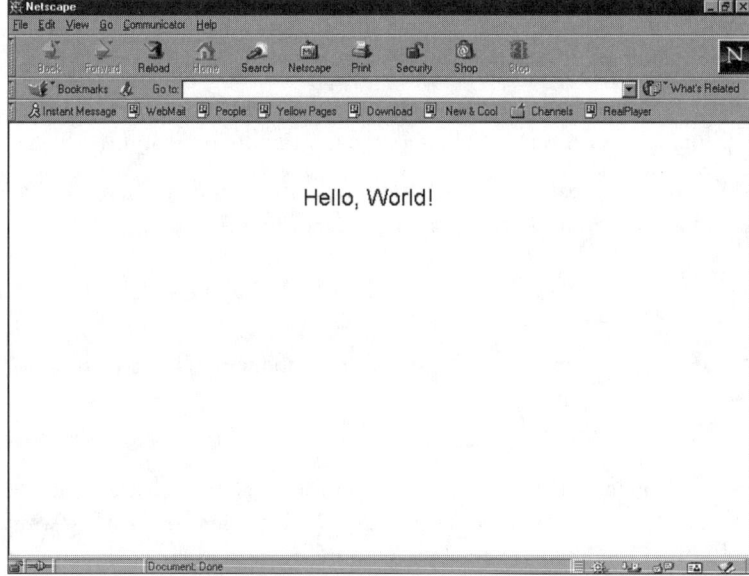

Figure 5.3

The same information in Internet Explorer. Compare this with Figure 5.2, and you'll find a minor difference in the size and a more significant difference in the placement of the text on the page.

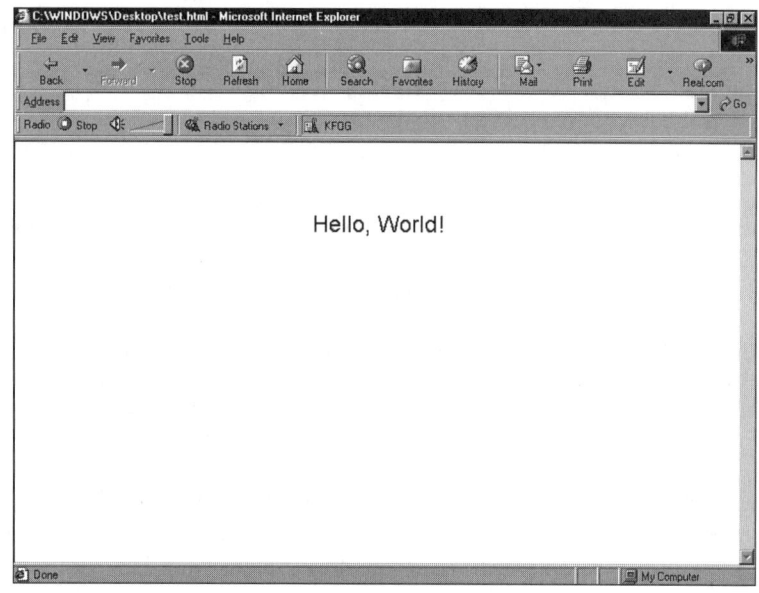

Caution

Because different browsers and platforms interpret and display browser-defined sizes differently, you will have to test your pages by using as many variations as possible to ensure that you are getting results that are satisfactory.

Another numeric type of value is known as *hexadecimal* code. This is the base-16 alphanumeric code that defines the range of available HTML colors. You've already seen an example of a hexadecimal color earlier, when I demonstrated the `bgcolor` and `text` attributes:

```
<body bgcolor="#ffffff" text="#000000">
```

The `ffffff` code translates into a background color of white, with the text value of `000000` as black.

→ To learn more about hex codes, **see** Chapter 25, "Color Concepts," **p. 527**.

Tip from

molly

Always include the hash # sign in each of your hexadecimal values.

There are other types of values of which to be aware. One such value is a relative or absolute link, meaning that a directory, series of directories, filename, or complete Web address can be included in certain attributes to fulfill a value:

```
<a href="http://www.molly.com/">Go to My Home Page</a>
```

PART

II

CH

5

This markup will create a link that, when clicked, goes to my home page. The a tag, or anchor tag, creates a link; the attribute is `href`, or hypertext transfer protocol reference; and the value is the URL, **http://www.molly.com/**.

Similarly, I can point to a directory and an image:

```
<img src="images/molly.gif" />
```

In this case, the tag is `img`, or image (which, again, is an *empty element* and must be terminated in XHTML), the attribute is `src` ("source"), and the value is a combination of the images directory and the specific file, `molly.gif`.

Another interesting value example is the companion value to the `alt` attribute. This attribute appears in image or object tags and offers a descriptive definition of the image or object for those individuals who cannot or do not want to see the image or object:

```
<img src="molly.gif" alt="picture of Molly" />
```

In this situation, you see that the value ascribed to the `alt` attribute is actually a self-defined series of words used to describe the picture. You also can see in this example how a tag can have multiple attributes with corresponding values.

→ To locate information on the anchor tag and its attributes, **see** Chapter 12, "Linking Pages with Standard Links," **p. 199**.

→ If you want to examine image syntax in detail, **see** Chapter 13, "Using Images in XHTML Documents," **p. 221**.

By now you probably have noticed that all values are preceded by an = symbol (the equal sign), and the value is within quotation marks. With the exception of hexadecimal values, which add a # (pound sign) to the alphanumeric value, this is a proper and consistent way of coding and identifying values within an XHTML statement.

SPECIAL CHARACTERS

There is a subset of information in XHTML that is referred to as the "special character set." This is XHTML syntax that creates punctuation and symbols necessary to content formatting.

Interestingly, many WYSIWYG programs *always* use special characters to invoke punctuation marks such as parentheses, quotations, or brackets. However, many hand coders simply type the punctuation and rarely is there any problem with a browser interpreting the ASCII, or text-based, character.

The best use for special characters is to create symbols or to clearly differentiate ASCII from XHTML.

Special characters look nothing like a standard HTML tag. A perfect example is the copyright symbol, which can be coded as

`&copy;`

The & symbol is the denotation for a special character's beginning, and the ; semicolon closes the character. This way, the browser knows not to display the literal word "copy," but interprets the entire piece as the actual © copyright symbol, as shown in Figure 5.4.

Figure 5.4
You can create the copyright symbol using a special character in XHTML.

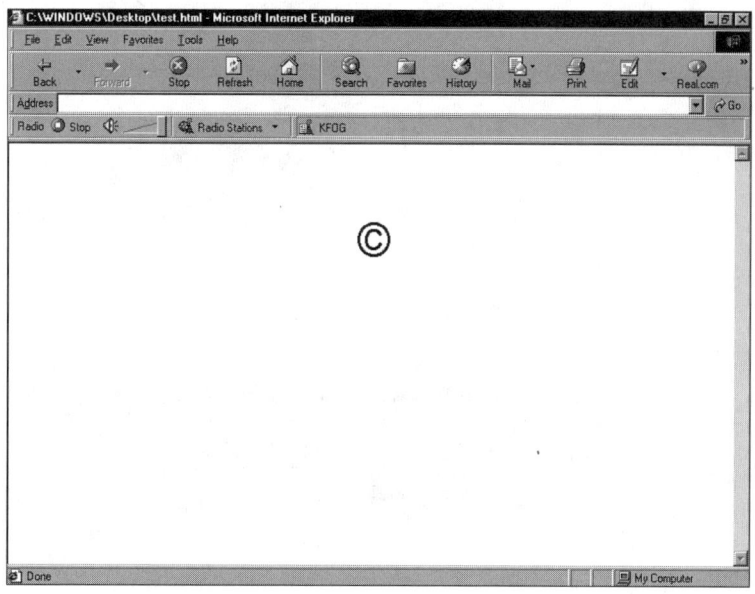

Sometimes, I want to show XHTML code examples on an XHTML page. Special characters allow me to do this—because otherwise the XHTML would be interpreted literally. If I type in `<img src="dude.gif" />` the browser isn't going to display that literal text information, but rather interpret the XHTML tag and go out looking for the image named `dude.gif`.

To make my syntax visually available to you, I would simply code the less-than and greater-than symbols as special characters, and then the literal string will be displayed rather than the XHTML:

`&lt;IMG src="dude.gif"&gt;`

Figures 5.5 and 5.6 clearly show why special characters are so handy.

Figure 5.5
Without special characters, the browser interprets the information as XHTML and displays the image.

Figure 5.6
With special characters, I can display an example of XHTML within an XHTML page.

The special character set is vast, sometimes with several codes representing the same character.

WELL-FORMED CODE

As you've already noticed, the exceptions and variations on these basic XHTML fundamentals sometimes appear to be vague.

This especially becomes problematic when using software applications that don't take the rules of XHTML into account and throw out syntactical rules. Someone studying the output of a WYSIWYG application will often learn *bad code*. In XHTML, this is especially problematic, because to be a valid XHTML document, the syntax rules must conform.

Does this mean browsers won't properly interpret bad code? Not at all. Browsers tend to be forgiving of lousy code. Just as you and I tend to understand vernacular speech, a browser recognizes most sloppy code. However, if you want to write proper XHTML documents, you've got to follow the rules!

 Wondering if there are really any hard and fast rules to the issue of structure and symmetry in coding pages? In some cases there are, but in most instances it is more a matter of ease of coding and speed of debugging; see "Line Length" in the "Troubleshooting" section near the end of this chapter.

However, every so often there's going to be one piece of bad code that will choke a browser completely. Imagine speaking with someone from a different part of the country. Although you might readily recognize what a person means when he or she says "Let's go have a pop" instead of "Let's go have a soda," you might not understand when they say "Hey, home, let's go chill." As the vernacular becomes more particular to a given person, or to follow the metaphor, a particular software program, the code gets harder and harder to understand.

You can avoid this problem by putting XHTML rules to work. This way, when you see something broken, you'll know it—and when you're searching for the reasons why nothing is displaying on a browser despite all the code you've created, you'll know how to go about troubleshooting the problem.

TROUBLESHOOTING

LINE LENGTH

Is there a limit to the number of characters on one line of code?

No. You can actually put the code for an entire page on one line. The browser knows how to parse the tags so the page appears as you've coded it. Just because you can do this, however, does not mean that you should. It is difficult to edit an XHTML file without any line breaks, and also leaves you open to coding errors.

DESIGNING FOR THE REAL WORLD

TROUBLESHOOTING YOUR MARKUP

The biggest benefit to looking at your code closely is that you're bound to catch other mistakes before they become glaring errors. When you're coding by hand, it's easy to put a closing tag in the wrong syntactical order (instead of) or using the > , instead of the < when you're typing quickly. In a large block of text, however, you might not notice the typo right away.

XHTML actually provides the opportunity for authors to create very streamlined, clean, error-free markup. Look carefully at your elements, attributes, and values. And, follow good XHTML coding practices. We'll take a look at the importance of well-formed documents in Chapter 6, which will aid you in writing trouble-free XHTML for the Web and beyond.

WELL-FORMED XHTML DOCUMENTS

In this chapter

UNDERSTANDING RIGOR AND WELL-FORMEDNESS

Standards are like glue. A high-quality glue will keep all the parts that need to remain bonded nice and snug. The lower the quality of the glue, the more separation and potential weakness enters the bond.

Rigor is a high-quality glue. Using specific and rigid rules, an author can write documents whose elements are strongly bonded to one another. When building sites with many documents, those documents adhere not only within themselves, but to other documents within the Web site.

WHY RIGOR AND WELL-FORMEDNESS MATTER

Why is it important to achieve rigor in document authoring? There are a lot of ideas regarding this, but some of the opinions I've heard regarding why we as authors should adhere to standards include

- The code within sites is consistent and therefore more easy to troubleshoot or share documents.
- It creates industry-wide compliance among authors, making it easier for people to move from company to company and maintain accuracy in the code they do.
- Compliance sends a strong and unified voice to software vendors that they, too, should create standards-aware products if they expect to be able to continue selling development products.
- Similarly, browser vendors are placed into the position of having to comply with standards *before* innovating. This means better, more stable results for authors trying to create documents across browsers.
- Code innovations can take place from a mature foundation instead of one still finding its walking legs. HTML itself is a prime example of what can happen when the foundation isn't mature. The syntax turned to chaos! And, although that was important for the rapid growth of *how* we work on the Web, slowing down and catching our breaths can make the future—which uses markup to extend to the wireless world and beyond—a lot more stable.
- You can learn something once, and then quickly pick up its applications. This is especially important where XML is concerned. If you know one XML application, it becomes much easier to learn XHTML, WML, SVG, and so on, because these applications are bonded to one another through the common glue of their meta-language, XML.

These ideas are just that, ideas. There is no rule here. Rather, the suggestion is to follow the rules to avoid problems when you don't know them.

COMPLICATIONS OF INCORRECT CODE

And, problems do indeed arise when rules aren't known, aren't followed, or are purposely broken.

Some of the very problems designers and developers are facing today have to do with weak foundations—bad glue.

If we look at all the reasons *to* follow standards, we can quickly see their destructive counterparts:

- Imagine that one or more of these individuals takes on a new job. He or she will find that entering a different authoring environment might mean complying with authoring practices completely different from the methods they've employed thus far. So, that individual now has to undo certain habits. Knowing the standards well to begin with will help ease this person into the new production methods rather than cause him great frustration and waste of time.

- Software vendors in the past years have been able to create software that creates markup that is as seemingly arbitrary from one package to the next. What's more, the code in these packages tends to be sloppy because it *can* be. Nothing compelling enough   such as an informed buying public—has existed to demand better products.

- The same sloppiness is inherent in most popular Web browsers. If any pro-standard argument is compelling enough, try the argument that says browsers must first adhere to the standards with which we're all working before adding innovative features. This gives us all a firm base to stand on, which we as developers and designers most certainly do not have at this time.

- Problems with code have led to chaos in the world of education and training. Pick up one book on HTML, and it tells you how to do something a certain way. Pick up another, it says to do it quite another way. Both books might be correct in theory, but in practice, the problems of inconsistency, messy code, and difficult troubleshooting all come in to play.

Rigor in XHTML 1.0 is one of the most critical parts of standards adherence. By following the methods set out in this chapter, you as an author become quite empowered to make the best possible decisions about how, and why, to code according to a given standard.

SYMMETRY AND WELL-FORMED DOCUMENTS

The concept of a *well-formed document* is critical to validation and conformance within XHTML 1.0. Well-formedness relates to the symmetrical relationship between elements in an XHTML document.

In HTML, this well-formedness does exist in a vague sense. One assumes that rules should be followed despite no formal discussion existing about a well-formed document. But, a self-perpetuating cycle of sloppy code practices leading to forgiving browsers, which in turn lead to even sloppier code practices has existed for far too long. A great place to begin getting rigor back into your authoring approach is to embrace XHTML's well-formedness concepts.

HORIZONTAL SYMMETRY

Horizontal symmetry is not an official or even highly accurate term, but it's a useful one I use describe the creation of well-formed elements within a document's content. This means most every tag you're going to use within the body of a document.

Let's say I'm creating a transitional document, and I want to add two tags to modify a bit of text, bold, `<b>...</b>` and italic, `<i>...</i>`, rendering that text both bold and italic.

Symmetry means opening and closing the tags in the proper order. First let me bold the text selection:

```
<b>My red balloon was swept out of my hands and into the sky.</b>
```

and now I'll add italics:

```
<i><b>My red balloon was swept out of my hands and into the sky.</b></i>
```

Because I approached the code methodically, I didn't run into a problem. I could have started with italics:

```
<i>My red balloon was swept out of my hands and into the sky.</i>
```

and then added the bold:

```
<b><i>My red balloon was swept out of my hands and into the sky.</i></b>
```

Either example is correct—it doesn't matter which tag comes first, the bold or the italic, as long as the tags resolve in *order*! What I *cannot* have is the following:

```
<b><i>My red balloon was swept out of my hands and into the sky.</b></i>
```

or

```
<i><b>My red balloon was swept out of my hands and into the sky.</i></b>.
```

These are syntactically incorrect, causing a disturbance in symmetry and therefore in well-formedness.

VERTICAL SYMMETRY

Vertical symmetry is the same concept, although I use it to describe elements that are mostly related to document structure in general.

See Listing 6.1, which shows a transitional XHTML document, properly formed.

LISTING 6.1   A TRANSITIONAL XHTML DOCUMENT

```
<?xml version="1.0"?>
<!DOCTYPE html PUBLIC "-//W3C//DTD XHTML 1.0 Transitional//EN"
"DTD/xhtml1-transitional.dtd">
<html xmlns="http://www.w3.org/1999/xhtml">
<head>
<title>A well-formed XHTML document</title>

</head>
<body>
```

LISTING 6.1   CONTINUED

```
</body>
</html>
```

Vertical symmetry relates to the logical open/close relationship between tags on the vertical axis. For example, my html tags encase my head tags and so forth. There is no overlap. Listing 6.2 is an example of asymmetrical, illegal code.

LISTING 6.2   ASYMMETRICAL, MALFORMED CODE

```
<?xml version="1.0"?>
<!DOCTYPE html PUBLIC "-//W3C//DTD XHTML 1.0 Transitional//EN"
    "http://www.w3.org/TR/xhtml1l/DTD/transitional.dtd">


<html xmlns="http://www.w3.org/1999/xhtml">
<head>

<title>Malformed Document</title>
</head>

<body>


</html>
</body>
```

See how my closing </html> tag comes, in this case, *before* my closing </body> tag? This is a major no-no! Will a browser forgive you? It very well might, but even if it does, the code is *not* considered XHTML, because it is not well-formed.

THE CONTAINER METHOD

If you learn to think about elements as containers, you avoid problems with symmetry. This becomes even more important when we are using troublesome elements, such as font, which as you know can be used in transitional XHTML 1.0 documents.

This tag, although deprecated in the HTML 4.0 standard, and not allowed in XHTML 1.0 strict, is in such wide conventional use—due to browser compatibility issues—that we must address it and its problems. Putting it aside for a more elegant approach such as style sheets is part of HTML 4.0's and XHTML 1.0's wisdom, but until we have widespread compliance, we have to be very, very careful of how we approach the idiosyncrasies of this tag. Learning symmetry well is one of the ways that you can avoid problems with font, as well as with other XHTML tags.

Figure 6.1 shows how symmetry works. Note in the top image that there are *no* intersecting lines. Each container is appropriately configured. However, when I have a piece of asymmetrical code and draw my lines, they intersect (see Figure 6.1). This method is a test, and proof, of horizontal symmetry.

Figure 6.1
Horizontal symmetry. If the lines don't intersect, the markup is well-formed. If the lines do intersect, they are malformed.

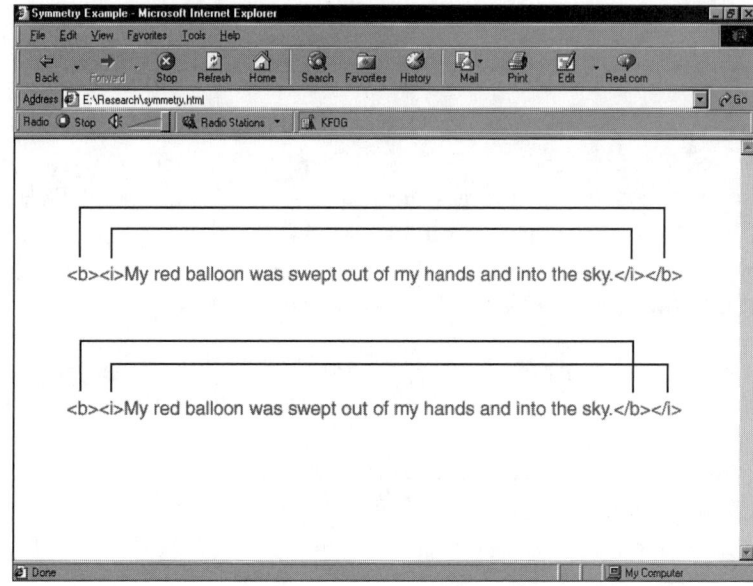

You can do this test with vertical symmetry, too. Figure 6.2 shows how.

Figure 6.2
Vertical symmetry. Clean lines, clean markup. Intersecting lines mean a malformed document.

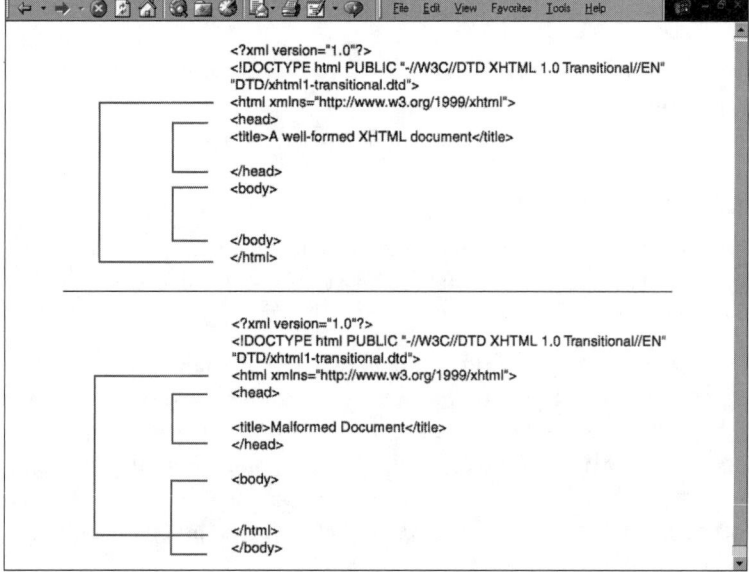

CASE SENSITIVITY

How case is managed in authoring also becomes part of the way documents are properly formed.

IN HTML

Tags and attributes can, in HTML, be in upper- or lowercase, depending upon personal tastes and needs. HTML itself is *not case sensitive*. As a result you can, in HTML

- Use all uppercase in tags and attributes
- Use all lowercase in tags and attributes
- Mix upper- and lowercase in tags and attributes

View the source on any arbitrary page out on the Web, and you'll see HTML tags and attributes in uppercase, lowercase, and mixed case, whereas attributes and values are in lowercase. Listing 6.3 shows an HTML 4.01 page using all three combinations.

LISTING 6.3   MIXED CASE IN HTML 4.01

```
<!DOCTYPE HTML PUBLIC "-//W3C//DTD HTML 4.0 Transitional//EN"
"http://www.w3.org/TR/REC-html40/loose.dtd">
<HTML>
<HEAD>
<TITLE>HTML Example of Case</TITLE>
</HEAD>
<BODY>
<P ALIGN="LEFT">These tags and attributes are all upper case</P>
<p align="right">These tags and attributes are all lower case</p>
<P align="center">These tags and attributes are all mixed case</P>
</BODY>
</HTML>
```

Ironically, HTML and browsers are so forgiving that you could even mix case within a given element and attribute:

```
<P AliGn="LefT"> . . . </p>
```

And this code will more than likely render properly.

IN XML

Of course, XML demands rigor. However, XML, unlike HTML, *is case sensitive*. This means that case is a critical component within your syntax. So, I can have an XML element that looks like this:

```
<desktop>

</desktop>
```

And I can use this code in the same document:

```
<DESKTOP>

</DESKTOP>
```

And I can add this element to the mix, too:

```
<DeskTop>

</DeskTop>
```

And all these elements are *individual, independent, and unique*, because XML is case sensitive.

In other words, desktop is not DESKTOP is not DeskTop.

IN XHTML 1.0

To create a method for XHTML, its authors decided to make all XHTML elements and attributes lowercase. This means XHTML is *case-specific*. You simply cannot use anything but lowercase markup in an XHTML document, and that is that. No mixed case, no upper-case. Only lowercase. Anything else departs from conforming XHTML code.

> **Note**
>
> You'll probably notice that the DOCTYPE is all uppercase, even though everything in an XHTML 1.0 document is supposed to be lowercase. The reason? The DOCTYPE declaration is not considered to be part of the XHTML markup. Rather, it is a separate piece of markup responsible for declaring the document itself.

ATTRIBUTE QUOTING

As with case, there are significant differences in the way that quotation marks are used in XHTML 1.0. Simply said, HTML is rather inconsistent, whereas in XHTML 1.0, rigorous use of quotes is the name of the day.

IN HTML

The use of quotations in HTML is inconsistent. For example, you could write

```
<div align="left">
```

or

```
<div align=left>
```

and either one is considered acceptable.

However, although I can confidently leave the quotations out from around a width="x" or align="center" attribute and value, making the width=x and align=center, there are many cases in which removing the quotations means trouble. Sometimes, an attribute will require a quote for a certain browser to understand it, or it won't render properly

One such instance is around hexadecimal values. In a body tag, for example, I can potentially render my HTML code unreadable by missing a quotation around those values. The same is true of any time I use a URL or directory/filename value for an anchor or image tag.

I've also seen this happen quite often with magic target names:

```
<a href="nextpage.html" target=_blank>
```

Another problem is partially quoting an attribute. Certainly, this happens in XHTML too; accidents, after all, do happen. However, when you aren't required to quote all attributes, it has been my experience that the problem occurs more frequently:

```
<p align="right>
```

Because there is *never* an instance in HTML where it's improper to quote attributes, I recommend anyone authoring HTML documents quote all attributes.

In XML and XHTML

In XML, all attribute values are quoted. Period. The same is true with XHTML. No matter your habits prior to writing XHTML 1.0, the bottom line is that you now *must quote all attribute values*.

MANAGING ELEMENTS

Element management in XHTML 1.0 also is very strict. There are two types of elements, as follows:

- **Non-Empty Elements**—These are elements that contain content within their open and closing tags, such as the paragraph element, the table data element, and the bold element.
- **Empty Elements**—These are elements that contain no data within them. In HTML, these are represented by one tag, such as a break, a horizontal rule, an image tag, or a meta tag.

Changes to the way elements are written is a very important part of the XHTML 1.0 standard.

→ More information on how to manage elements can be found in Chapter 9, "Formatting Text in XHTML," **p. 133**.

Non-Empty Elements

All non-empty elements must take a closing tag. So, if you've got a paragraph, you can't just use the open-tag technique, even though it was perfectly acceptable in HTML:

```
<p>In HTML, you didn't have to use a closing tag in a paragraph for it to be
conforming.
```

In XHTML:

```
<p>You must close your paragraphs in XHTML.</p>
```

The paragraph is quite commonly understood to have these two options. However, a common element that is non-empty and must now have a closing tag is the list item `<li>` element.

In HTML, an unordered list looks like this:

PART

II

CH

6

```
<ul>
<li>Item one
<li>Item two
<li>Item three
</ul>
```

Because the list item element is non-empty (there's content in that list!) you must use a closing tag in XHTML 1.0:

```
<ul>
<li>Item one</li>
<li>Item two</li>
<li>Item three</li>
</ul>
```

> **Note**
>
> Some people have asked me if using an end tag with paragraphs or list items changes the rendering of the content. Sometimes, it does. It depends upon the browser. However, these changes are pretty consistent and easy to get accustomed to. You still need to test your pages with a variety of browsers and platforms to get the best results.

EMPTY ELEMENTS

Empty elements also should be closed. You can close empty elements with a closing tag, but in most cases this just adds extra markup. So what you can do instead is to add a forward slash after the tag and before the closing bracket, like this:

```
<br/>
```

Now, because some browsers don't know how to render this, there's a little workaround that's been used to circumvent that problem. If you add a space before the slash, the browser will ignore the space and the slash, and just interpret a standard HTML `<br>`.

This results in the following:

```
<br />
```

and

```
<hr />
```

> **Note**
>
> Both are legitimate ways of coding in XHTML 1.0, but it is recommended that you use the space before the slash at this time to avoid browser interpretation problems.

The break and horizontal rule tags are pretty obviously empty elements. However, less obvious are elements that don't have closing companions but do contain detailed information. Three very good examples of this are the image tag `<img>`, the link tag `<link>`, and the meta tag, `<meta>`.

There is no difference in the way you'll close these tags in XHTML 1.0 from the way you close any empty element in a conforming XHTML document:

```
<img src="my.gif" />
```

and

```
<meta http-equiv="Content-Type" content="text/html; charset=iso-8859-1" />
```

and

```
<link rel="stylesheet" href="style/molly.css" />
```

Tip from

Naturally, there are other non-empty or empty elements in XHTML 1.0. Just follow the guidelines here to determine how to manage a given element. Typically, a tag that has no companion closing tag and contains no content outside of the opening tag will be an empty element. However, as in the case of the `<p>` and `<li>` tags, if there is no closing tag in HTML, but there is content after the opening tag, that tag is considered in XHTML 1.0 to be a non-empty element, and you should add a closing tag accordingly.

WHITESPACE

Spaces also can cause browser chokes. They are absolutely necessary in certain instances, absolutely disallowed in some instances, and positively ignored in other instances.

Spaces are absolutely necessary between a tag and an attribute, and an attribute and another attribute. `<body bgcolor="#ffffff">` *cannot* be coded as `<bodybgcolor="#ffffff">`. A browser won't know what to do with this information, because it can't separate the element name from the attribute name. It will think that you're trying to use a tag it doesn't understand, `bodybgcolor`, which of course doesn't exist.

Tip from

My good friend and long-time colleague Wil Gerken of *WeeklyWire* insists that browsers are stupid. His advice is to *never* let a browser think for itself. This means that you must always be careful to use proper syntax, eliminating any possibility that a browser will misinterpret your intentions.

Similarly, spaces are required between strings of attributes and values. `<body bgcolor="#ffffff" text="#000000">` *cannot* be coded as `<body bgcolor="#ffffff"text="#000000">`. The spaces are absolutely required to avoid browser code parsing problems.

Spaces are not recommended between an attribute and a value. `<body bgcolor="#ffffff">` *should not* be coded as `<body bgcolor = "#ffffff">`. This also might confuse a browser, which will be unable to identify the attribute and value as a unit that works together.

Additional spaces are completely ignored after the first logical space in body text. For example, if I have four spaces between the word "My" and the words "red balloon" in code, the browser will ignore the additional three spaces completely:

```
<p>My    red balloon was swept out of my hands and into the sky.</p>
```

PART

II

CH

6

In Figure 6.3, I've taken a snapshot of the way this code looks in Netscape. Look, Ma, only one space! The browser ignores everything beyond the logical space.

Figure 6.3
Despite the fact that I've entered four spaces in the code, the browser displays only one.

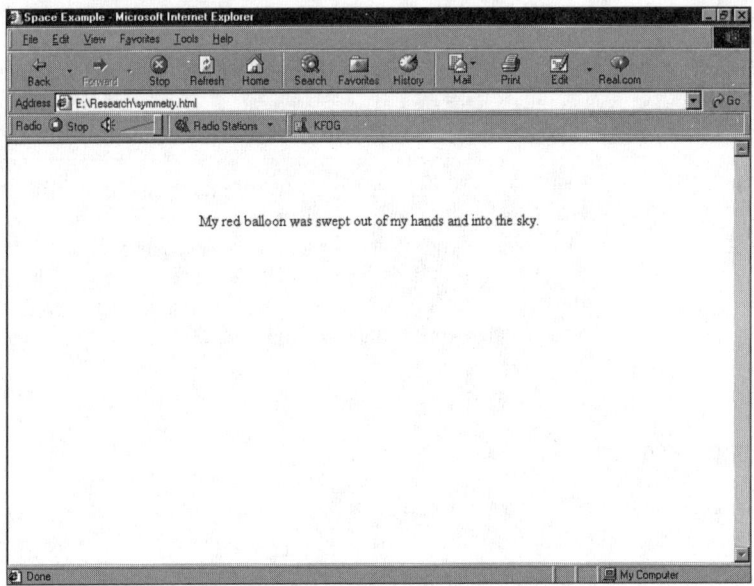

Another place spaces cause concern is between tags and content. In the following example, I hit my spacebar once within the bold tags for the first sentence. In the second sentence, I waited to tap my spacebar until after I coded the closing bold tag:

```
<p><b>This sentence </b>has a space</p>

<p><b>This sentence</b> has a space in the same place.</p>
```

In Figure 6.4, you'll see both sentences appear the same in the context of the browser. However, the spaces I placed into the code are different.

Tip from
molly

How do you avoid inconsistencies with this? My recommendation is to leave your spaces *outside* of the tags,

as shown in the second coded sentence. It's not wrong to do it within the code, but it is confusing. And although there is no noticeable difference in the output when using the `<b>` or `<i>` tags, you will notice a big difference when using the `<u>` tag. It's best to be consistent and keep your tags close to the text.

Spaces are a source of endless frustration for newcomers to XHTML authoring. I've had students stare at a page searching for the problem with their code and not be able to see that it's simply one missing space, or one additional space, where spacing rules must be put into place (okay, I'll admit it used to happen to me a lot, too)!

Figure 6.4
There's no visible difference here, until you look at the underlying code.

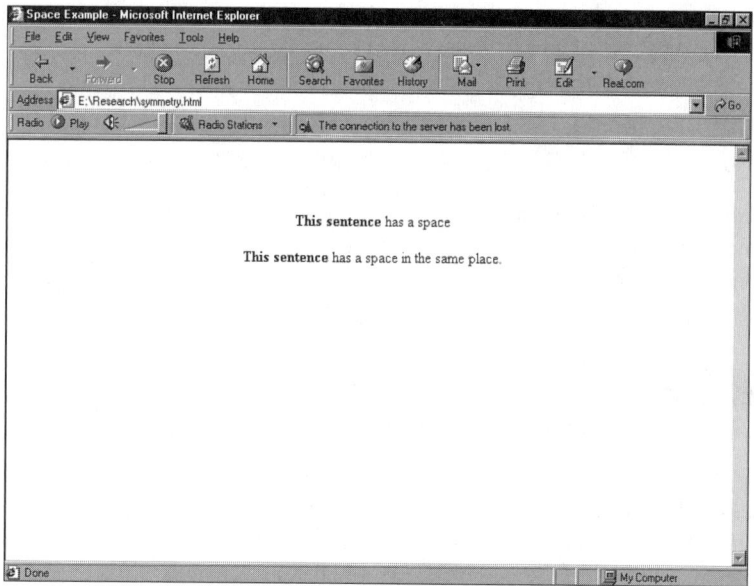

Take the hard-won advice of my many students and keep spaces *after* tags. After finding a space problem and seeing their work finally appear in the browser the way they *thought* it would, they now follow these guidelines. They're sure to keep you out of trouble.

And remember, it's often the browser, and not *you*, who has the problem. Put blame where it's due. Just keep your eyes peeled when trying to debug a site; it might be a space issue contributing to the code problem.

 Really need that space in there but just can't get it to work? Check out "Adding Spaces" in the "Troubleshooting" section near the end of this chapter for help.

TROUBLESHOOTING

ADDING SPACES

If using the spacebar doesn't insert additional spaces within text, how can I add them?

One of the special characters in HTML is a non-breaking space. It is coded as   and you can string as many of these in sequence as necessary.

DESIGNING FOR THE REAL WORLD

Learning proper XHTML syntax is essentially no different from understanding the rules of language.

Most English speakers know that saying "I ain't going to the store" is slang, and, although it's understandable, it ain't, um, isn't correct.

Although I might say "I ain't" in a casual or joking moment, I know that when I want to be formal and professional, I must say, "I'm not going to the store," because this is the correct, sophisticated use of the language.

Similarly, although you might have been forgiven your syntactical slang in HTML, if you use slang in XHTML, your documents will *not* be forgiven.

For this chapter's project, I'd like you to take an HTML page you've written in the past and make it a conforming XHTML document. If you don't have an HTML document, find one on the Web and rewrite it as an XHTML document. Then, use HTML Tidy to validate it and see if you've done the job properly!

Note

You can find HTML Tidy at `validator.w3.org/`. It's also available in some select programs such as HTML-Kit (see Chapter 4, "XHTML Tools.")

XHTML syntax is fairly simplistic. Although it has twists and turns, if you are educated enough in the English language to be reading and understanding this book, you've accommodated a much more complex syntactical system than XHTML. Rely on logic, and use the techniques in this chapter as a strong foundation for all your XHTML code. You can rest assured that the results will be sophisticated, correct, and professional.

STRUCTURING XHTML DOCUMENTS

In this chapter

UNDERSTANDING DOCUMENT STRUCTURE

Just as a human being is structured in a logical way, so is an XHTML document. If you study the shape of your spouse or child, you are likely to notice that they all have a similar structure—even if the *features* of their individual compositions are different.

When I look at myself in the mirror, I see my face, my hair, my eyes, my mouth—my head. And below my head is my body, with its particular physical attributes. My body can conceivably be divided into parts, too—upper body and lower body. Although my face and hair are different from yours, as is the shape of my upper and lower body, the *organization* of our physical beings is essentially the same.

XHTML documents mimic this arrangement. There is a head and a body. The head of an XHTML document contains features that are more mental than physical—occurring "behind the scenes" to accomplish or direct complex activities. I think of the XHTML body as being the domain of physical attributes—everything within the XHTML body is what is viewed, literally seen on the visible page.

Just as it would be an anomaly for an aspect of my head to manifest within the context of my body, or vice versa, so it is not logical to place the aspects of XHTML that function in the head into the body, and so forth.

This distinction is an important one, and is further broken down into parts within the head and body. There are divisions within the body, and there are special markers to help us label, or indicate, where certain features are to go.

Even for the more advanced coders among you, this basic concept is important. By keeping the document tags structured, you will avoid errors and enable yourself to power-code documents with efficiency and speed.

DOCUMENT DECLARATIONS AND ELEMENTS

The following declarations and elements are used to describe document formatting in this chapter:

- `<?xml>`—The XML declaration is used to define the document as an XML document and describe the XML version.
- `<!DOCTYPE>`—This is the document type declaration, and it is used to declare and define the document type.
- `<html>`…`</html>`—The HTML element, with its opening and closing tag, is used to begin the portion of the XHTML document that is written using HTML.
- `<head>`…`</head>`—The head tag denotes the head portion of an HTML document.
- `<title>`…`</title>`—Information placed within the title tag appears in the browser's title bar.

- **<body>...</body>**—This is the body of the HTML document, where all information that is to be visible on the screen is placed.

- **<!--...-->**—The comment tag is used for assisting coders with code navigation.

Note

The XML declaration is recommended but not required for valid XHTML 1.0 document structure. One reason many XHTML authors leave it out is because the XML declaration is not understood by many browsers, and will cause the code to render improperly or not render at all.

→ For more information about the XML declaration, **see** Chapter 5 "Defining XHTML Syntax," **p. 73**.

THE XHTML DOCUMENT SHELL

An *XHTML document shell* is how I tend to describe the combined tags that make up the head and body aspects of a page, with some specific tags that add to your page's basic functionality.

The shell defines the head and the body, as well as the skeletal system of the head and body. Listing 7.1 shows a complete and valid XHTML document shell for a strict XHTML document.

LISTING 7.1   THE HTML SHELL (TRANSITIONAL)

```
<?xml version="1.0"?>
<!DOCTYPE html PUBLIC "-//W3C//DTD XHTML 1.0 Strict//EN"
"http://www.w3.org/TR/xhtml1/DTD/xhtml1-strict.dtd">
<html xmlns="http://www.w3.org/1999/xhtml">
<head>
<title>Strict Document Sample</title>

</head>
<body>


</body>
</html>
```

You'll notice that the shell consists of declarations, elements, and attributes—all with opening and closing tags in place.

Tip

To ensure adherence to XHTML 1.0, you must include the appropriate XHTML document-type information.

PART

II

CH

7

The following sections examine the individual elements within the XHTML document.

HEAD STRUCTURE

Look closely at the document and you'll see that following the `<html>` tag there's a `<head>` tag, which is closed a few lines down. This is the head of your document. The information that goes into the head of a document includes the following:

- **Page title**—The `<title>` and corresponding `</title>` tag allow you to select a page title. This title does not appear in the body of an HTML page—in other words, when the document is viewed with a browser, this information will not be seen in the main viewing screen. Where it *will* often appear is within the title bar of the browser's interface. Note that you cannot add any other tags into a `title` element. However, you can use special characters, such as a copyright symbol, `&copy;`.

- **Scripting**—Any script that will be performed on a page, such as JavaScript is embedded into the head of a document, or linked to the document using the `link` tag, which appears in the document head. Remember, I said that much of the head is used for *mental* processes rather than visual ones. A script is a perfect example of this, as it is itself an invisible process, although its results will shape the action and behavior of a page.

- **Style**—For those authors interested in adding control and style to their pages, Cascading Style Sheets can be embedded into or linked to from a Web page. This information will appear within the head of an XHTML document.

- **The `link` element**—The `link` element provides information on relationships with other pages, such as external scripts, style, and accessible information.

- **Meta information**—The `meta` tag is a diverse and powerful tag that allows for a variety of mental rather than visual processes such as document author, search words, and special action items.

→ To read about special characters, **see** Chapter 5, "Defining XHTML Syntax," **p. 73**.

→ JavaScript is covered fully later; **see** Chapter 20, "Adding JavaScript to XHTML Documents," **p. 445**.

→ 'For more information about Style Sheets, **see** Chapter 18, "Cascading Style Sheets and XHTML," **p. 337** and Chapter 19, "Extensible Stylesheet Language (XSL)," **p. 419**.

For the purposes of this simple document outline, I've only included the `<title>` tag from this list of head possibilities because many pages will not require scripting, style, or `meta` information. But all pages should be titled. Therefore, I—and the W3C—consider the `<title>` tag a "must" for a basic XHTML template.

Within the `<title>` tag, you should place the name of your page. Get in the practice of working with a good description for your page title, keeping it simple but clear. Let's say I was making a home page for myself. I would title the page, simply, "Molly's Home Page."

```
<title>Molly's Home Page</title>
```

This information then appears in the browser's title bar. In Figure 7.1, I created a sample page with "Molly's Home page" within the `title` tags. Note how "Molly's Home Page" appears in the title bar? This is where your well-written title page description goes to work.

Figure 7.1
The title bar with Molly's Home Page can be seen along the top of the window in Netscape.

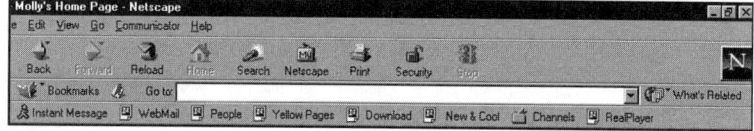

BODY STRUCTURE

The body of an XHTML document will include all the content information that you will be visually offering your audience. As you can tell from the shell, the `body` is left empty at this point, demonstrating only the available *space* for this information. One of your first jobs after creating the shell is to add `body` information such as the following:

- **Text**—The textual content of your site is placed in the `body`, using appropriate formatting to be readable and visually accessible for those who visit your page.

- **Images**—Whether using a header graphic to define a site's purpose, a photograph to enhance the text content, or a set of navigation buttons, images are an important part of what goes into the `body` of a document.

- **Links**—The heart and soul of the Web, links allow people to navigate your site as well as leave your site for Web destinations beyond. Links always go into the `body` of a page.

- **Multimedia and special, programmed events**—Shockwave, Flash, Java Applets, even inline video is managed by code placed in the `body` of an XHTML document.

Of course, there are many other elements that can be added within the body. We'll be taking a closer look at items such as lists, tables, and forms throughout the book.

→ For more information about textual content, **see** Chapter 9, "Formatting Text in XHTML," **p. 133**.

The `body` of an HTML document, like our bodies, ends up being larger and more physically varied than our heads. We accommodate this by preparing the shell with some space in which to work. Obviously, as we add information (see Figure 7.2), the `body` can become quite long.

PART

II

CH

7

Figure 7.2
Adding information to the body section as seen in Mozquito Factory.

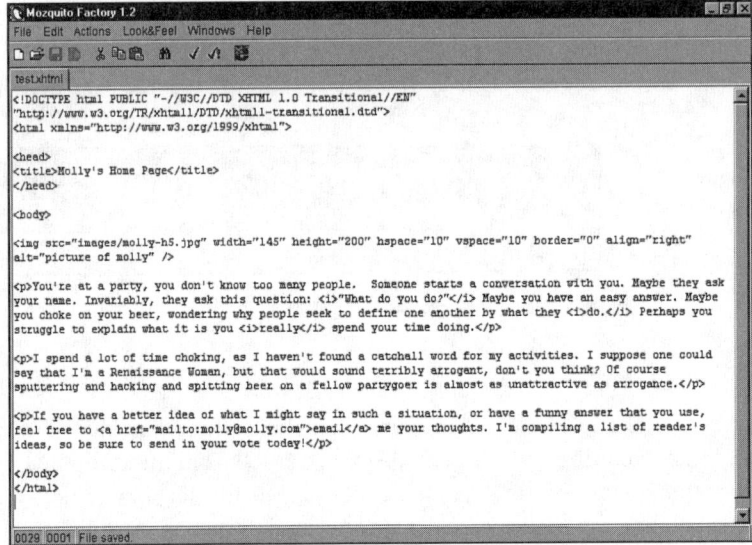

BUILDING AN XHTML SHELL

I'm going to step with you through the building of a simple XHTML document. The method I use, known as the *container method*, is something I recommend to help authors avoid missing tags. As discussed in Chapter 5, "Defining XHTML Syntax," XHTML is particularly concerned with keeping markup symmetry intact.

→ The container method and proper tag symmetry were introduced previously in Chapter 5; **see** "Defining XHTML Syntax," **p. 73**.

As you step through the process, you'll be coding in "containers":

1. Open the ASCII editor or editing environment of your choice (I'm using HomeSite).

2. Open a new file—it should be completely blank.

3. Enter the appropriate document version and type. I've chosen strict XHTML 1.0 for this exercise because nothing in the document is transitional in nature.

4. Add the opening and closing HTML tags with the appropriate namespace information. Then, add five blank lines in between the HTML tags. This creates your first container:

```
<!DOCTYPE html PUBLIC "-//W3C//DTD XHTML 1.0 Strict//EN"
"http://www.w3.org/TR/xhtml1/DTD/xhtml1-strict.dtd">
<html xmlns="http://www.w3.org/1999/xhtml">




</html>
```

4. Now add the head container directly beneath the opening HTML tag, consisting of the opening and closing head tags, with a carriage return in between:

```
<!DOCTYPE html PUBLIC "-//W3C//DTD XHTML 1.0 Strict//EN"
"http://www.w3.org/TR/xhtml1/DTD/xhtml1-strict.dtd">
<html xmlns="http://www.w3.org/1999/xhtml">
<head>

</head>


</html>
```

5. Next, introduce the title tag into the header tag by using both the opening and closing tag. My personal preference is to keep these on the horizontal, as follows:

```
<!DOCTYPE html PUBLIC "-//W3C//DTD XHTML 1.0 Strict//EN"
"http://www.w3.org/TR/xhtml1/DTD/xhtml1-strict.dtd">
<html xmlns="http://www.w3.org/1999/xhtml">
<head>
<title>          </title>
</head>


</html>
```

6. Go ahead and add the title to your page:

```
<!DOCTYPE html PUBLIC "-//W3C//DTD XHTML 1.0 Strict//EN"
"http://www.w3.org/TR/xhtml1/DTD/xhtml1-strict.dtd">
<html xmlns="http://www.w3.org/1999/xhtml">
<head>
<title> Document Exercise</title>
</head>


</html>
```

7. And finally, add the body tags directly below the closing head tag. Add some additional carriage returns if necessary to anticipate body information:

```
<!DOCTYPE html PUBLIC "-//W3C//DTD XHTML 1.0 Strict//EN"
"http://www.w3.org/TR/xhtml1/DTD/xhtml1-strict.dtd">
<html xmlns="http://www.w3.org/1999/xhtml">
<head>
<title> Document Exercise</title>
</head>
<body>

</body>
</html>
```

Figure 7.3 shows the shell within my editor. Check your code against this; you should be right on track.

Tip from

Save the file to a work folder, naming the file `xhtml_shell.html`. You'll want to keep this safe and separate because you'll be modifying it later in the chapter—and you can use it as you want for any future pages that you develop.

Figure 7.3
The XHTML within the Mozquito Factory editor shows how clean and easy to read your code is when you use the container method to create a shell.

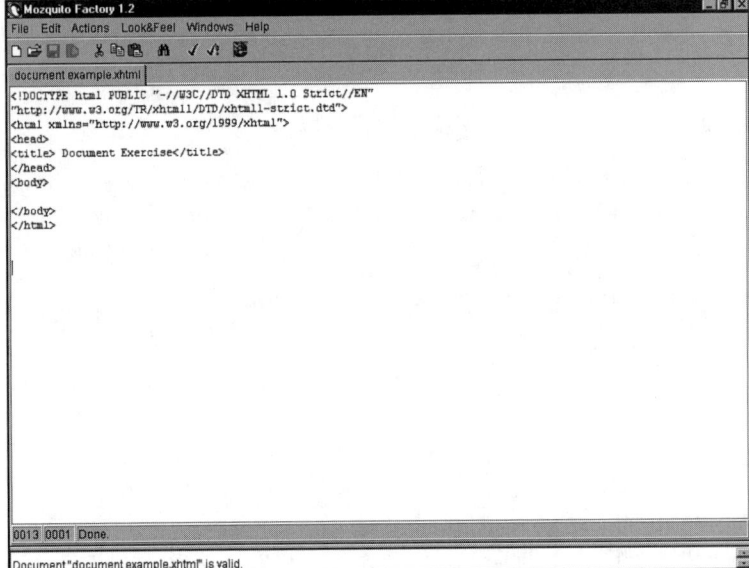

Is that all there is to an XHTML document? The simple answer is Yes! By understanding that there is a head and a body within the <html> opening and </html> closing tags, you've got the basic concept of document formatting down.

CLARITY AND ORIENTATION

Beyond the concerns that XHTML documents demand certain components to be valid and effective lies the concern that documents are neat, clean, and easy for people to decipher. This becomes especially important when more than one person is working on a given document. Committing to authoring documents that are clear and systematized is an important issue in professional document management.

A few helpful ways to do this include using comment tags, dividing documents into sensible divisions where necessary, and using techniques such as color coding where possible to assist in keeping markup well-organized.

COMMENTING SECTIONS IN AN XHTML DOCUMENT

Although there are no formal methods of dividing the body into custom sections by using standard tags, there is a conventional way of helping yourself manage such areas within a body, and, in fact, within the entirety of an XHTML document.

This is done using a specialty tag known as a *comment* tag. The comment tag is unlike any other tag in XHTML in that it follows none of the predetermined rules I described in Chapter 5. Still, the comment tag is an extraordinarily powerful tag that helps you, as well as those who work on your pages, maneuver through the code. This becomes especially helpful when your pages become extremely long and complex.

Here's a look at a comment tag in its simplest form:

```
<!- -     - ->
```

The tag is familiar in that it begins with a less-than sign and ends with a greater-than sign. The exclamation point is a marker that tells the browser to ignore the following informa-tion—as if it doesn't exist.

Placing a comment within this tag allows you to divide up your XHTML document. Here's a comment tag with a literal comment:

```
<!- - begin copyright information - ->
```

This comment tells me, or anyone viewing or working with my source code, that the copy-right information will appear after the tag. Comment tags are *never* displayed on a Web page, even if they appear within the body tag.

Comment tags can be used anywhere it makes logical sense to break up and mark an XHTML document. You also can use comment tags as a means of adding pertinent infor-mation to a page, such as the author's name, contact information, and update information. Comment tags can span multiple lines, with the opening tag on one line and the closing tag on any other line you want.

Tip from

Comment tags should serve to assist, not confuse, you and your assistants. Don't overuse them, but do use them where it seems necessary and important, particularly when dividing up the physical XHTML document.

I'm going now to revisit the simple shell I demonstrated earlier, this time adding comment tags to my needs and tastes (see Listing 7.2).

LISTING 7.2   ADDING COMMENT TAGS TO THE CODE

```
<! - - page design by: Molly E. Holzschlag   - - >
<! - - email molly@molly.com or visit http://www.molly.com/   - - >
<! - -   materials contributed by Molly.com, Inc. - - >
<! - - page last updated September 10th, 2000   - - >
<!DOCTYPE html PUBLIC "-//W3C//DTD XHTML 1.0 Strict//EN"
"http://www.w3.org/TR/xhtml1/DTD/xhtml1-strict.dtd">
<html xmlns="http://www.w3.org/1999/xhtml">
<head>
<title>MainStay Communications, Inc. - About the Company</title>
</head>

<! - - begin body information - - >
```

LISTING 7.2   CONTINUED

```
<body>

<! - - begin text content, and remember to close your paragraphs </p> - - >

<! - -  begin page footer: include copyright and mailto  - - >

</body>
</html>
```

If you study the previous example carefully, you'll see that I've included a variety of HTML information within the code. In the second comment tag, I place an email address and a URL:

```
<! - - email molly@molly.com or visit http://www.molly.com/ - - >
```

In a later comment tag, I make a note to others regarding a style preference. I actually typed in the literal tag, </p>,

```
<! - - begin text content, and remember to close your paragraphs </p> - - >
```

but the browser *will not see this* as XHTML code. Why? Because it is safely contained within a comment tag.

> **Note**
>
> Because browsers do not pay attention to what's within a comment tag, you can use these powerful, handy tags far beyond just describing a document's division. In fact, if you have a large section of text, an image, an object, or any combination thereof that you want to hide from the browser, placing that information within a comment tag will do the trick. This is useful when you cycle content on a page and don't want to keep multiple copies of a particular page.

Follow these steps to learn how to add some comment codes to your standard shell template:

1. Begin by opening the xhtml_shell.html file in your HTML editor.

2. At the top, add a comment tag as follows:

```
<! - -       - - >

<!DOCTYPE html PUBLIC "-//W3C//DTD XHTML 1.0 Strict//EN"
"http://www.w3.org/TR/xhtml1/DTD/xhtml1-strict.dtd">
<html xmlns="http://www.w3.org/1999/xhtml">
<head>
<title> Document Exercise</title>
</head>
<body>

</body>
</html>
```

3. Now add a literal comment, such as identifying yourself as the author of the document:

```
<! - - page authored by B. A. Coder - - >
<!DOCTYPE html PUBLIC "-//W3C//DTD XHTML 1.0 Strict//EN"
"http://www.w3.org/TR/xhtml1/DTD/xhtml1-strict.dtd">
<html xmlns="http://www.w3.org/1999/xhtml">
<head>
<title> Document Exercise</title>
</head>
<body>

</body>
</html>
```

4. Now add another comment tag denoting the beginning of the body area:

```
<!-- page authored by B. A. Coder -- >
<!DOCTYPE html PUBLIC "-//W3C//DTD XHTML 1.0 Strict//EN"
"http://www.w3.org/TR/xhtml1/DTD/xhtml1-strict.dtd">
<html xmlns="http://www.w3.org/1999/xhtml">
<head>
<title> Document Exercise</title>
</head>
<! - - begin body - - >
<body>

</body>
</html>
```

5. And add a comment tag showing where you plan to add your email and copyright information:

```
<!-- page authored by B. A. Coder -- >
<!DOCTYPE html PUBLIC "-//W3C//DTD XHTML 1.0 Strict//EN"
"http://www.w3.org/TR/xhtml1/DTD/xhtml1-strict.dtd">
<html xmlns="http://www.w3.org/1999/xhtml">
<head>
<title> Document Exercise</title>
</head>
<! - - begin body - - >
<body>
<! - - begin copyright and email information - - >

</body>
</html>
```

6. Compare your code to that shown in Figure 7.4

7. If the code is correct, save the file as html_comment.html.

Figure 7.4
Adding comment tags to the shell allows you, and those working on a project with you, to denote page sections, keep track of changes to a page, or make remarks on who made them.

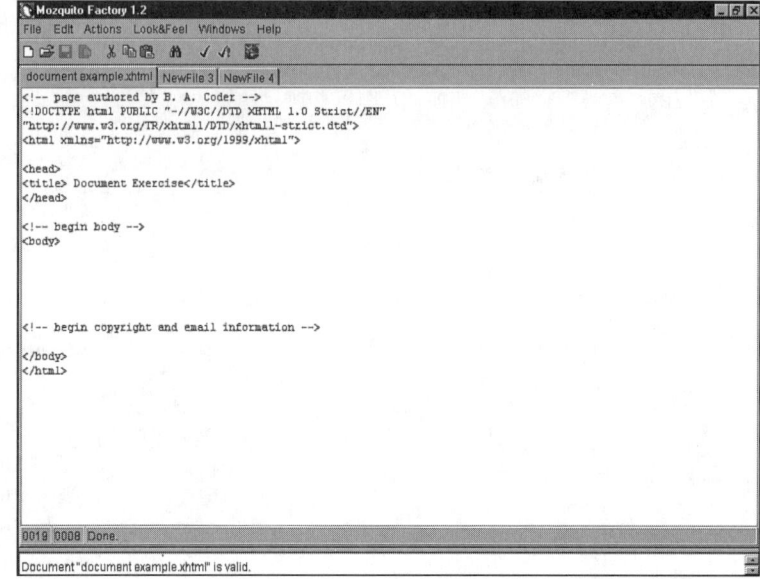

WRITING DOCUMENTS FOR CLARITY AND EASE OF USE

Another issue when writing XHTML documents is to be sure that you add plenty of visual space. This solves problems when navigating code because you can always find what you're looking for.

Different coders rely on different methods for cueing themselves with regard to clarity. I'll show you a few approaches here and point out which I prefer. You'll find out which methods you prefer as you work more with the language. Either way, the point is to make the process of coding easier on you, and ultimately, more fun.

Some of the methods of writing documents for ease of use include the following:

- **Flushing primary tags left**—This is putting all your main tags to the absolute left of the page. This helps keep you oriented on a page of code because the left is a natural place for our eyes to go—as readers of English, we are accustomed to moving our eyes to the left for visually oriented language clues.

- **Placing carriage returns between tags and content**—Adding visual space (also referred to as *whitespace*) between tags and content, as well as between tags and other tags, helps cushion, rest, and guide your eye to the next tag.

- **Indenting certain tags**—Some authors feel that indenting specific types of tags, such as table tags or table cell tags, helps them to navigate code more efficiently. This is not a personal favorite of mine; however, I've seen many authors use it effectively, and it just might suit your needs.

■ **Color coding tags**—Certain editors, editing environments, and Web page software applications allow you to color code tags. I love this feature; it is extremely helpful. Figure 7.5 shows the dialog box in HomeSite where I can set my own colors for specific tags. This way, if I'm looking for an image, I know to be on the lookout for a yellow tag. This is a great method of staying oriented within a page of code.

→ For more about editors and editing environments, **see** Chapter 4, "XHTML Tools," **p. 49**.

Figure 7.5
Setting up color coding in HomeSite allows the coder to easily create and edit code and stay oriented to the page without hunting around for certain tags.

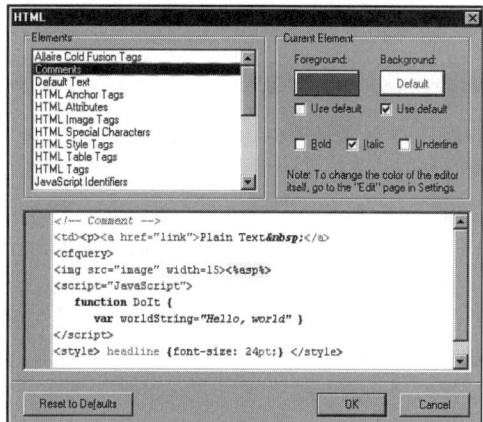

To get a good feel of how cluttered markup can frustrate the author—or anyone who might later have to take over maintaining a given page—I'm going to give you an example of poorly organized markup. Notice that the code and text in Listing 7.3 are all jammed together: no whitespace, no flushing. This makes it hard to find anything.

LISTING 7.3   CLUTTERED CODE

```
<p><img src="images/molly-h5.jpg" width="145" height="200" hspace="10" vspace="10"
border="0" align="right" alt="picture of molly" />
You're at a party, you don't know too many people. Someone starts a conversation
with you. Maybe they ask your name. Invariably, they ask this question:
<i>&quot;What do you do?&quot;</i> Maybe you have an easy answer. Maybe you choke
on your beer, wondering why people seek to define one another by what they
<i>do.</i> Perhaps you struggle to explain what it is you <I>really</I> spend your
time doing. </p>
<p>I spend a lot of time choking, as I haven't found a catchall word for my
activities. I suppose one could say that I'm a Renaissance Woman, but that would
sound terribly arrogant, don't you think? Of course sputtering and hacking and
spitting beer on a fellow partygoer is almost as unattractive as arrogance.</p>
<p>If you have a better idea of what I might say in such a situation, or have a
funny answer that you use, feel free to <a href="mailto:molly@molly.com">email</a>
me your thoughts. I'm compiling a list of reader's ideas, so be sure to send in
your vote today! </p>
```

Now let's take a look at the same code (see Listing 7.4) as I've hand-coded it.

LISTING 7.4   NEATER, CLEANER CODE

```
<img src="images/molly-h5.jpg" width=145 height=200 hspace="10" vspace="10"
border="0" align="right" alt="picture of molly" />
<p>You're at a party, you don't know too many people.  Someone starts a
conversation with you. Maybe they ask your name. Invariably, they ask this
question: <i>"What do you do?"</i> Maybe you have an easy answer. Maybe you choke
on your beer, wondering why people seek to define one another by what they
<i>do.</i> Perhaps you struggle to explain what it is you <i>really</i> spend your
time doing.</p>
<p>I spend a lot of time choking, as I haven't found a catchall word for my
activities. I suppose one could say that I'm a Renaissance Woman, but that would
sound terribly arrogant, don't you think? Of course sputtering and hacking and
spitting beer on a fellow partygoer is almost as unattractive as arrogance.</p>
<p>If you have a better idea of what I might say in such a situation, or have a
funny answer that you use, feel free to <a href="mailto:molly@molly.com">email</a>
me your thoughts. I'm compiling a list of reader's ideas, so be sure to send in
your vote today!</p>
```

My code flushes tags left, separates certain code from content, and adds carriage returns to create whitespace to help soothe and guide my eye as I work on the code. While these might seem to be subtle changes, I'm personally much happier with this kind of environment—I feel less constrained, less tense, and more capable of getting to the code I need to change, update, or remove.

 Concerned about how to manage existing, unruly code? See "Using Different Tools" in the "Troubleshooting" section near the end of this chapter.

Note   Some authors are concerned about adding space to their markup because they think that blank lines, tabs, and spaces will reflect on their visual page via the browser. This is simply not the case. You can have as many carriage returns between lines of code as you want, and the browser should ignore them—it's waiting for code, not space, to tell it what to do.

TROUBLESHOOTING

USING DIFFERENT TOOLS

If someone takes over a project that's been originated in a Web Page Editor such as FrontPage, is it worth taking the time to reformat the code to XHTML?

The first thing to consider before taking on such a large task is how the work is being used and updated. If a project entails moving back and forth from FrontPage, it's not worth reformatting the code because this will become a constant task. If the project will remain in a text-editing environment, it is definitely worth the effort. You will find that it's easier to make sense of the code and eliminate extraneous tags after it's in a workable and valid format.

DESIGNING FOR THE REAL WORLD

A STUDY IN CODING STYLES

You can learn a lot about XHTML and HTML coding by studying the code of others—that is, a lot about what to do and a lot more about what not to do. Even the most successful sites approach their code in different ways.

Whenever you see a site that appeals to you on some level—whether it be its simplicity or complexity—all you need to do is right-click the page and choose View Source. You'll instantly get an inside look into how the Web developer approaches his or her work. Also, you'll begin to see how HTML allows for a lot of sloppiness, whereas by virtue of its more rigorous nature, XHTML is neater and more precise.

For example, go to the Yahoo! site and view the source of their main page. You'll notice that the code is lumped together. There are no comments in the source. There also are some instances of overlapping tags, particularly `<font>` tags.

A visit to Excite yields slightly better code, from a readability standpoint. There are no carriage returns between blocks of code, but the tags are all flush left, making it much easier to analyze and tear apart. The Go Network site is similarly coded, with flush-left tags. Watch out for those overlapping tags, however!

Then, look at Lycos and Netcenter. Both are tagged flush left, and they've even separated blocks of code with carriage returns. Netcenter also has included comments to help the coders keep track of what goes where. Isn't it easier to make sense of the code on these sites?

For a peek at XHTML coding, see the very neatly structured code at the World Wide Web Consortium and the less neat but still well-organized markup at Stack Overflow.

As you navigate the Web, you'll find no shortage of examples to study. Just make sure those examples are good ones.

Note

Visit these pages for a look under the hood of the biggest sites on the Net:

Yahoo—`http://www.yahoo.com/`

Excite—`http://www.excite.com/`

Lycos—`http://www.lycos.com/`

Go Network—`http://www.go.com/`

Netscape Netcenter—`http://www.netcenter.com/`

Ebay—`http://www.ebay.com/`

Microsoft—`http://www.microsoft.com/`

Take a look at XHTML code:

World Wide Web Consortium—`http:://www.w3.org/`

Stack Overflow—`http://www.stackoverflow.com/`

PART

II

CH

7

MANAGING XHTML DOCUMENTS LOCALLY

In this chapter

THE IMPORTANCE OF FILE MANAGEMENT

Although this subject might seem quite basic to the intermediate reader, the reality is that significant problems arise when files are named improperly. The reason this is such a common occurrence is that many computer professionals are accustomed to working on one primary platform. For example, the designers among you will likely be most familiar with Macintosh computers, die-hard programmers and system administrators with UNIX and Linux, and IT professionals with Windows NT and Windows related software. Hobbyists also will typically fall into the Mac or Windows camps.

Files are managed differently on each platform. However, for files to be correctly rendered in a browser or located properly on a Web server, those files—and the directories in which they reside—must adhere to specific rules to be readable across all platforms. This chapter will review some file basics, and provide you with tips that will help reduce problems arising from cross-platform naming differences.

There are a wide variety of file types, but only a few are of immediate concern to people working with XHTML. Most of these files relate to the XHTML information itself, graphic files, specialty programming, or multimedia files. I won't go over all the extensions here, but I've provided several Notes with Web addresses that will enable you to explore this issue at greater length.

One of the difficulties I see time and again is that students of XHTML run into problems because of faulty file management. This chapter is intended to provide you with some simple and effective guidelines to managing your local files. I'll step away from discussion of standards or specific markup issues—the information in this chapter will help you no matter what level of XHTML or HTML you're working with. Topics covered include how to name your files, structure your file directories, save files, and address troubleshooting concerns.

NAMING CONVENTIONS

This is by far the biggest stumbling block for newcomers to XHTML. One of the main culprits is that people who come from a UNIX or Macintosh background, or who started using home computers with the release of Windows 95, are accustomed to using long filenames. These naming structures allow you to call a file just about anything you want, with no specific concern as to length, logic, or consistent relationship between a prefix and suffix (also referred to as an *extension*).

The primary problems with naming are

- **Improperly formed filenames**—To allow for global access, filenames must adhere to specific naming formats.
- **Unclear filenames**—Filenames get confusing if you don't create a system that clearly identifies, at least to you, what each file contains.
- **Names that are too long**—There's already enough length to many URLs—don't add to the problem by naming your file with an unreasonably long filename.

- **Names with no or improper prefixes and suffixes**—If you don't use the proper prefix and suffix locally, how will it work on the Internet? Get used to the available suffixes and use them.

⚠ *Unable to bring your site up once you've posted it to the Web? You might have incorrectly named your default file; see "Setting the Default Page" in the "Troubleshooting" section near the end of this chapter.*

IMPROPERLY FORMED FILENAMES

To avoid problems with badly formed filenames, follow these simple rules:

- **Don't use spaces**—Even if you're used to doing this on your local computer, you'll have trouble testing your files locally and running them on the Internet if you have a space in the name. In place of spaces, you can use underscores or hyphens.

- **Don't use any extraneous characters**—Stick to letters, numbers, underscores, and hyphens. Especially troublesome characters include apostrophes (as in "molly'swebsite"), dollar signs, percent signs, pound signs, parentheses, and so on, which might have special meanings for operating systems or Web software.

- **Put the "dot" in the right place**—Similarly, you should avoid using a period, or "dot," in any position other than between the prefix and suffix of a filename.

- **Name your files in all lowercase**—Even though at this point you're working locally and this won't trouble your individual computer, it's a good practice to get into early. Many servers still perceive filenames by case, meaning that `index.html`, `INDEX.html`, and `IndEX.html` are three different files! You'll avoid many a future headache by following this simple guideline.

UNCLEAR FILENAMES

One of the best ways to stay organized is to give your files understandable names. This becomes especially important when you begin managing many XHTML documents in a single project.

You can always assign a project a two- or three-letter code, and then give the filename a logical identifier. This is something I've gotten in the habit of doing on larger sites. For smaller sites, I stick to simple names.

The following is a series of filenames from my personal Web site:

```
index.html

new.html

books.html

bio.html

resume.html

contact.html
```

If I were going to have many, many files on that site, I might consider giving it a code, such as mh, for Molly Holzschlag. Then I would follow this up with a logical name and perhaps a numeric value to indicate a date or portion of a series:

```
index.html

mh_new.html

mh_books.html

mh_bio.html

mh_resume.html

mh_contact.html

mh_article1.html

mh_article2.html

mh_daily_1100.html
```

The important issue, as is so often the case in coding, is to be consistent. Pick a style that works for you and stick to it. You'll be happy that you did!

Note

Why do the documents in this example end in .html and not, say, .xml or .xhtml? For now, XHTML documents in use for common Web browsers and on common Web servers require the .html or a similar, understood suffix in order to render properly.

FILENAME LENGTH

Have you ever come across a URL so long that you couldn't copy it to send to a friend— even though the information at that location was really something to write about?

Avoid adding to the often-lengthy naming process on the Web by working with shorter filenames locally. This sets you up for a longer-term consistency rate with file-naming conventions.

I like to use the old DOS naming convention as a guide. DOS allows for a maximum of eight characters in the prefix. I recommend not exceeding the eight-character rule too much, or you start getting into filenames that are going to be too long.

Of course, DOS limits the suffix to three characters, which doesn't carry conceptually over to the Internet structure itself. You find out a bit more about this later when I discuss suffixes.

A good rule of thumb with filename length is to make the name sensible and logical without exceeding much more than eight characters in the prefix. Ten characters would be perfectly acceptable, but twenty characters would not.

Caution

Mac users need to understand the filename and length structure as much, if not more, than any computer user. The reason is that filenames exceeding these guidelines risk getting truncated, rendering the file unreadable by a browser.

CORRECT PREFIX AND SUFFIX NAMES

The only time a prefix name is going to matter is when a file goes live on the Internet. Locally, you can start with any name. However, plan ahead and find out what prefix your server will allow you to use for the first default page. Name that file accordingly, and you'll be prepared when the time comes to upload your pages.

The following are a few possible prefix choices:

```
index.html

default.html

welcome.html
```

Once again, certain operating systems have contributed to bad file-naming habits. On the Macintosh you're not required to put a suffix onto a filename. Will your file run? Not when you're trying to link to it—even local, poorly managed files will choke.

For standard HTML files, two primary options exist for the suffix: .html and .htm.

To find out which one you should use, do a bit of study regarding where you will ultimately place your work on the Internet. If your server requires .html as a suffix, that's what you should use. The .htm suffix is a carry-over from the three-letter suffix convention, and is found on Windows-based servers.

In most cases, you can use either one. As always, follow the consistency rule and choose one when the option is available. Never mix the two within a site—that spells trouble.

You'll run into a few other HTML-related extensions, but that won't affect you when working locally. Most of these extensions are related to server-side includes or backend processes such as Java Server Pages, CGI, and Perl, as well as Active Server Pages (ASP). They include variants such as

```
.jhtml

.htmlx

.shtml

.pl

.asp

.php

.cgi
```

Graphic files must be named properly at all times. For GIFs, always use the .gif extension, and for JPEGs, the .jpg (NOT .jpeg) extension.

A variety of other file types can be incorporated into your XHTML structure. Their suffixes vary depending upon the file type. When in doubt, consult the documentation for the suffix information, or check with the system administrator who manages the server on which your local documents will eventually be placed.

Note

Looking for filename information? Here are a few sites to help you out.

A great resource is available at `http://www.whatis.com/if.htm`. This is "Every File Format in the World" and, sure enough, you'll have every file format with its proper extension available to you, on demand.

Another Web resource that's helpful with filename extensions can be found at `http://www2.crosswinds.net/san-marino/~jom/filex/extensio.htm`.

One of the most complete lists of extensions and corresponding applications I've ever found can be viewed at `http://www-f.rrz.uni-koeln.de/themen/Graphik/ImageProcessing/fileext.html`.

FILE DIRECTORY STRUCTURE

As you already have noticed, working locally but thinking for the long term is a natural way to avoid problems. In terms of directory structure, it's good to set up a system that you can use consistently, whether you are managing your documents locally or on a server.

Tip from

molly

Think of directories as folders, and vice-versa. Depending on what operating system you're using, they are conceptually one and the same. Use the guidelines set out earlier for filenames for naming directories, helping you to avoid problems with naming that arise across platforms. Folder names should never have a dot or a filename suffix.

You can place all the files for a site into one directory. This is fine if you have only a few pages and graphic files. But when you start working with larger sites containing numerous XHTML documents, countless graphics, and other media, it becomes near to impossible to manage one directory of files.

Many designers share a conventional bit of wisdom when managing files. I'm going to follow this wisdom and ask you to follow along as I set up a series of folders to help you manage your data:

1. Create a new folder on your hard drive.
2. Give this folder an identifying name related to the site, such as webdesign.
3. Within that folder, create a subfolder.
4. Name that folder images.
5. Place any HTML files in the webdesign folder. This folder is considered your "root."
6. Place any images into the image subfolder.

Figure 8.1 shows the directory structure I just created.

Figure 8.1
A simple but effective directory structure.

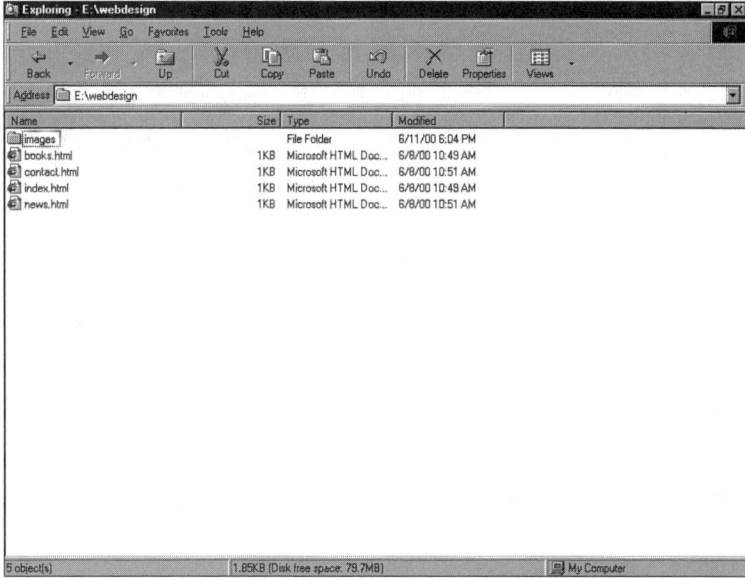

The topmost directory in any given structure is referred to as the *root directory*. Any directory within the root is referred to as a *subdirectory*. A *parent* directory is the directory immediately above any given subdirectory.

 Did you know that once your site is "live" on the Web, if you should happen to lose files from your hard drive you can still retrieve them? See "Lost Files" in the "Troubleshooting" section near the end of this chapter.

You can expand on this idea even further, if necessary. Let's say I want to have a number of subtopics within my primary topic of webdesign. I can break the information up into several subfolders, placing the XHTML and other documents within the appropriate, corresponding folder. If I want to have an articles subfolder, a scripts subfolder, and a media subfolder, I simply create those folders within the main folder (see Figure 8.2).

→ You'll need to follow the appropriate coding method when managing files in subdirectories. For information on how to do this, **see** Chapter 12, "Linking Pages with Standard Links," **p. 199.**

Figure 8.2
Multiple subfolders make large data management easy.

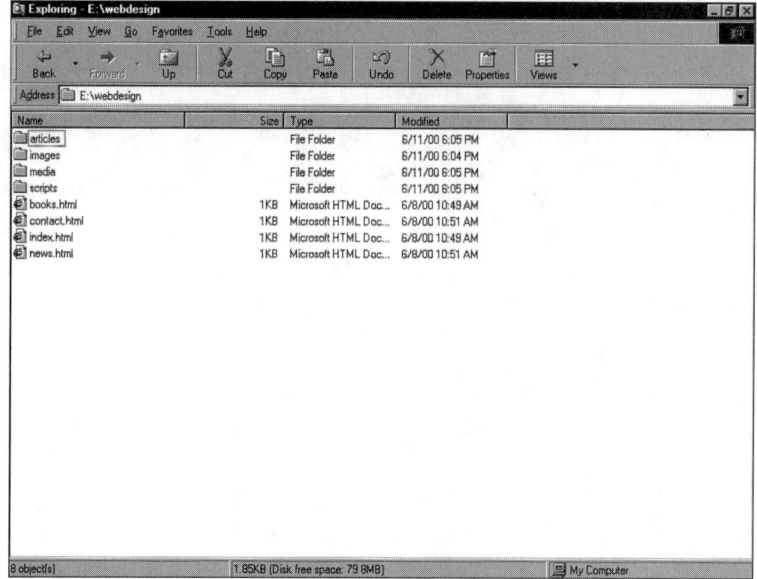

SAVING FILES

File management is easy, but it's also dangerous. It's possible to overwrite files, lose data, and save files to the wrong area of your computer. You also can run the risk of saving files improperly.

Follow these tips for general file management:

- **Save your work regularly**—Whenever I begin a new file, I immediately name it properly and save it to the correct location on my drive.

- **Back up your work!**—Whether you make a copy of the file to floppy disk, zip disk, or tape drive is no matter—just make sure you keep a copy! I can't express how many times I've worked for an hour just to lose all my sweat equity by making a critical mistake when saving the file.

- **Create your directory structure first, and save files to that area**—This way you'll know where your files are, setting up a logical structure upon which to form the linking of pages and page elements to a given XHTML document.

 If you've got the directory structure and file-naming issues handled, but are working with a team and having trouble knowing who is doing what because files are getting overwritten when different team members make changes, see "Version Control" in the "Troubleshooting" section near the end of this chapter.

Tip from
molly

> Many software programs automatically save (auto-save) data on a regular basis. I have this feature in most of my text editors. If you have such an option, be sure to set it to save files frequently. I usually do an auto-save about every five minutes. This means if I have a crash, I reduce data loss.

Another problem I see quite often has to do with saving files to the wrong format. Let's say you're in Photoshop, and you want to save a file as a JPEG, but you mistakenly select PCX. If you give the file the wrong suffix name the program will save the file improperly.

This problem holds true when saving XHTML files and related documents. It's important to remember that XHTML is saved in ASCII, or text format. If you save it, or transfer it as a binary file, the file will be corrupt. The same is true with binary formats—you can't try to save or transfer a GIF or JPEG file in ASCII, for example, because you will destroy the file's integrity.

TROUBLESHOOTING

SETTING THE DEFAULT PAGE

I created a Web page, but it doesn't appear when I type the domain name. What could be the problem?

You might have created your file with a name that is not recognized as a default by your Web server. A default Web page name is the filename used by your server to deliver a file when the URL or directory, but not a file name, is given. So, if I type in `http://www.molly.com/`, my server will know to send the default page for that location and directory, which is `index.html`. If you named the file `index.html`, for example, try renaming it `default.htm`. Alternatively, contact your Web service provider and ask for the default naming convention required by their servers.

LOST FILES

My hard disk crashed, and the local copy of the site I was working on is lost. I didn't make a backup. Can I recover lost files?

If your site is already live on the Web, you can recover the files from the server. Simply use your favorite FTP application to download the files. Be sure to preserve the directory structure so you don't wind up with broken links to repair. And be sure to create a backup in the future!

VERSION CONTROL

I am making revisions on a page, but now I want to revert to an earlier version of the page. How can I keep versions without renaming multiple files and constantly updating links?

Version control software will help manage your files. If you work on a development team, this software enables you to lock the other members of the team out of a particular file while you're working on it. You also can easily track revisions and revert to previous versions of a file. Version control software ranges from expensive, enterprise-level applications, such as Microsoft Visual SourceSafe, to home-developer applications, such as QVCS, a shareware package available on the Internet.

DESIGNING FOR THE REAL WORLD

SITE MAPPING

If you've been surfing the Web for some time, you've surely come across sites that contain a site map or index to help you navigate the site. Site maps not only help the end user, however. They also are a great planning exercise for your site. Working from a site map ensures that you have considered the future growth of the site and allows you to predetermine the subdirectories and filenames you want to use.

You can create a site map in several ways. The low-tech method is to simply use a blank sheet of paper and a pencil to draw boxes and lines. This process can quickly become cumbersome as you make changes and add to your site. Before you know it, the page gets so filled with lines and erasures that it's a jumbled mess.

A better solution is to design your site map right on the computer. If you have Microsoft Office, you can use the Organization Chart applet to create a hierarchical map of your site. This is useful in setting up a navigation structure for your site. Each of the major navigational headings can then become a subdirectory to organize your files.

If your site is more complex, with pages accessible from multiple links, a diagramming program such as Visio or SmartDraw better fits the bill. In these packages, you use stencils of boxes and other shapes to signify your pages and images and add lines and arrows to show the links between files. If you are only designing one site, this type of package might be overkill, but if you are involved in multiple projects, the software pays for itself in time saved.

The site-mapping tools you need also might already be on hand, depending on your development environment. Microsoft FrontPage and Adobe GoLive (see Figure 8.3) have site-mapping tools within their applications. These packages automatically track your links to both pages and images.

Figure 8.3
A site map in Adobe
GoLive.

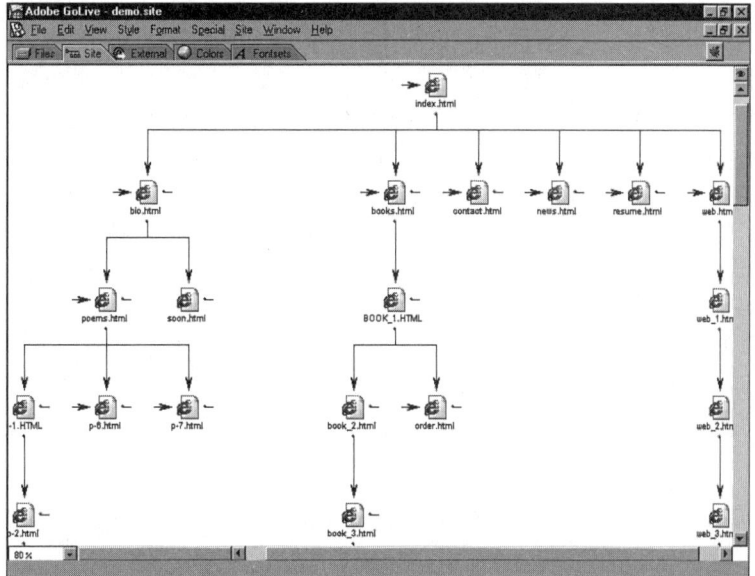

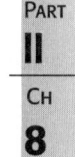

PART III

USING XHTML TO BUILD WEB PAGES

CHAPTER 9

FORMATTING TEXT IN XHTML

In this chapter

FORMATTING ELEMENTS

Text formatting is where XHTML is its most simplistic—and most powerful. After all, meta languages such as SGML that preceded XML (and therefore XHTML) were developed to format text-based documents and make them available on the Internet, with the major enhancement being the capability to hyperlink documents.

Most of the concepts in text formatting are straightforward, including standard headers, breaks, and paragraphs in strict XHTML 1.0 documents. Text styles such as bold, italic, and underlined text, color, and special formatting also can be added to transitional XHTML 1.0 documents.

The following tags are used to format text:

- `<h1>. . .</h1>`–`<h6>. . .</h6>`—The range of header tags used to denote paragraph and content headings and subheadings.
- `<br />`—The break tag, which is equivalent to one carriage return.
- `<p>. . .</p>`—The open/close approach to paragraph denotation.
- `<pre>. . .</pre>`—The preformatted text tag.
- `<b>. . .</b>`—The bold tag, for bolding text in transitional documents.
- `<i>. . .</i>`—The italics tag, for italicizing text in transitional documents.
- `<u>. . .</u>`—The underline tag, used for underlining text in transitional documents.

We also will examine the addition of color as well as several tags and special formatting, in addition to these standard text-formatting tags.

EXPLORING TEXT CONCEPTS

When approaching text content for a Web page, you should follow a number of helpful guidelines.

Just as you would prepare any professional text document, all Web-based text should be free of grammatical or spelling errors, appropriately written with the audience in mind, and follow a clear, concise pattern of development. A good structure to follow is to begin with an introduction, have several paragraphs that detail the content, and follow this with a conclusion, restating the intent of the communication.

The Web has certain visual constraints. It's important to keep in mind that extremely long pages of text are tiring on the eyes. Furthermore, keeping paragraphs short can be helpful in getting information across to page visitors, who tend not to stay on individual Web pages for very long periods of time.

→ For more information about the Web's visual environment, **see** Chapter 26, "Working with the Computer Screen," **p. 545**.

Following a logical arrangement of text is wise. For example, if you've structured your text well, you can highlight certain areas by using headers or text emphasis. There is a logical order for headers, beginning with the largest size and then moving into smaller sizes where necessary. When emphasizing text with bold, italic, or underlined styles, the important thing to remember is that a light touch is wise. Be consistent and logical, never deviating from the clean and precise output that is so necessary for effective Web communication.

WORKING WITH HEADERS

Headers help you denote specific areas of a document by titling that individual area. The header tag is an alphanumeric combination of an "h" plus a numeric value ranging from 1–6, 1 being the largest, and 6 being the smallest. As many seasoned authors already know, you can use headers to represent distinct layers of information within the natural progress of text. My page's title, for example, would be a large header, the first sub-section would be titled by using a header size one size smaller than the chapter head, and so forth.

PART
III
CH
9

Caution

Header tags seemingly work "backward," with the lowest value, "1," creating the largest visual header. Remember that this is a convention born of document formatting, where a larger header denotes the dominant level of concept, and so forth.

Header tags work simply by surrounding the text you want to use for titling with the appropriately sized tag:

```
<h1>Health Benefits of Exercise</h1>
```

Figure 9.1
Headers of size 1 are used most commonly when formatting the primary heading of a page.

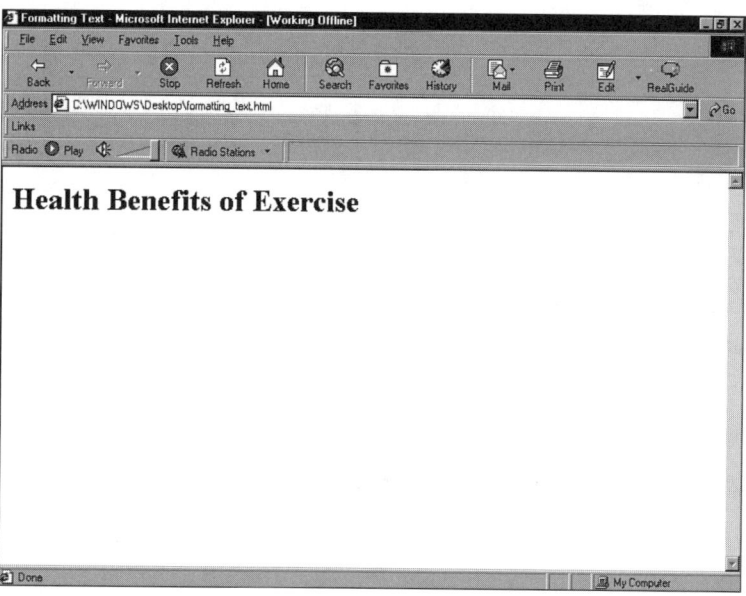

Simply change the numeric value to get a different size:

```
<h5>Other Benefits of Exercise</h5>
```

Figure 9.2 shows an example with a smaller header size.

Figure 9.2
Size 1 and size 5
headers compared.
The size 5 header will
appear quite small on
all browsers.

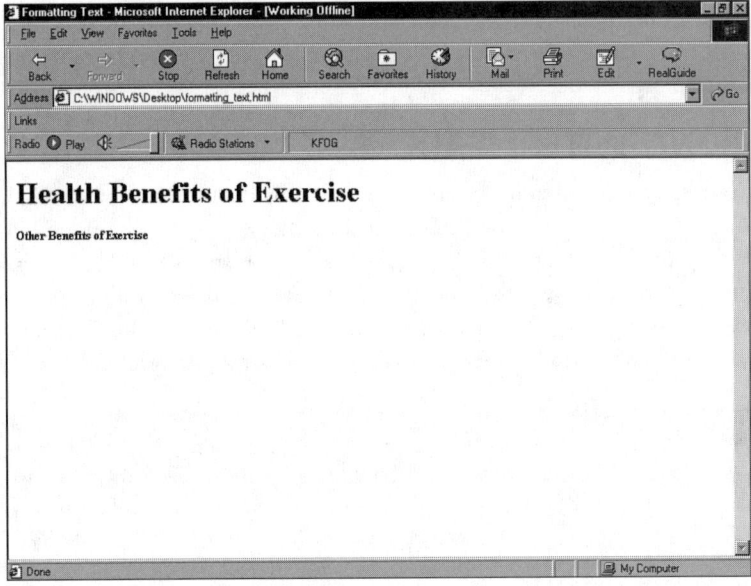

Note

Headers maintain relative consistency in size and appearance across browsers and platforms.

→ To read more about these concepts in detail, **see** Chapter 26, "Working with the Computer Screen," **p. 545**.

Tip from
molly

Use headers sparingly, and where absolutely necessary. Keeping to header sizes 1–3 is safest, because at smaller sizes, headers are hard to read.

Let's add a header to a paragraph of text:

1. Open one of your XHTML templates in a favorite editor:

```
<!DOCTYPE html PUBLIC "-//W3C//DTD XHTML 1.0 Transitional//EN"
"http://www.w3.org/TR/xhtml1/DTD/xhtml1-transitional.dtd">
<html xmlns="http://www.w3.org/1999/xhtml">

<head>
<title>   </title>
</head>

<body>
```

```
  </body>
</html>
```

2. Add a paragraph of text within the body area:

```
<!DOCTYPE html PUBLIC "-//W3C//DTD XHTML 1.0 Transitional//EN"
"http://www.w3.org/TR/xhtml1/DTD/xhtml1-transitional.dtd">
<html xmlns="http://www.w3.org/1999/xhtml">
<head>
<title>   </title>

</head>
<body>

<p>Exercise is an excellent way of improving your health. Medical studies
demonstrate that exercise can strengthen your heart and lungs, lower
your blood pressure, and help you maintain a healthy weight.</p>

</body>
</html>
```

3. Add a header:

```
<!DOCTYPE html PUBLIC "-//W3C//DTD XHTML 1.0 Transitional//EN"
"http://www.w3.org/TR/xhtml1/DTD/xhtml1-transitional.dtd">
<html xmlns="http://www.w3.org/1999/xhtml">
<head>
<title>   </title>

</head>
<body>

<h1>Health Benefits of Exercise</h1>

<p>Exercise is an excellent way of improving your health. Medical studies
demonstrate that exercise can strengthen your heart and lungs, lower
your blood pressure, and help you maintain a healthy weight.</p>

</body>
</html>
```

4. Title your page:

```
<!DOCTYPE html PUBLIC "-//W3C//DTD XHTML 1.0 Transitional//EN"
"http://www.w3.org/TR/xhtml1/DTD/xhtml1-transitional.dtd">
<html xmlns="http://www.w3.org/1999/xhtml">
<head>
<title>Health Benefits of Exercise</title>

</head>
<body>

<h1>Health Benefits of Exercise</h1>

<p>Exercise is an excellent way of improving your health. Medical studies
demonstrate that exercise can strengthen your heart and lungs, lower
your blood pressure, and help you maintain a healthy weight.</p>

</body>
</html>
```

5. Save your file.

6. View in your browser and check the results with Figure 9.3.

7. If they are similar, save your file.

Figure 9.3
Header, size 1, in relation to a paragraph of text, which is a default size (size 3).

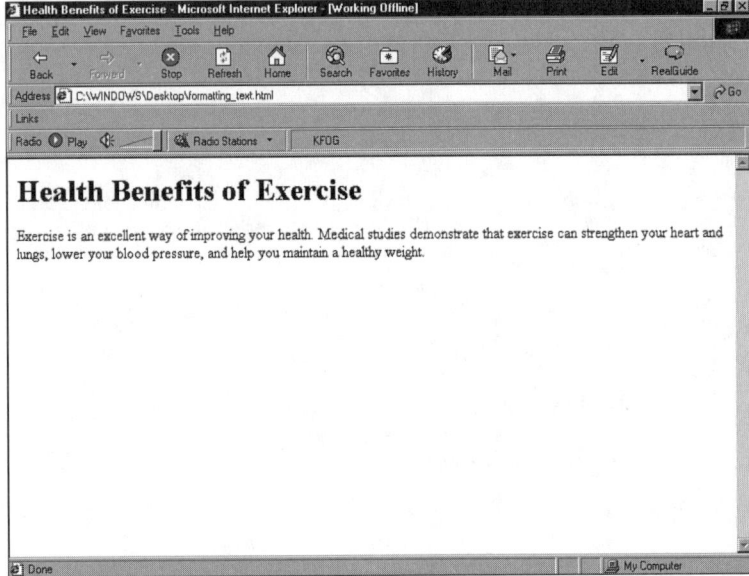

Headers are automatically left-aligned on a page, so if you want to center them, or align them to the right, the best way to do this is use an alignment method, which you can find later in this chapter.

INSERTING PARAGRAPHS AND BREAKS

By using the paragraph element, you can separate your paragraphs into discrete, visible blocks. The paragraph tag formats these blocks by invoking two carriage returns where you determine the end of your paragraph to be.

UNDERSTANDING THE PARAGRAPH TAG APPROACH

In HTML, there were two common paragraph-tagging styles. The first is to simply use the <p> tag before the natural beginning of a paragraph as shown in Listing 9.1.

LISTING 9.1   SINGLE <p> TAG BEFORE PARAGRAPH IN HTML

```
<HTML>
<HEAD>

<TITLE>Benefits of Exercise</TITLE>
</HEAD>
```

LISTING 9.1   CONTINUED

```
<BODY>

<H1>Health Benefits of Exercise</H1>
<P>Exercise is an excellent way of improving your health. Medical
studies demonstrate that exercise can strengthen your heart and
lungs, lower your blood pressure, and help you maintain a healthy
weight.

<P>Exercise can also assist with improving your mood. In fact, people who
exercise have demonstrated better self-esteem, stronger decision
making, and a generally more positive outlook on life.

</BODY>

</HTML>
```

As you've already guessed, this style—which was very popular among HTML authors—is not allowed in XHTML. Because a paragraph is a *non-empty element*, it must be closed with the </p> tag.

Aside from the clean and consistent code practices this formalization of paragraph formatting in XHTML provides, the technique becomes especially handy when you want to align text, or you want to add styles using a style sheet.

→ To learn how to work with style sheets, **see** Chapter 18, "Cascading Style Sheets and XHTML," **p. 377**.

Listing 9.2 shows the another code example, this time using the open/close paragraph style.

LISTING 9.2   THE OPEN AND CLOSE PARAGRAPH APPROACH

```
<!DOCTYPE html PUBLIC "-//W3C//DTD XHTML 1.0 Transitional//EN"
"http://www.w3.org/TR/xhtml1/DTD/xhtml1-transitional.dtd">
<html xmlns="http://www.w3.org/1999/xhtml">
<head>
<title>Health Benefits of Exercise</title>

</head>
<body>

<h1>Health Benefits of Exercise</h1>

<p>Exercise is an excellent way of improving your health. Medical studies
demonstrate that exercise can strengthen your heart and lungs, lower
your blood pressure, and help you maintain a healthy weight.</p>

<p>Exercise can also assist with improving your mood. In fact, people who
exercise have demonstrated better self-esteem, stronger decision making,
and a generally more positive outlook on life.</p>

</body>

</html>
```

WORKING WITH THE BREAK TAG

Sometimes you'll want to force a carriage return, and this can be done using the <br /> element. Breaks, unlike paragraphs, are *empty elements* and therefore are terminated with the XML convention of a slash />.

A great example of where you might want to use a break is when coding an address:

```
Natural Health Products<br />
1 Happy Trails Way<br />
Anytown, USA, 00000<br />
```

The break tag in each instance forces a carriage return to the next available line, with no extra lines in between (see Figure 9.4).

Figure 9.4
Using the break tag gives you added control over text placement and spacing on your Web page.

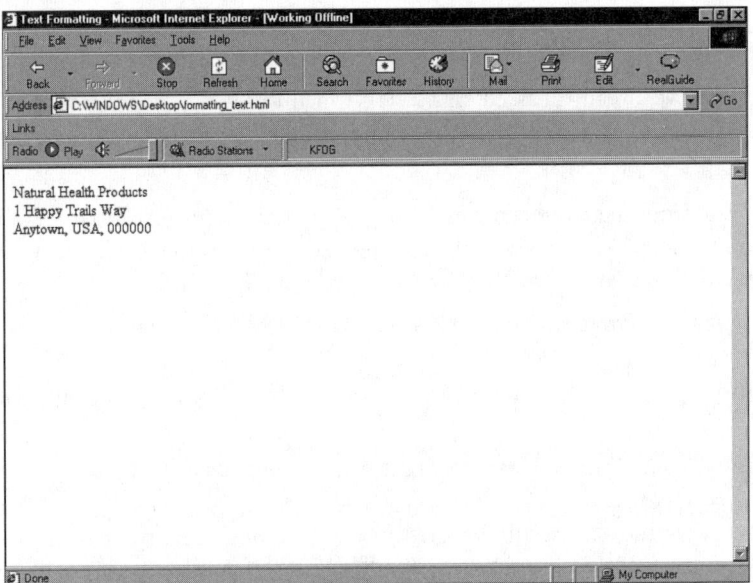

CREATING SPACE WITH BREAKS

Many people use breaks to create white space between elements, and even images or objects. Although not illegal per se, in strict documents, the preference is style sheets, and in transitional documents, table layouts. You also can consider using the pre, or preformatted text, element or employing the vspace attribute when working with images in transitional documents.

→ For information on how to use the vspace attribute, **see** Chapter 13, "Using Images in XHTML Documents," **p. 221**.

→ To find out how to use style sheets for positioning, **see** Chapter 18, "Cascading Style Sheets and XHTML," **p. 377**.

WORKING WITH THE PREFORMATTED TEXT TAG

The preformatted text tag, `<pre>`, and its companion closing tag, `</pre>`, were originally developed as a method of allowing columnar data in an HTML page. This was done before the advent of tables, and it was not an effective way of controlling data.

The tag works by including all the formatting you place within the tags—including carriage returns, spaces, and text—*without* the use of tags. In other words, you don't need a `<p>` tag to get a paragraph break, all you need to do is manually enter the paragraph tags, and so forth:

```
<pre>
This sentence is broken
Not by a break tag, but
By the preformatted carriage
Returns I've placed within
This section of code.
</pre>
```

Figure 9.5 shows how this code appears, complete with breaks.

PART

III

CH

9

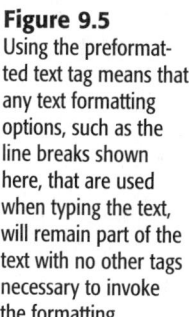

Figure 9.5
Using the preformatted text tag means that any text formatting options, such as the line breaks shown here, that are used when typing the text, will remain part of the text with no other tags necessary to invoke the formatting.

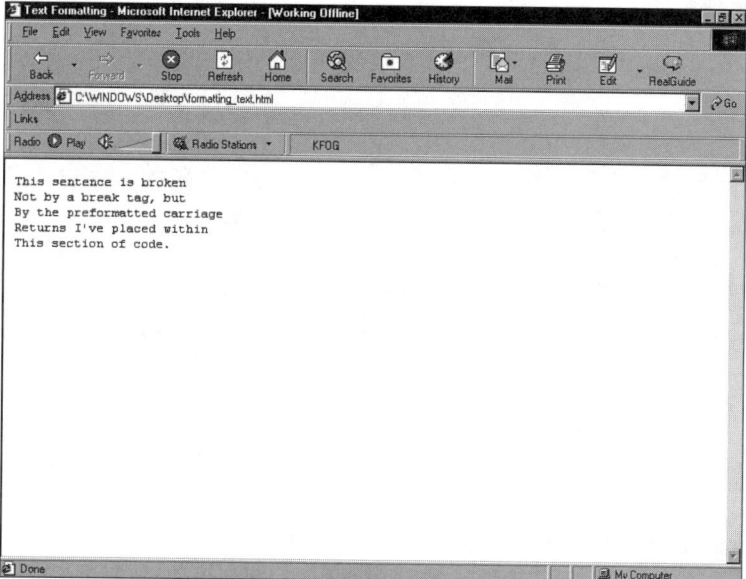

If you're very observant, you probably have noticed that the preformatted text tag does something else: it forces a fixed-width, or monospaced, font. This is different from the default font, and can be unattractive when the two are combined without forethought.

Tables have solved the irregularity problems caused when trying to arrange columnar material with the `pre` tag, and font tags and style sheets allow you to have infinitely more control over your fonts. The `pre` tag is still used from time to time to add space, however, and you can choose this option over or in addition to paragraphs and breaks when you want more space between elements on a page.

→ To learn more about creating columnar data with tables, **see** Chapter 14, "Laying Out Tables Within XHTML Documents," **p. 243**.

The preformatted text tag is still supported by all contemporary browsers, and can be confidently used for any of the tag's legal applications. However, choosing tables or sticking with paragraph and break tags is usually a more manageable choice than using the preformatted text tag.

USING TEXT STYLES

Writers and designers often want to draw attention to specific information within a text document. There are also conventional methods of formatting text information, such as creating bibliographic references.

Three main text styles can be used in XHTML 1.0 Transitional to accommodate these text formatting concerns: the bold, italic, and underline styles.

Caution

It's very important to maintain well-formed documents in XHTML. Frequent symmetry mistakes are made when employing text styles—especially when more than one style is being applied to a portion of text. So be careful to open and close your tags in the appropriate order.

The bold tag, or `<b>` (and its end tag, `</b>`) is simply placed around a set of text that you want to render in bold:

```
<p>Sally Forth sallies forth to <b>boldly</b> go where no one has
➥gone before.</p>
```

The same is true of italic tags, which use the `<i>` and closing `</i>` to achieve emphasis:

```
<p>Janet did a <i>terrific</i> job organizing this year's conference.</p>
```

The underline tags, with `<u>` and companion `</u>`, are no different:

```
<p>The novel I'm currently reading, <u>Fugitive Pieces</u>, is a poetic look at
the life of a Holocaust survivor.</p>
```

Caution

The underline element will not be included in XHTML 1.1. As such, the use of style sheets for underlining text is encouraged but not required.

In Figure 9.6, I've put each of these sentences together into an XHTML document and displayed them in my browser.

Caution

The use of underlined text should be approached with care. The reason for this is because links tend to be underlined, and people might mistake your underlined text for a link. Does this mean you should avoid underlining? I personally don't think so, but I do believe that it should be used only when necessary.

Figure 9.6
Bold, italic, and underlined text are all text formatting options, as seen here. However, you should use them for emphasis, and only where appropriate.

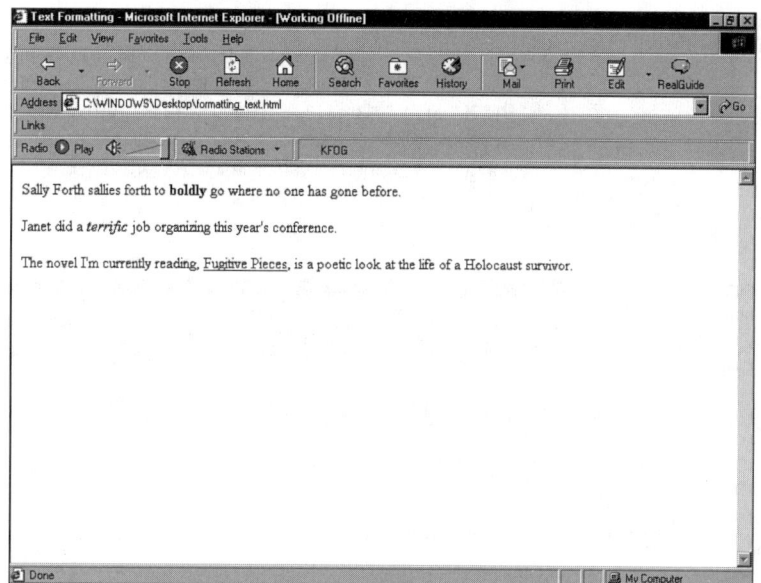

There are also tags related to bold and emphasis that will accomplish the same results. They are the ... and ... tags respectively.

Listing 9.3 shows a sample paragraph using standard bold and italics as well as the strong and emphasis options.

LISTING 9.3   USING THE Strong AND Emphasis ELEMENTS

```
<!DOCTYPE html PUBLIC "-//W3C//DTD XHTML 1.0 Transitional//EN"
"http://www.w3.org/TR/xhtml1/DTD/xhtml1-transitional.dtd">
<html xmlns="http://www.w3.org/1999/xhtml">
<head>
<title>Strong and Emphasis</title>
</head>
<body>

<p>People who <em>want</em> to be professional chefs usually learn by
apprenticing <strong>accomplished</strong> chefs, or by
attending an accredited culinary institute.</p>

<p>For those individuals <i>simply</i> interested in improving their
cooking skills, many <b>local</b> adult education and recreation
programs offer gourmet cooking classes.</p>

</body>
</html>
```

Figure 9.7 shows this code in the browser. You'll see that there is no visible difference between the two types as rendered in this browser.

It's interesting to point out that text formatting elements such as emphasis and italics are not dictated as appearing in italics by the standard. It's the browsers that make the decision to render the elements as you are seeing in Figure 9.7. Also, if you're authoring for multiple user agents, you may wish to use <em> and <strong> in order to have those agents render more accurately. For example, if you have a text-to-speech browser, that browser may read the text within a strong tag with a deeper voice.

Figure 9.7
Strong and emphasis are not visibly different from bold and italic.

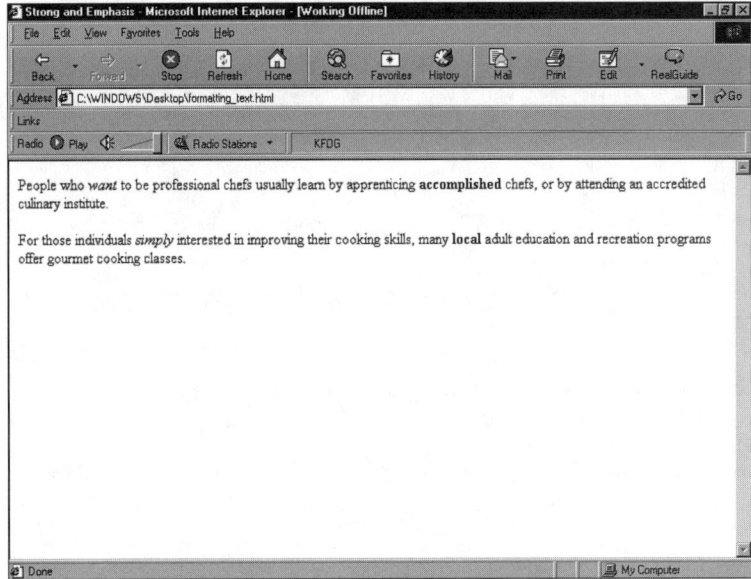

Use text styles sparingly. The point is to emphasize a few words or ideas on a page. More than this results in losing the impact that emphasis intends, so tread lightly. Furthermore, don't use italic, bold, or underline for long sections of body text—they are all more difficult to read for most people than standard weight text.

CREATING SPECIAL TEXT FORMATTING

Other, special types of text formatting are not as widely used, but do come in handy for certain kinds of text management. Of course, you can only use these in transitional XHTML 1.0 documents. In strict documents, this kind of control should be accomplished using style sheets.

If you want to make a section of text appear smaller than the surrounding body text, you can use the <small> tag:

```
<p>This text is normal, <small>whereas this text is smaller.
</small> This text is again normal.</p>
```

You can do the reverse by using the `<big>` tag:

```
<p>This text is normal, <big>whereas this text is bigger.</big>
This text is again normal.</p>
```

If you want to use superscript, which places the affected text slightly above the horizon line, you can use the `<sup>` element:

```
<p>This text is normal, <sup>whereas this text is superscripted.</sup> This
text is again normal.</p>
```

Subscript text, which appears below the horizon line, uses the `<sub>` tag:

```
<p>This text is normal, <sub>whereas this text is subscripted.</sub> This
text is again normal.</p>
```

And the editing convention known as strikethrough, can be achieved using the `<strike>` tag:

```
<p>This text is normal, <strike>whereas this text uses strikethrough.
</strike> This text is again normal.</p>
```

Figure 9.8 shows a screen shot of all these tags in action. You'll see that these really are specialty formats—most people rarely, if ever, have cause to use them.

PART

III

CH

9

Figure 9.8
Specialty formatting tags provide another element of control over the formatting and presentation of text on your Web page.

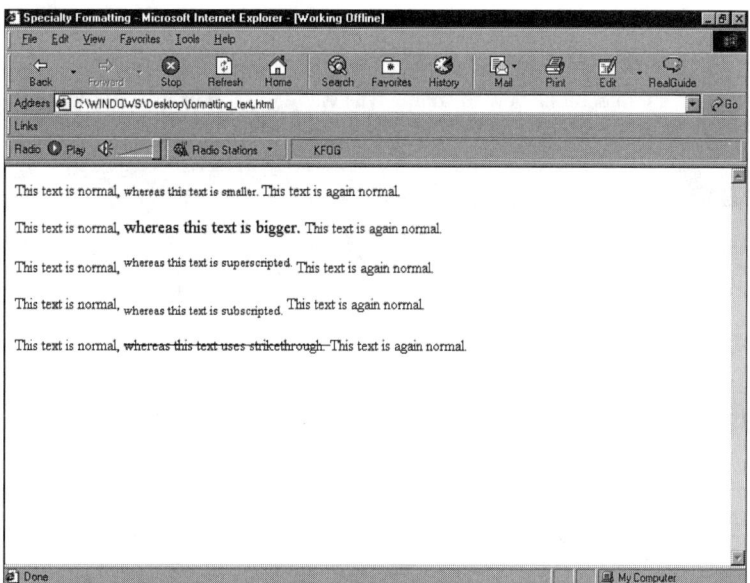

 Wondering what other specialty formatting tags you might use? See "Other Formatting Elements" in the "Troubleshooting" section near the end of this chapter.

ADDING COLOR, SIZE, AND TYPEFACES TO TEXT

One of the most problematic elements in HTML proved to be the font element. There are a few reasons as to why this is such a troublesome element, but two of the most compelling are

- For a specific font to display on a user's browser, that font must exist on his or her machine. This can severely limit choices for font faces, and also complicates HTML documents because of long strings of alternate font names included in the font tag attributes

- Every time you change the color, size, or font face, you must open and close the font tag. This also occurs within paragraphs and table cells. This causes an incredible amount of clutter within the document.

But, the realities for real-world designers who are trying to create well, the font element, despite all of its ugliness, works.

The font element gives you the most control available in HTML typography, which, as mentioned in the introduction to this chapter, is an area of great instability. With the FONT element, you can write your code to work with browsers that do not favor HTML 4.0 standards. You also can add style sheets to control typographic design.

→ For more information on how to control type with CSS, **see** Chapter 18, "Cascading Style Sheets and XHTML," **p. 377**.

> **Note**
>
> There is probably no more effective example of Transitional HTML 4.01 or XHTML 1.0 in use by professional coders today than just this issue: the deprecated font element used in combination with the favored CSS.

The font element uses the opening `<font>` and closing `</font>` tags, as shown in Listing 9.4.

LISTING 9.4   USING THE *font* TAG

```
<p><font>As soon as they had had enough to eat and drink they wanted music and
dancing, which are the crowning embellishments of a banquet, so a servant
brought a lyre to Phemius, whom they compelled perforce to sing to them. As
soon as he touched his lyre and began to sing Telemachus spoke low to Minerva,
with his head close to hers that no man might hear.</font></p>
```

Of course, if you were to load this into a browser, nothing would happen. You need some attributes to get color, size, and face into action.

FONT ELEMENT ATTRIBUTES

The following list defines the available attributes for the font element in XHTML 1.0 transitional.

- **size**—This attribute determines the font's size.
- **color**—Using this attribute, combined with a color, adds that color to the selection of text.
- **face**—This attribute allows HTML designers to write out the name of the typeface they want.

THE `size` ATTRIBUTE

Font sizing is fairly rudimentary, with whole-number values determining the size of the font. The default standard size is 3. Anything higher is going to be bigger and anything lower will be smaller.

The following is an example of a paragraph of text using font size:

```
<p><font size="5">As soon as they had had enough to eat and drink they wanted
music and dancing, which are the crowning embellishments of a banquet, so a
servant brought a lyre to Phemius, whom they compelled perforce to sing to
them. As soon as he touched his lyre and began to sing Telemachus spoke low to
Minerva, with his head close to hers that no man might hear.</font></p>
```

Figure 9.9 compares the default size of "3" to a size "5" paragraph.

Figure 9.9
The top paragraph is left at the default, and the bottom paragraph has a font size set to 5.

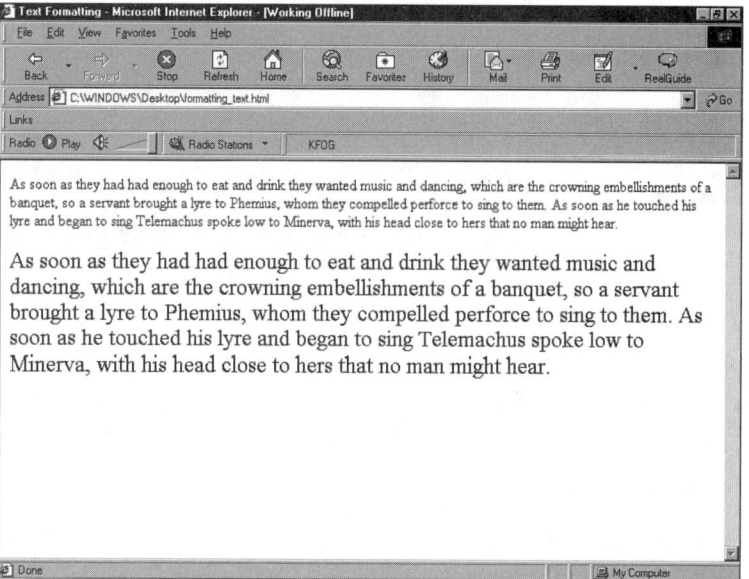

Anything much bigger than a size 5 is ungainly. Smaller sizes, such as 2, allow you to put more body text on a page, but you run the risk of making it difficult for people to read.

You also can use the minus and plus sign in front of a numeric value. The way this works is by adding the numeric size to the default (see Figure 9.10), as in the following:

```
<p><font size="-1"> As soon as they had had enough to eat and drink they wanted
music and dancing, which are the crowning embellishments of a banquet, so a
servant brought a lyre to Phemius, whom they compelled perforce to sing to
them. As soon as he touched his lyre and began to sing Telemachus spoke low to
Minerva, with his head close to hers that no man might hear.</font></p>
```

Figure 9.10
Subtract 1 from a standard default and you end up with a point size of 2.

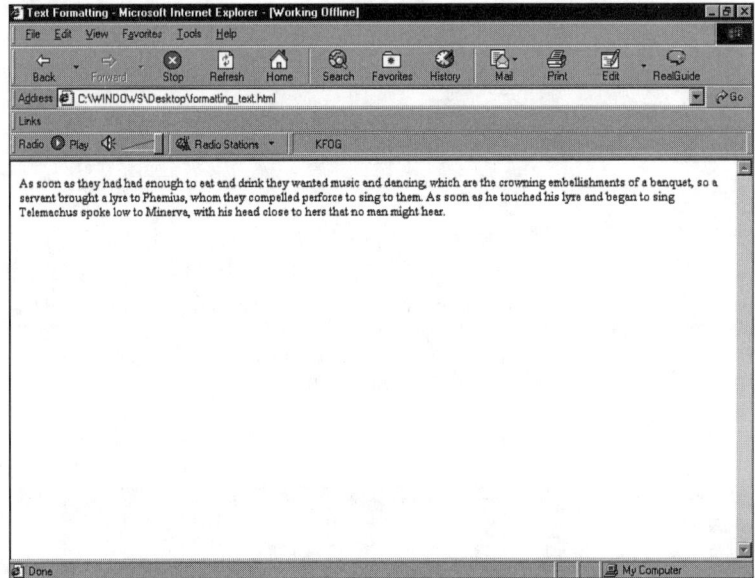

Note

The size attribute is essentially arbitrary because there's no standardization across browsers and platforms. This means that any size font will look different from one browser to another.

THE COLOR ATTRIBUTE

Understanding color theory and how color works on a computer screen and within a browser is very significant when it comes to selecting your text and link colors.

→ For a detailed explanation of color theory, **see** Chapter 25, "Color Concepts," **p. 527**.

The reason is two-fold:

- **Esthetic**—The quality of your page's design is always increased when you use color in a sophisticated fashion. It is important to learn how to make an individual palette that unifies your theme and sends a specific, visual message with each page you create.

- **Functional**—If you use colors that don't have enough contrast, your site visitors will have trouble reading your pages. You must choose colors that make visual as well as artistic sense.

⚠ *Are you unsure of how to get your link colors and background colors to work together? See "Matching Colors" in the "Troubleshooting" section near the end of this chapter.*

There are 136 predefined browser color names in general use, but only 16 of these color-names are found in HTML 4.01 and XHTML 1.0. Selecting from these colors, you can color text, links, and backgrounds.

Note

For a color chart that defines these colors by name, be sure to look for 136_colors.html online at `http://www.molly.com/molly/webdesign/136_colors.html`.

But the color names aren't broad enough for most developers, so professionals tend to work from the 216-color Web-safe palette to achieve visual stability when adding colors to links.

Note

This palette is viewable live at `http://www.molly.com/molly/webdesign/colorchart.html`.

An example of the `font` tag with the `color` attribute added looks like the following:

```
<p><font size="2" color="#999999"> As soon as they had had enough to eat and
drink they wanted music and dancing, which are the crowning embellishments of
a banquet, so a servant brought a lyre to Phemius, whom they compelled perforce
to sing to them. As soon as he touched his lyre and began to sing Telemachus
spoke low to Minerva, with his head close to hers that no man
might hear.</font></p>
```

By using Hexadecimal code, the base 16 equivalent of RGB (Red, Green, Blue) values, I've selected a gray color for my text.

→ For more about the Web-safe color palette, **see** Chapter 25, "Color Concepts," **p. 527**.

Note

For a good hexadecimal color chart visit `http://sdc.htrigg.smu.edu/HTMLPages/RGBchart.html` or download the nhue.gif file from `http://www.lynda.com/files/`. These charts put color selection and hexadecimal values right at your fingertips.

THE FACE ATTRIBUTE

If you want to add a font face to a selection of text, you can do so by using the `face` attribute and then defining a typeface name.

The following is an example of font code with the `face` attribute included:

```
<p><font face="arial">
As soon as they had had enough to eat and drink they wanted music and dancing,
which are the crowning embellishments of a banquet, so a servant brought a lyre
to Phemius, whom they compelled perforce to sing to them. As soon as he touched
his lyre and began to sing Telemachus spoke low to Minerva, with his head close
to hers that no man might hear.
</font></p>
```

Figure 9.11 shows the selection, and indeed, the face that appears is Arial regular.

Figure 9.11
The Arial typeface is in
the sans-serif family.

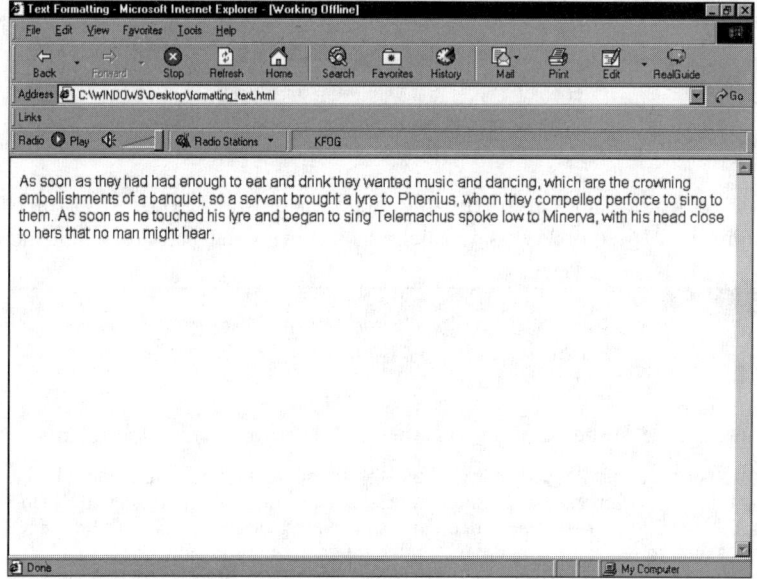

Sounds easy enough—and it is. The caveat—as I mentioned earlier—is that if the font isn't resident on your visitor's machine, he or she isn't going to see the font face that you're coding unless you provide some options.

Arial is a font native to Windows machines, but rarely, if ever, is it found on a Macintosh. Without that font being resident on the Macintosh, the browser will simply display the default font, which is normally set to Times. It's easy to see how quickly this can degrade any design you might have set out to create.

 Wondering if you really need to worry about whether a font is installed on your site visitor's machine? See "Using Other Fonts" in the "Troubleshooting" section near the end of this chapter.

The `face` attribute allows you to stack fonts into the value. The browser looks for the first font, and, if it doesn't find it, moves on to the next named font, and so on.

This stacking method gives you better control than just letting the browser do the thinking for you. You can put as many font names as appropriate and reasonable into the stack. This way, the browser will look for your preferred font and then for a similar font. In the case of the Macintosh, Helvetica is a sans-serif font that is similar to Arial.

```
<font face="arial, helvetica">
```

With this in the string, the browser looks for Helvetica if it cannot find Arial.

There's another option that you can add to the string as well. It's supported only by later Web browser versions, such as 4.0 and later. This allows you to put the generic family name into the string, as follows:

```
<font face="arial, helvetica, sans-serif">
```

Now the browser, if it cannot find Arial or Helvetica, will seek out the first sans-serif font that it can find on the resident machine and use that.

> **Note**
>
> The only two font names that are native to both Mac and Windows platforms are Courier and Times. Of course, many people add fonts to their systems. To get the best results, designers will use combinations of similar, common fonts to achieve the results desired.

Need to be sure that your corporate identity isn't lost by substituted fonts in your headers and other design elements? See "Need a Specific Font" in the "Troubleshooting" section near the end of this chapter.

This technique demonstrates clearly why it's so important to have an understanding of basic typography. You end up with ever so much more control.

Another important consideration is making sure you have a good understanding of what fonts are generally resident on standard machines. Table 9.1 shows the standard fonts that come loaded on Macintosh and Windows machines.

TABLE 9.1 COMPARISON OF RESIDENT FONTS ON WINDOWS AND MACINTOSH PLATFORMS

Windows	Macintosh
Arial	Chicago
Arial Black	Courier
Arial Narrow	Geneva
Arial Rounded MT Bold	Helvetica
Book Antiqua	Monaco
Bookman Old Style	New York
Century Gothic	Palatino
Century Schoolbook	Times
Courier	
Courier New	
Garamond	
Times New Roman	
Verdana	

It's a little daunting to think that the *only two fonts* that are completely cross-platform compatible are Times and Courier!

However, if you combine typographic knowledge with an understanding of the cross-platform limitations of fonts, you can gain some control over your documents.

Caution

You *must* remember that if a font face isn't available on a given machine, the default face will appear. Default is almost always a Serif font such as Times, unless the user has selected another font for his or her default.

Now you can put the `font face`, `color`, and `size` attributes together to come up with a singular style:

```
<p><font size="4" color="#666666" face="century schoolbook, times, serif">
As soon as they had had enough to eat and drink they wanted music and dancing,
which are the crowning embellishments of a banquet, so a servant brought a lyre
to Phemius, whom they compelled perforce to sing to them. As soon as he touched
his lyre and began to sing Telemachus spoke low to Minerva, with his head close
to hers that no man might hear.
</font></p>
```

Figure 9.12 shows the results: a size `"4"` dark gray type in the Century Schoolbook typeface.

Figure 9.12
The `font` tag with all attributes in action.

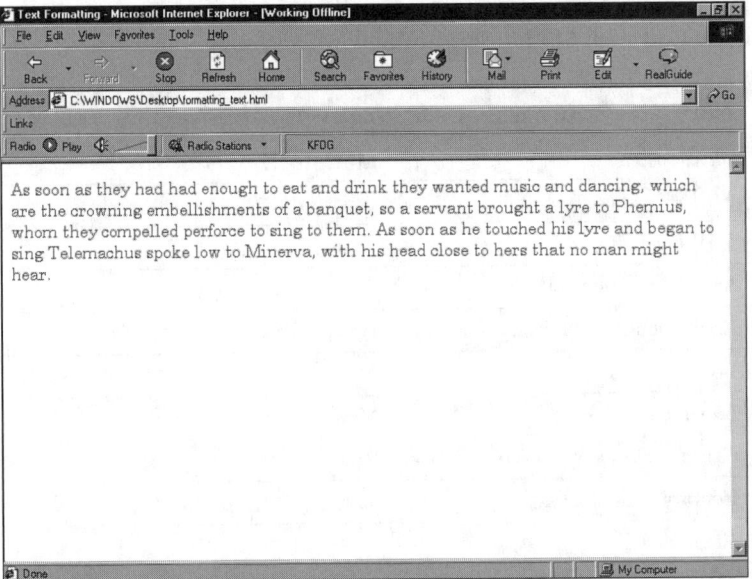

Note

If Web typography interests you, here are some resources to get you started:

DesktopPublishing.Com—A truly amazing place that contains thousands of resources, `http://www.desktoppublishing.com/`.

Microsoft's Typography on the Web—Excellent resource for all that's happening in Web typography, located at `http://www.microsoft.com/typography/web/default.htm`.

MANAGING COLOR FOR BACKGROUNDS, TEXT, AND LINKS

There are a number of specific attributes that can be added to the `<body>` tag to assist the browser in managing backgrounds, text, and link colors. Values for these attributes are either color names or hexadecimal codes, as described after the following attribute list:

- `text="x"`—This attribute tells the browser what color your default body text will be.

- `link="x"`—Without this attribute, browsers will usually use blue as a default link color, unless the user has configured another default link color into his or her browser. To maintain the integrity of your design, you should always use this attribute and set it to a value in step with your site palette—even if the color is blue.

- `vlink="x"`—This is the *visited* link. As with the link attribute, if you don't set this with a value, the browser will look for a default (usually purple), or a user-defined setting. For the same reasons as mentioned for using the `link="x"`, you should include an appropriate visited link color in your `body` string.

- `alink="x"`—Active link. This is a color that appears when the link is made active—when a mouse clicks it or passes over the link, depending on the browser you're using.

- `bgcolor="x"`—This sets the color that will fill your background. Browsers used to default to a very ugly gray, but now they usually default to white. Users can set this, too, so you always want to define it—even if you choose to use a background graphic (more on this in a bit).

- `background="url"`—Only use this attribute when you want to include a background graphic on your page.

Note

> Body controls, including the addition of background graphics, are very popular in HTML. However, these attributes have been deprecated in HTML 4.0 in favor of style sheets. As such, in XHTML, style sheets are the preferred method for achieving anything that has to do with presentation of material.

To add color to your XHTML transitional document using the `body` tag and the above attributes, simply use a color name or hexadecimal value with each of the desired attributes:

```
<body bgcolor="white" text="black" link="cyan" vlink="dark cyan"
alink="dark goldenrod">
```

or, for another color scheme in hexadecimal,

```
<body bgcolor="#999999" text="#FFFFFF" link="#660000"
vlink="#993300" alink="#CCCC99">
```

You also can add a background graphic:

```
<body bgcolor="#FFFFFF" text="#000000" link="#999999" vlink="#999999"
alink="#FFFFFF" background="images/gray_paper.gif">
```

Figure 9.13 shows a page with background color and links.

PART
III

CH
9

Figure 9.13
Background color and links.

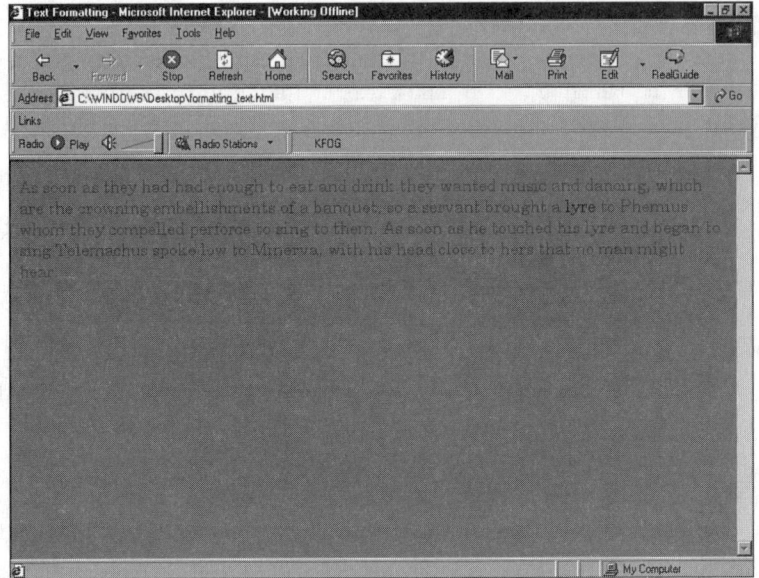

TROUBLESHOOTING

USING OTHER FONTS

Can't you assume that most computers are using Microsoft Word and, therefore, have certain other fonts installed?

Don't assume anything. Although Microsoft might lead the market in certain applications, there are still thousands of people using alternate packages. Also, not everyone installs the additional fonts that come with Microsoft or any other company's applications. The only fonts you can rely upon are those that come installed on the computer.

NEED A SPECIFIC FONT

If you need to use a specific font for headers to match a corporate identity, how can you ensure another font will not be substituted?

The only way to ensure that visitors will see your headers exactly as you intend is to create your headers in a graphics package and insert them as images into your HTML page. Even then, keep in mind that some visitors will be browsing without graphics, and will then only see the alternate text you code into your images, formatted in the default font.

DESIGNING FOR THE REAL WORLD

BEYOND BLACK AND WHITE

Choosing a palette for your Web site goes beyond choosing colors that work well together. Your color choices also work in conjunction with your images to create a tone for the site. If you're developing a site for "Sunny Days Farms," using blacks and grays would be incongruous with the name of the farm and the image it is likely to want to project.

A better example of how background and text colors can set a tone is funschool.com, a site with activities and games for children. In keeping with the name of the site and its target audience, the colors are bright and fun. There are more colors on the screen than I generally recommend, but they are used to good effect. When you enter, you immediately know that you are on a family site.

Although the site is brightly colored, funschool.com does not sacrifice readability. The contrast between the yellow background and blue text works well. The site also has the color convention of using black text on notes for parents and blue text to describe the child-oriented games and activities. The black connotes a more serious, adult tone, while the blue is playful.

PART

III

CH

9

Note

funschool.com–http://www.funschool.com

ADDING LISTS TO XHTML DOCUMENTS

In this chapter

USING LISTS

Lists are XHTML's way of helping to separate information into a logical series of items. Built on text-formatting styles, XHTML lists tend to be stable because browsers from early in the history of the language have supported them.

In this chapter, you'll get a chance to look at why lists are so valuable, learn how to use them, and to prepare for some of the special concerns to be aware of when using them.

COMMON LIST TAGS

The following tags are explored in this chapter:

- `<ul>...</ul>`—Unordered, or *bulleted* list.
- `<ol>...</ol>`—Ordered, or *numbered* list.
- `<li>...</li>`—List item tag.
- `<dl>...</dl>`—Definition list tag.
- `<dt>...</dt>`—Definition term, which is part of a definition list.
- `<dd>...</dd>`—Definition within a definition term.

THE VALUE OF LISTS

Why are lists so valuable? There are several important reasons, and as you work with XHTML both as a strict language and in the context of Web design, you'll see that, time and again, lists play an important role in the formatting of text documents.

Many times in this book I discuss the importance of being clear and concise when presenting information onscreen. Lists help you do just that—by clarifying important items, people are drawn directly to the information they must see, rather than having to wade through a lot of heavy text to find it.

Lists not only help clarify, but they logically order information, allowing you to guide your readers from one precise item to the next at a predetermined pace. This allows you to prepare your document content in such a way as to get people to the main ideas within that content quickly, and in the exact order you see fit.

Another powerful aspect of lists is that because they indent information, they create whitespace. This guides the eye toward important information, but also allows for a subtle but important design element to emerge: the flow, rather than the constraint, of space. Visual real estate is so precious on a computer screen that too much constrained information is detrimental to keeping people involved with the material.

Lists, then, strengthen a document logically, organizationally, and visually. This powerful combination can help every XHTML coder create pages with maximum impact.

→ For more information on how to maximize the visual impact of onscreen data, **see** Chapter 26,"Working with the Computer Screen," **p. 545**.

BULLETED (UNORDERED) LISTS

The bulleted list is probably the most commonly used to achieve logical organization within the text of an XHTML document. Bulleted lists place symbols rather than numeric values next to each list item. The default symbol of a standard, un-nested bulleted list is a disk.

→ For more information about list variations, **see** "List Attributes," **p. 174**.

Unordered lists begin and end with the <ul> and </ul> tags. As always, apply the container method when working with code, avoiding problems with well-formedness.

```
<ul>

</ul>
```

Now you need to put information between the tags. The most common information to use at this point is some unordered items, preceded by the list item <li> tags, as follows:

```
<ul>

<li>A pen</li>
<li>A glass of water</li>
<li>A small, yellow pad</li>

</ul>
```

This information appears as single line items preceded by a round bullet, as shown in Figure 10.1.

PART
II
CH
10

Figure 10.1
A bulleted, or unordered, list is commonly used to present small bits of information in a clean, orderly manner.

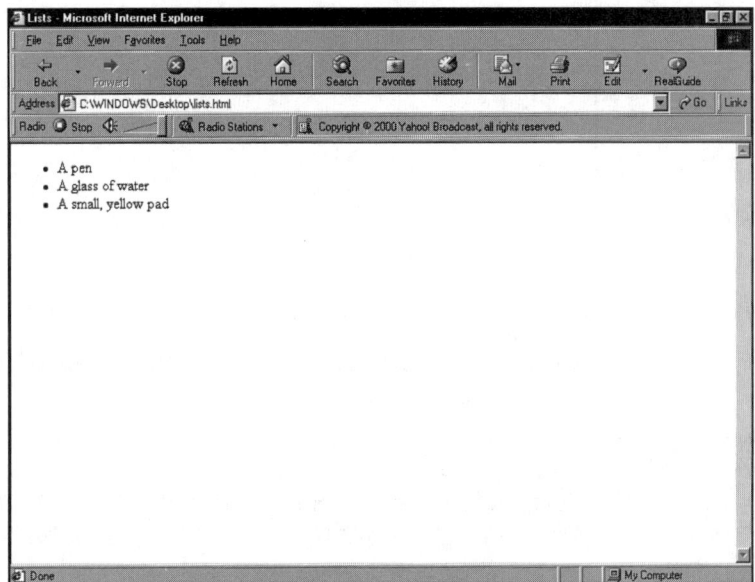

Experienced HTML coders will be aware that the closing link item tag, `</li>`, was rarely used in HTML. But, because of XHTML's rigorous syntax, the tag must now be closed to be a conforming XHTML document.

You'll notice that the browser naturally added a carriage return after each listed item. If you want more space between individual list items, you can add a break tag or two:

```
<ul>

<li>A pen<<br /><br />/li>

<li>A glass of water<br /><br /></li>

<li>A small, yellow pad<br /><br /></li>

</ul>
```

Figure 10.2 shows the additional space.

Figure 10.2
Additional space between line items can increase the readability of your list by providing additional whitespace—particularly if you are working with a smaller typeface.

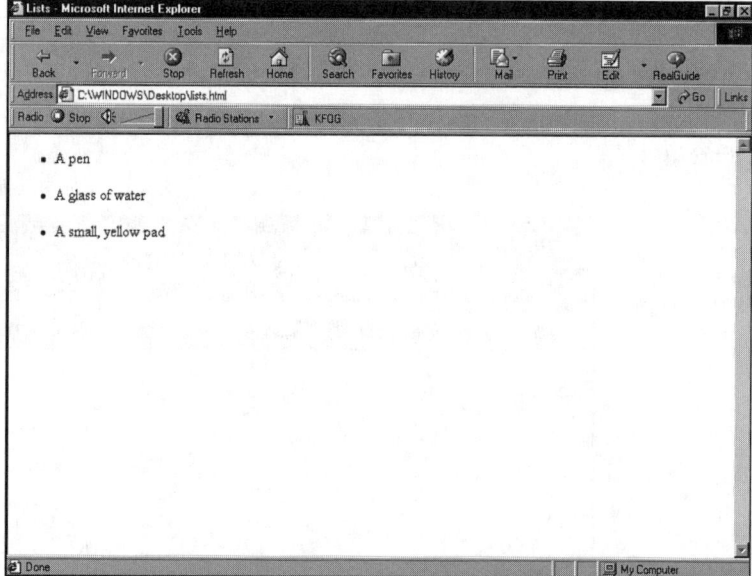

Different browsers interpret the amount of space between each line item differently. Therefore, if you choose to add a paragraph tag or other method of adding space between code, you'll need to check your work in a variety of environments.

Some coders use an indentation style to help them navigate code. Lists are one place where this can be done, as in the following:

➔ For an explanation of indentation style and other coding styles, **see** Chapter 5, "Defining XHTML Syntax," **p. 73**.

```
<ul>

        <li>A pen</li>
        <li>A glass of water</li>
        <li>A small, yellow pad</li>

</ul>
```

This indentation is a personal call—if you like the style and feel it will help you with speed and accuracy in your work, then go ahead and use it. My only concern is that you remain consistent in the style that you choose.

PART

II

CH

10

NUMBERED (ORDERED) LISTS

Ordered lists work exactly like bulleted lists, with the one exception being that instead of a round bullet being displayed by the line item tag, sequential numeric values are shown.

Begin with the container:

```
<ol>

</ol>
```

Use ordered lists wherever numeric ordering makes more sense than simple bullet points, as in the following:

```
<p>To get to Maple Drive follow these directions:</p>

<ol>

<li>Go to the first light on Main and take a left.</li>
<li>Drive 3 miles and turn right on High Street.</li>
<li>Follow High Street until you pass the Maple Elementary on your right.
Maple Drive is the first right after the school.</li>

</ol>
```

The numeric results are demonstrated in Figure 10.3. Note that standard numerals are displayed.

Figure 10.3
An ordered list presents information in a sequential manner.

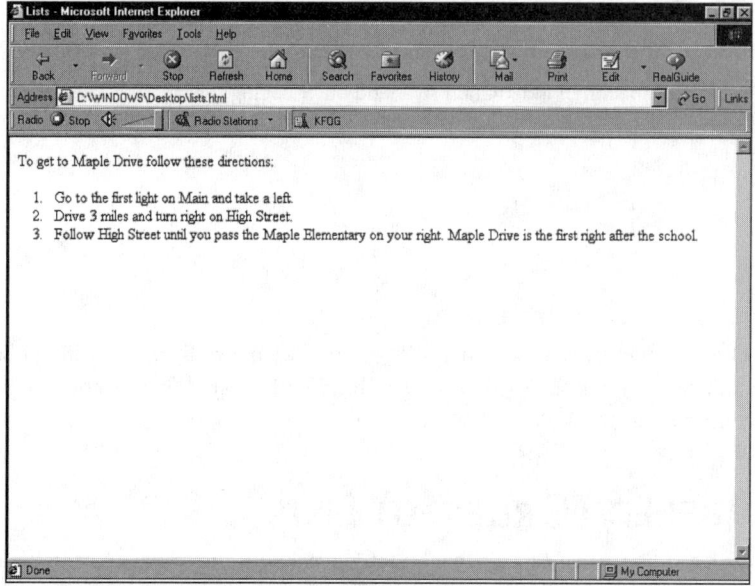

As with numbered lists, you can add extra space between each line item using paragraph or break tags. However, the same caution as to testing applies here, too.

 Want to use Roman numerals instead of standard numbers? See the "Troubleshooting" section near the end of this chapter for information on how to do just that.

Note

You can list as many items as you want to on a page, but you cannot stop a list and start another one and have it pick up at the numeric value where you left off. To set values on lists, you can use the value attribute, discussed in the "List Attributes" section toward the end of this chapter.

 Are you needing to use letters or Roman numerals for your lists rather than Arabic numbers? See "Alphabetical Lists" in the "Troubleshooting" section near the end of this chapter.

BUILDING A PAGE WITH LISTS

In this task, you'll build a page with both an ordered and unordered list:

1. Begin with an XHTML shell and title it **lists**:

```
<!DOCTYPE html PUBLIC "-//W3C//DTD XHTML 1.0 Transitional//EN"
"http://www.w3.org/TR/xhtml1/DTD/xhtml1-transitional.dtd">
<html xmlns="http://www.w3.org/1999/xhtml">
<head>
<title>Lists</title>
</head>
<body>
</body>
</html>
```

2. Now add an unordered container:

```
<!DOCTYPE html PUBLIC "-//W3C//DTD XHTML 1.0 Transitional//EN"
"http://www.w3.org/TR/xhtml1/DTD/xhtml1-transitional.dtd">
<html xmlns="http://www.w3.org/1999/xhtml">
<head>
<title>Lists</title>
</head>
<body>
<ul>

</ul>
</body>
</html>
```

3. Add several list items with a description and appropriate formatting:

```
<!DOCTYPE html PUBLIC "-//W3C//DTD XHTML 1.0 Transitional//EN"
"http://www.w3.org/TR/xhtml1/DTD/xhtml1-transitional.dtd">
<html xmlns="http://www.w3.org/1999/xhtml">
<head>
<title>Lists</title>
</head>
<body>
<ul>
<li>A reading lamp</li>
<li>A telephone</li>
<li>A clock</li>
<li>A computer</li>
<li>Stacks of paper</li>
<li>Books</li>
</ul>
</body>
</html>
```

4. Now separate the ordered list with a paragraph and add a new description:

```
<!DOCTYPE html PUBLIC "-//W3C//DTD XHTML 1.0 Transitional//EN"
"http://www.w3.org/TR/xhtml1/DTD/xhtml1-transitional.dtd">
<html xmlns="http://www.w3.org/1999/xhtml">
<head>
<title>Lists</title>
</head>
<body>
<p>What's on my desk:</p>
<ul>
<li>A reading lamp</li>
<li>A telephone</li>
<li>A clock</li>
<li>A computer</li>
<li>Stacks of paper</li>
<li>Books</li>
</ul>
<p>What's in my purse:</p>
</body>
</html>
```

5. Add the ordered list container:

```
<!DOCTYPE html PUBLIC "-//W3C//DTD XHTML 1.0 Transitional//EN"
"http://www.w3.org/TR/xhtml1/DTD/xhtml1-transitional.dtd">
<html xmlns="http://www.w3.org/1999/xhtml">
<head>
<title>Lists</title>
</head>
<body>
<p>What's on my desk:</p>
<ul>
<li>A reading lamp</li>
<li>A telephone</li>
<li>A clock</li>
<li>A computer</li>
<li>Stacks of paper</li>
<li>Books</li>
</ul>
<p>How to find my wallet:</p>
<ol>

</ol>
</body>
</html>
```

6. Add the list items:

```
<!DOCTYPE html PUBLIC "-//W3C//DTD XHTML 1.0 Transitional//EN"
"http://www.w3.org/TR/xhtml1/DTD/xhtml1-transitional.dtd">
<html xmlns="http://www.w3.org/1999/xhtml">
<head>
<title>Lists</title>

</head>
<body>

<p>What's on my desk:</p>

<ul>

<li>A reading lamp</li>
<li>A telephone</li>
<li>A clock</li>
<li>A computer</li>
<li>Stacks of paper</li>
<li>Books</li>

</ul>

<p>How to find my wallet:</p>

<ol>
<li>Go up the stairs.</li>
<li>Open the door to my office.</li>
<li>Climb over the mess.</li>
<li>Move all the papers off of my desk.</li>
```

```
<li>My wallet will be at the bottom of the pile.</li>
</ol>

</body>
</html>
```

7. Save the file as **lists.html** and compare it to Figure 10.4.

Figure 10.4
An unordered and ordered list on the same page. The unordered list is a random list of items; the ordered list describes a sequence of actions.

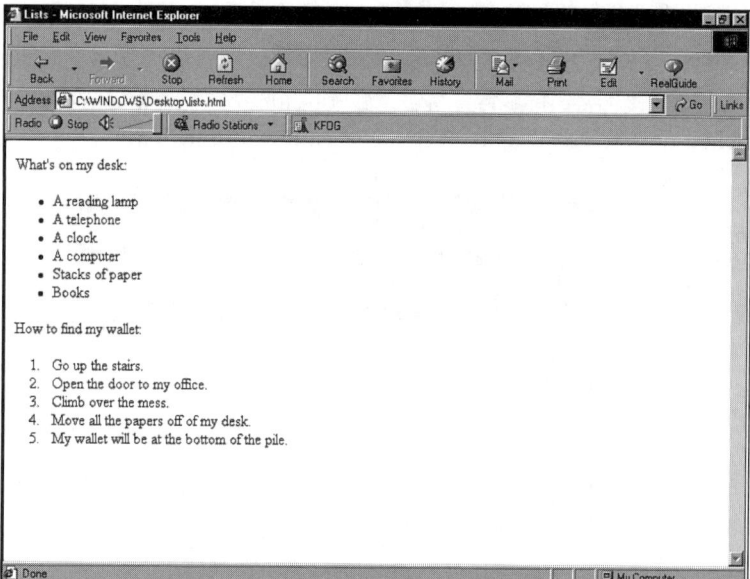

⚠ Want to know how to have lists with more than just plain round bullets? See "Alternate Bullets" in the "Troubleshooting" section near the end of this chapter for details.

DEFINITION LISTS

Definition lists come in handy when you want to offset information in dictionary-like style. These lists were created to manage such information as glossaries. The syntax for definition lists are a bit odd compared to the straightforward nature of ordered and unordered lists. Although the primary definition list tag, <dl>, and its required companion, </dl>, are standard, there are two unique internal tags that you can use: <dd> and <dt>.

Begin with the <dl> container:

```
<dl>

</dl>
```

Then, you add a definition term:

```
<dl>
```

PART
II

CH
10

```
<dt>element</dt>

</dl>
```

and then, the definition itself:

```
<dl>

<dt>element</dt>
<dd>an element can be considered the "command center" of code formatting.</dd>

</dl>
```

Figure 10.5 shows these tags in action. As with ordered and unordered lists, the tags used in definition lists also assume breaks between the information.

Figure 10.5
The definition list tags enable you to create a glossary-type list on your site.

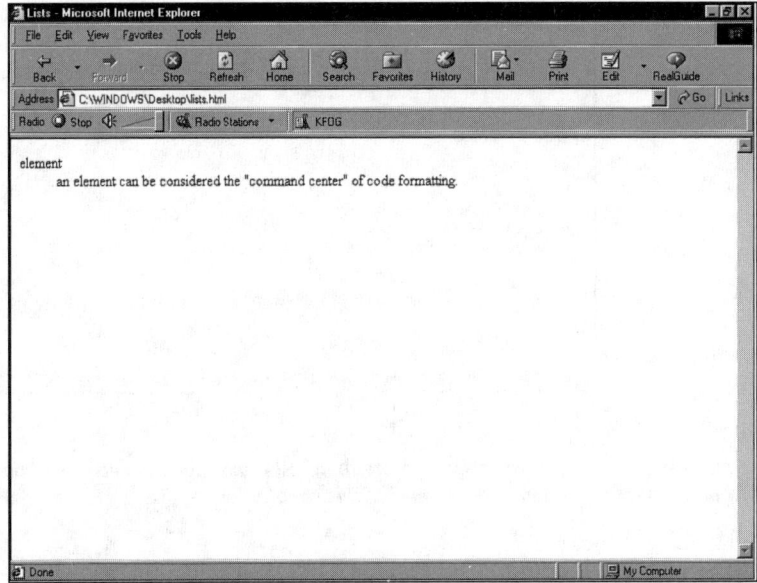

Several complications and additional issues must be addressed when working with lists. These include nesting lists, using lists for purposes other than their original intent, and working with list attributes.

ADVANCED LIST TECHNIQUES

There are several techniques that you can use to manipulate lists and list attributes more effectively. They include nesting lists, using lists for indentation, and altering list attributes.

NESTING LISTS

Nesting is the act of putting one container within another. Do you remember those magical Chinese boxes from childhood, where you would open one only to find another, identical but smaller, inside the first? This concept is akin to the process of nesting.

Lists can be nested, creating an outline style of information. When nesting lists, it's important to remember XHTML's well-formedness, or you can run into problems.

Let's build an unordered list with one level of nesting:

1. Open a basic XHTML shell in your favorite editor and title it **nested lists**.

```
<!DOCTYPE html PUBLIC "-//W3C//DTD XHTML 1.0 Transitional//EN"
"http://www.w3.org/TR/xhtml1/DTD/xhtml1-transitional.dtd">
<html xmlns="http://www.w3.org/1999/xhtml">
<head>
<title>Nested Lists</title>

</head>
<body>


</body>
</html>
```

2. Add the unordered list tags using the container method:

```
<!DOCTYPE html PUBLIC "-//W3C//DTD XHTML 1.0 Transitional//EN"
"http://www.w3.org/TR/xhtml1/DTD/xhtml1-transitional.dtd">
<html xmlns="http://www.w3.org/1999/xhtml">
<head>
<title>Nested Lists</title>

</head>
<body>

<ul>

</ul>

</body>
</html>
```

3. Add several list items:

```
<!DOCTYPE html PUBLIC "-//W3C//DTD XHTML 1.0 Transitional//EN"
"http://www.w3.org/TR/xhtml1/DTD/xhtml1-transitional.dtd">
<html xmlns="http://www.w3.org/1999/xhtml">
<head>
<title>Nested Lists</title>

</head>
<body>

<ul>
```

```
<li>Chocolate</li>
<li>Coffee</li>
<li>Sugar</li>

</ul>

</body>
</html>
```

4. Now, add another unordered list container *beneath* a list item (I've indented this one for the sake of clarity):

```
<!DOCTYPE html PUBLIC "-//W3C//DTD XHTML 1.0 Transitional//EN"
"http://www.w3.org/TR/xhtml1/DTD/xhtml1-transitional.dtd">
<html xmlns="http://www.w3.org/1999/xhtml">
<head>
<title>Nested Lists</title>

</head>
<body>

<ul>

<li>Chocolate
      <ul>

      </ul>

<li>Coffee</li>
<li>Sugar</li>

</li>

</ul>

</body>
</html>
```

5. Place several list items within that container:

```
<!DOCTYPE html PUBLIC "-//W3C//DTD XHTML 1.0 Transitional//EN"
"http://www.w3.org/TR/xhtml1/DTD/xhtml1-transitional.dtd">
<html xmlns="http://www.w3.org/1999/xhtml">
<head>
<title>Nested Lists</title>

</head>
<body>

<ul>

<li>Chocolate

      <ul>
      <li>unsweetened</li>
        <li>semi-sweet</li>
        <li>dark</li>

      </ul>
```

```
<li>Coffee</li>
<li>Sugar</li>

</li>
</ul>

</body>
</html>
```

6. View the file and check it against Figure 10.6.

7. Save the file as **nested_list.html**.

Figure 10.6
You'll notice that your nested list has a different kind of bullet from the primary level list. This is the browser's way of helping you and your page visitors distinguish between lists and sub-lists.

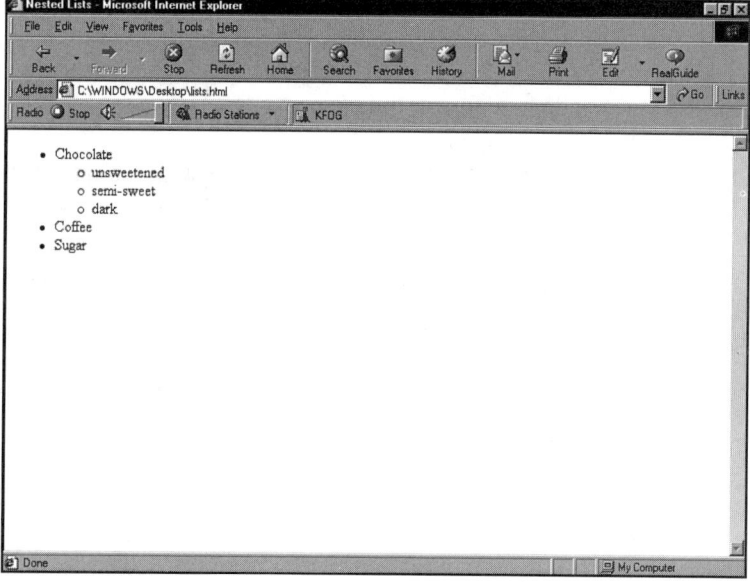

If you want to do the same thing with an ordered list, simply change the unordered tags to ordered tags, as shown in Listing 10.1.

LISTING 10.1   NESTED LISTS

```
<!doctype html public "-//W3C//DTD XHTML 1.0 Transitional//EN"
"http://www.w3.org/TR/xhtml1/DTD/xhtml1-transitional.dtd">
<html xmlns="http://www.w3.org/1999/xhtml">
<head>
<title>Nested Lists</title>
</head>

<body>

<p>The three most important food groups in order of importance:</p>
```

```
<ol>
<li>Chocolate
    <ol>
        <li>Buy the chocolate.</li>
        <li>Unwrap it quickly.</li>
        <li>Eat it immediately!</li>
    </ol>

<li>Coffee</li>
<li>Sugar</li>
</li>
</ol>

</body>
</html>
```

If you view this code in a browser, as I did (see Figure 10.7), you'll notice that the nested numeric list is *not* differentiated with another numeric system. The listing simply starts over, but is indented under the primary reference.

Figure 10.7
A nested, ordered list is displayed with the same formatting but with numbers rather than bullets.

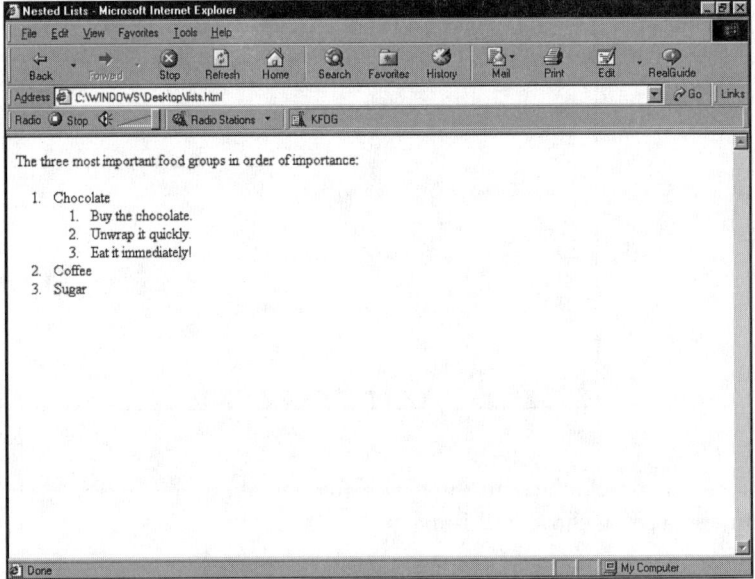

You can combine list types, too. Listing 10.2 shows the same list, but with the primary level as unordered, and the secondary level as ordered.

LISTING 10.2   MIXING NESTED LISTS

```
<!doctype html public "-//W3C//DTD XHTML 1.0 Transitional//EN"
"http://www.w3.org/TR/xhtml1/DTD/xhtml1-transitional.dtd">
<html xmlns="http://www.w3.org/1999/xhtml">
<head>
```

LISTING 10.2   CONTINUED

```
<title>Nested Lists: Mixed Lists</title>
</head>

<body>

<ul>

<li>Chocolate
<ol>
        <li>Buy the chocolate.</li>
        <li>Unwrap it quickly.</li>
        <li>Eat it immediately!</li>
   </ol>


<li>Coffee</li>
<li>Sugar</li>
</li>
</ul>

</body>
</html>
```

In this case, the bullets appear in the primary list, and the numerals in the secondary.

Try one more exercise, this time adding a third nested list to the original, unordered nested example:

1. Open nested_list.html in your editor.

2. Add a third-level unordered list container:

```
<!doctype html public "-//W3C//DTD XHTML 1.0 Transitional//EN"
"http://www.w3.org/TR/xhtml1/DTD/xhtml1-transitional.dtd">
<html xmlns="http://www.w3.org/1999/xhtml">
<head>

<title>Nested Lists: Three Deep</title>
</head>

<body>

<ul>

<li>Chocolate

    <ul>
        <li>unsweetened                 <ul>

                    </ul>
        </li>
        <li>semi-sweet</li>
        <li>dark</li>
    </ul>

    <li>Coffee</li>
```

```
<li>Sugar</li>
</li>
</ul>

</body>
</html>
```

3. Add the list items:

```
<!doctype html public "-//W3C//DTD XHTML 1.0 Transitional//EN"
"http://www.w3.org/TR/xhtml1/DTD/xhtml1-transitional.dtd">
<html xmlns="http://www.w3.org/1999/xhtml">
<head>

<title>Nested Lists: Three Deep</title>
</head>

<body>

<ul>

<li>Chocolate

    <ul>
        <li>unsweetened
            <ul>
                        <li>Hershey's</li>
                <li>Cadbury's</li>
                        <li>Toblerone</li>

                </ul>
        </li>
          <li>semi-sweet</li>
          <li>dark</li>
    </ul>

<li>Coffee</li>
<li>Sugar</li>
</li>
</ul>

</body>
</html>
```

4. Compare the file to Figure 10.8.

5. Save the file as **3nested_lists.html**.

You'll see that your third list now has a square, rather than round, symbol, to help differentiate the levels of information. If you were to do this example with an ordered list, the same results for double lists would apply: The third list will take on numeric values, beginning from 1, but with no differentiation in type.

Figure 10.8
Nested list with three
sections.

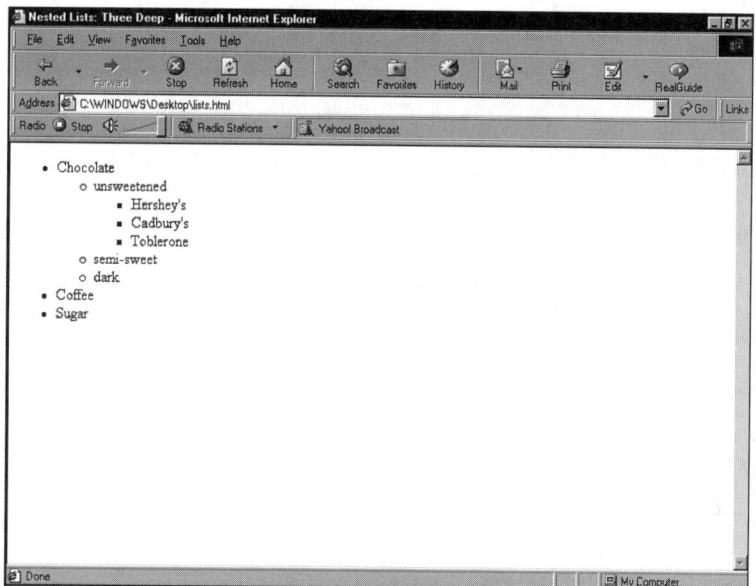

USING LISTS FOR INDENTING ITEMS

Frustrated by a lack of control, particularly in the early days of HTML, coders got clever and saw that they could exploit certain aspects of tags to get results that were never intended by that tag.

A prime example of this is lists. You might have noticed that all lists naturally create indentations to achieve the logical placement of specific items. So some coders, and some software applications, exploit lists to achieve indentation.

Look at this little snippet of code I took from a WYSIWYG editor:

```
<P><UL>
</UL>
<P>
```

What on earth is this, you might be thinking? Well, it's an empty list within a paragraph—a poor attempt at adding an indent, exploiting list properties.

The problems with this are threefold. First, you're using a tag for which it was never intended—setting yourself up for possible problems with certain browsers. Second, there are much more stable and appreciable ways of indenting information with HTML 4.0. Finally, it's not acceptable to do this in XHTML, which asks for rigor in syntax. Superfluous code of this nature is simply unallowed.

→ To find other methods of indenting content, **see** Chapter 14, "Laying Out Tables Within XHTML Documents," **p. 243**, and Chapter 18, "Cascading Style Sheets and XHTML," **p. 377**.

LIST ATTRIBUTES

Some people want to be able to control the order or visual appearance of list elements. This can be done by using several list attributes, including value and type.

If I want to pick up where I left off with an ordered list, I can add a numeric value to the list item:

```
<ol>

<li value="30">This is item 30</li>
<li>this is 31</li>
<li>and so forth</li>

</ol>
```

I can change the visual appearance of my bullets using the type attribute in the list item, as follows:

```
<ul>

<li type="disc">This bullet appears as a disc</li>
<li type="circle">This appears as a circle</li>
<li type="square">and this bullet appears as a square</li>

</ul>
```

Figure 10.9 shows these attributes at work.

Figure 10.9
Adding value and type to lists can help to differentiate your list items, especially when nesting one or more lists.

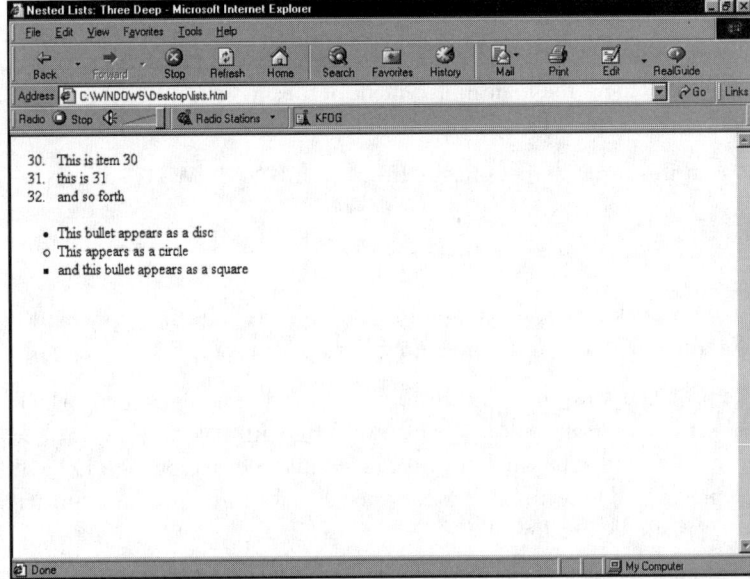

Some people do use the type attribute with list items, and it is supported by contemporary browsers. In fact, the type attribute can be replaced with style sheets, which in strict XHTML 1.0 is the way to go.

TROUBLESHOOTING

ALPHABETICAL LISTS

How do you create a list in alphabetical, rather than numerical, order?

You can use the type attribute within your ordered list element to specify alphabetical order or even Roman numeration, but this is a deprecated attribute in strict DTDs. The best method is to use style sheets to define classes for lists. These classes can specify alphabetical or Roman numerical order, as well as other formatting information.

→ To learn more about style sheets and Web typography, **see** Chapter 18, "Cascading Style Sheets and XHTML," **p. 377**.

ALTERNATE BULLETS

What about all the lists on the Web that use fancy bullets?

There are several different ways to break content into a list. Many of these methods do not use the <ol> or <ul> tags, however, and instead use tables and/or images to give the appearance of a bulleted list format.

→ To find more information on creating tables, **see** Chapter 14, "Laying Out Tables Within XHTML Documents," **p. 243**.

→ To learn how to prepare images, **see** Chapter 29, "Creating Professional Web Graphics," **p. 595**.

DESIGNING FOR THE REAL WORLD

USING LISTS: DINOSAURIA AND *PUBLISHER'S WEEKLY*

As mentioned throughout this chapter, lists help create a flow to your Web pages. They also provide built-in whitespace to make the page easier on the eyes. As with all things XHTML, lists need to be used in proper balance with the rest of your content. If you break your content down into too many bulleted items, you risk losing depth in your subject matter as everything becomes a "sound bite."

Lists don't necessarily have to be used as a series of one-liners, however. The Dinosauria uses lists to divide larger chunks of information. The bullets allow your eyes to easily jump from topic to topic, while each item provides a complete explanation of a particular dinosaur myth.

Lists also make great jumping-off points. The *Publisher's Weekly* Bestsellers site makes excellent use of XHTML lists. The list items are nested in a table, creating a two-column list.

This opens up even more whitespace than a standard, one-column list. Also, each item on the list is a link to another area on the site. The main page is left uncluttered and easy to navigate, with the real meat of the site's content left to internal pages.

Note

The Dinosauria–`http://www.ucmp.berkeley.edu/diapsids/dinosaur.html`

***Publisher's Weekly* Bestsellers**–`http://www.publishersweekly.com/bestsellersindex.asp`

ALIGNING TEXT USING XHTML

In this chapter

ALIGNING TEXT

The way text appears on a page is important to both readability and esthetics. *Alignment*—also known as *justification*—describes how the text is positioned both in relation to itself, and in relation to other objects on a page. Alignment plays a large role in the way text looks, determining where and how that text is placed.

The problem for Web designers who want to use XHTML is that alignment is the domain of style sheets, and in the strictest XHTML interpretations, must be relegated to them. However, alignment can be used properly in XHTML if you're writing transitional documents. Because alignment is pretty common for current Web developers, and style sheets are not completely ready for all markets, I'm including this information for your use. Just keep in mind that all documents with the forms of alignment described here must conform to the XHTML *transitional* DTD.

→ To recap the DTDs in XHTML, **see** Chapter 5, "Defining XHTML Syntax," **p. 73.**

Typically, text is justified to the left (at least with most Western languages). This means it begins at the flush-left margin of the page. Along the right side, the text is uneven. This is referred to as *ragged right*.

However, there are other alignment options that you'll want to use. For shorter sections of text, you can right-align or center the text. This can add emphasis to the text in question, as well as break up the space to provide a bit of visual respite from the standard justification.

> **Note**
>
> You can use several methods to control text alignment. There are common XHTML tags, attributes, and values of which you should be aware. It's important to remember that because alignment is really a layout process rather than a formatting process, style-sheet alignment is recommended over the elements described herein.

→ To learn how to align text using style sheets, see Chapter 18, "Cascading Style Sheets and XHTML," **p. 377.**

Before getting to the actual tags, take a look at what values or types of alignment are available:

- **Default**—When no alignment is specified for text, browsers cause it to default to the standard flush left, ragged right (see Figure 11.1).
- **Left**—This is the same as browser default. However, you can use left as a fixed value with alignment. This is especially helpful when you're using another kind of alignment on the page and want to secure anything that you want to appear as left-justified.
- **Right**—Right alignment is the flushing of text to the right margin leaving a ragged left margin, as shown in Figure 11.2. Right alignment is an interesting special effect, but generally should be used as enhancement, not standard body text.
- **Center**—The centering of text, like right justification, creates a visual effect (see Figure 11.3). It's important not to overuse centering. Many novice designers use a lot of

centered text. What they're really after is whitespace and visual texture, because centering creates a more interesting look. However, it is difficult to read for any length of time.

- **Justify**—Justification is the spacing of text so that each margin is flush rather than
  ragged. Compare Figure 11.4 to the left, or default, justification in Figure 11.1 to get
  an idea of the difference.

Figure 11.1
Default or flush-left
alignment.

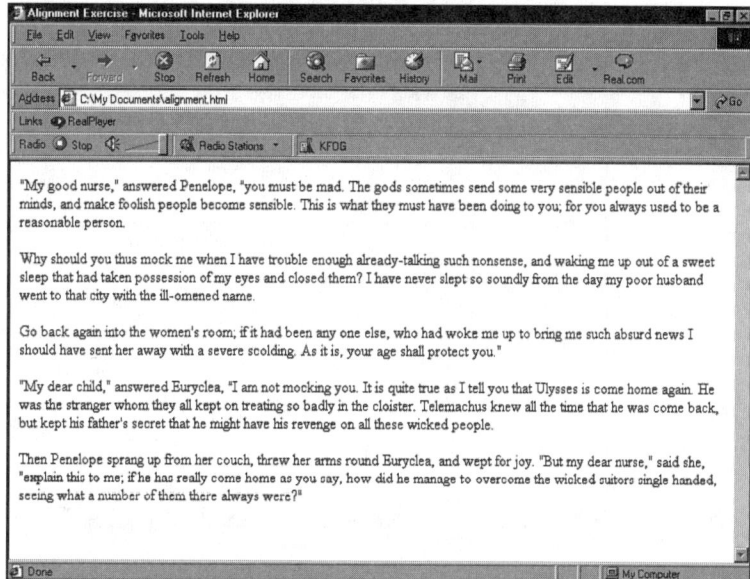

Figure 11.2
Right alignment. Note
ragged left margin.

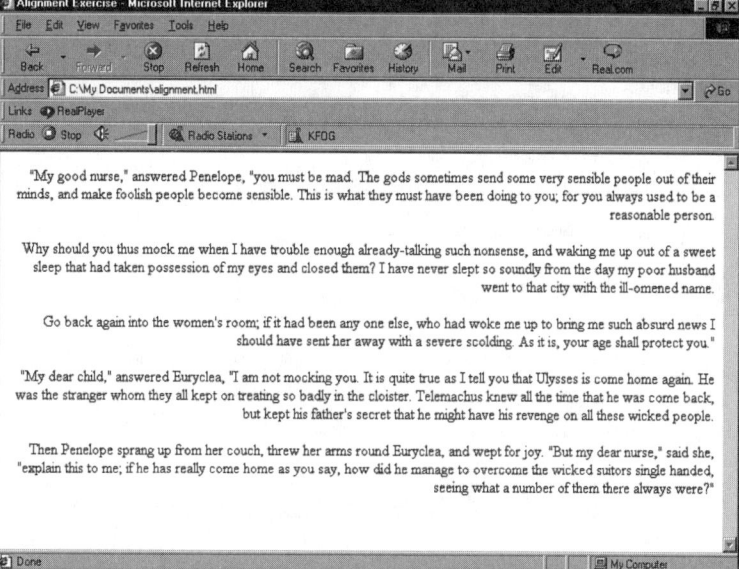

Warning

The `justify` attribute is only available for Internet Explorer and Netscape 4.0 and later. If you choose to use it, your alignment reverts to the default left in browsers that cannot read it.

Figure 11.3
Centered text. Centering should be used for emphasis, not for body text.

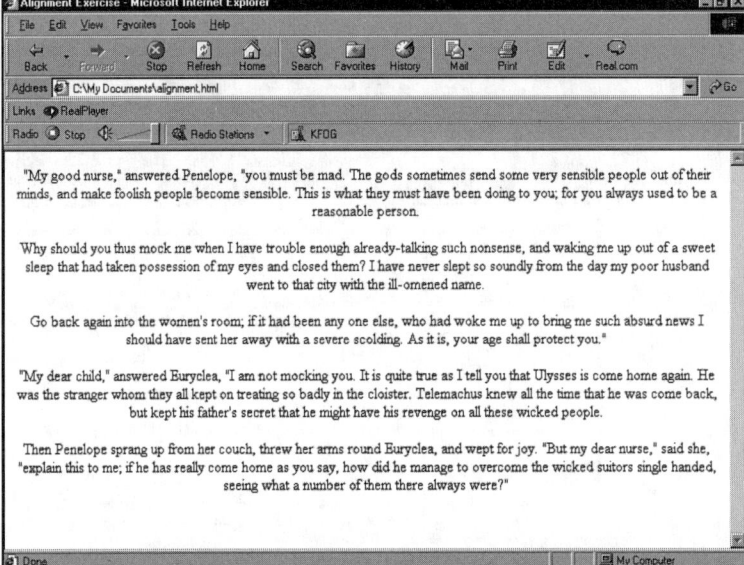

Figure 11.4
Justified text has flush left and right margins. You can see clearly how each line is flush left and right.

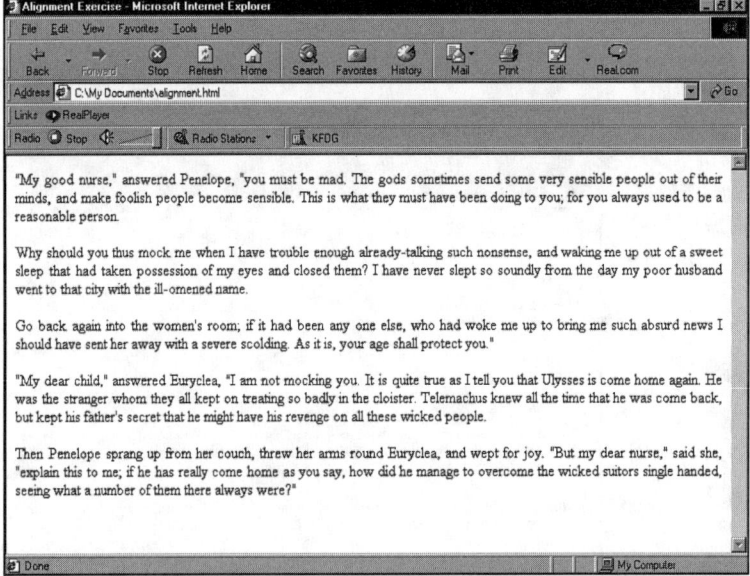

Alignment with Style

As mentioned, style sheets are the preferred method in strict XHTML 1.0 for many layout concerns. Text alignment can be controlled with style sheets.

The appropriate syntax for aligning text with style sheets is as follows:

```
text-align: value
```

Your value can equal left, center, right, or justify just as with standard HTML tagging.

USING THE div ELEMENT

The div element is a powerful tool for a number of reasons. Not only can it be used to divide sections of an HTML document and align information within that section, but also it is one of the pillars of cascading style sheets.

Using the div element, whether for simple document formatting or for more advanced applications, has become one of the primary methods of controlling Web documents since HTML 4.0.

To align text by using the div element, you'll need to select one of the alignment attributes discussed in the previous section.

Note

You'll see that I've added the blockquote element to many of the examples in this chapter. Although this element has lost emphasis since the HTML 4.0 standard in favor of style sheet positioning, it's a simple and effective way to block sections of text attractively within a page that isn't using style sheets. It's important to realize that blockquote was never intended for this purpose, but it's become a conventional method of gaining margins and attractive spacing of text. It is acceptable in transitional XHTML 1.0. However, it's not acceptable in strict XHTML to do this. Many experts are encouraging people away from the use of blockquote even in transitional documents.

If you have a section of text that you want to center, you apply the div tags to the document in a step-by-step fashion, adding formatting along the way:

1. Begin with a transitional XHTML shell:

```
<!DOCTYPE html PUBLIC "-//W3C//DTD XHTML 1.0 Transitional//EN"
"http://www.w3.org/TR/xhtml1/DTD/xhtml1-transitional.dtd">
<html xmlns="http://www.w3.org/1999/xhtml">
<head>
<title>Alignment Exercise </title>
</head>
<body>


</body>
</html>
```

2. Add the text for the page:

```
<!DOCTYPE html PUBLIC "-//W3C//DTD XHTML 1.0 Transitional//EN"
"http://www.w3.org/TR/xhtml1/DTD/xhtml1-transitional.dtd">
<html xmlns="http://www.w3.org/1999/xhtml">
<head>
<title>Alignment Exercise </title>
</head>
<body>
The Odyssey, by Homer

Book XXIII

"My good nurse," answered Penelope, "you must be mad. The gods sometimes send
some very sensible people out of their minds, and make foolish people become
sensible. This is what they must have been doing to you; for you always used
to be a reasonable person.

Why should you thus mock me when I have trouble enough already-talking such
nonsense, and waking me up out of a sweet sleep that had taken possession of
my eyes and closed them? I have never slept so soundly from the day my poor
husband went to that city with the ill-omened name.

Go back again into the women's room; if it had been any one else, who had woke
me up to bring me such absurd news I should have sent her away with a severe
scolding. As it is, your age shall protect you."

"My dear child," answered Euryclea, "I am not mocking you. It is quite true as
I tell you that Ulysses is come home again. He was the stranger whom they all
kept on treating so badly in the cloister. Telemachus knew all the time that
he was come back, but kept his father's secret that he might have his revenge
on all these wicked people."

Then Penelope sprang up from her couch, threw her arms round Euryclea, and
wept for joy. "But my dear nurse," said she, "explain this to me; if he has
really come home as you say, how did he manage to overcome the wicked suitors
single anded, seeing what a number of them there always were?"

</body>
</html>
```

3. Format the text to your needs:

```
<!DOCTYPE html PUBLIC "-//W3C//DTD XHTML 1.0 Transitional//EN"
"http://www.w3.org/TR/xhtml1/DTD/xhtml1-transitional.dtd">
<html xmlns="http://www.w3.org/1999/xhtml">
<head>
<title>Alignment Exercise </title>
</head>
<body>

<head>
<title>Alignment Exercise</title>
</head>
<body>

<h2>The Odyssey, by Homer</h2>
```

```
<b>Book XXIII</b><br />
<blockquote>
<p>"My good nurse," answered Penelope, "you must be mad. The gods sometimes
send some very sensible people out of their minds, and make foolish people
become sensible. This is what they must have been doing to you; for you always
used to be a reasonable person.</p>

<p>Why should you thus mock me when I have trouble enough already-talking such
nonsense, and waking me up out of a sweet sleep that had taken possession of
my eyes and closed them? I have never slept so soundly from the day my poor
husband went to that city with the ill-omened name. </p>

<p>Go back again into the women's room; if it had been any one else, who had
woke me up to bring me such absurd news I should have sent her away with a
severe scolding. As it is, your age shall protect you." </p>

<p>"My dear child," answered Euryclea, "I am not mocking you. It is quite true
as I tell you that Ulysses is come home again. He was the stranger whom they
all kept on treating so badly in the cloister. Telemachus knew all the time
that he was come back, but kept his father's secret that he might have his
revenge on all these wicked people." </p>

<p>Then Penelope sprang up from her couch, threw her arms round Euryclea, and
wept for joy. "But my dear nurse," said she, "explain this to me; if he has
really come home as you say, how did he manage to overcome the wicked suitors
single handed, seeing what a number of them there always were?" </p>

</blockquote>
</body>
</html>
```

4. Now add the opening and closing div tags around the text you want to align:

```
<!DOCTYPE html PUBLIC "-//W3C//DTD XHTML 1.0 Transitional//EN"
"http://www.w3.org/TR/xhtml1/DTD/xhtml1-transitional.dtd">
<html xmlns="http://www.w3.org/1999/xhtml">
<head>
<title>Alignment Exercise </title>
</head>
<body>

<div>
<h2>The Odyssey, by Homer</h2>
<b>Book XXIII</b><br />
</div>

<blockquote>
<p>"My good nurse," answered Penelope, "you must be mad. The gods sometimes
send some very sensible people out of their minds, and make foolish people
become sensible. This is what they must have been doing to you; for you always
used to be a reasonable person.</p>

<p>Why should you thus mock me when I have trouble enough already-talking such
nonsense, and waking me up out of a sweet sleep that had taken possession of
my eyes and closed them? I have never slept so soundly from the day my poor
husband went to that city with the ill-omened name. </p>
```

```
<p>Go back again into the women's room; if it had been any one else, who had
woke me up to bring me such absurd news I should have sent her away with a
severe scolding. As it is, your age shall protect you." </p>

<p>"My dear child," answered Euryclea, "I am not mocking you. It is quite true
as I tell you that Ulysses is come home again. He was the stranger whom they
all kept on treating so badly in the cloister. Telemachus knew all the time
that he was come back, but kept his father's secret that he might have his
revenge on all these wicked people." </p>

<p>Then Penelope sprang up from her couch, threw her arms round Euryclea, and
wept for joy. "But my dear nurse," said she, "explain this to me; if he has
really come home as you say, how did he manage to overcome the wicked suitors
single handed, seeing what a number of them there always were?" </p>

</blockquote>
</body>
</html>
```

5. Type the attribute and center value into the opening div tag:

```
<!DOCTYPE html PUBLIC "-//W3C//DTD XHTML 1.0 Transitional//EN"
"http://www.w3.org/TR/xhtml1/DTD/xhtml1-transitional.dtd">
<html xmlns="http://www.w3.org/1999/xhtml">
<head>
<title>Alignment Exercise </title>
</head>
<body>

<div align="center">
<h2>The Odyssey, by Homer</h2>
<b>Book XXIII</b><br />
</div>

<blockquote>
<p>"My good nurse," answered Penelope, "you must be mad. The gods sometimes
send some very sensible people out of their minds, and make foolish people
become sensible. This is what they must have been doing to you; for you always
used to be a reasonable person.</p>

<p>Why should you thus mock me when I have trouble enough already-talking such
nonsense, and waking me up out of a sweet sleep that had taken possession of
my eyes and closed them? I have never slept so soundly from the day my poor
husband went to that city with the ill-omened name. </p>

<p>Go back again into the women's room; if it had been any one else, who had
woke me up to bring me such absurd news I should have sent her away with a
severe scolding. As it is, your age shall protect you." </p>

<p>"My dear child," answered Euryclea, "I am not mocking you. It is quite true
as I tell you that Ulysses is come home again. He was the stranger whom they
all kept on treating so badly in the cloister. Telemachus knew all the time
that he was come back, but kept his father's secret that he might have his
revenge on all these wicked people. </p>

<p>Then Penelope sprang up from her couch, threw her arms round Euryclea, and
wept for joy. "But my dear nurse," said she, "explain this to me; if he has
```

```
really come home as you say, how did he manage to overcome the wicked suitors
single handed, seeing what a number of them there always were?" </p>

</blockquote>
</body>
</html>
```

6. Save your document as div_center.html.

7. View the page in your browser.

The text header should now be center-aligned and the body text default left, as in my example shown in Figure 11.5.

Figure 11.5
Using the div element to center the alignment of the header enables me to leave the rest of the page defaults at the original left alignment.

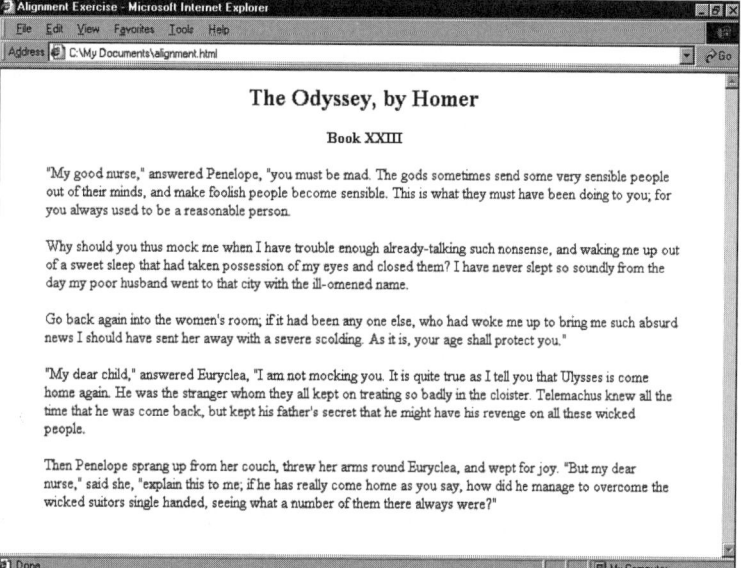

Note

Many HTML authors use the <center> tag to center text. This element has been deprecated in the HTML 4.0 standard, and therefore in the XHTML 1.0 strict standard as well. Although it is still considered part of the transitional interpretation, it was deprecated primarily due to its lack of flexibility: No attributes or values can be added to it. Choosing the <div> element or other elements discussed in this chapter for centering text is a more sophisticated choice. The centering of text with the div tag renders the same visual results to the text or images in question as the center element did.

If you want to alter your selection of text and make it align to the right, change the code to reflect the `right` value (see Listing 11.1).

LISTING 11.1   ALIGNING TO THE RIGHT

```
<!DOCTYPE html PUBLIC "-//W3C//DTD XHTML 1.0 Transitional//EN"
"http://www.w3.org/TR/xhtml1/DTD/xhtml1-transitional.dtd">
<html xmlns="http://www.w3.org/1999/xhtml">
<head>
<title>Alignment Exercise </title>
</head>
<body>

<div align="right">
<h2>The Odyssey, by Homer</h2>
<b>Book XXIII</b><br />
</div>

<blockquote>
<p>"My good nurse," answered Penelope, "you must be mad. The gods sometimes
send some very sensible people out of their minds, and make foolish people
become sensible. This is what they must have been doing to you; for you always
used to be a reasonable person.</p>

<p>Why should you thus mock me when I have trouble enough already-talking such
nonsense, and waking me up out of a sweet sleep that had taken possession of
my eyes and closed them? I have never slept so soundly from the day my poor
husband went to that city with the ill-omened name. </p>

<p>Go back again into the women's room; if it had been any one else, who had
woke me up to bring me such absurd news I should have sent her away with a
severe scolding. As it is, your age shall protect you." </p>

<p>"My dear child," answered Euryclea, "I am not mocking you. It is quite true
as I tell you that Ulysses is come home again. He was the stranger whom they
all kept on treating so badly in the cloister. Telemachus knew all the time
that he was come back, but kept his father's secret that he might have his
revenge on all these wicked people. </p>

<p>Then Penelope sprang up from her couch, threw her arms round Euryclea, and
wept for joy. "But my dear nurse," said she, "explain this to me; if he has
really come home as you say, how did he manage to overcome the wicked suitors
single handed, seeing what a number of them there always were?" </p>

</blockquote>
</body>
</html>
```

Figure 11.6 shows the header with right alignment as formatted with the `div` element. The remaining text defaults to the left.

Figure 11.6
Using the div element here results in right alignment of the header with all text outside of the element defaulting to the left.

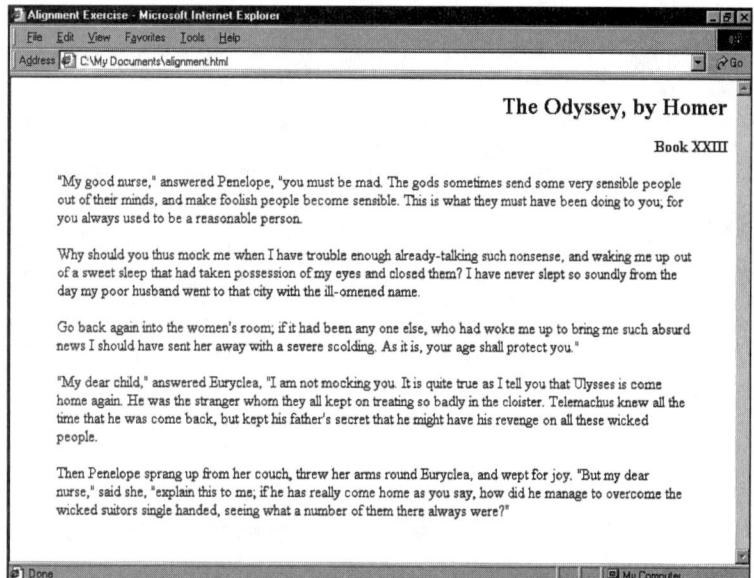

Similarly, by changing the value to justify, you can use the div element to justify the text. In the code sample shown in Listing 11.2, I've justified the entire page of text, making the entire page a single division.

LISTING 11.2   JUSTIFYING TEXT

```
<!DOCTYPE html PUBLIC "-//W3C//DTD XHTML 1.0 Transitional//EN"
"http://www.w3.org/TR/xhtml1/DTD/xhtml1-transitional.dtd">
<html xmlns="http://www.w3.org/1999/xhtml">
<head>
<title>Alignment Exercise </title>
</head>
<body>

<h2>The Odyssey, by Homer</h2>
<b>Book XXIII</b><br />
<div align="justify">


<blockquote>
<p>"My good nurse," answered Penelope, "you must be mad. The gods sometimes
send some very sensible people out of their minds, and make foolish people
become sensible. This is what they must have been doing to you; for you always
used to be a reasonable person.</p>

<p>Why should you thus mock me when I have trouble enough already-talking such
nonsense, and waking me up out of a sweet sleep that had taken possession of my
eyes and closed them? I have never slept so soundly from the day my poor
husband went to that city with the ill-omened name. </p>
```

```
<p>Go back again into the women's room; if it had been any one else, who had
woke me up to bring me such absurd news I should have sent her away with a
severe scolding. As it is, your age shall protect you." </p>

<p>"My dear child," answered Euryclea, "I am not mocking you. It is quite true
as I tell you that Ulysses is come home again. He was the stranger whom they
all kept on treating so badly in the cloister. Telemachus knew all the time
that he was come back, but kept his father's secret that he might have his
revenge on all these wicked people. </p>

<p>Then Penelope sprang up from her couch, threw her arms round Euryclea,
and wept for joy. "But my dear nurse," said she, "explain this to me; if he has
really come home as you say, how did he manage to overcome the wicked suitors
single handed, seeing what a number of them there always were?" </p>

</blockquote>
</div>
</body>
</html>
```

Figure 11.7 demonstrates the attractive, tight look of justified text.

Figure 11.7
Justified text is clean and attractive.

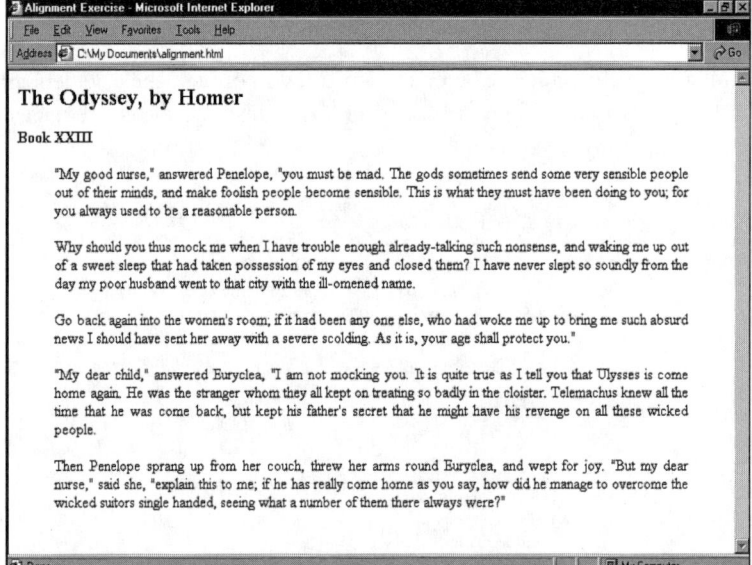

USING THE paragraph ELEMENT TO ALIGN TEXT

You also can use the starting and ending paragraph tags, combined with the same attributes as found within the `<div>` tag, to create the exact same type of alignment.

Once again, left is the standard default for paragraphs, so you will rarely, if ever, use this attribute with a paragraph tag.

In the following stepped example, you'll align text to the center using the open/close paragraph tags:

1. Begin with a transitional XHTML shell:

```
<!DOCTYPE html PUBLIC "-//W3C//DTD XHTML 1.0 Transitional//EN"
"http://www.w3.org/TR/xhtml1/DTD/xhtml1-transitional.dtd">
<html xmlns="http://www.w3.org/1999/xhtml">
<head>
<title>Alignment Exercise </title>
</head>
<body>


</body>
</html>
```

2. Add your text selection:

```
<!DOCTYPE html PUBLIC "-//W3C//DTD XHTML 1.0 Transitional//EN"
"http://www.w3.org/TR/xhtml1/DTD/xhtml1-transitional.dtd">
<html xmlns="http://www.w3.org/1999/xhtml">
<head>
<title>Alignment Exercise </title>
</head>
<body>

The Odyssey, by Homer
Book XXIV

"Happy Ulysses, son of Laertes," replied the ghost of Agamemnon, "you are
indeed blessed in the possession of a wife endowed with such rare excellence
of understanding, and so faithful to her wedded lord as Penelope the daughter
of Icarius. The fame, therefore, of her virtue shall never die, and the
immortals shall compose a song that shall be welcome to all mankind in honour
of the constancy of Penelope.

How far otherwise was the wickedness of the daughter of Tyndareus who killed
her lawful husband; her song shall be hateful among men, for she has brought
disgrace on all womankind even on the good ones."

Thus did they converse in the house of Hades deep down within the bowels of
the earth. Meanwhile Ulysses and the others passed out of the town and soon
reached the fair and well-tilled farm of Laertes, which he had reclaimed with
infinite labour. Here was his house, with a lean-to running all round it,
where the slaves who worked for him slept and sat and ate, while inside the
house there was an old Sicel woman, who looked after him in this his
country-farm. When Ulysses got there, he said to his son and to the other two:

"Go to the house, and kill the best pig that you can find for dinner.
Meanwhile I want to see whether my father will know me, or fail to recognize
me after so long an absence."
</body>
</html>
```

PART

II

CH

11

3. Format the text with paragraphs and other formatting you want to use:

```
<!DOCTYPE html PUBLIC "-//W3C//DTD XHTML 1.0 Transitional//EN"
"http://www.w3.org/TR/xhtml1/DTD/xhtml1-transitional.dtd">
<html xmlns="http://www.w3.org/1999/xhtml">
<head>
<title>Alignment Exercise </title>
</head>
<body>

<h2>The Odyssey, by Homer</h2>
<b>Book XXIV</b><br />

<blockquote>
<p>"Happy Ulysses, son of Laertes," replied the ghost of Agamemnon, "you are
indeed blessed in the possession of a wife endowed with such rare excellence
of understanding, and so faithful to her wedded lord as Penelope the daughter
of Icarius. The fame, therefore, of her virtue shall never die, and the
immortals shall compose a song that shall be welcome to all mankind in honour
of the constancy of Penelope.</p>

<p>How far otherwise was the wickedness of the daughter of Tyndareus who
killed her lawful husband; her song shall be hateful among men, for she has
brought disgrace on all womankind even on the good ones."</p>

<p>Thus did they converse in the house of Hades deep down within the bowels of
the earth. Meanwhile Ulysses and the others passed out of the town and soon
reached the fair and well-tilled farm of Laertes, which he had reclaimed with
infinite labour. Here was his house, with a lean-to running all round it,
where the slaves who worked for him slept and sat and ate, while inside the
house there was an old Sicel woman, who looked after him in this his country-
farm. When Ulysses got there, he said to his son and to the other two:</p>

<p>"Go to the house, and kill the best pig that you can find for dinner.
Meanwhile I want to see whether my father will know me, or fail to recognize
me after so long an absence."</p>

</blockquote>
</body>
</html>
```

4. Now, add the center align value to the section you want to center:

```
<!DOCTYPE html PUBLIC "-//W3C//DTD XHTML 1.0 Transitional//EN"
"http://www.w3.org/TR/xhtml1/DTD/xhtml1-transitional.dtd">
<html xmlns="http://www.w3.org/1999/xhtml">
<head>
<title>Alignment Exercise </title>
</head>
<body>
<h2>The Odyssey, by Homer</h2>
<b>Book XXIV</b><br />

<blockquote>
<p>"Happy Ulysses, son of Laertes," replied the ghost of Agamemnon, "you are
indeed blessed in the possession of a wife endowed with such rare excellence
```

```
of understanding, and so faithful to her wedded lord as Penelope the daughter
of Icarius. The fame, therefore, of her virtue shall never die, and the
immortals shall compose a song that shall be welcome to all mankind in honour
of the constancy of Penelope.</p>

<p align="">How far otherwise was the wickedness of the daughter of Tyndareus
who killed her lawful husband; her song shall be hateful among men, for she
has brought disgrace on all womankind even on the good ones."</p>

<p>Thus did they converse in the house of Hades deep down within the bowels of
the earth. Meanwhile Ulysses and the others passed out of the town and soon
reached the fair and well-tilled farm of Laertes, which he had reclaimed with
infinite labour. Here was his house, with a lean-to running all round it,
where the slaves who worked for him slept and sat and ate, while inside the
housethere was an old Sicel woman, who looked after him in this his country-
farm. When Ulysses got there, he said to his son and to the other two:</p>

<p>"Go to the house, and kill the best pig that you can find for dinner.
Meanwhile I want to see whether my father will know me, or fail to recognize
me after so long an absence."</p>
</blockquote>
</body>
</html>
```

5. Save the file as p_align.html.

6. Compare your file to the example I've captured in Figure 11.8. Your alignment might appear slightly different than mine if you've set your font size or resolution differently than I have, but the type of alignment you see should be the same.

Figure 11.8
Center alignment with the paragraph element. The p element controls only what is immediately within the scope of the paragraph, whereas the div element can control the alignment of multiple paragraphs.

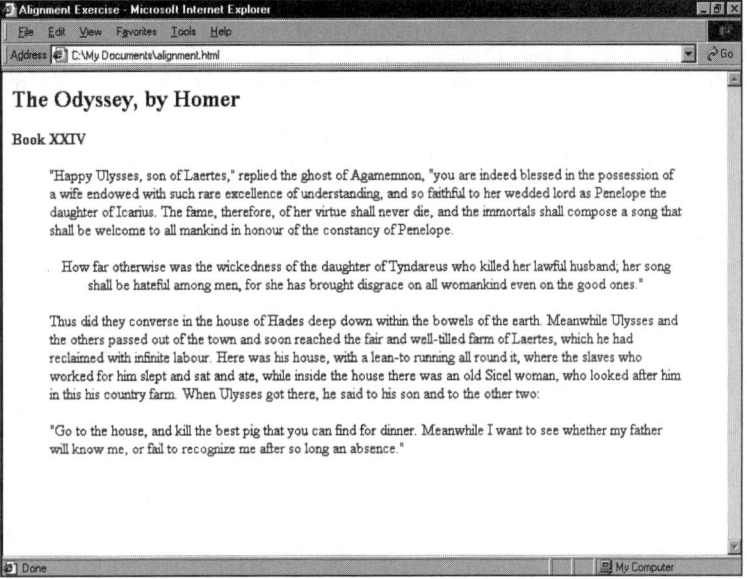

As with the div element, you can simply change the value to create another alignment style (see Listing 11.3).

LISTING 11.3   USING THE `<p>` ELEMENT FOR ALIGNMENT

```
<!DOCTYPE html PUBLIC "-//W3C//DTD XHTML 1.0 Transitional//EN"
"http://www.w3.org/TR/xhtml1/DTD/xhtml1-transitional.dtd">
<html xmlns="http://www.w3.org/1999/xhtml">
<head>
<title>Alignment Exercise </title>
</head>
<body>
<h2>The Odyssey, by Homer</h2>
<b>Book XXIV</b><br />

<blockquote>
<p>"Happy Ulysses, son of Laertes," replied the ghost of Agamemnon, "you are
indeed blessed in the possession of a wife endowed with such rare excellence of
understanding, and so faithful to her wedded lord as Penelope the daughter of
Icarius. The fame, therefore, of her virtue shall never die, and the immortals
shall compose a song that shall be welcome to all mankind in honour of the
constancy of Penelope.</p>

<p align="right">How far otherwise was the wickedness of the daughter of Tyndareus
who killed her lawful husband; her song shall be hateful among men, for she has
brought disgrace on all womankind even on the good ones."</p>

<p>Thus did they converse in the house of Hades deep down within the bowels of
the earth. Meanwhile Ulysses and the others passed out of the town and soon
reached the fair and well-tilled farm of Laertes, which he had reclaimed with
infinite labour. Here was his house, with a lean-to running all round it, where
the slaves who worked for him slept and sat and ate, while inside the house
there was an old Sicel woman, who looked after him in this his country farm.
When Ulysses got there, he said to his son and to the other two:</p>

<p>"Go to the house, and kill the best pig that you can find for dinner.
Meanwhile I want to see whether my father will know me, or fail to recognize
me after so long an absence."</p>

</blockquote>
</body>
</html>
```

As you can see in Figure 11.9, the paragraph where I've added the right value to the align attribute is right-aligned as expected.

Figure 11.9
Right alignment using the paragraph element. Use this approach sparingly, as the resulting ragged left can be difficult to read.

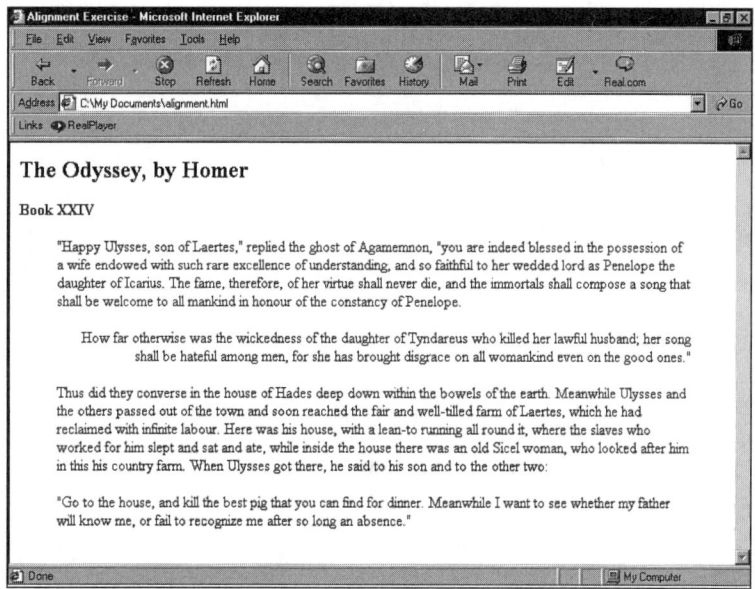

However, because the paragraph element only influences individual paragraphs, you would have to add the value to *every* opening paragraph tag to format an entire page to that value (see Listing 11.4).

LISTING 11.4 ALIGNING A FULL PAGE OF TEXT WITH THE paragraph ELEMENT, INCLUDING THE ALIGNMENT IN EACH OPENING PARAGRAPH TAG

```
<!DOCTYPE html PUBLIC "-//W3C//DTD XHTML 1.0 Transitional//EN"
"http://www.w3.org/TR/xhtml1/DTD/xhtml1-transitional.dtd">
<html xmlns="http://www.w3.org/1999/xhtml">
<head>
<title>Alignment Exercise </title>
</head>
<body>
<h2>The Odyssey, by Homer</h2>
<b>Book XXIV</b><br />

<blockquote>
<p align="right">"Happy Ulysses, son of Laertes," replied the ghost of
Agamemnon, "you are indeed blessed in the possession of a wife endowed with
such rare excellence of understanding, and so faithful to her wedded lord as
Penelope the daughter of Icarius. The fame, therefore, of her virtue shall
never die, and the immortals shall compose a song that shall be welcome to all
mankind in honour of the constancy of Penelope.</p>

<p align="right">How far otherwise was the wickedness of the daughter of Tyndareus
who killed her lawful husband; her song shall be hateful among men, for she has
brought disgrace on all womankind even on the good ones."</p>
```

```
<p align="right">Thus did they converse in the house of Hades deep down within
the bowels of the earth. Meanwhile Ulysses and the others passed out of the
town and soon reached the fair and well-tilled farm of Laertes, which he had
reclaimed with infinite labour. Here was his house, with a lean-to running all
round it, where the slaves who worked for him slept and sat and ate, while
inside the house there was an old Sicel woman, who looked after him in this
his country farm. When Ulysses got there, he said to his son and to the other
two:</p>

<p align="right">"Go to the house, and kill the best pig that you can find for
dinner. Meanwhile I want to see whether my father will know me, or fail to
recognize me after so long an absence."</p>

</blockquote>
</body>
</html>
```

Although this technique works and is perfectly legal code, it is somewhat cumbersome. In a case such as this, I would choose using the div element to manage the page's alignment. I would re-code the page as shown in Listing 11.5.

LISTING 11.5 USING THE div ELEMENT—A MORE ELEGANT SOLUTION FOR LONGER SECTIONS OF TEXT

```
<!DOCTYPE html PUBLIC "-//W3C//DTD XHTML 1.0 Transitional//EN"
"http://www.w3.org/TR/xhtml1/DTD/xhtml1-transitional.dtd">
<html xmlns="http://www.w3.org/1999/xhtml">
<head>
<title>Alignment Exercise </title>
</head>
<body>
<h2>The Odyssey, by Homer</h2>
<b>Book XXIV</b><br />

<div align="right">

<blockquote>
<p>"Happy Ulysses, son of Laertes," replied the ghost of Agamemnon, "you are
indeed blessed in the possession of a wife endowed with such rare excellence
of understanding, and so faithful to her wedded lord as Penelope the daughter
of Icarius. The fame, therefore, of her virtue shall never die, and the
immortals shall compose a song that shall be welcome to all mankind in honour
of the constancy of Penelope.</p>

<p>How far otherwise was the wickedness of the daughter of Tyndareus who killed
her lawful husband; her song shall be hateful among men, for she has brought
disgrace on all womankind even on the good ones."</p>

<p>Thus did they converse in the house of Hades deep down within the bowels of
the earth. Meanwhile Ulysses and the others passed out of the town and soon
reached the fair and well-tilled farm of Laertes, which he had reclaimed with
infinite labour. Here was his house, with a lean-to running all round it, where
the slaves who worked for him slept and sat and ate, while inside the house
there was an old Sicel woman, who looked after him in this his country farm.
When Ulysses got there, he said to his son and to the other two:</p>
```

```
<p>"Go to the house, and kill the best pig that you can find for dinner.
Meanwhile I want to see whether my father will know me, or fail to recognize
me after so long an absence."</p>

</blockquote>

</div>
</body>
</html>
```

Figure 11.10 shows the results

Figure 11.10
All-over alignment with the div element streamlines the code across longer sections of text.

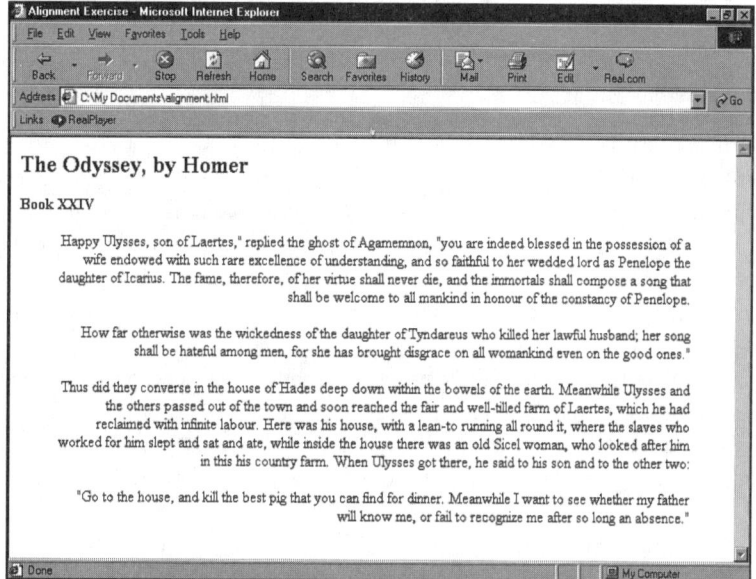

NESTING THE div ELEMENT

The div element can be nested. This is a convenient way to apply alignment—and style—to divisions within divisions of a document.

Remember those nested boxes, where you would open one, then another, and finally another smaller one inside of that one? This is the concept of nesting. As with nesting lists, the nesting of divisions can help you gain a lot of control over the format of your HTML document with ease.

In Listing 11.6, I have first applied right alignment to the entire page; in other words, I've placed an opening div tag at the top of the text, and a closing div tag at the end of the text. This formats the entire page align-right.

Because I wanted to center a section, I simply added the div tags with the align="center" attribute and value around that individual section. The alignment is applied *only* to that section, but the browser understands that this is a nested element, and reverts back to the original right-alignment after the centered section is closed.

 Trying to decide if the `div` *tag is right for you? See, "Backward Compatibility" in the "Troubleshooting" section near the end of this chapter.*

LISTING 11.6   NESTING THE div ELEMENT

```
<!DOCTYPE html PUBLIC "-//W3C//DTD XHTML 1.0 Transitional//EN"
"http://www.w3.org/TR/xhtml1/DTD/xhtml1-transitional.dtd">
<html xmlns="http://www.w3.org/1999/xhtml">
<head>
<title>Alignment Exercise</title>
</head>
<body>

<div align="right">
<h2>The Odyssey, by Homer</h2>
<b>Book XXIII</b>

<blockquote>
<p>"My good nurse," answered Penelope, "you must be mad. The gods sometimes
send some very sensible people out of their minds, and make foolish people
become sensible. This is what they must have been doing to you; for you always
used to be a reasonable person.</p>

<p>Why should you thus mock me when I have trouble enough already-talking such
nonsense, and waking me up out of a sweet sleep that had taken possession of my
eyes and closed them? I have never slept so soundly from the day my poor
husband went to that city with the ill-omened name.</p>

        <div align="center">
    <p>Go back again into the women's room; if it had been any one else, who had
    woke me up to bring me such absurd news I should have sent her away with a
    severe scolding. As it is, your age shall protect you."</p>
        </div>

<p>"My dear child," answered Euryclea, "I am not mocking you. It is quite true
as I tell you that Ulysses is come home again. He was the stranger whom they
all kept on treating so badly in the cloister. Telemachus knew all the time
that he was come back, but kept his father's secret that he might have his
revenge on all these wicked people.</p>

<p>Then Penelope sprang up from her couch, threw her arms round Euryclea, and
wept for joy. "But my dear nurse," said she, "explain this to me; if he has
really come home as you say, how did he manage to overcome the wicked suitors
single handed, seeing what a number of them there always were?"</p>
```

```
</div>
</blockquote>
</body>
</html>
```

In Figure 11.11 you'll see the influence of the `<div align="center">` tag. I've highlighted it so you can see the difference in formatting with ease.

Figure 11.11
Right justification and a centered division on the same page.

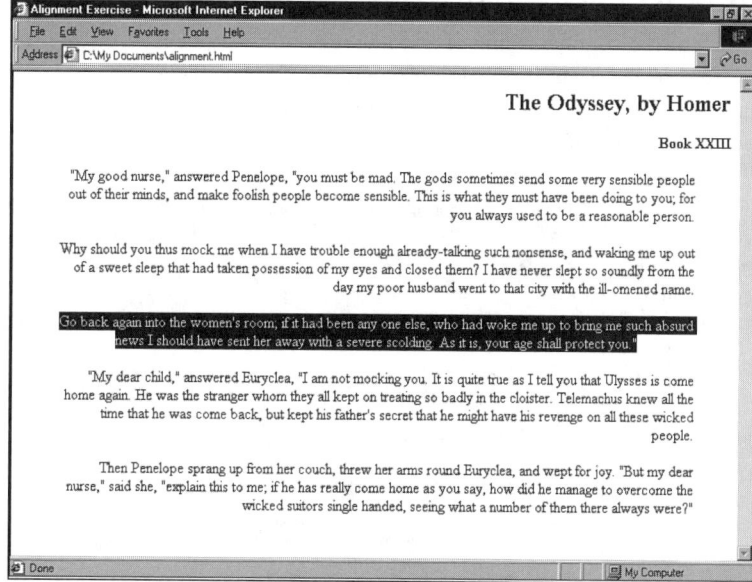

→   For more information on alignment styles for images and objects **see** Chapter 13, "Using Images in XHTML Documents," **p. 221**.

TROUBLESHOOTING

OTHER FORMATTING ELEMENTS

I've occasionally seen the `<tt>` element in use. What does it do?

The `<tt>` element forces any text within its opening and closing tags to appear in a "type-writer" (monospaced) font. This can be used much as the deprecated `<code>` element—formatting sections of text such as code listings in the monospace style. In both instances, style sheets are favored over these presentation options.

BACKWARD COMPATIBILITY

I want to use the `div align="center"` option to center text. Won't older browsers have trouble interpreting this?

PART
II
CH
11

The simple answer is yes; older browsers will ignore the div method of alignment. However, most browsers in use today can manage it. If it's imperative to have a section of text centered in as many browsers as possible, you can opt for using the `<p align="center">` option, or use the rather clumsy but effective combination of either p or div and the deprecated center tag.

DESIGNING FOR THE REAL WORLD

Figure 11.12 contains a mix of alignment options. Use what you've learned in this chapter to recreate the page. It is unimportant as to whether you use div or p alignment; rather, the end visual result is what you're after. Of course, check your syntax to be sure your code is well-formed, transitional XHTML.

Figure 11.12
Match this! This page can be recreated using the alignment methods found in this chapter. Come up with the same look on your own.

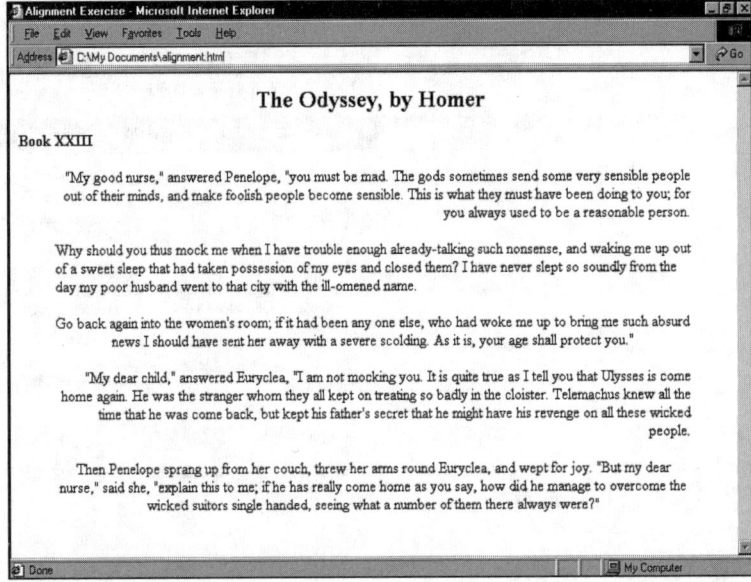

LINKING PAGES WITH STANDARD LINKS

In this chapter

LINKS ARE THE WEB'S VERY ESSENCE

I have a friend, Joe, who lives in Tucson, Arizona. I have another friend, Jo, who lives in Southeast Asia. Before the advent of the Internet, the two would probably have had little opportunity to meet—to *link* together and form a relationship.

Linking—it's the essence of the Web. Without it, the concept would be reduced to the publication of text documents on the Internet. Linking is what takes you beyond the framework of not only a single document to other, related documents, but farther beyond and into the human potential of relating ideas as well as people.

Originally referred to as *hyperlinking*, the technical method to offer linking opportunities to documents also has expanded to include more than just text links. In fact, today's Web uses a variety of media and objects that are active links. Another term, *hypermedia*, has been added to include this aspect.

If you attempt to picture this vast network of linked information—from text documents to entertainment Web sites, to personal home pages to people—you can begin to see what a complex Web is woven by this seemingly simple act of linking.

And, although the XHTML syntax for linking is fairly straightforward, there are some details you must become familiar with to harness the Web's potential and facilitate the opportunities that linking allows.

Such issues include working with the anchor element, using relative and absolute links, and managing specialty links, such as those used to link from one point on a page to another or to email.

THE anchor ELEMENT

If the essence of the Web can be defined as linking, the essence of linking can most certainly be exemplified by the XHTML element at its core—the anchor, which uses the <a> . . . </a> anchor tags.

This element is what allows one XHTML document to attach, or anchor itself, to another. That other document can be nearby, or it can be far away—much like my friends Joe and Jo. If each had a Web site located in his native area, those sites could be attached, or anchored, to each other using the anchor element.

Caution

You can easily link to another's site if you know the proper address. Most people are happy if you link to their sites; however, some sites want to know who is linking to them and why. Out of consideration for others, get in touch instead of linking to them without express permission.

To function properly, the anchor element must employ attributes and values. Typically, and at the most basic, the common attribute is href, or *hypertext reference*. This is followed by a value, most often consisting of a URL, *Uniform Resource Locator*.

URI Versus URL

You'll often see references to URLs and URIs. You may be wondering whats up with that! Well, URL stands for Uniform Resource Locator and is specific to Web addresses. URI stands for Uniform Resource Identifier. A URI is an address describing *any* point of contact on the Internet. Trend has it that URIs have become the way of describing addresses. It's really a catch-all phrase, though. So, for the sake of familiarity *and* clarity, I use URL here and throughout the book.

In this case, I'm going to use the URL of Macmillan USA's Web site:

```
<a href="http://www.mcp.com/">
```

Between this string of tag, attribute, and value, and the closing tag, *any text or object* that is placed there will be considered "hot." This means it is a clickable link that takes you from the page you're on to the page to which the anchor refers:

```
<a href="http://www.mcp.com/">Click on this to go Macmillan USAs Home Page</a>
```

This link (see Figure 12.1) will then take you to the Macmillan Web site (see Figure 12.2).

Figure 12.1
The hyperlink to Macmillan's page.

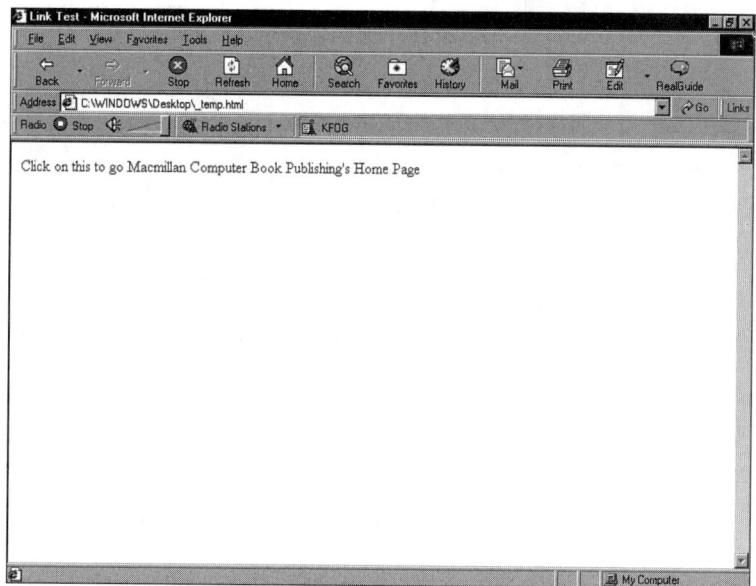

Anchor tags create links, and there are two kinds of links of note: *absolute* and *relative*. Many of you are familiar with these linking techniques already, but for those of you who want clarification, I'll go over them in the following sections.

Figure 12.2
Click the link, and the
referred page loads.

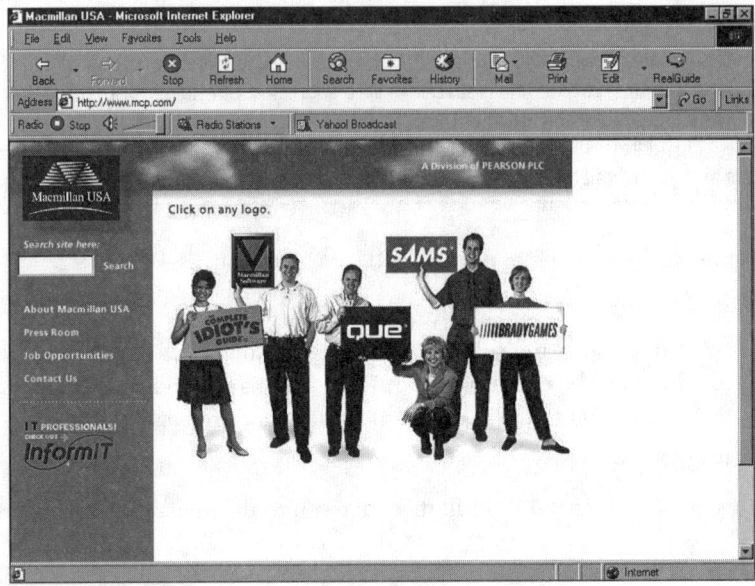

ABSOLUTE LINKING

The example we just looked at, which used a complete URI as its value, is referred to as an *absolute* link. This means that you use *absolutely the entire* Web address, not just a part of it. You must include the beginning `http:` information, as well as the domain. This will then take you to that Web site's default home page.

 Concerned about linking to other people's pages? How about having other people link to yours? See "Reciprocal Link Refusal" in the "Troubleshooting" section near the end of the chapter for more information.

Absolute linking is important when addressing anchors to sites other than your own—in other words, sites that reside on other servers. The use of the absolute address allows your browser to query the correct server and actually go to a specific file on that server if you code your anchor to do so. Joe, and his site in Arizona, will require an absolute link to Jo's site in Southeast Asia.

Tip from

Linking off of your site is what the Web is all about. Still, you should be sure to place your offsite links wisely. Creating a special links page or linking within the text can be effective. What you want to avoid is linking within the first paragraph of any page's text—you could lose your site visitors and never see them again!

→ For a detailed look at structuring Web sites, **see** Chapter 24, "Effective Page Design," **p. 513**.

If you want to refer to a particular section within a Web site, you will have to include relevant directories. In this example, I want to send you to the Que imprint area of the Macmillan Web site, so I use the following URL as my value:

```
<a href="http://www.mcp.com/que/">Que</a>
```

This URL takes you to the default page set up for searching MCP's catalogs. Now if there's a specific page within an area on a Web site, you can code the reference with a specific page's filename:

```
<a href="http://www.mcp.com/que/authors_bio_holzsclag_que.cfm">
Read about Que Author Molly E. Holzschlag</a>
```

This link takes you directly to my page on the Macmillan USA Que Imprint site (see Figure 12.3).

Figure 12.3
Following my specific page link, I end up on my author page at Que.

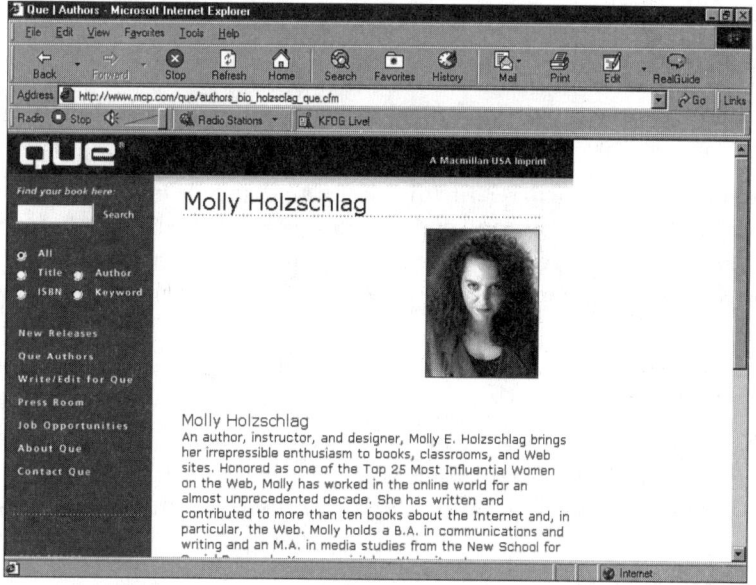

PART
III

CH
12

Caution Although current versions of browsers allow you to eliminate the http:// and simply type in www.mcp.com to access a site, this by no means suggests that you can drop the http:// code from an absolute URL in XHTML code. In fact, if you do so, you'll wind up with an ineffective link.

RELATIVE LINKING

Now let's say that Joe and Jo are going to set up housekeeping in the same house. However, Joe is in the study, and Jo is in the living room. We want to link them up, but do we need to specify a direct address—an absolute link—as we did when they were half a world away from one another? No! After all, they're already at the same address.

Relative linking allows you to link to files residing at the same address, on the same server. The files can be in the same directory as one another, or they might be in another directory. In either case, there are methods of linking *relatively* (in relation to) rather than absolutely to these files.

If you are linking from one page to another page within a site, and both files reside in the same directory, all you need to do is state the *hypertext reference* value as the filename:

```
<a href="jo.html">Jo's Home Page</a>
```

Where things get a bit more complex is when you want to link to a document in another directory on that server. Let's say I had my XHTML page in my main folder, but I had a subfolder called "Jo" where I've placed the file, jo.html. I then have to place the path to that file into the hypertext reference, as follows:

```
<a href="jo/jo.html">Jo's Home Page</a>
```

Now the browser knows to look under the jo directory, rather than in the same directory as the original document.

You will always have to refer to the exact path to the file from your initial page. If I had a subfolder in the jo directory called "stories," and I wanted to link from my first document in the main folder, I have to include the entire path to the file I want to have the browser load. In this instance, I want to load the file travels1.html. The syntax would then look like the following:

```
<a href="jo/stories/travels1.html">Read About Jo's Adventures in Southeast
Asia</a>
```

Now what happens if you are on Jo's Home Page (jo.html), but you want to link back up to the main page? In relative linking, you use the .. (double dot) to take you to the folder above the subfolder. So from jo.html to the index.html in the main folder, I have to code the following:

```
<A href="../index.html">Go Back Home</a>
```

This now takes me to the top parent directory, where my index.html file exists.

Follow these steps to create a relative link:

1. On your computer, create a folder and name it **root**.

2. Open root and create a subfolder, named **articles**.

3. Create an XHTML page as follows:
   ```
   <!DOCTYPE html PUBLIC "-//W3C//DTD XHTML 1.0 Transitional//EN"
   "http://www.w3.org/TR/xhtml1/DTD/xhtml1-transitional.dtd">
   <html xmlns="http://www.w3.org/1999/xhtml">
   <head>
   <title>Relative Link Example</title>
   </head>
   <body>
   ```

```
<p>This page will appear in the root directory. If I want to link it to
an article in the "articles" directory, I would use relative linking.</p>


</body>
</html>
```

4. Save this file in the root folder as **index.html** (see Figure 12.4).

Figure 12.4
The root directory is now ready for subdirectories and documents.

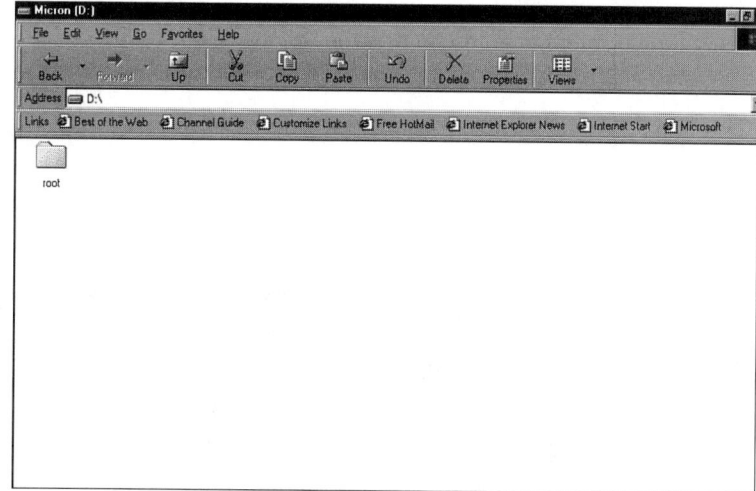

Now you have an index page within the root directory. You have to have something to link to for relative linking to work.

1. Open your editor and code the following page:

```
<!DOCTYPE html PUBLIC "-//W3C//DTD XHTML 1.0 Transitional//EN"
"http://www.w3.org/TR/xhtml1/DTD/xhtml1-transitional.dtd">
<html xmlns="http://www.w3.org/1999/xhtml">
<head>
<title>Sample Article I</title>
</head>
<body>

<p>This page will appear in the article directory.</p>


</body>
</html>
```

2. Save this page as **article1.html** in the article directory.

Follow these steps to add the link to the original document:

1. Open index.html in your editor and add the following syntax:

PART

III

CH

12

```
<!DOCTYPE html PUBLIC "-//W3C//DTD XHTML 1.0 Transitional//EN"
"http://www.w3.org/TR/xhtml1/DTD/xhtml1-transitional.dtd">
<html xmlns="http://www.w3.org/1999/xhtml">
<head>
<title>Relative Link Example</title>
</head>
<body>

<p>This page will appear in the root directory. If I want to link it to
an article in the "articles" directory, I would use relative linking.</p>

<p>If you <a href="articles/article1.html">Click This Link</a> the
articles1.html
page will load. This is a relative link example!</p>

</body>
</html>
```

2. Save the file.

3. Check your link. It should load `article1.html`, as shown in Figure 12.5.

Figure 12.5
Clicking my first relative link loads the sample article page.

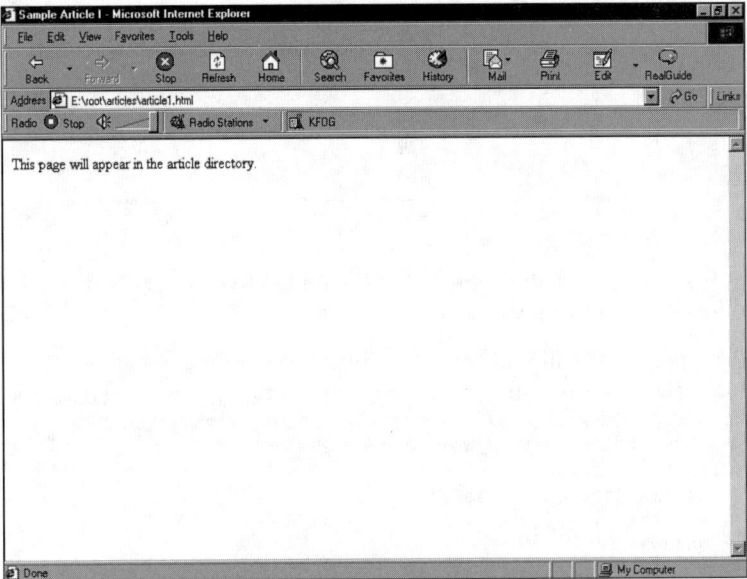

If you want to link back to the index, follow these steps:

1. Open the `artciles1.html` file in your editor and add the following relative link:

```
<!doctype html public "-//W3C//DTD XHTML 1.0 Transitional//EN"
"http://www.w3.org/TR/xhtml1/DTD/xhtml1-transitional.dtd">
<html xmlns="http://www.w3.org/1999/xhtml">
<head>
<title>Sample Article I</title>
</head>
<body>
```

```
<p>This page will appear in the article directory.</p>

<p>If you <a href="../index.html">Click Right Here</a> you'll return to the
index
page. This link is also a relative link!</p>

</body>
</html>
```

2. Save the file and test the link. I just did, and the `index.html` file loaded into my browser (see Figure 12.6).

Figure 12.6
When I click the link, it loads the referring file. The link returns me to the home page, located in the root directory.

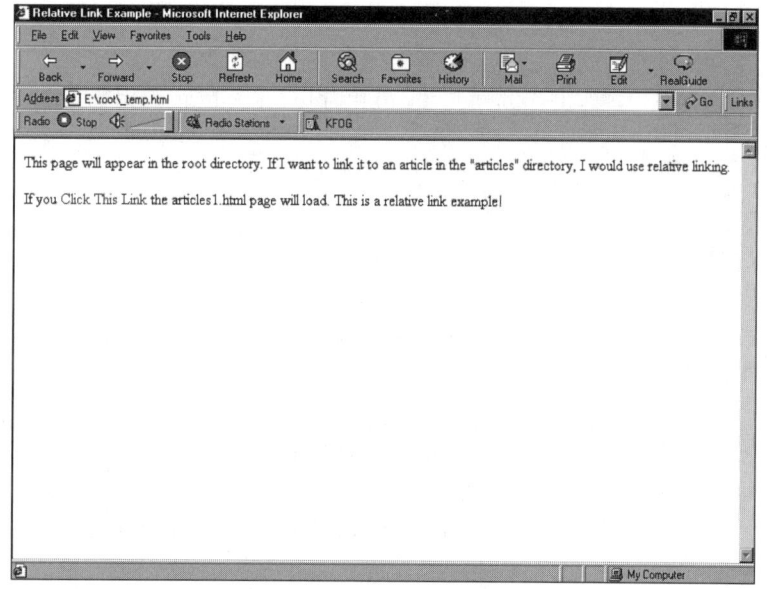

PART

III

Сн

12

Relative linking is simple and powerful. You will use this form of linking every time you are working locally or on the same server, unless you choose to link out to the Internet at large.

 Want to troubleshoot links? See the "Troubleshooting" section near the end of this chapter.

In Listing 12.1, I show our sample article page with an external, absolute link added.

LISTING 12.1   RELATIVE LINKING

```
<!doctype html public "-//W3C//DTD XHTML 1.0 Transitional//EN"
"http://www.w3.org/TR/xhtml1/DTD/xhtml1-transitional.dtd">
<html xmlns="http://www.w3.org/1999/xhtml">
<head>
<title>Sample Article I</title>
</head>
<body>
```

LISTING 12.1   CONTINUED

```
<p>This page will appear in the article directory.</p>


<p>If you <a href="../index.html">Click Right Here</a> you'll return to the index
page. This link is also a relative link!</p>

<p>If you decide to visit the Macmillan USA's site, you can do so by
<a href="http://www.mcp.com/">Clicking Right Here!</a></p>


</body>
</html>
```

When two sites each contain a link to the other, the term used to define this is *reciprocal linking*. The concept of *reciprocity* is an important one because it can promote the flow of traffic between Web sites, a helpful aspect in marketing sites.

LINKING IMAGES

So far, the examples used in this chapter show hypertext links. In other words, it's *text* that is active. However, as mentioned earlier, a variety of media—particularly images—can be made "hyper," or linkable.

Using images as links is easy to do, too. All that is necessary is to place the image within the context of the anchor tag, and that image will become hyper—anchored to the relative or absolute link that you've designated:

```
<a href="computers.html"><img src="computer_image.gif" alt="image of a
computer"/></a>
```

In Figure 12.7, you'll see the computer image. If I click the image, it will take me to the `computers.html` page.

Tip from

A border surrounding images is not always esthetically pleasing. To remove the border, you can add the `border="0"` attribute and value to the `img` code.

Here's the modified code:

```
<a href="computers.html"><img src="computer_image.gif" border="0" alt="image of a
computer"/></a>
```

The link now has no border (see Figure 12.8).

Figure 12.7
A linked image automatically appears with a border around it to indicate that the image is acting as a link.

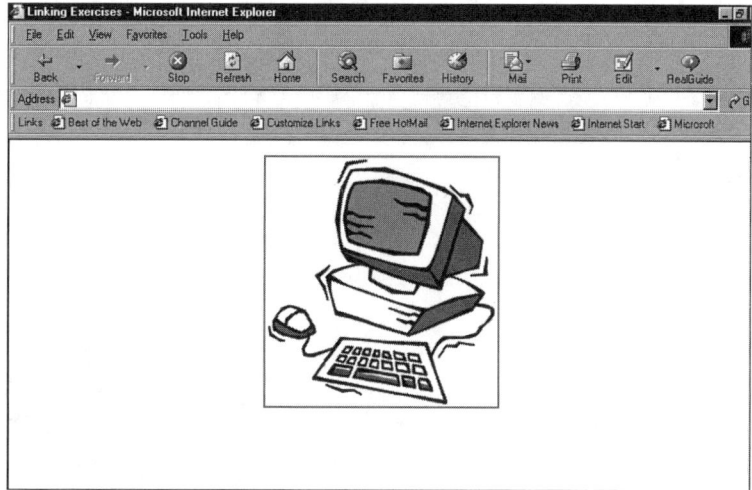

Figure 12.8
The same linked image without the border is much more appealing to the eye and won't disturb the visual quality of the overall design of the page the way links with borders tend to do.

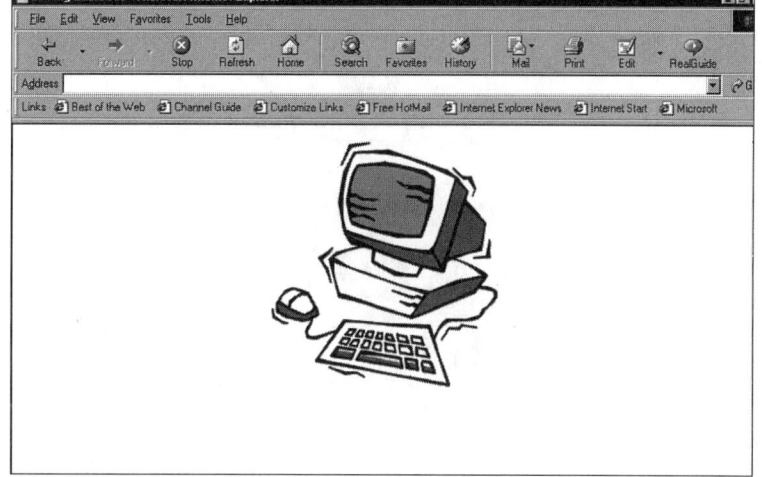

PART

III

CH

12

INTRA-PAGE LINKING

A helpful method of navigating within a page is to use a process called *intra-page linking*. Figure 12.9 shows a site for the Ramada Inn in Tucson, Arizona. You can see that there are three links to the left of the photo, each pointing to a specific topic that appears not on *another* page, but on the same page as those links.

If I click the Amenities link, I'm taken to the Amenities page, which contains a range of information regarding the hotel. What happens if I want a quick route back to the top of the page? Well, the little "up" arrow (see Figure 12.10) provides just that—an intra-page link that takes me back to the offerings on that page.

Figure 12.9
Ramada Inn intra-page links enable their site visitors to quickly get to the information they want without scrolling up and down the page to locate it.

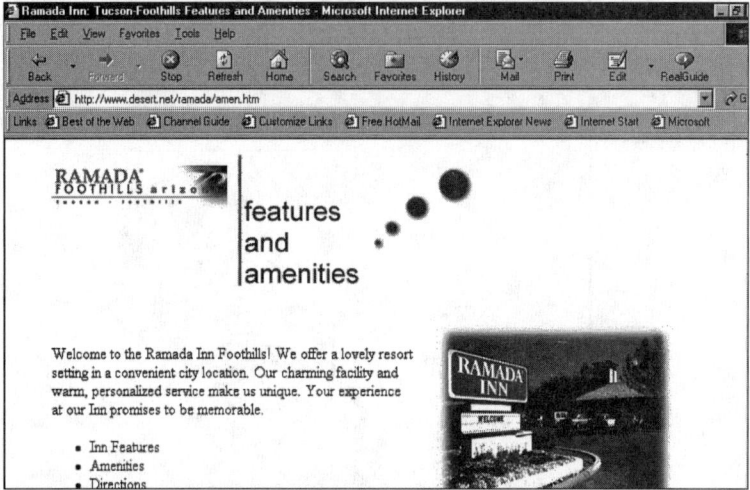

Figure 12.10
The arrow link offers a quick return to the top of the Web page.

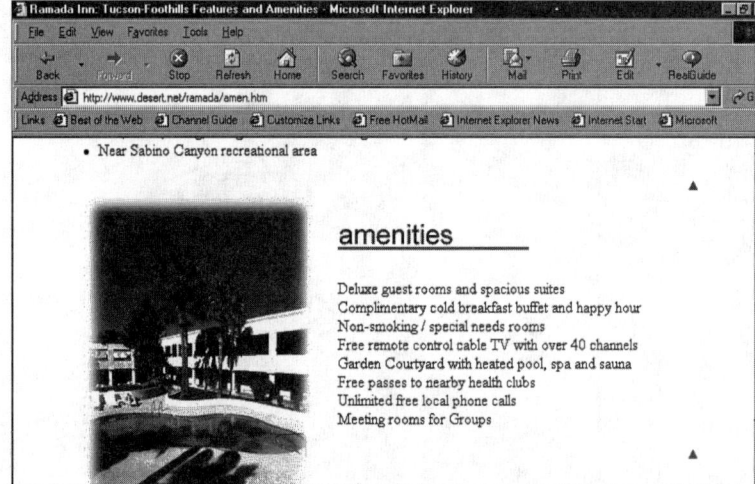

Intra-page linking is convenient for visitors, and helps coders organize pages in a succinct, sensible fashion. Here's a look at the link that takes us from the top of the page to the directions:

```
<a href="#direct">directions</a>
```

As you can see, it looks like a regular, relative link. The only difference is that instead of a filename, there's a pound sign followed by a single word.

Because we have no file to link to, we have to create somewhere for this link to go. This is called a *named target*. It looks like the following:

```
<a name="direct"><img src="direct.gif" alt="amenities" width="200" height="42"
border="0" /></a>
```

In this case, the anchor tag names a point on the page for the initial link to the *named target*. The anchor can be text or, as shown in this example, a graphic. So, when I click the initial link, Directions, I'm taken to the target anchor.

To help you understand this method, here is an exercise for intra-page linking:

1. In your HTML editor, build a simple shell:

```
<!doctype html public "-//W3C//DTD XHTML 1.0 Transitional//EN"
"http://www.w3.org/TR/xhtml1/DTD/xhtml1-transitional.dtd">
<html xmlns="http://www.w3.org/1999/xhtml">
<head>
<title>Intra-Page Link Example</title>
</head>
<body>

</body>
</html>
```

2. To the shell, add several link items:

```
<!doctype html public "-//W3C//DTD XHTML 1.0 Transitional//EN"
"http://www.w3.org/TR/xhtml1/DTD/xhtml1-transitional.dtd">
<html xmlns="http://www.w3.org/1999/xhtml">
<head>
<title>Intra-Page Link Example</title>
</head>
<body>

<p>Gentle Ben's Gem Shop Offers Amethyst, Aquamarine, and Rose Quartz.</p>

</body>
</html>
```

3. Now add text that will make a natural target for those items:

```
<!doctype html public "-//W3C//DTD XHTML 1.0 Transitional//EN"
"http://www.w3.org/TR/xhtml1/DTD/xhtml1-transitional.dtd">
<html xmlns="http://www.w3.org/1999/xhtml">
<head>
<title>Intra-Page Link Example</title>
</head>
<body>

<p>Gentle Ben's Gem Shop Offers Amethyst, Aquamarine, and Rose Quartz.</p>

<h1>Amethyst</h1>
<p>Amethyst is a beautiful gem, with clear as well as purple coloration that ranges
in depth and intensity. The depth of the purple color relates to the age of the
gem. The older the gem, the deeper the color can get.</p>

<h1>Aquamarine</h1>
<p>It's almost as if the depths of the ocean are reflected in this gem. From clear
crystal to the purest aqua, this is a breathtaking gemstone.</p>

<h1>Rose Quartz</h1>
<p>Rosy pink and smooth, Rose quartz is favored by many gem collectors for use
```

PART

III

CH

12

```
in
making jewelry as well as figurines. It is thought to have powerful healing
properties where the heart is concerned. Some say that keeping a piece of Rose
Quartz near you will help bring a perfect love into your life.</p>

</body>
</html>
```

4. Now let's name the first target "amethyst":

```
<h1><a name="amethyst">Amethyst</a></h1>
```

5. When you're finished, move back up to the top list, and link the word *amethyst* to the target you just created:

```
Gentle Ben's Gem Shop Offers <A href="#amethyst">Amethyst</A>, Aquamarine, and
Rose Quartz.
```

6. Save your file as **intra_link.html** and check the link in your browser.

Now that you've stepped through the first natural intra-page link instance in our example, you can go ahead and finish the page. Listing 12.2 shows the final code.

LISTING 12.2 INTRA-PAGE LINKING

```
<!doctype html public "-//W3C//DTD XHTML 1.0 Transitional//EN"
"http://www.w3.org/TR/xhtml1/DTD/xhtml1-transitional.dtd">
<html xmlns="http://www.w3.org/1999/xhtml">
<head>
<title>Intra-Page Link Example</title>
</head>
<body>

<p>Gentle Ben's Gem Shop Offers <a href="#amethyst">Amethyst</a>,
<a href="#Aquamarine">Aquamarine</a>, and <a href="#rose">Rose Quartz</a>.</p>

<h1><a name="Amethyst">Amethyst</a></h1>
<p>Amethyst is a beautiful gem, with clear as well as purple coloration that ranges
in depth and intensity. The depth of the purple color relates to the age of the
gem. The older the gem, the deeper the color can get.</p>

<h1><a name="Aquamarine">Aquamarine</a></h1>
<p>It's almost as if the depths of the ocean are reflected in this gem. From clear
crystal to the purest aqua, this is a breathtaking gemstone.</p>

<h1><A name="rose">Rose Quartz</a></h1>
<p>Rosy pink and smooth, Rose quartz is favored by many gem collectors for use in
making jewelry as well as figurines. It is thought to have powerful healing
properties where the heart is concerned. Some say that keeping a piece of Rose
Quartz near you will help bring a perfect love into your life.</p>

</body>
</html>
```

You can compare your page to mine, as shown in Figure 12.11.

Figure 12.11
Intra-page linking
exercise.

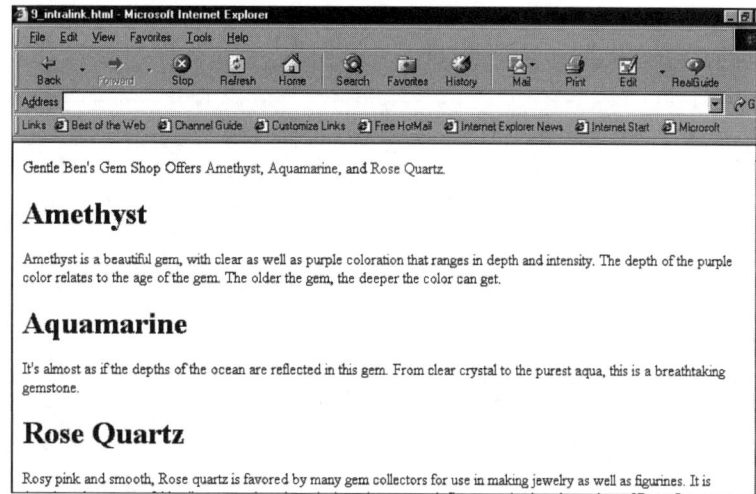

And what of the little "back to top" image? It works exactly the same way. Here's the named target at the top of the page:

```
<a name="top">welcome</a>
```

And here's the code for the linked arrow:

```
<a href="#top"><img src="uparrow.gif" alt="click here and go to top" width="20"
height="12" border="0" align="right" /></a>
```

Many people rely heavily on this method to organize their sites. It can be a powerful, easy way to set up intra-page navigation, and offers the site visitor easy methods of moving around a page.

Caution

Although intra-page linking can be an XHTML coder's best helper in organizing material within a page, it's important to keep the length of pages to a reasonable size. You will see pages on the Internet that scroll for many screens—even with intra-page linking this is not an ideal situation. Keep to no more than five or six total screens per page, with three screens being best. This way, your users don't have to scroll forever to find information.

MAIL LINKS

A convenient way of enabling Web site visitors to reach you via your Web page is to provide a link to your email address. This can be managed using the anchor tag and a reference known as mailto.

The following is an example:

```
<a href="mailto:molly@molly.com">Send an e-mail to Molly</a>
```

Click the link, and your browser calls up a mail program that automatically lets you type in an email to the designated account.

Tip from

Mail links can be used around images, too. Simply use the `mailto:` code and addressing as shown in this section, and place an image rather than text between the open anchor tag and the closing tag.

Figure 12.12 shows how doing this in Internet Explorer pulls up my default mail reader, Eudora.

Figure 12.12
With `mailto:`, the browser launches a default mail reader.

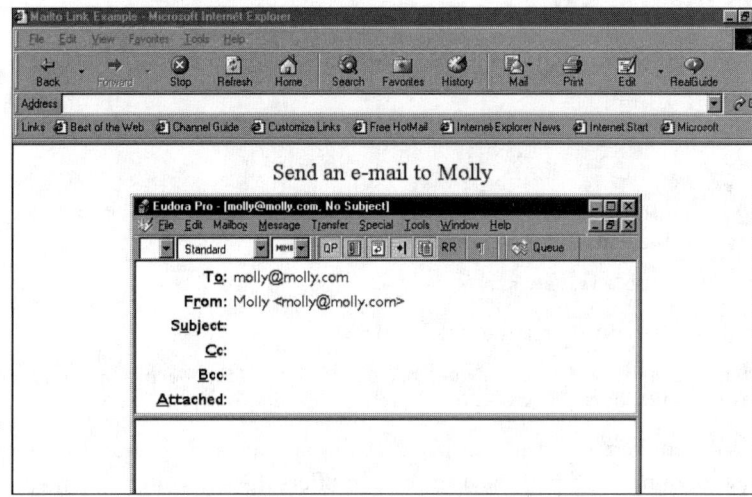

Tip from

Using forms is another popular way to offer mail links to site visitors, and there are other methods to choose from as well.

→ For more about creating and managing forms, **see** Chapter 16, "Working with Standard Forms," **p. 319**.

Because mail links are such an effective method of getting people to contact you, many individuals like to put a `mailto:` link on every page of their site. This can be done discreetly in the footer information. In Figure 12.13, the footer information for the Ramada Inn site shown earlier in this chapter reflects this convenience.

Figure 12.13
`mailto:` is often used on every page to make it more convenient for the site visitor to contact the site owner.

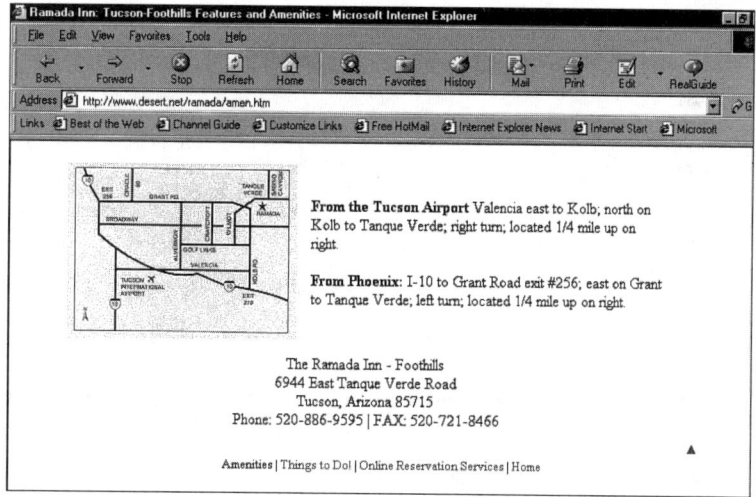

USING MULTIPLE LINKS ON A PAGE

Pages can have multiple link styles. There's no limit to how many links or the type of links you can have on a single page. It is wise to balance your links throughout a page so that they make sense.

Follow these steps to create a page that uses every kind of link covered in this chapter: absolute, relative, intra-page, and `mailto`:

1. In your HTML editor, create a shell:

```
<html>
<head>
<title>Link Mania</title>
</head>

<body>


</body>
</html>
```

2. Now set up some text for a variety of link styles:

```
<html>
<head>
<title>Link Mania</title>
</head>

<body>

<p>Select from these options:</p>


<ol>
<li>See a mailto: link</li>
```

```
<li>Shoot to a named anchor</li>
<li>How about a relative link?</li>
<li>Check out an absolute link</li>
</ol>

<p>Since my first online experience, I've been enraptured with the Internet.
When
the World Wide Web came along, I thought "this is so cool!"</p>

<p>One of the reasons I really, really like the Web is because you can link to
the
rest of the world in a variety of ways. For example, if you wanted to have a
page that let people send me email, all I'd have to do is set up an email
link, like this one.</p>

<p>Or, if I want to link to another document in the same site, I can have a
relative link.</p>

<p>Absolute links are particularly cool, because they take you away from one
site
to another site of interest. In fact, if you click here, you can go visit one
of
my favorite sites!</p>

</body>
</html>
```

3. Add the relative, absolute, and `mailto:` links:

```
<html>
<head>
<title>Link Mania</title>
</head>

<body>

<p>Select from these options:</p>

<ol>
<li>See a mailto: link</li>
<li>Shoot to a named anchor</li>
<li>How about a relative link?</li>
<li>Check out an absolute link</li>
</ol>

<p>Since my first online experience, I've been enraptured with the Internet.
When
the World Wide Web came along, I thought "this is so cool!"</p>

<p>One of the reasons I really, really like the Web is because you can link to
the
rest of the world in a variety of ways. For example, if you wanted to have a
page that let people send me email, all I'd have to do is set up an email
link, <a href="mailto:molly@molly.com">like this one</a>.</p>

<p>Or, if I want to link to another document in the same site, I can have a <a
href="new_page.html">relative</a> link.

<p>Absolute links are particularly cool, because they take you away from one
```

```
site
to another site of interest. In fact, if you click here, you can go visit one
of
my <a href="http://www.filmvault.com/filmvault/">favorite sites!</a></p>

</body>
</html>
```

4. Now set up your named targets:

```
<html>
<head>
<title>Link Mania</title>
</head>

<body>

<p>Select from these options:</p>

<ol>
<li>See a mailto: link</li>
<li>Shoot to a named anchor</li>
<li>How about a relative link?</li>
<li>Check out an absolute link</li>
</ol>

<p>Since my first online experience, I've been enraptured with the Internet.
When
the <a name="namedanchor">World Wide Web</a> came along, I thought "this is so
cool!"</p>

<p>One of the reasons I really, really like the Web is because you can link to
the
rest of the world in a variety of ways. For example, if you wanted to have a
page that let people send me email, all I'd have to do is set up an email link,
<a name="mailto"><a href="mailto:molly@molly.com">like this one</a>.</a></p>

<p>Or, if I want to link to another document in the same site, I can have a <a
name="relative"><a href="new_page.html">relative</a>link.</a>

<p>Absolute links are particularly cool, because they take you away from one
site
to another site of interest. In fact, if you click here, you can go visit one
of
my <a name="absolute"><a href="http://www.filmvault.com/filmvault/">favorite
sites!</a></a>

</body>
</html>
```

5. Finally, add your intra-page links:

```
<html>
<head>
<title>Link Mania</title>
</head>

<body>

<p>Select from these options:</p>
```

```
<ol>
<li><a href="#mailto">See a mailto: link</a></li>
<li><a href="#namedanchor">Shoot to a named anchor</a></li>
<li><a href="#relative">How about a relative link?</a></li>
<li><a href="#absolute">Check out an absolute link</a></li>
</ol>

<p>Since my first online experience, I've been enraptured with the Internet.
When
the <a name="namedanchor">World Wide Web</a> came along, I thought "this is so
cool!"</p>

<p>One of the reasons I really, really like the Web is because you can link to
the
rest of the world in a variety of ways. For example, if you wanted to have a
page that let people send me email, all I'd have to do is set up an email
link, <a name="mailto"><a href="mailto:molly@molly.com">like this
one</a>.</a></p>

<p>Or, if I want to link to another document in the same site, I can have a <a
name="relative"><a href="new_page.html">relative</a> link.</a></p>

<p>Absolute links are particularly cool, because they take you away from one
site
to another site of interest. In fact, if you click here, you can go visit one
of
my <a name="absolute"><a href="http://www.filmvault.com/filmvault/">favorite
sites!</a></a>

</body>
</html>
```

6. Save your file as **linkmania.html** and test it in your browser. Click each link and watch it work.

You can compare your page to mine, shown in Figure 12.14.

Figure 12.14
The Link Mania page. Save this exercise as it will be a good reference should you run into questions about how to properly code links.

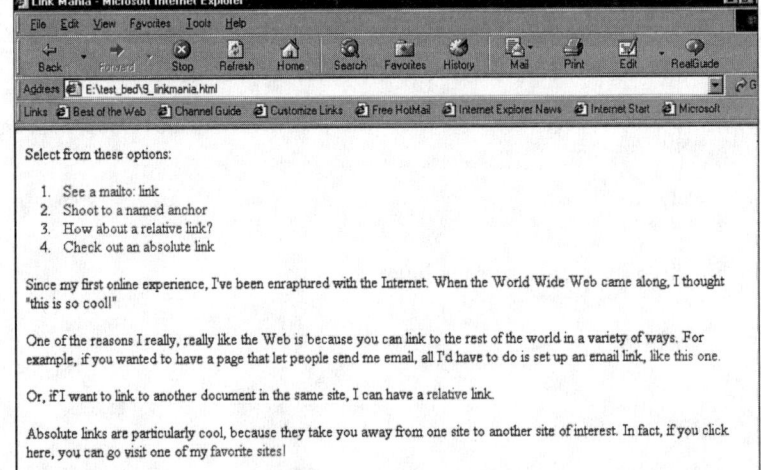

TROUBLESHOOTING

LINKING TO FILES IN DIFFERENT FOLDERS

What is the syntax for linking from a page in one subdirectory to a page in a different subdirectory?

If you are linking from, say `molly_books.html` within the books subdirectory to `molly_music.html` within the music subdirectory, the link would look as follows:

```
<a href="../music/molly_music.html">Molly's Music</a>
```

Notice that you have told the browser to go back up one level (the `../`) and then look in the music subdirectory. For more on this refer to the section on relative links.

RECIPROCAL LINK REFUSAL

Why would someone turn down an opportunity for their site to gain more exposure through a link on another site?

In most cases, Web developers are honored when you choose to link to their site. There are some instances when this is not the case. Some Web hosting services charge based on the number of server hits per month. If the site that adds the link is extremely popular, this can result in extra fees for the linked site because of the extra hits. In some cases, the extra hits are enough to cause the server to crash if it is not able to handle such a high-usage load.

DESIGNING FOR THE REAL WORLD

ABOUT ABOUT.COM

If you've read anything about the Internet in the past year, you've surely read something about portal sites. Most of the large portal sites started out as search engines and expanded their offering to encourage visitors to stay on the site longer. Yahoo! and Excite have added clubs and user communities that enable members to chat or post on message boards about their favorite topics.

About.com has taken a slightly different approach. About has created communities, called guide sites, within which visitors can search for sites of interest. Each About community serves almost as a custom search engine for a particular topic. The links within each community are chosen by a guide—the community leader.

A look at an About guide site shows examples of just about every type of linking imaginable. There are, of course, relative links to and from the various pages within the guide site. There are also links to other related guide sites. Note, however, that even though the other guide sites are part of About, they have a unique URL, requiring absolute links to be used. The sites also have links to other About services, requiring more absolute links, and links to the various recommended sites elsewhere on the Web.

Each guide site also contains a link to email the guide, using a `mailto:` link. Finally, there is a `mailto:` form, which enables you to send information about the site to a friend just by filling in their email address.

About.com—`http://www.about.com/`

Yahoo!—`http://www.yahoo.com/`

Excite—`http://www.excite.com/`

USING IMAGES IN XHTML DOCUMENTS

In this chapter

MOVING TOWARD DESIGN

Adding images to a Web page is the first step in moving away from simple document formatting and into the world of design. Images add identity, color, shape, and presence. The proper use of images is a powerful and important aspect of the Web, yet one that eludes many Webmasters.

In this chapter, you'll learn how to add images to your pages by using XHTML.

There are several ways to position an image on a page. You can use transitional XHTML tags that are moving out in favor of style sheets, you can use tables, and you can choose to use CSS style sheet positioning.

In this chapter, the focus is on strict and transitional XHTML tags. Although more advanced methods are exciting and troublesome in turn, the designer can always rely on conventional XHTML and historical HTML wisdom to manage images. That's the focus here—making sure that your foundation skills are in place *before* sending you off into the less-stable and more-complex methods of image control.

→ You can learn about other methods of placing images in related chapters. To learn how you can use tables to control the position and appearance of images on a page, **see** Chapter 14, "Laying Out Tables with XHTML Documents," **p. 243**.

→ For a discussion on how to accomplish similar results with style sheets, **see** Chapter 18, "Cascading Style Sheets and XHTML" **p. 377**.

THE img ELEMENT IN XHTML

You'll begin by using the img element to place images on a page. This element is considered an empty element, and therefore must take a terminating symbol in XHTML as follows:

```
<img />
```

To display an image, the `<img />` tag requires a source that is called with the src= attribute. The source directs the HTML to get the image in question:

```
<img src="guitar.gif" />
```

This string alone is sufficient to add an image to your page, provided the image resides in the same location as the referring document. However, good behavior dictates that we add the alt attribute for accessibility purposes:

```
<img src="guitar.gif" alt="molly's guitar" />
```

We'll discuss more about the alt attribute and additional img attributes throughout the chapter.

Typically, XHTML developers place images in a specific directory below the root XHTML directory. This directory is aptly named *images* or *graphics*, depending on your preference. If your image resides in such a subdirectory and your XHTML page is in the root directory, you'll need to address the source appropriately, by using relative linking:

```
<img src="images/guitar.gif alt="molly's guitar" />
```

→ For a discussion on the management of files, **see** Chapter 8, "Managing XHTML Documents Locally," **p. 119**.

→ To get insight into how to manage relative links, **see** Chapter 12, "Linking Pages with Standard Links," **p. 199**.

Caution

Some people will link to an image that resides off their site by using an absolute URL to reach the location of an image. This is not a recommended practice for several reasons. One consideration is that you risk a bad connection and the image might never load any time you go off your own server. Another concern is ownership: If that graphic element isn't yours and you link to it without the owner's express permission, you could be in violation of copyright.

Images always go within the body section of an XHTML document. Listing 13.1 shows a transitional XHTML page with a graphic.

LISTING 13.1   ADDING AN IMAGE TO AN HTML PAGE

```
<!DOCTYPE html PUBLIC "-//W3C//DTD XHTML 1.0 Transitional//EN"

"http://www.w3.org/TR/xhtml1/DTD/xhtml1-transitional.dtd">

<html xmlns="http://www.w3.org/1999/xhtml">

<head>

<title>Adding an Image to an XHTML Page</title>

</head>

<body>

<img src="guitar.gif alt="molly's guitar" />

</body>

</html>
```

Figure 13.1 shows the results. You'll notice that the image appears on the left of the page. It has no special position, other than that determined according to the browser's default settings.

In transitional XHTML, you can add attributes to the img tag that will control the action and the appearance of an image on a page.

PART

III

CH

13

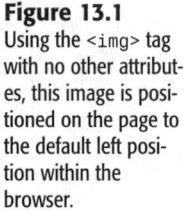

Figure 13.1
Using the `<img>` tag with no other attributes, this image is positioned on the page to the default left position within the browser.

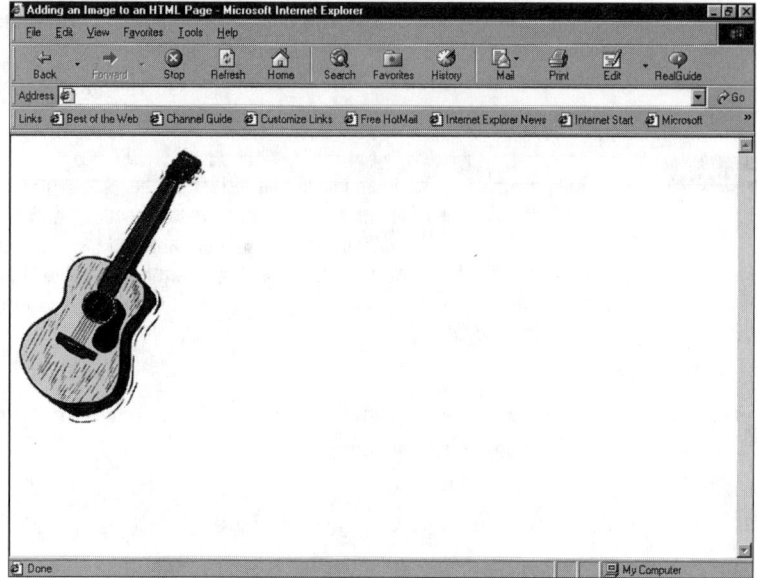

IMAGE TAG ATTRIBUTES

A variety of attributes can be added to an `img` tag to control the way a browser manages the image. These attributes include the following:

- `src="x"`—As mentioned, this is the source attribute, and is used with either an absolute or relative URL that points to the location of the image.

- `width="x"`—This allows a browser to predetermine the width, in pixels, that your image requires.

- `height="x"`—Along with the `width` attribute, the browser can prepare the necessary space for your image in advance. This controls the way your images are loaded on a page.

- `border="x"`—To add or remove a border, use this attribute, where `"x"` is a numeric value.

- `align="x"`—You can align an image horizontally and vertically on a page by using this attribute.

- `alt="description of image"`—The powerful `alt` attribute allows you to describe the image to text-only browsers, tagging the image before it loads onto a page, and allows a ToolTip to appear with the description as a mouse passes over the image.

- `hspace="x"`—*Horizontal space* is used to add space, with a numeric value, around the horizontal axis of the image.

- `vspace="x"`—*Vertical space* controls the spacing of the image along the vertical axis.

Note

What if your image can't be described by a short `alt` description? Rather than add an excessively long `alt` attribute, use the `longdesc` attribute instead. A value for `longdesc` is not a text description at all, but a URL that points to a web page where the image is described in further detail. Here's an example:

```
<img src="guitar.gif" longdesc="image1_description.html" />
```

Caution

Remember that anything involving layout is considered to be *presentation*, not formatting. And, because the most strict XHTML markup demands that presentation and formatting be separated, you cannot use any presentation attributes related to the `img` element in an XHTML page conforming to the strict XHTML 1.0 DTD. You can, however, use these attributes and their corresponding values in a transitional XHTML document.

→ For information on the `ismap` and `usemap` attributes that are used in imagemaps, **see** Chapter 30, "Designing Specialty Graphics," **p. 623**.

The following sections take a more in-depth look at these attributes and how they work.

width **AND** height

The best advice I can give you regarding these attributes is twofold:

- Always, always, include `width` and `height` in your `img` tag in a transitional XHTML document. This helps the browser manage the image data throughout the page and may result in the page being rendered more promptly.
- Never, never, use inaccurate `width` and `height` values for any image except for single pixel GIFs. Standard image values must *always* be exact, or you'll cause your browser to abnormally stretch or minimize an image.

You might be thinking: "But Molly, I've seen people create thumbnails of large images by making the `width` and `height` values smaller. I thought that was a clever idea!" It's clever, and it's very problematic.

This is because your large image *still* has to download to the browser. Let's say you have 5 images of 50KB each, and you resize them on your page by using the `width` and `height` attributes. You haven't resized the image by doing this—only the *appearance* of the image. Your browser must retrieve all 250KB of those images even though it will display them as smaller than their actual dimensions. The weight remains the same—and your site visitors might not remain on your site waiting for the downloads.

Following the rules, this code shows my guitar image with the proper width and height:

```
<img src="images/guitar.gif" alt="molly's guitar" width="200" height="284" />
```

To find the exact `width` and `height` of your image, look at it in your imaging program. The image size is available there (see Figure 13.2).

PART
III

CH
13

Figure 13.2
Image *width* and *height* information can be found by checking the image in a graphics software program, such as what is seen here in Adobe Photoshop.

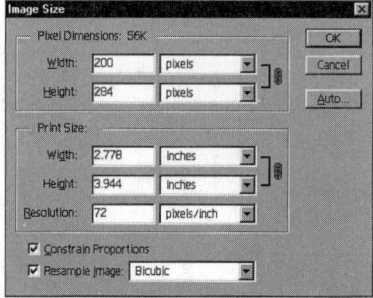

Tip from
molly

Another way to determine the `width` and `height` of your image is to open the graphic in Netscape. The image's dimensions are noted along the top bar of the interface.

→ For information on various imaging programs, **see** Chapter 27, "Web Graphic Tools and Professional Tools," **p. 561**.

→ When you design your graphics, you should size them appropriately for the Web. To learn how to do this properly, **see** Chapter 29, "Creating Professional Web Graphics," **p. 595**.

IMAGE BORDERS

Borders around images were once the default of most Web browsers, particularly if the image was linked. The default now is to have no border. This isn't an accident—borders around images constrain the image.

→ To learn why borders around images are problematic, **see** Chapter 26, "Working with the Computer Screen," **p. 545**.

To ensure that your graphics always appear without borders, it's wise to include a value of `"0"` with the `border` attribute:

```
<img src="images/guitar.gif" width="200" height="284" border="0" alt="molly's
guitar" />
```

This string protects your image from appearing with borders in older browsers or browsers that still use a border as its default if no border information is included in the `img` string.

If you really want a border around an image, you can set it by setting a numeric value in the `border` attribute:

```
<img src="images/guitar.gif" width="200" height="284" border="4" alt="molly's
guitar" />
```

Figure 13.3 shows the image with the border.

Borders pick up the color of your text if they are not linked. If they are linked, borders appear in either the browser defaults of blue for an unvisited link, purple for a visited link, the user's custom colors, or the `link` and `vlink` colors that you personally specify within the `body` tag or style sheet.

Figure 13.3
This figure shows the guitar image with a border value of "4".

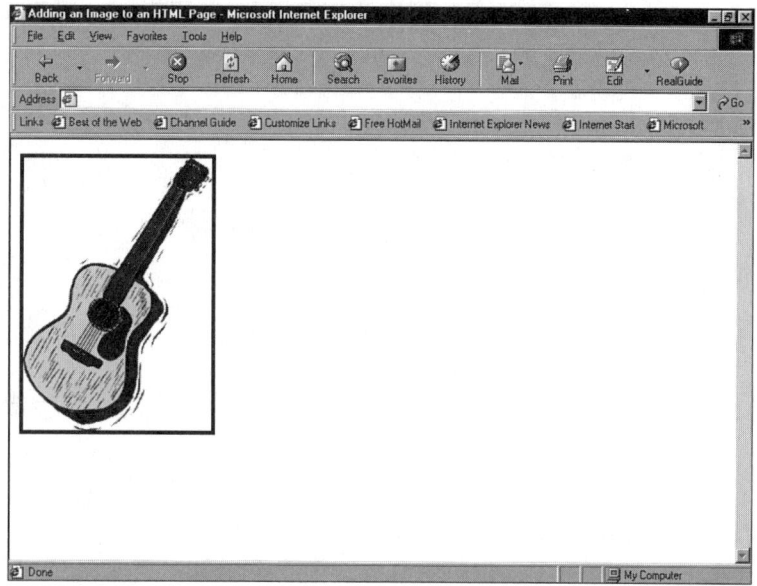

ALIGNMENT

There are a number of ways to align your image. On the horizon line, the default value is left for a solitary object. You also can set the alignment to a value of left (this is important when wrapping text, discussed in the "Floating Images" section later in this chapter) or a value of right:

```
<img src="images/guitar.gif" alt="molly's Ggitar" width="200" height="284"
border="0" align="right" />
```

In Figure 13.4, you can see that this alignment value has caused the image to appear along the right side of the browser.

→ To center images, you must use another method such as the div tag; for information on how to manage centering of text and media, **see** "Aligning Text," **p. 178** or "Using the div Element," **p. 181.**

Although the horizontal alignment values of left and right are likely to be used most frequently, you also can use the align attribute to align an image vertically:

```
<img src="little_guitar.gif" alt="little guitar" align="top" />
```

Standard, cross-browser values for this include the following:

- **top**—This puts the image along the topmost part of the horizon line.
- **middle**—The image is aligned with the middle or baseline of the horizon.
- **bottom**—With this value, the image is aligned with the bottom of the horizon line.

I've set up an example of each of these, which you can see in Figure 13.5.

PART
III

CH
13

Figure 13.4
Using the `align` attribute with a value of `"right"` I've successfully aligned this image to the right rather than default left of the browser.

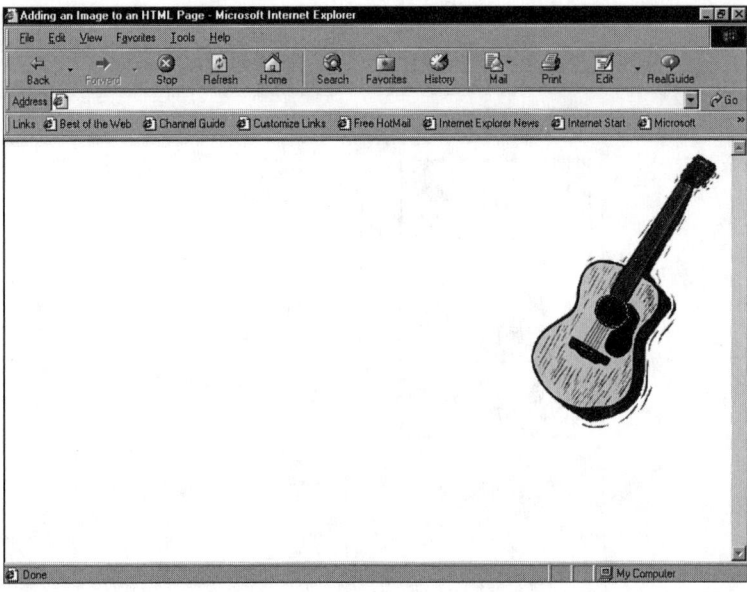

Figure 13.5
Vertical-alignment of an image. Note the way the image relates to the text.

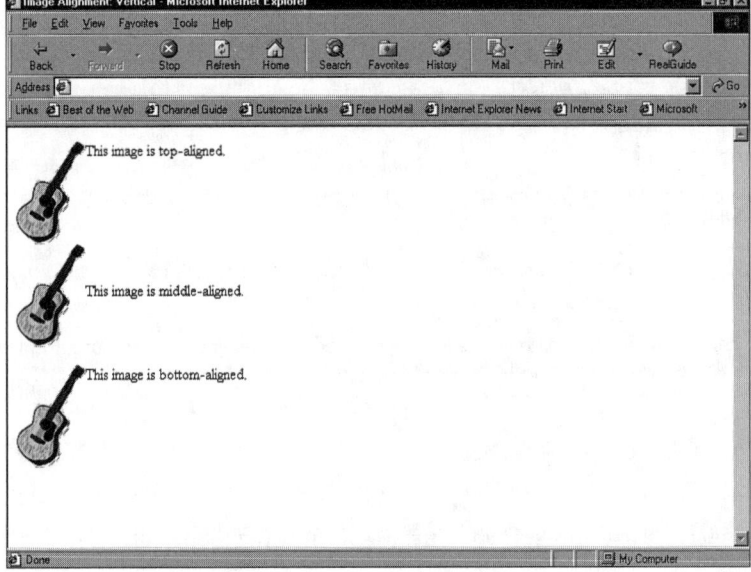

There are several other browser-specific, conventional alignment values, rather than standard methods. I've included the following here for your information:

- **texttop**—Aligns with the top of highest text or image on that line.
- **absmiddle**—Aligns with the *absolute* middle of the highest surrounding text or image.

- **baseline**—Aligns to the bottom.

- **absbottom**—Aligns the bottom of the image with the lowest image or text along the line.

These are sometimes helpful, but because they are browser-specific, they are not standard. In fact, vertical alignment of images by using the `align` attribute is reserved for instances when the need for precise alignment is desired. In XHTML 1.0, such alignment is handled with tables in transitional documents and style sheets in transitional and strict documents.

→ To learn more about CSS, **see** Chapter 18, "Cascading Style Sheets and XHTML," **p. 377**.

THE alt ATTRIBUTE

This important attribute allows you to write out a description of the image. For example, because my guitar image is actually a drawing rather than a photo, I could describe the image as a "drawing of a guitar" as follows:

```
<img src="images/guitar.gif" width="200" height="284" border="0"
alt="drawing of a guitar" />
```

For those individuals without graphics—whether using text browsers due to blindness, limited Internet resources, or for those individuals who surf the Web with graphics turned off—the `alt` attribute provides a great way to describe the visual nature of what's going on (see Figure 13.6). In XHTML 1.0, you'll need the `alt` attribute in strict documents in order to be compliant.

Figure 13.6
The `alt` description appears when image loading is turned off.

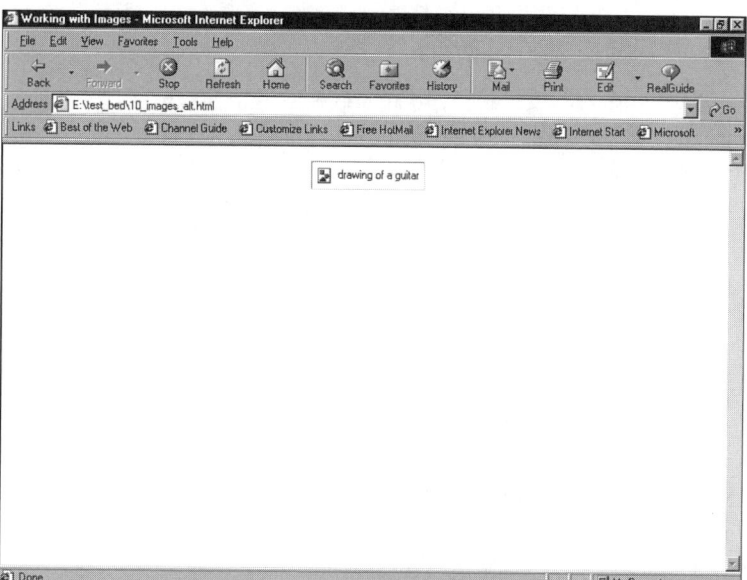

The `alt` description appears in two other instances. One is as a page is loading graphics. The description shows up before the associated graphic is loaded. This is a helpful way of keeping visitors interested in what's coming. Descriptions defined with this attribute also appear when a mouse passes over a given image (see Figure 13.7). Also thought to be helpful, others and I *sometimes* find the extra visual information annoying. It's a compromise—one I'm willing to make at this point to provide people with the most extensible support possible.

Figure 13.7
The alt description also appears when a mouse passes over the image.

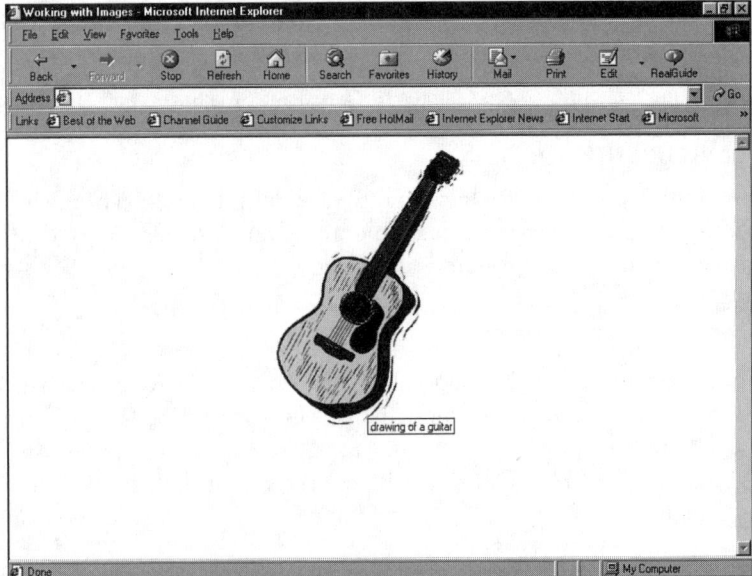

You should use this attribute with an appropriate text value, with one exception: when an image is a single-pixel graphic used for fixing graphic placement. In this case, the alt attribute should be left blank by leaving the attribute in, but placing no value within the quotes:

```
<img src="images/spacer.gif" width="20" height="1" border="0" alt="" />
```

Tip from

Why add an alt attribute with quotes and no value? Well, when you do this, there will be *no demarcation* of the image in a text-based environment. If you don't use this clever technique, [inline] appears where the graphic should be.

HORIZONTAL AND VERTICAL SPACE

Values for hspace and vspace are numeric. For demonstration purposes, I'm going to use values that are a bit exaggerated for these attributes:

```
<img src="images/guitar.gif" width="200" height="284" border="1" align="right"
alt="drawing of a guitar" hspace="100" />
```

Compare Figure 13.8 and Figure 13.9. In Figure 13.8, I use no horizontal spacing; in Figure 13.9, I use the horizontal spacing value of `"100"`. I've added a border of `"1"` to the image so that you can easily see how this puts space between the text and the image.

Figure 13.8
Normal spacing between text and image.

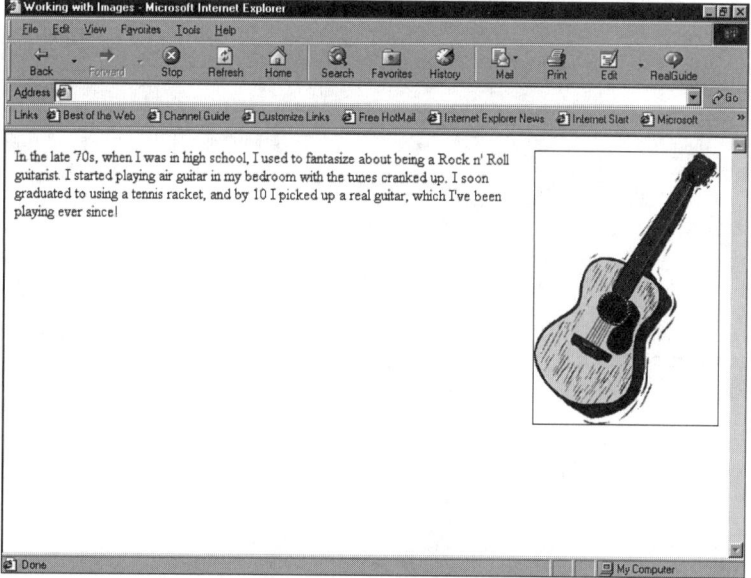

Figure 13.9
Horizontal space added between text and image.

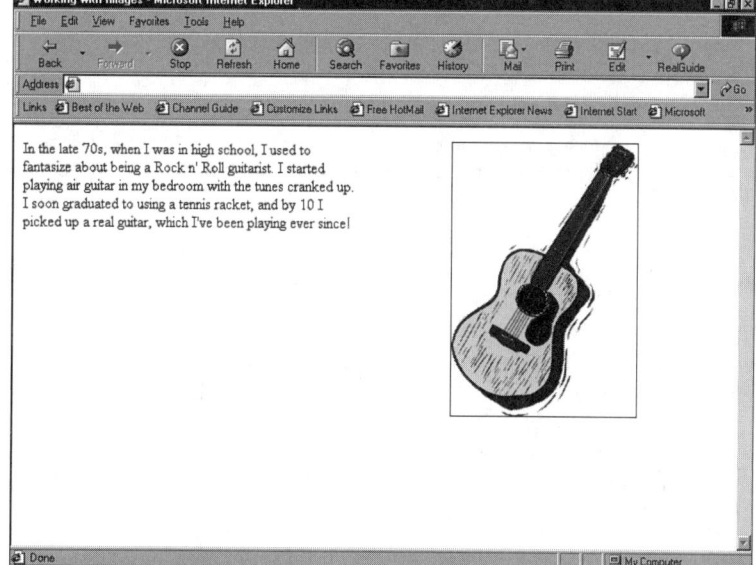

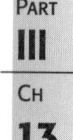

PART

III

Cʜ

13

Now compare Figure 13.8 and Figure 13.10, where I've used a vertical spacing of `"40"`. Here's the code:

```
<img src="images/guitar.gif" width="200" height="284" border="0" align="right"
alt="drawing of a guitar" vspace="40" />
```

Figure 13.10
In this case, vertical space appears between text and image, providing necessary white space in between. Without that space, the text and image would be too close together, making the text difficult to read and diminishing the unique importance of the image.

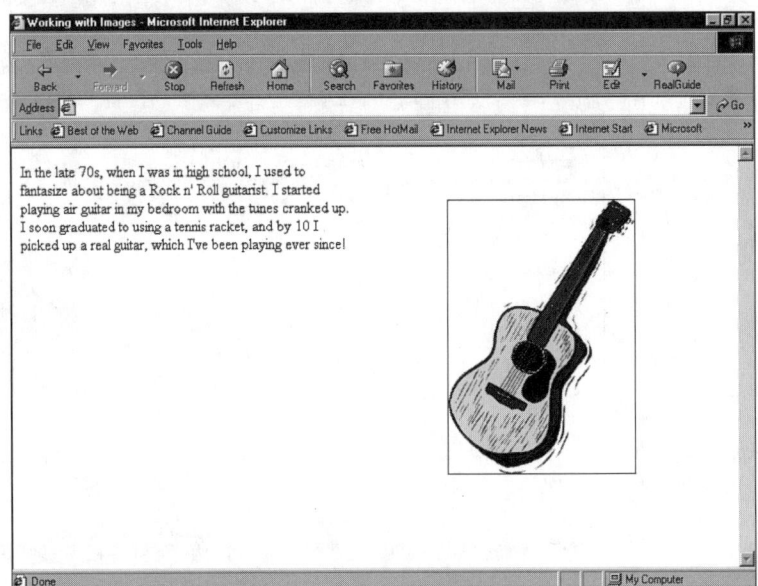

Using the hspace and vspace attributes is particularly helpful when wrapping text around images. This is called *dynamic* text wrapping, or *floating* images. You'll learn more about this technique in the next section.

 What if you want to use a horizontal line to help create space between text or images, but don't want to use an image file for the line? See "Horizontal Rules" in the "Troubleshooting" section near the end of this chapter.

FLOATING IMAGES

Using a combination of attributes within the img tag, you can achieve attractive, dynamic layout of graphics and text. Although tables and style sheets are perhaps more sophisticated ways of addressing this matter, you're likely to have plenty of need for this technique.

To float images, you first must align the image. Even if you want to place your image to the left, which is typically the default position, you must use the align attribute to achieve this technique.

Listing 13.2 shows an XHTML page with text and a left-aligned image.

LISTING 13.2   FLOATING IMAGE AND DYNAMIC TEXT

```
<!DOCTYPE html PUBLIC "-//W3C//DTD XHTML 1.0 Transitional//EN"
"http://www.w3.org/TR/xhtml1/DTD/xhtml1-transitional.dtd">
<html xmlns="http://www.w3.org/1999/xhtml">
<head>
<title>Floating Image and Dynamic Text: Left</title>
</head>
<body>
s<img src="images/little_guitar.gif" width="75" height="107" border="0"
align="left" alt="drawing of a guitar" />
In my other life, I'm a guitar player and vocalist. I've been singing since I
was a child, and was formally trained as a vocalist.  spent many years singing
soprano in a variety of school choirs and other music organizations.  My first
instrument was the piano, which I like but never had the discipline to achieve
any level worthy of impressing anyone!  In the late 70s, when I was in high
school, I used to fantasize about being a Rock n' Roll guitarist. I started
playing air guitar in my bedroom with the tunes cranked up.  I soon graduated
to using a tennis racket, and by 10 I picked up a real guitar, which I've been
playing ever since! I've been playing in a duo named  Courage Sisters, with my
music partner, Patti Sundberg, for the last several years. We play a variety of
original, acoustic music typically comprised of two guitars and two voices.
We're especially known for complex harmonies.
</body>
</html>
```

Figure 13.11 shows the left-aligned image and the text that wraps *dynamically* around the graphic.

Note

The word *dynamic* is used frequently but often improperly in the Web design field. In the case of text wrapping, dynamic refers to the fact that the text naturally finds its way around the image, taking up whatever available space exists. Let's say I viewed the page in Figure 13.11 at 1,024×768 resolution. The text will move into the extra space, continuing to wrap around the image. With style sheets or tables, the positioning is *absolute*. This means that the text and image would be fixed, regardless of the viewing circumstance.

I also can have my image aligned to the right. Listing 13.3 is the same image and text, but the alignment is now right, with the text wrapping around the image from the left.

Figure 13.11
A left-aligned image with text wrapping. This dynamic approach to relating text and visual objects creates a natural flow that is both visually appealing and easy on the eyes.

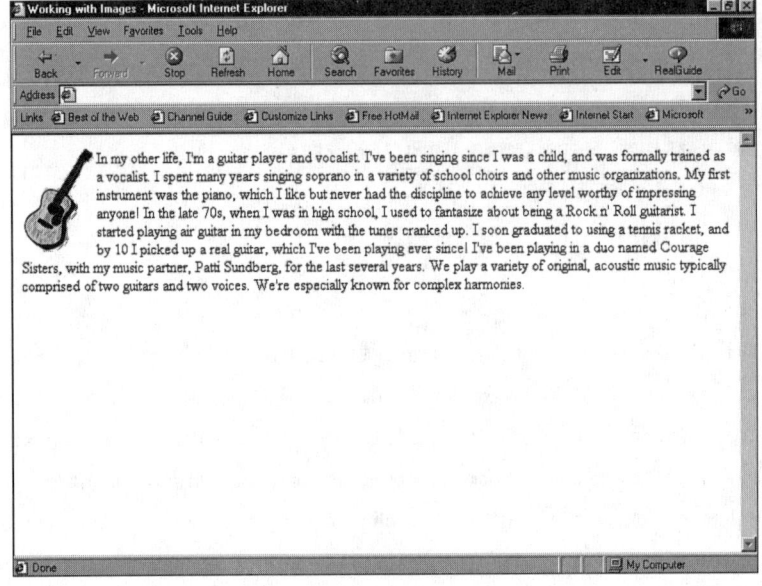

LISTING 13.3   RIGHT-ALIGNED FLOATING IMAGE AND DYNAMIC TEXT

```
<!DOCTYPE html PUBLIC "-//W3C//DTD XHTML 1.0 Transitional//EN"
"http://www.w3.org/TR/xhtml1/DTD/xhtml1-transitional.dtd">
<html xmlns="http://www.w3.org/1999/xhtml">
<head>
<title>Floating Image and Dynamic Text: Right</title>
</head>
<body>
<img src="images/little_guitar.gif" width="75" height="107" border="0"
align="right" alt="drawing of a guitar" />
In my other life, I'm a guitar player and vocalist. I've been singing since I
was a child, and was formally trained as a vocalist.  spent many years singing
soprano in a variety of school choirs and other music organizations.  My first
instrument was the piano, which I like but never had the discipline to achieve
any level worthy of impressing anyone!  In the late 70s, when I was in high
school, I used to fantasize about being a Rock n' Roll guitarist. I started
playing air guitar in my bedroom with the tunes cranked up.  I soon graduated
to using a tennis racket, and by 10 I picked up a real guitar, which I've been
playing ever since! I've been playing in a duo named  Courage Sisters, with my
music partner, Patti Sundberg, for the last several years. We play a variety of
```

LISTING 13.3 CONTINUED

```
original, acoustic music typically comprised of two guitars and two voices.
We're especially known for complex harmonies.
</body>
</html>
```

Figure 13.12 shows the right-aligned image and floating text.

Figure 13.12
Right alignment and text wrap. If you're using a square image with no padding or with a distinct border, be sure to add `hspace` and `vspace`.

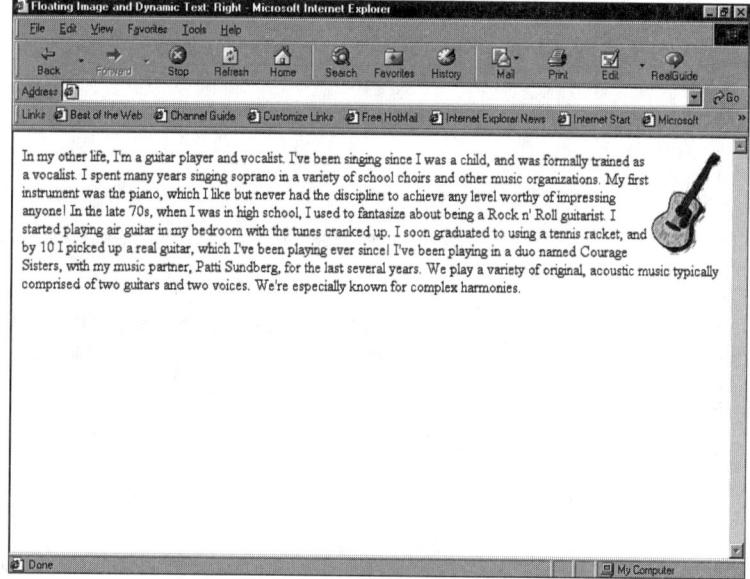

You might notice that the text bumps into the edges of the image a bit. It's slightly less noticeable in this particular instance because my image is angled and has some whitespace around it. However, if you're using a regular photograph, square image, or image with a border, alignment and text wrapping without the use of `hspace` and `vspace` can make a page looked cramped and cluttered (see Figure 13.13).

To avoid this problem, add a numeric value of about 5–15 to each of the spacing attributes:

```
<img src="images/little_guitar.gif" width="75" height="107" border="0"
align="right"
alt="drawing of a guitar" hspace="15" vspace="10" />
```

This adds a nice amount of whitespace (see Figure 13.14), and makes the image and text relationship more harmonious and readable!

PART
III

CH
13

Figure 13.13
Bordered image and text are too close, cramping the page's style.

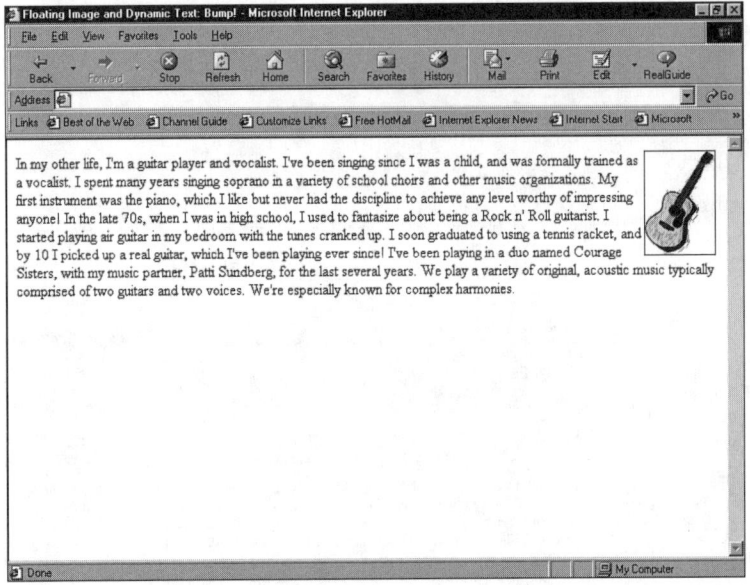

Figure 13.14
More whitespace makes the text more readable.

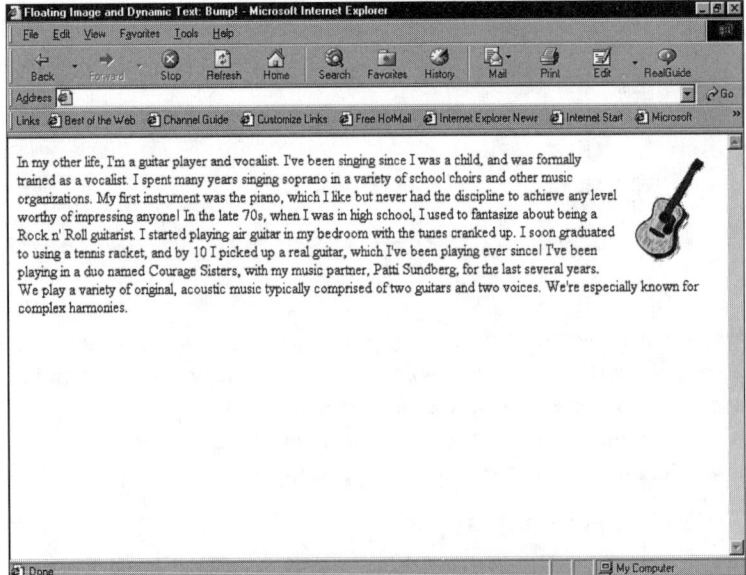

Tip from

molly

Want to put some distance between an aligned graphic and another element, such as another image or text? To break out of the dynamic wrapping, use a `<br />` tag with the `clear="all"` attribute and value.

```
<img src="guitar.gif alt="molly's guitar" align=right />
<br clear=all />
```

→ For more about text alignment and wrapping, **see** "Aligning Text," **p. 178**.

ALIGNING MULTIPLE IMAGES

As Web pages become more complex, you'll want to effectively place images so they look balanced and in proportion to other elements on the page. Let's walk through a page that has a graphic header, an image, and dynamic text:

1. Begin in your editor with a standard shell:

```
<!DOCTYPE html PUBLIC "-//W3C//DTD XHTML 1.0 Transitional//EN"
"http://www.w3.org/TR/xhtml1/DTD/xhtml1-transitional.dtd">
<html xmlns="http://www.w3.org/1999/xhtml">
<head>
<title>An Excerpt from Homer's Odyssey</title>
</head>
<body>

</body>
</html>
```

2. Add the text and page formatting:

```
<!DOCTYPE html PUBLIC "-//W3C//DTD XHTML 1.0 Transitional//EN"
"http://www.w3.org/TR/xhtml1/DTD/xhtml1-transitional.dtd">
<html xmlns="http://www.w3.org/1999/xhtml">
<head>
<title>An Excerpt from Homer's Odyssey</title>
</head>
<body>

<p>A maid servant then brought them water in a beautiful golden ewer and poured it
into a silver basin for them to wash their hands, and she drew a clean table
beside them. An upper servant brought them bread, and offered them many good
things of what there was in the house, the carver fetched them plates of all
manner of meats and set cups of gold by their side, and a man-servant brought
them wine and poured it out for them.</p>

<p>Then the suitors came in and took their places on the benches and seats.
Forthwith men servants poured water over their hands, maids went round with the
bread-baskets, pages filled the mixing-bowls with wine and water, and they laid
their hands upon the good things that were before them.</p>

<p>As soon as they had had enough to eat and drink they wanted music and
dancing,
which are the crowning embellishments of a banquet, so a servant brought a lyre
to Phemius, whom they compelled perforce to sing to them. As soon as he touched
his lyre and began to sing Telemachus spoke low to Minerva, with his head close
to hers that no man might hear.</p>

</body>
</html>
```

3. Add the header image, aligned right, with all the appropriate attributes. I used the `<br clear="all" />` trick to break out of the right alignment:

```
<!DOCTYPE html PUBLIC "-//W3C//DTD XHTML 1.0 Transitional//EN"
"http://www.w3.org/TR/xhtml1/DTD/xhtml1-transitional.dtd">
<html xmlns="http://www.w3.org/1999/xhtml">
<head>
<title>An Excerpt from Homer's Odyssey</title>

</head>
<body>

<img src="images/odyssey_hed.gif" width="350" height="50" border="0"
align="right" alt="an excerpt from homer's odyssey" />
<br clear="all" />

<p>A maid servant then brought them water in a beautiful golden ewer and poured
it
into a silver basin for them to wash their hands, and she drew a clean table
beside them. An upper servant brought them bread, and offered them many good
things of what there was in the house, the carver fetched them plates of all
manner of meats and set cups of gold by their side, and a man-servant brought
them wine and poured it out for them.</p>

<p>Then the suitors came in and took their places on the benches and seats.
Forthwith men servants poured water over their hands, maids went round with the
bread-baskets, pages filled the mixing-bowls with wine and water, and they laid
their hands upon the good things that were before them.</p>

<p>As soon as they had had enough to eat and drink they wanted music and
dancing,
which are the crowning embellishments of a banquet, so a servant brought a lyre
to Phemius, whom they compelled perforce to sing to them. As soon as he touched
his lyre and began to sing Telemachus spoke low to Minerva, with his head close
to hers that no man might hear.</p>

</body>
</html>
```

4. Add the image you intend to float with all the necessary attributes, including `<br
clear="all" />`, which forces anything that comes after the image to the next available
line:

```
<!DOCTYPE html PUBLIC "-//W3C//DTD XHTML 1.0 Transitional//EN"
"http://www.w3.org/TR/xhtml1/DTD/xhtml1-transitional.dtd">
<html xmlns="http://www.w3.org/1999/xhtml">
<head>
<title>An Excerpt from Homer's Odyssey</title>

</head>
<body>

<img src="images/odyssey_hed.gif" width="350" height="50" border="0"
align="right" alt="an excerpt from homer's odyssey" />
<br clear="all" />


<p>A maid servant then brought them water in a beautiful golden ewer and poured
it
into a silver basin for them to wash their hands, and she drew a clean table
```

```
beside them. An upper servant brought them bread, and offered them many good
things of what there was in the house, the carver fetched them plates of all
manner of meats and set cups of gold by their side, and a man-servant brought
them wine and poured it out for them.</p>

<p><img src="images/schooner2.jpg" width="270" height="140" border="0"
align="right" hspace="5" vspace="5" alt="image of schooner" /></p>

<p>Then the suitors came in and took their places on the benches and seats.
Forthwith men servants poured water over their hands, maids went round with the
bread-baskets, pages filled the mixing-bowls with wine and water, and they laid
their hands upon the good things that were before them.</p>

<p>As soon as they had had enough to eat and drink they wanted music and
dancing,
which are the crowning embellishments of a banquet, so a servant brought a lyre
to Phemius, whom they compelled perforce to sing to them. As soon as he touched
his lyre and began to sing Telemachus spoke low to Minerva, with his head close
to hers that no man might hear.</p>

</body>
</html>
```

Figure 13.15 shows the page. Notice how there's plenty of whitespace, balance between the graphics and the text, and the text and images flow naturally along the page.

Figure 13.15
Images and text define the two most critical elements of visual design.

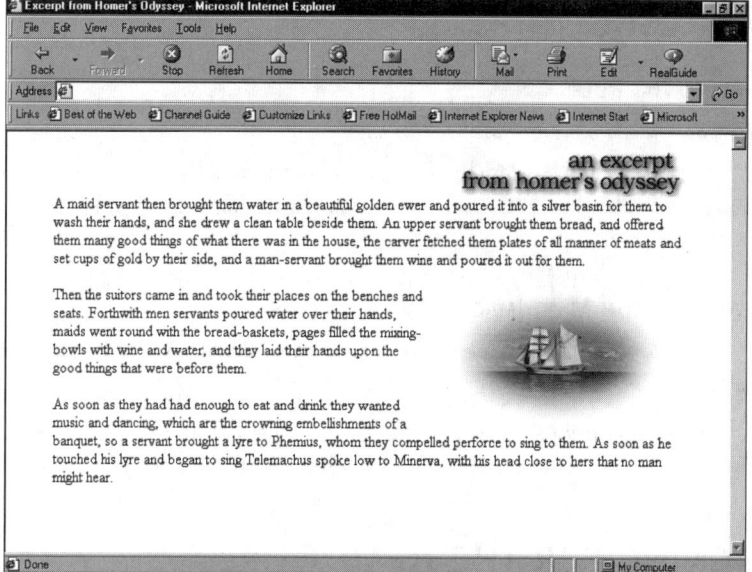

PART

III

CH

13

This technique demonstrates not only the appeal images add to a Web page, but the strong relationship that exists between text and images.

 What do you do if you want more control over laying out multiple images than this method provides? See "Working with Many Images" in " Troubleshooting" section near the end of this chapter.

LINKING IMAGES

Images, like text, can be linked. Making an image "hot" is a common practice and a foundational part of navigation.

Linking images is easy. All you need to do is surround the code for the image with the standard linking element, the <a>, or anchor element.

→ For more about links, **see** Chapter 12, "Linking Pages with Standard Links," **p. 199**.

The following is a sample linked image:

```
<a href="index.html"><img src="images/home_button.gif" width="50" height="100"
border="0" alt="follow this link  to go home" /></a>
```

Tip from

molly

If you want an image to clearly be noted as a link, you can set the border to a numeric value to show the link border. With the border set to off ("0"), this image will appear seamless with the rest of the page. A smoother, more consistent design is achieved by leaving borders off—my preferred method.

→ Another method of linking images is with imagemapping. To read more about this method, **see** Chapter 30, "Designing Specialty Graphics," **p. 623**.

TROUBLESHOOTING

HORIZONTAL RULES

How do you add a horizontal rule to a page?

There is an XHTML element for generic horizontal rules, the <hr /> tag. For graphical horizontal rules, however, you use the standard image tags to insert the graphic, as explained in this chapter.

WORKING WITH MANY IMAGES

What happens when I have numerous images that I'd like to lay out with greater control? How can I do that more effectively than with these simplistic techniques?

You have two options. The first, and most realistic in the current browser environment, is the use of tables. You can also use style-sheet positioning to achieve more complex layouts.

DESIGNING FOR THE REAL WORLD

EXHIBITING YOUR WORK

Now that you know how to use images on your Web pages, you can use those skills to create a gallery on your site. Although your photos or images might or might not be of the same quality as Christopher Burkett's, you can share your visions with the world.

Christopher Burkett is a renowned photographer. His Web site displays some of his best work (don't miss a look at "Summer Heather Garden"). The site is simple and easy to navigate, letting the power of Burkett's photographs send the message of the site. Each thumbnail image links to a larger image of the same work. This enables visitors to see several images at once and choose the specific works they want to see in more detail. The thumbnails also load quickly, because they are very small in size. By clicking a thumbnail, the visitor is accepting the longer download time of a larger image.

You can do the same for your galleries. Simply create two versions of your images, one at a very small scale and lower quality, the other on a larger scale and higher quality. Add the small images to your page. Then link each of those images to the higher-quality version. Some Web designers choose to set the larger image against the same background and navigational elements as the rest of the site to maintain a consistent look. Others simply link to the image, which then displays against a plain background without any navigational elements. Personally, I would recommend adding at least a "back" link to help visitors navigate easily.

Note

Visit Christopher Burkett's Web site at `http://www.christopherburkett.com/`.

Artistic images on the Web add culture and visual appeal to the slick, information-rich, and often commercial focus of today's Web site. Using the Web to display art is a wonderful opportunity to balance the way we use the Web—and to share and promote your artistic works.

PART

III

CH

13

LAYING OUT TABLES WITHIN XHTML DOCUMENTS

In this chapter

THE IMPORTANCE OF TABLES

Tables were originally introduced to provide a way to table data. As simple as that might seem, it only took a few weeks for savvy coders to realize that the grid system created by tables could be used as a means of controlling the entire layout of pages.

This realization grew beyond a means and into a convention—soon, the vast majority of sites on the Web came to embrace tables as their underlying structure. The entire infrastructure of most sites uses tables for graphic placement, color arrangement, and text layout control.

The XHTML standard, in its strict interpretation, recommends that tables as a grid system should be set aside. In their place, the hope is that people will have XHTML markup documents combined with some form of style. The absolute positioning available with cascading style sheets steps far beyond the scope of tables, ideally allowing pixel-by-pixel control of objects on a page.

→ For information on using CSS, **see** Chapter 18, "Cascading Style Sheets and XHTML," **p. 377**.

But, as you by now are aware, the reality of broad-spectrum XHTML design with style sheets is limited to those specialty sites where the audience is known to have compliant software. But, many browsers fall short of complying with the current code standards available. And, because so many site visitors are using browsers that still do not support style sheets, or support them inadequately, style sheets for truly interoperable positioning aren't an option. However, tables still are.

Note

Even if you've been coding tables for some time, I encourage you to work through this chapter with me. You'll discover tips and insights that might help you troubleshoot problems or refine your current coding style.

Therefore, understanding tables as a layout tool is imperative. Furthermore, as the transition is made from table layout to absolute positioning, a knowledge of how tables work will be extremely helpful to those Webmasters who are required to make those changes.

Caution

An important concern for table-based designs involves ensuring that users who are accessing the information with alternative devices can properly display the information. For text-only browsers and screen readers used by many visually disabled, as well as those individuals accessing via PDAs and cell phones, you may have to streamline tables considerably, using fewer graphics and more consideration as to structure.

TABLE ELEMENTS

The first step in becoming aware of how best to use tables as a fundamental tool in Web design is to understand the basic tags used to create them.

There are really only three absolutely critical tags required to create a table. These are:

- `<table>...</table>`—The main table tag, denoting the beginning and subsequent end of a table.
- `<tr>...</tr>`—The table row tag, and its companion closing tag.
- `<td>...</td>`—The table data, or table cell. This tag is used to define individual table cells.

Caution

> Many people get confused between the role of table rows and cells. I encourage XHTML students to think of table rows as the horizontal axis, and table cells as the vertical, columnar information. Every time you create a row, you're creating a horizontal control. Each new row creates a new horizontal section. Similarly, each time you add a table cell, you're adding a vertical column to the table.

Certainly, there's more to it than these three simple tags, but before we explore the attributes of `table` tags, you'll want to build a table for practice.

THE BASIC TABLE

Before you begin, set up a workshop folder on your computer—you will use this to save files that you make for future use. Again, I encourage experienced coders to walk through these steps to learn a highly methodical, clean approach to creating great table layouts.

1. In your favorite editor, set up a transitional XHTML template, with the `<html>`, `<head>`, `<title>`, and `<body>` tags in place:

```
<!DOCTYPE html PUBLIC "-//W3C//DTD XHTML 1.0 Transitional//EN"
"http://www.w3.org/TR/xhtml1/DTD/xhtml1-transitional.dtd">
<html xmlns="http://www.w3.org/1999/xhtml">
<head>
<title>     </title>
</head>
<body>


</body>
</html>
```

2. In between the `<title>` tags, type the page's title, `Table Exercise I`:

```
<!DOCTYPE html PUBLIC "-//W3C//DTD XHTML 1.0 Transitional//EN"
"http://www.w3.org/TR/xhtml1/DTD/xhtml1-transitional.dtd">
<html xmlns="http://www.w3.org/1999/xhtml">
<head>
<title> Table Exercise I</title>
</head>
<body>


</body>
</html>
```

PART

III

CH

14

3. Now, add the `<table>` tag below the `<body>` tag. This alerts the HTML browser interpreting your code that a table is beginning. Using the container method, place the closing `</table>` tag above the `</body>` tag:

```
<!DOCTYPE html PUBLIC "-//W3C//DTD XHTML 1.0 Transitional//EN"
"http://www.w3.org/TR/xhtml1/DTD/xhtml1-transitional.dtd">
<html xmlns="http://www.w3.org/1999/xhtml">
<head>
<title> Table Exercise I</title>
</head>
<body>

<table>


</table>

</body>
</html>
```

4. Directly underneath the `<table>` tag, place the `<tr>` tag. This defines the beginning of your first table row. Directly above the `</table>` tag, place the closing `</tr>` tag:

```
<!DOCTYPE html PUBLIC "-//W3C//DTD XHTML 1.0 Transitional//EN"
"http://www.w3.org/TR/xhtml1/DTD/xhtml1-transitional.dtd">
<html xmlns="http://www.w3.org/1999/xhtml">
<head>
<title> Table Exercise I</title>
</head>
<body>

<table>
<tr>


</tr>
</table>

</body>
</html>
```

5. Move down to the line below the opening `<tr>`, and type in the tag to determine the starting point of your first table cell, `<td>`. Below this, add a line of text, and then close the cell with the `</td>` closing tag:

```
<!DOCTYPE html PUBLIC "-//W3C//DTD XHTML 1.0 Transitional//EN"
"http://www.w3.org/TR/xhtml1/DTD/xhtml1-transitional.dtd">
<html xmlns="http://www.w3.org/1999/xhtml">
<head>
<title> Table Exercise I</title>
</head>
<body>

<table>
<tr>

<td>This is my first table cell.</td>
```

```
</tr>
</table>

</body>
</html>
```

6. Repeat step 5, adding a second table cell (remember, cells determine columns):

```
<!DOCTYPE html PUBLIC "-//W3C//DTD XHTML 1.0 Transitional//EN"
"http://www.w3.org/TR/xhtml1/DTD/xhtml1-transitional.dtd">
<html xmlns="http://www.w3.org/1999/xhtml">
<head>
<title> Table Exercise I</title>
</head>
<body>

<table>
<tr>

<td>This is my first table cell.</td>

<td>This is my second table cell.</td>

</tr>
</table>

</body>
</html>
```

7. Save this HTML file as `table_exercise_1.html`.

8. Compare the file to Figure 14.1.

Figure 14.1
The final product is a table with two cells. The data looks as though it is simply placed on a single line, but actually, each sentence is in a different cell.

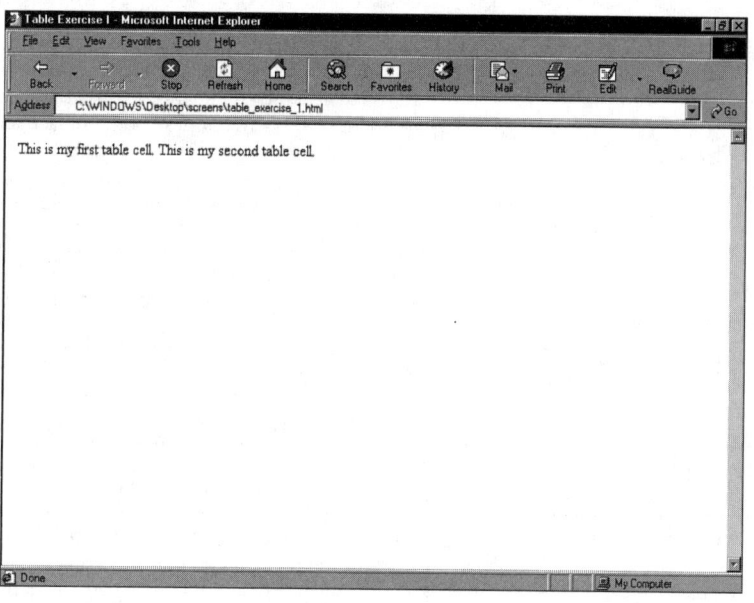

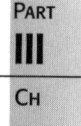

As every XHTML document has a foundational template, so does a table layout. This simple exercise can be seen as a simple table grid template.

Tip from

You'll notice I've kept the closing `</td>` tag on the same line as the opening tag and the data. This is a good practice to get into doing, because it will keep your cells tight and help you avoid gaps in fixed-table designs.

Note

It's important to remember that while I'm focusing on how tables are used for grid layouts, tables can, and do, serve their original function: the tabling of data. You can use the same techniques covered in this chapter to assemble spreadsheet style information as well as understand the grid concepts offered.

TABLE ATTRIBUTES

The `<table>` tag has a variety of related attributes and values that turn it from a simple tag into the control tower of table layouts. Because many of these attributes are style related, using them is most appropriate when authoring documents as transitional rather than strict XHTML 1.0.

Following are some of the more common attributes for the `table` tag.

TABLE 14.1   COMMON TABLE ATTRIBUTES

Attribute and Value	Results
`align="x"`	To align tables on a page, you can use this attribute. Options allow `"x"` to equal `left`, `center`, or `right`. Because browsers default alignment to the left, and it's commonplace to center tables by using other tags such as the `div` tag, the only really effective use of this attribute is when you specifically want an entire table placed to the center or far right of the browser field.
`border="x"`	The `"x"` is replaced with a value from 0 on up. This value defines the width of the visual border around the table (see the tip directly after this list to show how to turn borders into a handy design tool).
`cellspacing="x"`	Cellspacing defines the amount of space between each individual table cell (in other words, between visual columns and rows). The `"x"` requires a value from 0 on up.
`cellpadding="x"`	This attribute calls for the space around the edges of each cell within the table—its literal "padding."
`width="x%" or width="x"`	To define the width of a table, you can choose to use a number that relates to the percentage of browser space you want to span, or a specific numeral that will be translated into pixel widths.

→ For an overview of how to align text and objects, including tables, **see** Chapter 9, "Formatting Text in XHTML," **p. 133**.

Tip from

molly

While working with tables for page layout, you'll find it extremely helpful to turn on borders by adding a value of "1" to the border attribute to see the grid you are creating. Then turn them off to see the results without the borders.

⚠ *Aren't there other table tags and attributes? See "Other Table Tags," in the "Troubleshooting" section near the end of this chapter.*

BORDERS

Borders and width are primary control attributes and values for a table. Borders are most powerful for grid design when turned completely off, because this is what gives us the invisible control for our layout. However, there are instances in which you might like to have a table border, such as when you are laying out information in a spreadsheet-style fashion.

Caution

When used as design elements, borders around tables cause a site to appear visually constrained, creating a sense of claustrophobia for site visitors. Although the instinct to place a border around a table is probably born from a desire to keep things neat and orderly, the results are usually problematic. My recommendation is to use table borders only as a power tool while building the site. Later you'll want to set them to a value of "0". The exception to this is when you're creating data that is meant to be tabled and requires the borders to make sense, or has a subtle border appropriate for your overall design.

TABLE WIDTH

Table width is an important issue—one that bears close examination. The reason is because the width of tables will determine how a table interacts with a browser and the dimension settings of your computer screen.

The maximum viewing space for true cross-Web browser, cross-platform, computer design is 585–600 pixels × 295 pixels per screen. When coding widths by pixel (referred to as *fixed design* or *fixed-width design*), this means that anything larger forces a horizontal scrollbar to appear on screens set to a 640×480 resolution. This is a general design problem and should generally be avoided.

Many developers argue that 800×600 resolution is a highly popular screen resolution in use by Web site visitors. I am finding this to be the case with my site. My sites statistics are showing that the largest percentage of my visitors are using 800×600 resolution. The remainder is split between lower and higher resolutions.

I have several reasons why I often prefer the very conservative rule of 585–600 pixels wide per screen when designing strictly fixed tables (as opposed to percentage based, or dynamic tables), but it's important to express that these are *my* reasons and recommendations.

- If you design tables with fixed design for lower screen resolution and the majority of individuals visiting are at higher resolutions, you can still make the site attractive using design-savvy techniques.

- If 100 people are visiting my site per day, and 13 users come in at lower resolution, I want to accommodate them without the horizontal scroll.

- Often, people using lower resolutions have vision problems. Low resolution means objects appear larger on the page. I want to accommodate these individuals appropriately.

- Tables using percentages rather than pixels (referred to as *dynamic table designs*) can be employed where and when appropriate to avoid the problem altogether.

Depending on your audience and your preference, you might choose to set your fixed-width designs to higher resolutions. I have nothing against that; I just tend to be a little conservative in my thinking in this regard, although I find myself becoming more flexible—depending upon the audience—as time goes on.

Note

If you're designing for small-screen access such as PDAs and cell phones, the restrictions on fixed table widths are even *more* conservative because of the very low resolution of these devices. The resolution of such devices varies greatly, so check with the device manufacturers for specific resolution information and adjust your table widths accordingly.

Note

For the purposes of the examples in this chapter, I'm going to stick to 585–600 pixel widths whenever creating a table that will be used as a grid system for the entire screen.

CREATING A FIXED-WIDTH TABLE

When do you choose to use pixels, and when are percentages a better choice? Pixels give you more control over your page, but you have to be careful and watch your math. This means that every width within a table must add up precisely. You'll see how this realistically unfolds as you work through the stepped exercises in this chapter.

Percentages are powerful when you want to create a dynamic table—a table that opens up to the entirety of the available screen space. This sounds like a better option, but because you do lose control and design integrity, the technique should only be used in specific instances. We'll now get a feel for adding the primary attributes of border and width to the `<table>` tag.

1. Begin by opening the file `table_exercise_1.html` in your HTML editor. Change the title to Table Exercise II. You should see the following:

```
<!DOCTYPE html PUBLIC "-//W3C//DTD XHTML 1.0 Transitional//EN"
"http://www.w3.org/TR/xhtml1/DTD/xhtml1-transitional.dtd">
<html xmlns="http://www.w3.org/1999/xhtml">
<head>
```

```
<title> Table Exercise II</title>
</head>
<body>

<table>
<tr>

<td>This is my first table cell.</td>

<td>This is my second table cell.</td>

</tr>
</table>

</body>
</html>
```

2. The first attribute you're going to add is the border, which you need to set to a numeric value of "1":

```
<!DOCTYPE html PUBLIC "-//W3C//DTD XHTML 1.0 Transitional//EN"
"http://www.w3.org/TR/xhtml1/DTD/xhtml1-transitional.dtd">
<html xmlns="http://www.w3.org/1999/xhtml">
<head>
<title> Table Exercise II</title>
</head>
<body>

<table border="1">
<tr>

<td>This is my first table cell.</td>

<td>This is my second table cell.</td>

</tr>
</table>

</body>
</html>
```

3. Now add the width in pixels:

```
<!DOCTYPE html PUBLIC "-//W3C//DTD XHTML 1.0 Transitional//EN"
"http://www.w3.org/TR/xhtml1/DTD/xhtml1-transitional.dtd">
<html xmlns="http://www.w3.org/1999/xhtml">
<head>
<title> Table Exercise II</title>
</head>
<body>

<table border="1" width="585">
<tr>

<td>This is my first table cell.</td>

<td>This is my second table cell.</td>

</tr>
```

```
    </table>

    </body>
    </html>
```

4. Save your file as `table_exercise_2.html` and view it using your browser. It should match Figure 14.2.

Note that in this instance the border is visible, showing you the grid that you've created.

Figure 14.2
The result of this exercise is a table with two visible cells spanning 585 pixels.

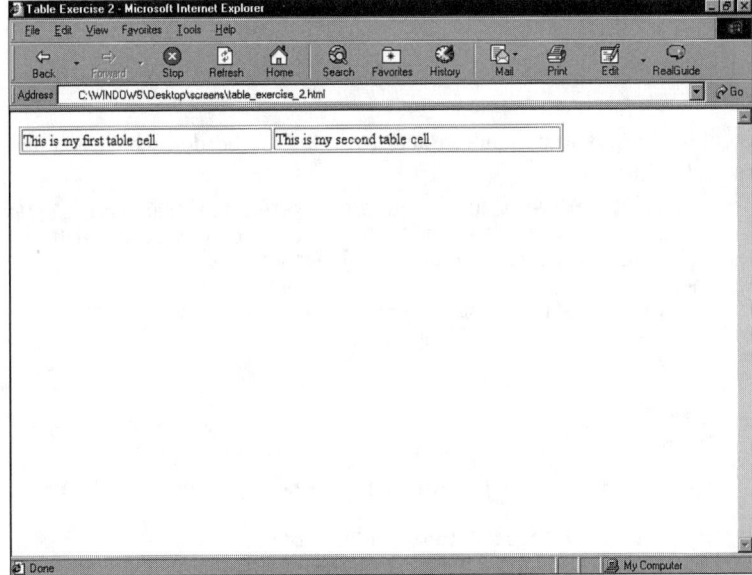

PADDING

Cellpadding and spacing are sometimes helpful because they can aid in the addition of whitespace when coding tables without borders. In a desire to gain and maintain control of your layouts, however, cellpadding and spacing become problematic.

The following examples show code using these techniques so that you can visualize how they work. Let's begin with cellpadding, demonstrated in Listing 14.1.

LISTING 14.1   CELLPADDING

```
<!DOCTYPE html PUBLIC "-//W3C//DTD XHTML 1.0 Transitional//EN"
"http://www.w3.org/TR/xhtml1/DTD/xhtml1-transitional.dtd">
<html xmlns="http://www.w3.org/1999/xhtml">
<head>
<title>Cellpadding</title>
</head>
<body>
```

LISTING 14.1   CONTINUED

```
<table border="1" cellpadding="20">
<tr>

<td>This is my first table cell.</td>

<td>This is my second table cell.</td>

</tr>
</table>

</body>
</html>
```

Figure 14.3 shows the results of this table. Note how far apart the border is from the text. This is the result of the padding.

Figure 14.3
Cellpadding within a table adds whitespace between the cell border and its contents so that even when borders are not used, the information on your page won't appear too close to each other giving a cramped feeling on the page.

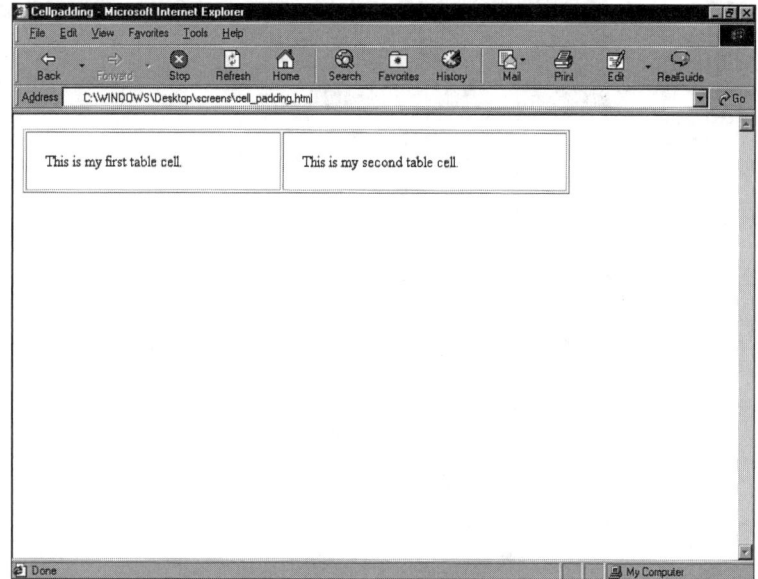

Listing 14.2 shows you cellspacing only.

LISTING 14.2   CELLSPACING

```
<!DOCTYPE html PUBLIC "-//W3C//DTD XHTML 1.0 Transitional//EN"
"http://www.w3.org/TR/xhtml1/DTD/xhtml1-transitional.dtd">
<html xmlns="http://www.w3.org/1999/xhtml">
<head>
<title>Cellspacing</title>
</head>
<body>

<table border="1" cellspacing="20">
```

PART
III

CH
14

LISTING 14.2   CONTINUED

```
<tr>

<td>This is my first table cell.</td>

<td>This is my second table cell.</td>

</tr>
</table>

</body>
</html>
```

In Figure 14.4, you'll notice that the text is now encased in the cell's border, but there's plenty of space between the cell itself and the edge of the table.

Figure 14.4
In contrast to cell-padding, cellspacing within a table adds space between the cell border and the table border.

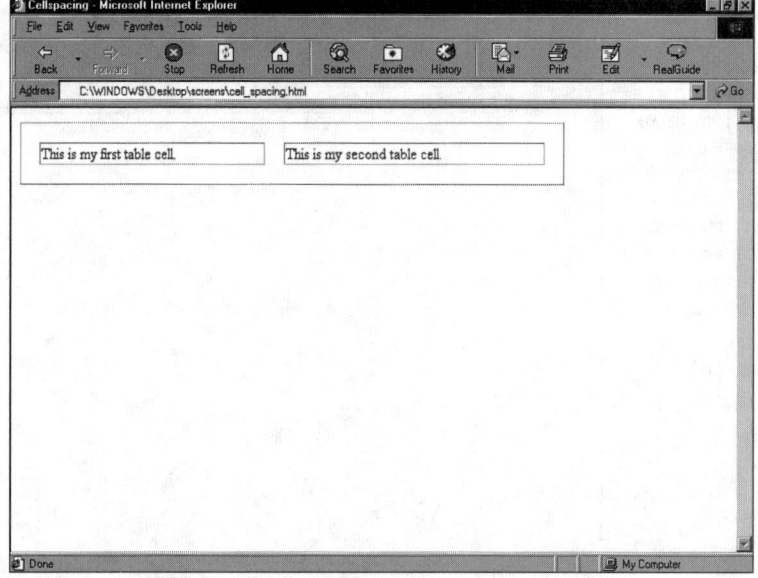

Listing 14.3 shows an example with both cellpadding and cellspacing in action at the same time.

LISTING 14.3   CELLPADDING AND SPACING TOGETHER

```
<!DOCTYPE html PUBLIC "-//W3C//DTD XHTML 1.0 Transitional//EN"
"http://www.w3.org/TR/xhtml1/DTD/xhtml1-transitional.dtd">
<html xmlns="http://www.w3.org/1999/xhtml">
<head>
<title>Cellpadding</title>
</head>
<body>
```

LISTING 14.3   CONTINUED

```
<table border="1" cellpadding="20" cellspacing="20" width="585">
<tr>

<td>This is my first table cell.</td>

<td>This is my second table cell.</td>

</tr>
</table>

</body>
</html>
```

Now there is padding and spacing, giving the text some breathing room within the cell, and some space between the cell's border and the remainder of the table (see Figure 14.5).

Figure 14.5
Cellpadding and cellspacing work together to help give your page a nice, organized look with plenty of whitespace to aid readability.

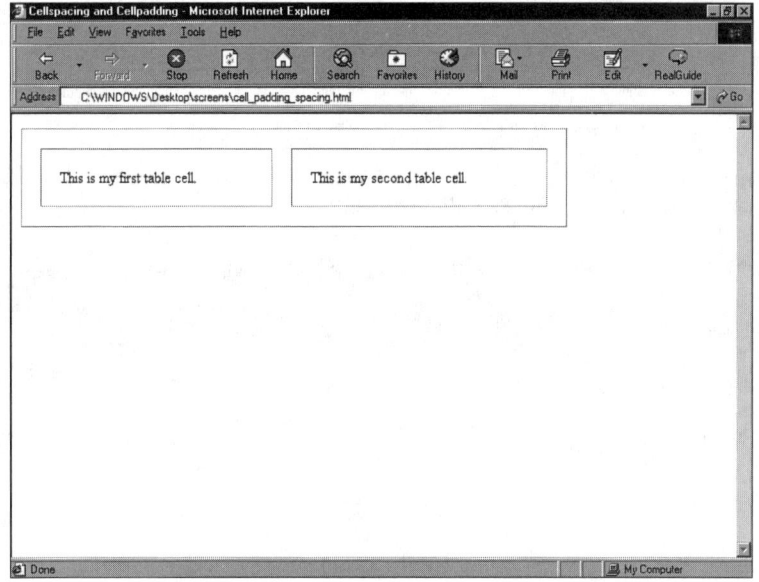

So far, you can't see any problems with the amount of padding and spacing I've added to this example. However, what happens if I added more text, or, as in Listing 14.4, more table cells?

LISTING 14.4   CARELESS MATH FORCES A HORIZONTAL SCROLL AT 640×480

```
<!DOCTYPE html PUBLIC "-//W3C//DTD XHTML 1.0 Transitional//EN"
"http://www.w3.org/TR/xhtml1/DTD/xhtml1-transitional.dtd">
<html xmlns="http://www.w3.org/1999/xhtml">
<head>
<title>Cellspacing</title>
```

PART
III

CH

14

LISTING 14.4   CONTINUED

```
</head>
<body>

<table border="1" cellspacing="20" cellpadding="20" width="585">
<tr>

<td>This is my first table cell. This is my first table cell.</td>

<td>This is my second table cell. This is my second table cell.</td>

<td>This is my third table cell. This is my third table cell.</td>

<td>This is my fourth table cell. This is my fourth table cell.</td>

<td>This is my fifth table cell. This is my fifth table cell.</td>

<td>This is my sixth table cell. This is my sixth table cell.</td>

<td>This is my seventh table cell. This is my seventh table cell.</td>
</tr>
</table>
</body>
</html>
```

The width of the table (585 pixels) cannot accommodate the amount of padding, so a horizontal scrollbar appears (see Figure 14.6).

Figure 14.6
The cellpadding and cellspacing values conflict with the table width causing an undesired horizontal scrollbar to appear.

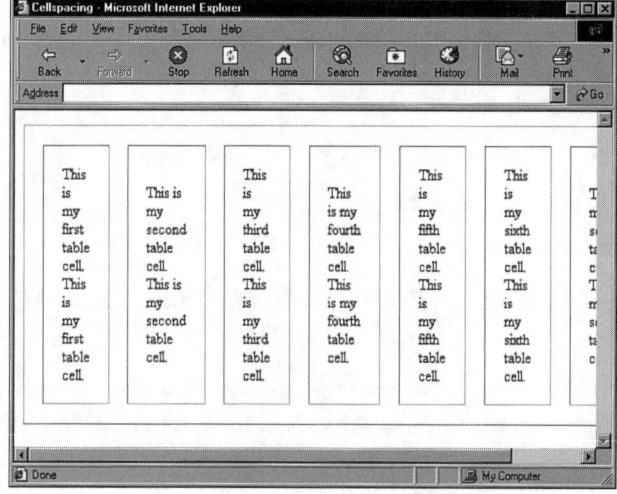

One solution to this problem is to always be sure that you subtract the total amount of the padding and spacing from the maximum pixel width defined. Also, you'll want to fix the widths of each individual cell, as you'll learn later in this chapter when you examine table cell attributes.

However, the best way to avoid disturbing problems with padding and spacing is to *use them sparingly and with forethought* (see Figure 14.7). There are better methods of adding white-space to tables that allow you to control your design with greater precision, as well.

Figure 14.7
The padding and spacing are removed, and all seven cells are accommodated within 585 pixels when the screen is set to full size.

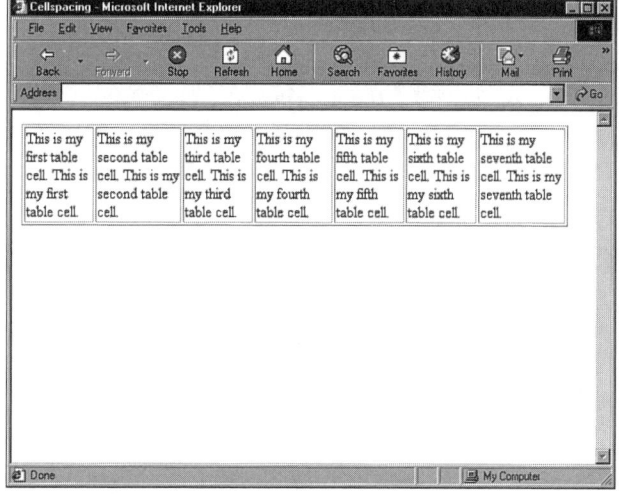

COLUMN SPAN

Spanning columns enables you to create interesting grids and to manage areas of space within a table more completely. The attribute is as follows:

■ `colspan="x"` — colspan refers to the number of columns the cell you are working with will span.

Column span works by allowing the table to span a set amount of columns (remember, columns are created with cells). If you don't use the colspan attribute, the table will try to compensate for any undesignated space.

Consider Listing 14.5, which you'll recognize as a standard table sample with two rows. The top row contains four cells set to a width of 100 pixels each, and the bottom row has two—one with a width of 100 pixels, another with a width of 300 pixels.

LISTING 14.5   STANDARD TABLE WITH ROWS AND COLUMNS

```
<!DOCTYPE html PUBLIC "-//W3C//DTD XHTML 1.0 Transitional//EN"
"http://www.w3.org/TR/xhtml1/DTD/xhtml1-transitional.dtd">
<html xmlns="http://www.w3.org/1999/xhtml">
<head>
<title>Column Span</title>
</head>
<body>
```

PART

III

CH

14

LISTING 14.5   CONTINUED

```
<table border="1" cellspacing="0" cellpadding="0" width="400">
<tr>

<td width="100" valign="top" align="left">
This is my first table cell in the top row.</td>

<td width="100" valign="top" align="left">
This is my second table cell in the top row.</td>

<td width="100" valign="top" align="left">
This is my third table cell in the top row.</td>

<td width="100" valign="top" align="left">
This is my fourth table cell in the top row.</td>

</tr>

<tr>

<td width="100" valign="top" align="left">
This is my first table cell in the bottom row.</td>

<td width="300" valign="top" align="left">
This is my second table cell in the bottom row.</td>

</tr>

</table>
</body>
</html>
```

Logically speaking, the browser should know to set the first table cell in the bottom row to 100 pixels and then stretch, or *span*, the remaining cell to reach across the full 300 pixels available. But this doesn't happen. Instead, the browser applies a blank space (see Figure 14.8) to a section of that row.

The colspan attribute allows you to tell the browser how to manage that space and avoid this problem.

To do this, you have to subtract the number of available cells from the *total sum* of possible columns. Because you have a total of four cells, or columns, in the top row, you have to use that as the amount from which to subtract. You have one cell in the bottom row already, so the second cell, which will span the remainder of the row, must take a colspan of "3". Subtract the first cell from the total available columns to get this value (see Listing 14.6).

Figure 14.8
Without `colspan`, the browser gets confused!

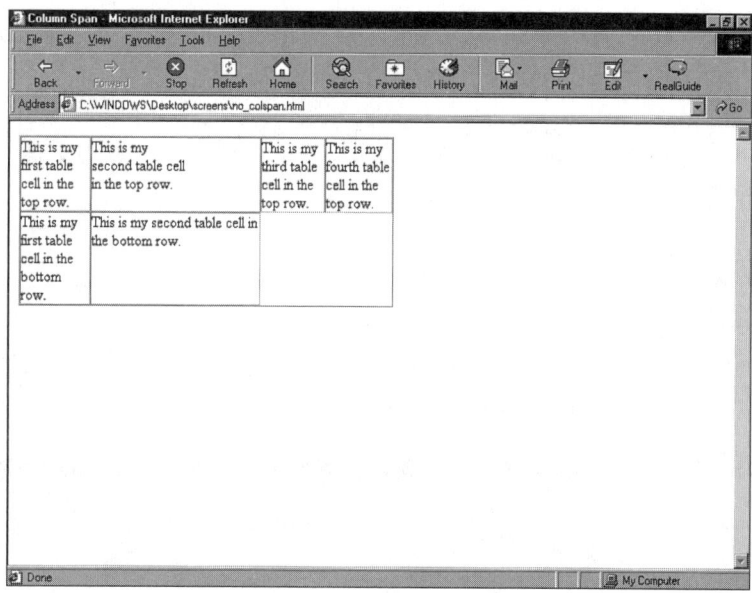

LISTING 14.6 SPANNING COLUMNS

```
<!DOCTYPE html PUBLIC "-//W3C//DTD XHTML 1.0 Transitional//EN"
"http://www.w3.org/TR/xhtml1/DTD/xhtml1-transitional.dtd">
<html xmlns="http://www.w3.org/1999/xhtml">
<head>
<title>Column Span</title>
</head>
<body>

<table border="1" cellspacing="0" cellpadding="0" width="400">
<tr>

<td width="100" valign="top" align="left">
This is my first table cell in the top row.</td>

<td width="100" valign="top" align="left">
This is my second table cell in the top row.</td>

<td width="100" valign="top" align="left">
This is my third table cell in the top row.</td>

<td width="100" valign="top" align="left">
This is my fourth table cell in the top row.</td>

</tr>

<tr>

<td width="100" valign="top" align="left">
```

PART

III

CH

14

LISTING 14.6 CONTINUED

```
This is my first table cell in the bottom row.</td>

<td width="300" colspan="3" valign="top" align="left">
This is my second table cell in the bottom row.</td>

</tr>

</table>
</body>
</html>
```

When I add the colspan attribute and value to the second cell, the browser will now render the table accordingly (see Figure 14.9).

Figure 14.9
The colspan attribute solves the problem.

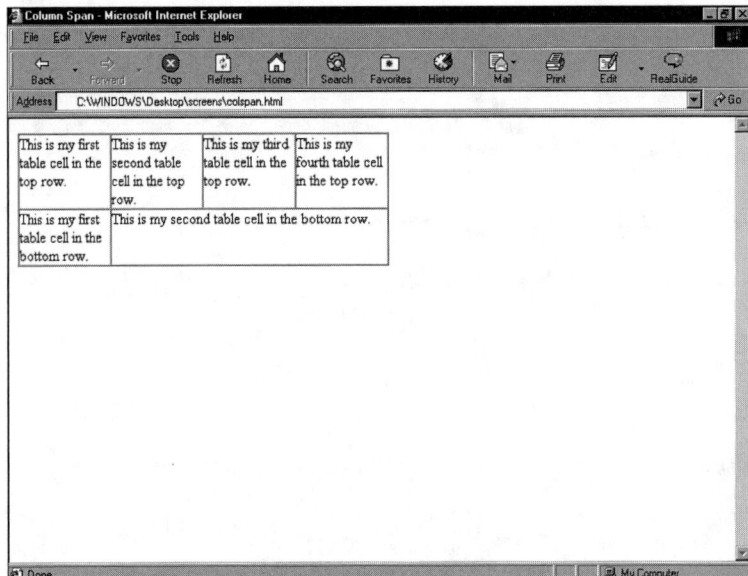

ROW SPAN

Rowspan works in exactly the same way, but is applied to the rows.

- **rowspan="x"**—As with colspan, rowspan refers to the span of the cell, in this case how many rows the cell stretches.

The code in Listing 14.7 shows two rows, each with three cells.

LISTING 14.7 A TABLE WITH ROWS AND CELLS

```
<!DOCTYPE html PUBLIC "-//W3C//DTD XHTML 1.0 Transitional//EN"
"http://www.w3.org/TR/xhtml1/DTD/xhtml1-transitional.dtd">
```

LISTING 14.7   CONTINUED

```
<html xmlns="http://www.w3.org/1999/xhtml">
<head>
<title>Row Span</title>
</head>
<body>

<table border="1" cellspacing="0" cellpadding="0" width="300">
<tr>

<td width="100" valign="top" align="left">
This is my first table cell in the top row.</td>

<td width="100" valign="top" align="left">
This is my second table cell in the top row.</td>

<td width="100" valign="top" align="left">
This is my third table cell in the top row.</td>

</tr>

<tr>

<td width="100" valign="top" align="left">
This is my first table cell in the bottom row.</td>

<td width="100" valign="top" align="left">
This is my second table cell in the bottom row.</td>

<td width="100" valign="top" align="left">
This is my third table cell in the bottom row.</td>

</tr>

</table>
</body>
</html>
```

Figure 14.10 shows the simple table that this code creates.

Now, let's say you want to have the first cell in the top row, width of 100 pixels, span both rows, creating a vertical column. To do this, you have to first remove a column from the bottom row, because you're going to essentially stretch the first cell across that space. Then, you need to add the rowspan attribute and value to the first cell in the top row.

The way you get rowspan value is by simply counting the number of rows you want to span—in this case, "2".

Listing 14.8 is resulting code.

PART
III

CH
14

Figure 14.10
The result of Listing 14.7 is a table with two rows and three cells in each row.

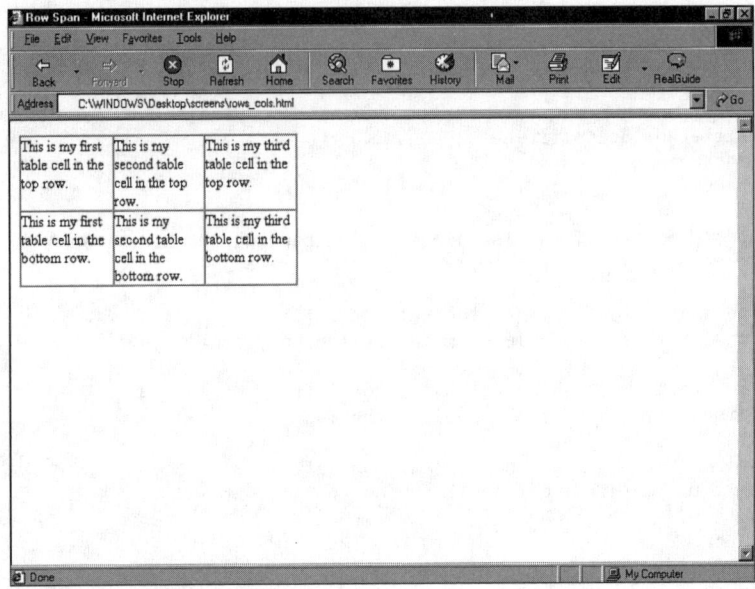

LISTING 14.8   SPANNING ROWS

```
<!DOCTYPE html PUBLIC "-//W3C//DTD XHTML 1.0 Transitional//EN"
"http://www.w3.org/TR/xhtml1/DTD/xhtml1-transitional.dtd">
<html xmlns="http://www.w3.org/1999/xhtml">
<head>
<title>Row Span</title>
</head>
<body>

<table border="1" cellspacing="0" cellpadding="0" width="300">
<tr>

<td width="100" rowspan="2" valign="top" align="left">
This is my first table cell, and it spans two rows.
</td>

<td width="100" valign="top" align="left">
This is my second table cell in the top row.
</td>

<td width="100" valign="top" align="left">
This is my third table cell in the top row.
</td>

</tr>

<tr>

<td width="100" valign="top" align="left">
This is my second table cell in the bottom row.
</td>
```

LISTING 14.8   CONTINUED

```
<tr width="100" valign="top" align="left">
This is my third table cell in the bottom row.
</td>

</tr>

</table>
</body>
</html>
```

Figure 14.11 shows the table with the first cell now spanning two rows.

Using these attributes can get fairly complex, particularly when you have a table with many rows, and many cells within those rows. The rule of thumb when working with these attributes is to rely on the mathematical formulas described in this chapter.

Figure 14.11
Similar to how the `colspan` attribute enables you to span columns within the table, the `rowspan` attribute allows you to span rows.

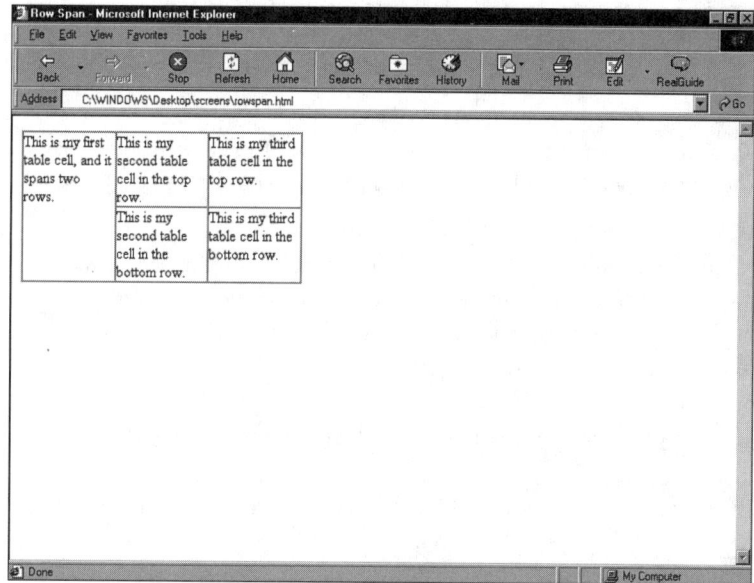

Remember that a table data cell creates a column. Because I have five table data cells in this table, I have to account for five individual cells

I'm going to span the second cell, and I want it to stretch from the cell's beginning along the full measure of the table. Therefore, I will use a value of `"3"` to create the span. This can be very confusing, because it really appears that there are now only three total columns and the logical span for this cell would be `"2"`. The trick is to always count the cell you are working from as being the first part of a span. Then you simply add to that number to reach the total amount of cells, without getting confused by the visual results.

PART

III

CH

14

Fix your table width, make sure that your table cells total the appropriate width, and when using colspan and rowspan attributes, measure how many cells or rows need to be spanned appropriately.

TABLE AND TABLE CELL ALIGNMENT

As I mentioned, rows make up a table's horizontal axis, and cells its vertical axis. There are ways to control alignment in both. The following section will describe how.

HORIZONTAL ALIGNMENT

The only two attributes ever used within rows include align, which controls the row's spatial alignment, and valign, which determines the vertical placement of all the data within a row. While these attributes are considered legal, they don't offer the kind of control available in attributes related to the table and td elements, so they are rarely used.

Note

To understand table rows best, think of them as the horizontal structure of the grid, whereas table cells will be the columnar, or vertical, structure of that grid.

To show you some of the control issues related to row attributes, take a look at Listing 14.9. The border value is set to "1" and cellpadding and cellspacing are added, so you can see the rows clearly.

When viewed in my browser (see Figure 14.12), you'll notice how the valign attribute used in the first two rows doesn't even apply. Furthermore, although the align attribute in the third row does in fact center the text within that row, the fourths row's table cell alignment value *overrides* that of the row.

LISTING 14.9   ROW ATTRIBUTES ARE OFTEN INCONSISTENT

```
<!DOCTYPE html PUBLIC "-//W3C//DTD XHTML 1.0 Transitional//EN"
"http://www.w3.org/TR/xhtml1/DTD/xhtml1-transitional.dtd">
<html xmlns="http://www.w3.org/1999/xhtml">
<head>
<title>Table Row Attributes and Values</title>
</head>
<body>

<table border="1" cellspacing="10" cellpadding="10" width="100%">
<tr valign="top">

<td>This is my first table row.</td>

</tr>

<tr valign="bottom">
<td>This is my second table row.<td>

</tr>
```

LISTING 14.9   CONTINUED

```
<tr align="middle">
<td>This is my third table row, middle alignment.</td>
</tr>

<tr align="middle">
<td align="right">This is my fourth table row.</td>

</tr>
</table>
</body>
</html>
```

Figure 14.12
Row attributes are inconsistent.

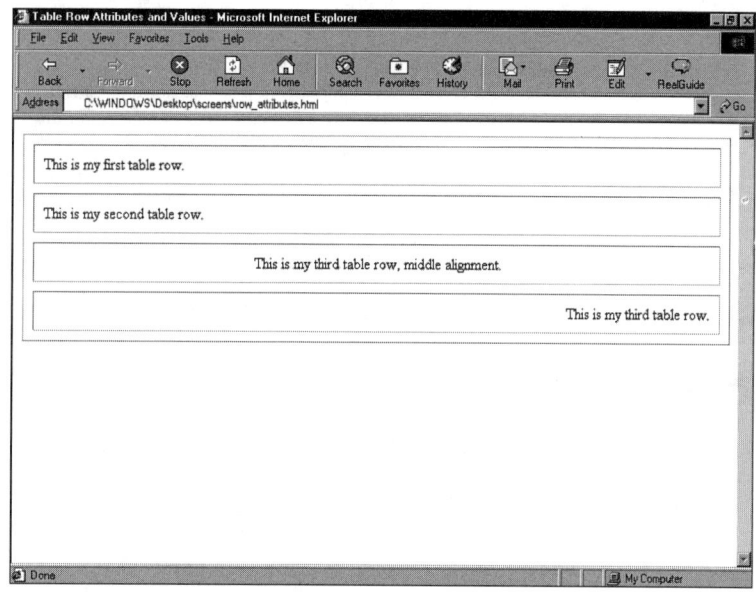

Tip from

It has long been my experience that row attributes do not necessarily lend themselves to strong control over tables. The greatest control comes from the relationship between table tags and attributes and table cell tags.

In the previous example, I've demonstrated an instance where practical wisdom can override the standard to become a convention. It's important to know that you can use attributes within rows, and many coders do. It's perfectly legal, but not always the easiest way to accomplish your table goals.

VERTICAL ALIGNMENT

The essence of table design really relies on the table cell, or td tag. This tag has a variety of important attributes that can be applied for maximum table control. The attributes and values are added to specific sections, depending upon what type of control they offer.

PART

III

CH

14

Primary attributes and values should generally be placed in all table cells. Column and row spanning attributes and values are more useful in specific grid designs, and specialty attributes such as `height`, and `bgcolor`, are generally used in more advanced or specialized table design.

PRIMARY ATTRIBUTES

Table 14.2 shows the primary attributes for the table cell tag.

TABLE 14.2 TABLE CELL ATTRIBUTES

Attribute and Value	Results
`width="x%"` or `width="x"`	Setting a percentage width with x% will make the cell dynamic within the context of the table. Fixing the cell width to a pixel value fixes that cell within the table. For example, you can have dynamic cells in a fixed design and vice versa.
`align="x"`	When you use this attribute within a table cell, the data inside the cell will align with the literal value you assign to the attribute. In other words, a `<left>` value will left-justify the text or graphic you place within the cell, the `<center>` value will center the information, and a value of `<right>` will justify the information to the right of the cell.
`valign="x"`	The vertical alignment of a table cell will place the information therein to the `top`, `middle`, or `bottom` of the cell.

Note

I'll mention again that I personally believe primary attributes and related values should be placed in all table cell tags. Making sure that the browser is given as much possible information stabilizes the table and creates more realistic cross-browser, cross-platform XHTML design.

Listing 14.10 shows a table with three cells, each cell being completely defined with primary attributes.

LISTING 14.10 DEFINING THE ATTRIBUTES IN EVERY CELL

```
<!DOCTYPE html PUBLIC "-//W3C//DTD XHTML 1.0 Transitional//EN"
"http://www.w3.org/TR/xhtml1/DTD/xhtml1-transitional.dtd">
<html xmlns="http://www.w3.org/1999/xhtml">
<head>
<title>Table Cell Attributes and Values</title>
</head>
<body>

<table border="1" cellspacing="0" cellpadding="0" width="585">
<tr>

<td width="250" valign="top" align="left">
This is my first table cell. Its width is 250 pixels, the information within it
is vertically aligned to the top of the cell, and is justified to the left of
the cell.</td>
```

LISTING 14.10   CONTINUED

```
<td width="250" valign="middle" align="right">
This is my second table cell. It, too, has a width of 250 pixels. The
information within this cell is aligned to the middle of the cell, and is
justified to the right.</td>

<td width="90" valign="bottom" align="middle">
This is my third table cell. Its values are completely different than the prior
cells.</td>

</tr>
</table>
</body>
</html>
```

Figure 14.13 shows how the table cell attributes are much more consistent.

Figure 14.13
These table cells help to clarify just how cells are a critical component of object placement.

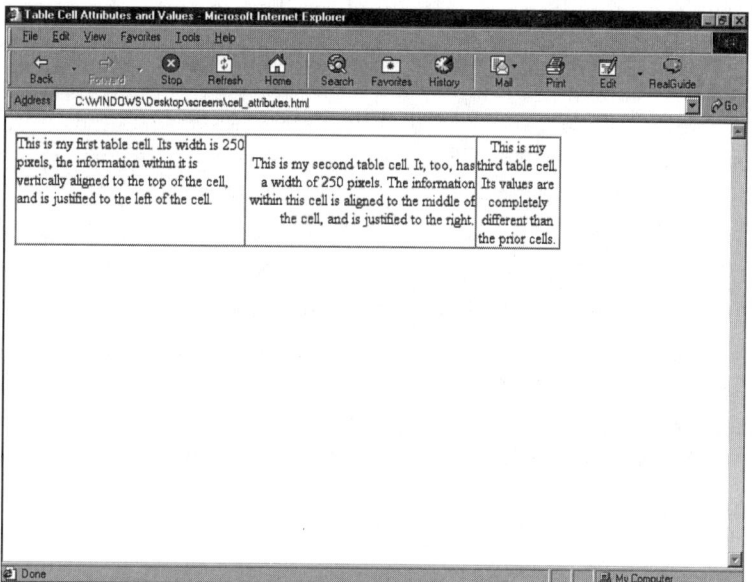

In the first cell, the information is vertically aligned to the top of the cell, and justified to the left. The second cell's data is vertically aligned to the middle of the cell and justifies right. Finally, the third cell's content, which is vertically aligned to the bottom of the cell, also is centered. Each cell is fixed to the width called for within the cell and within the table tag itself.

Note

When you don't add attributes to a tag, browsers will seek the default. Table borders default to 0, cell padding and cellspacing to 1. Alignment defaults to the left, and width becomes dynamic, meaning that the width of a table and the cells within adapt to the combination of browser space and the data you've placed within the cells.

PART
III

CH
14

This control relationship between the table cell and the table tag is the most powerful aspect of table coding. Carefully working with this relationship is certain to help you create stable, compatible tables that allow you to firmly secure your data and design.

> **Note**
>
> In transitional XHTML 1.0, background color can be added to individual table cells using the `bgcolor="x"` (where "x" is a named or hexadecimal color) attribute color also can be achieved using style sheets, which of course is the preferred idealistic method when dealing with XHTML 1.0 in its strictest sense.

MAXIMIZING TABLE POWER/MINIMIZING CODE

In just a few chapters, you're going to read about an aspect of cascading dtyle sheets known as *absolute positioning*. Using this feature within XHTML, you can separate style and layout from the content of an XHTML document. The advantage of positioning in this way is that it is, in fact, as absolute as positioning any element on a Web page can get.

As you already are aware, however, what works in the strict interpretation of XHTML is not necessarily what works in the real world. Or at least, not yet. And, because tables and frames have a longer history than CSS, it's a given that designers will naturally lean toward what works and what is interoperable across platforms and browsers.

Furthermore, although style sheet positioning is preferred for layout within the standard in strict XHTML, XHTML has by no means given up on tables as a viable and acceptable method for layout. On the shirttails of this attitude ride some new tags for tables.

When you're creating page layouts, the idea is to take available visual space and control it. Tables allow you to do that and to do it fairly well. However, the rules are a bit complex. So, in this section, I'm going to show you how to take the information you learned earlier in this chapter, and systematically demonstrate how to create powerful page layouts.

Before you jump in, however, let me show you some of the capabilities that are associated with using tables for layout purposes:

- **Placement of graphics**—When you're designing a page without tables, you can left-align, center, or right-align a graphic. You also can control a graphic to some limited degree on the vertical axis. But what you can't do is take graphics and put them at close-to-specific, fixed points onto your page. With tables, you can (of course, you can ideally do this even better with CSS).
- **Control of space**—Without tables, you can control margins. What you can't do is make elegant columns for text and graphics, or divide a page into specific areas—particularly vertical sections—for use in navigation or textual design. You can, however, control this space using tables.
- **Dynamic Flow**—Creation of pages that flow dynamically to the resolution of the screen, yet maintain a more complex layout than available with more basic XHTML techniques.

It's undeniable that the use of tables provides some of the most powerful options within the developer's toolkit. But, you need to have the ability to visualize how tables work as a layout system. Without knowing how the pieces will ultimately fit together, you can end up with slipshod, faulty work.

SEEING THE GRID

Many designers begin their designs with a sketch or graphical mockup. Some do both, sketch out some ideas first and then refine them in a layer-based imaging program such as Photoshop. This approach allows you to not only move objects around, but also—most imperative to designing with tables—to *see the grid*. As a result, you can create a design completely free of the logical constraints of XHTML. Then, you can look at the design to see how you need to slice it up to create the supporting grid that will position the text and images where you want them.

Figure 14.14 shows a splash page design mockup. To a fairly adept eye, it will be obvious that this design cannot be achieved without the use of either a very large graphic or some combination of graphics and tables.

Figure 14.14
Splash page mockup
as seen in Photoshop.

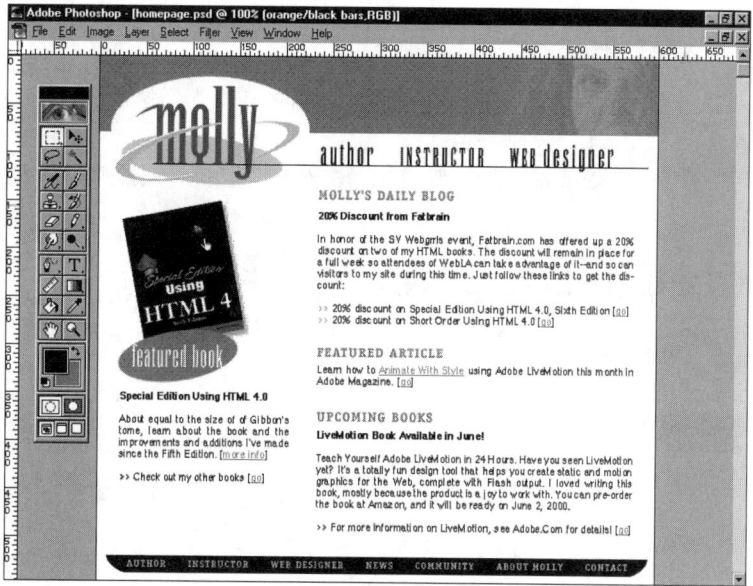

Figure 14.15 shows guides in Photoshop that I've denoted as being the grid I want to create. Using guides isn't the only way to create grids, however; you can use other ways, too. As long as you are following syntactical rules, there isn't a right or a wrong way per se.

PART

III

CH

14

Tip from

Always go with the least complex coding solution that provides the kind of control necessary for your design. Reduce extraneous rows, cells, nesting, and spanning. If you see an easier way to accomplish a table layout, your tables will render more quickly and page weights will be less hefty.

Figure 14.15
Final design displayed with table borders set to "1".

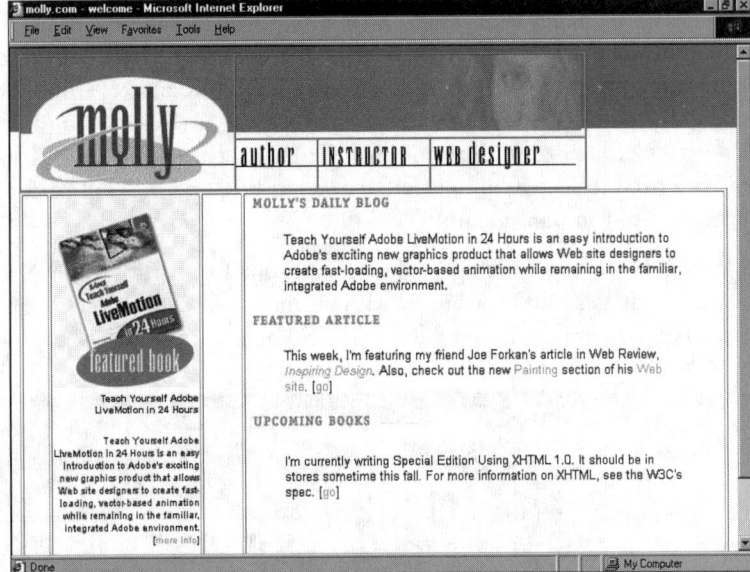

USING FIXED AND DYNAMIC DESIGN

Beyond seeing the grid is the next designer challenge: deciding whether a design should be *fixed* or *dynamic*.

Note

In this case, *dynamic* refers to the capability of the design to adapt to any variable. In most instances, this variable will be screen resolution.

Fixed designs are created for a specific resolution. *Fixed-width* layouts require very accurate measurement on the designer's part. You must work within the parameters of the resolution—585×295 pixels per screen for the lowest common denominator—and ensure that each section is mathematically fixed within those parameters (see Table 14.3). This is particularly important concerning width, because vertical scrolling is much more acceptable than horizontal scrolling.

TABLE 14.3 SCREEN MEASUREMENTS BY COMMON RESOLUTION (IN PIXELS)

Screen Resolution	Screen Measurement
640×480	585×295
800×600	745×415
1,024×768	969×583
1,280×1,024	1,225×839

Dynamic layouts, however, stretch to meet the resolution of the screen. These layouts rely on percentages or wildcards, essentially saying "put this information here, but this information can take up whatever screen space is available."

The Origin of Fixed Screen Widths

Screen measurements are lower than their corresponding resolution because additional screen space gets eaten up by the browser. Open your favorite Web browser, and you'll see menus on the top, a scrollbar to the right, a status bar along the bottom, and even a thin margin to the left. All these elements eat away at the available screen space.

There are differences between platforms, too, and the way people use computers! Windows browsing software appears to take up slightly less space, and typically speaking, Windows users open their Windows to the parameters of the available desktop. Macintosh browsing software can eat a little more space on the horizontal—about 10 pixels' worth. Mac users tend not to open their browsing windows to the full desktop space.

Because it's impossible to control what users do with their software, the numbers evolve from the desire to offer the best-case scenario for each resolution, avoiding horizontal scrolls wherever possible.

Of fixed and dynamic tables, I use fixed or combinations of fixed and dynamic designs the most. This tends to be true of people who have some background in visual design, because they are used to having more specific control over elements when working in the print medium.

However, dynamic design might well be the preferred choice depending on the scenario. You should know how to do both, and how to combine the two for maximum flexibility.

APPLYING A FIXED TABLE DESIGN

In the earlier grid example, I showed you a design that has a left functional margin and an area of body text. One way to approach this design is to use a table. The grid that I drew showed four total columns. The first column manages the left navigation; the second, the whitespace between the navigation and the body text; the third, the body of the document; and the fourth, a precise amount of whitespace.

→ For more information on working with background designs, **see** Chapter 29, "Creating Professional Web Graphics," **p. 595.**

To fix this page to a 640×480 resolution (with a 585×295 per screen recommendation), follow these steps:

1. Determine how much space is necessary for each section. (For my page, I want 125 pixels for my navigational margin, 10 pixels of whitespace between the margin and my text, and a right margin of 45.)

2. Add up these sections. (In my example, I get a total of 180 pixels. Subtract that number from 585. I end up with 405 pixels available for my body area.)

3. Fix this information into the table. To do so, create a table with the fixed width of 585 pixels. Then create four cells, each with the appropriate number of fixed pixels for each cell.

Listing 14.11 shows the HTML code necessary to create the grid.

LISTING 14.11 HTML CODE FOR A FIXED, LEFT-MARGIN TABLE

```
<!DOCTYPE html PUBLIC "-//W3C//DTD XHTML 1.0 Transitional//EN"
"http://www.w3.org/TR/xhtml1/DTD/xhtml1-transitional.dtd">
<html xmlns="http://www.w3.org/1999/xhtml">
<head>
<title>Fixed, left-Margin Table</title>
</head>

<body>
<table border="0" width="585" cellpadding="0" cellspacing="0">
<tr>
<td width="125" align="left" valign="top"></td>

<td width="10" align="left" valign="top"></td>

<td width="405" align="left" valign="top"></td>

<td width="45" align="left" valign="top"></td>

</tr>
</table>
</body>
</html>
```

In coding the opening <table> tag, note that I included the border, cellpadding, and cellspacing attributes along with the width. This approach goes back to the "don't let the browser do the thinking for you" concept.

Along the same lines, every table cell includes the correct width but also the default "left" alignment and top alignment. (You can set these attributes as you ultimately need them to be set; they are the conventions I typically begin with.)

The example in Listing 14.11 isn't the entire picture. Although later generation (4.0 and above) browsers in both the IE and Netscape varieties tend to respect cell widths, you *always* run the risk of a collapsing or drifting table cell unless you fix that cell. One way to do so is to incorporate a graphic into the cell design. My navigation buttons, for example, are all 125 pixels wide, so the cell to the left is going to be sturdy. What about my other cells, however? I either have to do the same thing with a specific graphic, or include a single pixel, transparent GIF (known as a spacer GIF) stretched to the width of the table to ensure that it really *is* fixed.

How to Make a Spacer GIF

In Photoshop or your favorite imaging program, create an image that is 1×1 pixel. Fill the image with a color (I use white). Now, index the color and reduce the bits to the lowest number your imaging program allows. Export the file as a GIF, but before saving, remove all the color and be sure that the image is not interlaced. Save this file as `spacer.gif` and place it in your images directory. You can now call upon it at any time.

Listing 14.12 shows the code with the navigation buttons and spacer graphics in place.

LISTING 14.12   FIXED, LEFT-MARGIN DESIGN WITH SPACER GRAPHICS INCLUDED

```
<!DOCTYPE html PUBLIC "-//W3C//DTD XHTML 1.0 Transitional//EN"
"http://www.w3.org/TR/xhtml1/DTD/xhtml1-transitional.dtd">
<html xmlns="http://www.w3.org/1999/xhtml">
<head>

<title>Fixed, left-Margin Table</title>
</head>
<body background="images/bluebak.gif">
<table border="0" width="585" cellpadding="0" cellspacing="0">
<tr>
<td width="125" align="left" valign="top">

<p><a href="new.html"><IMG src="images/new.gif" border="0" width="125"
height="30" alt="what's new"></a></p>

<p><a href="about.html"><IMG src="images/about_us.gif" border="0" width="125"
height="30" alt="About Us"></a></p>

<p><a href="products.html"><IMG src="images/products.gif" border="0" width="125"
height="30" alt="products"></a></p>

<a href="contact.html"><IMG src="images/contact.gif" border="0" width="125"
height="30" alt="contact"></a>
</td>

<td width="10" align="left" valign="top">
<img src="images/spacer.gif" border="0" width="10" height="1" alt="" /></td>

<td width="405" align="left" valign="top"><IMG src="images/company_header.gif"
border="0" width="405" height="50" Âalt="welcome to the company" />
</td>

<td width="45" align="left" valign="toptop">
<img src="images/spacer.gif" border="0" width="45" height="1" alt="" />
</td>
</tr>
</table>
</body>
</html>
```

In Figure 14.16, you can see the results. This table will not collapse, because every cell is mathematically accounted for. In Figure 14.17, the table's border is set to 1 so that you can see the grid.

Caution

When using spacer images in a table, be sure to include an `alt` attribute in the image, and leave the attribute value undeclared. The reason you should do this is so that screen readers for the visually disabled will ignore the spacer image. If you don't do this, the word "image" will be repeated to the user over and over again.

Figure 14.16
Fixed, left-margin table design. This popular design method is used throughout the Web as a method of keeping navigation and content in specific, familiar locations.

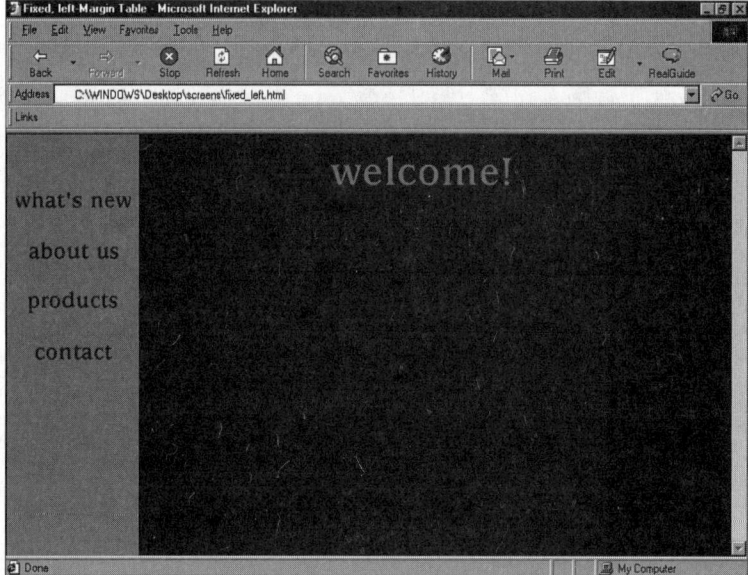

If you want to reverse the process—say you want to fix a table with a right margin—you prepare it exactly the same way. Mark off the exact widths of each section—whether it be whitespace, a navigation area, or a body text area—and do the math.

Of course, one of the problems with designing to the lowest common resolution occurs when someone comes along viewing the page at a higher resolution. In the case of fixed tables, more whitespace is visible at the right and bottom of the page. The design will be set into the left x- and y-axes snugly. Because this design is so prevalent on the Web, most individuals are not distracted by it.

Tip from
molly

If you want to balance whitespace around fixed table designs in transitional XHTML 1.0, center the table using the `div` element. It won't be noticeable at low resolution, but at higher resolutions you'll end up with the empty space flowing around the fixed table instead of weighing heavily on one side of the page.

Figure 14.17
This table has a border attribute set to 1 so that you can see the grid—note the cells where the spacer GIFs fill in.

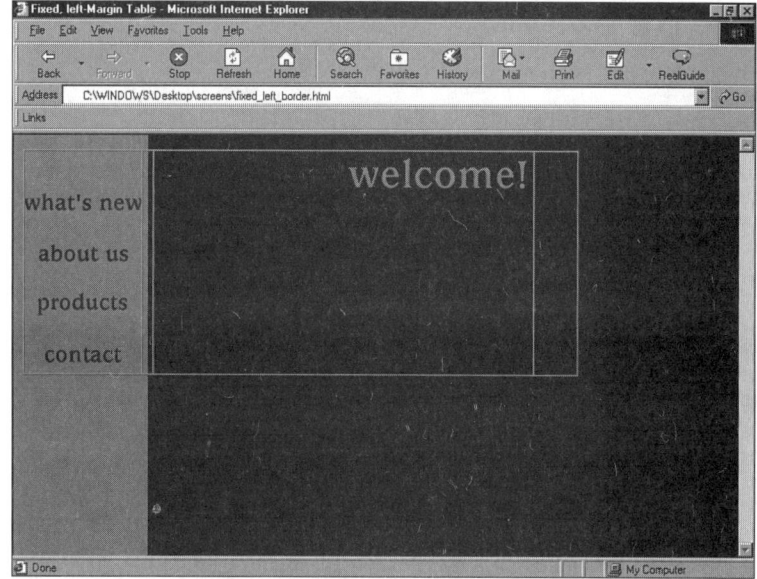

→ To learn more about how to work with the div element **see** Chapter 11, "Aligning Text Using XHTML," **p. 177.**

Stick to this process for fixed designs and you'll never force a horizontal scrollbar!

Tip from

In fixed design, you must never exceed a cell's parameters. In other words, if you have a cell that is 125 pixels wide, but you put a 200-pixel–wide graphic in it, you will cause the table to render improperly.

WORKING WITH DYNAMIC TABLE DESIGN

To create tables that stretch to accommodate any space, you can make them dynamic by using a percentage for widths instead of a fixed layout. Dynamic tables come in handy when designing tables that contain some graphical information, but are more loosely designed.

Listing 14.13 shows a dynamic table. I've made the entire table dynamic—placing a 100% value in the <table> tag itself (both height and width) and creating four dynamic columns of 25% each. What's powerful about this table is that it will adjust to the dimensions of the available space, no matter what.

PART

III

CH

14

LISTING 14.13   A DYNAMIC TABLE

```
<!DOCTYPE html PUBLIC "-//W3C//DTD XHTML 1.0 Transitional//EN"
"http://www.w3.org/TR/xhtml1/DTD/xhtml1-transitional.dtd">
```

LISTING 14.13   CONTINUED

```
<html xmlns="http://www.w3.org/1999/xhtml">
<head>
<title>Dynamic Table</title>
</head>
<body>
<table border="1" width="100%" height="100%" cellpadding="1" cellspacing="1">
<tr>
<td width="25%" align="left" valign="top">text</td>

<td width="25%" align="left" valign="top">text</td>

<td width="25%" align="left" valign="top">text</td>

<td width="25%" align="left" valign="top">text</td>
</tr>
</table>
</body>
</html>
```

In Figure 14.18, you can see the table at full resolution. If I make the browser window smaller (see Figure 14.19), the table automatically adjusts. If I did this with a fixed table, however, I would obscure all the information that fell outside the exact pixel range of my browser window size.

Figure 14.18
A dynamic table at 800×600 resolution.

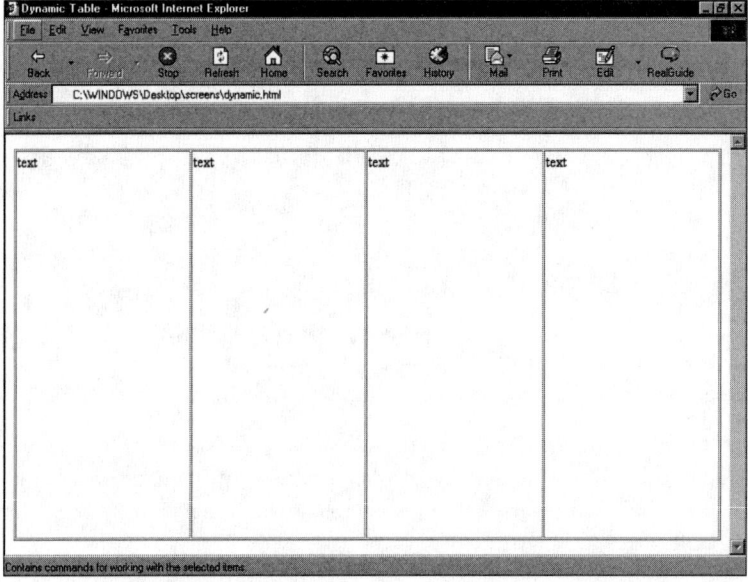

The greatest challenge with dynamic table design, however, is that you lose the integrity of the fixed grid that allows you to stabilize a precision design within it.

Figure 14.19
Dynamic tables readjusted to browser size fill only the available space.

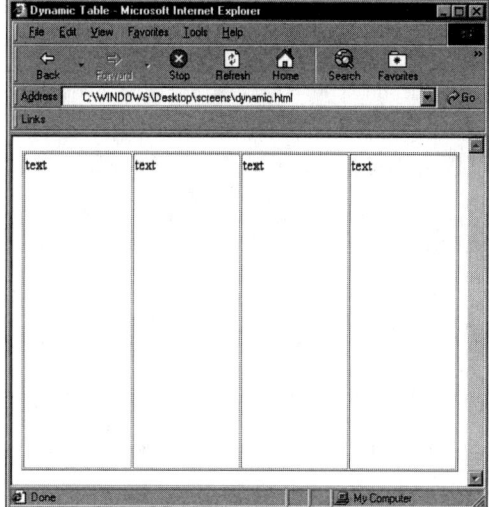

COMBINATION FIXED AND DYNAMIC TABLE DESIGN

One way to reach for the best of both worlds is to combine fixed and dynamic approaches. The wisdom here, however, is to ensure that only one cell is fixed to a percentage width, and that width should be 100%. This approach helps you maintain the shape of the layout but allows for dynamic positioning of text.

This approach works well, for example, if I have a left and right margin I want to keep fixed, but I want to keep the center, body area dynamic. I could achieve this effect by fixing the cells to the left and right using both a fixed width cell and spacer GIF set to the dimensions of the cell, but leaving the center cell dynamic. Listing 14.4 shows an example of this effect.

LISTING 14.14   FIXED AND DYNAMIC CELLS

```
<!DOCTYPE html PUBLIC "-//W3C//DTD XHTML 1.0 Transitional//EN"
"http://www.w3.org/TR/xhtml1/DTD/xhtml1-transitional.dtd">
<html xmlns="http://www.w3.org/1999/xhtml">
<head>
<title>Fixed and Dynamic Table</title>
</head>
<body background="images/decorative.gif" text="#FFFFFF">
<table border="0" width="100%" cellpadding="0" cellspacing="0">
<tr>

<td width="75" align="left" valign="top">img src="images/spacer.gif" border="0"
width="75" height="1" alt="" /></td>

<td width="100%" align="left" valign="top">
<p>A maid servant then brought them water in a beautiful golden ewer and poured
it into a silver basin for them to wash their hands, and she drew a clean table
beside them. An upper servant brought them bread, and offered them many good
```

PART

III

CH

14

Listing 14.14   Continued

```
things of what there was in the house, the carver fetched them plates of all
manner of meats and set cups of gold by their side, and a man-servant brought
them wine and poured it out for them.</p>

<p>Then the suitors came in and took their places on the benches and seats.
Forthwith men servants poured water over their hands, maids went round with the
bread-baskets, pages filled the mixing-bowls with wine and water, and they laid
their hands upon the good things that were before them.</p>

<p>As soon as they had had enough to eat and drink they wanted music and
dancing, which are the crowning embellishments of a banquet, so a servant
brought a lyre to Phemius, whom they compelled perforce to sing to them. As
soon as he touched his lyre and began to sing Telemachus spoke low to Minerva,
with his head close to hers that no man might hear.</p></td>

<td width="50" align="left" valign="top"><IMG src="images/spacer.gif" border="0"
width="50" height="1" alt="" />
</td>
</tr>
</table>
</body>
</html>
```

In this case, you have the advantage of being able to fix margins. Here, you can accommodate a left, decorative background and whitespace to the right (see Figure 14.20). You also can allow for the dynamic wrapping of text (see Figure 14.21).

Figure 14.20
Fixed margins over a decorative background allow for better positioning of the text so it does not run into the decorative margin design.

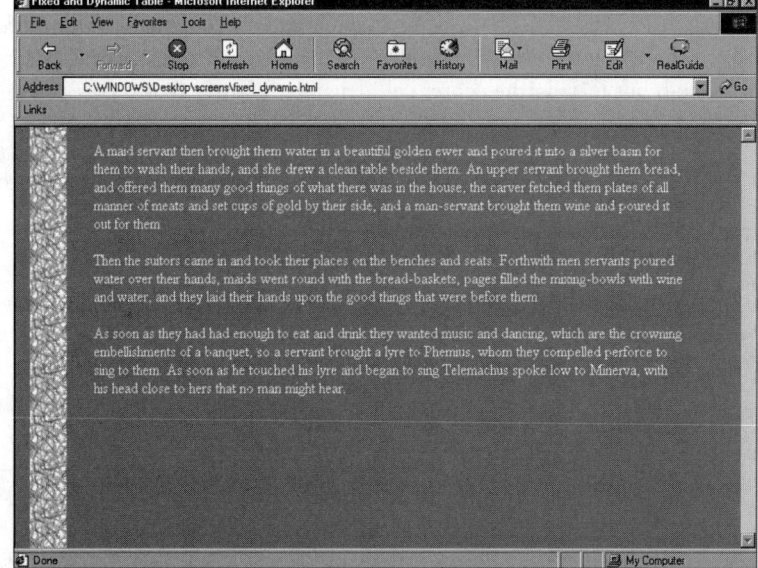

Tip from
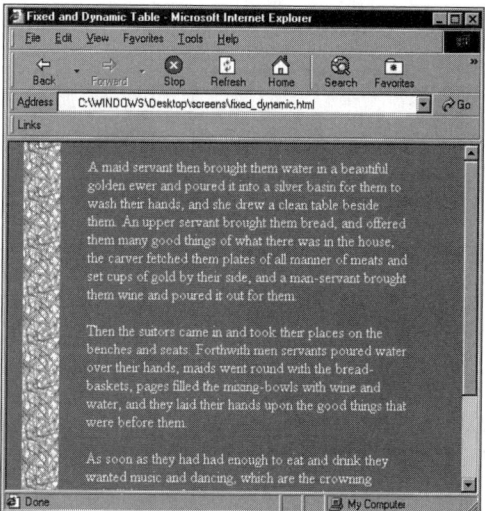

What happens when you have a fixed table design, but you want it to be available for a variety of resolutions? If you're that committed to providing people with perfection at any resolution, you can create separate designs and route browsers by resolution using JavaScript.

→ To use the JavaScript Route-by-Res script to have site visitors automatically routed to resolution-specific pages, **see** Chapter 20, "Adding JavaScript to XHTML Documents," **p. 445**.

Figure 14.21
The fixed and dynamic combination readjusted. Note how the design adjusts to the screen space, without the appearance of a horizontal scrollbar.

NESTING AND STACKING TABLES

To create complex layouts using tables, you can often employ column and row spanning. Spanning provides options that help designers break from strict column and row design and add some visual diversity.

However, sometimes this technique is limited or cannot provide you with the control you're after. Say you want to create a layout that manages a background margin tile, yet you want to have central sections broken up. And, within those sections, you want to add swatches of background design or color.

One method of enabling complex table design is to nest tables. In this process, you put a table within a table to achieve the layout you require.

Here's the rule: Any table cell within a table can accept a complete, new table. Doing so creates a nest:

```
<td>
    <table>
    <tr>
```

```
        <td>      </td>
        </tr>
        </table>
</td>
```

You can take the nest even further:

```
<td>
        <table>
        <tr>

        <td>

<table>

                <tr>

                <td>      </td>
                </tr>
                </table>

        </td>
        </tr>
        </table>
</td>
```

Nesting tables is one of the keys to complex table design. After you've learned the basics, nesting can help you get control over space within space.

 Creating great tables, but finding that they take too long to download to the visitor's browser? See "Reducing Fat Table Code" in the "Troubleshooting" section near the end of this chapter.

Caution

Use nesting creatively, but use it wisely. Nesting anything beyond three levels is a good indicator that you need to go back and examine your grid, looking for a more simple approach to the layout.

You also can stack tables. In this process, you take more than one table and place it above another. The advantage of stacking is that you can separate particular sections of a page, revert to standard XHTML in between, return to a table, or combine any variety of options to create varied design.

Listing 14.15 demonstrates a set of stacked tables with a numbered list between the two tables.

LISTING 14.15   STACKED TABLES

```
<!DOCTYPE html PUBLIC "-//W3C//DTD XHTML 1.0 Transitional//EN"
"http://www.w3.org/TR/xhtml1/DTD/xhtml1-transitional.dtd">
<html xmlns="http://www.w3.org/1999/xhtml">
<head>
<title>Stacked Table Example</title>
</head>
<body background="images/flocked.gif" text="#FFFFCC">
<table border="0" width="595" cellpadding="0" cellspacing="0">
<tr>
<td width="100" align="left" valign="top">
<h3>An Excerpt from Homer's Odyssey</h3></td>

<td width="495" align="left" valign="middle">
<p>A maid servant then brought them water in a beautiful golden ewer and poured
it into a silver basin for them to wash their hands, and she drew a clean table
beside them.<p></td>

</tr>
</table>

<p>Then the suitors came in and took their places on the benches and seats:</p>

<ul>
<li>Men servants poured water over their hands</li>
<li>maids went round with the bread-baskets</li>
<li>pages filled the mixing-bowls with wine and water</li>
</ul>

<p>and they laid their hands upon the good things that were before them.</p>
<table border="0" width="595" cellpadding="0" cellspacing="0">
<tr>
<td width="595" align="left" valign="top">
<img src="images/lyre.gif" width="100" height="69" border="0" ALT="lyre image"
align="left" hspace="10" Vspace="10" />

<p>As soon as they had had enough to eat and drink they wanted music and
dancing, which are the crowning embellishments of a banquet, so a servant
brought a lyre to Phemius, whom they compelled perforce to sing to them.  As
soon as he touched his lyre and began to sing Telemachus spoke low to Minerva,
with his head close to hers that no man might hear.</p></td>

</tr>
</table>
</body>
</html>
```

Figure 14.22 shows the results.

PART
III

CH
14

Figure 14.22
Stacked table design.

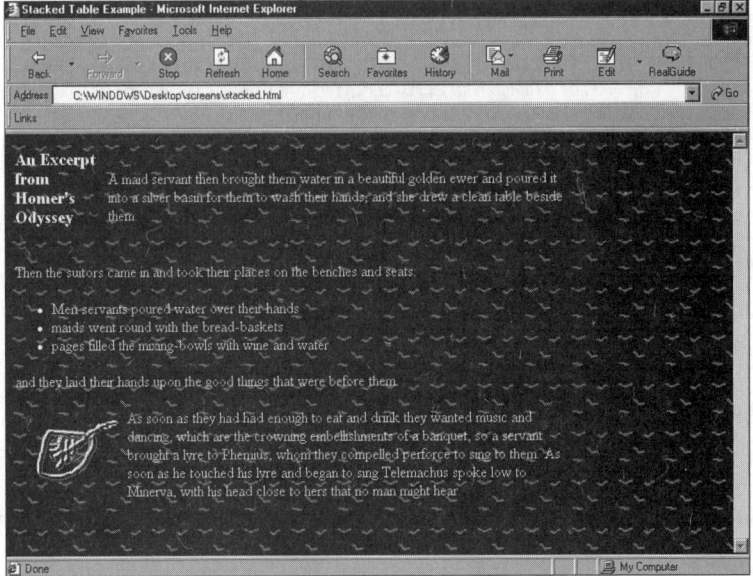

ALIGNING TABLES

Aligning tables provides you with additional power over the way your table designs are laid out in relation to the screen, as well as in relation to other elements on the page. To align a table horizontally on a page, use the div element, with a left, center, or right value:

```
<div align="right">

<table>
<tr>
<td><p>This table is aligned to the right of the available browser space, but the
cell information will not be right aligned, unless I add an alignment attribute
to, or within, the cell itself.</p></td>
</tr>
</table>
</div>
```

Note

Recall that the align attribute within table tags typically aligns the information within a table, not the table itself.

You can align tables vertically, too. To do so, use the height attribute combined with a middle alignment in a table cell:

```
<table height="100%">
<tr>

<td valign="middle">
<p>Content goes here</p>
</td>
```

```
</tr>
</table>
```

You also can combine width and height (see Figure 14.25) to combine vertical and horizontal alignment:

```
<table height="100%" width="100%" border="1">
<tr>

<td valign="middle">
<p>Content goes here</p>
</td>
</tr>
</table>
```

Figure 14.23
A table that is both horizontally and vertically aligned to 100% width and height will take up the entire screen space. Note that with a middle cell alignment, the content appears in the center of the table.

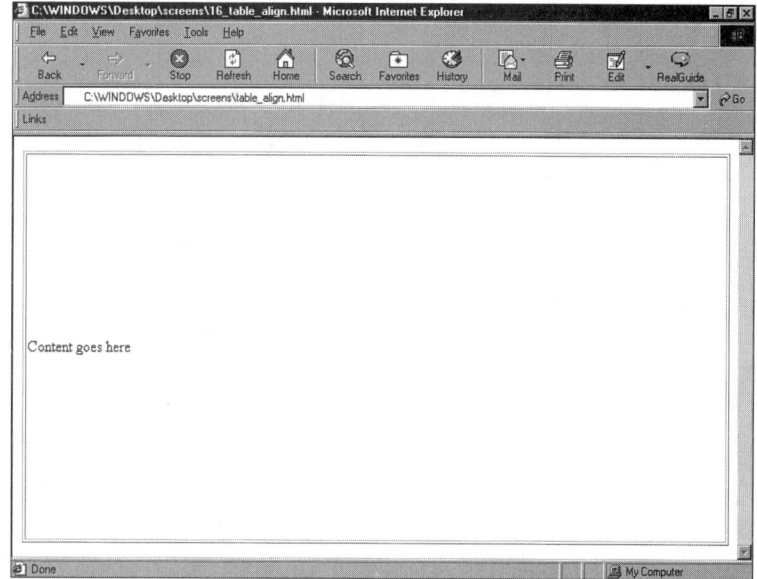

SLICING GRAPHICS FOR PLACEMENT IN A TABLE

One of the more interesting uses of tables is to create a grid system for the placement of graphics. This approach is sensible when you want to animate sections of a larger image or to place images in otherwise difficult-to-reach places on the browser page, such as slightly left of center. Instead of using one really big graphic to accommodate this look, designers slice the graphics, keeping the overall weight down and the load time faster.

→ For more information on working with graphics, **see** Chapter 29, "Creating Professional Web Graphics," **p. 595**, and Chapter 30, "Designing Specialty Graphics," **p. 623**.

In Figure 14.24, I've captured an image that is built using numerous pieces.

PART

III

CH

14

Figure 14.24
An image that is actually made up of several sliced images.

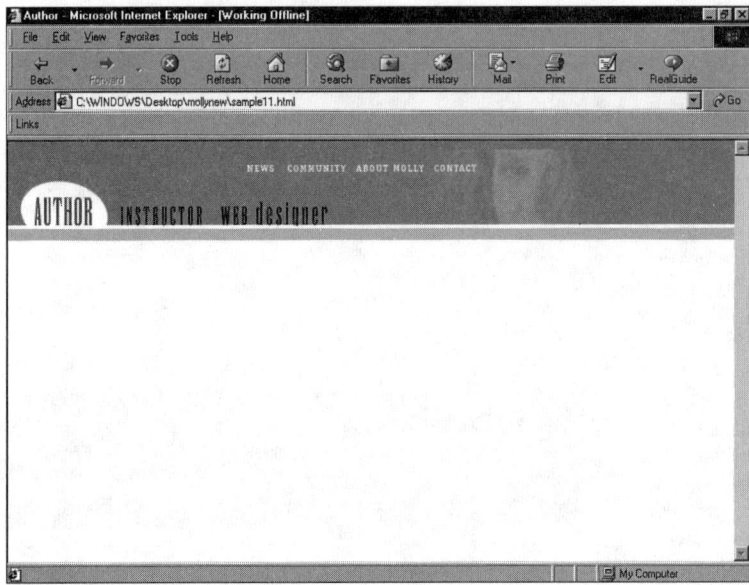

If this image had been created as one graphic, it would have weighed a lot more and have been more difficult to lay out properly. By slicing the image and placing it within a table, the weight of the image is reduced, and so is the page's load time.

Listing 14.17 shows the table code for the image.

LISTING 14.17   SLICING A GRAPHIC

```
<!DOCTYPE html PUBLIC "-//W3C//DTD XHTML 1.0 Transitional//EN"
    "http://www.w3.org/TR/xhtml11/DTD/transitional.dtd">
<html xmlns="http://www.w3.org/1999/xhtml">
<head>
<title>Author</title>
</head>
<body bgcolor="#FFFFFF" background="images/molly_inner_bak.gif"
text="#000000" link="#FF9900" vlink="#CC6600" alink="#99CC00"
topmargin="8">
<table width="600" border="0" cellpadding="0" cellspacing="0">

<tr>
<td valign="top" align="left" width="282"><a href="news.html">
<img src="images/news_top.gif" align="left" width="282" height=
"27" border="0" alt="news" /></a></td>
<td valign="top" align="left" width="72"><a href=
"http://www.webwithmolly.com/"><img src=
"images/community_top.gif" width="72" height="27" border="0" alt=
"community" /></a></td>
<td valign="top" align="left" width="83"><a href="about.html">
<img src="images/about_top.gif" width="83" height="27" border="0"
alt="about molly" /></a></td>
<td valign="top" align="left" width="56"><a href="contact.html">
<img src="images/contact_top.gif" width="56" height="27" border=
```

LISTING 14.17 CONTINUED

```
"0" alt="contact" /></a></td>
<td valign="top" align="left" width="107" rowspan="2"><img src=
"images/face_right.gif" width="107" height="82" border="0" alt=
"face" /></td>
</tr>

<tr>
<td valign="top" align="left" width="340" rowspan="2" colspan=
"2"><img src="images/author_hed.gif" width="340" height="55"
border="0" alt="author" /></td>
<td valign="top" align="left" width="83"><img src=
"images/spacer.gif" width="83" height="1" border="0" alt="" />
</td>
<td valign="top" align="left" width="56"><img src=
"images/face_block.gif" width="56" height="55" border="0" alt=
"" /></td>
</tr>

</table>
</body>
</html>
```

Figure 14.25 shows the page with the borders set to "1", so you can see the underlying grid.

Figure 14.25
The table grid for the sliced images is seen here.

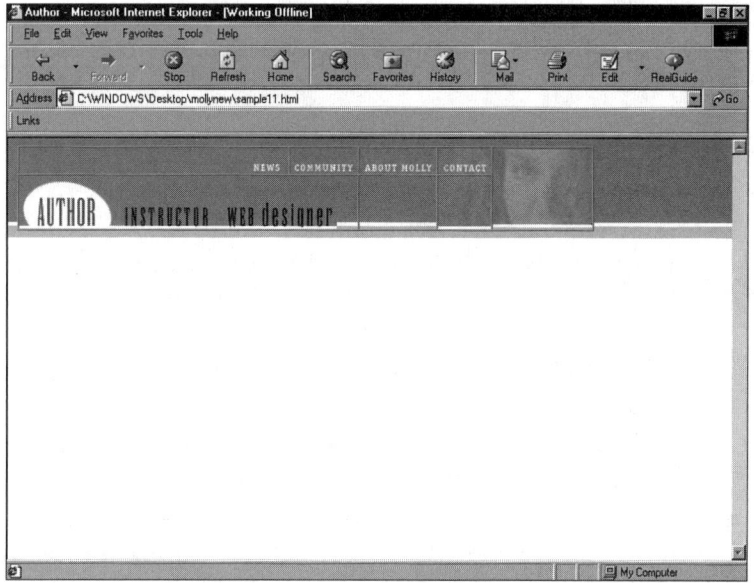

Tip from molly

When tabling sliced images, you often need to make sure that sequential cells are on the same line of code for the cells to line up properly. Use *no* padding or spacing in the table; otherwise, you cannot line up individual graphics.

More and more tools are becoming available to help with this process. Macromedia Fireworks and Adobe LiveMotion are prime examples. Many designers create grid systems in Photoshop and then slice the larger image into separate images.

→ For more information on Fireworks, LiveMotion and other imaging tools, **see** Chapter 27, "Web Graphic Tools and Professional Tools," **p. 561**.

TROUBLESHOOTING

OTHER TABLE TAGS

Aren't there any other table tags?

Yes, there are several other tags. Many of them, such as caption, can be used to assist in making tables more accessible to special needs audiences. Another is the th element, which stands for Table Header. These are similar to cells but automatically place any text into bold. In table-based grid design, you see these additional tags quite infrequently. However, you can use them when you're creating a table for the display of tabular data. The th will then denote the headers, as well as allow for better aural rendering for voice browsers.

→ For a discussion of table tags specific to access issues, **see** Chapter 2, "XHTML Foundations," **p. 23**.

DISAPPEARING TABLES

I've built a table, but it isn't appearing on the page. What's wrong?

This is often the result of a missing tag, usually a closing </td>, </tr>, or </table> tag. Check your syntax!

REDUCING FAT TABLE CODE

How can I keep my tables streamlined so that they load quickly and orderly?

Tables can be notoriously fat—filled with extraneous code that is ultimately unnecessary for the success of that table. Part of this problem emanates from WYSIWYG software, as these applications use tables to lay out every piece of information on a page! Some of this comes from coders who are after precision but might not readily see a more simple approach. Here are some pointers on getting your tables lean and mean:

- Begin with the vertical rather than horizontal arrangement. It's *amazing* how this orientation will change the way your table layouts are designed! Look for how many are absolutely necessary to support the page.

- After you've determined your columns, then *and only then* look at the rows and rigorously work to minimize them. Do you need more than one row? Are you certain? If so, how many do you need to accomplish the layout? Reach for standard XHTML elements instead of table elements where you can. Can you use a break tag or two to get the whitespace instead of adding a row? If so, do it!

- Print out a copy of your layout and draw the table grid onto the page. Try a few times to see if you can reduce extraneous code but maintain the table integrity.

- Reduce the number of tables in the layout, if possible. Is there anyway you can reasonably incorporate the contents of the page into only one table?

Less is almost always more in XHTML and Web development. This concept is especially true when working with tables.

Note   If an attribute, element, or table technique is absolutely necessary to accomplish a table design, leave it in! Some layouts are going to be complex and weigh more than others. However, following these steps will ensure that you get the slimmest possible code no matter the situation.

DESIGNING FOR THE REAL WORLD

DESIGN FIRST, THEN PLAN THE TABLE

One of the problems many Web developers face is how to create innovative designs within the constraints of table grids. This is one of the reasons that style sheet positioning is so idealistic and appealing.

When working to create great designs, do the design work first, and then and only then begin to solve the table necessary to lay out the design.

One way to do this is to first sketch your design ideas out on paper. After you have a sketch, you can move to Photoshop to lay out the design. After you're satisfied with the layout, you can then begin to solve the table problem.

I'll teach you more about this in the next chapter, but I want you to start out by creating a design—first by sketching it, then by laying it out in Photoshop (or the imaging software you typically use for graphic layout). I want you to think outside the box—literally! Don't try to force the design into the context of tables. Just let the design flow naturally from you.

No matter your level of experience, this is a great exercise to help you come up with innovative designs. In fact, I'm going to do the exercise with you. Here's what I did:

1. I first took out my sketch pad, and I made several sketches. I chose the one with which I was most satisfied.
2. Using the sketch as a guide, I opened up my favorite imaging program, Photoshop. You can use whatever imaging program you are most comfortable with.
3. One by one, I laid out the elements of the design carefully, placing the header, background, and navigation on separate layers so I could make adjustments to them at a later time.
4. I saved my file with the layers intact using Photoshop's native format, PSD.

After you have your design mocked up, follow these steps:

1. Print out the mockup. This gives you an opportunity to move away from the screen and think creatively.

2. Draw a table grid directly over your design. Do this several times (see Figure 14.26), trying out different approaches and ideally minimizing the table's complexity (see Figure 14.27).

Figure 14.26
This attempt is logical, but overly complex.

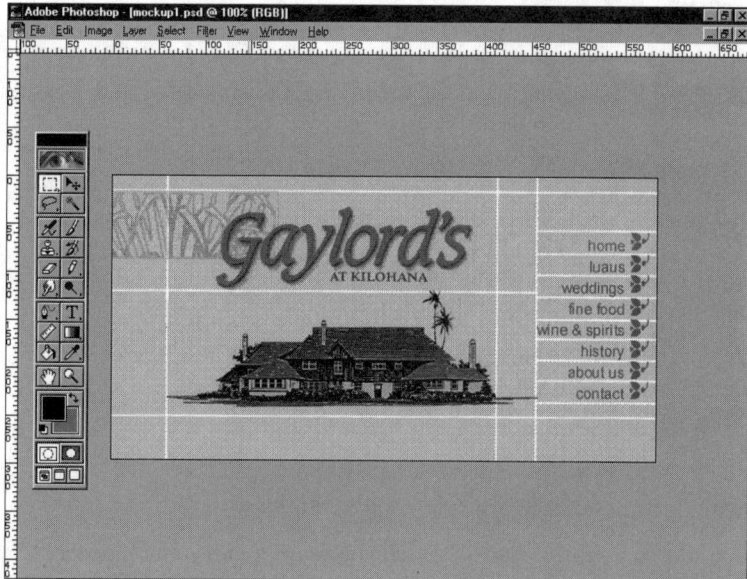

Figure 14.27
A simple, elegant approach to the table design—two columns, two rows. The graphics will be placed on a solid background, and I'll use break tags to gain space where necessary.

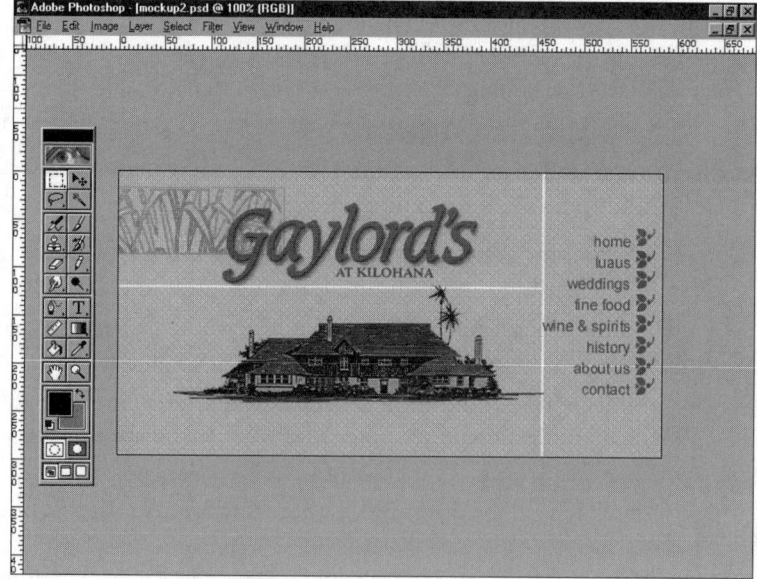

3. Move back to your imaging program and set up guides, measuring each table element carefully.

Note

Depending on the style of graphics and background, you can often keep graphics whole without slicing. This is especially true when your graphics contain very few colors, or you don't require movement via GIF animation in a portion of the design.

Now you can generate the graphics and code the table. Ideally, you've worked this process through rigorously enough so that your table is streamlined—achieving what it needs without being too complicated and weighty.

PART

III

CH

14

CHAPTER **15**

WORKING WITH FRAMES

In this chapter

TO FRAME OR NOT TO FRAME

Frames have been both a source of frustration and empowerment for Web site designers and visitors alike. The frustration comes from a number of concerns. First, frames divide the available browser space, which is preciously restricted to begin with. Frames, particularly in their bordered manifestation, literally take what is a small, contained space and break that space up into smaller, even more contained spaces (see Figure 15.1).

Figure 15.1
Bordered frames break up the screen's visible space.

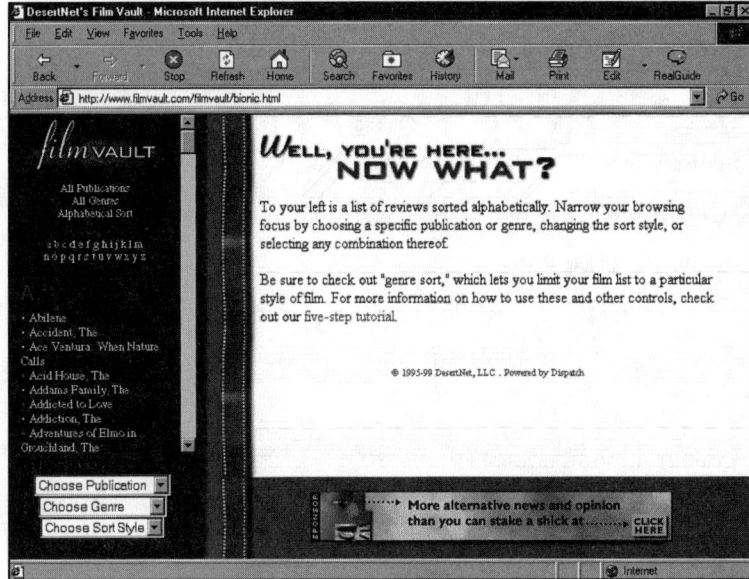

→ For information about available screen space, **see** Chapter 26, "Working with the Computer Screen," **p. 545**.

Using frames requires an understanding of accessibility options for the site to be made useful to blind and disabled site visitors. This makes frames an unfortunate choice for specific audiences unless the author knows what he or she is doing. Frames also make it more difficult to bookmark pages within a site, or to refer to specific pages within a framed structure via a URL. Finally, frames force the designer to write more code, because they require more actual pages of code per visible page.

Because of these difficulties, only the most technologically adept, design-literate of coders can use frames as part of a design well, and even then at the risk of upsetting visitors to the pages they built.

But frames also are empowering from a design perspective. One aspect of this empowerment is that designers can keep sections of a page static whereas other parts of the page can be used to display other pages. Particularly handy for fixed navigation, this is a common approach to the development of menu bars and other, specialty areas that are to remain in place.

Note

Frames were formally adopted as standard in HTML 4.0. Frames carry over into XHTML 1.0 with their own DTD. In XHTML 1.1, frames will become a separate module.

The most juicy bit of news is that frames, particularly of the border*less* variety, give designers another method to create a grid system upon which to base their design (see Figure 15.2).

Figure 15.2
Borderless frames create a design system similar to what is available when using tables, however with other capabilities such as keeping sections of the design static.

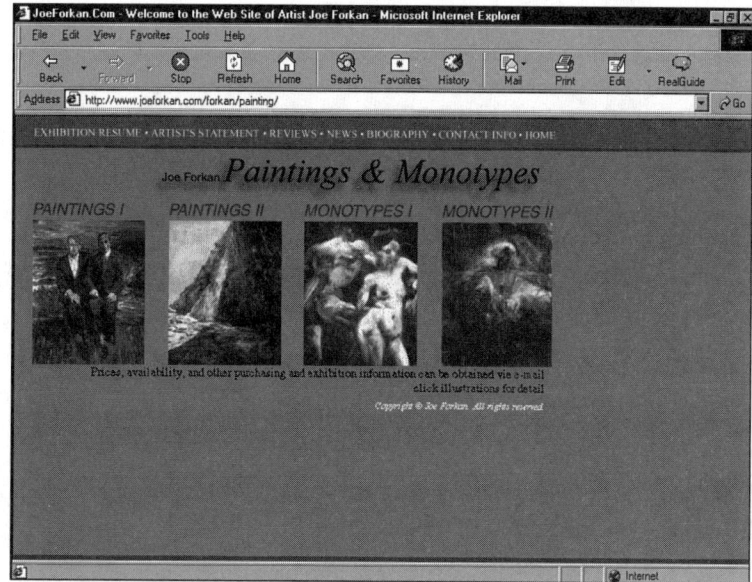

→ To see if tables are a better option for your particular design needs, **see** Chapter 14, "Laying Out Tables Within XHTML Documents," **p. 243**.

This system expands frames from their original role as an organizational tool to include page format and design control. With borderless frames, as with borderless tables, individual sections of a page can be defined and controlled.

But where tables can only be used on a page-by-page basis, frame technology introduces the static concept, discussed previously, and the aspect of *targets* allowing a variety of powerful controls.

Webmasters and site designers can now make better choices about how to employ frames. Whether the choice is to use borders for an attractive interface or to create pages with frames as the silent and strong foundation beneath a complex and multifaceted design, the Web designer is ultimately empowered by having these choices.

No matter how you feel about frames, it's a good idea to know the ropes in terms of coding them. This way, you always have the option to use them if you like or to set them aside if you feel their use is problematic for your audience.

Concerned with issues related to linking to other Web sites from within your frames page? See "Using Frames to Contain Other Sites," in the "Troubleshooting" section near the end of this chapter.

UNDERSTANDING FRAME STRUCTURE

Before I introduce the practical aspects of how to design a framed page, I want to demonstrate a fundamental aspect of frame design. Much like tables, frames are built by thinking in columns and rows. Tables, as described in Chapter 14, "Laying Out Tables Within XHTML Documents," get a bit complex with the ways columns and rows are spanned, creating a technological blur between horizontal and vertical reference points. Frames approach the issue in a much clearer way. A column is always a vertical control, a row a horizontal one.

Moreover, the syntax is clear. Rows are created using the rows attribute, columns use the cols attribute. Both columns and rows can be set to a value by using pixels *or* percentages. For example, cols="240, *" calls for a left column with a *width* of 240 pixels, and the right column, denoted by the asterisk, will be the *dynamic remainder* of the available viewing space.

To add more columns, simply define each one in turn. For example, if I wanted to create four columns of equal percent, the syntax would read cols="25%,25%,25%,25%". The results of this sequence are shown in Figure 15.3.

Figure 15.3
Here the frame columns have been designed in equal sizes using percentages, and the borders are turned on.

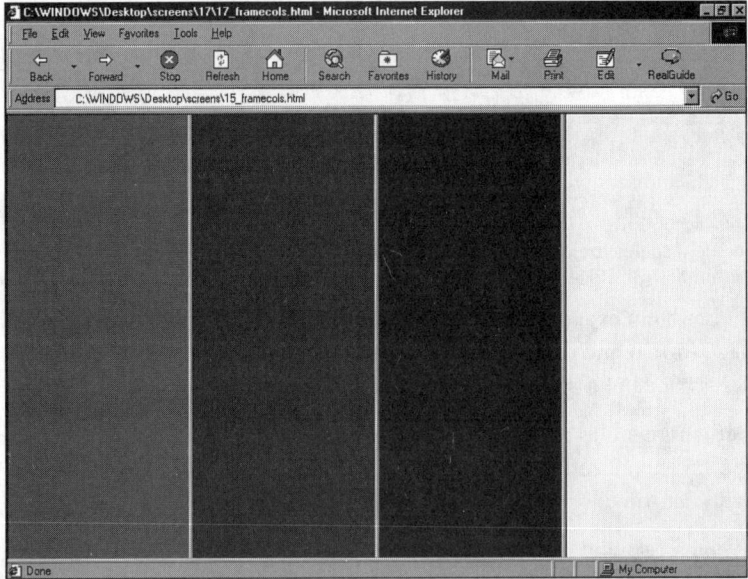

Similarly, if I wanted to create rows rather than columns, I would simply change the syntax to rows="240, *", and the results would be a top row with a *height* of 240 pixels. To create four individual rows of equal percent, I would call for rows="25%,25%,25%,25%", as demonstrated in Figure 15.4.

Figure 15.4
Four individual rows
of 25% each.

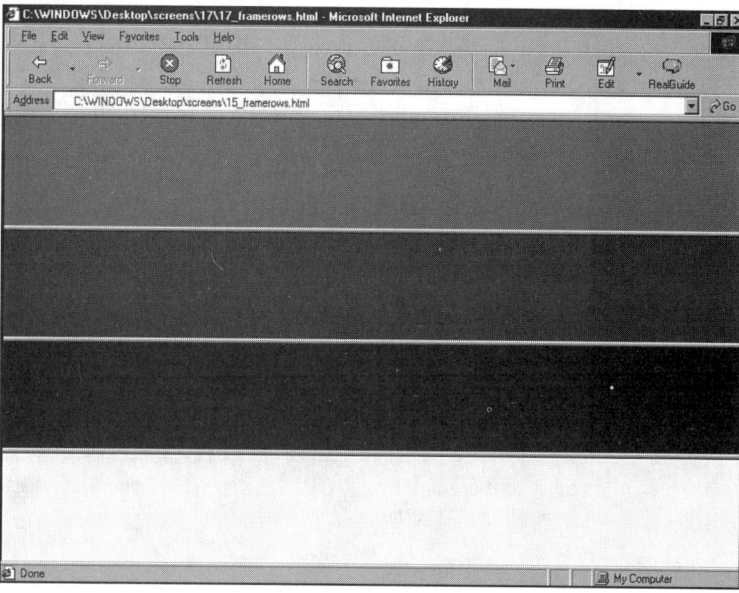

To create combinations of columns and rows, the values are simply stacked into the appropriate tags and pages of the framed site.

THE FRAMESET

As with tables, there are only three components absolutely necessary to build a framed page. Yes, frames can get a bit complicated, depending on the ways you want to employ them, but at the most basic level, all framed sites begin with the factors introduced here.

Any framed page requires a controlling XHTML document that gives the instructions on how the framed page is to be set up. This control is called the *frameset*. Then, an XHTML page is required for each individual frame.

Tip from
molly
Remember your sums! A framed page requires one XHTML page per each individually defined area *plus* one XHTML page for the control, or *frameset*, page.

The frameset page is the control page of your framed site. In it, you'll argue primarily for the rows or columns you want to create and the HTML pages that will fill those rows or columns. This is done using two major tags:

- `<frameset>`—This tag defines the frame, and its basic arguments define rows and columns. The frameset information is closed with a corresponding `</frameset>` tag.

- **`<frame>`**—The `frame` tag arranges individual frames within the frameset. This includes the location of the XHTML document required to fill the frame, using the `src="x"` (where x assigns the relative or absolute URL to the location of the XHTML page). A variety of other `<frame>` tag attributes will be covered later in the chapter.

It's important to remember that the `<frameset>` tag is a conceptual replacement for the `<body>` tag in the frameset HTML page. Therefore, in a simple frameset (as in one without `noframes` in place), *no body tags* should appear.

> **Note**
>
> XHTML 1.0 requires you to identify the frameset document by including the version information. This means you'll need to insert
>
> ```
> <!DOCTYPE html PUBLIC "-//W3C//DTD XHTML 1.0 Frameset//EN"
> "http://www.w3.org/TR/xhtml1/DTD/xhtml1-frameset.dtd">
> ```
>
> into an XHTML 1.0 frameset. You'll find that individual pages within the framed site can use either strict or transitional XHTML 1.0, depending upon your needs. Be sure to refer to the appropriate DTD accordingly.

BUILDING A FRAMED PAGE

In this case, we're going to build a two-column page, with the left column serving as a simple menu that could eventually be used to guide a visitor through the site.

First, you'll create the page for the left, or menu, column:

1. In your editor, type the following:
   ```
   <!DOCTYPE html PUBLIC "-//W3C//DTD XHTML 1.0 Strict//EN"
       "http://www.w3.org/TR/xhtml1/DTD/strict.dtd">
   <html xmlns="http://www.w3.org/1999/xhtml">
   <head>
   <title>Menu</title>
   </head>
   <body>

   <p><a href="about.html">About the Company</a></p>

   <p><a href="clients.html">Company Clients</a></p>

   <p><a href="contact.html">Contact Company</a></p>

   </body>
   </html>
   ```

2. Save the file as `menu.html`.

3. View the file in your browser to see how it looks before you apply the frameset to it.

4. Now create the main page of XHTML:
   ```
   <!DOCTYPE html PUBLIC "-//W3C//DTD XHTML 1.0 Strict//EN"
       "http://www.w3.org/TR/xhtml1/DTD/strict.dtd">
   <html xmlns="http://www.w3.org/1999/xhtml">
   ```

```
<head>
<title>Main Page</title>
</head>
<body>
<p>Welcome to The Company! We specialize in a variety of high
quality services. Our clients encompass just about everyone who
is anyone.</p>
</body>
</html>
```

5. Save the file as main.html.

6. View the file in your Web browser to see what it looks like before adding the frameset command file.

Now you'll create the frameset.

1. Open your XHTML editor and begin a new page. Type the following container:

```
<!DOCTYPE html PUBLIC "-//W3C//DTD XHTML 1.0 Frameset//EN"
"http://www.w3.org/TR/xhtml1/DTD/xhtml1-frameset.dtd">
<html xmlns="http://www.w3.org/1999/xhtml">
<head>
<title>Frame Control</title>
</head>
<frameset>
</frameset>
</html>
```

2. Now you'll want to add the columns or rows. In this instance, I'm using columns:

```
<!DOCTYPE html PUBLIC "-//W3C//DTD XHTML 1.0 Frameset//EN"
"http://www.w3.org/TR/xhtml1/DTD/xhtml1-frameset.dtd">
<html xmlns="http://www.w3.org/1999/xhtml">
<html xmlns="http://www.w3.org/1999/xhtml">
<head>
<title>Frame Control</title>
</head>
<frameset cols="240, *">
</frameset>
</html>
```

3. The individual frames with their corresponding XHTML pages are added by using the frame tag:

```
<!DOCTYPE html PUBLIC "-//W3C//DTD XHTML 1.0 Transitional//EN"
    "http://www.w3.org/TR/xhtml1/DTD/transitional.dtd">
<html xmlns="http://www.w3.org/1999/xhtml">
<head>
<title>Frame Control</title>
</head>
<frameset cols="240, *">
<frame src="menu.html" />
<frame src="main.html" />
</frameset>
</html>
```

4. Save the document as index.html.

5. Load the frameset page into your browser and view the results. Does it match Figure 15.5? If it does, congratulations!

Figure 15.5
This figure displays a simple, framed page.

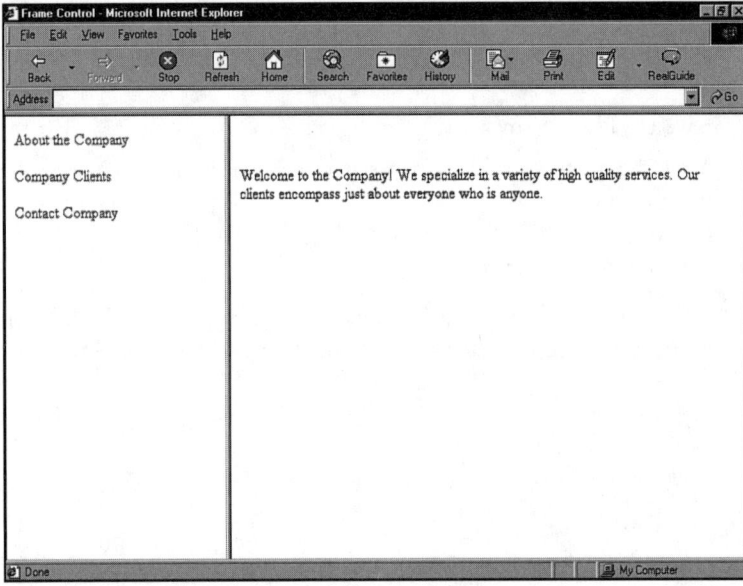

Note

You might have noticed that the `<frame>` tag is an exception to the open/close rule, as there is no counterpart `</frame>` tag. All the information for individual frames is placed within the tag and it is considered closed when the XML convention of angle/right-angle bracket "/>" is reached.

Tip from

Pages not matching the examples? Look over your syntax carefully. It's amazing how tiny mistakes can create total XHTML havoc.

SETTING frameset AND frame TAG ATTRIBUTES

There are several powerful attributes available to the `<frameset>` and `<frame>` tags.

The following list covers those used for the `<frameset>`.

- `cols="x"`—As covered earlier, this attribute creates columns. An `"x"` value is given for each column in the framed page, and will be either a pixel value, a percentage value, or a combination of one of those plus the `"*"`, which creates a *dynamic* or *relative size* frame—the remainder of the framed space.

- `rows="x"`—This attribute is used to create rows in the same fashion that the column attribute is used.
- `border="x"`—The `border` attribute is used by Netscape Navigator 3.0, 4.0, and later to control border width. Value is set in pixel width.
- `frameborder="x"`—frameborder is used by the Internet Explorer browser to control border width in pixels. Netscape Navigator 3.0, 4.0, and later uses the attribute with a yes or no value.
- `framespacing="x"`—Used originally by Internet Explorer, this attribute controls border width.

Use the following tag attributes with the `<frame>` tag:

- `frameborder="x"`—Use this attribute to control frameborders around individual frames. Netscape Navigator requires a yes or no value, whereas Internet Explorer will look for a numeric pixel width value.
- `marginheight="x"`—Argue a value in pixels to control the height of the frame's margin.
- `marginwidth="x"`—This attribute argues for a frame's margin width in pixels.
- `name="x"`—This critical attribute allows the designer to name an individual frame. Naming frames permits *targeting* by links within other XHTML pages. Names must begin with a character or numeral.
- `noresize`—Simply place this attribute in your string if you don't want to allow re-sizing of a frame. This fixes the frame into the position and disallows a visitor to alter the size of a frame. You'll note that this is an interesting attribute in that it takes is own name as a value: `noresize="noresize"`.
- `scrolling="x"`—By arguing `"yes"`, `"no"`, or `"auto"`, you can control the appearance of a scrollbar. A `"yes"` value automatically places a scrollbar in the frame, a `"no"` value ensures that no scrollbar ever appears. The `"auto"` argument turns the power over to the browser, which will automatically place a scrollbar in a frame should it be required.
- `src="x"`—The `"x"` value is replaced with the relative or absolute URL of the XHTML page you want to place within the frame at hand.
- `title="x"`—To add a human-readable description of the frame's function, use the title attribute with a descriptive value, such as `title="navigation frame"`. This is a particularly useful means of ensuring accessibility for those with disabilities.

So many choices—ultimately lending to a lot of control with frame-based design.

EXPLORING A FRAME WITH MARGIN, RESIZE, AND SCROLL CONTROLS

Listing 15.1 shows the code for a framed page with `marginheight`, `marginwidth`, `noresize`, and `scrolling` attributes.

LISTING 15.1   FRAMESET WITH marginheight, width, resize, AND scrolling ATTRIBUTES

```
<!DOCTYPE html PUBLIC "-//W3C//DTD XHTML 1.0 Frameset//EN"
"http://www.w3.org/TR/xhtml1/DTD/xhtml1-frameset.dtd">
<html xmlns="http://www.w3.org/1999/xhtml">
<head>
<title>Frame With Numerous Controls</title>
</head>
<frameset cols="240, *">
<frame src="menu.html" marginheight="5" marginwidth="5" noresize=
"noresize" scrolling="auto" />

<frame src="main.html" marginheight="15" marginwidth="15"
noresize="noresize" scrolling="auto" />
</frameset>
</html>
```

The first issue to be aware of is that this is a frameset, and therefore no body tag is used. Instead, the frameset tag and its companion closing tag are placed around the internal information.

Within the frameset tag, I've coded for a left frame of 240 pixels, and I've used the "*" value to allow for the right frame to be dynamic.

Following this information are the two strings of syntax for each of the corresponding frames. The left frame information is placed first, and then the right frame information is coded underneath.

In the first frame instance, I've named the source, and I've added margin information of height and width at 5 pixels each. This gives me a bit of whitespace around any of the information appearing within that frame. I've chosen the noresize option, and set scrolling to auto so that at lower resolutions individuals will see a scrollbar should it become necessary.

I'm of the opinion that a "yes" value for scrolling rarely looks good, but is extremely useful when the frame in question contains a long document. A "no" value is most valuable for fixed-column frames used for menus.

If you do your math and are absolutely certain that you have allowed for enough viewing area to contain the HTML information, use the "no" value. Setting scrolling on "auto" is usually the favorable choice, because it allows the browser to make the decision. An "auto" value is especially favorable wherever you've argued for *dynamic* or *relative size* (a "*" value) rows and columns.

Resizing is similar in concept. Although offering it can foul up your attractive, well-thought-out framed pages, resizing can be valuable when you want to give your visitor ultimate control. In this case, I've decided to not allow my visitor that control.

The second frame is coded exactly the same way, with the one distinction of more whitespace allotted to the area via the margin controls.

TARGETING WINDOWS

To effectively use frames, a designer must decide where link options will load. For example, in the frame page you've developed so far in this chapter, I've guided you to create a menu on the left, and a larger frame field on the right. This is a natural start for effective design using frames.

There are two basic ways to link, or *target*, HTML pages to specific windows:

- Combine `target` and `name` attributes to specifically target windows.
- Use a magic target name.

`target` and `name` attributes allow you to add more HTML pages to your framed site and to target a specific window by naming that window and targeting the link.

> **Note**
>
> A *magic target* name is a special name reserved by browsers to perform a distinct function.

CREATING A FRAME USING `target` AND `name` ATTRIBUTES

Naming the target is the best place to start. Using the same frameset code in Listing 15.1 shown previously, I've added a name to the right, or "main," frame:

```
<!DOCTYPE html PUBLIC "-//W3C//DTD XHTML 1.0 Frameset//EN"
"http://www.w3.org/TR/xhtml1/DTD/xhtml1-frameset.dtd">
<html xmlns="http://www.w3.org/1999/xhtml">
<head>
<title>Frames with Targets and Names</title>
</head>
<frameset cols="240, *">
<frame src="menu.html" marginheight="5" marginwidth="5" noresize=
"noresize" scrolling="auto" />
<frame src="main.html" name="right" marginheight="15"
marginwidth="15" noresize="noresize" scrolling="auto" />
</frameset>
</html>
```

After the target window has a name, the target must be added to the link. In the menu file, I'm going to specify the target, as follows:

```
<!DOCTYPE html PUBLIC "-//W3C//DTD XHTML 1.0 Strict//EN"
    "http://www.w3.org/TR/xhtml1/DTD/strict.dtd">
<html xmlns="http://www.w3.org/1999/xhtml">
<head>
<title>Menu</title>
</head>
<body>
<a href="about.html" target="right">About the Company</a>

<p> <a href="clients.html" target="right">Company Clients</a></p>

<p> <a href="contact.html" target="right">Contact Company</a></p>
```

```
<p></p>
</body>
</html>
```

As long as I've created each of the pages referred to in the links, each click of the link on this menu will load the appropriate page into the right frame (see Figure 15.6).

Figure 15.6
Targeting the right frame causes the pages referred to in the links to appear in that frame.

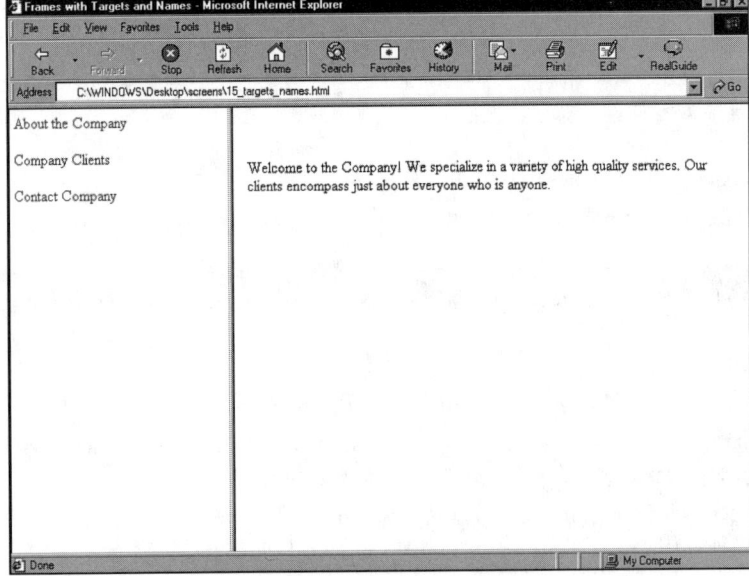

Tip from molly

Want all of a site's pages to load into the same window? Follow the name and target convention. Within each document you want to load into that window, use the <base> tag. To load all pages within the framed site you are building would be to place this syntax within the <head> of *every* page to be loaded in that window: <base target="right">.

Caution

When using the <base> tag, remember that you are creating a default. This means that if you have any other targets, they will override the default.

MAGIC TARGET NAMES

There are several predefined target names that will cause certain actions to occur when a target link is created.

- **target="_blank"**—The "_blank" argument causes the targeted document to open in a completely new browser window.

- `target="_self"`—The targeted document will load in the same window where the originating link exists.

- `target="_parent"`—This will load the targeted document into the link's parent frameset.

- `target="_top"`—Use this attribute to load the link into the full window, over-riding any existing frames.

You'll notice that magic target names always begin with an underscore to avoid problems.

The following are issues to bear in mind when using magic target names:

- You should avoid naming standard targets with anything other than an accepted alphanumeric character. An underscore, or any other symbol, will be ignored.

- The magic target name "_blank" always forces a new browser window to open. Be careful to use this only when a new window is absolutely necessary, otherwise you run the risk of angering Web site visitors, who, depending upon their settings, might end up with numerous, resource-draining browser windows on the desktop.

- The `target="_top"` attribute and value is usually the right choice when a link takes the visitor out of your framed site into a new site. Some coders like the idea of keeping external sites inside their own site by targeting the remote site into a local frame, allowing the native site's menu or advertisement to remain live while surfing elsewhere. This is not only considered an annoyance, but might get you into legal trouble. Avoid this at all costs unless you have express permission from the site you are incorporating within your own. See the "Troubleshooting" section for more information on this topic.

You can now put your magic to use and try out a magic target name exercise:

1. Begin by opening your editor. You'll need to create two more pages to target. Copy the following:

```
<!DOCTYPE html PUBLIC "-//W3C//DTD XHTML 1.0 Strict//EN"
    "http://www.w3.org/TR/xhtml1/DTD/strict.dtd">
<html xmlns="http://www.w3.org/1999/xhtml">
<head>
<title>Magic Targets: About</title>
</head>
<body>
<h2>About the Company</h2>

<p>This page has information about the company.</p>
</body>
</html>
```

2. Save the file as `about.html`.

3. Open another blank editing page and enter the following:

```
<!DOCTYPE html PUBLIC "-//W3C//DTD XHTML 1.0 Strict//EN"
    "http://www.w3.org/TR/xhtml1/DTD/strict.dtd">
<html xmlns="http://www.w3.org/1999/xhtml">
<head>
```

```
<title>Magic Targets: Clients</title>
</head>
<body>
<h2>Clients</h2>

<p>This page has information about the clients.</p>
</body>
</html>
```

4. Save this file as `clients.html`.

5. Now create another:

```
<!DOCTYPE html PUBLIC "-//W3C//DTD XHTML 1.0 Strict//EN"
    "http://www.w3.org/TR/xhtml1/DTD/strict.dtd">
<html xmlns="http://www.w3.org/1999/xhtml">
<head>
<title>Magic Targets: Contact</title>
</head>
<body>
<h2>Contact</h2>

<p>This page will be set up with a contact form.</p>
</body>
</html>
```

6. Save this page as `contact.html`.

7. Open the `menu.htm` file you made earlier. This is the file where the *links* to the pages that will be targeted appear. You should see the following:

```
<!DOCTYPE html PUBLIC "-//W3C//DTD XHTML 1.0 Strict//EN"
    "http://www.w3.org/TR/xhtml1/DTD/strict.dtd">
<html xmlns="http://www.w3.org/1999/xhtml">
<head>
<title>Menu</title>
</head>
<body>
<p><a href="about.html">About the Company</a></p>

<p><a href="clients.html">Company Clients</a></p>

<p><a href="contact.html">Contact Company</a></p>
</body>
</html>
```

8. You're going to add the syntax first for the "about" page, which we'll make target over the menu frame. The syntax is as follows:

```
<A href="about.html" target="_self">About the Company</A>
```

Save the file, open the frameset page, and in the menu frame you will notice that About is now hot. Click that link and watch how `about.html` loads into the menu frame.

9. Return to your HTML editor and add the following syntax to the clients reference:

```
<A href="clients.html" target="_blank">Company Clients</A>
```

10. Save the file, and open the frameset page in your browser. Clients is now hot. When you click this choice, you'll note how `clients.html` is loaded into an entirely *new* browser window (see Figure 15.7).

11. Finally, add a link to the contact page itself:

```
<!DOCTYPE html PUBLIC "-//W3C//DTD XHTML 1.0 Strict//EN"
    "http://www.w3.org/TR/xhtml1/DTD/strict.dtd">
<html xmlns="http://www.w3.org/1999/xhtml">
<head>
<title>Magic Targets: Contact</title>
</head>
<body>
<h2>Contact</h2>

<p>This page will be set up with a contact form.</p>

<p><a href="menu.html" target="_top">Reload the Menu Only</a></p>
</body>
</html>
```

12. Click the link, which loads the menu page over the contact form.

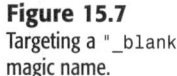

Figure 15.7
Targeting a "_blank"
magic name.

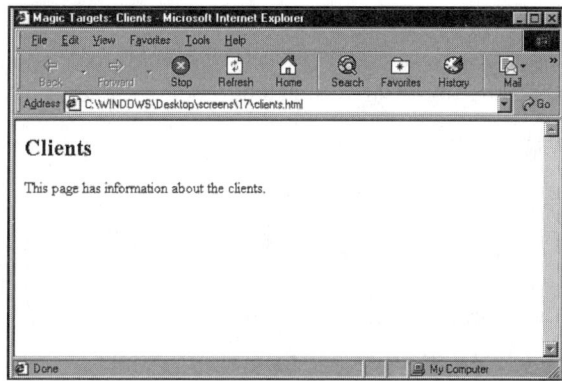

You've now tackled some of the most difficult aspects of coding for frames. I encourage you to try a few variations using targets and attributes of your own selection. You'll learn a lot from experimentation, and have fun in the process.

WORKING WITH BORDERLESS FRAMES

Choosing to use borderless frames is a critical issue because using, or not using, borders, is the point where the designer makes decisions about how to use frame technology as a format tool. Removing borders makes formatting a page seamless, and this is a powerful as well as a currently popular method of designing pages.

The first rule in cross-browser design is to know which browsers you are attempting to reach. With borderless frames, that rule is clarified by the fact that only certain browsers, and certain browser versions, interpret borderless frames in the correct manner.

The first thing to remember is that borderless frames are not supported in the Netscape and Microsoft browsers earlier than the 3.0 version.

The challenge of borderless frames doesn't lie in the coding per se, but in the differences in the way popular browsers interpret the code, or require the code to read.

Fortunately, there's a workaround: You can stack attributes within tags, and if a browser doesn't support that attribute or its value, it will ignore it and move on to the attribute and related value that it does interpret.

In HTML 4.0 and XHTML 1.0, coding borderless frames are easy. You simply add the attribute and value `frameborder="0"` within the `<frame>` tag.

However, browsers without strict HTML 4.0 support, which includes most popular browsers before their 4.0 and later versions, require a little jostling to get the borderless effect.

The Netscape browser (3.0+) allows for borderless frames when

- The `border` attribute is set, in pixels, to a numeric value of `"0"`.
- The `framespacing` attribute is assigned a `"no"` value.

Microsoft's Internet Explorer, browser version 3.0, produces borderless frames if

- The `frameborder` attribute is set, in pixels, to a numeric value of `"0"`.
- The `framespacing` attribute is assigned a width, in pixels, to a numeric value of `"0"`.

If it seems like there's a conflict, well, there really isn't, because each browser either requires a different attribute to control width, or a different value to control spacing. It looks confusing, but if you stack attributes, you can easily create borderless frames that will be read by both browsers without difficulty.

This technique results in two legal syntax options:

```
<frameset frameborder="0" framespacing="0" border="0">
```

or

```
<frameset frameborder="no" framespacing="0" border="0">
```

Either one is correct, and it's just a matter of personal preference as to which you'll use. Remember to add your columns and rows to the string to create a full range of frameset arguments.

Because you already have a fully operational framed page, you can simply add the appropriate syntax to the frameset string to achieve a borderless effect (see Listing 15.2).

LISTING 15.2 CODING BORDERLESS FRAMES

```
<!DOCTYPE html PUBLIC "-//W3C//DTD XHTML 1.0 Frameset//EN"
"http://www.w3.org/TR/xhtml1/DTD/xhtml1-frameset.dtd">
<html xmlns="http://www.w3.org/1999/xhtml">
<head>
<title>Borderless Frames</title>
</head>
<frameset frameborder="0" framespacing="0" border="0" cols="240,
```

LISTING 15.2   CONTINUED

```
*">
<frame src="menu.html" marginheight="5" marginwidth="5" noresize=
"noresize" scrolling="auto" />
<frame src="main.html" marginheight="15" marginwidth="15"
noresize="noresize" scrolling="auto" />
</frameset>
</html>
```

View the results in both Netscape Navigator 3.0 or later or Internet Explorer 3.0 or later. Your results should match Figure 15.8.

Figure 15.8
A borderless frame gives a cleaner and more professional look to your pages.

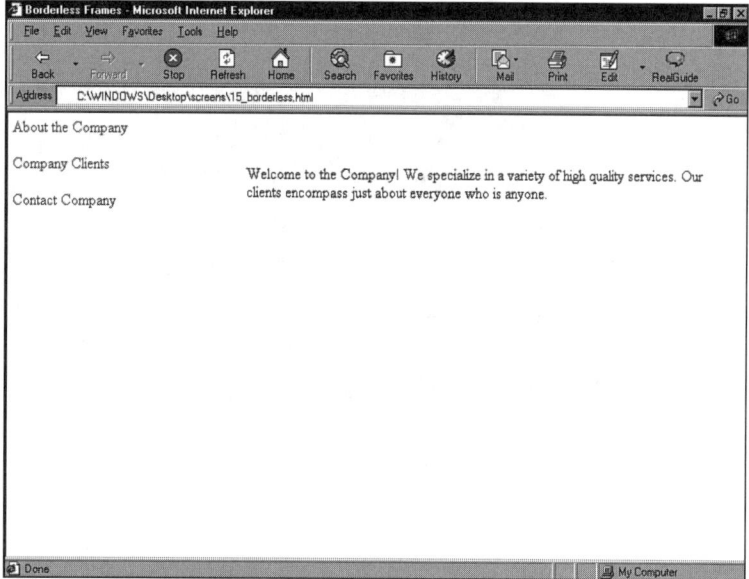

ADVANCED FRAME CONCEPTS

Frames are problematic; there's no denying that. For one thing, they require extra work from you, the designer. For each framed page, you have to code, design, and manage more than one page.

Next, frames upset people. As discussed earlier in the chapter, part of the reason is that frames break up space. So, unless you're using borderless frames, the visual clutter they add to a page is detrimental.

Another headache is that they are more difficult to search for, prepare for searches, and print out.

So how do you design a sophisticated, advanced frame-based page? The absolutely, positively, most imperative place to begin is to determine whether your site really needs frames at all. If you can create the same layout with basic HTML or tables, then do it that way.

There's only one really, really good reason to use frames in a page's design, and that is to create an interface that has both static and active parts (see Figure 15.9). In other words, say you want your company logo to dominate the user experience, and you have a standard navigation bar that you want to always be present. Put them in frames. This approach makes sense because the user's experience becomes enhanced rather than problematic.

Figure 15.9
An elegant site that uses frames with static navigation (top) and active parts (center).

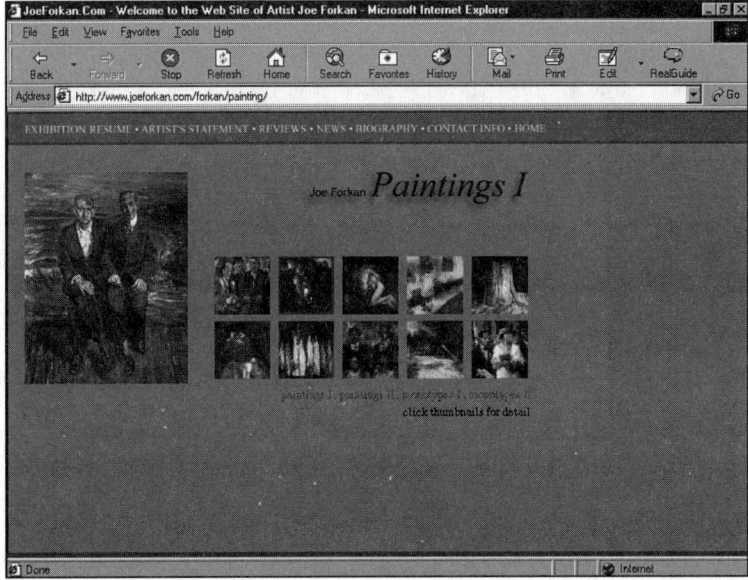

I also recommend that you use borderless frames. They reinforce the fact that you're using the frames not to constrain design, but to create perpetual information.

You also can use frames for design, such as when creating bleeding or blurred edges. These techniques can't be achieved without frames unless you use background graphics, which limit your options. However, you should never use more frames than absolutely necessary to achieve your goal—especially in the primary body section of your layout. Can you create a page with seven columns and five rows? Absolutely! Unless you can tell me why that's important other than as an exercise to understand how to create such a page, I don't think you should do it.

Finally, the use of tables within the framed pages—especially the content pages—can give you maximum design power when you're laying out complex sites.

Listing 15.3 shows the frameset for the frame design in Figure 15.9. The top frame handles the navigation, and the central frame handles content. A bottom frame handles a bleed along the bottom. Note that the `<noframes>` tag is also employed.

LISTING 15.3   SOPHISTICATED FRAMESET DESIGN

```
<!DOCTYPE html PUBLIC "-//W3C//DTD XHTML 1.0 Frameset//EN"
"http://www.w3.org/TR/xhtml1/DTD/xhtml1-frameset.dtd">
<html xmlns="http://www.w3.org/1999/xhtml">
<!— frames —>
<head>
<title>Frameset Design</title>
</head>
<frameset rows="30,3,*,5" frameborder="no" border="0"
framespacing="0">
<frame name="topnav" src="top_nav.html" marginwidth="0"
marginheight="0" scrolling="no" frameborder="0" noresize=
"noresize" />
<frame name="topline" src="topline.html" marginwidth="0"
marginheight="0" scrolling="no" frameborder="0" noresize=
"noresize" />
<frame name="main" src="main.html" marginwidth="0" marginheight=
"0" scrolling="auto" frameborder="0" noresize="noresize" />
<frame name="bottom" src="bottom.html" marginwidth="0"
marginheight="0" scrolling="no" frameborder="0" noresize=
"noresize" />
<noframes>
<body>
<p>Welcome to the online portfolio of the illustration,
cartooning, and painting of Joe Forkan. This site is
predominantly visual and requires frames.</p>

<p>Visitors without graphic or frames support can email Joe
Forkan for more information at <a href=
"mailto:joe@joeforkan.com">joe@joeforkan.com</a></p>

<p>Thank you for visiting!</p>
</body>
</noframes>
</frameset>
</html>
```

Frames, as with tables, can be fixed (see Figure 15.10), or allowed to stretch dynamically to fit a specific resolution or screen size. Similarly, you can combine the techniques to achieve a combination of fixed and dynamic frame design.

To make frames dynamic, use percentages rather than numeric values when you're creating your rows or columns:

```
<frameset rows="50%,25%,25%">
<frame src="red.html" noresize="noresize" scrolling="no" />
<frame src="black.html" noresize="noresize" scrolling="no" />
<frame src="yellow.html" noresize="noresize" scrolling="no" />
</frameset>
```

Note that I've split the browser area into three sections (see Figure 15.11). You can split the area into as many sections as you like, actually; however, the concern is to always add up to 100%. This way, when you resize the browser (see Figure 15.12), the frames will dynamically adjust.

Figure 15.10
Remember that fixing frame widths becomes more important as you add more than two frame columns or rows. Fixing the frames helps secure each frame in place.

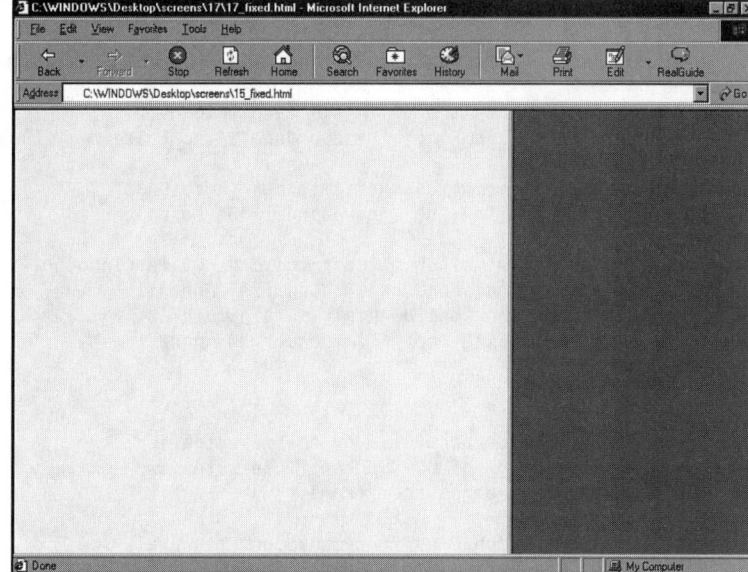

To make a portion of a frame fixed and another dynamic, you use the * (asterisk symbol) in place of a numeric value or percentage. This symbol simply means that the browser should evaluate what space is available and flex to accommodate that space:

```
<frameset rows="*,150, 150">
<frame src="red.html" noresize="noresize" scrolling="no" />
<frame src="black.html" noresize="noresize" scrolling="no" />
<frame src="yellow.html" noresize="noresize" scrolling="no" />

</frameset>
```

Figure 15.11
Dynamic frames adjust to the available screen space of the browser, making the design more compatible across a variety of environments.

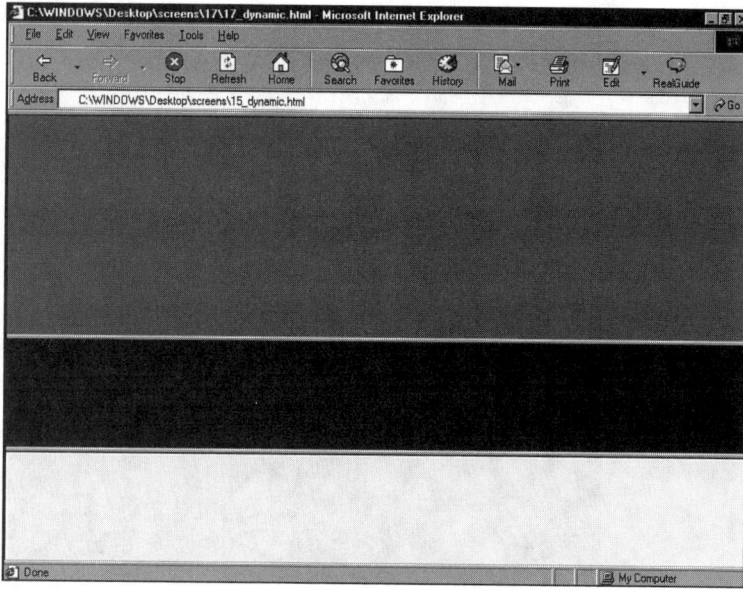

Figure 15.12
Dynamic frames adjusted to the browser or resolution size.

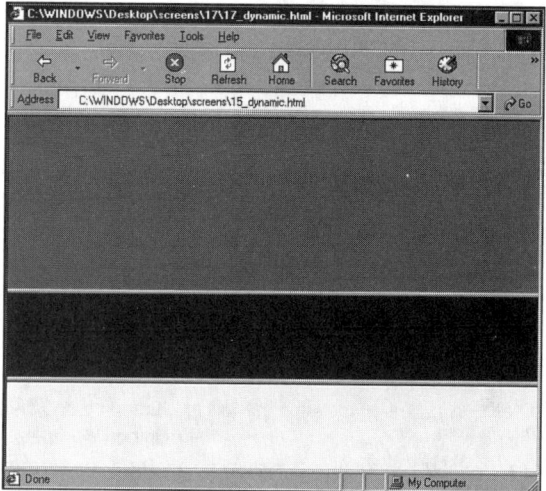

Figure 15.13 shows the results full-frame. In 15.14, I've once again collapsed the browser. Note that the top row stays fixed at 250 pixels, but the bottom row is dynamic.

Figure 15.13
Combination of fixed and dynamic frames. The top row is fixed at 150, and the bottom is dynamic.

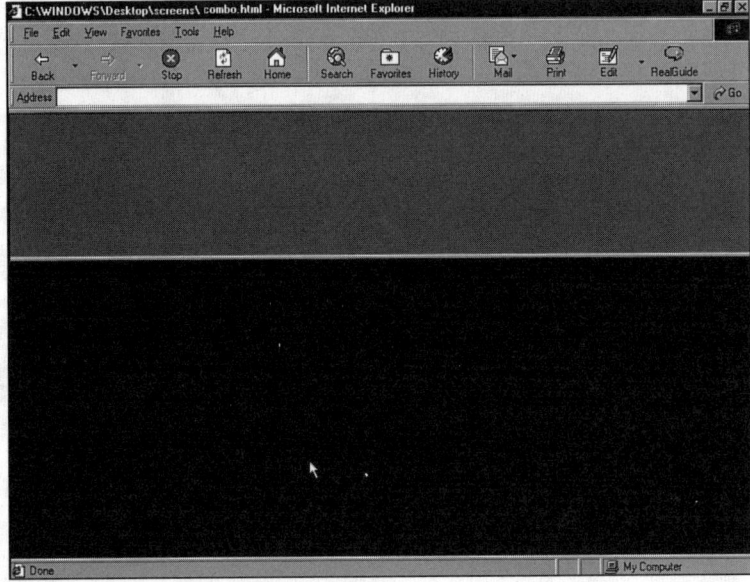

Figure 15.14
After I resized the browser, the dynamic portion collapsed but the top, fixed row remained intact.

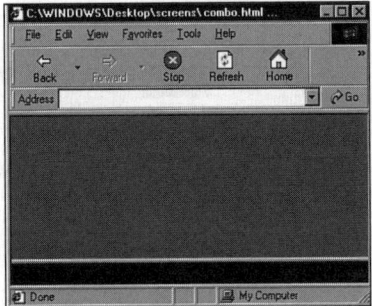

Tip from
molly

> Frame design is most elegant when borders are turned off and the use of graphics and layout within the framed pages is maximized. More important, however, frame design should never be frivolous. You should always use frames for a good reason, such as when you want static navigation, banner, or branding areas, or you are using borderless frames for fixed layout.

COMBINING ROWS AND COLUMNS

There are instances in frame-based layouts where you'll want to reserve two or more static sections with some in rows and some in columns. A good example of this is when you'd like your navigation to appear in one static portion of the page, and headers, footers, or ads in another static portion. Perhaps your navigation runs along the left, and your ad runs along the top, with your content in the right bottom section.

To accomplish this, a combination of rows and columns are used in a frameset nest. Listing 15.4 shows how this is done.

LISTING 15.4   COMBINING ROWS AND COLUMNS

```
<!DOCTYPE html PUBLIC "-//W3C//DTD XHTML 1.0 Frameset//EN"
"http://www.w3.org/TR/xhtml1/DTD/xhtml1-frameset.dtd">
<html xmlns="http://www.w3.org/1999/xhtml">
<framset rows="100, *">
<frame src="top.html">
   <frameset cols="200, *">
   <frame src="nav.html">
   <frame src="main.html">
   </frameset>
</frameset>
```

Figure 15.15 shows the results.

Figure 15.15
Nesting framesets for combination rows and columns.

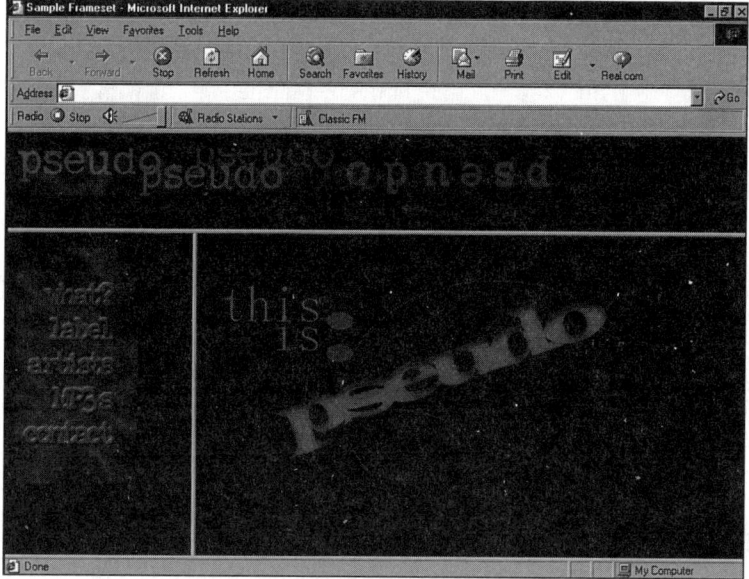

> **Caution**
>
> Be absolutely sure you close each nest with the closing `</frameset>` element or your browser may not render the nested frames properly.

WORKING WITH INLINE FRAMES (I-FRAMES)

Originally introduced by Internet Explorer 3.0, I-Frames—*inline*, or *floating* frames—were officially adopted in HTML 4.0. This is good news because they're very effective when put to appropriate use. The bad news, however, is that they aren't supported by Netscape 4.61 and other browsers. Because Netscape 6.0 promises to be compliant with standards, they should be supported there. However, early tests with the pre-release version showed no such support.

I-Frames work a bit differently from standard frames. First, you don't create a separate frameset for the frame. You place the I-Frame information directly inline in any standard HTML or XHTML page.

Here's a snippet of I-Frame syntax:

```
<iframe width="350" height="200" src="text.html">

</iframe>
```

This syntax looks a bit like an `image` or `object` tag in action, and in fact, it works in a similar way, too, with the width and height defined in the tags. As with standard frames, you can add scrolling and border attributes:

```
<iframe width="350" height="200" src="text.html" scrolling="no"
frameborder="0">

</iframe>
```

You can align and space inline frames just as you would an image:

```
<iframe width="350" height="200" src="text.html" scrolling="no"
frameborder="0" align="right" hspace="10" vspace="10">

</iframe>
```

> **Note**
>
> Inline frames support the `name` attribute, as well as magic target names.

Figure 15.16 shows a page using an I-Frame.

Figure 15.16
Inline frames can be placed anywhere on a page. Unlike standard frames, they do not require a frameset, but as with standard frames, I-Frames do require an additional HTML page to work.

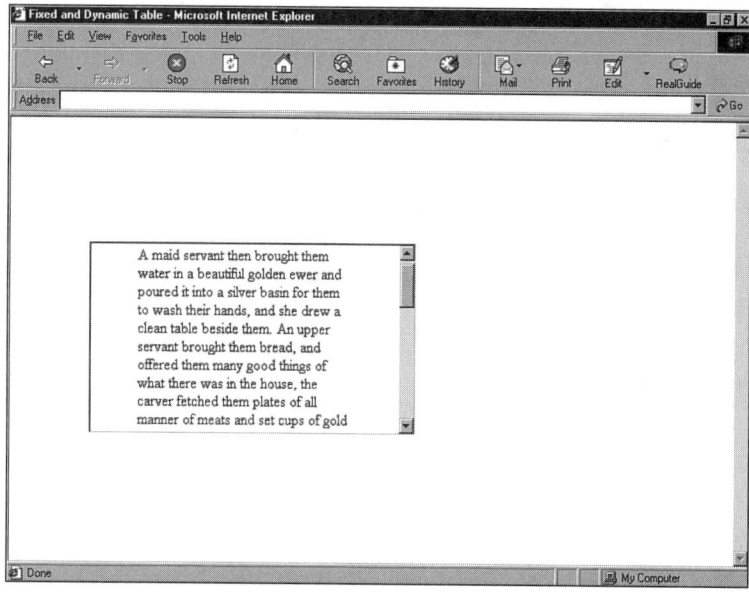

THE noframes TAG AND ACCESSIBILITY

One of the most important considerations when designing with frames is, as mentioned earlier, ensuring that individuals who cannot use frames, such as the blind or mobility impaired, can still have access to important information on a Web site.

The Internet, with its vast wealth of information and communications opportunities, has been empowering for a wide variety of individuals with different needs and circumstances world-over.

Sadly, the graphically rich environment of the Web is at best cumbersome and at worst inaccessible to people who use screen readers, special access tools, or who are accessing sites at slower speeds than those to which we are accustomed.

Note

It's important to point out that tables also are problematic in terms of accessibility, but slightly less so. Tables can be read fairly well by line-based browsers assuming they are coded properly. Graphical browsers used with screen readers often do not perceive table columns as separate entities and therefore will read right across columns. However, frames, without the noframes element in use, are inaccessible in either case.

Keeping to the current trends *and* incorporating no-frame and text access addresses cross-browser issues by enabling not only those who *require* text access, but those who prefer it as well.

One of the ways to achieve this in a framed site is by employing the logical <noframes> tag. This is placed in the *frameset*. Critical information can then be provided at the same URL as the frameset page, and an entirely accessible site can be formed by using the same pages as the framed site. See Listing 15.3 for a sample of frame code that includes full use of the noframes tag, and follow the steps in the "Designing for the Real World" section below to create accessible frames.

TROUBLESHOOTING

USING FRAMES TO CONTAIN OTHER SITES

What if I want to keep part of my site available at all times? Can I just link the external site into one of my own frames?

Can you? Technically speaking, yes. Legally speaking? Questionable. People have argued over this very issue and the general sense is that if doing this isn't exactly illegal, it is a complete lack of etiquette. What's more, it doesn't make experienced Web visitors very happy—when I get to a site I want to experience *that* site, not a hybrid. Newcomers to the Web might be completely confused by this action as well. There have even been court cases in which framed content has been considered copyright infringement when incorporated into someone else's site. So, I recommend you never do this.

PRINTING FRAMES

How can I make my framed pages easily printable?

Provide a link to a printable format or a downloadable text, XHTML, or even PDF (Portable Document Format) file available so that individuals who want to print out portions of your site can do so with ease.

DESIGNING FOR THE REAL WORLD

BUILDING ACCESSIBLE FRAMED PAGES

You'll do this using the <noframes> tag, as described earlier in the chapter. To do so, follow these steps:

1. Create a frameset in your XHTML editor:

```
<!DOCTYPE html PUBLIC "-//W3C//DTD XHTML 1.0 Frameset//EN"
"http://www.w3.org/TR/xhtml1/DTD/xhtml1-frameset.dtd">
<html xmlns="http://www.w3.org/1999/xhtml">
<head>
<title>Frame with noframes Element</title>
</head>
```

```
<frameset frameborder="0" framespacing="0" border="0" cols="240,
*">
<frame src="menu.html" marginheight="5" marginwidth="5" noresize=
"noresize" scrolling="auto" />
<frame src="main.html" name="right" marginheight="15"
marginwidth="15" noresize="noresize" scrolling="auto" />

</frameset>
</html>
```

2. Add the `<noframes>` tag and its companion `</noframes>` in the following fashion:

```
<!DOCTYPE html PUBLIC "-//W3C//DTD XHTML 1.0 Frameset//EN"
"http://www.w3.org/TR/xhtml1/DTD/xhtml1-frameset.dtd">
<html xmlns="http://www.w3.org/1999/xhtml">
<head>
<title>Frames with NOFRAMES Element</title>
</head>
<frameset frameborder="0" framespacing="0" border="0" cols="240,
*">
<frame src="menu.html" marginheight="5" marginwidth="5" noresize=
"noresize" scrolling="auto" />
<frame src="main.html" name="right" marginheight="15"
marginwidth="15" noresize="noresize" scrolling="auto" />
<noframes>
</noframes>
</frameset>
</html>
```

3. Now add all the HTML syntax necessary to create a fully functional page within the `<NOFRAMES>` tag:

```
<!DOCTYPE html PUBLIC "-//W3C//DTD XHTML 1.0 Frameset//EN"
"http://www.w3.org/TR/xhtml1/DTD/xhtml1-frameset.dtd">
<html xmlns="http://www.w3.org/1999/xhtml">
<head>
<title>Frames with noframes Element</title>
</head>
<frameset frameborder="0" framespacing="0" border="0" cols="240,
*">
<frame src="menu.html" marginheight="5" marginwidth="5" noresize=
"noresize" scrolling="auto" />
<frame src="main.html" name="right" marginheight="15"
marginwidth="15" noresize="noresize" scrolling="auto" />
<noframes>
<body>
<p>Welcome. We're happy to provide this non-frames access to our
Web site. If you prefer to view our site using frames, please
upgrade your browser to a recent one that fully supports frames.
Otherwise, please visit our <a href="index_noframes.html">
non-framed</a> version of this site.</p>
</body>
</noframes>
</frameset>
</html>
```

4. Save the page. You've now made the page completely accessible to non-frame browsers.

The results of this exercise will be a framed site accessible to text-based line browsers such as Lynx Or voice browsing software used by people with visual impairments.

Tip from

molly

Because you can format an entire XHTML document within the `noframes` element, consider using the index page as the Welcome page to your site. From there, link to internal pages that are external to the frame design.

CHAPTER 16

WORKING WITH STANDARD FORMS

In this chapter

THE IMPORTANCE OF FORMS

Forms are one of the oldest and most flexible methods of allowing your site visitors to interact with your site, and ultimately, you. Whether you're providing a method of collecting feedback for the site's improvement, collecting demographic information, or receiving orders for products on your site, forms are the interface through which you are most likely to interact with your audience.

Unlike more static XHTML methods, forms depend upon a relationship between the site visitor and the page you create *as well as* scripts residing on the Web server.

Typically, this relationship is helped along by a server application. Server applications can be any number of technologies, including CGI (Common Gateway Interface) and Perl scripts, Microsoft Active Server Pages (ASP), JavaServer Pages (JSP), servlets, PHP, or Allaire's ColdFusion. These applications act as the conduit through which the information passes, and hands off the information server-side for processing.

> **Note**
>
> Server technologies differ. Because of the various methods of processing forms, you will have to work with your ISP (Internet Service Provider) or systems administrator to find out some information about your server and how it will process the feedback forms.
>
> See the "Designing for the Real World" section at the end of this chapter for an example of how feedback forms are processed on my personal Web site.

Forms can encompass a wide range of functions, including the simple gathering of a user's name, address, and contact information, which is then sent to an email address (often referred to as a *mailto* form), to the creation of games based on user input.

In this chapter, I'm going to focus specifically on how to create a mailto form interface—how to prepare it for processing, create input fields, and control the behavior of various form elements. Combine your learning from this chapter with the information gathered from your ISP, and you will be able to put this as well as a variety of other forms to work.

USING PROPER FORM SYNTAX

Forms employ tags and special elements to enable diverse input options to be displayed and made functional by the form. The special elements are known as *controls*, and I'll be showing you how to make the most out of setting up and using your form controls.

FORM ELEMENTS AND ATTRIBUTES

There are two key form elements and associated attributes that you'll need to know to create forms.

- `<form>...</form>`—The foundational element of all forms. Form accepts a variety of attributes. The two most critical are `action`, which combines with a URL to the form processor, and `method`, which takes the value of `get` or `post`, depending upon the way the form technology is set up.

- **`<input />`**—The input element is responsible for managing the input controls that will be placed within the tag, which only has an opening with no associated closing tag. Commonly used attributes for the `<input>` tag are as follows:

  `type="x"`—This specifies the type of control being called upon. See the "Controls" section for details.

  `name="x"`—The `name` attribute names the control.

  `value="x"`—Value describes the input control. This is optional with all controls except for `radio`.

  `size="x"`—The width of the input control in pixels. Sometimes the number of characters determines the size of the control, as is the case with the `text` and `password` controls.

  `maxlength="x"`—The maximum number of input characters allowed in an input control.

  `checked="x"`—This option pre-selects a given radio button or checkbox within a form.

  `src="x"`—Allows you to determine the location of an image to be used for graphical button elements within the form.

  `alt="x"`—Specifies alternative text for graphical buttons.

- **`<textarea>...</textarea>`**—This element creates a text input area. It's the same in concept as a control, but it is managed using an element instead of an attribute. The attributes it accepts are `name` (see previous), `rows="x"`, where *x* defines the number of lines in the box, and `cols="x"`, where *x* specifies the width of the box.

- **`<select>...</select>`**—The `select` element creates a menu. It can be a drop-down menu or a text list menu, depending upon the way you define the attributes of the element. You can add the `multiple` attribute if you'd like to have a site visitor be able to choose more than one option in the list menu.

- **`<option>...</option>`**—This element defines each individual list item within a `select` menu. Both the opening and closing tags are required. Note that the end tag in HTML 4.0 was *optional* with the `option` element, but is necessary in XHTML.

Note

Rows and columns in a text area do not constrain the amount of data allowed. For example, if I have a text area that is 40 columns wide and 20 rows high, I can type into that box continuously. Scroll bars will become available to help me work within the box most effectively.

CONTROLS

Controls define the kind of input option that will appear onscreen. Controls are syntactically an XHTML *attribute value* and are placed in the value position of the `type` attribute within an `<input />` tag statement.

The controls available include

- **text**—Creates an input text box that consists of a single line. Width of the box is controlled by the size attribute.

- **password**—Exactly like text, except the characters input by the site visitor will reflect back as asterisks. No additional security is added by using this option; it's merely a display feature.

- **checkbox**—Creates a box that can be checked. You can have multiple check boxes in a selection, and all of them might be checked if applicable.

- **radio**—This creates a radio button. You can have as many as you want in a given subject area, but only one can be selected.

- **submit**—This control creates the familiar "Submit" button, which appears as a raised button with a push-button look. The word on the control can be customized using the value attribute.

- **reset**—The same in appearance and customization features as submit, this control will clear the form so the site visitor can re-enter his or her answers.

- **file**—This creates a file selection control. The site visitor can then select a file for upload from the local hard drive.

- **hidden**—Hidden controls are those that don't render in the browser. They are used to insert information for the recipient of the form data. For example, this can be used to send additional information to a form processing script, such as script version information. However, "hidden" in this context only means that the information is not rendered. It's still viewable in the source.

- **image**—Allows for the insertion of a custom image. This gives the designer the ability to use a graphic for submit and reset instead of the default option.

- **button**—Creates a push button. These must be associated with a script to work, because there is no built-in action for them.

Note

> There is also a button element, which can be used to create graphical options for Submit with a slightly different interpretation. It creates a visible button and allows for the insertion of an image and descriptive content. This approach is used less than the standard <input /> tag plus the button control.

→ For more information, **see** "Customizing Submit with Images," later in this chapter.

BUILDING A FORM

The exercises in the following sections will focus on the design of a form. I'll first review the foundational elements of the form. Each subsequent section will then examine how a specific control can be used to enhance or customize the form to your design needs.

A form can begin anywhere within the body of an XHTML document. You'll use the <form> tag and its companion closing tag </form> to indicate the beginning and end of the document.

1. Open an XHTML template that you've created, or an existing XHTML page where you'd like to introduce a form.

2. Add the form tag and its companion closing tag. Make sure to leave several spaces in between so you can effectively add form elements to come.

```
<form>

</form>
```

3. To set up the way in which your form sends information to the server, you'll need to add the method attribute and an appropriate value. Values are get and post.

```
<form   method="post">

</form>
```

Note

To get, or to post, that is the question! The get and post values help determine the way in which data is sent to the server. The difference is that get appends the form's data to the URL specified in the action. On the other hand, post sends the information separately.

4. Naturally, you'll want to ensure that the data you send goes to the correct place for processing. To do this, you'll use the action attribute, combined with the path to the script on the server that will help perform the action.

```
<form   method="post" action="http::://www.myserver.com/apps/cgi-bin/mailscript">
" "
</form>
```

Tip from

molly

Check with your ISP for both the method of preference (get or post) and the location and name of the script available. This will help you properly fill out your method and action attributes.

This bare-bones form can be considered a form template. Just as this book describes how to power-code from an XHTML template and table template, you can use this code as the foundation for all your forms.

ADDING A TEXT FIELD

At this point, you'll want to begin adding areas where people can input data in to the form. One of the most common input areas is known as a *Text Field* (also referred to as a *Text Box*). You will use text fields for information that is entered on a single line, such as a name, address, phone number, and email address.

You'll set up the text field by using the `<input />` tag and the `type` attribute. Fields are defined by the type attribute's value. There are also a number of additional attributes and values you'll want to add to your text field, including name, size, and the maximum number of characters the box will allow.

1. Within the form, add the `input` tag, `type` attribute, and `text` value.

```
<form  method="post" action="/cgi-bin/mailscript">

""

<input type="text" />

</form>
```

2. Add the descriptive text that will appear on the page, and give the field a name.

```
<form  method="post" action="/cgi-bin/mailscript">


First Name: <input type="text" name="firstname" />

</form>
```

Note

The name is necessary so that when the form comes back, the recipient will understand the information related to it. For example, if you name this field "firstname," the processed form results, as they appear in your email,will look something like firstname: Janey.

3. You can set the size (width) of the text field by using the `size` attribute and a numeric value.

```
<form  method="post" action="/cgi-bin/mailscript">


First Name: <input type="text" name="firstname" size="25" />

</form>
```

Note

The size value will stretch the text field to the size of *visible* characters it will hold. Size in this case is not measured in pixels.

4. Text fields can receive more characters than their visual size. For example, if I set the size of the field to be 25, I can still allow the page visitor to input 100 characters if I so choose.

```
<form  method="post" action="/cgi-bin/mailscript">


First Name: <input type="text" name="firstname" size="25" maxlength="100" />

</form>
```

5. Continue adding as many text fields as your form requires, modifying the attributes to your needs and tastes.

```
<form  method="post" action="/cgi-bin/mailscript">


First Name: <input type="text" name="firstname" size="25" maxlength="100" />
<br />

Last Name: <input type="text" name="lastname" size="25" maxlength="100" />
<br />

Email: <input type="text" name="email" size="25" maxlength="100" />

</form>
```

PART

III

CH

16

Note

In this case, I've added line breaks between the lines, formatting the form's input areas using XHTML as I go.

Tip from

molly

If you'd like to use the text fields for passwords and have the "*" character echoed rather than the actual characters, use "password" in place of "text" for the type attribute.

Check your work against Figure 16.1, which displays the information you've added to the form so far.

Figure 16.1
This unfinished form contains three text fields, complete with name and maxlength attributes.

MAKING A CHECK BOX

Text fields are powerful, but sometimes you'll want to offer a group of choices to your site visitor to make. Checkboxes will help you set up these choices and then take the user's selection to the server for processing. You'll use the <input /> tag as before, but this time your type value will be checkbox.

1. Add the first choice, in this case an age range.

```
<form  method="post" action="/cgi-bin/mailscript">


First Name: <input type="text" name="firstname" size="25" maxlength="100" />
<br />

Last Name: <input type="text" name="lastname" size="25" maxlength="100" />
<br />

Email: <input type="text" name="email" size="25" maxlength="100" />

<p>Age:</p>

<p>25 - 35</p>

</form>
```

2. Type in the input tag and the proper attributes.

```
<form  method="post" action="/cgi-bin/mailscript">


First Name: <input type="text" name="firstname" size="25" maxlength="100" />
<br />

Last Name: <input type="text" name="lastname" size="25" maxlength="100" />
<br />

Email: <input type="text" name="email" size="25" maxlength="100" />

<p>Age:</p>

<p>25 - 35 <input type="checkbox" name="25-35" /></p>

</form>
```

3. Continue to add check boxes as necessary. You can even pre-select a check box for your site visitor by using the checked attribute.

```
<form  method="post" action="/cgi-bin/mailscript">


First Name: <input type="text" name="firstname" size="25" maxlength="100" />
<br />

Last Name: <input type="text" name="lastname" size="25" maxlength="100" />
<br />

Email: <input type="text" name="email" size="25" maxlength="100" />
```

```
<p>Age:</p>

<p>25 - 35 <input type="checkbox" name="25-35" /></p>

<p>36 - 40 <input type="checkbox" name="36-40" checked="checked" /></p>

</form>
```

Note

Check boxes also allow you to set up choices where an individual can check more than one box. For example, if you were setting up a selection of choices of films seen in the past six months, you'd want your site visitors to check as many as apply to them. In this case, I can actually choose more than one age group if I wanted to do so. If you want to purposely limit the way a user can input information, you'll choose a radio button instead of a check box.

In Figure 16.2, I've taken a screen shot of the form as it is so far, with text boxes and check boxes.

Figure 16.2
The form now contains check boxes. When completed and activated, site visitors will be able to click the check box most appropriate to them.

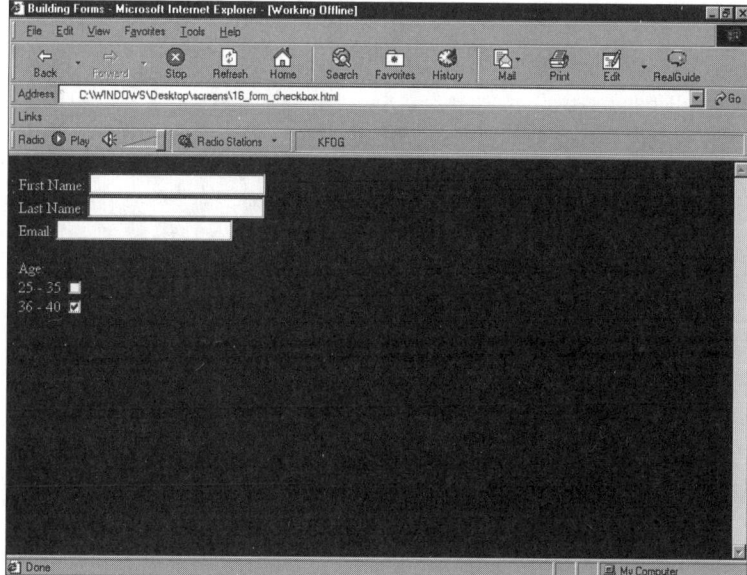

Caution

In HTML, the checked attribute appeared alone. This is referred to as *attribute minimization,* which is not allowed in XML, and therefore, in XHTML. So, instead of simply typing "checked" to indicate a box is checked, you must use the full attribute value pair, checked="checked" to have a conforming document. The bad news is that some older Web browsers don't understand this method. I recommend you, well, check your work!

ADDING A RADIO BUTTON

As with check boxes, radio buttons allow you to make a selection. However, radio buttons will automatically move to the point of selection. Unlike check boxes, they do not allow more than one choice.

1. Add the selection options required in your form. I'm using gender in my example.

```
<form  method="post" action="/cgi-bin/mailscript">


First Name: <input type="text" name="firstname" size="25" maxlength="100" />
<br />

Last Name: <input type="text" name="lastname" size="25" maxlength="100" />
<br />

Email: <input type="text" name="email" size="25" maxlength="100" />

<p>Age:</p>

<p>25 - 35 <input type="checkbox" name="25-35" /></p>


<p>36 - 40 <input type="checkbox" name="36-40" checked="checked" /></p>

<p>Gender:</p>

<p>Male</p>

<p>Female</p>

<p>Prefer not to say</p>

</form>
```

2. Using the input tag, add the type attribute, radio value, and attributes of your choice.

```
<form  method="post" action"/cgi-bin/mailscript">

First Name: <input type="text" name="firstname" size="25" maxlength="100" />
<br />

Last Name: <input type="text" name="lastname" size="25" maxlength="100" />
<br />

Email: <input type="text" name="email" size="25" maxlength="100" />

<p>Age:</p>

<p>25 - 35 <input type="checkbox" name="25-35" /></p>


<p>36 - 40 <input type="checkbox" name="36-40" checked /></p>

<p>Gender:</p>
```

```
<input type="radio" name="male" /> Male
<input type="radio" name="female" checked="checked"  />Female

" " " " " "

<input type="radio" name="undisclosed" />Prefer not to say

</form>
```

Note   Radio buttons also can contain the "checked" attribute. Once the user clicks another radio button, the previous button will clear and the user's new choice will be selected instead.

The form now contains both radio and check box options (see Figure 16.3).

Figure 16.3
With both check boxes and radio buttons, the form is beginning to become both more technically and visually complex.

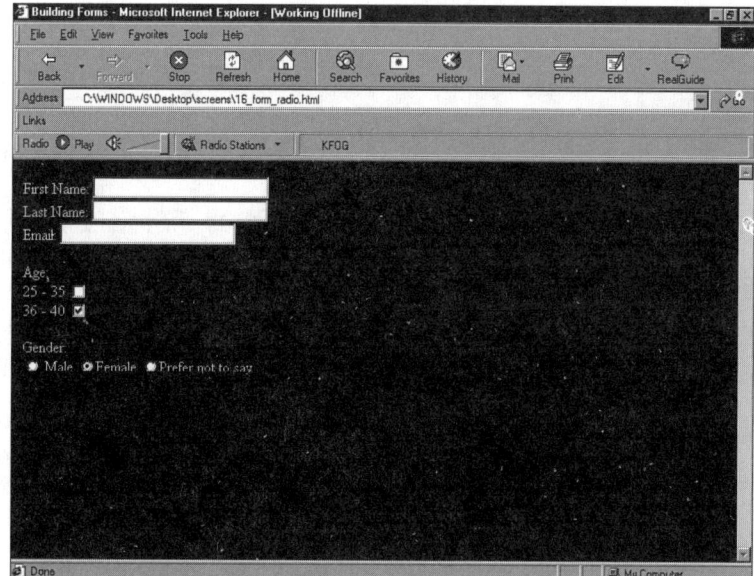

MAKING A MENU LIST

Another powerful method of offering form selections for your visitors is a menu with options. These are especially helpful when you have numerous items in a list, such as a list of states or countries.

Drop-down lists are created by using the select element and individual option tags. There are several attributes that can modify both, which will be explained as we step through the process.

1. In the area where you'd like to place your drop-down list, input your display text, and the opening and closing select tags.

```
<form  method="post" action="/cgi-bin/mailscript">
```

```
State:
<select>


</select>

</form>
```

2. If you'd like to set the size by items, you can do so by using the size attribute. If you give the numeric value of "4," four items will be shown in the resulting drop-down menu.

```
<form  method="post" action="/cgi-bin/mailscript">

State:
<select size="4">


</select>

</form>
```

If you have four items and specify a size of four, the menu will be displayed as a list box, with all options fully visible onscreen.

If you specify a numeric value that is less than the total available options, a scrollbar will appear in the menu. Leaving this attribute out is the popular method of choice as it creates the familiar drop-down style menu.

→ To create a drop down menu for navigation, **see** Chapter 20, "Adding JavaScript to XHTML Documents," **p. 445**.

3. You also can allow for multiple items to be selected. To do this, add the multiple= "multiple" attribute and attribute value.

```
<form  method="post" action="/cgi-bin/mailscript">


State:
<select multiple="multiple">


</select>

</form>
```

4. Now, add the option tag and the first option. Here I've added the name attribute to the option tag. This ensures that the form results will display the selected option.

```
<form  method="post" action="/cgi-bin/mailscript">


State:
<select size="4" multiple="multiple">
<option value="arizona">Arizona

</select>

</form>
```

5. Continue adding options as necessary. You can use the `selected` attribute for the option which you'd like to have set as the default menu selection.

```
<form  method="post" action="/cgi-bin/mailscript">


State:
<select>
<option value="arizona">Arizona</option>
<option value="california">California</option>
<option value="nevada" selected="selected">Nevada</option>
</select>

</form>
```

Figure 16.4 shows two menu variations. The first is the drop-down menu (you'd need to click on the arrow to see the other options), the second is a list menu (all the options are visible). The list variation was created by ensuring that the number of list items and the size of the menu are equal.

Figure 16.4

Two variations on a menu theme: The left menu is a drop-down menu, and the right menu is a list menu. The code difference is in the attributes used to describe the `select` and `option` elements.

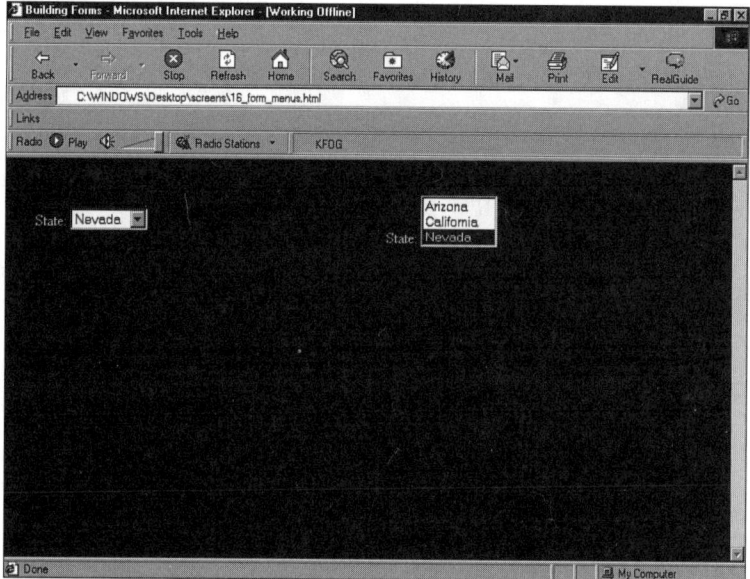

Note

As with the `checked` attribute, `selected` was minimized in HTML. In XHTML, you must write out the full attribute value pair, `selected="selected"` or your document will not be well formed.

PART

III

CH

16

CREATING A TEXT AREA

Text fields are handy for one-line sections of input. However, if you want to give your visitors more room to add their own feedback and thoughts, you can accommodate them by providing them with a text area.

Text areas are created using the <textarea> tag, and its companion closing </textarea> tag. You'll also add attributes including rows and cols to determine the amount of rows and columns in your text area, respectively.

1. In the portion of the form where you'd like to add the text area, type in the display text and opening and closing textarea element tags.

```
<form  method="post" action="/cgi-bin/mailscript">


First Name: <input type="text" name="firstname" size="25" maxlength="100" />
<br />

Last Name: <input type="text" name="lastname" size="25" maxlength="100" />
<br />

Email: <input type="text" name="email" size="25" maxlength="100" />

<p>Age:</p>

<p>25 - 35 <input type="checkbox" name="25-35" /></p>


<p>36 - 40 <input type="checkbox" name="36-40" checked="checked" /></p>

<p>Gender:</p>

<input type="radio" name="male" /> Male
<input type="radio" name="female" checked="checked" />Female


<input type="radio" name="undisclosed" />Prefer not to say

<p>State:</p>
<select>
<option name="arizona">Arizona</option>
<option name="california">California</option>
<option name="nevada" selected="selected">Nevada</option>
</select>

<p>Do you have additional concerns?</p>

<textarea>



</textarea>

</form>
```

2. To set the rows (how high the text area will be), add the row with a numeric value.

```
<form  method="post" action="/cgi-bin/mailscript">


First Name: <input type="text" name="firstname" size="25" maxlength="100" />
<br />

Last Name: <input type="text" name="lastname" size="25" maxlength="100" />
<br />

Email: <input type="text" name="email" size="25" maxlength="100" />

<p>Age:</p>

<p>25 - 35 <input type="checkbox" name="25-35" /></p>


<p>36 - 40 <input type="checkbox" name="36-40" checked="checked" /></p>

<p>Gender:</p>

<input type="radio" name="male" /> Male
<input type="radio" name="female" checked="checked" />Female


<input type="radio" name="undisclosed" />Prefer not to say

<p>State:</p>
<select>
<option value="arizona">Arizona</option>
<option value="california">California</option>
<option value="nevada" selected="selected">Nevada</option>
</select>

<p>Do you have additional concerns?</p>

<textarea rows="5">

</textarea>

</form>
```

3. To set the width in characters, use the cols attribute with a numeric value. I've also set a "name" attribute so the script can identify the purpose of the textarea.

```
<form  method="post" action="/cgi-bin/mailscript">


First Name: <input type="text" name="firstname" size="25" maxlength="100" />
<br />

Last Name: <input type="text" name="lastname" size="25" maxlength="100" />
<br />

Email: <input type="text" name="email" size="25" maxlength="100" />

<p>Age:</p>

<p>25 - 35 <input type="checkbox" name="25-35" /></p>
```

```
<p>36 - 40 <input type="checkbox" name="36-40" checked /></p>

<p>Gender:</p>

<input type="radio" name="male" /> Male
<input type="radio" name="female" checked="checked" />Female

<input type="radio" name="undisclosed" />Prefer not to say

<p>State:</p>
<select>
<option value="arizona">Arizona</option>
<option value="california">California</option>
<option value="nevada" selected="selected">Nevada</option>
</select>

<p>Do you have additional concerns?</p>

<textarea name="feedback" rows="5" cols="25">

</textarea>

</form>
```

Figure 16.5 shows the form.

Note

Setting the `name` attribute enables the script to decipher what the information within the textarea is. Note also that if you place content within the textarea, that content will display to the site visitor. Some Web authors use this as a means to cue the site visitor to type something into the area, such as "type comments here."

Figure 16.5
The form with the text area displayed. Despite the small size of the text area, the site visitor can input as much information as he or she wants. A scrollbar will appear if necessary.

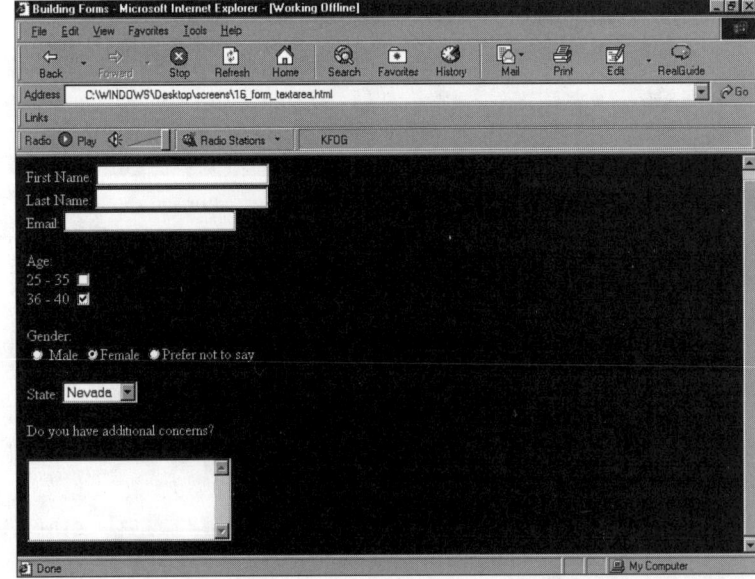

Wondering if you'll need more than one text area on your form? See, "Multiple Text Areas" in the "Troubleshooting" section near the end of this chapter for some helpful information.

PROVIDING RESET AND SUBMIT BUTTONS

With the bulk of your form designed, it's time to offer the ability of the page visitor to submit the form, or reset the form data and start over.

1. To add a submit button, use the input tag with the type attribute. The value "submit" will create the button.

```
<form  method="post" action="/cgi-bin/mailscript">


<input type="submit" />

</form>
```

2. You can customize what the submit button says by adding a value.

```
<form  method="post" action="/cgi-bin/mailscript">


<input type="submit" value="send it!" />

</form>
```

3. The reset button works using the same logic. Simply use the reset value in the type attribute to create a reset button. If you'd like to customize how the button is labeled, use the value attribute.

```
<form  method="post" action="/cgi-bin/mailscript">


<input type="submit" value="send it!" />

<input type="reset" value="do it over" />

</form>
```

Figure 16.6 shows the results of our completed form, which is fully designed but will not function until properly connected with the server-side script.

Tip from

If you want your forms to be very neat and organized, use tables to lay out the form's input controls.

If you'd like to use an image to customize your Submit and Reset buttons, you can do so by first creating the image, and then following one of two options.

→ For more information on creating images, **see** Chapter 29, "Creating Professional Web Graphics," **p. 595**.

Figure 16.6
Here you see the final form with the Submit and Reset buttons. I've customized the labels to express my own personality and needs.

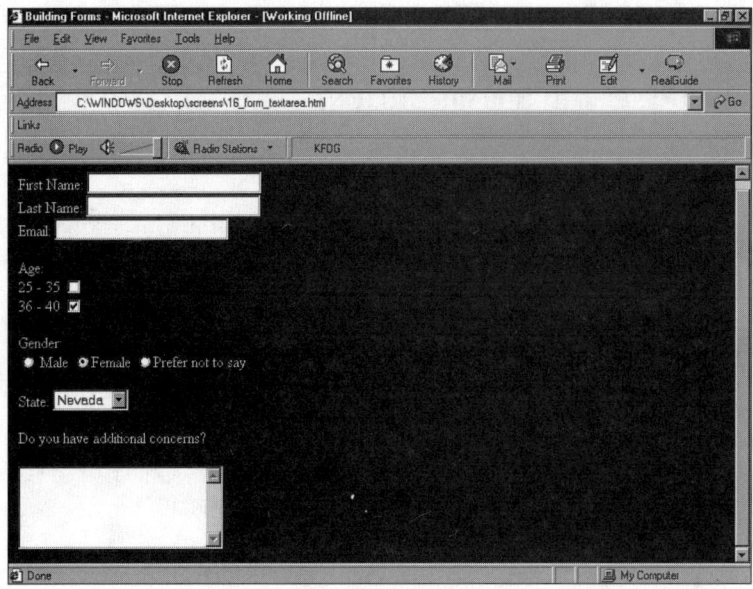

The first option is to insert the image directly into the Submit or Reset control, as follows:

```
<input type="image" src="images/go.gif" width="50" height="25" alt="go"
value="submit" />
```

This will result in a seamless look, with the button fitting into the design of the page.

Caution

While you can use an image for `submit`, this technique will unfortunately not work for `reset`.

The second option is to use the `button` element. This sets the image *into* the submit button:

```
<button name="submit" value="submit" type="submit">
Send <img src="images/go.gif" width="50" height="25"  alt="go"></button>
```

As mentioned in the note early in this chapter, the second option is rarely used. Figure 16.7 shows an example of both styles.

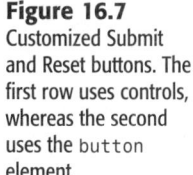

Figure 16.7
Customized Submit and Reset buttons. The first row uses controls, whereas the second uses the `button` element.

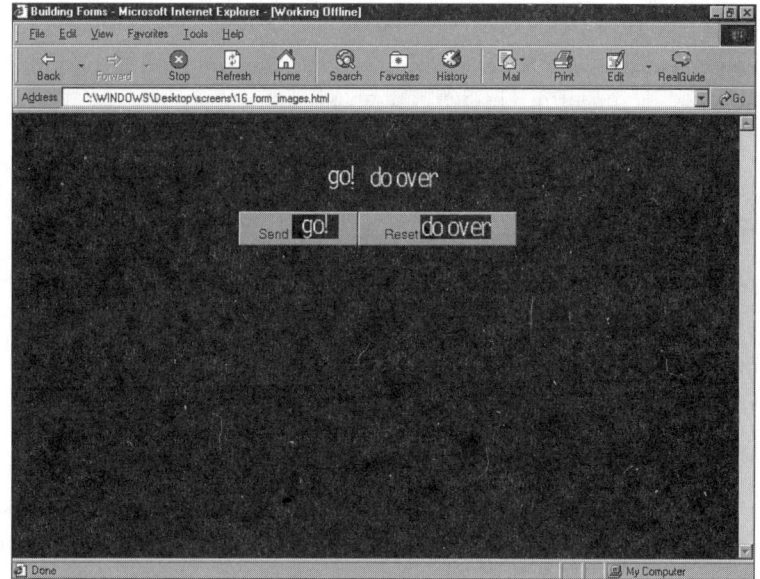

TROUBLESHOOTING

MULTIPLE TEXT AREAS

Can you add more than one text area to a page?

You can use multiple text areas on a page, depending upon your needs. However, determine *before* building your form what elements are necessary. This will result in a more organized, logical form that is easy for your site visitors to use.

DESIGNING FOR THE REAL WORLD

METHOD, ACTION, AND HIDDEN FIELDS AT MOLLY.COM

The following syntax is taken from the contact form on my Web site. I want to have you look closely at two issues. First, let's examine the form's method and action attributes.

```
<form method="post" action="http://opus1.com/htbin/mailto">
```

As you can see, `"post"` is the preferred method for my ISP. Also, the action points to a specific script on the server. The first part of the URL is the ISP's address (`opus1.com`), the directory `htbin` is the location of the script, and `mailto` is the name of the script. This simple syntax is what connects my form to the server's script so any information entered into the form can be processed and sent to me via email.

Another real-world issue is the use of *hidden fields*. These are `input` entries that use the `type="hidden"` attribute and value to invisibly include them within the form. The first entry in my form is as follows:

```
<input name="from" type="hidden" value="site visitor" />
```

This information will insert the words "site visitor" into the FROM line of any email processed by the form. This next example is similar:

```
<input name="subject" type="hidden" value="Feedback: Molly's Web Site" />
```

In this case, the SUBJECT line of email from this form will clearly note that it is in regards to Feedback: Molly's Web Site.

Hidden fields are very powerful. I can use this information to create filters within my email program so all incoming mail from this form goes directly to a specific box. This helps me stay organized, and discriminate between information coming from my personal versus any other Web sites I have.

CHAPTER 17

ANOTHER APPROACH TO XHTML FORMS USING XHTML-FML

In this chapter   *By Christian Jarolim and Cassandra Greer*

CREATING DYNAMIC FORMS

Although basic forms can offer basic options, what happens when you want to go beyond the basics? Standard Web form markup has basically not been updated since its inception—despite the increasing demands of a growing Internet. This means that it is up to you to manually enhance the functionality of your forms through scripting. But not everyone is a JavaScript expert and the list of standard code shortcomings is endless. Bottom line? You can really enhance a site if you have something better than standard forms.

XHTML-FML

To solve the problem of inadequate forms, the World Wide Web Consortium's HTML working group is currently working on the next generation of Web forms, *XHTML Extended Forms*, or simply *XForms*. XForms are not yet a standard, but this does not keep us from having better forms now.

As you already know, XHTML was designed to allow extensions to be developed. Mozquito Technologies has taken advantage of this feature and has developed the Forms Markup Language, XHTML-FML. XHTML-FML is a prelude to XForms. The Forms working group at the W3C has just defined requirements for XForms.

> **Note**   For more information on XForms, see www.w3.org/MarkUp/Forms/.

XHTML-FML already provides solutions for several key XForms requirements. With the help of the Mozquito Matrix, this powerful extension to XHTML is operational in current version 4 and 5 browsers.

EXTENDING XHTML

An important aspect of XHTML-FML is the way in which XHTML has been extended to include the *Forms Markup Language* (FML). Before, it was considered harmful to extend HTML with proprietary extensions.

In reality, it is only natural for tools to develop and be refined in response to changing needs. The W3C is currently working on extending XHTML safely, by defining a Modularization Framework. This upcoming W3C recommendation redefines XHTML as a set of modules. Each module reflects a component of XHTML such as an image module, a table module, a text module, and so on.

→ For further information on modularization, **see** Chapter 21, "XHTML Modularization", **p. 471**.

These modules can be combined like plug and play. It will be possible to define your own "XHTML conforming modules" that can be combined with existing XHTML modules to create a new member of the family. As you are already aware, the XHTML family has three members: XHTML 1.0 document types "strict," "transitional," and "frameset." More family members can be created by combining XHTML modules which conform to the strict W3C conformance rules. A new markup language must conform to these rules to be called

XHTML-*MyML*. XHTML-FML is the first family member, which conforms to these rules, defines new functionality and still works within the existing Web architecture, thanks to Mozquito.

EXPLORING THE LIMITS OF FORMS

XHTML-FML has immediate benefits for authors who want to construct sophisticated Web forms and dynamic Web pages using a markup language rather than tiresome cross-browser scripting. Imagine you have lots of content. There are two ways to manage that content. One is to set up one large document and the other is to divide the content into logical units and create a type of slide show. With XHTML-FML and its <x:toggle> element, you can use both ways together: create one file and set up a slide show with easy-to-read content and a good navigation.

Then there's the problem of repetitive code. In ordinary XHTML you often have to repeat sections of code over and over again. In XHTML-FML you can set up a template for that repeated code. This makes the file much smaller and therefore easier to maintain.

XHTML-FML also provides run-time calculations. The <calc> tag even enables you to create small shops independent of a server environment.

You can set up required fields and input validation within your page. This avoids annoying roundtrips to the server because the user is prompted to enter mandatory data before he or she can submit the file to the server.

There is much more to XHTML-FML. Here's what this chapter will explain:

- How to Get Started with XHTML-FML
- Advantages of Mozquito Forms Over HTML Forms
- Creating Dynamic Forms with XHTML-FML
- Advanced XHTML-FML Techniques
- Real World Example: The "Shop in a Page"

GETTING STARTED USING XHTML-FML

Because you can author extremely complex and multifunctional Web pages with XHTML-FML, it is necessary to plan carefully. You need to consider not only how to set your file/form/Web site but what files you need to maintain and update in the future.

So far XHTML-FML can only be displayed as stand-alone exported .html files. This is the reason for code that is created for use on platform-independent browsers version 4 and higher (Microsoft Internet Explorer and Netscape Navigator) and therefore might become quite large in content and functionality increase. So you should consider first which features to implement.

A Web site is not just a tool for delivering information but also a platform for communicating a certain atmosphere and identity. This is done more and more with sound, but most Web designers and companies are still quite traditional in their approach: They work out and then stick to a certain corporate design. When it comes to forms, such a corporate design is hard to maintain because forms are not usually designed to look nice. They just need to get the job done. With XHTML and styles you can work around this and find a solution that fits both your needs and your visitors' and customers' sense of taste.

THE AUTHORING ENVIRONMENT

Because XHTML-FML is leading-edge technology, you need a special authoring environment, the Mozquito Factory, which can be found at www.mozquito.org/factory/. You also can use your favorite text editor, but you should avoid WYSIWYGs, because as of this writing, they do not yet contain options for XHTML tags.

As soon as you've installed "Mozquito Factory" you can start. The Mozquito Factory is a set of tools working in the background and a text editor providing some special functionality like checking your files for well-formedness and validity.

Here's a closer look at the advantages of Mozquito Forms over HTML Forms:

- **Multiple screen pages in a single file**—A standard XHTML document can be of any length. A document that contains more information than a single screen page will automatically get scrollbars. With FML, you can define any number of screen pages in a single document. You can build slide shows, multi-page forms or any other Web page that needs to be dynamically updated. Because everything is defined as a single file, every page appears without having to be requested from the server separately. This feature allows you to maintain local state throughout a series of pages. The <toggle> tag is also a scalable mechanism that has often proven to be more powerful than frames.

- **Avoid repetition of code**—Documents often contain the same chunks of markup code over and over again. With XHTML-FML, you can define any combination of tags as a <template> within the XHTML-FML document. A template can be inserted with the <insert> tag at any point in the target document. The same template can be used multiple times, and you can modify parts of the template each time it is inserted. The document is therefore smaller and much easier to maintain.

- **Compute and display field calculations at run-time**—Imagine an order form where you could display the "total sum" of the selected items immediately. Before FML, calculations on the client using the values of the form fields were only possible through scripting. But now, the <calc> tag can be wrapped around any form field able to reference other form fields or other calc elements. This results in interdependent field calculations. In addition, the value of a <textoutput> tag appears to the user as normal text but internally behaves like any other form field. Changing the value of a textoutput will dynamically update the displayed text. This lets you display the "total sum" as just plain text, unchangeable by the user, yet its value can be submitted back to the server with the rest of the form.

■ **Input validation made easy**—Text input form fields allow a text string to be entered. It is often a good idea to limit the type of data entered by the user. Today, we often see forms submitted to the server and then sent back again because some of the fields were not filled out correctly. These annoying "round-trips" to the server can be avoided. Input validation can now occur immediately while the user fills out a form. For this, we have added two new attributes to the `<textinput>` element. If validation is set to "strict," the user is forced to enter the kind of data specified in the `ctype` (content type) attribute. For example, if the `ctype` of a field is set to "email," then the field will only accept email addresses.

Note

You can find more information at the Mozquito Web site, `www.mozquito.com/`.

CREATING DYNAMIC FORMS WITH XHTML-FML

To start with, let's have a look at a minimal XHTML-FML document, as shown in Listing 17.1.

LISTING 17.1   MINIMAL XHTML-FML DOCUMENT EXAMPLE

```
<?xml version="1.0"?>
<!DOCTYPE html PUBLIC "-//OVERFLOW//DTD XHTML-FML 1.0//EN"
"http://www.mozquito.org/dtd/xhtml-fml1.dtd">
<html xmlns="http://www.w3.org/1999/xhtml"
xmlns:x="http://www.mozquito.org/xhtml-fml">
  <head>
    <title>XHTML-FML - Feedback Form</title>
    <meta name="generator" content="Mozquito Factory 1.3" />
  </head>
  <body>

    <x:form>
      ...
    </x:form>

  </body>
</html>
```

The most important difference to plain XHTML 1.0 documents is the definition of an additional XML namespace in the `html` root tag:

`xmlns:x=http://www.mozquito.org/xhtml-fml`

The Forms Markup Language namespace is now available in this document using the prefix x.

All FML tags are now identified by the prefix x in front of the element name, (`<x:form>` in the above document).

A BASIC FEEDBACK FORM

In this section, you'll be introduced to a basic feedback form, which asks for the name, e-mail address of the person filling out the form, as well as a message.

The first thing you need to do is define your form using the FML form container (`<x:form>`) in the document body. This tag is similar to the standard `<form>` tag in HTML 4.0. `<x:form>...</x:form>`.

Now we'll introduce you to the XHTML-FML tag `<x:textinput>`, which creates an input field for a single line of text. This tag is similar to the `<input type="text">` tag used in HTML 4.0.

Now let's begin by defining a single `textinput` for requesting a page visitor's name.

Start your text editor or the Mozquito Factory and type or download the following code from Que's Web site. You can open a new document template in the Mozquito Factory, or if you prefer, use your own editor and copy the code from Listing 17.2. If you're using Mozquito Factory, open the file `template1.txt` in the templates sub-directory in the Mozquito Factory, and then add the code shown in Listing 17.2.

LISTING 17.2 ADDING STYLE TO A BASIC XHTML-FML FORM TEMPLATE

```
<?xml version="1.0"?>
<!DOCTYPE html PUBLIC "-//OVERFLOW//DTD XHTML-FML 1.0//EN"
"http://www.mozquito.org/dtd/xhtml-fml1.dtd">
<html xmlns="http://www.w3.org/1999/xhtml" xmlns:x="http://www.mozquito.org/xhtml-
fml">
  <head>
    <title>XHTML-FML - Feedback Form</title>
    <meta name="generator" content="Mozquito Factory 1.3" />

    <style type="text/css">
      <![CDATA[

      body { font-family: arial,sans-serif; }

      ]]>
    </style>
  </head>
  <body>
    <x:form>

      Your name:
      <x:textinput id="name" /><br />

    </x:form>
  </body>
</html>
```

If you're using Mozquito Factory, click on the browser icon on the toolbar or CTRL-D to view the results on your browser.

Using your own editor, save the document as `feedbackform.html`.

Navigate to the folder where you saved the document and double-click on the file.

Figure 17.1 shows an example of a basic feedback form using XHTML-FML.

Figure 17.1
A basic feedback form using XHTML-FML.

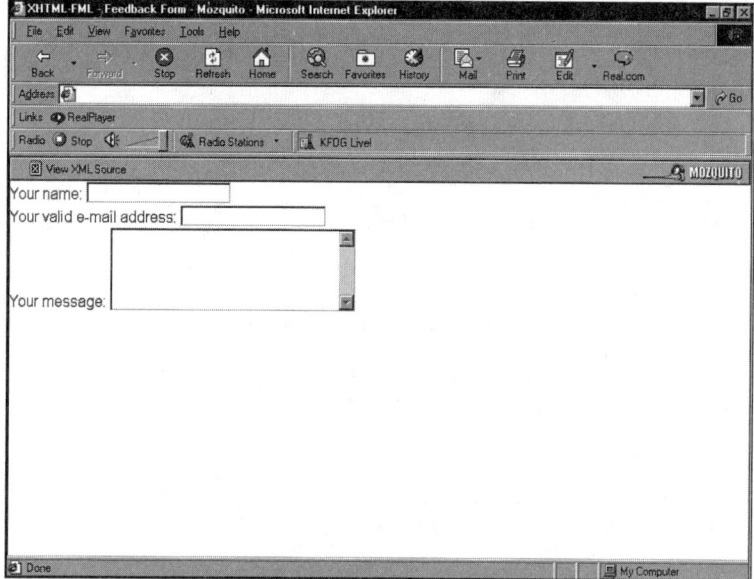

PART

III

CH

17

Let's deconstruct and add to this code. First, you'll notice a style sheet to the template found inside the document head:

```
<style type="text/css">
  <![CDATA[

  body { font-family: arial, sans-serif; }

  ]]>
</style>
```

In the document body, you use the `<x:textinput>` tag to create a `textinput` box. XHTML-FML form controls such as `textinput` must always appear inside an FML form container `<x:form>` in the document body.

```
<x:form>

  Your name:
  <x:textinput id="name" /><br />

</x:form>
```

The `textinput` field has an ID with the value "name".

Then, you'll add another `textinput` field for the email address and a `textarea` field using the XHTML-FML tag:

```
<x:textarea />:
```

```
<x:form>

  Your name:
  <x:textinput id="name" size="20" /><br />

  Your valid e-mail address:
  <x:textinput id="email" size="20" /><br />

  Your message:
  <x:textarea id="message" /><br />

</x:form>
```

Using the `size` attribute, you specify the width of the `textinput` field in characters.

Then you add attributes to make sure that the email address is checked for correct syntax when it is entered into the `textinput` field:

```
<x:form>

  Your name:
  <x:textinput id="name" size="20" /><br />

  Your valid e-mail address:
  <x:textinput id="email" size="20" ctype="email" validation="strict" /><br />

  Your message:
  <x:textarea id="message" /><br />

</x:form>
```

Once you've copied the code, save the document and double-click the file again, or send the document to the browser from within the Mozquito Factory.

Now enter an incorrect email address into the form (that is, @test). Once you attempt to exit this form control, you will get the alert shown in Figure 17.2.

Figure 17.2
A basic feedback form using XHTML-FML.

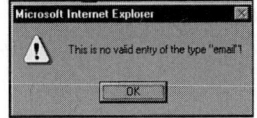

Click "OK." The incorrect email address will disappear and the cursor will be reactivated, allowing input again.

This example introduces two new attributes, which let this happen. The first one is `ctype` (Content Type), with the value "email." This key word advises Mozquito to check the entered data to see whether a user entered a correctly formed email address. You can only check whether an address is actually valid by sending a message to that address.

ADDITIONAL CONTENT TYPES

In addition to the `ctype` value "email", there are other content types available also. Here is a list of current content types:

- **text**—(for non-numeric text strings)
- **num**—(for numbers only)
- **date**—(for dates of type: DD.MM.YY / DD.MM.YYYY / DD/MM/YY / DD/MM/YYYY)
- **url**—(a complete URL such as http://www.domain.com/)
- **www**—(a URL without the referrer, www.domain.com)
- **email**—(an email address as in : john@doe.com)
- **creditcard**—(for the 15 or 16 digits of a credit card number)
- **expiredate**—(for the card expiry date of the type MM/YY)

Additional content types are being added regularly. Look for updates at the Mozquito Web site.

The other attribute you have been introduced to is `validation`. It lets you choose between two levels of validation: `strict` and `loose`.

You used `strict` for the value of the validation attribute in the previous example. This means that once the page visitor hits the OK button in the validation alert, the incorrect data is deleted. If validation is set to `strict`, the page visitor must either enter data matching the validation criteria or no data at all.

When validation is set to `loose`, the incorrect data still remains in the form control after the alert has appeared. The page visitor is informed that the data is incorrect but can still proceed and leave the data as it is.

SUBMITTING FORMS

The next step is to add the functionality needed to submit the information to your server.

Listing 17.3 shows the source code of a form ready to be processed.

PART

III

CH

17

LISTING 17.3   SOURCE CODE OF A FORM READY TO BE PROCESSED.

```
<x:form id="feedbackform" action="http://www.mozquito.org/servlets/Echo"
method="post">

   Your name:
   <x:textinput id="name" size="30" send="yes" /><br />

   Your valid e-mail address:
   <x:textinput id="email" size="30" ctype="email" validation="strict" send="yes"
/><br />

   Your message:
   <x:textarea id="name" size="30" send="yes" /><br />

   <x:button value="Submit" onclick="submit:feedbackform" />

</x:form>
```

In the code in Listing 17.3, you have given the form an action to do or submit. The value of the action attribute is the URL where the data is submitted. This can be a program or script of any kind running on a server. We have used the Mozquito Echo Service located at `http://www.mozquito.org/servlets/Echo` that displays the submitted data on an XHTML page.

Another addition is the send attribute on both `textinput` fields and the `textarea` field in the form. You need to explicitly set the send attribute to the value yes if the form control should send its value to the server.

When you design feature-rich Web forms in XHTML-FML, many of your form controls will be used for things like navigation or for their values to other form elements in the same document and therefore do not need to send their value to the server. In the end only a few form controls will need to send their values to the server, so form elements do not send their values automatically.

The `<x:button>` tag creates a push button. You used this tag in the previous example for the submit button. The `value` attribute holds the text being displayed on the button.

With the event handler `onclick`, we can specify what should happen if the page visitor pushes the button. In this case, we want to submit the information the form's user inserts, and we use the submit action statement as the value of the `onclick` attribute:

`submit:FormID`

After the submit key word and the colon, the ID of the form that we want to submit must be given. In our example we say `submit:feedbackform`, because we have given our form the ID `feedbackform`.

This is especially handy when working with multiple forms inside a single XHTML-FML document. You could ask the page visitor whether he or she wants to fill out this address form or a different form, all defined in a single XHTML-FML document, and then only submit the one chosen.

Figure 17.3 shows the results.

Figure 17.3
The form with a submit button.

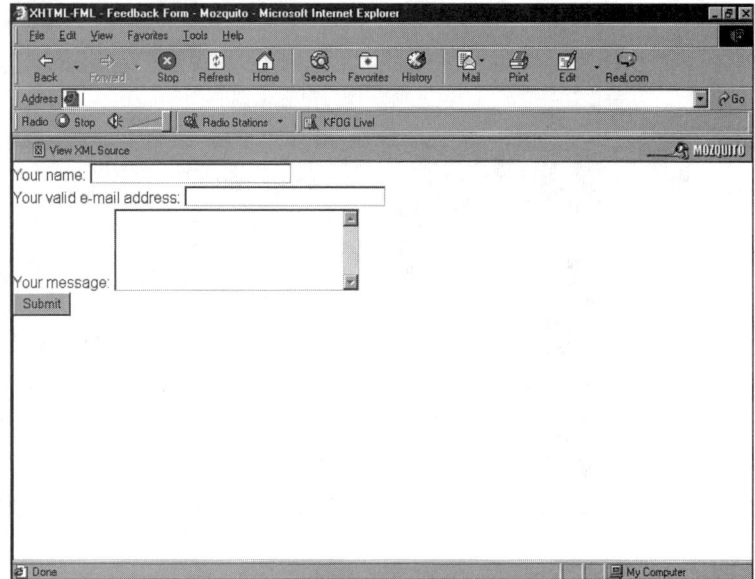

REQUIRING MANDATORY FIELDS

In certain cases, you'll want to make sure the form can be submitted only after certain form controls or fields have been filled out. Examples of this include the name, a correct email address, and a message from the page visitor. To add these mandatory fields, you'll use the mandatory attribute for each mandatory field (Listing 17.4).

LISTING 17.4   ADDING MANDATORY FIELDS

```
<x:form d="feedbackform" action="http://www.mozquito.org/servlets/Echo">

   Your name:
   <x:textinput id="name" size="30" send="yes" mandatory="yes" /><br />

   Your valid e-mail address:
   <x:textinput id="email" size="30" ctype="email" validation="strict" send="yes"
      mandatory="yes" /><br />

   Your message:
   <x:textarea id="message" send="yes" mandatory="yes" /><br />

   <x:button value="Submit" onclick="submit:feedbackform" />

</x:form>
```

In your browser, an alert page from Mozquito.Com will now appear when the submit button is pushed but some of the mandatory fields aren't filled in (see Figure 17.4).

Figure 17.4
If a mandatory field isn't filled in by a visitor, an alert will be generated.

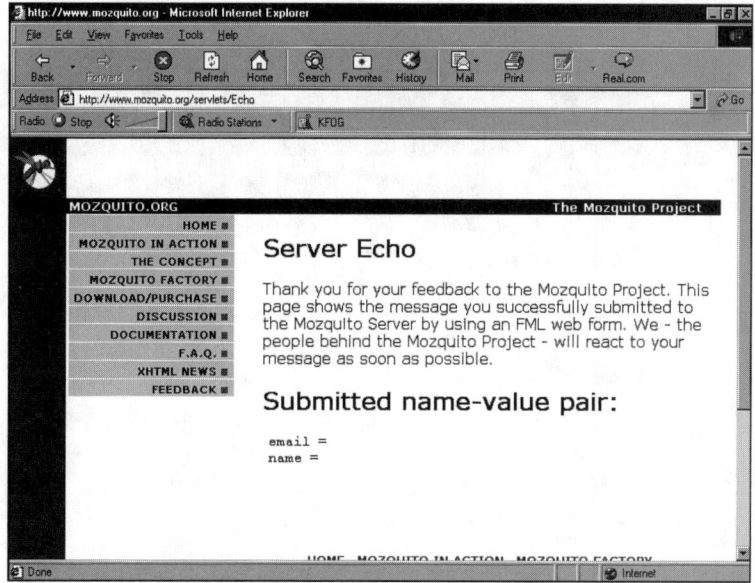

By default, the alert lists the IDs of the fields that were left blank. The form can only be submitted when *all* form controls with mandatory set to yes contain valid entries.

> **Caution**
>
> A form control ID might not always clearly indicate which form control needs to be filled. The text appearing with the form control on the screen page is viewed as its label, not the ID. However, in the document source, this text isn't clearly associated with the form control.

To attach an alert to a specific form control, mandatory is set to yes and the form control has a label. In this instance, the alert will show a list of labels instead of Ids (see Figure 17.5).

Figure 17.5
Using alert boxes for mandatory forms.

Listing 17.5 shows these changes in the source.

LISTING 17.5: IDENTIFYING MANDATORY FORM ELEMENTS WITH LABELS

```
<x:form id="feedbackform" action="http://www.mozquito.org/servlets/Echo">

  <x:label for="name">Your name</x:label>:
  <x:textinput id="name" size="30" send="yes" mandatory="yes" /><br />

  <x:label for="email">Your valid e-mail address</x:label>:
  <x:textinput id="email" size="30" ctype="email" validation="strict" send="yes"
     mandatory="yes" /><br />

  <x:button value="Submit" onclick="submit:feedbackform" />

</x:form>
```

The `<x:label>` tag uses the `for` attribute to associate itself to another form control. The value of the `for` attribute is the same as the associated form control's ID.

The only thing you have to do now to use it online is to check your file for well-formedness and validity, and to use the Mozquito Factory to automatically generate the JavaScript `.html` file.

CREATING AN ONLINE SURVEY

Online help Web developers get a little more information from site visitors. Besides, people really enjoy filling out surveys.

In the next XHTML-FML example you are going to ask a specified target audience about their communication habits. We've kept this short because it's an example, but you can customize the survey to your liking.

Before setting up a survey, you should decide what to ask. You might choose to ask your visitors about how they use your site:

- Which services do you use now, how often and from where?
- Which services would you like to use, from where and how often?

Let's say that they'll answer these questions, and in turn, your site will reward them with a free test drive of your services, on our example—three months unified messaging.

To start with, set up the empty XHTML-FML template you were introduced to in the last example. Then, set up four screens welcome screen, first question, second question, and a "Thank You" screen. Listing 17.6 shows the code.

LISTING 17.6 SETTING UP A SURVEY

```
<?xml version="1.0"?>
<!DOCTYPE html PUBLIC "-//OVERFLOW//DTD XHTML-FML 1.0//EN"
"http://www.mozquito.org/dtd/xhtml-fml1.dtd">
<html xmlns="http://www.w3.org/1999/xhtml"
xmlns:x="http://www.mozquito.org/xhtml-fml">
  <head>
    <title>XHTML-FML - Online Survey</title>
    <meta name="generator" content="Mozquito Factory 1.3" />
    <style type="text/css">
      <![CDATA[

.content { position:absolute; left:140; top:90 }
h1,h2,p { font-family:Verdana,Arial,Helvetica,sans-serif; }

      ]]>
    </style>
  </head>
  <body>
    <x:form id="survey"
            action="http://www.mozquito.com/servlets/Echo"
            method="post">
      <div class="content">
        <h1>Online Survey</h1>
        <x:toggle id="pages">

          <x:tg id="page1">
            <h2>Welcome!</h2>
            <x:button value="go to survey"
                      onclick="toggle:pages,page2" />
          </x:tg>

          <x:tg id="page2">
            <h2>What do you use now?</h2>
            <x:button value="move on"
                      onclick="toggle:pages,page3" />
          </x:tg>

          <x:tg id="page3">
            <h2>What do you want to use in future?</h2>
            <x:button value="move on"
                      onclick="toggle:pages,page4" />
          </x:tg>

          <x:tg id="page4">
            <h2>Thanks for your help</h2>
            <x:button value="submit"
                      onclick="submit:survey" />
          </x:tg>

        </x:toggle>
      </div>
    </x:form>
  </body>

</html>
```

Once you've set up this code, check it in your browser. Your results should match ours, as shown in Figure 17.6.

Figure 17.6
Setting up page one of the survey.

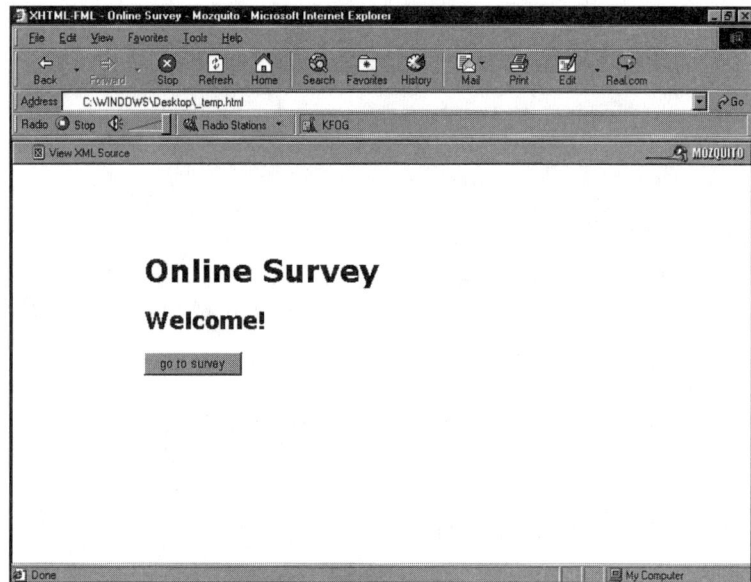

WORKING WITH TOGGLE

The code we introduced in Listing 17.6 serves as an introduction to a new concept known as the "toggle." Toggle allows you to switch between XHTML-FML elements and even whole sets of content.

The basic construction of a toggle is very simple. Below, we show an example that will let you switch between a `textinput` element and a `textoutput` element. On your browser this will show up as a `textinput` field that switches, when filled, into text, and back into a `textinout` field again as soon as you click on the text:

```
<x:form>
  <x:toggle id="example" shared="yes">
    <x:textinput id="number1"
                 onchange="toggle:example,number2" />

    <x:textoutput id="number2"
                  onclick="toggle:example,number1" />
  </x:toggle>
</x:form>
```

Note

A toggle needs an ID and encloses at least two other XHTML-FML elements.

If you want to switch from one element to another, you need an action statement, which tells the form what to do:

```
onclick="toggle:example,number1")
```

In the online survey, you use another new tag: <x:tg> (togglegroup).

This is also a toggle and can contain other XHTML-FML elements as well as all XHTML elements, and so it is the best choice for switching contents:

```
<x:tg id="page2">
  <h2>What do you use now?</h2>
  <x:button value="move on" onclick="toggle:pages,page3" />
</x:tg>
```

The enclosed button switches the toggle with the ID "pages" from one set of displayed content (enclosed in the <x:tg> tags) to another with the ID "page3."

ADDING CONTENT

The next step in our survey will be to add content. This happens similarly to the example form in the Feedback Form section. Listing 17.7 shows the code.

LISTING 17.7 ADDING CONTENT TO THE SURVEY

```
<?xml version="1.0"?>
<!DOCTYPE html PUBLIC "-//OVERFLOW//DTD XHTML-FML 1.0//EN"
"http://www.mozquito.org/dtd/xhtml-fml1.dtd">
<html xmlns="http://www.w3.org/1999/xhtml"
xmlns:x="http://www.mozquito.org/xhtml-fml">
  <head>
    <title>XHTML-FML - Online Survey</title>
    <meta name="generator" content="Mozquito Factory 1.3" />
    <style type="text/css">
      <![CDATA[

.content { position:absolute; left:140; top:90 }
h1,h2,h3,p,div { font-family:Verdana,Arial,Helvetica,sans-serif; }

      ]]>
    </style>
  </head>
  <body>
    <x:form id="survey" action="http://www.mozquito.com/servlets/Echo"
method="post">
      <div class="content">
        <h1>Online Survey</h1>
        <x:toggle id="pages">

          <x:tg id="page1">
            <h2>Welcome!</h2>
            <p>
              Welcome to ACME Messaging, Inc, the best
              messaging service on the Internet. With our
              service you can connect everywhere with E-Mail,
              Voicemail, Faxes and Phone Messages from one In-
              Box.
```

LISTING 17.7   CONTINUED

```
            </p>
            <p>
               With this survey we want to ask you about your
               communication habits and what
method would
               like to use, when it comes to communication via   the Internet.
            </p>
            <p>
               As soon as you complete this form, you'll get
               free access to our full service for
               three months as a little "thanks" for your help.
            </p>
            <x:button value="go to survey"
                      onclick="toggle:pages,page2" />
         </x:tg>

         <x:tg id="page2">
            <h2>What do you use now?</h2>
            <table cellspacing="0" cellpadding="0" border="0">
               <tr>
                  <td align="right">
                     How often do you use your phone?
                  </td>
                  <td>
                     <x:pulldown id="now_often_phone" send="yes">
                        <x:option>choose</x:option>
                        <x:option id="always"
                           value="always">always</x:option>


                        <x:option id="often"
                           value="often">often</x:option>
                        <x:option id="sometimes"
                           value="sometimes">sometimes</x:option>
                        <x:option id="never"
                           value="never">never</x:option>
                     </x:pulldown>
                  </td>
               </tr>
               <tr>
                  <td align="right">
                     How often do you use your cellular?
                  </td>
                  <td>
                     <x:pulldown id="how_often_cellular"
                        send="yes">
                        <x:option>choose</x:option>
                        <x:option id="always"
                           value="always">always</x:option>

                        <x:option id="often"
                           value="often">often</x:option>
                        <x:option id="sometimes"
                           value="sometimes">sometimes</x:option>
                        <x:option id="never"
```

LISTING 17.7   CONTINUED

```
              value="never">never</x:option>
            </x:pulldown>
          </td>
        </tr>
        <tr>
          <td align="right">
            How often do you use your e-mail?
          </td>
          <td>
            <x:pulldown id="now_often_email" send="yes">
              <x:option>choose</x:option>
              <x:option id="always"
                value="always">always</x:option>
              <x:option id="often"
                value="often">often</x:option>
              <x:option id="sometimes"
                value="sometimes">sometimes</x:option>
              <x:option id="never"
                value="never">never</x:option>
            </x:pulldown>
          </td>
        </tr>
      </table>
      <x:button value="move on"
              onclick="toggle:pages,page3" />
  </x:tg>

  <x:tg id="page3">
    <h2>How often do you want to use what in
    future?</h2>
    <table cellspacing="0" cellpadding="0" border="0">
      <tr>
        <td align="right">
          How often will you use your phone in future?
        </td>
        <td>
          <x:pulldown id="future_often_phone"
            send="yes">
            <x:option>choose</x:option>
            <x:option id="always"
              value="always">always</x:option>
            <x:option id="often"
              value="often">often</x:option>
            <x:option id="sometimes"
              value="sometimes">sometimes</x:option>
            <x:option id="never"
              value="never">never</x:option>
          </x:pulldown>
        </td>
      </tr>
      <tr>
        <td align="right">
          How often will you use your cellular in future?
        </td>
        <td>
```

LISTING 17.7   CONTINUED

```
          <x:pulldown id="future_often_cellular"
            send="yes">
            <x:option>choose</x:option>
            <x:option id="always"
              value="always">always</x:option>
            <x:option id="often"
              value="often">often</x:option>
            <x:option id="sometimes"
              value="sometimes">sometimes</x:option>
            <x:option id="never"
              value="never">never</x:option>
          </x:pulldown>
        </td>
      </tr>
      <tr>
        <td align="right">
          How often will you use your e-mail in future?
        </td>
        <td>
          <x:pulldown id="future_often_email"
            send="yes">
            <x:option>choose</x:option>
            <x:option id="always"
              value="always">always</x:option>
            <x:option id="often"
              value="often">often</x:option>
            <x:option id="sometimes"
              value="sometimes">sometimes</x:option>
            <x:option id="never"
              value="never">never</x:option>
          </x:pulldown>
        </td>
      </tr>
    </table>
    <x:button value="move on"
      onclick="toggle:pages,page4" />
  </x:tg>

  <x:tg id="page4">
    <h2>Thanks for your help</h2>
    <p>
        We want to say Thank you for helping us with this
        survey and give you three months of free access
        to our ACME services. Please answer the following questions to
receive your account.

    </p>
    <h3>Do you want your personal ACME account?</h3>
    <table cellspacing="0" cellpadding="0" border="0">
      <tr>
        <td align="right">name: </td>
        <td>
          <x:textinput id="name" send="yes"
            mandatory="yes" />
        </td>
      </tr>
      <tr>
```

PART

III

CH

17

LISTING 17.7   CONTINUED

```
                <td align="right">e-mail: </td>
                <td>
                  <x:textinput id="email" validation="strict"
                    ctype="email" send="yes" mandatory="yes" />
                </td>
              </tr>
              <tr>
                <td align="right">cellphone: </td>
                <td>
                  <x:textinput id="cellphone"
                    validation="strict" ctype="num" send="yes"
                    mandatory="yes" />
                </td>
              </tr>
            </table>
            <x:button value="submit" onclick="submit:survey" />
          </x:tg>

        </x:toggle>
      </div>
    </x:form>
  </body>
</html>
```

There you are! Your online survey sample is now complete. Try it in your browser.

ADVANCED XHTML-FML TECHNIQUES

As you've seen with the examples in this chapter, with XHTML-FML, traditional forms get a big boost. In this section, you'll get a few short but sweet examples of how you can use XHTML to get real interactivity *without* relying on a server.

REAL TIME CALCULATION

Imagine an online shop or a currency calculator. If you wanted to set up pages like this before XHTML-FML, you needed a server to process the calculations.

With XHTML-FML, you can set up calculations right on the page itself, using the following code:

- **<x:calc>**—The calc element by itself has no display. If a form control is nested inside a calc, the form controls value is the same as the calc's value.
- **term="x"**—The term attribute specifies the mathematical expression. The expression is declared by using the ID of form controls together with mathematical operands.
- **digits="x"**—The digits attribute is used to specify how the resulting value of the calc is being rounded, for example, a value of 2 rounds up the calc's value to two digits after the comma.

Here's a sample:

```
<x:textoutput id="sum" value="22.07"/> +
<x:textinput id="extra" size="5"/> =
<x:calc id="calcsum" digits="2" term="sum + extra">
  <x:textoutput id="total"/>
</x:calc>
```

Figure 17.7 shows the results.

Figure 17.7
Using XHTML-FML for client-side, real-time calculations.

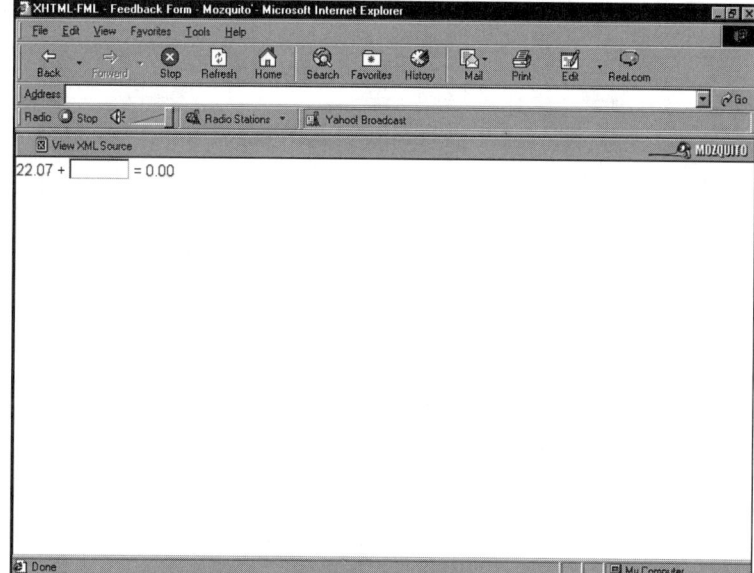

"LEARNING" PULL-DOWNS

Another benefit of XHTML-FML is something we call "open-ended lists." These lists are found in a simple pull-down, which has an item called "Please enter...." The visitor can add items just by clicking on the "Please enter..." text and typing the new item.

Listing 17.8 shows the code for an open-ended list.

LISTING 17.8   OPEN ENDED LISTS

```
<x:label for="countries">Country</x:label>:
<x:toggle id="openlist" shared="yes">
  <x:pulldown id="countries" send="yes" mandatory="yes">
    <x:option>Please choose:</x:option>
    <x:option value="Canada">Canada</x:option>
    <x:option value="Finland">Finland</x:option>
    <x:option value="France">France</x:option>
    <x:option value="Germany">Germany</x:option>
    <x:option value="India">India</x:option>
```

LISTING 17.8   CONTINUED

```
    <x:option value="Israel">Israel</x:option>
    <x:option value="Japan">Japan</x:option>
    <x:option value="The Netherlands">The
      Netherlands</x:option>
    <x:option value="United Kingdom">United Kingdom</x:option>
    <x:option value="USA">USA</x:option>
    <x:option value="Please enter..."
onclick="toggle:openlist">Other...</x:option>
  </x:pulldown>
  <x:textinput size="20" id="more"
onchange="toggle:openlist" />
</x:toggle>
```

The pulldown has become the content of the toggle element. Only the first element inside `<x:toggle>`, the pulldown, is displayed when the document is loaded into the browser.

As this example shows, you can use this feature whenever you need open-ended listings.

LABELS

The `<x:label>` tag is helpful if you want to display good-looking error messages or prompts. It displays content you want instead of the ID of the submitted element. It contains the attribute `for="x"`, which is the pointer to the tag it is addressing:

```
<x:label for="mail">Your e-mail</x:label><br/>

<x:textinput id="mail" ctype="email" validation="strict" />
```

Figure 17.5, which is the dynamic form example discussed earlier, shows labels in action.

SENDING CONTENT FROM ONE ELEMENT TO ANOTHER

Using `setval` you can send the value of an XHTML-FML element to another:

```
<x:form>
  <h1>calc</h1>
  <x:pulldown id="choose"
    onchange="setval:calc01;reset:calcsum">
    <x:option>choose</x:option>
    <x:option value="25">25</x:option>
    <x:option value="50">50</x:option>
    <x:option value="75">75</x:option>
  </x:pulldown>
  <x:textoutput id="calc01" /> +
  <x:textoutput value="13" id="extra" /> =
  <x:calc id="calcsum" digits="2" term="calc01 + extra"
    send="yes">
    <x:textoutput id="total" />
  </x:calc>
</x:form>
```

In this example, there is a pull-down that sends its value to a textoutput used in the calculation below. This functionality is useful for things like complex shopping carts, where you want to display changing content. It's also a helpful method anytime you want to share an element's value with other elements.

PUTTING ADVANCED XHTML CONCEPTS TO WORK: SHOP IN A PAGE

The last real world example in this chapter on XHTML-FML is what we call a "Shop in a Page." You let your customers browse through a series of products, each with a picture and product details, as well as the calculation of the total sum of the orders.

You'll first create a table containing one row and three cells. The first row in the table serves as the header and contains all the details for a specific product: number of orders, product name, a short description, unit price and the calculated sum.

→ For more information on working with tables, **see** Chapter 14, "Laying Out Tables Within XHTML Documents," **p. 243**.

PART

III

CH

17

In the first table cell, you use the open ended lists from the online survey in Listing 17.7. The pull-down menu restricts the visitor to numbers for the number of orders. This is why you have to add validation to the textinput field for amounts higher than 5. These are the steps for creating the table:

1. Use num as the value of ctype to restrict entries other than numbers:

```
<x:form>

  <table bgcolor="lightgrey">
    <tr>
      <td>
        <x:toggle id="openqty" shared="yes">
          <x:pulldown id="quantity" send="yes">
            <x:option value="0">0</x:option>
            <x:option value="1">1</x:option>
            <x:option value="2">2</x:option>
            <x:option value="3">3</x:option>
            <x:option value="4">4</x:option>
            <x:option value="5">5</x:option>
            <x:option value="6" onclick="toggle:openqty">+...</x:option>
          </x:pulldown>
          <x:textinput size="5" onchange="toggle:openqty" ctype="num"
validation="strict" />
        </x:toggle>
      </td>
      <td>
        White Socks
      </td>
      <td>
        A pair of white tennis socks, 85% acrylic, 15% stretch nylon.
      </td>
    </tr>
  </table>

</x:form>
```

2. Now add two more cells in the table for the calculations at the end of the row:

```
<td>
  $ <x:textoutput id="unitprice" value="1.95" send="yes" />
</td>
<td>
  $
  <x:calc id="sum" term="unitprice * quantity" send="yes">
    <x:textoutput />
  </x:calc>
</td>
```

3. Check your work in a browser. Compare it to our results in Figures 17.8 and 17.9.

Figure 17.8
With 0 products checked, the total is $0.00.

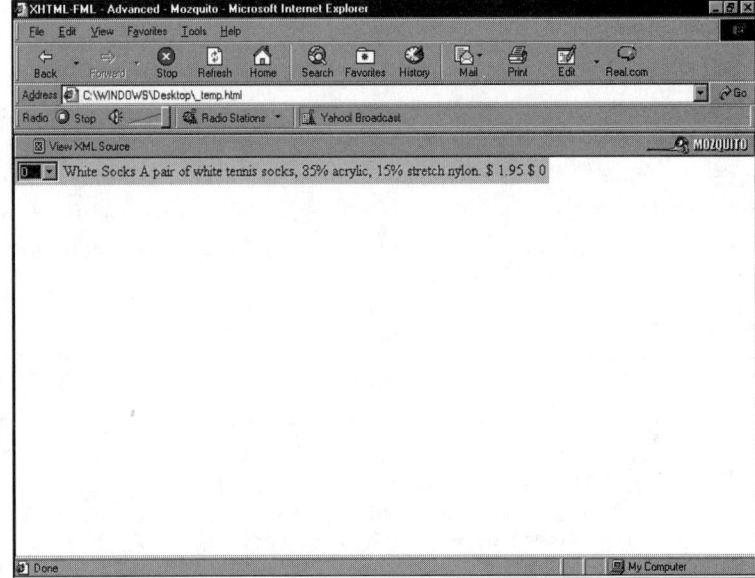

In this code, you've worked with the advanced tag, `<x:calc>`. By itself, this element has no display. Instead, the `calc` element is wrapped around other FML form elements. In this example, you see another text output field inside `calc`. The element inside will automatically inherit the calculated value of the `calc` element. The value of the `textoutput` field is always the same as the value of the `calc` element.

The value of the `calc` element changes depending on the `term` attribute. The value of `term` is any mathematical expression with numbers and the IDs of other FML form controls. The term you use in the example is

```
unitprice * quantity
```

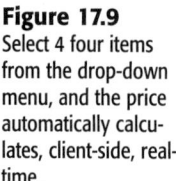

Figure 17.9
Select 4 four items from the drop-down menu, and the price automatically calculates, client-side, real-time.

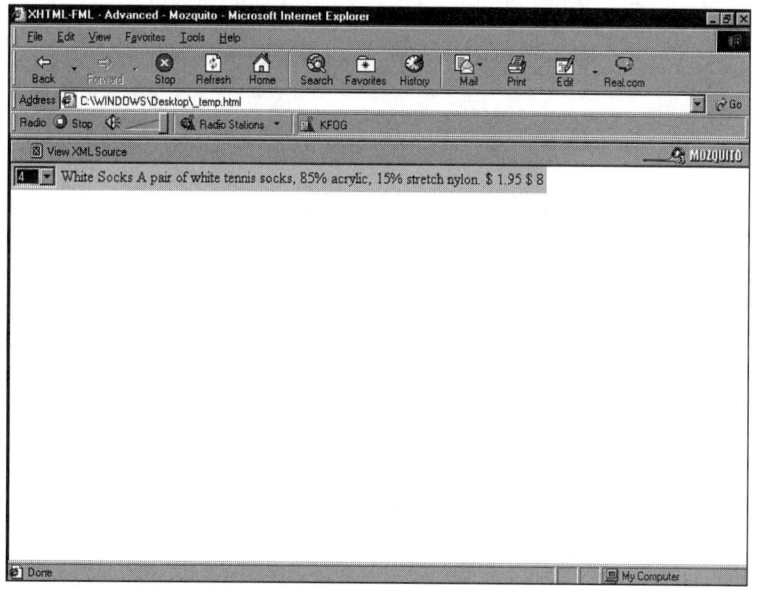

You reference the form control for quantity (the open-ended pulldown list) and the `textoutput` field, which uses the unit price as its value ($ 1.95).

If one of the two referenced form-control values is changed due to interaction with the page visitor, the `calc` element value will be updated automatically using the calculation defined in the `term` attribute.

Because the `textoutput` field inside the `calc` element immediately inherits the new `calc` element's value, we get to see the result directly on the screen.

You might have noticed that the calculated sum is always rounded up to a whole number. We can prevent this from happening by telling the `calc` element to round up by two digits to the right of the decimal point with the `digits` attribute:

```
<x:calc id="sum" term="unitprice * quantity" send="yes" digits="2">
  <x:textoutput />
</x:calc>
```

The next question is how to order more than one product. So far, only one table row for a single product order has been defined.

To order several different products, you need to add rows to the table, copying the above row and pasting it into the document source several times.

In conventional forms, this would have two problematic results:

- The source code would become very complex due to endlessly repeating code for each row.
- If we wanted to change something that affects all the products afterward (for instance adding an additional cell) we would have to go through the entire document source and add each cell individually.

If you use XHTML-FML you can avoid both. Only small parts of the code change. In your example, the text for the product name and description and the unit price change between multiple table rows. All the other tags would remain the same.

You can do this with the tag: `<x:template>`

Just define the table containing the single table row as a *template*. Then you can *insert* the template as often as you like in the source code.

Take the table out of the form container `<x:form>` and put it inside the `<x:template>` tag, instead. Then use `<x:insert>` to insert the template whereever you want within the form. Listing 17.9 is what the source now looks like in the body of the document.

LISTING 17.9   USING X:FORM AND X:INSERT

```
<x:template id="product">
  <table bgcolor="lightgrey">
    <tr>
      <td>
        <x:toggle id="openqty" shared="yes">
          <x:pulldown id="quantity" send="yes">
            <x:option value="0">0</x:option>
            <x:option value="1">1</x:option>
            <x:option value="2">2</x:option>
            <x:option value="3">3</x:option>
            <x:option value="4">4</x:option>
            <x:option value="5">5</x:option>
            <x:option value="6" onclick="toggle:openqty">+...</x:option>
          </x:pulldown>
          <x:textinput size="5" onchange="toggle:openqty" ctype="num"
validation="strict" />
        </x:toggle>
      </td>
      <td>
        White Socks
      </td>
      <td>
        A pair of white tennis socks, 85% acrylic, 15% stretch nylon.
      </td>
      <td>
        $ <x:textoutput id="unitprice" value="1.95" send="yes" />
      </td>
      <td>
        $
        <x:calc id="sum" term="unitprice * quantity" send="yes" digits="2">
          <x:textoutput />
        </x:calc>
```

LISTING 17.9   CONTINUED

```
      </td>
    </tr>
  </table>
</x:template>

<x:form>

  <x:insert id="WhiteSocks" template="product" />
  <x:insert id="RedSocks" template="product" />

</x:form>
```

Templates by themselves are not shown visually. The `insert` tag lets you insert the contents of a template at the location of the insert tag in the document source. The `template` attribute references the ID of the template you want to insert.

Something to consider: What if you want to change parts of the template before it is inserted a second time?

You can define variable parts within a template. This can be done by enclosing parts of the template within pipes, | |. The text enclosed in pipes inside a template can be changed when inserting the template.

To avoid inserting the exact same row twice, change the source to that found in Listing 17.10.

LISTING 17.10   AVOIDING MULTIPLE ROWS

```
<x:template id="product">
  <table bgcolor="lightgrey">
    <tr>
      <td>
        <x:toggle id="openqty" shared="yes">
          <x:pulldown id="quantity" send="yes">
            <x:option value="0">0</x:option>
            <x:option value="1">1</x:option>
            <x:option value="2">2</x:option>
            <x:option value="3">3</x:option>
            <x:option value="4">4</x:option>
            <x:option value="5">5</x:option>
            <x:option value="6" onclick="toggle:openqty">+...</x:option>
          </x:pulldown>
          <x:textinput size="5" onchange="toggle:openqty" ctype="num"
validation="strict" />
        </x:toggle>
      </td>
      <td>
        |title|
      </td>
      <td>
        |description|
      </td>
      <td>
        $ <x:textoutput id="unitprice" value="|price|"
send="yes" />
```

PART

III

CH

17

LISTING 17.10   CONTINUED

```
      </td>
      <td>
          $
        <x:calc id="sum" term="unitprice * quantity" send="yes" digits="2">
          <x:textoutput />
        </x:calc>
      </td>
    </tr>
  </table>
</x:template>

<x:form>

  <x:insert id="WhiteSocks" template="product">
    <x:prop name="title">White Socks</x:prop>
    <x:prop name="description">A pair of white tennis socks,
        85% acrylic, 15% stretch nylon.</x:prop>
    <x:prop name="price">1.95</x:prop>
  </x:insert>
  <x:insert id="RedSocks" template="product">
    <x:prop name="title">Red Socks</x:prop>
    <x:prop name="description">A pair of red socks, 70% nylon, 30%
cotton.</x:prop>
    <x:prop name="price">2.49</x:prop>
  </x:insert>

</x:form>
```

Check your work in the browser, and you'll now see that the two rows are different (see Figure 17.10).

Figure 17.10
Adding cells to Shop in a Page

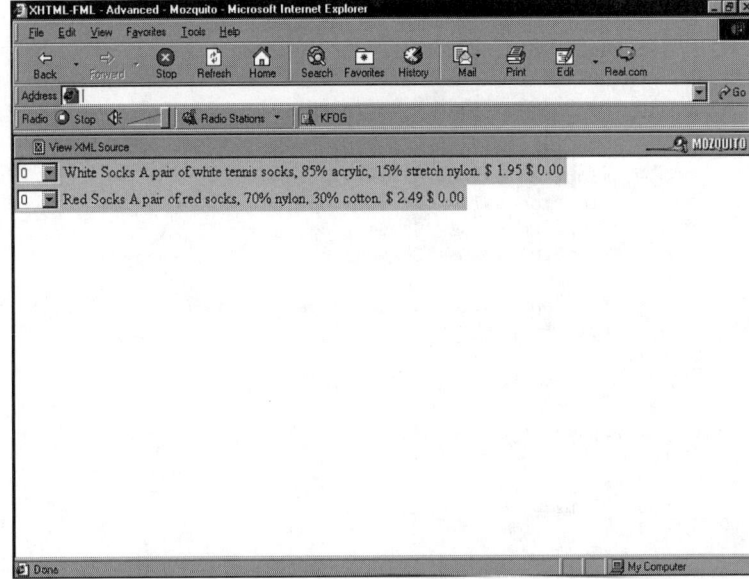

By enclosing title, description and price in the template source with pipes, you can use the prop tag inside the insert element to replace these space holders with specific content. Now reference the space holders by using the pipe-enclosed text as the value of the prop tag name attribute. The content of the prop element replaces the text enclosed by pipes. Adding more products is now very simple: Just add more inserts.

Displaying the total sum of the order at the bottom of the table is your next step. Leave the template aside for now and focus on the form container <x:form>:

```
<x:form>

  <x:insert id="WhiteSocks" template="product">
    <x:prop name="title">White Socks</x:prop>
    <x:prop name="description">A pair of white tennis socks, 85% acrylic, 15%
stretch
nylon.</x:prop>
    <x:prop name="price">1.95</x:prop>
  </x:insert>
  <x:insert id="RedSocks" template="product">
    <x:prop name="title">Red Socks</x:prop>
    <x:prop name="description">A pair of red socks, 70% nylon, 30%
cotton.</x:prop>
    <x:prop name="price">2.49</x:prop>
  </x:insert>

  <p>Total: $
    <x:calc id="total" term="WhiteSocks.sum + RedSocks.sum" digits="2" send="yes">
      <x:textoutput />
    </x:calc>
  </p>

</x:form>
```

Now you use the calc element the same way you did for multiplying the number of a single product ordered by the unit price, except for one difference: The term now uses names that are the combination of two IDs separated by a dot. In XML, all IDs must be unique. If the templates are copied without automatically changing all the element IDs in the template on insertion, there would be no way to address these tags, because they would have duplicate names.

The IDs in the template are prefixed with the ID of the specific insert tag. The first row you insert gets the ID prefix WhiteSocks, the ID of the insert tag. If you recall, you gave the calc element, which multiplies the number of a single product ordered by the unit price, the ID sum. The ID is then WhiteSocks.sum.

When products are ordered from the Shop in a Page, not only the price of each product but also the total sum of all the products is now calculated immediately.

Instead of showing all the products on one screen page, you can use XHTML-FML to create a slideshow, showing each product one at a time. Just use the <x:toggle> tag in FML to toggle between two (or more) products. You have already used toggle to create open-ended lists, but now use it for client-side persistency throughout a series of screen pages. Create client-side persistency simply by defining multiple screen pages inside a single XHTML-FML document. Page visitors can quickly and easily flip from one product page to the next, because all the information is already on the browser. Normally, this would only be possible with a combination of frames, cookies, and script.

Let's make a few changes inside <x:form> to the source of the Shop in a Page (see Listing 17.11).

LISTING 17.11   TOGGLING BETWEEN PRODUCTS

```
<x:form>

  <div align="center">

    <x:toggle id="show">
      <x:insert id="WhiteSocks" template="product">
        <x:prop name="title">White Socks</x:prop>
        <x:prop name="description">A pair of white tennis socks, 85% acrylic, 15%
stretch nylon.</x:prop>
        <x:prop name="price">1.95</x:prop>
      </x:insert>
      <x:insert id="RedSocks" template="product">
        <x:prop name="title">Red Socks</x:prop>
        <x:prop name="description">A pair of red socks, 70% nylon, 30%
cotton.</x:prop>
        <x:prop name="price">2.49</x:prop>
      </x:insert>
    </x:toggle><br />

    <p>Total: $
      <x:calc id="total" term="WhiteSocks.sum + RedSocks.sum" digits="2"
send="yes">
        <x:textoutput />
      </x:calc>
    </p>

    <x:button value="Back" onclick="toggle:show,-" />
    <x:button value="Next" onclick="toggle:show,+" />

  </div>
</x:form>
```

You nested both inserts inside a toggle element with the ID, and added two buttons.

For better layout, you can also add a div element to center everything on the screen. Although you don't change much in the source, it makes a huge difference in the browser for each page, as follows:

- **The first page**—When the document is loaded onto the browser, only the first product is shown, because the first element inside the toggle element is always shown first. This is the insert tag inserting the template you defined for a single product. By clicking the Next button, we watch the second product dynamically appear.

- **The second page**—The area for calculating the total as well as the buttons reappear at the same position on the next page because they are defined outside of the `toggle` element in the document source. Mozquito remembers all the field values not shown on the screen, so you can still calculate the total sum of the products, although you only see one product at a time.

- **The Back button**—This brings you back to the first product, the white socks. Use the action statement `toggle:show` as the value of the `onclick` event handler in the `button` element. By putting a comma and a minus sign after the ID of the toggle element, you toggle backward through the elements inside the toggle. By using a plus sign, you move forward.

Let's add a heading and an image to each product. Because you already inserted the template containing the table with the product information, you simply need to add a heading and an image before the table in the template. You also define the value of the `src` attribute of the image as a property, so you can then specify the filename with an additional `<prop>` tag when inserting the template. Listing 17.12 shows the minor changes to the source.

LISTING 17.12   ADDING A HEADING AND AN IMAGE FOR EACH PRODUCT

```
<x:template id="product">
  <h1>|title|</h1>
  <x:img src="images/|image|" width="340" height="206" alt="|title|" preload="yes"
/>
  <table bgcolor="lightgrey">
    <tr>
      <td>
        <x:toggle id="openqty" shared="yes">
          <x:pulldown id="quantity" send="yes">
            <x:option value="0">0</x:option>
            <x:option value="1">1</x:option>
            <x:option value="2">2</x:option>
            <x:option value="3">3</x:option>
            <x:option value="4">4</x:option>
            <x:option value="5">5</x:option>
            <x:option value="6" onclick="toggle:openqty">+...</x:option>
          </x:pulldown>
          <x:textinput size="5" onchange="toggle:openqty" ctype="num"
validation="strict" />
        </x:toggle>
      </td>
      <td>
        |title|
      </td>
      <td>
        |description|
      </td>
      <td>
        $ <x:textoutput id="unitprice" value="|price|" send="yes" />
      </td>
      <td>
        $
```

Listing 17.12 Continued

```
        <x:calc id="sum" term="unitprice * quantity" digits="2" send="yes">
          <x:textoutput />
        </x:calc>
      </td>
    </tr>
  </table>
</x:template>

<x:form>

  <div align="center">

    <x:toggle id="show">
      <x:insert id="WhiteSocks" template="product">
        <x:prop name="title">White Socks</x:prop>
        <x:prop name="description">A pair of white tennis socks, 85% acrylic,
          15% stretch nylon.</x:prop>
        <x:prop name="price">1.95</x:prop>
        <x:prop name="image">white.jpg</x:prop>
      </x:insert>
      <x:insert id="RedSocks" template="product">
        <x:prop name="title">Red Socks</x:prop>
        <x:prop name="description">A pair of red socks, 70% nylon, 30%
cotton.</x:prop>
        <x:prop name="price">2.49</x:prop>
        <x:prop name="image">red.jpg</x:prop>
      </x:insert>
    </x:toggle><br />

    <x:button value="Back" onclick="toggle:show,-" />
    <x:button value="Next" onclick="toggle:show,+" />

    <p>Total: $
      <x:calc id="total" term="WhiteSocks.sum + RedSocks.sum" digits="2"
send="yes">
        <x:textoutput />
      </x:calc>
    </p>

  </div>

</x:form>
```

We also re-use the title property as the content of the heading as well as the value of the alt attribute of the image. If you check the page in the browser, you'll find what we did in Figure 17.11.

Figure 17.11
Adding headers and images.

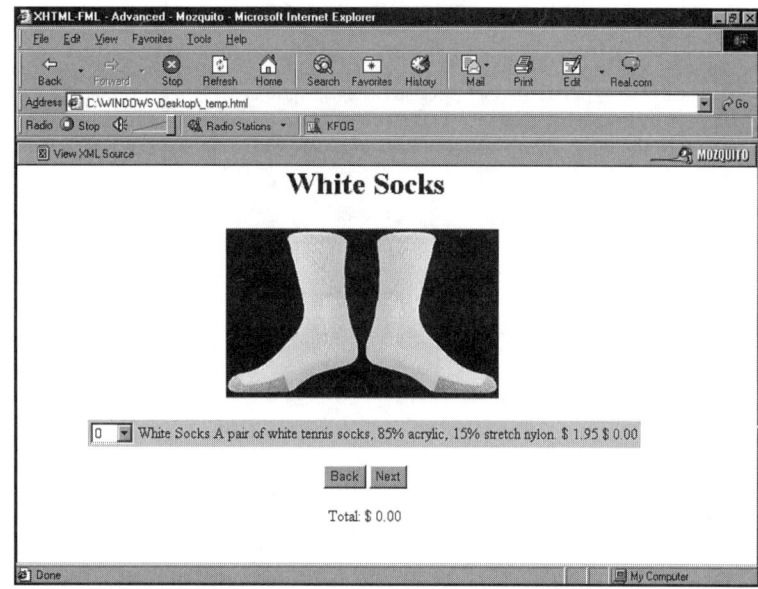

Flipping to the next page, you immediately see the next image with the filename red.jpg, showing red socks. Normally, this second image would be loaded from the server the moment you toggled to the next page. But by adding preload="yes" to the FML image tag <x:img>, you tell your XHTML-FML document to preload all the images into the document at the initial loading of the site. This ensures that visitors receive a document containing multiple pages and as well as all the images all at once, so they can browse the document offline. The preload attribute is the primary difference between the FML image tag <x:img> and the XHTML image tag <img>.

Now add an address form to your product catalog. The address form can be extended with additional fields for credit card information. Here you can do this by creating a third screen page containing the address form with the credit card details. Just add the address form after the two insert elements inside the toggle.

Because the address form contains more than one element, you'll need to group these elements into a single toggle group. This will ensure that all the elements in the address form appear at the same time, not just one at a time. The additions to the toggle section in the source can be found in Listing 17.13.

LISTING 17.13   ADDING AN ADDRESS FORM

```
<x:toggle id="show">
  <x:insert id="WhiteSocks" template="product">
    <x:prop name="title">White Socks</x:prop>
    <x:prop name="description">A pair of white tennis socks, 85% acrylic, 15%
stretch
nylon.</x:prop>
    <x:prop name="price">1.95</x:prop>
    <x:prop name="image">white.jpg</x:prop>
  </x:insert>
  <x:insert id="RedSocks" template="product">
    <x:prop name="title">Red Socks</x:prop>
    <x:prop name="description">A pair of red socks, 70% nylon, 30%
cotton.</x:prop>
    <x:prop name="price">2.49</x:prop>
    <x:prop name="image">red.jpg</x:prop>
  </x:insert>
  <x:tg>
    <table>
      <tr>
        <td><x:label for="name">Your name</x:label>:</td>
        <td><x:textinput size="30" id="name" send="yes" mandatory="yes" /></td>
      </tr>
      <tr>
        <td><x:label for="email">Your valid e-mail address</x:label>:</td>
        <td><x:textinput id="email" size="30" ctype="email" validation="strict"
send="yes"
              mandatory="yes" #47;></td>
      </tr>
      <tr>
        <td><x:label for="countries">Country</x:label>:</td>
        <td>
          <x:toggle id="openlist" shared="yes">
            <x:pulldown id="countries" send="yes" mandatory="yes">
              <x:option>Please choose:</x:option>
              <x:option value="Canada">Canada</x:option>
              <x:option value="Finland">Finland</x:option>
              <x:option value="France">France</x:option>
              <x:option value="Germany">Germany</x:option>
              <x:option value="India">India</x:option>
              <x:option value="Israel">Israel</x:option>
              <x:option value="Japan">Japan</x:option>
              <x:option value="The Netherlands">The Netherlands</x:option>
              <x:option value="United Kingdom">United Kingdom</x:option>
              <x:option value="USA">USA</x:option>
              <x:option value="Please enter..."
onclick="toggle:openlist">Other...</x:option>
            </x:pulldown>
            <x:textinput size="20" id="more" onchange="toggle:openlist" />
          </x:toggle>
        </td>
      </tr>
      <tr>
        <td><x:label for="state">State / Province</x:label>:</td>
        <td><x:textinput size="30" id="state" mandatory="yes" send="yes"/></td>
      </tr>
```

LISTING 17.13   CONTINUED

```
        <tr>
          <td><x:label for="postal-code">ZIP / Postal code</x:label>:</td>
          <td><x:textinput size="30" id="postal-code" mandatory="yes" send="yes"
/></td>
        </tr>
        <tr>
          <td><x:label for="city">City</x:label>:</td>
          <td><x:textinput size="30" id="city" mandatory="yes" send="yes" /></td>
        </tr>
        <tr>
          <td><x:label for="address">Street / Address</x:label>:</td>
          <td><x:textarea id="address" mandatory="yes" send="yes" rows="3"
cols="30" /></td>
        </tr>
      </table>

  </x:tg>
</x:toggle><br />
```

The toggle group element `<x:tg>` can hold any number of tags, but because these tags are now a group, they will be shown at the same time on the screen.

Your Shop in a Page is now ready for action! And, as you can see from these examples, XHTML-FML can indeed make a Web page more than a Web page. The boring static forms of the past can now be powerful tools for interacting with your page visitors, thanks to the extensibility of XHTML. Try XHTML-FML out yourself and see what kind of difference it can make in the quality of your site.

Note

Mozquito keeps up-to-date tutorials and software on their Web site. Your mission is to visit and try out any of the tutorials that best suit your needs and curiosity.

ADDING STYLE AND SCRIPTING

CHAPTER **18**

CASCADING STYLE SHEETS AND XHTML

In this chapter

STYLE SHEETS AND XHTML

This chapter will introduce you to style sheets, and teach you how to implement them in your pages. All of the information in this chapter is as applicable to HTML as it is to XHTML. However, there are a few important things to bear in mind when it comes to using CSS with XHTML:

- Because XML describes CSS as CDATA (content data), style in XML and XHTML are supposed to be marked up using the CDATA element. However, because most current HTML browsers will choke on the CDATA element, your pages might be rendered unreadable, or displayed in odd ways:

```
<style type="text/css">
<!--
/* <![CDATA[ */

BODY
{
color: white;
background-color:black;
}

/* ]]> */ -->
</style>
```

So, it's important to remember this method, but set it aside unless you're working on pages that will be rendered in XML-compliant browsers only.

- Although you can use any of the style methods (linked, embedded, or inline) in XHTML 1.0 transitional documents, it is *highly recommended* that you begin to use linked style sheets only, avoiding any rendering problems and truly living up to the "separate document formatting from presentation" concept inherent to HTML 4.0 and XHTML 1.0.

- In a strict XHTML 1.0 document, use a linked document.

Tip from

Be sure to test your documents. This is especially true when you use style, as you'll want to be sure you get as consistent results as possible.

STYLE SHEET BASICS

Cascading style sheets (CSS) is the broad term used to refer to several methods of applying style elements to XHTML pages. In this case, think of a style as any kind of design element, including typeface, background, text, link colors, margin controls, and placement of objects on a page.

Why should you use style sheets if markup can do at least some of this work by itself? The developers of HTML originally intended for it to be only a formatting language, responsible for the basic layout of a page, including body, headers, paragraphs, and a few specific items such as bulleted lists. Web designers and browser developers are the ones who have pushed and pulled at HTML to make it accommodate aspects of style, and XHTML has inherited this legacy.

To gain some separation between HTML's original function as a formatting tool but still offer a powerful addition to the designer's toolbox in terms of style, cascading style sheets were developed. In fact, as of the HTML 4.0 standard, many of the style-oriented tags (such as the font tag) were deprecated (considered undesirable) in favor of CSS.

Caution

Web browsers don't fully support CSS. Although Internet Explorer introduced CSS in the Windows 3.0 browser version, it had some bugs with the implementation. Netscape, in a rush to meet the competition, built Navigator 4.0 to be CSS compliant. But the compliance is very incomplete at best. Add to this the fact that many Web visitors do not keep up-to-date with the latest and greatest browsers, and the reality of following XHTML's strict standard is still to be carefully considered.

SEPARATING PRESENTATION FROM STRUCTURE

Until cascading style sheets entered the picture, HTML was missing an important element. Although some control of style with headers and font tags is possible, these techniques are limited because of the limitations of HTML. In many ways, style sheets provide a long-awaited solution for many of HTML's restrictions. The results are better font control, color management, margin control, and even the addition of special effects such as text shadowing. Another powerful benefit is the ability to control multiple pages within a site from a single sheet, and use multiple types of style sheets in a sequence for very precise control.

Note

You can find a significant source for information on style sheets at the World Wide Web Consortium's site at `http://www.w3.org/Style/`.

The logic and power of style sheets outweigh the current problems with browser support, and for this reason, designers clearly must learn the concepts and techniques and be at the ready to employ them where necessary.

UNDERSTANDING THE CASCADE

One of the powers of style sheets is that there is a hierarchy of elements. For example, you can combine inline, embedded and linked styles, or any number of individual types of style sheets, for maximum control. Say you have a large site that you're controlling with a single style sheet. However, you have a page on which you want to alter some of the styles. No problem! You can simply place the modified style as an embedded sheet within the individual page. The browser will first look for the embedded style and apply that information. Whatever isn't covered in the embedded sheet the browser will seek out in the linked sheet.

PART
IV

CH
18

You also can override both styles by adding an inline style. When all three forms are in place, the style-sheet–compliant browser looks for that style first, then the embedded style, and then the linked sheet; it reads the information in that order.

I've created a page with a link, an embedded sheet, and some inline styles, as you can see in Listing 18.1.

LISTING 18.1 LINKED, EMBEDDED, AND INLINE STYLES APPLIED TO THE SAME PAGE

```
<?xml version="1.0"?>
<!DOCTYPE html PUBLIC "-//W3C//DTD XHTML 1.0 Transitional//EN"
"http://www.w3.org/TR/xhtml1/DTD/xhtml1-transitional.dtd">
<html xmlns="http://www.w3.org/1999/xhtml">
<head>
<title>Combination Style Sheet Example</title>

<link rel=stylesheet href="mystyle_1.css" type="text/css" />

<style>

<!--

p {
font: 13pt verdana;
}

-->

</style>
</head>

<body>

<h1 style="font-family: garamond; font-size: 22pt;">
A Midsummer Night's Dream</h1>

Act I Scene I<br />

<p>Either to die the death or to abjure <br />
For ever the society of men. <br />
Therefore, fair <a href="hermia.html">Hermia</a>,

question your desires; <br />
Know of your youth, examine well your blood, <br />
Whether, if you yield not to your father's choice, <br />
You can endure the livery of a nun, <br />
For aye to be in shady cloister mew'd, <br />
To live a barren sister all your life, <br />
Chanting faint hymns to the cold fruitless moon. <br />
Thrice-blessed they that master so their blood, <br />
To undergo such maiden <a href="pilgrim.html">pilgrimage</a>; <br />

But earthlier happy is the rose distill'd, <br />
Than that which withering on the virgin thorn <br />
Grows, lives and dies in single blessedness.
```

LISTING 18.1   CONTINUED

```
</p>

<body>
</html>
```

In Figure 18.1, you can see the concept of cascade in action—with the inline style overpowering the embedded style, and so forth. In a sense, the linked sheet becomes the default.

Figure 18.1
In this case, I combined style methods to achieve the page's look and feel.

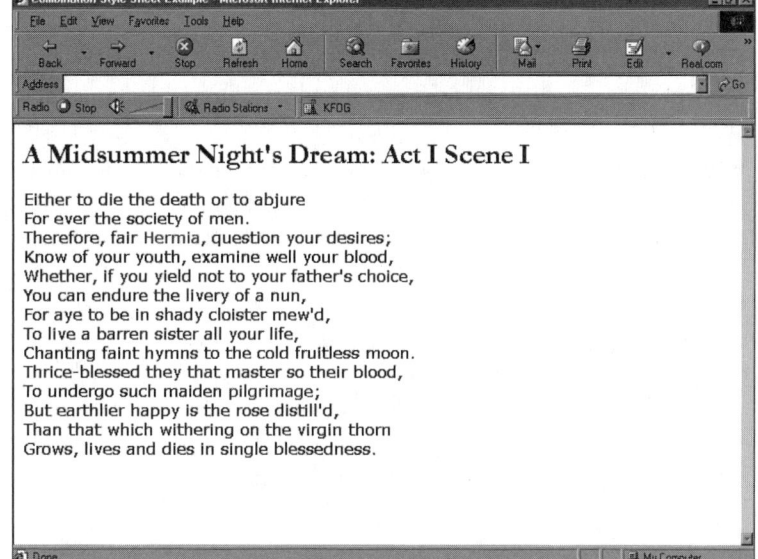

Tip from
molly

Whenever possible, streamline the style sheets in a cascade. If you can accomplish the same results using a single linked sheet or an embedded sheet, do so. Use the cascade concept whenever you need to override a linked sheet at specific points in the style relationship, such as linked to embedded to inline, or linked to inline, embedded to inline and so forth.

Another example of a cascade concept within CSS is the use of multiple external sheets in the same document:

```
<head>
<link rel="stylesheet" type="text/css" href="molly1.css" />
<link rel="stylesheet" type="text/css" href="molly2.css" />
<link rel="stylesheet" type="text/css" href="molly3.css" />
</head>
```

The *last* style sheet in the list will override what isn't in the middle one, and the middle one will override what isn't in the first one. This is another example of cascade.

STYLE SHEET SYNTAX

If you recall the discussion about XHTML syntax, sentences require specific elements, as do mathematical equations. Style sheets are similar to both in that if their syntax does not follow a specified order, they might not function properly.

→ For a refresher on XHTML syntax, **see** Chapter 5, "Defining XHTML Syntax," **p. 73**.

Whatever method you choose to deliver your style to XHTML documents, the syntax is going to be similar in all cases. Style sheets, like sentences, are made up of very specific parts. These parts include the following:

- **Selectors**—Selectors represent the elements that receive the properties and values you assign. Selectors are usually standard XHTML elements, such as a header, h1, or a paragraph, p. Style sheets allow for modified selectors, including classes, which are discussed later in the chapter.

- **Properties**—A property describes the appearance of the elements corresponding to a selector. For example, if you have a paragraph, p, as a selector, properties you include will define that selector. Margins, fonts, and backgrounds are some property concepts. Style sheets contain many properties, and you can use a variety of properties to define a selector.

- **Values**—Values describe properties. Say you have a level one header, h1, as your selector, and you've included a type family, type-family, as a property. The face that you actually define is the value of that property.

Properties and values combined make up a *declaration*. A selector and a declaration make up a *rule*, as shown here:

```
h1 {
type-family: garamond, times, serif;
}
```

Note that the curly brackets are used to contain the declaration. This syntax is only true for embedded or linked styles. Whenever using inline style, you use quotations to contain your declaration. Selectors aren't defined in this case, as the application of the declaration is inherent to the tag to which the style is being applied:

```
<h1 style="type-family: garamond, times, serif;">This text will
be defined by the declaration</h1>
```

Any time you have multiple declarations, you'll end each individual declaration with a semicolon (;). In the case of a single declaration, it's not necessary to use the semicolon.

Tip from

Even though a semicolon is unnecessary when ending a single style declaration, many working developers, WYSIWYG programs, and XHTML editors use the semicolon anyway. This can reduce errors, and I use the final semicolon myself when coding style sheets.

STYLE SHEET METHODS

Style can be delivered to an XHTML document by a variety of methods.

You can use these three types of style sheets:

- **Inline**—This method allows you to take any XHTML tag and add a style to it. Using the inline method gives you maximum control over any aspect of a Web page. Say you want to control the look and feel of a specific paragraph. You could simply add a `style="x"` attribute to the paragraph tag, and the browser would display that paragraph using the style values you added to the code.
- **Embedded**—Embedding allows for control of a full page of XHTML. Using the `<style>` tag, which you place within the `<head>` section of an XHTML page, you can insert detailed style attributes to be applied to the entire page.
- **Linked**—Also referred to as an "external" style sheet, a linked style sheet provides a powerful way for you to create master styles that you can apply to an entire site. You create a main style sheet document using the `.css` extension. This document contains the styles you want a single page or even thousands of pages to adopt. Any page that links to this document takes on the styles called for in that document.

In the following examples, you'll see a variety of syntaxes that will look unfamiliar if you are new to style sheets. Bear with me through these examples. You first need to understand the methods used to apply style. Then I'll provide a closer look at style sheet syntax itself. Finally, you'll have a chance to go through some exercises that will help you put both the method and the syntax to work.

PART

IV

CH

18

INLINE STYLE

You can add inline style to any XHTML element that makes sense. Such tags include paragraphs, headers, horizontal rules, anchors, and table cells. Each is a logical candidate for inline style. Here's a standard paragraph:

```
<p>The text in this paragraph will display as text using the
default font.</p>
```

The following example uses the paragraph tag along with the `style` attribute to achieve inline style:

```
<p style="font: 13pt verdana">The text in this paragraph will display as 13 point
text using the
verdana font.</p>
```

Figure 18.2 shows two paragraphs, one with the standard default typeface for a Windows machine (Times) and one with the Verdana typeface applied.

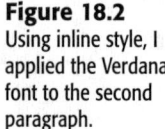

Figure 18.2
Using inline style, I applied the Verdana font to the second paragraph.

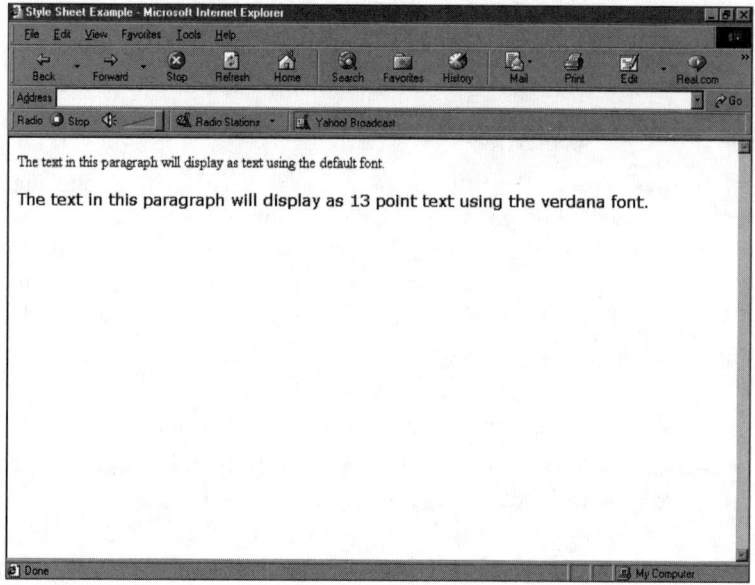

Two elements can help you apply inline style to sections of a page. These elements are particularly useful not only for style sheets, but also later when you combine style sheets with dynamic events through DHTML. They are the division, or div element, and the span element.

→ To read more about the div element, **see** Chapter 11, "Aligning Text Using XHTML," **p. 177**.

div and span specify a defined range of text, so everything in between them adopts the style you want to use. The primary difference between div and span is that div is a block level element, meaning it can contain all other XHTML elements, whereas span can only be used inline. For example you can align a table with div, but you couldn't do the same with span. Another major difference is that div forces a line break after the division, whereas span does not. For this reason, span is especially useful within sentences or paragraphs, and div is most appropriate when used to define larger sections of text, including paragraphs, headings, lists, and nested elements.

Tip from
molly

Use span to modify the style of any portion of text shorter than a paragraph.

The following is an example of the division element at work:

```
<div style="font-family: garamond; font-size: 14pt;">

<p>All of the text within this section is 14 point Garamond.</p>
</div>
```

This example shows the <span> tag:

```
<p><span style="color: #999999">This text appears in the color gray, with no line
break after the closing span tag </span> and the rest of the text.</p>
```

Figure 18.3 shows the combined results of the div and span elements with style attributes applied.

Figure 18.3
Adding inline style to a paragraph with the div and span tags gives you precise control over fonts and colors, as seen in this example.

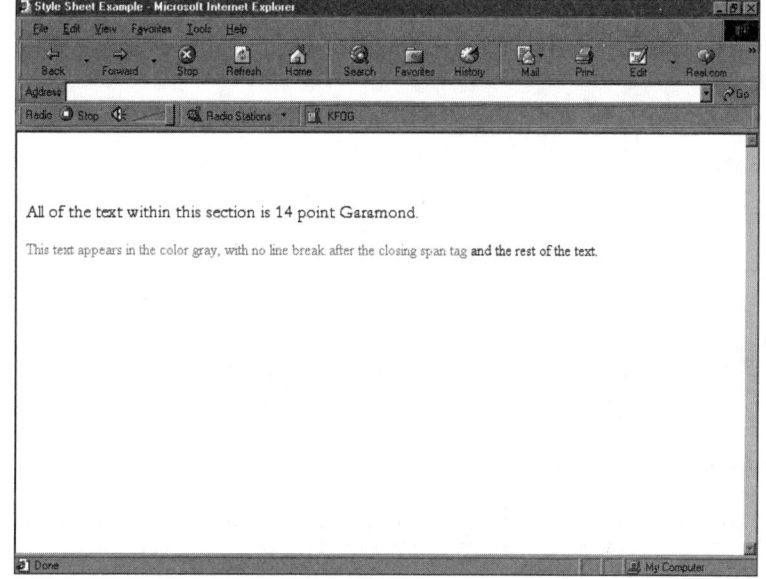

EMBEDDED STYLE

Embedded styles use the style element, which you place within the head section of an HTML document, as shown in Listing 18.2.

LISTING 18.2   USING THE style ELEMENT

```
<?xml version="1.0"?>
<!DOCTYPE html pUBLIC "-//W3C//DTD XHTML 1.0 Transitional//EN"
"http://www.w3.org/TR/xhtml1/DTD/xhtml1-transitional.dtd">
<html xmlns="http://www.w3.org/1999/xhtml">
<head>
<title>Embedded Style Sheet Example I</title>

<style>

<!--

body {
background: #FFFFFF;
color: #000000;
}
h1 {
```

LISTING 18.2   CONTINUED

```
font: 14pt verdana; color: #CCCCCC;
}
p {
font: 13pt times;
}
a {
color: #FF0000; text-decoration: none;
}

-->

</style>
</head>
<body>

<h1>a Midsummer Night's Dream: Act I Scene I</h1>

Either to die the death or to abjure <br />
For ever the society of men. <br />
Therefore, fair <a href="hermia.html">Hermia</a>, question your desires; <br />
Know of your youth, examine well your blood, <br />
Whether, if you yield not to your father's choice, <br />
You can endure the livery of a nun, <br />
For aye to be in shady cloister mew'd, <br />
To live a barren sister all your life, <br />
Chanting faint hymns to the cold fruitless moon. <br />
Thrice-blessed they that master so their blood, <br />
To undergo such maiden <a href="pilgrim.html">pilgrimage</a>; <br />


But earthlier happy is the rose distill'd, <br />
Than that which withering on the virgin thorn <br />
Grows, lives and dies in single blessedness.

</body>
</html>
```

Tip from molly

To ensure that your embedded style sheet is hidden from older browsers, you can place comment tags such as `<!-- style sheet goes here -->` around the sheet. Begin the comment tag underneath the `<style>` tag and end the comment immediately before the `</style>` tag.

As you can tell from the preceding example, an XHTML document using a style sheet begins to look quite a bit different from older HTML standards, but following the logic is not difficult. In this case, the page's body calls for a background color, a text color, an h1 font style, a paragraph style, and a link style.

Figure 18.4 shows the results of the embedded style sheet in Listing 18.2.

Figure 18.4
In this case, I used embedded style to add color and type styles to the page.

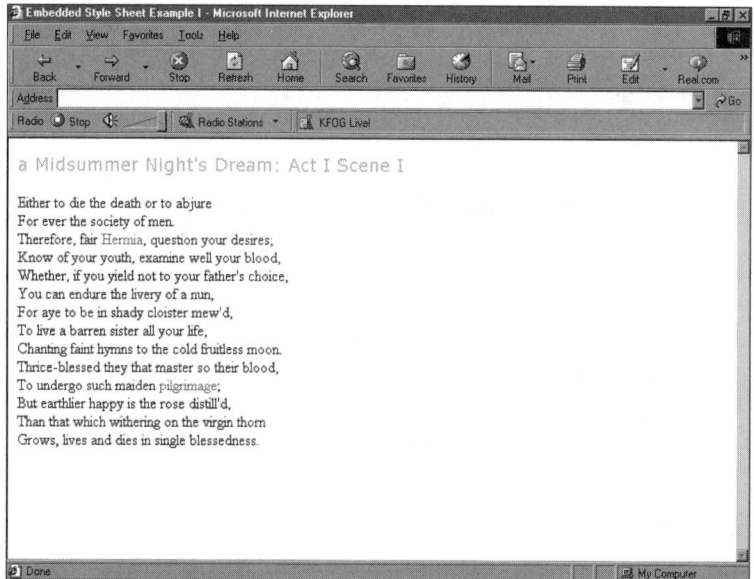

Notice how the level one heading, h1, calls for a font using the font's name as well as a literal point size. This figure is a prime example of one reason why cascading style sheets are so powerful: Not only can you choose to control sizing in points, but you also can use pixels (px), percentages (75%), and centimeters (cm).

Another interesting aspect of this style sheet includes the difference in fonts as defined by the header and paragraph style; they're different in color and face. With style sheets, the days of having an XHTML page littered with font tags are limited. Style is handled in a nice, compact fashion.

The <a> (anchor) tag in the style sheet shows yet another handy piece of syntax. The text-decoration: none string forces underlining to be removed from links, allowing for clean, attractive design results.

LINKED STYLE SHEETS

Linked style sheets, also called *external* style sheets, extend the form of embedded style. Using the same code contained within the style element as you saw in the embedded sample, you can place this information in a separate document. You then can save the document with the file extension .css. You should be sure that this document is either in the root directory with the XHTML files that you intend to have it affect or that you code the link properly when linking to the sheet.

→ To read more about directory structure and linking, **see** Chapter 8, "Managing XHTML Documents Locally," **p. 119**, and Chapter 12, "Linking Pages with Standard Links," **p. 199**.

PART
IV

CH
18

The power of linked style is that you can link all the pages in a site that you want to have influenced by the style to this single sheet. You can link only one page, or one thousand pages to a single style sheet.

Listing 18.3 shows the syntax for a linked, or external, style sheet.

LISTING 18.3 A LINKED STYLE SHEET

```
body {
background: #000000;
color: #FFFFCC;
}
h1 {
font: 14pt Garamond; color: #CCCCCC;
}
p {
font: 13pt arial;
}
a {
color: #FF0000; text-decoration: none;
}
```

Caution

Style sheets should not contain any HTML tags, simply the selectors, properties, and values.

Now, you can take this style sheet and step through the process of making it into an actively linked external sheet:

1. Make sure that you have a standard XHTML page that has been coded and saved to a directory. Here's my page, saved to a directory as linked_style1.html:

```
<?xml version="1.0"?>
<!DOCTYPE html PUBLIC "-//W3C//DTD Xhtml 1.0 Transitional//EN"
"http://www.w3.org/TR/xhtml1/DTD/xhtml1-transitional.dtd">
<html xmlns="http://www.w3.org/1999/xhtml">
<head>
<title>Linked Style Sheet Example</title>

</head>
<body>

<h1>A Midsummer Night's Dream: Act I Scene I</h1>

Either to die the death or to abjure <br />
For ever the society of men. <br />
Therefore, fair <a href="hermia.html">Hermia</a>, question your desires;

<br />
Know of your youth, examine well your blood, <br />
Whether, if you yield not to your father's choice, <br />
You can endure the livery of a nun, <br />
For aye to be in shady cloister mew'd, <br />
To live a barren sister all your life, <br />
Chanting faint hymns to the cold fruitless moon. <br />
```

```
Thrice-blessed they that master so their blood, <br />
To undergo such maiden <a HREF="pilgrim.html">pilgrimage</a>; <br />


But earthlier happy is the rose distill'd, <br />
Than that which withering on the virgin thorn <br />
Grows, lives and dies in single blessedness.

</body>
</html>
```

2. Open your text or XHTML editor, and type the code shown in Listing 18.3.

3. Save the file as `mystyle_1.css`.

4. place this file in the directory where the `linked_style1.html` file resides.

5. Reopen `linked_style1.html`.

6. Add the following link element in the `head` section of the XHTML document:

```
<?xml version="1.0"?>
<!DOCTYPE html PUBLIC "-//W3C//DTD Xhtml 1.0 Transitional//EN"
"http://www.w3.org/TR/xhtml1/DTD/xhtml1-transitional.dtd">
<html xmlns="http://www.w3.org/1999/xhtml">
<head>
<title>Linked Style Sheet Example</title>
<link rel=stylesheet href="mystyle_1.css" type="text/css" />

</head>
<body>

<h1>A Midsummer Night's Dream: Act I Scene I</h1>

Either to die the death or to abjure <br />
For ever the society of men. <br />
Therefore, fair <a href="hermia.html">Hermia</a>, question your desires;

<br />
Know of your youth, examine well your blood, <br />
Whether, if you yield not to your father's choice, <br />
You can endure the livery of a nun, <br />
For aye to be in shady cloister mew'd, <br />
To live a barren sister all your life, <br />
Chanting faint hymns to the cold fruitless moon. <br />
Thrice-blessed they that master so their blood, <br />
To undergo such maiden <a href="pilgrim.html">pilgrimage</a>; <br />


But earthlier happy is the rose distill'd, <br />
Than that which withering on the virgin thorn <br />
Grows, lives and dies in single blessedness.

</body>
</html>
```

7. Save the file.

8. View the file in a style-sheet–compliant browser. It should match the results shown in Figure 18.5.

PART

IV

CH

18

Figure 18.5
Any page containing
this link adopts the
styles defined in
mystyle_1.css.

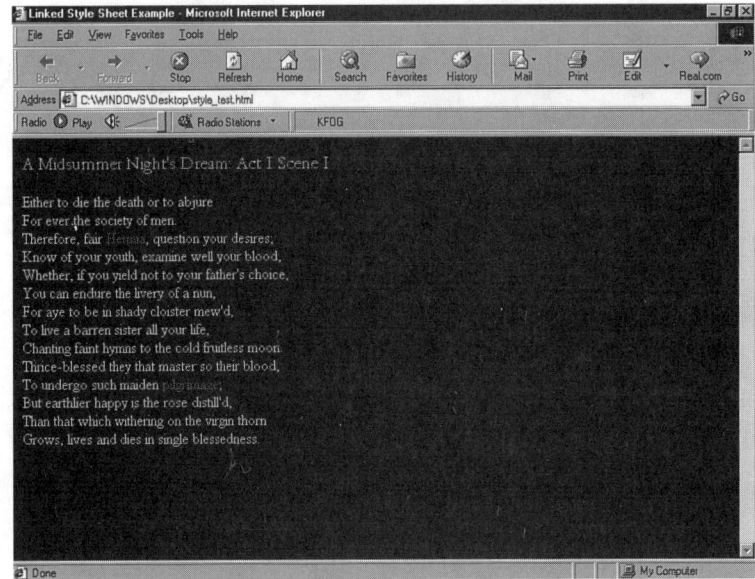

If you want to have 1,000 XHTML pages globally affected by this one style sheet, you can do so by linking them to this page. Then, if you want to make style adjustments to those 1,000 pages, you simply have to change the *one* file—mystyle_1.css.

INHERITANCE

The term *cascading* refers primarily to the fact that not only can you use multiple styles in an individual XHTML

page, but also that the style-sheet–compliant browser will follow an order—a cascade—to interpret style information. You therefore can use all three style types, and the browser will interpret the linked styles first; embedded, second; and inline, last. Even though you might have master styles applied to an entire site, you can control aspects of individual pages with embedded styles and individual areas within those pages with inline styles.

 Are you having problems with your cascade? See "Cascade Woes," in the "Troubleshooting" section near the end of this chapter.

Another aspect of CSS is *inheritance*. This concept defines specific elements as being parents, and elements within those elements as children. Take for example the body element. This element contains all other markup that affects the way the content of the page is displayed. Elements within the body are considered *children* of the body element.

This concept continues down the markup hierarchy, referred to as a *tree*. Think of it as a family tree, in fact. So, if you have a paragraph, the elements within that paragraph are the *children* of that parent, and so on.

Inheritance specifies that unless you command otherwise, a particular style will be inherited by a child of a parent. For example, if you specify a specific text color in a paragraph tag, all tags within that paragraph will inherit that color unless you state otherwise.

 Have you created your style sheets and still aren't seeing the results as you thought you would? See "Troublesome Browsers," in the "Troubleshooting" section near the end of this chapter.

EXPLORING CLASS AND GROUPING

Two other interesting aspects of style sheets include class and grouping. *Class* refers to ways of breaking down your style rules into very precise pieces. Whenever you want some of the text on your pages to look different from the other text, you can create what amounts to a custom-built XHTML tag. Each type of specially formatted text you define is called a *style class*.

For example, suppose you want two different kinds of h1 headings in your documents. You can create a style class for each one by putting the following text in the style sheet:

```
<style>

<!--

h1.serif {
font: 24pt Century Schoolbook
}
h1.sans {
font: 18pt Arial
}

-->

</style>
```

You then assign the class serif or sans inline to achieve the results.

Grouping is achieved when style properties and values are condensed, resulting in tighter rules. Consider the following class example:

```
p.1 {
font: arial;
font-size: 13pt;
line-height: 14pt
}
```

In this example, all paragraphs with the class of 1 will show up as a 13-point Arial font with a line height of 14 points. If you apply grouping to this class, you end up with the following results:

```
p.1 {font: 13pt/14pt arial}
```

The design will be the same, either way. Notice, however, that you place the font size first, the line height after the forward slash, and then the name of the font.

> **Caution**
>
> Grouping requires a specific syntactical order to work properly. With type, the font size comes first, the line height comes second, and then the font name is included.

WORKING WITH CLASSES

To get the most variation in style, assign classes to individual XHTML tags. You do so very simply by adding a named extension to any XHTML tag.

If you have two headers and two paragraph styles that you want to add attributes to, you can name each one and assign styles to the individual paragraphs. You then can call on the name within the specific XHTML tag in the body of the document, as shown here:

```
<style>

<!--

h1.left {
font: arial 14pt;
color: #FF0033;
text-align: left
}

H2.right {
font: arial 13pt;
color: #FF6633;
text-align: right
}

-->

</style>
```

In the XHTML, you place the class name:

```
<h1 class="left">This is my Left Heading</h2>
```

All the `h1` headers that you name `class="left"` will have the `h1.left` class properties. Similarly, the `H2.right` headers named `class="right"` will have the properties defined for that class.

In Listing 18.4, I show an XHTML page with the embedded style sheet and class combination used to achieve the page style.

LISTING 18.4   WORKING WITH CLASSES

```
<?xml version="1.0"?>
<!DOCTYPE html PUBLIC "-//W3C//DTD Xhtml 1.0 Transitional//EN"
"http://www.w3.org/TR/xhtml1/DTD/xhtml1-transitional.dtd">
<html xmlns="http://www.w3.org/1999/xhtml">
<head>
```

LISTING 18.4 CONTINUED

```
<title>style sheet sample: class</title>
<style>

<!--

p.center {
font-family: garamond, times, serif;
font-size: 14pt;
text-align: center;
}

p.right {
font-family: verdana, helvetica, sans-serif;
font-size: 13pt;
text-align: right;
}

p.name {
font-family: garamond, times, serif;
font-size: 10pt;
text-align: center;
text-weight: bold;
text-style: italic;
}

-->

</style>

</head>

<body>

<p class="center">
Brain researchers estimate that your unconscious data base outweighs the
conscious on an order exceeding ten million to one. This data base is the
source of your hidden, natural genius. In other words, a part of you is much
smarter than you are. The wise people regularly consult that smarter part.
</p>

<p class="right">
Crazy people who are productive are geniuses. Crazy people who are rich are
eccentric. Crazy people who are neither productive nor rich are just plain
crazy. Geniuses and crazy people are both out in the middle of a deep ocean;
geniuses swim, crazy people drown. Most of us are sitting safely on the shore.
Take a chance and get your feet wet.
</p>

<p class="name">
-- Michael J. Gelb
</p>
</body>
</html>
```

Figure 18.6 shows class in action.

Figure 18.6
Using classes, I varied the paragraph alignment and text appearance on this page.

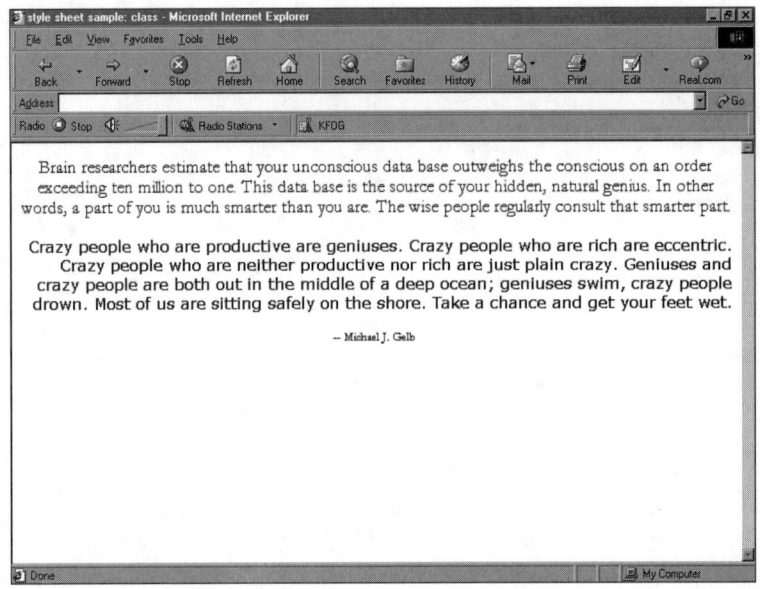

If you'd like to create a custom class, you can do so by simply naming the class—it doesn't have to be attached to a familiar XHTML selector. For example, let's say I'd like to have the style assigned to "right" in the previous example be globally useful to *any* XHTML tag rather than just a paragraph tag. In this case, you'd write the style code as follows:

```
.right {
font-family: verdana, helvetica, sans-serif;
font-size: 13pt;
text-align: right;
}
```

Then, you'd add the style to any tag you like using the custom class. The information contained within that tag will pick up the style information described using the `right` _custom class.

USING GROUPING

To group style sheets, you can do the following:

- Group multiple selectors
- Group properties and values

Say you want to assign the same properties to a number of header styles. One reason you might do so is to force all headers to update to a single style after being linked to the sheet.

Without grouping, the code would look like this:

```
<style>

<!--
```

```
h1 {
font-family: arial;
font-size 14pt;
color: #000000;
}

h2 {


font-family: arial;
font-size 14pt;
color: #000000;
}

h3 {


font-family: arial;
font-size 14pt;
color: #000000;
}

-->

</style>
```

Here's the same example grouped:

```
h1, h2, h3 {


font-family: arial;
font-size 14pt;
color: #000000;
}
```

The processes of grouping properties and grouping values are similar in concept. Without grouping, an example of properties and values within the body would look like this:

```
body {
font-family: arial, san-serif;
font-size: 13pt;
line-height: 14pt;
font-weight: bold;
font- style: normal;
}
```

With grouping, you can simply name the attribute font: and then stack the arguments like this:

```
body {
font: bold normal 13pt/14pt arial, san-serif;
}
```

To exemplify how order in grouping works, you can group margins using the margin: property. However, you must follow the property with the top, right, left, and bottom margin values in that order. Be sure to specify all these values when grouping; otherwise, you'll end up with the same value applied to all:

```
body {
margin: .10in .75in .75in .10in;
}
```

Note that no commas appear between the values. However, the declaration can end with a semicolon.

Listing 18.5 describes a style sheet using class and grouping.

LISTING 18.5 CLASS AND GROUPING

```
<?xml version="1.0"?>
<!DOCTYPE html PUBLIC "-//W3C//DTD XHTML 1.0 Transitional//EN"
"http://www.w3.org/TR/xhtml1/DTD/xhtml1-transitional.dtd">
<html xmlns="http://www.w3.org/1999/xhtml">
<head>
<title>Class and Grouping</title>

<style>

<!--

body {
margin: 0.10in 0.50in 0.50in;
}

h1.left {
font: 16pt ZapfChancery;
text-align: left;
}

h2.right {


font: 14pt ZapfChancery;
text-align: right;
color: #FF0033;
}

p.left {
font: 13pt/11pt garamond;
text-align: left;
}

p.right {
font: 13pt arial;
text-align: right;
margin: 0in .75in .50in;
}

a {


text-decoration: none;
font-weight: bold;
}
```

LISTING 18.5 CONTINUED

```
-->
</style>

</head>
<body>

<h1 class="left">A Midsummer Night's Dream</h1>

<p class="left">
Either to die the death or to abjure
For ever the society of men.
</p>

<p class="right">
Therefore, fair <a href="hermia.html">Hermia</a>,


question your desires;
Know of your youth, examine well your blood,
Whether, if you yield not to your father's choice,
You can endure the livery of a nun,
For aye to be in shady cloister mew'd,
To live a barren sister all your life,
Chanting faint hymns to the cold fruitless moon.
</p>

<p class="left">
Thrice-blessed they that master so their blood,
To undergo such maiden <a href="pilgrim.html">pilgrimage</a>;


But earthlier happy is the rose distill'd,
Than that which withering on the virgin thorn
Grows, lives and dies in single blessedness.
</p>

<h2 class="right">From Act I, Scene I</h2>

</body>
</html>
```

Figure 18.7 shows the combination of class and grouping.

More Style Resources

You will definitely require more information about style sheets if you find that you are using them regularly in your design work. Up-to-date style-sheet resources are available on the Web, and many books address working with styles.

A primary online resource for style sheet information is the World Wide Web Consortium's style sheet section at `http://www.w3c.org/Style/`. In this area, you can find the complete specification and latest information on XHTML style sheets.

Because Microsoft's Internet Explorer pioneered popular browser support of style sheets, Microsoft has accumulated some excellent references on its developer site at `http://msdn.microsoft.com/default.asp`.

Another powerful style reference is the Web Review Style Sheets Reference Guide at `http://style.webreview.com/`. This page contains general information, and links to Eric Meyer's excellent style compatibility browser charts.

Figure 18.7
By combining class and grouping, you can achieve concise code and varied style.

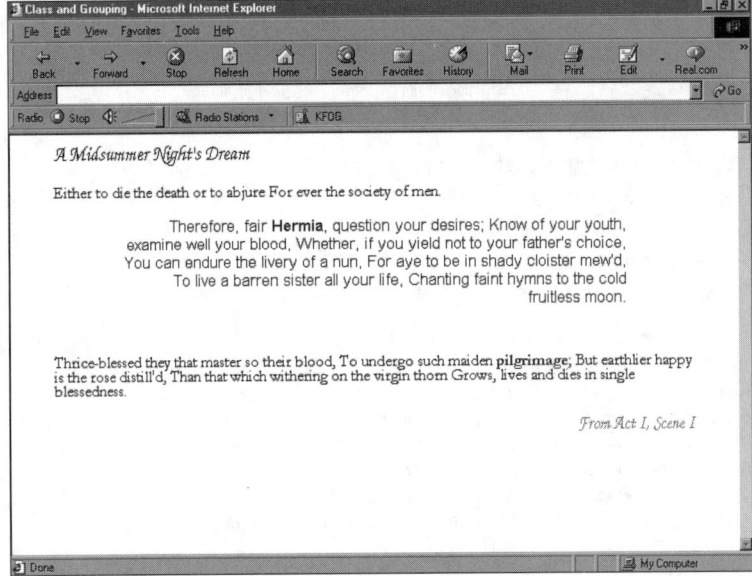

USING STYLE SHEETS

First, I'll detail style sheet properties, and then you'll have the opportunity to apply style to your pages.

There are numerous style sheet properties that cover text, space, color, fonts, and positioning. They pose many more issues than can easily be taught in one chapter. However, to get you off to a working start, I've included some useful style sheet properties and values here.

Many design elements of controlling page layout, margins, indents, and text alignment can help bring a sophisticated look to your pages.

Properties can be very helpful when you're designing with style sheets. I've included some of the most commonly used in Table 18.1.

TABLE 18.1 STYLE SHEET PROPERTIES

Property	Results
margin-left	To set a left margin, use a distance in points, inches, centimeters, or pixels. The following sets a left margin to three-fourths of an inch: {margin-left: .75in;}.

TABLE 18.1   CONTINUED

Property	Results
margin-right	For a right margin, select from the same measurement options as provided for the margin-left attribute. Here's an example: {margin-right: 50px;}.
margin-top	You can set top margins using the same measurement values as for other margin attributes. Consider this example: {margin-top: 20pt;}.
text-indent	Again, points, inches, centimeters, or pixel values can be assigned to this attribute, which serves to indent any type of text. Consider this example: {text-indent: 0.5in;}.
text-align	This long-awaited feature allows for justification of text. Values include left, center, and right, as shown in this example: {text-align: right;}.

Text alignment is a powerful layout tool, and designers will enjoy being able to place text in a variety of alignments without having to rely on tables, divisions, or other, less graceful, XHTML workarounds that existed in the past.

Caution

Cascading style sheets allow for negative values for margin properties. These values allow the designer to overlap areas of a page's design, which is a powerful capability with no existing relative in standard XHTML. However, browser support is still sketchy regarding negative values, so they should be used with care.

→ For a complete look at XHTML alignment as well as examples of style sheets, **see** Chapter 9, "Formatting Text in XHTML," **p. 133**.

PART

IV

CH

18

APPLYING MARGINS WITH STYLE

In the following exercise, you can get started using margins with style:

1. Open your XHTML editor.

2. Create a standard shell:

```
<?xml version="1.0"?>
<!DOCTYPE html PUBLIC "-//W3C//DTD XHTML 1.0 Transitional//EN"
"http://www.w3.org/TR/xhtml1/DTD/xhtml1-transitional.dtd">
<html xmlns="http://www.w3.org/1999/xhtml">
<head>
<title>Style Sheet Exercise</title>

</head>
<body>


</body>
</html>
```

3. Add a selection of text:

```
<?xml version="1.0"?>
<!DOCTYPE html PUBLIC "-//W3C//DTD XHTML 1.0 Transitional//EN"
"http://www.w3.org/TR/xhtml1/DTD/xhtml1-transitional.dtd">
```

```
<html xmlns="http://www.w3.org/1999/xhtml">
<head>
<title>Style Sheet Exercise</title>

</head>
<body>

"The most beautiful thing we can experience is the mysterious; It is the source
of all true art and science"
<br />
-- Albert Einstein


</body>
</html>
```

4. Add the style elements into the head of the document:

```
<?xml version="1.0"?>
<!DOCTYPE html PUBLIC "-//W3C//DTD XHTML 1.0 Transitional//EN"
"http://www.w3.org/TR/xhtml1/DTD/xhtml1-transitional.dtd">
<html xmlns="http://www.w3.org/1999/xhtml">
<head>
<title>Style Sheet Exercise</title>

<style>

<!--


-->

</style>

</head>
<body>

"The most beautiful thing we can experience is the mysterious; It is the source
of all true art and science"
<br />
-- Albert Einstein


</body>
</html>
```

5. Add the following margin syntax alongside the body selector within the style section:

```
body {
margin-left: 2.75in;
margin-right: 2.75in;
margin-top: 2.75in;
margin-bottom: 2.75in;
}
```

6. Save the file as style_margin.html.

7. View the file in your browser. It should be similar to my example in Figure 18.8.

Figure 18.8
Here, I applied a margin of 2.75 inches to the left, right, top, and bottom of the quote. Note that a scrollbar has appeared to accommodate the overlap the bottom margin causes. Try a number of measurements on your own!

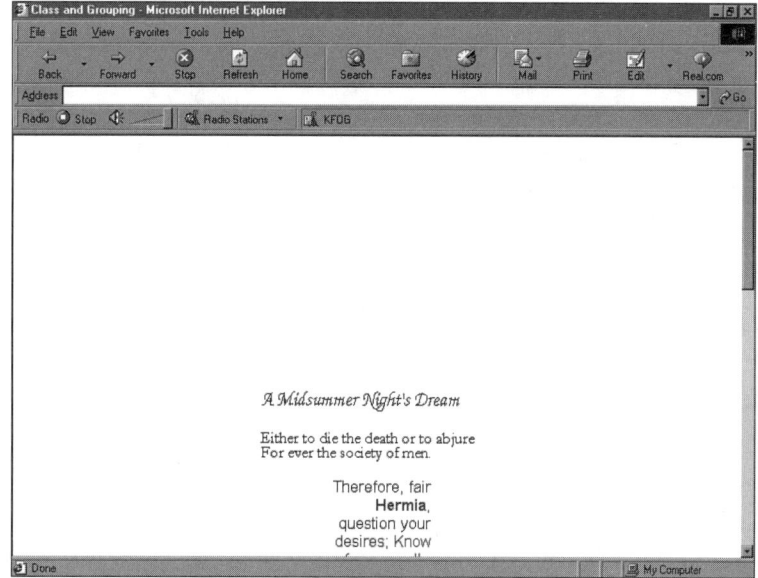

Note

Although I added the margin values to the entire page with the body attribute in Figure 18.8, you can add margins to *any* XHTML tag you want. For example, if you want to control the headers with different margins, place the margin values in the string next to the header of your choice. Similarly, you can adjust margins on individual paragraphs by adding the margin values you seek to the p element.

In Listing 18.6, I've created an embedded style sheet that includes margins, text alignment, and indents.

LISTING 18.6   MARGINS, ALIGNMENT, AND INDENTATION

```
<?xml version="1.0"?>
<!DOCTYPE html PUBLIC "-//W3C//DTD XHTML 1.0 Transitional//EN"
"http://www.w3.org/TR/xhtml1/DTD/xhtml1-transitional.dtd">
<html xmlns="http://www.w3.org/1999/xhtml">
<head>
<title>Margins, Alignment, Indents</title>

<style>

<!--

body {
margin-left: 1.00in;
margin-right: 1.00in;
margin-top: 1.00in;
```

LISTING 18.6 CONTINUED

```
margin-bottom: 1.00in;
}

h2 {

text-align: center;
}

p {
text-align: justify;
text-indent: .50in;
}

-->

</style>

</head>
<body>

<h2>A Midsummer Night's Dream</h2>

<p>Either to die the death or to abjure
For ever the society of men.</p>

<p>Therefore, fair <a href="hermia.html">Hermia</a>, question your desires;


Know of your youth, examine well your blood,
Whether, if you yield not to your father's choice,
You can endure the livery of a nun,
For aye to be in shady cloister mew'd,
To live a barren sister all your life,
Chanting faint hymns to the cold fruitless moon.</p>

<p>Thrice-blessed they that master so their blood,
To undergo such maiden <a href="pilgrim.html">pilgrimage</a>;



But earthlier happy is the rose distill'd,
Than that which withering on the virgin thorn
Grows, lives and dies in single blessedness.</p>

</body>
</html>
```

You can see the style results in Figure 18.9.

You can create more detailed layouts if you study style sheets further; for example, you can add and control white space and also the placement and alignment of elements, overlays, and special effects.

Figure 18.9
On this page, I used style sheets to control margins, alignment, and indentation.

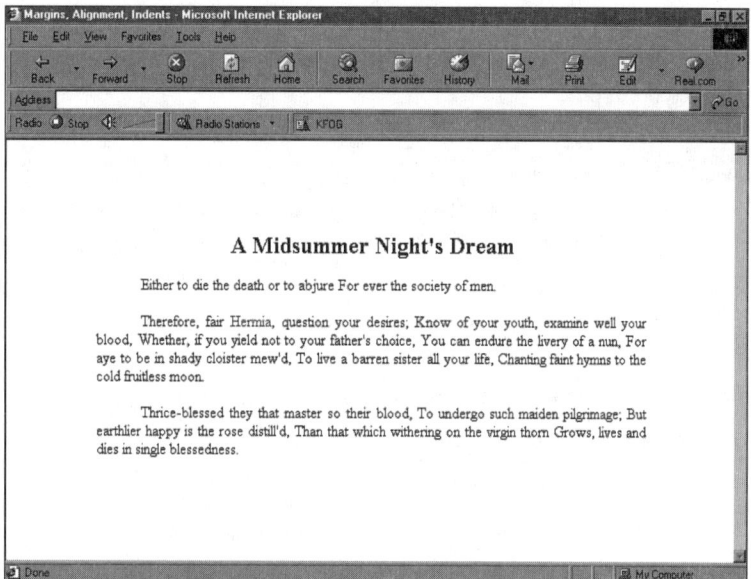

DISPLAYING TEXT WITH CSS

Setting type using style sheets is one of the most exciting design aspects of XHTML. Not only do you have the ability to call for many type styles to appear on a page or a site, but you also have the control that only the methods of style allow.

This control becomes especially important when you're creating large sites. Instead of having to work with multiple, worrisome <font> tags and attributes, with XHTML you can create a single style sheet that defines all the styles required for the entire site, including a variety of links, specialty links, anchors, and lists.

Instead of the <font> tag, you now can use the style sheet property font-family. You can then add a variety of values along with it, or you can use classes and grouping to fully flex the power of type through the use of style sheets. What's more, you can add a wide variety of typographic conventions to type that extend far above and beyond the font element, providing you with extended options and more refined design results.

The Trouble with Fonts

The reality of font support in style sheets is much the same as those issues encountered by the designer when employing the <font> tag and its attributes. The specific typeface must be available on the computer viewing your page. And, as with the <font> tag, style sheets do allow you to stack any number of typefaces so that you can maximize the chances that your browser will pick up a typeface that you want your audience to see.

If the people viewing your pages don't have Arial, for example, they'll probably have Helvetica, and so forth. Although these typefaces have some minor differences, they are similar enough to be considered workable in the context of style-sheet design.

STYLE SHEET FONT FAMILIES

Style sheets recognize five font families, attempting to address the major family groups available in typography.

Note

In XHTML, font categories, or master families, are simply referred to as *families*. This terminology is one of the confusing differences found between the technology of the Web and the older, venerable typographic standards.

For style sheets, five font categories, or master families, are defined, as shown in Table 18.2.

TABLE 18.2 FONT CATEGORIES

Font Category	Description
Serif	Serif faces are those faces with strokes. These strokes are said to aid in readability; therefore, serif typefaces are often very popular for printed body text. Some examples of serif faces include Times, Garamond, and Century Schoolbook.
Sans Serif	These typefaces tend to be rounded and have no strokes. Common sans-serif faces include Helvetica, Arial, Avant Garde, and Verdana.
Script	A script face is one that looks similar to cursive writing or handwriting. Common script typefaces include Park Avenue and Lucida Handwriting.
Monospace	These faces look like typewriter fonts. They are called monospace fonts because each letter within the face takes up the same width as another. For example, the letter w, which is wider in most faces than an i, is actually the same width in a monospace font. Courier is the common monospace font found on both the Windows and Macintosh platforms.
Fantasy	Referred to by most typographers as *decorative*, the fonts available in this category are best used for headers and artistic text rather than body text. Decorative fonts include Whimsy and party.

To apply a family inline, you follow a stacking convention such as is found with the <font> tag. You do so in all cases of style, whether using the inline, embedded, or linked methods.

Here's an inline example:

```
<p style="font-family: arial, helvetica, sans-serif">
In this selection, the browser will search the user's computer for the Arial
font. If it's found, it will be displayed. If it isn't found, it will look for
Helvetica. If neither is found, the browser will display the first sans-serif
typeface available.
</p>
```

In Listing 18.7, I've taken this paragraph and added it to an HTML page with other text that has no style or font information added.

LISTING 18.7   STYLE APPLIED TO A SINGLE PARAGRAPH

```
<?xml version="1.0"?>
<!DOCTYPE html PUBLIC "-//W3C//DTD XHTML 1.0 Transitional//EN"
"http://www.w3.org/TR/xhtml1/DTD/xhtml1-transitional.dtd">
<html xmlns="http://www.w3.org/1999/xhtml">
<head>

<title>style sheet sample</title>
</head>

<body>
<p>This paragraph has no style or font information added to it. Therefore, it
relies on the browser's own defaults for a typeface. You'll see this paragraph
appear in Times</p>

<p style="font-family: arial, helvetica, sans-serif">
In this selection, the browser will search the user's computer for the Arial
font. If it's found, it will be displayed. If it isn't found, it will look for
Helvetica. If neither is found, the browser will display the first sans-serif
typeface available.</p>
</body>
</html>
```

Figure 18.10 shows the difference between the first paragraph, with only the browser's defaults to figure out what typeface to include, and the second paragraph, where the typeface is controlled by style.

PART

IV

CH

18

Figure 18.10
The default font compared to the Arial font created with style sheets.

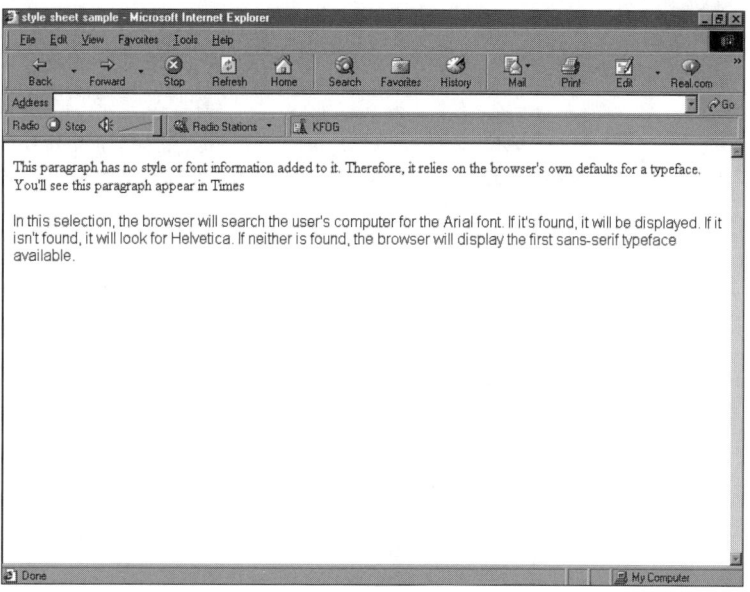

Caution

You are always in some danger that you'll lose control with typefaces, particularly those within the Fantasy family. The Fantasy fonts are installed by individuals rather than shipped with the computer in question.

TYPE PROPERTIES AND VALUES

You can apply a range of properties to typefaces using style sheets, and you can apply an admirable selection of values to those properties. I'll focus on the most immediate and familiar here so that you can get started quickly using them in your designs.

As with standard XHTML fonts, properties are available to control size and color. With style sheets, unlike XHTML fonts, you also can control the weight and style of a typeface, as well as line height, also known as *leading*, which is the measurement between individual lines of set type.

You can accomplish sizing by using the font-size property or using grouped properties.

Type size in style sheets can be defined using points, pixels, inches, centimeters, millimeters, and picas. For Web designers, points or pixels are going to be the most natural choice, although this choice ultimately depends on your preferences.

 Want to develop sites using style exclusively? Find out when you can in "The Advantage of Intranet Design" in the "Troubleshooting" section near the end of this chapter.

Caution

Although having so many size options is undeniably exciting, using measurements other than points can create some serious problems. One of these problems is the no-print phenomenon found when pixels are used as a measurement rather than points. Although the type will appear in style sheet browsers, such as Internet Explorer 3.0 and higher and Netscape 4.0 and higher, type defined in pixels might not print. For the sake of stability and consistency, I recommend using points as a preferred measurement when you're setting type using style sheets.

The following is an example of inline style setting the size of the typeface in points:

```
<p style="font-family: century schoolbook, times, serif; font-size: 24pt;">

"The most beautiful thing we can experience is the mysterious; It is the source
of all true art and science"<br />
-- Albert Einstein

</p>
```

Figure 18.11 shows how the font face and size are applied to this quote.

Figure 18.11:
Using inline style, I applied the Century Schoolbook font at 24 points.

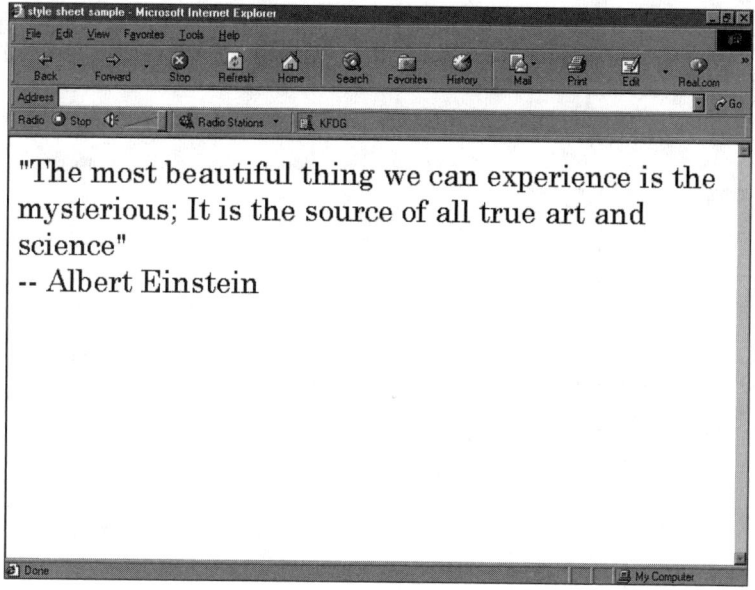

In this instance, I've set up a style sheet that can be embedded into a single page or linked to from a page. The style then affects any standard paragraphs on that page:

```
<style>

<!--

p{

font-family: arial, helvetica, sans-serif;
font-size: 14pt;

    }

-->

</style>
```

In Figure 18.12, you can see the embedded style sheet in action. The text is now made up of 14-point Arial text.

Style sheets rely on standard browser color techniques. In other words, you'll use hexadecimal—and preferably browser-safe—colors for the best results.

Note

You can use RGB (Red, Green, Blue) values in style sheets, too. Most hand coders stick with hex, whereas some WYSIWYG programs use the RGB values instead.

→ To learn about hexadecimal color, **see** Chapter 25, "Color Concepts," **p. 527**.

Figure 18.12
Here, an embedded
style sheet set the text
to 14-point Arial.

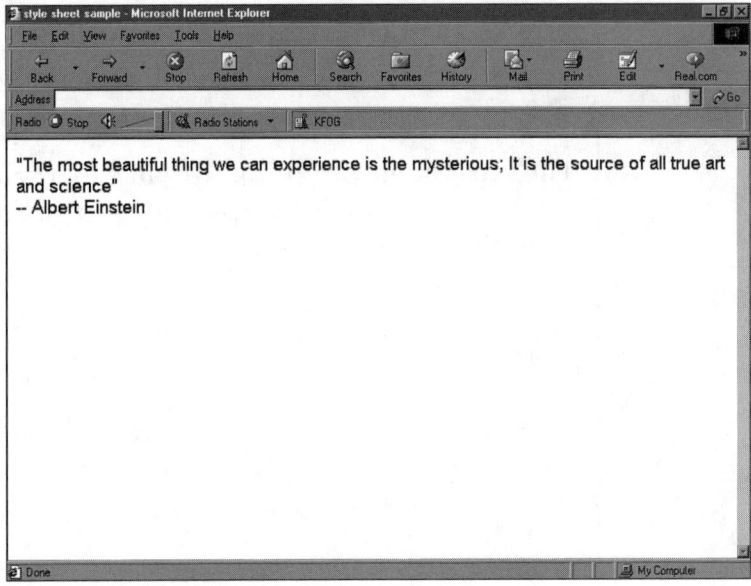

You can add color, like all style properties, to any reasonable XHTML tag using inline, embedded, or linked sheet methods, with the color property.

In Listing 18.8, I use color, type selection, and type size within the style element.

LISTING 18.8   EMBEDDED STYLE WITH FACE, SIZE, AND COLOR

```
<?xml version="1.0"?>
<!DOCTYPE html PUBLIC "-//W3C//DTD XHTML 1.0 Transitional//EN"
"http://www.w3.org/TR/xhtml1/DTD/xhtml1-transitional.dtd">
<html xmlns="http://www.w3.org/1999/xhtml">
<head>

<title>style sheet sample: embedded</title>
<style>

p {
font-family: garamond, times, serif;
font-size: 18pt;
color: #CC9966;
}

</style>

</head>

<body>
<p>Brain researchers estimate that your unconscious data base outweighs the
conscious on an order exceeding ten million to one. This data base is the
source of your hidden, natural genius. In other words, a part of you is much
smarter than you are. The wise people regularly consult that smarter part.</p>
```

LISTING 18.8   CONTINUED

```
<p>"Crazy people who are productive are geniuses. Crazy people who are rich are
eccentric. Crazy people who are neither productive nor rich are just plain
crazy. Geniuses and crazy people are both out in the middle of a deep ocean;
geniuses swim, crazy people drown. Most of us are sitting safely on the shore.
Take a chance and get your feet wet."</p>

<p align="left">
-- Michael J. Gelb
</p>
</body>
</html>
```

Figure 18.13 shows the results.

Figure 18.13
The font face is Garamond, the color is sienna (which will show up as gray in the figure but sienna if you test the code in your browser), and a font size of 18 points.

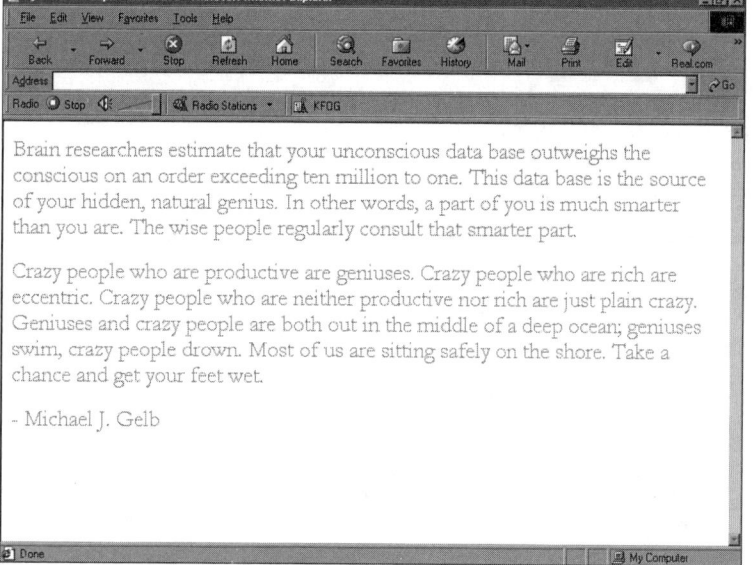

Weight is how thick or thin a typeface is. The Arial face, for example, has variations in weight including black (a very heavy face), bold, light, and so forth.

Because typefaces have different variants, unless you are absolutely sure that visitors to your site have a specific typeface, you generally should apply a value that is going to be available to all typefaces you are using. The one near-global value for typefaces is bold.

⚠ *Having trouble with inline style? See "Come on Inline!" in the "Troubleshooting" section near the end of this chapter.*

The primary purpose, then, for the font-weight property is to make a given typeface bold.

Here's an example of weight applied inline:

```
<p style="font-family: arial, helvetica, sans-serif; font-weight: bold;
font-size: 14pt; color=#CCCCCC;">
"I studied the lives of great men and famous women, and I found that the men and
```

women who got to the top were those who did the jobs they had in hand, with everything they had of energy and enthusiasm." — Harry S. Truman</p>

You also can apply weight to an embedded or linked sheet. In Listing 18.9, I've applied the bold to a header size 1 but have left the paragraph at a standard weight.

LISTING 18.9 USING THE `font-weight` PROPERTY IN A HEADER

```
<?xml version="1.0"?>
<!DOCTYPE html PUBLIC "-//W3C//DTD XHTML 1.0 Transitional//EN"
"http://www.w3.org/TR/xhtml1/DTD/xhtml1-transitional.dtd">
<html xmlns="http://www.w3.org/1999/xhtml">
<head>

<title>style sheet sample: embedded</title>

<style>

<!--

h1 {
font-family: helvetica, arial, sans-serif;
font-weight: bold;
color: #CC9966;
}
p {
font-family: garamond, times, serif;
color: #999999;
}
-->
</style>

</head>

<body>
<h1>Quotations from Michael J. Gelb</h1>
<p>"Brain researchers estimate that your unconscious data base outweighs the
conscious on an order exceeding ten million to one. This data base is the source
of your hidden, natural genius. In other words, a part of you is much smarter
than you are. The wise people regularly consult that smarter part."</p>

<p>"Crazy people who are productive are geniuses. Crazy people who are rich are
eccentric. Crazy people who are neither productive nor rich are just plain
crazy. Geniuses and crazy people are both out in the middle of a deep ocean;
geniuses swim, crazy people drown. Most of us are sitting safely on the shore.
Take a chance and get your feet wet."</p>

</body>
</html>
```

Figure 18.14 shows the results.

Figure 18.14
The header and paragraph in this example take on different styles as defined by an embedded sheet.

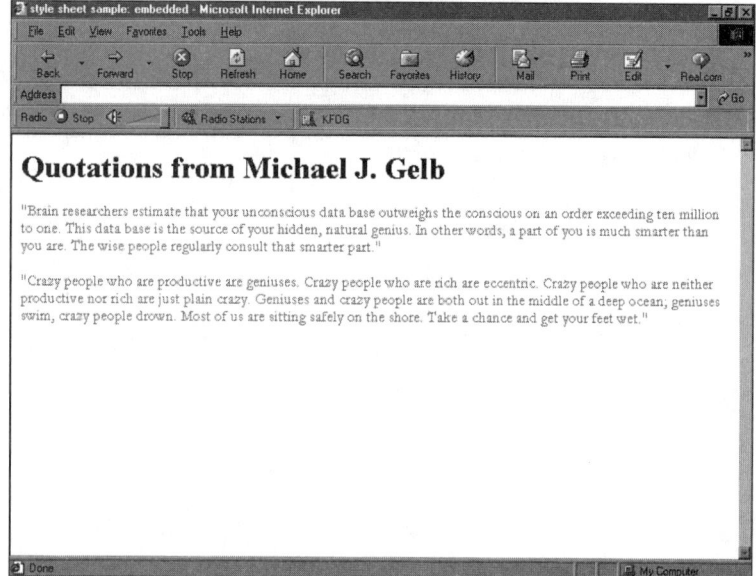

APPLYING FONT STYLE

In this context, *style* refers to the slant of a given typeface. The two styles are italic and oblique. As with weight variations, oblique is a rare option and should be used cautiously. However, italic style is available in most typefaces, so you're pretty safe using it wherever you require italics.

The following is an example of inline font style:

```
<p style="font-family: century schoolbook, times, serif; font-style: italic;
font-size: 14pt; color=#999999;">

"I studied the lives of great men and famous women, and I found that the men and
women who got to the top were those who did the jobs they had in hand, with
everything they had of energy and enthusiasm." -- Harry S. Truman</p>
```

Figure 18.15 shows this passage in Century Schoolbook 14-point italic.

Caution

As I've said several times throughout this book, you should use italic and bold sparingly. Their primary function in body type is to emphasize passages of text. Excessive use of bold or italic compromises readability.

Leading is the space between individual lines of text. Normal default leading is usually the same or very near to the point size of the type being used. For example, when you have 12-point type, the leading is going to look very natural at 12 points, too.

To control leading with style sheets, you can use the `line-height` property. Its value is numeric, in whatever measurement you're using. As I've mentioned, I prefer points for a number of reasons.

Figure 18.15
Applying italic with the `font-style` property.

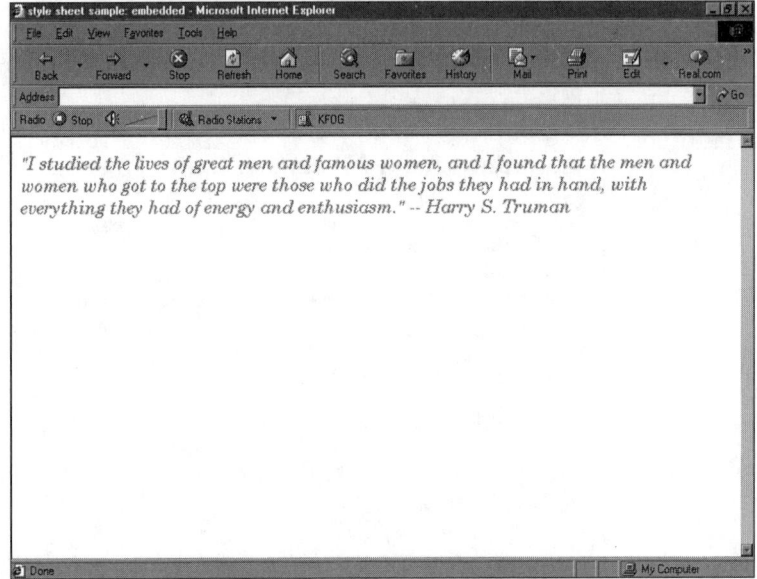

Listing 18.10 shows normal default line height, followed by a larger value, and in the last paragraph, the line height is a smaller value, making the distance between the lines shorter.

LISTING 18.10   ADDING LINE HEIGHT

```
<?xml version="1.0"?>
<!DOCTYPE html PUBLIC "-//W3C//DTD XHTML 1.0 Transitional//EN"
"http://www.w3.org/TR/xhtml1/DTD/xhtml1-transitional.dtd">
<html xmlns="http://www.w3.org/1999/xhtml">
<head>

<title>A Midsummer Night's Dream</title>

</head>

<body>
<p style="font-family: courier new, courier, monospace; font-size: 12pt;
color: #999999;">
Call you me fair? that fair again unsay.
Demetrius loves your fair: O happy fair!
Your eyes are lode-stars; and your tongue's sweet air
More tuneable, than lark to shepherd's ear,
When wheat is green, when hawthorn buds appear.</p>

<p style="font-family: courier new, courier, monospace;
font-size: 12pt; line-height: 18pt; color: #999999;">
Sickness is catching: O, were favour so,
Yours would I catch, fair Hermia, ere I go;
My ear should catch your voice, my eye your eye,
My tongue should catch your tongue's sweet melody.</p>
```

LISTING 18.10   CONTINUED

```
<p style="font-family: courier new, courier, monospace;
font-size: 12pt; line-height: 9pt; color: #999999;">
Were the world mine, Demetrius being bated,
The rest I'd give to be to you translated.
O, teach me how you look, and with what art
You sway the motion of Demetrius' heart.</p>

</body>
</html>
```

Figure 18.16 shows how leading affects each paragraph.

Figure 18.16
Leading, or line height, is applied to this selection of text.

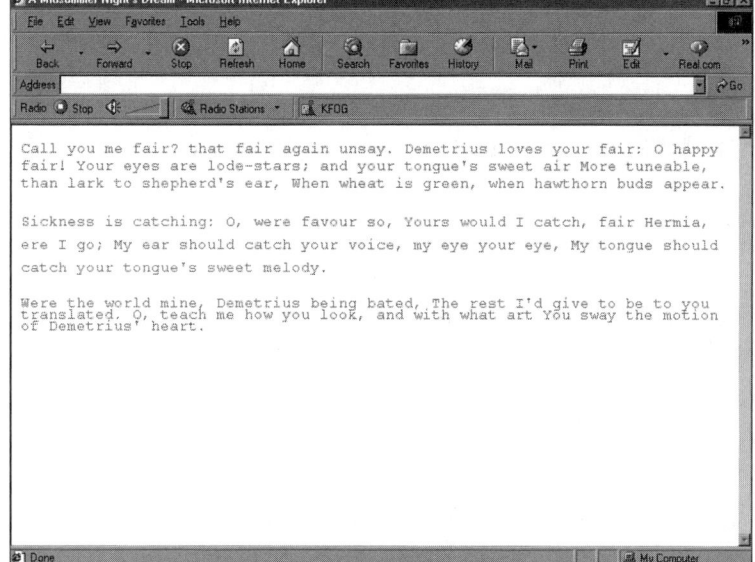

PART

IV

Ch

18

You also should be aware of several other type options, including the following:

- **text-decoration—This property is extremely useful for** turning off link underlining within an anchor. To do so, set text-decoration to a value of none. The values of underline, italic, and line-through are also supported.

- **background**—If you want to place a color or image behind text, you can do so by using this property. Either use a hexadecimal color or a URL (address) where that address points to a background image tile. Note that you can assign this option not only to the <body> tag, but also to any tag or span of text to "highlight" an area on a page.

Listing 18.11 demonstrates a page with the use of text decoration and background.

LISTING 18.11   TEXT DECORATION AND BACKGROUND SETTINGS

```
<?xml version="1.0"?>
<!DOCTYPE html PUBLIC "-//W3C//DTD XHTML 1.0 Transitional//EN"
"http://www.w3.org/TR/xhtml1/DTD/xhtml1-transitional.dtd">
<html xmlns="http://www.w3.org/1999/xhtml">
<head>

<title>A Midsummer Night's Dream</title>

</head>

<body>

<p style="font-family: courier new, courier, monospace; font-size: 12pt; color:
#999999;">
Call you me fair? that fair again unsay.
<a href="demetrius.html" style="text-decoration: line-through;">Demetrius</a>

loves your fair: O happy fair!
Your eyes are lode-stars; and your tongue's sweet air
More tuneable, than lark to shepherd's ear,
When wheat is green, when hawthorn buds appear.
Sickness is catching: O, were favour so,
Yours would I catch, fair <a href="hermia.html"
style="text-decoration: none">Hermia</a>, ere I go;


My ear should catch your voice, my eye your eye,
My tongue should catch your tongue's sweet melody.</p>

<p style="background: #000000; font-family: courier new, courier, monospace; font-
size: 12pt; color: #FFFFFF">
Were the world mine, Demetrius being bated,
The rest I'd give to be to you translated.
O, teach me how you look, and with what art
You sway the motion of Demetrius' heart.</p>

</body>
</html>
```

In Figure 18.17, you can see that the first link has been struck through. The second link, however, has no strikethrough. Finally, I've used black to set a background against the final paragraph. This trick can be very handy when you're creating sidebars or offsetting text for emphasis.

Figure 18.17
The first link in this case has a strikethrough. Notice also the black background achieved behind the bottom paragraph.

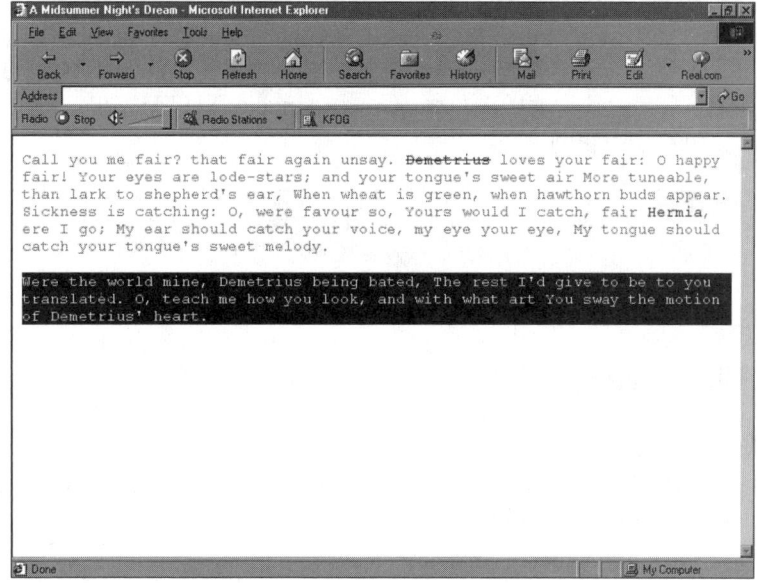

STYLE SHEET EVOLUTION

Are you having fun yet? I hate to be a spoilsport, but I'm here to let you know that despite the great control style sheets can offer you typographically, you still encounter the problem of cross-browser interoperability.

The ugly truth remains that if you want to appeal to the widest Web audience and keep your designs intact, you need to design across browsers. However, if you combine the font element and style sheets, you can create pages that look good for those browsers that support fonts and even better for those visitors who have style-sheet–enabled browsers.

Another issue is the ever-chaotic state of affairs at the World Wide Web Consortium (W3C). At this writing, the style sheet recommendation is level CSS2. The additions to the recommendation add a lot of functionality, without changing anything too significant in the basic concepts in CSS1.

However, XSL, which is the style sheet component to XML, is a different story. This style sheet language is also under development, adding more spice to the style soup.

As of May 12, 1998, cascading style sheets version II (CSS2) became the recommendation from the World Wide Web Consortium. Although few properties have been altered, much has been added. These additions include advanced positioning and—most specific to this chapter—downloadable fonts. This feature will most certainly aid you in getting the look and feel you're after without having to rely on the lick-and-a-promise method of stacking typefaces into the style sheet or font element.

XSL, or the eXtensible Style Language, has been added to the W3C's working draft of languages. XSL works with XML to modify style within XML pages. The draft specifies that XSL is to be seen as a supportive piece to CSS in that although CSS affects XHTML documents, XSL works with XML to create and modify XHTML documents, creating a chain of powerful style options.

> **Note**
>
> For more information on both CSS2 and XSL, a visit to the World Wide Web Consortium at `http://w3.org/style/` is in order.

TROUBLESHOOTING

TROUBLESOME BROWSERS

I've put together a style sheet and checked the syntax. The style is picked up by IE, but not Netscape. What's the problem?

Netscape 4.0 and above (excluding Netscape 6.0, which is still in pre-release) is much less style-sheet-compliant than Microsoft IE 5.0 and later. In fact, Microsoft IE had some CSS support with its 3.0 version, and it's improved from that point forward. Netscape 6.0 remedies much of these support concerns, but the version difference can be frustrating! The best recommendation I have is to not rely on style sheets if you want the best consistency for a wide range of even compliant browsers.

CASCADE WOES

I've got a linked style sheet, an embedded style sheet, and an inline style set to cascade. Something isn't working right. How can I fix it?

The best way to troubleshoot problems in a cascade is to comment out any embedded and inline style, and unlink from the linked style sheet. Test the page without any style. Are there any errors? If not, go ahead and add the inline style back in and test. Does it work? If so, add the embedded style sheet. Does the linked style override the embedded style that it's supposed to? If not, look carefully at your code for any errors. If so, go ahead and look at the page with the linked style only. If you are error free at this point, with no problems in either the XHTML or CSS code, it's likely there is a compatibility or non-compliance issue with the browser you're using.

THE ADVANTAGE OF INTRANET DESIGN

I'm creating an intranet design for my company, which uses Microsoft Internet Explorer 4.0 and above exclusively. Can I use style sheets for text design with strict XHTML?

The advantage of designing for closed sites where you have definitive information about the browsers in use is that making decisions regarding style sheets and strict XHTML becomes easy. You immediately see whether or not your users can support them, and after you have that information, you can decide how best to code the pages you create.

COME ON INLINE!

I want to set only one letter of a word to a different font size and style, achieving a "drop-cap" effect. How can I do this effectively?

Use inline style with the span element and the styles discussed in this chapter. Avoid using div tags as these will force a break.

DESIGNING FOR THE REAL WORLD

MAKING COMPLEX STYLE SIMPLE

A couple years ago, I developed a site for the Microsoft Network. One of the interesting challenges was working with the variety of links that we needed to accomplish the design. Each link had a different combination of type style, color, and other features. Obviously, we could never do this using conventional HTML, nor could you do it with XHTML, either. The answer? Style sheets! Listing 18.12 shows the resulting sheet in detail.

LISTING 18.12   STYLE SHEET FOR LARGE SITE

```
.plumlink{color:#666699;font:9pt arial,helvetica,sans-serif;font-weight:bold;
text-decoration:none;}

A.plumlink:hover{color: #339999;}

.topLinks{color:#003333;font:9pt arial,helvetica,sans-serif;}
A.topLinks:hover{color:#ff9933;}

.LgBodyLinks{color:#669999;font:11pt arial,helvetica,sans-serif;
text-decoration:none;font-weight:bold;}

A.LgBodyLinks:hover{color: #ff9933;}

.BodyLinks{color:#669999;font:9pt arial,helvetica,sans-serif;font-weight:bold;
text-decoration:none;}

A.BodyLinks:hover {color: #ff9933;}

.smBodyLinks{color:"#003333";font:8pt arial,helvetica,sans-serif;
text-decoration:none;}

A.smBodyLinks:hover{color:#ff9933;}

.FeatureLinks{color:#336666;font:14pt arial,helvetica,sans-serif;
font-weight: bold;text-decoration:none;}

A.FeatureLinks:hover {color: #ff9933;}

.ULBodyLinks{color:#669999;font:9pt arial,helvetica,sans-serif;
font-weigh:=bold;}

A.ULBodyLinks:hover {color: #ff9933;}
```

LISTING 18.12   CONTINUED

```
.ULplainBodyLinks{color:#669999;font:9pt arial,helvetica,sans-serif;}

A.ULplainBodyLinks:hover {color: #ff9933;}

.ga{color:#6699CC;font:9pt arial, helvetica, sans-serif;font-weight:bold;
text-decoration:none;}

A.ga:hover {color:#339966;}
.navLinkExt{color:#003333;font:9pt arial, helvetica, sans-serif;
font-weight:bold;}

A.navLinkExt:hover {color:#ff9933;}

.navLink{color:#003333;font:11pt arial, helvetica, sans-serif;
text-decoration:none;font-weight:bold;}

A.navLink:hover {color:#ff9933;}

.navLinkActive{color:#666699;font:12pt arial, helvetica, sans-serif
;text-decoration:none;font-weight:bold;}

A.navLinkActive:hover {color:#ff9933;}

.horBar{color:#ffffff;font:9pt arial, helvetica, sans-serif;
text-decoration:none;font-weight:bold;}

A.horBar:hover{color:#ff9933;}

.bl{color: #666666;font:8pt arial, helvetica, sans-serif;}

.bql{color: #666666;font:8pt arial, helvetica, sans-serif;}
```

We then linked to this sheet, and wherever we wanted to apply a given style, we simply added its class to a tag or area within our markup as follows:

```
<a href="home.html" class="navLink">This link will be bold, no underline,
11 point sans-serif, with the hexadecimal color of #003333.</a>
```

Of course, when you create complex style, you don't have to link to a sheet; you can always use a style to set the typographic elements of selected areas of text within a page (using the div and span elements) or apply a single style sheet to one page only.

CHAPTER 19

EXTENSIBLE STYLESHEET LANGUAGE (XSL)

In this chapter

by Kynn Bartlett

UNDERSTANDING XSL

In the previous chapter, you learned one way to separate presentation from structure, using cascading style sheets (CSS). Now we'll look at a different way in which form and content can be separated—a very "XML" way of presenting styles.

Extensible Stylesheet Language (XSL) was developed by the World Wide Web Consortium to serve two functions—to create an XML-based syntax for expressing style, and to provide a way to transform from one XML language to another. When we speak of XSL, we're actually talking about three related W3C specifications:

- **XSL Formatting Objects (XSL-FO)**—an XML vocabulary for describing how an XML document should be displayed
- **XSL Transformations (XSLT)**—a template-based language for changing the structure of an XML document or converting it to a different XML-based dialect
- **XPath**—a "sub-language" used by XSLT to identify specific parts of an XML document

> **Note**
>
> XSL-FO is defined by a very long specification (over 500 pages when printed) at `http://www.w3.org/TR/xsl/` and it is still in development as a W3C Working Draft. XSLT became a W3C Recommendation on 16 November 1999 and can be found at `http://www.w3.org/TR/xslt/`; the XPath specification was formalized on the same date and is located at `http://www.w3.org/TR/xpath/`.

Unlike cascading style sheets, an XSL style sheet is not simply a set of additional presentational styles added onto a Web page. Instead, when using XSL you are creating an entirely new document formed by applying the XSLT document to your XML document. This new document can be in any XML-based language, such as XHTML, WML, or XSL-FO.

→ For more on WML, the Wireless Application Protocol Markup Language, **see** Chapter 34, "Overview of Alternative Devices, Languages, and Protocols," **p. 683.**

Because XSL Transformations can be used with any XML-based language, you can use XSL with your XHTML files as easily as you can with any other well-formed XML documents.

FORMATTING OBJECTS

The XSL Formatting Objects language offers an alternative to the use of HTML and CSS as a formatting language, one that is based on XML syntax. As you might have noticed, the syntax for CSS is not very similar to that of XHTML or other XML-based markup languages. Selectors and rules are defined in a very "non-XML" manner.

To remedy this, the XSL-FO specification was created to allow presentational styles to be defined as XML markup. There are several advantages to this, including better processing by advanced browsers (which have to speak only one type of language instead of two), compatibility with XML-based tools, and ease of transformation to and from XML-based languages.

Unfortunately, the XSL-FO standard is still in development and is not yet supported by any mainstream browsers, which means that applying XSL-FO in practice is still a ways off as I write this. However, by being aware of what XSL-FO is and how it's used, you can be prepared for future browser releases that do implement the standard.

XSL-FO tags look very similar in appearance to XHTML tags, and serve some of the same functions as the presentational markup found in XHTML 1.0 Transitional and earlier versions of HTML. XSL-FO tags are identified by the `fo:` prefix to indicate the XSL-FO namespace, which has the URI **http://www.w3.org/1999/XSL/Format**. In addition to the tags, XSL-FO also defines a number of attributes which affect the styles of those tags. Many of these attributes will be very familiar from CSS, as they serve roughly the same function as CSS rules.

Short listings of XSL-FO tags and attributes are provided in Tables 19.1 and 19.2. The XSL-FO specification, as noted before, is very long and contains many more tags and elements than these, allowing for a fine degree of control over how your page is displayed.

TABLE 19.1   COMMON XSL-FO TAGS

XSL-FO tag	Function
`fo:block`	Define a rectangular block, such as a paragraph or a heading (like `<div>`)
`fo:external-graphic`	Include an inline graphic (like `<img>`)
`fo:inline`	A in-line section of text (like `<span>` or `<b>`)
`fo:list-block`	The container for list items
`fo:list-item`	A container for each item in a list, that holds the label and body
`fo:list-item-body`	The content of a list item
`fo:list-item-label`	The name or number of a list item
`fo:simple-link`	Identifies something to be used as a hypertext link
`fo:title`	Give a title to a page

TABLE 19.2   COMMON XSL-FO ATTRIBUTES

XSL-FO attribute	Function
`background-color`	Sets a background color
`background-image`	Sets a background image
`border-left-color`	Sets the color of the left border
`border-bottom-width`	Sets the width of the bottom border
`font-family`	Sets the font
`font-weight`	Sets the boldness
`height`	Sets the height
`max-height`	Defines a maximum height
`min-height`	Defines a minimum height
`text-align`	Sets text alignment

To use XSL-FO to format your page, you will need to make use of XSL Transformations to change your Web page from an ordinary XHTML (or XML) document into a document written in XSL-FO.

XSL-FO

When would you use XSL-FO? Formatting objects have been designed to allow a large degree of control over the layout, and are really meant to be used in situations such as printing a book. Their applicability to Web use is very limited, even discounting the lack of browser support. Håkon W Lie, the author of the cascading style sheets specification and Chief Technology Officer at Opera Software, went so far as to suggest "Formatting Objects Considered Dangerous" in an April 1999 essay. His argument is that XSL-FO (called XFO in his essay) when used on the Web ignores the semantics of a document in favor of pure presentation, damaging the accessibility and usability of the Web. You can read his essay online at

`http://www.operasoftware.com/people/howcome/1999/foch.html`.

TRANSFORMATIONS

The XSL Transformations language plays a very important role in the XML family—it serves as a translator, converting between one dialect of XML and another. For this reason, XSLT is crucial to the adoption of XML as a universal data communications language. Applications for XSLT range from business to business e-commerce to wireless Web networking.

Because XHTML is defined according to the rules for XML, you can use XSLT with your XHTML files to change them into other XML-based languages. You can also use XSLT to display XML files, using your knowledge of XHTML to good effect by converting the XML into XHTML. Alternate presentations of your page can be created by applying an XSLT style sheet for WAP phones or other specialized Web access devices. You can even extract specific information from your XHTML files and create a completely different view of the same content by applying XSLT and XPath.

XSL Transformations are based upon templates. The tags that comprise these templates are a combination of XSLT tags—identified by the XSLT namespace and most often by the `xsl:` prefix—and of the tags belonging to the "target" XML-based language. So if you are converting an XML document to XHTML, your templates will consist of XSLT tags mixed in with XHTML tags.

Note

Because of the way namespaces work in XML, it's not as important that the tags be prefixed by `xsl:`, but rather that they start with some namespace prefix that references the XSLT namespace, which is identified by `xmlns:xsl="http://www.w3.org/1999/XSL/Transform`. As long as the namespace identifier is `http://www.w3.org/1999/XSL/Transform`, it doesn't matter what the prefix is—but for most cases, and for the purposes of this chapter, using `xsl:` makes the most sense.

Each XSLT template consists of two parts—a pattern to match, and the tags of the template itself. Patterns are defined using the XPath syntax, which includes wildcards such as * as well as functions and expressions for greater flexibility.

A very important concept in XSL is the representation of a document as nodes in a tree. This way of thinking about XML data will be familiar to you if you have a computer science background or if you've worked with the HTML DOM before.

In brief, you can think of a document as a tree-like structure—like a family tree in genealogy. At the top of the tree is the "root node," and each subsequent part of the document is a child node of the root—or a child of a child of the root, or further descendants. For XSLT purposes, nodes are of several important types. Element nodes consist of one element in the document, and its children are the content contained by the tags that comprise the element, plus one node for each attribute. The content in an element node can be other elements or text nodes. Attribute nodes can't have any elements.

When XSL Transformations occur, there are three trees involved. The first is the source tree—the original file, written in an XML-based language (which might be XHTML, or might not). The second is the transformation tree, which is the XSLT file. The third is the result tree, created by applying the XSLT to the source tree. To create the result tree, you will have to build it up from the templates in the transformation tree and decorate it—like a holiday tree—with the content in the source tree.

XSLT PARSERS

The actual assembly of the result tree occurs when the source document and the XSLT style sheet are combined by an XSLT parser. The XSLT parser reads in the source tree and the transformation tree, and produces a result tree according to the instructions encoded in the XSLT templates.

When using XSLT in a Web environment, there are two places where this parsing can occur—the client side in the user's browser, or the server side.

CLIENT-SIDE PARSING

For XSLT parsing to happen in the browser, the Web browser must be able to understand both XML and XSLT. Currently, only Microsoft's Internet Explorer 5.0 (and higher) has support for XSLT parsing, although future releases of Mozilla might include XSLT.

Note

Early versions of Internet Explorer contain a version of Microsoft's XML/XSL parser based on a draft version of the XSL specification which is not in compliance with the later W3C Recommendation. Newer versions of the MSXML package are available from Microsoft which adhere more closely to the XSL standard; you should download the latest version from `http://msdn.microsoft.com/` if you intend to work with client-side XSLT. Further information on using MSXML with XSLT can be found in the unofficial MSXML FAQ at `http://www.netcrucible.com/xslt/msxml-faq.htm`.

Parsing XSLT on the client side is quite similar in procedure to using cascading style sheets. You need to add a tag in the XML (or XHTML) document that tells the browser where to find the XSLT style sheet. To set an XSLT style sheet in Internet Explorer 5, use the following:

```
<?xml-style sheet type="text/xsl" href="transform.xsl" ?>
```

Naturally, you'll want to fill in the name of your style sheet file instead of `transform.xsl`. Note that this tag doesn't follow the normal rules for XML and XHTML tags—it's actually a processing instruction, and those are marked by the `<?` and `?>` at the beginning and end of the tag. There are no closing tags for processing instructions.

Unfortunately, the limited number of browsers supporting XSLT makes it difficult to rely on client side parsing of XSLT. One solution is to use scripting to detect the browser type and serve up XSLT for client side parsing only when Internet Explorer 5 is recognized. In other cases, an XHTML page would be sent—possibly generated by an XSLT parser on the server.

SERVER-SIDE PARSING

When you do server side processing of XSLT, you are creating the output file on the server, and the XSLT style sheet never actually gets seen by the Web user—just the end result. This means that the Web browser doesn't have to understand XML and XSLT at all, as long as you send it a result file that is in a language it can understand. For example, you can send XHTML to desktop Web browsers, or WML to WAP-enabled phones.

Server side parsing can occur when you process a request from a Web browser; this is dynamic application of the style sheet. When a request is received from the browser, the Web server selects a style sheet (if there's more than one available) and formats the XML file, sending the result back to the user's browser on the fly. This approach is more flexible and allows for greater customizing of the result to fit the user, and is compatible with data-base-driven Web designs.

You can also apply style sheets on the server in a "batch" mode, or when the content is updated. This lets you generate static pages based on templates, with the content stored separately in XML files and the pages recreated whenever the content is updated. In effect, you are using a content management system based on XSLT. The advantage over dynamic application is in speed, but you lose out on some of XSLT's flexibility and power.

In this chapter, I present source files, XSLT style sheets, and result files for each example. The result files were generated using the second method described above; this way I can display the resulting XHTML. In practice, you will find yourself using client-side parsing, dynamic server-side parsing, and batch server-side processing on different projects as your needs vary.

There are a number of different XSLT parsers available, including offerings from Microsoft, IBM, the Apache Group, and others. I've generated the examples using Saxon, a Java-based XSLT parser engine, available from **http://users.iclway.co.uk/mhkay/saxon/**. Because it's written in Java, it runs on a variety of computers including Windows desktop machines. A comprehensive list of XSL-related software, including parsers, is located at `http://www.xmlsoftware.com/xsl/`.

CREATING XSL STYLE SHEETS

To create an XSLT style sheet, you'll need to know several things. First you need to understand the original format of your source document. It has to be compatible with XML, and you'll need to know what it consists of. You can't create an XSLT style sheet without knowing your document's structure. Is it in an XML content description language? In XHTML?

You'll also need to specify what kind of output you're generating. Will it be XHTML for Web browsers, XSL-FO for high end printing machinery, WML for WAP phones, or another XML-based format for business-to-business data transfer? In this chapter, our examples will concentrate on XHTML.

EXPLORING XSLT SYNTAX

As an XML vocabulary, XSLT syntax should be very familiar to you. It is composed of well-formed, structured tags, some of which serve as containers for other tags and content, and some of which are empty tags. Attributes set on the tags control their behavior. XSLT tags are identified by the use of `xsl:` before the tag name, to indicate the use of the XSLT namespace.

A short listing of common XSLT elements is shown in Table 19.3. The full specification for XSLT is available online at `http://www.w3.org/TR/xslt/`.

PART
IV

CH
19

TABLE 19.3 COMMON XSLT ELEMENTS	
Element	Function
`<xsl:style sheet>`	Define an XSLT style sheet; the wrapper around all XSL content
`<xsl:strip-space>`	Directs the parser to ignore spaces in XML/XHTML documents
`<xsl:output>`	Specify the format and properties of the result document
`<xsl:template>`	Define an XSLT template
`<xsl:value-of>`	Insert the value of a source XML node
`<xsl:for-each>`	Define a section that is repeated one per matching source node
`<xsl:apply-templates>`	Apply templates to the specified nodes
`<xsl:sort>`	Define an order by which templates will be applied
`<xsl:comment>`	Create a comment in the result tree

As you look at the examples later in this chapter, I'll explain the use and syntax of each tag.

STRUCTURE OF AN XSL DOCUMENT

To examine what an XSLT style sheet looks like, we'll take a look at a typical application of XSLT—formatting an online book.

In Listing 19.1, you can see a very simple way to describe a chapter of a book in XML. The file consists of a `<book>` element which contains a `<title>`, an `<author>`, and one or more `<chapters>`. Each `<chapter>` has a `<chapnum>` (which tells the chapter number), a `<title>` for the chapter, and one or more `<para>` tags containing paragraphs of text.

> **Note**
>
> For an example of XML and XHTML used to present electronic book texts, see the HTML Writers Guild's Gutenberg at HWG, at **http://www.hwg.org/gutenberg/**. This is a project to encode some of the great works of history in an XML format that allows rendering and transformation into the data formats of the 21st Century.

LISTING 19.1   A SIMPLE WAY TO DESCRIBE A BOOK CHAPTER IN XML

```
<book>
 <title>A Tale of Two Cities</title>
 <author>Charles Dickens</author>
 <chapter>
  <chapnum>I</chapnum>
  <title>The Period</title>
  <para>
   It was the best of times, it was the worst of
   times, it was the age of wisdom, it was the age of
   foolishness, it was the epoch of belief, it was the epoch
   of incredulity, it was the season of Light, it was the
   season of Darkness, it was the spring of hope, it was the
   winter of despair, we had everything before us, we had
   nothing before us, we were all going direct to Heaven, we
   were all going direct the other way—in short, the period
   was so far like the present period, that some of its
   noisiest authorities insisted on its being received, for
   good or for evil, in the superlative degree of comparison
   only.
  </para>
  <para>
   There were a king with a large jaw and a queen with
   a plain face, on the throne of England; there were a king
   with a large jaw and a queen with a fair face, on the
   throne of France. In both countries it was clearer than
   crystal to the lords of the State preserves of loaves and
   fishes, that things in general were settled for
   ever.
  </para>
 </chapter>
</book>
```

Because this isn't written in XHTML, it won't be much use in a browser that displays just XHTML. So it will need to be transformed for use in a Web environment. Listing 19.2

shows a style sheet which has been written to change the XML into XHTML. Read over this sample code and notice how the style sheet consists of both `xsl:` tags and familiar XHTML tags.

LISTING 19.2   A SAMPLE XSLT DOCUMENT FOR PRESENTING A CHAPTER FROM AN ONLINE BOOK

```
<xsl:stylesheet
 xmlns:xsl="http://www.w3.org/1999/XSL/Transform"
 version="1.0"
 xmlns="http://www.w3.org/1999/xhtml">

 <xsl:strip-space elements="*"/>
 <xsl:output indent="yes"/>

 <xsl:template match="/">
  <html>
   <head>
    <title>
      <xsl:value-of select="book/title" />
    </title>
   </head>
   <body>
    <xsl:apply-templates select="book/*" />
   </body>
  </html>
 </xsl:template>

 <xsl:template match="title">
  <h1>
   <xsl:apply-templates/>
  </h1>
 </xsl:template>

 <xsl:template match="chapnum">
  <h1>
   Chapter
   <xsl:apply-templates/>
  </h1>
 </xsl:template>

 <xsl:template match="author">
  <h2>
   Written By
   <xsl:apply-templates/>
  </h2>
 </xsl:template>

 <xsl:template match="para">
  <p>
   <xsl:apply-templates/>
  </p>
 </xsl:template>

</xsl:stylesheet>
```

You should be able to recognize some patterns in the code sample, such as the use of `<xsl:template>` and `<xsl:apply-templates>`, and the match and select attributes.

xsl:stylesheet

The `<xsl:stylesheet>` is a container that contains the XSLT style sheet. The attributes on `<xsl:stylesheet>` apply to the whole style sheet and define how the rest of the tags should be interpreted. The version attribute specifies that we are writing to the 1.0 specification of XSLT. (There is only one version right now, but in the future there might be additional releases.)

The `xmlns:xsl` attribute defines the `xsl:` prefix as referring to tags in the XSLT namespace. The `xmlns` attribute—with no `:xsl` suffix—indicates that the default namespace for non-XSLT tags is XHTML.

If you are writing your own XSL, you will probably not need to change these attributes on the `<xsl:stylesheet>` tag, with the exception of the `xmlns` attribute. If you are writing a style sheet to transform to something besides XHTML, you will change this to the appropriate namespace reference.

An `<xsl:stylesheet>` can contain two types of tags—further instructions about how to apply the transformations, and templates for matching.

xsl:strip-space AND xsl:output

To indicate that extra whitespace in the source document—such as indentations—should be ignored, use the `<xsl:strip-space>` tag as shown here, with the attribute `elements="*"` to show that this applies to all elements in the source tree. If you don't do this, you might run into problems with "whitespace nodes" that get counted as invisible text elements in your source tree. `<xsl:strip-space>` is always an empty element.

You use the `<xsl:output>` tag to provide details on how the final result tree's output should appear. In this case, I've specified the attribute `indent="yes"`, which will make our resulting document listings much more readable. Like `<xsl:strip-space>`, `<xsl:output>` is an empty tag.

xsl:template AND xsl:apply-templates

An XSLT style sheet is primarily composed of `<xsl:template>` instructions. A template is composed of two things—a pattern that matches what the template is applied to, and the body of the template itself. To tell the XSLT processor to apply templates to portions of the source document, you use the `<xsl:apply-templates>` tag.

When the XSLT processor begins applying the style sheet to the source document, the first thing it looks for is a template that matches the root node. If it doesn't find it, then there's not much to process. The root node is indicated by `match="/"`—the `"/"` is an XPath expression which means "the root of the source document."

Other templates match specific tags in the source tree—for example, the second template in Listing 19.2 will only match `title` tags. Different tags will pass by this template.

The root template is used to start building the result tree. The contents of the root template form the basic structure of the result document, and any XSLT tags in the root template are applied to flesh out that structure and insert content from the source document.

To tell the processor to match against certain tags in the source tree and insert the output into the result tree a given location, the `<xsl:apply-templates>` tag is used. The tag `<xsl:apply-templates select="book/*" />` indicates that matches should be found for specific tags in the source document, and that the results of applying those templates should be placed at the point in the result tree where the `<xsl:apply-templates>` is located.

The expression `select="book/*"` is more Xpath—in this case, it means "select all children of the `<book>` element from the source tree, and apply any templates that match." Whenever you apply a new template, the "current location" in the mode switches to be at that location in the source tree, which means that XPath expressions are relative to the new current node.

You can think of each template as one hole in a child's toy that has holes cut out in the shape of squares, triangles, stars, and circles of various sizes. Some parts of the source tree will match one or more templates, and some will simply not fit in any of the holes.

DEFAULT TEMPLATES IN XSLT

If a selected node of the source tree matches more than one template, the first one matched will be used. If the node matches none of the templates, then the default template will be used. XSLT defines a default template for all nodes that inserts the value of the node—which is the text content, not including any attributes, of the node and all its children nodes—at the appropriate location in the result tree.

In Listing 19.3, we use the default template in this manner to get the text of the `<title>` element. The second template calls `<xsl:apply-templates/>` with no select parameter, which means "match all the children of this node"—but the only child node of `<title>` is the text node consisting of the title text itself. Because the value of a text node is the text, this gives us what we want.

xsl:value-of

Another way to get the value of a node is to use the `<xsl:value-of>` tag. The `select` attribute is an XPath expression to identify the specific part of the source document whose value you would like to insert.

APPLYING THE STYLE SHEET

So what does this style sheet do? Take a look at Listing 19.3, which is the result of applying the XSLT style sheet in Listing 19.2 to the source document in Listing 19.1.

LISTING 19.3   THE XHTML CREATED BY APPLYING THE XHTML STYLE SHEET TO THE XML DOCUMENT

```
<?xml version="1.0" encoding="utf-8" ?>
<html xmlns="http://www.w3.org/1999/xhtml">
  <head>
   <title>A Tale of Two Cities</title>
  </head>
  <body>
   <h1>A Tale of Two Cities</h1>
   <h2>
   Written By
   Charles Dickens</h2>
   <h1>
   Chapter
   I</h1>
   <h1>The Period</h1>
   <p>
   It was the best of times, it was the worst of
   times, it was the age of wisdom, it was the age of
   foolishness, it was the epoch of belief, it was the epoch
   of incredulity, it was the season of Light, it was the
   season of Darkness, it was the spring of hope, it was the
   winter of despair, we had everything before us, we had
   nothing before us, we were all going direct to Heaven, we
   were all going direct the other way—in short, the period
   was so far like the present period, that some of its
   noisiest authorities insisted on its being received, for
   good or for evil, in the superlative degree of comparison
   only.
   </p>
   <p>
   There were a king with a large jaw and a queen with
   a plain face, on the throne of England; there were a king
   with a large jaw and a queen with a fair face, on the
   throne of France. In both countries it was clearer than
   crystal to the lords of the State preserves of loaves and
   fishes, that things in general were settled for
   ever.
   </p>
   </body>
</html>
```

As you can see, the result document is XHTML, and consists of the content from the XML document and the structure and tags from the XHTML document. Figure 19.1 shows the results as they appear in a browser.

UNDERSTANDING XPATH REFERENCES

XPath is the language used in XSLT select and match attributes (and a few other places) to identify specific parts of the source document. If the source document is thought of as a tree, XPath can be thought of as instructions on how to traverse that tree and reach a specific branch or leaf of the tree.

Figure 19.1
The XHTML result document displayed in a Web browser.

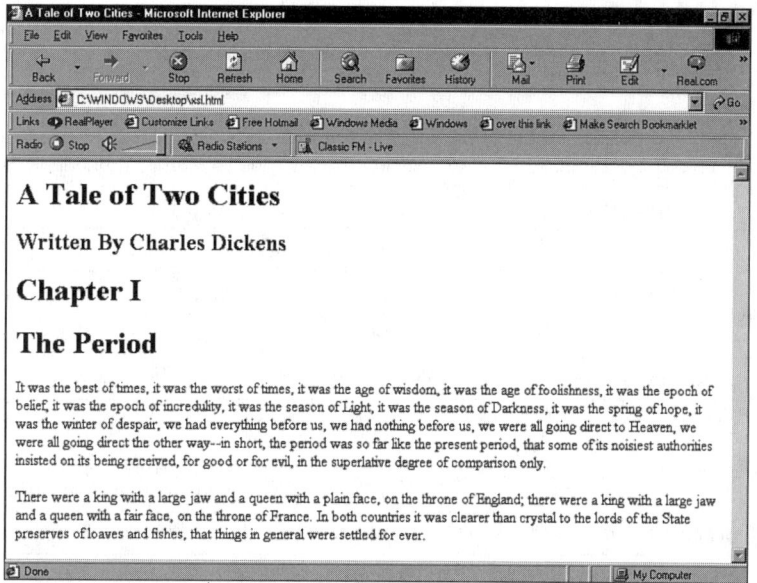

XPath syntax is similar to that used to describe file systems. The root node is called /, and subnodes are named and separated by slashes. The XPath expression "car/make/year" can be read as "the node named year, which is a subnode of make, which is a subnode of car."

Several simple functions are also built into XPath, such as count(), which calculates how many children there are in a given set of nodes.

A list of XPath syntax and functions are given in Table 19.4 and will be explained when used in examples in this chapter.

PART
IV

CH
19

TABLE 19.4   XPATH SYNTAX AND FUNCTIONS

XPath Expression	Matches
/	Root node
.	Current node
..	Parent node of current node
grape	Subnode "grape"
grape/lime	Subnode "lime" of subnode "grape"
grape/*	All children of subnode "grape"
/grape	Node "grape" that is a direct child of the root node
@tangerine	Attribute "tangerine" of current node
@*	All attributes of current node

TABLE 19.4   CONTINUED

XPath Expression	Matches
grape@tangerine	Attribute "tangerine" of "grape" subnode
grape/lime@tangerine	Attribute "tangerine" of "lime" subnode of "grape" subnode
..@tangerine	Attribute "tangerine" of parent node
//	Any number of intervening nodes
grape//lime	All nodes "lime" which have "grape" as an ancestor
[]	Introduces a predicate expression
grape[lime]	Node "grape" that has a child "lime"
grape[lime='Key']	Node "grape" that has a child "lime" whose value (text content) is "Key"
grape[@tangerine]	Node "grape" that has an attribute "tangerine"
grape[@tangerine="3"]	Node "grape" that has an attribute "tangerine" whose value is 3
count(grape/*)	The number of children of subnode "grape"

TRANSFORMING XHTML WITH XSLT

As I noted before, XSLT can be used with XHTML as easily as it can be used with any other XML-based language. As it's a language to transform documents, XSLT is especially good for producing alternate versions of your pages, as well as inserting presentational markup or CSS to style unformatted XHTML Strict.

USING CSS AND XSLT WITH XHTML

Although they approach style from different perspectives, cascading style sheets and Extensible Stylesheet Language are not incompatible at all, and they can be used together to produce sophisticated styling techniques.

When you generate an XHTML document using XSLT, you can create embedded style sheets, reference external CSS documents, or insert CSS into style attributes. Let's look at a simple example of how to do this.

In Listing 19.4, I've created an XHMTL document that consists of just a plain table with some data. This table is a listing of the Tibetan Mastiff dogs owned by the Bartlett family. The name, sex, and age of each dog is included in this data table. (I've used the th element—table header—to identify which line of the table is a header for the rest.)

→ For more information on tables, **see** Chapter 14, "Laying Out Tables Within XHTML Documents," **p. 243**.

LISTING 19.4 A RATHER ORDINARY XHTML TABLE LISTING TIBETAN MASTIFF DOGS OWNED BY ONE FAMILY

```
<html>
<head>
<title>A Simple Data Table</title>
</head>
<body>
<table>
 <tr>
  <th>Dog Name</th>
  <th>Sex</th>
  <th>Age</th>
 </tr>
 <tr>
  <td>Angie</td>
  <td>female</td>
  <td>10</td>
 </tr>
 <tr>
  <td>Xena</td>
  <td>female</td>
  <td>2</td>
 </tr>
 <tr>
  <td>Sunny</td>
  <td>male</td>
  <td>7</td>
 </tr>
 <tr>
  <td>Kim</td>
  <td>male</td>
  <td>10</td>
 </tr>
 <tr>
  <td>Nying</td>
  <td>female</td>
  <td>10</td>
 </tr>
 <tr>
  <td>Perkyi</td>
  <td>female</td>
  <td>5</td>
 </tr>
</table>
</body>
</html>
```

When you display this in a Web browser, as in Figure 19.2, you can see that all the information is presented—but it's not very exciting. How can this presentation be spiced up using XSLT? Let's try a very simple set of transformations to reformat the page.

Figure 19.2
This very basic XHTML table contains important content, but it is quite plain to look at.

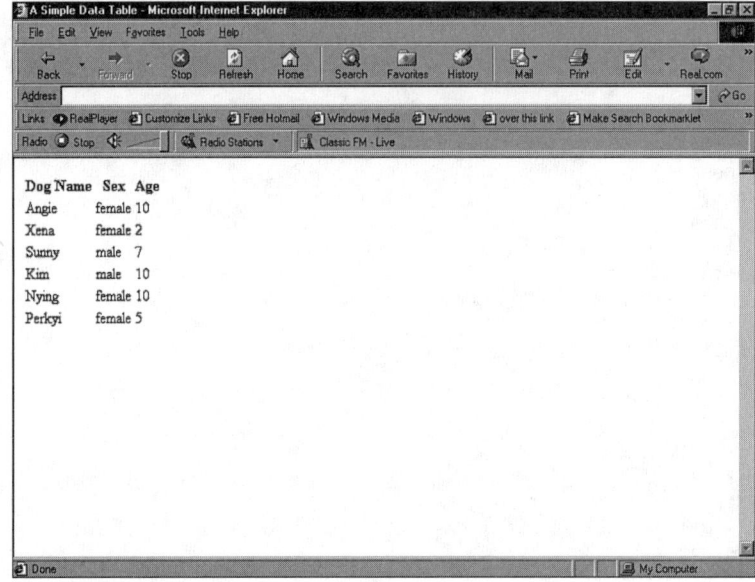

The XSLT style sheet I created for this page will not only reformat the table, it will also reorder the data and insert a header. The style sheet is shown in Listing 19.5.

LISTING 19.5 AN XSLT STYLE SHEET TO TRANSFORM THE TABLE OF DOGS INTO A MORE PRESENTABLE FORMAT

```
<xsl:stylesheet
 xmlns:xsl="http://www.w3.org/1999/XSL/Transform"
 version="1.0"
 xmlns="http://www.w3.org/1999/xhtml">

<xsl:strip-space elements="*"/>
<xsl:output indent="yes"/>

<xsl:template match="/">
 <html>
  <head>
   <title>Bartlett Dogs</title>
   <style type="text/css">
    <xsl:comment>
     <![CDATA[
     p.note { font-family: Arial, sans-serif;
          border: 5px solid blue;
          padding: 3px;
          width: 585px; }
     ]]>
    </xsl:comment>
   </style>
  </head>
  <body>
```

LISTING 19.5   CONTINUED

```
      <h1 style="font-family: Arial;">
      Bartlett Family Tibetan Mastiffs
      </h1>
      <p class="note">
      Our dogs are listed in order from oldest to
      youngest.
      </p>
      <xsl:apply-templates select="html/body/*" />
      </body>
     </html>
    </xsl:template>

    <xsl:template match="table">
     <table border="0" width="585" cellspacing="4"
         style="background-color: green; font-family: Arial;">
      <xsl:apply-templates select="tr[th]" />
      <xsl:apply-templates select="tr[td]" >
       <xsl:sort select="td[position()=3]"
           data-type="number" order="descending" />
      </xsl:apply-templates>
     </table>
    </xsl:template>

    <xsl:template match="tr">
     <tr>
      <xsl:apply-templates />
     </tr>
    </xsl:template>

    <xsl:template match="th">
     <th align="left"
      style="background-color: white; font-weight: bold;">
      <xsl:apply-templates />
     </th>
    </xsl:template>

    <xsl:template match="td">
     <td align="left" style="background-color: yellow;">
      <xsl:apply-templates />
     </td>
    </xsl:template>
   </xsl:stylesheet>
```

PART

IV

CH

19

This style sheet includes a number of XSLT and XPath functions that you haven't seen before, such as CDATA, xsl:comment, predicates in XPath selections, xsl:sort, and the XPath position() function.

xsl:comment AND CDATA

To prevent our CSS from being interpreted as text by older browsers, I need to wrap the embedded style sheet in comments inside the `<style>`...`</style>` tags. To do this, I had to use the xsl:comment tag—if I just used normal `<!— comments —>` they would be interpreted as comments in the XSLT document, and not actual markup to be passed along in the result document. If you want a comment to appear in your results, use the `<xsl:comment>` tag as shown here.

I also used the CDATA tag to enclose the text of the style sheet. CDATA is an XML instruction that basically says "pass this along as is—don't bother to check to see if it's markup, well formed, or anything else." Whenever you are using embedded style sheets in your XSLT document, you want do use both `xsl:comment` and CDATA as shown so that it appears correctly in your result document. This is also how you want to embed scripts (such as Javascript) in your XSLT style sheet.

➜ For more on embedded cascading style sheets, **see** Chapter 18, "Cascading Style Sheets and XHTML," **p. 377.**

XPATH PREDICATES

In the template that matches `table`, you'll notice that I used two `xsl:apply-templates`—one with `select="tr[th]"` and one with `select="tr[td]"`. This is an example of XPath predicates at work —a predicate is indicated by square brackets following an XPath expression, and refines the selection.

In the first case, `tr[th]` means "select all `tr` elements which contain a th element." In the second, `tr[td]` means "select all `tr` elements which contain a td element." The effect of this is that the table rows containing a header are included first, and then the table rows containing table data.

`xsl:sort` AND `position()`

In many cases, `xsl:apply-templates` will be an empty element and you will open and close it at the same time, with `<xsl:apply-templates />`. However, if you wish to sort the way in which you apply your templates, you can use `xsl:apply-templates` as a container, one which can only contain the `<xsl:sort>` tag.

The `select` attribute for `<xsl:sort>` is an XPath expression to identify what you use as your key for sorting. In this example, I've said to use the `td` attribute—and I added a predicate, `[position()=3]`. That predicate means that the third `td` child object should be matched, which in this case is the "age" column for our dogs. The XPath `position()` function calculates the position in the list of child nodes. The other attributes of `<xsl:sort>` are `data-type`, which can be "text" or "number", and `order`, which takes the values "ascending" or "descending."

So what does all this produce? The resulting XHTML file is shown in Listing 19.6, and Figure 19.3 displays that file in a Web browser. Notice that the dogs are sorted by age!

LISTING 19.6 THE XHTML FILE PRODUCED BY THE PRECEDING XSLT FILE

```
<?xml version="1.0" encoding="utf-8" ?>
<html xmlns="http://www.w3.org/1999/xhtml">
  <head>
   <title>Bartlett Dogs</title>
   <style type="text/css"><!—
```

LISTING 19.6   CONTINUED

```
p.note { font-family: Arial, sans-serif;
         border: 5px solid blue;
         padding: 3px;
         width: 585px; }

   —></style>
  </head>
  <body>
   <h1 style="font-family: Arial;">
     Bartlett Family Tibetan Mastiffs
    </h1>
   <p class="note">
     Our dogs are listed in order from oldest to
     youngest.
    </p>
   <table border="0" width="585" cellspacing="4" style="background-color: green;
font-family: Arial;">
     <tr>
      <th align="left" style="background-color:
        white; font-weight: bold;">Dog Name</th>
      <th align="left" style="background-color:
        white; font-weight: bold;">Sex</th>
      <th align="left" style="background-color:
        white; font-weight: bold;">Age</th>
     </tr>
     <tr>
      <td align="left" style="background-color:
        yellow;">Angie</td>
      <td align="left" style="background-color:
        yellow;">female</td>
      <td align="left" style="background-color:
        yellow;">10</td>
     </tr>
     <tr>
      <td align="left" style="background-color:
        yellow;">Kim</td>
      <td align="left" style="background-color:
        yellow;">male</td>
      <td align="left" style="background-color:
        yellow;">10</td>
     </tr>
     <tr>
      <td align="left" style="background-color:
        yellow;">Nying</td>
      <td align="left" style="background-color:
        yellow;">female</td>
      <td align="left" style="background-color:
        yellow;">10</td>
     </tr>
     <tr>
      <td align="left" style="background-color:
        yellow;">Sunny</td>
      <td align="left" style="background-color:
        yellow;">male</td>
      <td align="left" style="background-color:
```

PART

IV

CH

19

LISTING 19.6 CONTINUED

```
      yellow;">7</td>
    </tr>
    <tr>
     <td align="left" style="background-color:
      yellow;">Perkyi</td>
     <td align="left" style="background-color:
      yellow;">female</td>
     <td align="left" style="background-color:
      yellow;">5</td>
    </tr>
    <tr>
     <td align="left" style="background-color:
      yellow;">Xena</td>
     <td align="left" style="background-color:
      yellow;">female</td>
     <td align="left" style="background-color:
      yellow;">2</td>
    </tr>
   </table>
  </body>
</html>
```

Figure 19.3
A little XSLT and CSS adds style to the boring data table, and even sorts the dogs by age!

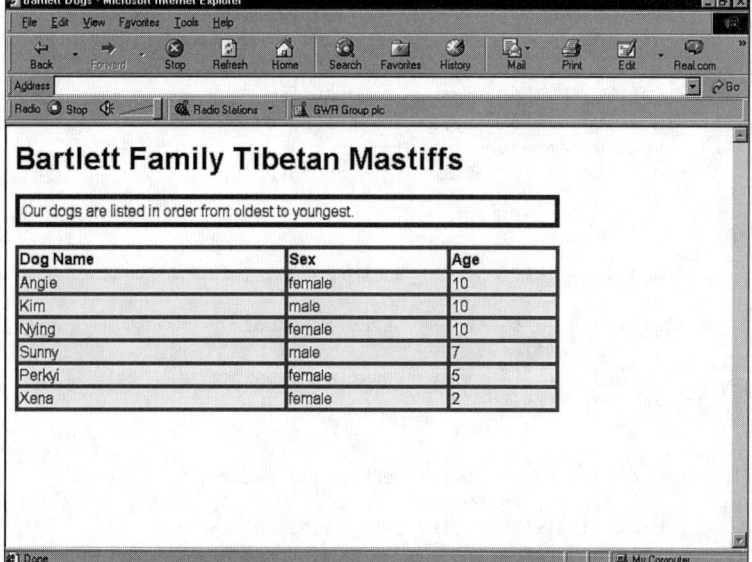

CREATING ALTERNATE CONTENT VIEWS

XSL Transformations can accomplish a lot more than simply presenting the existing structure of the page in a new light—the ability to completely transform the source document means that XSLT can be used to create completely different views of the same information. For example, a page with navigation graphics can be reformatted to use text and CSS, a set of layout tables can be converted to frames, markup can be simplified for hand-held access devices, or a data table can be summarized in text paragraphs.

I'll take the same data I used before—the table of Tibetan Mastiffs shown in Listing 19.6—and apply a different style sheet that will create a completely different representation of the content.

The new XSLT style sheet is designed to provide a different structure on the same content, and is shown in Listing 19.7.

LISTING 19.7   A NEW XSLT STYLE SHEET

```
<xsl:stylesheet
 xmlns:xsl="http://www.w3.org/1999/XSL/Transform"
 version="1.0"
 xmlns="http://www.w3.org/1999/xhtml">

<xsl:strip-space elements="*"/>
<xsl:output indent="yes"/>

<xsl:template match="/">
 <html>
  <head>
   <title>Summary Report on Bartlett Dogs</title>
  </head>
  <body>
   <h1>
    Summary of Dogs
   </h1>
   <p>
    The Bartletts have
    <xsl:value-of select="count(html/body/table/tr[td])" />
    dogs.
   </p>
   <p>
    They have
    <xsl:value-of
     select="count(html/body/table/tr[td='female'])" />
    female dogs and
    <xsl:value-of
     select="count(html/body/table/tr[td='male'])" />
    male dogs.
   </p>
   <p>
    The male dogs are:
   </p>
   <ul>
    <xsl:for-each select="html/body/table/tr[td='male']">
     <li>
      <xsl:value-of select="td[position()=1]"/>
      --
      <xsl:value-of select="td[position()=3]"/>
      years old
     </li>
    </xsl:for-each>
```

LISTING 19.7   CONTINUED

```
      </ul>
      <p>
       For more about Tibetan Mastiffs, please see
       <a href="http://www.tibetanmastiffs.com">
        http://www.tibetanmastiffs.com
       </a>
      </p>
     </body>
    </html>
   </xsl:template>

</xsl:stylesheet>
```

`count()` AND MORE XPATH PREDICATES

In the first paragraph, I used the XPath `count()` function. This function takes an XPath expression—`html/body/table/tr[td]`— and returns a numeric value, which is inserted into the result document by the `<xsl:value-of>` tag. This XPath expression identifies all table rows that have a `td` element, and counts them —which tells me how many dogs are in the data table. Later, I use the predicates `[td='male']` and `[td='female']` to only select dogs of a certain gender.

`xsl:for-each`

In this example, I used `<xsl:for-each>` instead of calling `<xsl:apply-templates>`. The `xsl:for-each` element defines a section of XSLT that is executed once for each node in the select of the `<xsl:for-each>` tag, and that block of XSLT is treated as if it were a template itself. You can use `<xsl:for-each>` for simple loops in this manner.

When we apply our XSLT style sheet, we get the XHTML document presented in Listing 19.8. Figure 19.4 shows how it looks in a browser. Compare this to the original document. You can see how much the structure has changed and how XSLT has provided a different way of looking at the same content.

LISTING 19.8   THE RESULTS OF APPLYING THE XSLT STYLE SHEET (LISTING 19.7) TO THE TABLE OF DOGS (LISTING 19.6).

```
<?xml version="1.0" encoding="utf-8" ?>
<html xmlns="http://www.w3.org/1999/xhtml">
  <head>
   <title>Summary Report on Bartlett Dogs</title>
  </head>
  <body>
   <h1>
     Summary of Dogs
    </h1>
   <p>
    The Bartletts have
    6
    dogs.
```

LISTING 19.8   CONTINUED

```
  </p>
<p>
  They have
  4
  female dogs and
  2
  male dogs.
 </p>
<p>
  The male dogs are:
 </p>
<ul>
  <li>Sunny
    --
    7
    years old
   </li>
  <li>Kim
    --
    10
    years old
   </li>
 </ul>
<p>
  For more about Tibetan Mastiffs, please see
  <a href="http://www.tibetanmastiffs.com">
   http://www.tibetanmastiffs.com
   </a>
 </p>
 </body>
 </html>
```

Figure 19.4
By using XPath to identify specific content in our XHTML file, we're able to create a new page that summarizes the original page.

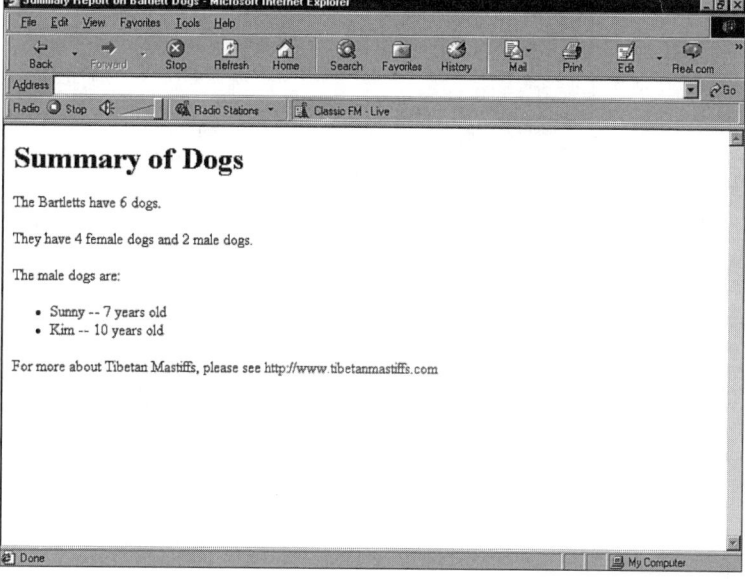

XSLT IN THE REAL WORLD

ADAPTING WEB PAGES FOR SPECIFIC AUDIENCES

One of the biggest challenges of Web design for the 21st Century is making content accessible to everyone, including people with disabilities who use assistive technologies such as screenreaders or Braille terminals. One approach is to create pages that degrade gracefully and offer text alternatives to graphic content. This strategy has worked well and made the World Wide Web much more usable by people with special needs.

The advent of XSLT offers the opportunity to use different approach—the chance to make Web sites that can actually "morph" to meet the specific needs of its users. One company who is applying this approach is Edapta, Inc. of San Diego, California (Figure 19.5). Edapta has applied XSL technology to solving the accessibility problems of the Web, and has come up with some interesting results.

Figure 19.5
Edapta, Inc. home page.

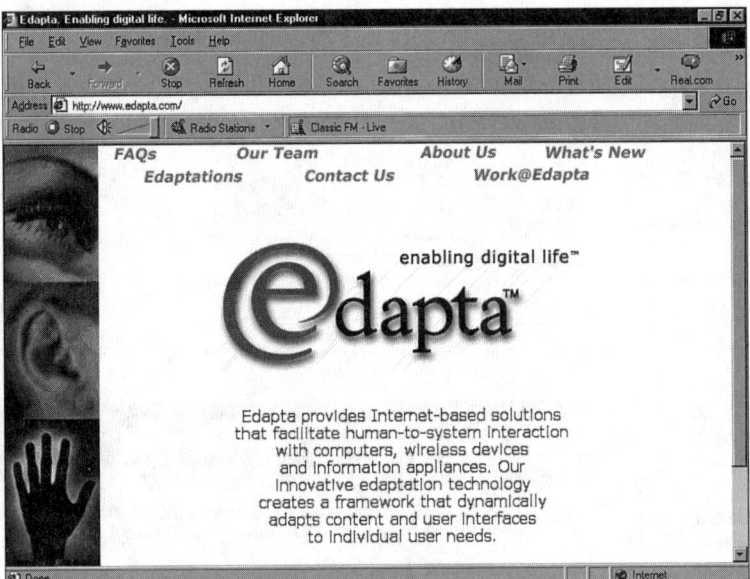

Starting with a Web site written in XML or XHTML, Edapta's XSLT-based software can transform the site for each user, presenting a user interface that is optimized for their capabilities and preferences. For example, users of screenreaders – programs that read screen output aloud – experience Web pages in a linear fashion. Edapta's software can create a new interface that puts the main content up front and the navigation at the bottom, along with creating a short index with anchors at the start of the page, optimized for screenreader use.

This same technique can be used to create alternate interfaces for any other access device, from a TV set-top box to a hand-held PDA. Through applying XSLT style sheets, access can be guaranteed for a wide number of Web users.

Note

More information on Edapta's site morphing technology can be found at `http://www.edapta.com/`.

CHAPTER 20

ADDING JAVASCRIPT TO XHTML DOCUMENTS

In this chapter

SCRIPTING AND XHTML

This chapter will introduce you to JavaScript, and teach you how to use it in your pages. As with Chapter 18, "Cascading Style Sheets and XHTML," all the information in this chapter is as applicable to HTML as it is to XHTML.

And, as with style, there are a very similar rules to bear in mind when it comes to using JavaScript with XHTML:

- Because XML describes JavaScript as CDATA (content data), scripting in XML and XHTML should be marked up using the CDATA element if you're going to embed the script into the document. As you've already read in the CSS chapter, this element is incompatible with most browsers:

```
<script>
<!--
/* <![CDATA[ */

your script goes here
 /* ]]> */ -->
</script>
```

Embedded scripts are the most commonly used in current HTML practices.

- For your XHTML pages to validate with embedded JavaScript, you should denote your documents as being transitional XHTML 1.0 documents.

- It is *highly recommended* that you begin to use linked scripts only, avoiding any rendering problems and confusion.

- In a strict XHTML 1.0 document, use a linked script.

THE POWER OF SCRIPTING

The power of JavaScript has become extremely significant to Web developers. Used originally to enhance sites with cool stuff, JavaScript has become a sophisticated method of addressing many previously confounding site development concerns.

JavaScript is a scripting language that was originally derived from Netscape's LiveScript. Sun Microsystems, developer of the Java language, took an interest in this powerful script and, along with Netscape, made some adjustments and re-introduced the script under the new name JavaScript.

Unlike Java, which can be used to develop entirely standalone applications, JavaScript works primarily with Web pages. Furthermore, Java programs for the Web known as *applets* can demand significant resources from an individual's computer and browser. JavaScript, on the other hand, is usually included within the HTML file and interpreted line-by-line by the browser.

JavaScript is used most frequently to:

- Add visual functions such as alert boxes and pop-up windows
- Create animations
- Detect browser, browser version, and platform

Note

JavaScript is also one of the fundamental cornerstones of Dynamic HTML, along with Cascading Style Sheets (CSS). You'll have the opportunity to work with both of those topics.

In this chapter, I'll first explain the fundamental elements of JavaScript—objects, operators, statements, and functions. Then, I'll offer a variety of helpful JavaScripts, showing you how to add an alert box, drop-down navigation menu, pop-up window, and mouseover animation, and how to detect and route Web browsers for cross-browser design.

UNDERSTANDING JAVASCRIPT

JavaScript isn't XHTML, but it works with it. JavaScript, however, is a general-purpose scripting language.

Some general JavaScript rules to remember include the following:

- JavaScript is case sensitive.
- It's possible that even if someone is using a JavaScript-enabled browser, the JavaScript is turned off—so you need to plan your designs to be non–JavaScript-compliant too.
- JavaScript code should always be commented out so older browsers don't display the code.

Different programming languages vary in syntax and keywords. Syntax is the exact structure of statements in the language, and keywords are the built-in terms that the language is designed to understand. They all have one core concept in common, though: Every programming language works by following a list of instructions.

It's really no different from many of the things you already do in day to day life. When a friend tells you how to get to her house, you follow the directions she gives you—turning left here, driving past a particular store, turning right there, and so forth—until you have completed the list of instructions to travel between your home and hers.

When you go to the grocery, you're following a program too. If you wrote it out step by individual step, it might look something like the following:

1. Leave house
2. Get in car

3. Drive to grocery

4. Park car

5. Get out of car

6. Enter grocery

JavaScript works the same way.

You create a list of very specific instructions that will be followed by a Web browser sequentially when it accesses your Web page or when a site visitor takes an action, such as a moving or clicking the mouse. When all those instructions are strung together and interpreted in order, a task is performed.

JAVASCRIPT PLACEMENT

In HTML, JavaScript appears right in the individual HTML file and fits within the `<script>` and `</script>` tags. In XHTML, you need to add the CDATA element for strict, conforming documents. But, because the CDATA element is unreadable by most Web browsers, be sure to either make your document a transitional XHTML 1.0 document, or link to the script using the `link` element.

To embed a script, place the script within the script (and CDATA if you're using it) into the `head` element on your XHTML page. You also will often include pieces of JavaScript within tags to control *intrinsic* (inline) events.

Tip

> You also should use comment tags around your code so browsers that don't support JavaScript won't try to write the code to the page.

Listing 20.1 shows the structure of a typical XHTML document including the JavaScript tags.

LISTING 20.1 AN XHTML DOCUMENT WITH JAVASCRIPT TAGS

```
<?xml version="1.0"?>
<!DOCtype html PUBLIC "-//W3C//DTD XHTML 1.0 Transitional//EN"
"http://www.w3.org/TR/xhtml1/DTD/xhtml1-transitional.dtd">
<html xmlns="http://www.w3.org/1999/xhtml">
<head>
<title>     </title>

<script language="JavaScript">


<!--
Hide the script from non-JS browsers
javascript code goes here
//-->


</script>
```

LISTING 20.1   CONTINUED

```
</head>
<body>
</body>

</html>
```

Note

You'll see that although the opening portion of the comment tag, `<!--`, looks like any standard comment tag, the closing portion is different from what is used in commenting non-script based XHTML (`-->`). The closing portion for comment scripting is `//-->`. This is an important distinction.

OBJECTS AND OPERATORS IN JAVASCRIPT

Objects and operators perform the same roles in JavaScript that nouns and verbs do in human languages. *Objects* are the things (windows, page elements, and so on), whereas *operators* tell JavaScript what kind of actions should take place.

You should know that the DOM considers each element on every Web page a separate object. The window where you view the page is an object, the title of the page is an object, as is the body. Even things like headings, paragraphs, and images are objects. With the DOM, each object can be accessed and manipulated with JavaScript.

PROPERTIES AND OPERATORS

One of the most important things about objects is that they have *properties*. Properties for a paragraph object, for instance, include such things as font size, font color, and so on. You can use JavaScript to change the values in those properties, so you can change the font color in a paragraph by simply resetting it in a line of program code. Likewise, you can alter the properties of any element in the same way.

Operators are the key to making changes. As the name implies, they are used to perform operations on objects. Those operations include things like adding, subtracting, multiplying, and dividing values. Table 20.1 shows the basic JavaScript arithmetic operators.

TABLE 20.1   COMMONLY USED JAVASCRIPT ARITHMETIC OPERATORS

Operator	Function
+	Addition
-	Subtraction
*	Multiplication
/	Division
++	Increment
--	Decrement

PART

IV

CH

20

The first four are used in normal math. If you want to add two values, you use value1 + value2. If you want to multiply two values, you use value1 * value2. It's the same with subtraction and division, except of course for the symbols used.

The increment and decrement operators, though, are unique to programming, and they follow a very special syntax. I'll revisit them shortly. In addition to the basic arithmetic operators, there are others. One of the most common operators is the equals sign (=). You'll be using it a lot. In JavaScript, it's called the *assignment operator* because it's used to assign a value to an object or a *variable*. Variables are names you create to hold values.

Technically, a variable is a value that changes during the course of your program, but you can use a variable to hold an unchanging value (like *pi*) as well. In that case, you have a situation that would give language purists a fit—the variable contains a *constant*. In either case, the syntax is the same.

Before you can use a variable, you have to declare it. Although you simply can declare its existence without assigning any particular value to it, it's a common practice to both declare it and assign it an initial value at the same time. That's called *initializing a variable*. The following are a couple of examples. The first is a simple variable declaration, whereas the second shows how you initialize a variable:

```
var bananaCost
```

```
var orangeCost = 3
```

In both cases, the variable is available for use in your script. You can go right ahead and use them without further ado. But the variable bananaCost has no value as yet, so you'll have to include something in your script to take care of that little detail before you can do anything useful with it.

The other variable, orangeCost, already contains a value, so you could do things with it like the following:

```
orangeCost + 5
```

Because the variable orangeCost contains the value 3, this would be the same thing as saying 3 + 5.

There are a bunch of variations on the assignment operator that let you perform commonly used combinations of math and assignment. For example, it's not unusual at all to have an expression like value = value + 7 or value = value / 2.

In the first case, you've got an expression that increases a value by 7 every time it's executed; in the second case, you divide the value by 2 every time you execute that expression. If you want to use a shorthand version of that kind of expression, you can use the *compound assignment operators*. They're specifically designed for the purpose. Table 20.2 shows the basic JavaScript compound assignment operators.

TABLE 20.2   COMMONLY USED JAVASCRIPT COMPOUND ASSIGNMENT OPERATORS

Operator	Function
+=	Addition compound assignment
-=	Subtraction compound assignment
*=	Multiplication compound assignment
/=	Division compound assignment

You use these in place of expressions like the ones in the preceding paragraph. Table 20.3 compares expressions that use compound assignment operators with the equivalent expressions that use both arithmetic operators and the normal assignment operator.

TABLE 20.3   COMPARISON OF COMPOUND ASSIGNMENT OPERATORS AND NORMAL APPROACH

Compound Expression	Normal Expression
value += 7	value = value + 7
value -= 7	value = value - 7
value *= 7	value = value * 7
value /= 7	value = value / 7

Now that you've been introduced to variables and assignments, it's time to take a look at the increment and decrement operators (++ and --). The increment operator adds 1 to a value. The decrement operator subtracts 1 from a value. They're especially useful when you need to establish a countup or countdown situation.

Of course, you always can use something like count = count + 1 or even count += 1, but its easier to just say count++ instead. Also, it's readily apparent that you're in a countup or countdown when you see either the increment or the decrement operator.

Now for the special syntax of the increment and decrement operators. You can place them either before or after the variable they apply to (++count or count++), and it matters very much where you put them. When they're placed before the variable, the increment or decrement operation takes place before the expression that they're a part of is interpreted. When they're placed after, the expression is interpreted first. Take the following two examples:

```
total = ++count
total =   count++
```

Assume the variable count holds the value 4 before these lines are executed. In the first case, the value of count will be increased by 1 before its value is assigned to the variable total. In that case, the value in total will be 5 and the value in count will also be 5. In the second case, the value of count is assigned to the variable total first, and then count is incremented.

PART

IV

CH

20

The result is that total holds the original value of 4, but the count now holds a value of 5. This can make a huge difference in your program. Which one you end up using depends on how you want your program to work, but you need to keep the difference in mind or you'll end up with results other than those you had in mind.

CREATING LOGICAL RELATIONSHIPS

You can write perfectly good programs by using only the assignment and arithmetic operators, but you don't get into the real power until you start using the logical and comparison operators. Logical operators look at the relationship between values, and comparison operators compare values to tell if a comparison is true or false. This seemingly simple capability is the key to truly sophisticated programs. Tables 20.4 and 20.5 show the JavaScript logical and comparison operators.

TABLE 20.4   COMMONLY USED JAVASCRIPT COMPARISON OPERATORS

Operator	Function
==	Equality
!=	Inequality
>	Greater than
<	Less than
>=	Greater than or equal to
<=	Less than or equal to

TABLE 20.5   JAVASCRIPT LOGICAL OPERATORS

Operator	Function
&&	AND
||	OR
!	NOT

Each comparison operator tests for different conditions. If the condition is met, the operator returns a value of true (numerically, 1); if it's not met, the operator returns a value of false (numerically, 0).

The equality operator (==) tests to see if two values are the same. The inequality operator (!=) tests to see if two values are different. Greater than (>) and less than (<) check to see if a value is higher or lower than another one; greater than or equal to (>=) and less than or equal to (<=) do the same thing, but will also return true if the value tested is equal.

The logical operator, AND (&&), checks to see if two conditions are both true. If either one of them is false, it will return false. The OR operator (||), on the other hand, works a bit differently. It checks to see if either one of two conditions are true. If either one of them is true, it will return `true`. Only if both of them are `false` will it return `false`. The NOT operator (!) simply reverses the truth or falsehood of anything to which it's applied.

Caution
The similarity between the comparison equality operator (==) and the assignment operator (=) is one of the most common sources of programming errors. It's not at all unusual for even professional programmers to unconsciously use the assignment operator when testing for equality.

STATEMENTS AND FUNCTIONS IN JAVASCRIPT

Statements are the sentences of JavaScript. They combine objects and operators into instructions to perform actions. A statement is a single action, although it can depend on conditions, and ends in a semicolon (;). The following are some examples of simple statements:

```
petNumber = cats + dogs;
timeLeft = timeHad - timeUsed;
userName = "Elmer Fudd";
```

In addition to the statements you create yourself from scratch, JavaScript has a number of built-in statements you can use in your scripts.

THE if STATEMENT

One of the most widely used is the `if` statement. `if` statements test to see if a condition is `true` and, if it is, they perform some action. If it isn't `true`, nothing happens.

```
if (carPrice < 20000) {buyIt();}
```

The curly braces ({}) are used to contain the statement that gets executed if the condition evaluates as `true`. They act much like the start tags and end tags in XHTML, and you always have to have evenly matched pairs of braces. This will become more important later as you get into more complex structures that involve multiple statements.

Caution
Leaving out a brace, either at the beginning or end of a statement, is another common cause of programming errors.

Although a simple `if` statement is often placed on a single line like the previous example, it's not unusual to see it on multiple lines, with each element of it separated for easy reading like the following:

```
if (carPrice < 20000)
    {
    buyIt();
    }
```

This way, the condition the `if` statement is testing is listed first, followed by the action to be performed if it turns out to be `true`.

THE if...else STATEMENT

There's also a variant of the if statement called the if...else statement. Like the if statement, it tests to see if a condition is true, but it offers an alternative action if the statement is false:

```
if (carPrice < 20000)
    {
    buyIt();
    }
else
    {
    forgetIt();
    }
```

LOOPS

Another critical built-in statement type that JavaScript programmers use a lot are known as *loops*. Loops keep the program running in circles, doing little or nothing until some condition is met.

Loops are common to many programming languages. For example, if you're playing a computer game, the program is doing things while in a loop that's waiting for you to move the joystick or press the fire button (or fly your plane into a mountain). If you're using a word processor, it sits there waiting in a loop until you use the mouse or the keyboard.

The most common loop is the for loop, and it makes heavy use the increment and decrement operators. The for loop uses a counter variable that's set to some particular starting value (often 0 or 1). It checks to see if that counter variable has reached a specified limit and then performs a specified action. Next, it increments or decrements the counter variable and starts all over again. The following is what a typical for loop looks like:

```
for (counter=1; counter<=10; counter++)
    {
    doSomething();
    }
```

The various parts of this break down into the following steps:

1. Start the counter value at 1.
2. Test to see if the counter value is less than or equal to 10.
3. Perform the function named doSomething().
4. Add 1 to the counter value.
5. Go back to step 2. If the counter value is greater than 10, the loop is finished. Otherwise, steps 3 through 5 are repeated.

The upshot of all this is that you use the for loop in this example to perform the same action 10 times in a row. You could just as easily set the counter variable to a value of 10, say that the action should be repeated as long as the condition counter>=1 is met, and use the negation operator (counter--) to count down instead of using the increment operator (counter++) to count up.

There's another statement that's very similar to the `for` loop, called the `while` loop. They both repeat themselves until some condition is met. The difference between the two is that the `for` loop has a built-in variable and a requirement for that variable to either increase or decrease. The `while` loop, on the other hand, has only the condition itself, with no guarantee that the condition will ever change. The following is a typical `while` loop:

```
while (counter<=10)
    {
    doSomething();
    }
```

As you can see, you need something else in the program to change the condition. Assuming the counter value is less than or equal to `10` when the `while` loop starts, the loop will never end unless that value is changed by the function `doSomething()`. The possibility of an endless loop where no action is taken and the program runs on and on is one of the reasons why most programmers use `while` loops a lot less often than `for` loops.

FUNCTIONS

The actions in the preceding statements look a little different from what you've seen so far. They have those funny parentheses after them. They're actually instructions to perform entire sets of statements, called functions. If statements are sentences, functions are paragraphs, collections of statements. Where a single statement performs a single action, functions combine several statements together to perform a number of actions in a sequence.

You name functions so you can execute the entire sequence of statements at once by just invoking the name of the function. This is known as *calling a* function, and you'll come to appreciate its simplicity.

Technically, a function can consist of as little as one statement, but they normally include several at a time. The following is a typical function:

```
function getSleep()
    {
    turnOffLights = true;
    bed = "yes";
    }
```

You have to start with the keyword `function` so JavaScript knows what you're defining. As with `if` statements, you need to be sure to place the statements that compose the function within curly braces, and you have to make certain that you have an equal number of opening and closing braces flanking the statements. When the function is called by your script, both of the statements will be performed one right after the other.

Although the preceding example used a pair of simple assignment statements, functions can include much more complex statements as well:

```
function getSleep()
    {
    if (doneWithWork = true)
        {
        turnOffLights = true;
```

```
        bed = "yes";
        knockOff();
        }
    else
        {
        turnOffLights = false;
        bed = "not yet";
        keepGoing();
        }
    }
```

This time, the function consists of an `if...else` statement that includes conditional testing resulting in the assignment of one or another value to two variables and the possibility of one or another of two different functions being called. It's not unusual for one function to be called from within another one. The ability to do so enables you to write code that is easily understandable because it can be broken down into several basic functions, each of which is called as needed.

Caution

It's perfectly possible to call a function from inside itself as well as from inside another one. This is called *recursion,* and it's a risky thing to do. Recursion can quickly crash a JavaScript program. It can happen even when you don't do it deliberately. If function A calls function B which, in turn, calls function A, function A then calls B again, which calls A again, and so on.

JavaScript has a set of built-in functions, too, which can make your life a lot easier. In the mock program for going to the grocery that you saw earlier in this chapter, one of the instructions was "Drive to grocery." If that's all you were told to do, you'd know already, without further instructions, that you had to put the key in the ignition, start the car, use the gearshift, the steering wheel, the accelerator pedal, and the brake pedal to perform that task.

That's the way it is with JavaScript's native functions, too. All you have to do is tell JavaScript that you want a pop-up window, for instance, and it'll make one for you. You don't have to tell it how to do it, because it already knows how.

JAVASCRIPT APPLICATIONS

Here, you'll look at how to create a simple message box. From there, you'll look at animating graphics and, lastly, you'll take a look at a series of sophisticated browser tests.

Note

The following scripts contain many of the processes described in the language basics sections of this chapter. For example, you might well recognize functions and operators at work. However, I chose to present the code without defining its anatomy. My objective is to familiarize you with JavaScript enough so that you can identify aspects of the language and use scripts freely. To learn more about writing JavaScript on your own, pick up a copy of Joe Burns' *JavaScript Goodies* from Que.

SIMPLE MESSAGE BOX

This JavaScript (see Listing 20.2) allows you to type anything you like into the message box and have it returned to you by using an *alert box*. This is a box that pops up and stays until the visitor clicks OK.

The use of a message box like this isn't particularly functional, but it does demonstrate, in very simple terms, a function, a variable, and an alert command. Furthermore, it shows how JavaScript interacts with various aspects of HTML, in this case, a simple form.

LISTING 20.2   SIMPLE MESSAGE BOX

```
<?xml version="1.0"?>

<!DOCtype html PUBLIC "-//W3C//DTD XHTML 1.0 Transitional//EN"
"http://www.w3.org/TR/xhtml1/DTD/xhtml1-transitional.dtd">
<html xmlns="http://www.w3.org/1999/xhtml">

<head>

<script language="JavaScript">

<!-- Hide JavaScript
function MsgBox (textstring) {
alert (textstring) }
// - End hide JavaScript - -->

</script>
</head>
<body>
<br />
<br />
<br />
<br />

<div align="center">
<form>
<input name="text1" type="text" />
<input name="submit" type="button" value="Click Me!"
onClick="MsgBox(form.text1.value)" />
</form>
</div>

</body>
</html>
```

Figure 20.1 shows type that's been entered into the box, and Figure 20.2 shows the resulting alert button.

Figure 20.1
I've typed "Hello, World :)" into the text box. No action will take place until I click the Submit button.

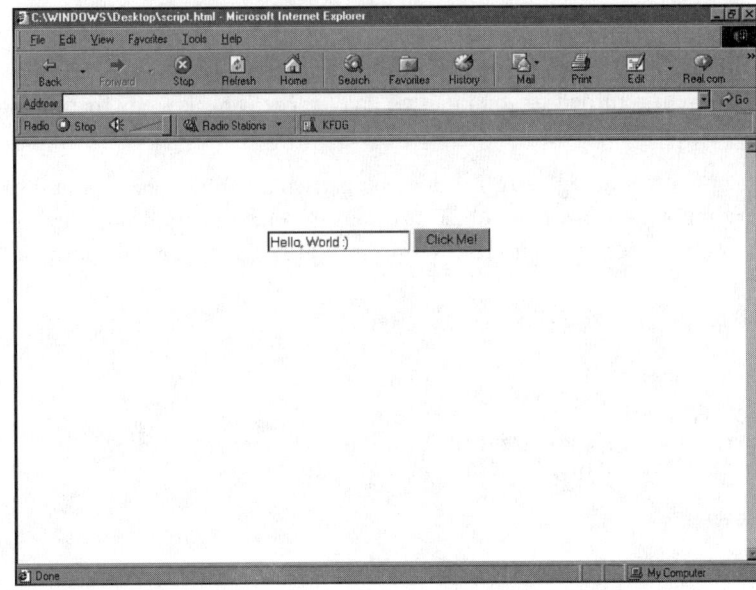

DROP-DOWN MENU NAVIGATION

Using drop-down menus takes the relationship between JavaScript and XHTML to a more sophisticated and useful level than the simple message box example. You create the drop-down menu in XHTML and control its actions with JavaScript (see Listing 20.3).

I'll use the standard `select` object with option tags holding the names of different Web sites for the menu. The value attributes of the `option` elements will be the URLs of the Web sites.

→ For a description of the select and option tags, **see** Chapter 16, "Working with Standard Forms," **p. 319**.

Figure 20.2
The alert button appears after I select Click Me!. The browser has responded to the onClick JavaScript function.

LISTING 20.3 JAVASCRIPT DROP-DOWN MENU NAVIGATION

```
<?xml version="1.0"?>
<!DOCTYPE html PUBLIC "-//W3C//DTD XHTML 1.0 Transitional//EN"
"http://www.w3.org/TR/xhtml1/DTD/xhtml1-transitional.dtd">
<html xmlns="http://www.w3.org/1999/xhtml">
<head>
<title>JavaScript Drop Down Menu</title>

<script language="JavaScript">
<!-- Hide the script from non-JS browsers
function goToLink(form)
```

LISTING 20.3 CONTINUED

```
    {
location.href = form.options[form.selectedIndex].value;
    }
//-->
</script>
</head>

<body>
<br />
<br />
<br />
<br />

<div align="center">
<form name="URLmenu">
<select name="choices">
<option value="http://www.molly.com/">Molly.com</option>
<option value="http://www.webreview.com/">Web Review</option>
<option value="http://www.webtechniques.com/">Web Techniques Magazine</option>
<option value="http://www.mcp.com/">Macmillan Computer Publishing</option>
<option value="13_message_alert.html">Message alert page</option>
</select>
<input type="button" value="Go!" onclick="goToLink(this.form.choices)" />
</form>
</div>

</body>
</html>
```

Figure 20.3 shows the drop-down menu. When the user clicks the GO button, he or she will end up at the selected URL.

Figure 20.3
Here is an example of a JavaScript drop-down menu navigation. Select your location in the text box and click GO!.

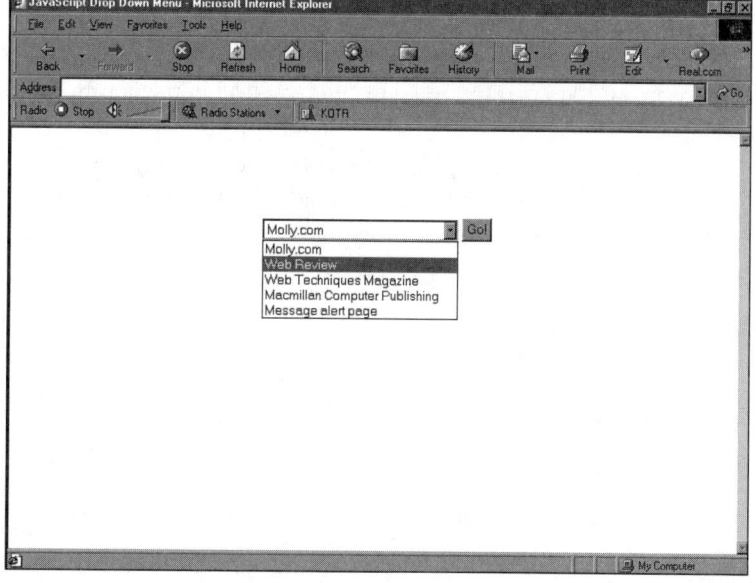

The form included in this menu is a standard piece of XHTML. The JavaScript comes in when a user clicks the button. At that point, the goToLink function is called. The value in the parentheses (this.form.choices) uses a JavaScript shortcut for the name of the form object. this refers to the current object.

The choices part is the name of the select element. When this is passed to the goToLink function, it takes a look to see which of the options in that element have been selected, and then takes the value of that option and makes it the current URL of the Web page.

JavaScript not working? See "Got Script?" in the "Troubleshooting" section near the end of this chapter.

POP-UP WINDOW

The Pop-Up Window is one of the mainstays of JavaScript functionality. It can be used any time you want to have a customized XHTML page pop-up to display some element, such as a help menu.

You can control a variety of attributes in this script, such as whether or not there is a toolbar or status bar in the window, by setting them to 1 (or yes) or 0 (or no).

To install this script, follow these simple steps:

1. Type this script into the head of an HTML document where you'd like to have a pop-up window:

   ```
   <script language="JavaScript">
   <!--//BEGIN Script

   function new_window(url) {

   link =
   window.open(url,"Link","toolbar=0,location=0,directories=0,status=0,menubar=0,
   scrollbars=0,resizable=0,width=200,height=250,left=80,top=180");

   }
   //END Script-->
   </script>
   ```

2. Create the XHTML file you'd like to have load in the pop-up window. Name and save the file.

3. Type this line of JavaScript into the script of your original document, where your_popup.html is the name of your pop-up XHTML file:

   ```
   <a href="javascript:new_window('your_popup.html')">click me</a>
   ```

4. Save your file and test the page.

Figure 20.4 shows the pop-up in action.

Figure 20.4
This JavaScript pop-up window is handy for adding additional information such as a help page or code sample without having to invoke an entirely new browser window.

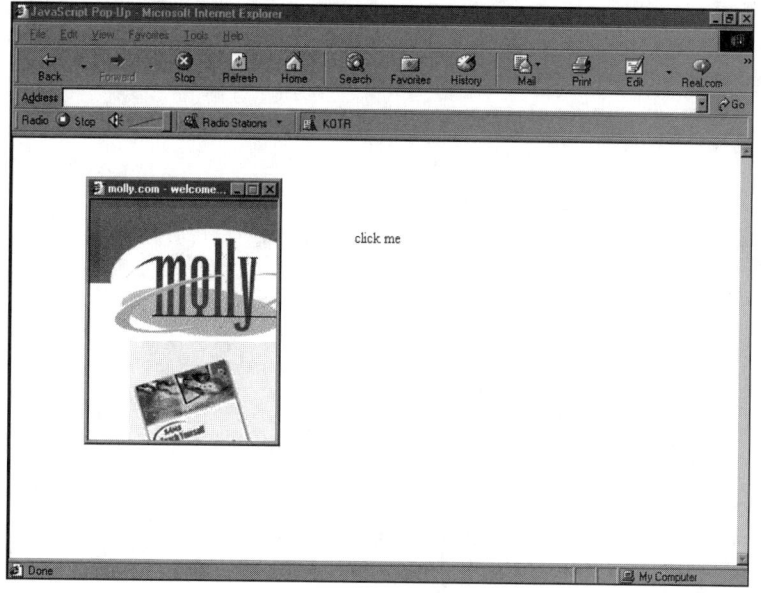

Tip

As helpful as pop-up windows can be, they also can be overused (especially when made automatic and used for advertising). My advice is to use them where they enhance the site: providing help, additional navigation, and code samples. Try to avoid automating pop-ups on page load, and reserving them for user-initiated tasks, such as in the example just provided.

JavaScript Mouseovers

An extremely popular use for Web sites, the JavaScript mouseover and pre-load image application is actually quite simple (see Listing 20.4). However, you will need to create graphic buttons to work with this example.

→ Learn to design mouseover buttons, **see** Chapter 29, "Creating Professional Web Graphics," **p. 595**.

LISTING 20.4   MOUSEOVER CODE

```html
<html>
<head>
    <title>Mouseover</title>
<script language="javascript">
<!--
// browser test:
bName = navigator.appName;
bVer = parseInt (navigator.appVersion);
if (bName == "Netscape" && bVer >= 3) version = "n3";
else if (bName == "Netscape" && bVer == 2) version = "n2";
else if (bName == "Microsoft Internet Explorer" && bVer >= 3) version = "n3";
else version = "n2";
```

LISTING 20.4   CONTINUED

```
// end of browser test

// preload universal images:

// If it is Netscape 3 browser
if (version== "n3") {

b0off = new Image(); b0off.src = "images/new_off.gif";

b0on = new Image(); b0on.src = "images/new_on.gif";

}

function hiLite(imgDocID,imgObjName) {
    if (version == "n3") {
        document.images[imgDocID].src = imgObjName;
        }
    }

function hiLiteOff(imgDocID,imgObjName) {
    if (version == "n3") {
        document.images[imgDocID].src = imgObjName;
        }
    }

//-->

</script>
</head>

<script bgcolor="#000000">
<br />
<br />
<br />
<br />

<div align="center">
<a href="new.html" onmouseover="hiLite('b0','images/new_off.gif')"
onmouseout="hiLiteOff('b0','images/new_on.gif')">
<img src="images/new_off.gif" name="b0" width="81" height="94" border="0"
alt="what's new" /></a>
</div>

</script>
</html>
```

Tip

Use an imaging program with layers to easily create your multiple mouseover images and avoid shifting of text location.

→ For general information on working with imaging programs, **see** Chapter 29, "Creating Professional Web Graphics," **p. 595.**

→ To learn advanced graphic techniques, **see** Chapter 30, "Designing Specialty Graphics," **p. 623.**

You can add as many images to this code as you like, following these steps:

1. Add the image to the image list in the code:

   ```
   b1off = new Image(); b1off.src = "images/about_off.gif";

   b1on = new Image(); b1on.src = "images/about_on.gif";
   ```

2. Add the HTML referencing the new image:

   ```
   <a href="about.html" onmouseover="hiLite('b1','images/about_off.gif')"
   onmouseout="hiLiteOff('b1','images/about_on.gif')">
   <img src="images/about_off.gif" name="b1" width="81" height="94" border="0"
   alt="about us" /></a>
   ```

You can complete this process until you have as many images as you want.

Finding incorrect or missing graphics when testing your script? See "The Wrong Image," in the "Troubleshooting" section near the end of this chapter.

BROWSER TESTING AND ROUTING

In the mouseover example, you probably noticed code referencing browsers. This is browser testing, also known as *browser sniffing* or *browser detection*:

```
// browser test:
bName = navigator.appName;
bVer = parseInt (navigator.appVersion);
if (bName == "Netscape" && bVer >= 3) version = "n3";
else if (bName == "Netscape" && bVer == 2) version = "n2";
else if (bName == "Microsoft Internet Explorer" && bVer >= 3) version = "n3";
else version = "n2";
// end of browser test
```

Although certainly the visual functions and esthetic applications of JavaScript hold an important role in design, it is the browser detection that has empowered developers greatly. The reason for this is that designers can ensure that the right design goes to the right browser.

Because both Netscape Navigator and Microsoft Internet Explorer have slightly different capabilities, it can be advantageous to determine which one of the major browsers a visitor to your Web site is using.

Tip

Web designers might want to please both of their audiences, creating two different versions of their sites, one that exploits the expanded capabilities of Navigator and one that exploits the expanded capabilities of Internet Explorer, and then using browser detection and routing to send the site visitor to the site optimized for their situation.

First you can decipher the browser's header. The following is one way of doing just that:

```
<form name="browserHeader">
<input type="button" name="status" value="View Browser Header Info"
```

PART

IV

CH

20

```
onClick="alert('\nBrowserName: ' + navigator.appName + '\nBrowser Version: ' +
parseInt(navigator.appVersion) + '\n\nUser Agent Info:\n' + navigator.userAgent)"
/>
</form>
```

You can now put this information together and do some browser detection/routing. The most common need for detection/routing is to send Netscape users one way and Microsoft IE users the other.

This example sends anyone using Internet Explorer 3.0 and above one way, and anyone using Netscape 3.0 and above another way, and other browsers, or non-JavaScript–supported browsers a third way.

```
<script language="JavaScript">
function browserRouting() {
  bName = navigator.appName;
  bVer = parseInt(navigator.appVersion);
  if (bName == "Netscape" && bVer >= 3) parent.location='net.html'
    else if (bName == "Microsoft Internet Explorer" && bVer >= 2) parent.location
Â='ie.html'
      else parent.location='other.html';
}
</script>
```

In this case, you'll have to create three corresponding pages, net.html, ie.html, and other.html. The JavaScript then will redirect the visitor to the page for their browser.

Another browser detect and route that is important in today's Web design world is to route by screen resolution. The "Route by Res" script allows you to do just that.

→ For a closer look at screen resolution concerns, **see** Chapter 26, "Working with Computer Screen," **p. 545**.

You'll need to first create a selection of documents that are designed specifically for a given resolution. I created three files, one for 640×480 resolution (640.html), one for 800×600 res (800.html), and one for high res (1024.html).

Then, you'll add the code in Listing 20.5 to the head portion of the default index page.

LISTING 20.5   ROUTE BY RESOLUTION

```
<script LANGUAGE="JavaScript">
<!-- Begin
function redirectPage() {
var url640x480 = "640.html";
var url800x600 = "800.html";
var url1024x768 = "1024.html";
if ((screen.width == 640) && (screen.height == 480))
window.location.href= url640x480;
else if ((screen.width == 800) && (screen.height == 600))
window.location.href= url800x600;
else if ((screen.width == 1024) && (screen.height == 768))
window.location.href= url1024x768;
else window.location.href= url640x480;
}
// End -->
</script>
```

In the opening body tag of the XHTML document, add the following statement:

```
<body onload="redirectPage()">
```

Save the page as a default or index page, using the appropriate extensions.

> **Note**
>
> The default page should contain content prepared for individuals who do not have JavaScript available or enabled.

Test the script by changing your screen's resolution several times and reloading the page each time. Using this script, you can create designs optimized to the resolution dimensions of your audience.

> **Note**
>
> You don't need to name the files literally in this script. It will automatically load the appropriate XHTML page if you've named them according to my lead.

TROUBLESHOOTING

GOT SCRIPT?

The code is correct, but the script isn't working. What's the problem?

If you've checked carefully for syntax errors and are certain that your script is free and clear of any bugs, the problem is probably due to one of two reasons:

- **JavaScript is disabled or unavailable in your browser**—To check to be sure JavaScript is running, look in your browser's preferences and make sure JavaScript is available and enabled.

- **Your browser doesn't support the JavaScript version or syntax in use**—There are differences between browser versions and support for JavaScript versions and syntax. This is most clearly demonstrated in the differences between Netscape and Internet Explorer, but the problems arise between versions as well. Internet Explorer 3.0 and below simply does not have the JavaScript sophistication found in the 4.0 and 5.0 versions, whereas Netscape has almost always been ahead of the game where JavaScript (excluding the use of JavaScript for DHTML and Style Sheets) is concerned.

THE WRONG IMAGE

I've used the mouseover script in this section, but the wrong image was loading upon mouseover. Then, I thought I had fixed the code, but no image showed up when I tested the mouseover. What's wrong?

It's very likely that you've named your image files incorrectly either in the script section of the document, or inline with the image name attribute, or both. Look carefully through your code to determine where the misnaming might have occurred.

DESIGNING FOR THE REAL WORLD

JAVASCRIPT AND STYLE SHEETS

JavaScript goes hand-in-hand with Cascading Style Sheets. It can be used to access and act on any CSS attribute. There's a slight difference in the way the names of the attributes are handled in JavaScript, though. Fortunately, the conversion is simple and follows a strict rule.

Where property names in CSS are always in lowercase and the words are separated by hyphens, you drop the hyphens in JavaScript and capitalize the beginning of every word except the first one. For example, the CSS attribute `font-family` would be `fontFamily` in JavaScript. Three-word attributes are done the same way; the CSS attribute `page-break-after` would be `pageBreakAfter` in JavaScript.

Let's assume you want to change the font size of a paragraph with JavaScript. Follow these steps:

1. Select an existing XHTML page where you'd like to have a style sheet.

```
<?xml version="1.0"?>
<!DOCTYPE html PUBLIC "-//W3C//DTD XHTML 1.0 Transitional//EN"
"http://www.w3.org/TR/xhtml1/DTD/xhtml1-transitional.dtd">
<html xmlns="http://www.w3.org/1999/xhtml">
<head>

<title>JavaScript and Style</title>
</head>

<script>

<Aahref="http://www.molly.com/">Vist Molly's Web page!</a>


</script>
</html>
```

2. Build a style sheet containing the a selector and add type attributes:

```
<html>
<head>
<title>JavaScript and Style</title>
<style>
<!--
a    font: 14pt Garamond;
     text-decoration: none
}
-->
</style>
</head>

<script>

<a onclick = "this.style.fontSize='24'" href="http://www.molly.com/">Vist
Molly's Web page!</a>

</script>
</html>
```

3. Add the following JavaScript to any link where you'd like to have the change occur:

```
<a href="http://www.molly.com/">Vist Molly's Web page!</a>
```

4. Save and test your file.

The font-size property set by the Cascading Style Sheet for this XHTML page would be overridden when someone clicked this link. This example uses a single JavaScript statement that's contained within the element it affects. As you might recall from the section on drop-down menus, that's the secret of the shortcut this. this refers to the current object. CSS attributes can be changed in regular JavaScript functions as well, but you need to use the full name of the affected object to access and change its attributes.

Note
Due to browser inconsistencies, this example might not work in many browsers, including Netscape 4.6 and below. It will work admirably well in Internet Explorer 4.0 and above, which supports a wider range of mouse-related events.

ADVANCED XHTML CONCEPTS AND APPLICATIONS

CHAPTER **21**

XHTML MODULARIZATION

In this chapter   *by Christan Jarolim and Cassandra Greer*

THE NEED FOR MODULARIZATION

Imagine a really nice online shop, a shop you can access just as well on your cellular phone as you can on your desktop PC or your handheld device. But wait! A cell phone has very different technical requirements for interacting with the Internet from your handheld device does, or even your desktop PC.

Right now, shopping on your cell phone is not exactly convenient and for most, not even possible. You might be tempted to think that the answer is to deal with each of these platforms is to write separate interfaces for each. But that is a real pain in the neck. It requires not only separate interfaces but also separate maintenance for the life of each application. It is simply a ton of work that shouldn't be necessary.

The Internet has changed incredibly in the past 10 years. What used to be basically a forum for information exchange for academics and computer geeks has become the non-plus-ultra of today's entertainment.

During the history of the Web, interfaces have developed from simple presentation to incorporating all sorts of bells and whistles. You can actually see a distinct divergence in Web development. First, there is the tried and true yet static presentational markup language, HTML. And then there is the growing world of proprietary languages and plug-ins for achieving sensation effects and user interaction.

Basically, Web design has gotten out of control. Remember, computers are supposed to make our lives easier, not more difficult. All these new languages and technologies are making it impossible for every designer to keep up on all the latest developments. Once you actually become an expert in latest design technique, it could already be passé.

We now have a way of closing this gap between need and acquiring new skills. HTML has been updated and revised into the Extensible HyperText Markup Language Version 1.1 (XHTML 1.1). It is currently under discussion by the W3C, and is expected to be brought into the recommendation phase, possibly by the time this book has been published. As you can see from its name, this new language is meant to be extended. This means that anyone can add to it in order to make it suit their needs. This also means it can be extended to include not only new presentational markup but also markup that incorporates the latest functionality.

This is done with modules. This idea of modularization lets you create basic language extensions that provide cross-platform access to the Internet.

This chapter will discuss a number of aspects related to modularization: what it is, why it is important, how it is done, and what it means for the future of the World Wide Web.

WHAT IS XHTML MODULARIZATION?

XHTML Modularization is the concept that enables you to extend XHTML's reach on emerging platforms. You can create a new set of markup tags that work in conjunction with other XHTML module tags.

XHTML itself is defined as a set of basic modules:

- The structure module
- The basic text module
- The hypertext module
- The list module

There are also a few other extensible modules that will be discussed later in the chapter.

Note

In addition to these basic modules, there are specific rules, which allow you to create your own XHTML modules and use them in combination with or instead of the already existing XHTML modules. These rules were developed by the W3C HTML Working Group and can be found at `http://www.w3.org/TR/xhtml-building/`.

Why has XHTML been modularized? Remember the idea of diverging technology on the Web? That gulf between presentational markup and the interactive but complicated bells and whistles? With XHTML we can bring these two camps back together.

Because XHTML has a modular framework, not-yet-developed technologies can be added to XHTML whenever necessary and can be made available throughout the World Wide Web. The coolest thing is that these modules are compatible with each other. A current example WML, the Wireless Markup Language, an application of XML that accommodates cell phone interfaces in the World Wide Web.

→ Read more about WML in Chapter 34, "Overview of Alternative Devices, Languages, and Protocols," **p. 683** and in Chapter 36, "Pagers, Cell Phones, and Other Wireless Devices," **p. 711**.

XHTML Basic is being developed to simplify the transfer of essentially data between different platforms. Also currently in development is XForms, an extension to XHTML that extends the function and capability of the existing forms module to a level normally only available with scripting and applets. Currently implemented is the Forms Markup Language, XHTML-FML, for forms and Web applications.

→ For further information about XHTML Basic, **see** Chapter 23, "XHTML Basic," **p. 35**.

Another major problem we have on the Web is the fact that new devices are continually being invented and developed. Considering the astounding number and types of devices that have appeared on the market in only the last ten years, we really can't predict what kind of cool devices will be available in the next 10 years. The potential is mind-boggling. One thing is for sure: The term "one size fits all" definitely no longer applies when it comes to accessing the Internet. HTML as it is just doesn't cut it any longer.

Adaptation is the key to future device interface inter-compatibility. But how do you adapt technology to each device?

Let's take a look at the challenges each device presents in relation to the others.

A cell phone can't offer the same experience as a desktop computer, so there has to be different ways for presenting information for each of them. To understand what I mean, just take a look at the screen of your cellular and imagine trying to view that Web site you just built for one of your customers (see Figure 21.1).

Figure 21.1
Text information on a cell phone.

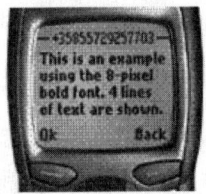

Even if you have a handheld with a browser, you will use a Web site differently from using your desktop's browser (see Figure 21.2).

Figure 21.2
Browsing on a hand-held device.

Now think about an online shop. Of course, it would be nice to have the shop available on every imaginable device. But on a device with a small display, limited memory, and processing speed as well as low bandwidth, you can only show few if any images. You also need to provide your visitors with different navigation than on a device with a large display and greater bandwidth.

Your customers will have different online needs depending on whether they are using their cell phone while waiting at a bus stop or sitting in the office in front of a desktop computer or lounging at home surfing on the TV.

Each device has its own technical requirements and is used in different ways and in different situations.

There are several ways to approach delivering such information. The first, which we call "the path of thorns," is to plan for every version of every desktop browser, for every model of every handheld or cell phone.

This means you will have to set up and maintain the content separately for each device and each of its user agents you want to give access to your content. You will achieve good results by meeting the requirements for each device. But the disadvantage is that you need many more resources (time, manpower, knowledge, money). One person can do only so much!

Another approach is to set up a server and device-specific template pages, and then adapt your content to meet the requirements of each device you want to reach. As a result, there will be Web sites especially made for each device, but updating the content for all the devices at once will be much easier.

Both of these ways have their disadvantages, but they work. And with both, you can adapt content to any device you want if it has a browser. But with XHTML Modularization, there's a better way, and that's to plan for all the devices you want accessed. Set up and maintain one site and define how each device should access it.

This means that you don't need more resources than you can afford. In addition, every device is provided with the same basic content and functions and they can deliver, perhaps via a server, additional device-specific content and functionality. There is just one site covering all the tools to be maintained.

For this you need a module-based markup language like XHTML. To set up such a language, you need to follow some rules to make it extensible and usable for more than one purpose.

XHTML MODULES

An XHTML Module is designed in such a way that it can tell any browser how best to display site content, regardless of what kind of browser it is, and regardless of what kind of hardware requirements happen to limit the content in size and function. To make this easier, XHTML is currently partitioned into two module sections:

- **Abstract Modules**—An abstract module defines a type of data that is distinct from others within the document type. One example of an abstract module would be frames, and another would be forms.

- **DTD Modules**—A document type definition module details elements, attributes, and content declarations. In XHTML 1.0, there are only three DTDs. But modularization of XHTML enables the development of unique DTDs using a DTD module.

ABSTRACT MODULES

XHTML Abstract Modules define the XHTML elements, their attributes, and the rules concerning what kind of data a specific element can contain and how these elements can be nested (the content models).

The Abstract Modules are broken down into basic, presentational, forms, tables, and modules that identify various media types, as described in the following section.

BASIC MODULES

These modules cover the basics of an XHTML document:

- **The Structure Module**—This delivers the structure for the XHTML document and, together with the document type (DOCTYPE) declaration and the XML declaration, builds its framework. The elements included in this module are `html`, `head`, `title`, and `body`.

- **The Basic Text Module**—This defines the text container elements, their attributes, and content modules.
- **The Hypertext Module**—This consists of the a element, which defines hypertext links to other resources.
- **The List Module**—This provides elements for unordered lists, ordered lists, and definition lists. The elements are ul, ol, li, dl, dt, and dd.
- **The Applet Module**—This module delivers the applet element if an applet is used.

PRESENTATIONAL MODULES

Presentational modules describe the presentation of text within an XHTML document:

- **The Presentation Module**—This provides elements (b, big, g, hr, i, small, sub, sup, tt), their attributes, and a minimal content model for simple presentation-related markup.
- **The Edit Module**—This module defines elements (del, ins) and attributes for use in editing-related markup.
- **The BDO Module**—This defines an element (bdo) that can be used to declare the bi-directional rules for the element's content.

THE FORMS MODULE

As the name implies, this module exists to support forms:

- **The Basic Forms Module**—This module defines two content sets: Form with form and Formctrl with input, select, and textarea. The Form content set defines the block in which the elements of the Formctrl content set can work as they are supposed to. This module basically represents the forms concept found in HTML 3.2.
- **The Forms Module**—This provides all of the forms features found in HTML 4.0. This module also defines two content sets: The Form content set with form and fieldset and the Formctrl content set with input, select, textarea, label and button. As you see, this module contains also all the content sets and their elements as seen above in the Basics Forms Module. It is a superset of the Basic Forms Module, and therefore, these modules might not be used together in a single document.

THE TABLES MODULE

Modules in this group are used for creating tables:

- **The Basic Tables Module**—This provides table-related elements (caption, table, td, th, tr), but only in a limited form.
- **The Tables Module**—This provides all of the table-related elements (caption, table, td, th, tr, col, colgroup, tbody, thead, tfoot). They are accessed easier by non-visual user agents. Like we saw in the Forms Module, this module is a superset of the Basic

Tables Module. You cannot use both the Basic Tables Module and the Tables module together.

ADDITIONAL MODULES

A number of additional modules exist to control media and scripting:

- **The Image Module**—This provides basic image embedding, and may be used in some implementations independently of client side image maps.

- **The Client-Side Image Map Module**—This provides the elements a&, area, img&, map, and object& for client side image maps. It requires that the Image Module (or another module that supports the img element) is included.

- **The Server-Side Image Map Module**—This provides support for image-selection and transmission of selection coordinates. It requires that the Image Module (or another module that supports the img element) is included.

- **The Object Module**—This provides the elements object, param for the inclusion of objects of general-purpose.

- **The Frames Module**—This provides the frame-related elements frameset, frame, noframes, a&, area&.

- **The Iframe Module**—This defines an element that can be used to define a base URL against which relative URIs in the document will be resolved.

- **The Intrinsic Events Module**—These are the attributes onblur, onfocus, onreset, onsubmit, onload, onunload, onchange, onselect and are used in conjunction with the elements (a&, area&, form&, body&, label&, input&, select&, textarea&, button&) that can have specific actions occur when certain events are performed by the user.

- **The Meta-Information Module**—This defines the meta element that describes information within the XHTML documents head element.

- **The Scripting Module**—This defines the elements script and noscript that are used to contain information pertaining to executable scripts or the lack of support for executable scripts.

- **The Stylesheet Module**—This enables the processing of style sheets and is used to define the layout of an XHTML document and the appearance of its elements.

- **The Link Module**—This defines an element that can be used to define links to external resources. These resources often enhance the user agent's ability to process the associated XHTML document.

- **The Base Module**—This defines an element that can be used to define a base URL against which relative URIs in the document will be resolved.

- **The Legacy Module**—This defines elements and attributes that have been earmarked as deprecated by the W3C in previous versions of HTML and XHTML. While the use of these elements and attributes is no longer encouraged, they facilitate the step from backwards compatibility to current standards.

PART

V

CH

21

XHTML DTD MODULES

To display a XHTML Web page, a browser needs an XHTML Document Type Definition (DTD). The DTD is a separate document that defines the rules and functionality of an XHTML page. It is a kind of "user's guide" for the browser, telling it how to properly display the respective Web page.

Because it is a document of its own and because it describes the rules and the functions of a modular markup language, the DTD is also based on a series of modules:

- **The XHTML Character Entities Module**—This defines a collection of named character entities made available by the respective XHTML DTD.
- **The XHTML Modular Framework Module**—This consists of a set of support modules, which define tools to simplify the definition of XHTML DTD content models.
- **The XHTML Module Implementations Module**—This contains the formal definition of each of the XHTML Abstract Modules as a DTD module and therefore is a type of "template" describing how to write a Document Type Definition.
- **The XHTML DTD Support Modules**—These are elements of the XHTML DTD that are hidden from regular users but need to be understood when creating other XHTML family members (for example, XHTML-FML).

XHTML VALIDATION

One of the main points you have to consider when you write an XHTML Web page is whether it is valid XHTML according to the DTD you have chosen (XHTML Strict, XHTML Transitional, or XHTML Frameset).

This might seem like a pain. Before, you could just write markup and not bother about the rules as long as the browsers displayed a page more or less like you wanted. But considering the benefits you receive for XHTML validation, it is worth it to check.

XHTML is a cleaner version of HTML 4.0. It is defined in the Extensible Markup Language, XML. XML is not a markup language like HTML is, but is a set of rules for defining markup languages.

Using human language as an analogy, you can say that XML is similar to an alphabet made up of 26 unique units and the guideline that words are separated by white space. Just as English, French, and German share a basic, standard alphabet, XHTML modules will all be written using XML. Different languages suited to different situations can then emerge using this "alphabet."

Once you have mastered the basic set of XML rules, it's easy to understand, learn, and implement any other XML-based markup language. Switching between these languages will be no big deal at all.

The fact that HTML has become an XML application results in a number of benefits.

Having a widely available mechanism for checking whether a document conforms to these rules is the important part of the story. There is a rapidly growing array of XML parsers available for XML documents. In conjunction with a corresponding DTD, these parsers can check to see whether an XML document (such as a XHTML Web page) is authored correctly.

As you have most likely noticed, desktop browsers have gotten ever bigger and slower in the past few years. This is because the browsers have been including every possible DTD in an attempt to accommodate all the different versions of HTML as well as sloppy code. A huge amount of resources is wasted in the process.

Because HTML has now become a part of XML, validation is one of XHTML's great new features, helping you write proper markup. With validation, you literally ask the people who defined the markup language to assist you. The checking takes place within some XHTML editors while authoring a Web page—you don't have to constantly load the page into a browser just to see if the document is authored correctly. Plus, since there are only a relatively few rules that the browser needs for checking the code, the browser becomes much less of a hard disk and memory hog. The browser can be more efficient and therefore faster.

In the future, it's possible that some browsers will simply not display Web pages that are not valid.

Browser manufacturers and users will welcome a reduction in browser size and the days of browser bloat will fade away like a bad dream.

A browser that is only required to render valid XHTML pages will not only be lean enough to operate faster on your desktop but will also operate in environments lacking high amounts of memory and CPU power such as cell phones, pagers, handhelds, and so on.

There are various tools currently available with which you can validate your documents currently. The W3C has a Validation Service at **validator.w3.org**/ and you can use the Mozquito Factory (on the CD-ROM) for validation directly on your desktop.

DEVICES AFFECTED BY XHTML MODULARIZATION

We discussed above how content can be delivered to different devices. Here's a short overview of the kinds of devices currently available and how they might be used in the near future:

■ **Digital Television**—DTV has come to our homes already, in the form of set-top boxes, Web broadcast, and so on. With a set-top box connected to a modem, the TV becomes interactive with the outside world. Tests researching bi-directional communication via the TV set are already being run, but the infrastructure for this has yet to be built.

■ **Smart Phones**—Modern life requires certain devices for functioning to full capacity. One of these devices is the phone. In the near future, there will be very few people without a cell phone, because most people will want to be available all the time. This idea goes both ways, however. People want to have access to information and services at any time. Customers available anywhere anytime is a huge challenge and opportunity for all types of online services. The future of these Smart phones is not totally decided: Cellular phones are getting smaller every month. But the clutter factor is motivating phone manufacturers to prepare for even smarter phones, which incorporate the functions of other handheld devices, integrating many systems into one. These smart phones will need to support the upcoming Web standards. We'll see whether or not cellular displays become smaller or larger. But whatever happens, the size of the display and the bandwidth will stay far below the standards we're used to on desktop computers.

- **Handheld Devices**—It is doubtful whether they will ever be as popular as, say, desktop computers. The reason for this is that cellular phones are becoming more and more "intelligent" and could eventually elbow out handheld devices. Most cell phones can already serve as day planners, manage addresses, and—of course—phones. Some of them can already send e-mail and browse through the World Wide Web.

- **Two-Way Pagers**—Pagers used to receive only one way but now they can send and receive email and information from the Web. But again they might be elbowed out by cell phones, which already have the same functionality.

- **Desktop Browsers**—These browsers are standard and will continue to play an important role for Web designers. As XHTML becomes more widespread, the differences between platforms and their browsers will hopefully disappear and we can start to forget about cross-browser authoring and concentrate on creating better Web pages and sites without worrying too much about the platform.

- **Car Navigation Systems**—People love their cars but getting from place to place as quickly, safely, and efficiently as possible has always been top priority. Current navigation systems the most current information via satellites. What is stopping us from using that same satellite link to browse the Internet for local hotels, restaurants, or entertainment when we are on the road?

- **Printers**—Let's not forget those devices we don't normally associate with Web interactivity. What if there was a browser so small that it would work on any amount of memory? Through Modularization, it could become a standard to set up your printing device (or any other you use within your environment) via an XHTML-based driver directly connected to the World Wide Web.

Right now, there are a zillion device-dependent software environments that cannot be linked together without serious grief and pain, if at all. The average Web designer is normally in no position, time and resource-wise, to even attempt it.

If you want to set up content for, let's say, a Car Navigation System, your cellular phone, or your Palm Pilot, you will have to use a proprietary software environment provided by the respective manufacturers. It's basically a given that you will struggle to master most the more advanced device functions advertised in those glossy computer magazine ads.

You have to use very clever server environments to achieve this level of functionality and accessibility. Using these environments, as well as setting up and maintaining a site especially designed for a single device, is a lot of work, but currently, it is the only way to reach your goal.

What if you wanted to tell a potential customer via a message sent to a cell phone that you have new content on your site? What if you also wanted to let him see a preview of that new information in advance via fax so he knows what to look for when he's back at his desk? You'd need to set up three special server add-ons and adapt the respective content so it can be accessed in three different ways (via a cellular browser, via a server based fax service, that can be triggered using your cell phone and via the conventional way—a Web site).

There are more and more extensions and even fellow XHTML family member languages emerging from the work of several groups. These languages include, the Forms Markup Language (XHTML-FML), XForms, and SMIL, and are designed for or will be adapted to meet your future needs.

→ To learn more about XHTML-FML **see** Chapter 17, "Another Approach to XHTML Forms Using XHTML-FML," **p. 339,** and to learn more about SMIL **see** Chapter 38, "Synchronized Multimedia Integration Language," **p. 767.**

EXTENDING XHTML IN REAL LIFE

Extending XHTML will be the ultimate challenge for client manufacturers, document authors and content providers when they realize they need to provide more than just presentational markup for their customers. Anyone can use the extensible architecture of XHTML to set up document types that meet their needs. Of course, they will have to follow the rules of XHTML Modularization to be integrated within the growing number of XHTML family members.

To become XHTML family members, modules will have to share certain characteristics:

- **Standards**—They must implement methods defined by the W3C.
- **Unique Identifiers**—They must use unique identifiers to tell the client agent (for example, a browser) that it should use the exchanged module that is found in a certain DTD instead of the original module.
- **Required Modules**—They will need a minimum set of modules: the Basic Structure Module, the Hypertext Module, the Basic text module, and the List module within the respective DTD.
- **Namespaces**—Additional elements and attributes have to be defined in their own unique XML namespaces.
- **Validation**—Documents written with this language must validate against their DTD.

Let's take a look at an example of how XHTML Modularization is being used today.

XHTML BASIC

One good example of modularization is XHTML Basic, which is essentially XHTML for Small Information Appliances.

PART
V

CH

21

Note

The XHTML Basic documentation can be found at `www.w3.org/TR/WD-xhtml-basic-20000210/`.

XHTML Basic is a reduced form of XHTML to fit the needs of all kinds of devices. The starting point of its design is a common subset of XHTML modules (basic text, hyperlinks, basic forms, basic tables, images and meta information) which all kinds of device dependent markup languages like WML (the Wireless Markup Language—used to present content on mobile phone user agents) need.

The purpose for having a common subset of features here is not to limit future XHTML family member features, but to have one common base, from where these new XHTML subsets can emerge using the features of XHTML Modularization.

As a result a content creator will design for as many devices (that is, mobile phones, televisions, PDAs, vending machines, pagers, car navigation systems, mobile game machines, digital book readers, and smart watches) as he wants without needing to set things up more than once.

XHTML Modularization is used here in two respects: first to set up the central part of XHTML Basic and second to extend it and build on it.

A first step in the right direction could be to extend it with a more general events module, so events are not dependent on infrastructure of a certain kind. This extension process—no matter whether it concerns events or extended forms—can only be done by improving and/or adding modules to the XHTML basic modules.

APPLYING XHTML MODULARIZATION

Initially considered a part of a Web authoring tool (Mozquito) to create better Web forms, the Forms Markup Language (XHTML-FML) became the basis for creating very powerful, interactive and dynamic Web applications with just plain markup.

Here's the story: The first working draft of FML actually had nothing to do with XHTML. It was created by Web designers who were tired of the antiquated forms module in HTML. Then the Mozquito people realized that this developing markup language could become a family member of the XHTML standard developing at that time. So they sent their ideas to the Web standards body, the W3C, and asked for some feedback on it.

The reaction was quite unexpected. Stack Overflow (now Mozquito Technologies) was invited to work with the HTML Working Group on this new standard, specifically on improving the forms module, which had not been changed since 1993.

The result was XHTML-FML, the Forms Markup Language. It is a test case for new forms standards preceding the up and coming XForms as well as the base for real interactivity with a visitor's Web page.

All this was made possible through XHTML Modularization. Without it, we couldn't have freely created a method of markup that we feel addresses specific needs of developers like us.

Modularization gives *any* developer the opportunity to do exactly what we did: author custom markup that truly embraces the concepts of extensibility.

The following examples will show you what XHTML-FML looks like in the context of creating a module.

Caution

Although XHTML-FML follows the standards, current browsers do not support XHTML-FML markup as is. Unfortunately, current browsers do not fully implement the current standards but hopefully this will change in the near future. The code is written in an editor and then generated by the Mozquito Matrix into an HTML compatible file that current browsers can handle. To see the following examples of code in action it is necessary to either install the trial version of the Mozquito Factory from the CD included in this book or download it from `www.mozquito.com/`.

To extend the functionality of XHTML so it meets a Web author's needs, Stack Overflow made major changes to several existing modules. They replaced the Forms Module and the Image Module with improved ones and also created new modules (the Toggle Module, the Template Module, and the Calc Module).

The improved forms module that Stack Overflow created unique syntax:

```
<x:form id="snoop" action="server/servlets/Snoop" method="post">
  <x:radio send="true">
    <x:item value="item01" onchange="submit:snoop">
      first item
    </x:item>
    <x:item value="item02" onchange="submit:snoop">
      second item
    </x:item>
  </x:radio>
</x:form>
```

Similarly, we made changes to the image module so that it can do image pre-loading via a `preload` attribute:

```
<x:img id="example.gif" preload="yes" with="120" height="92" alt="example" />
```

We added three completely new modules. The Toggle module allows multiple pages within one document without needing a server. It is quite easy to work with. You create a toggle container, give it an ID, and then put in the XHTML-FML elements you want to be toggled. Then you set up an action trigger (in this case, a button), and there it is:

```
<x:form id="toggle">
  <x:toggle id="page">
    <x:tg>page 1</x:tg>
    <x:tg>page 2</x:tg>
    <x:tg>page 3</x:tg>
  </x:toggle>
  <x:button onclick="toggle:page" value="switch the content" />
</x:form>
```

The Template module allows you to avoid repetitive code of any kind. It also is not too complicated. You just create a template container, give it an ID and put the code, that

PART

V

CH

21

otherwise would be repeated, in it. Then you go to the place, where there the repetitive code parts would otherwise be and set your insert markers:

```
<x:template id="foo">
  <h3 style="color:blue">I am defined in a template and inserted
<em>here</em></h3>
</x:template>

...
<x:insert template="foo"/>
<x:insert template="foo"/>
```

The Calc Module allows real time calculation without the need for a server during the calculation. Again this is not complicated. You just need to define your calculation.

```
<x:textoutput id="sum" value="22.07"/> +
<x:textinput id="extra" size="5"/> =
<x:calc id="calcsum" digits="2" term="sum + extra">
  <x:textoutput id="total"/>
</x:calc>
```

XHTML-FML *event handlers* are attribute-like command string containers used within XHTML-FML elements:

```
<x:button onclick="toggle:page" value="switch the content" />
```

XHTML-FML elements use so-called *action statements*. Together with their event handlers, they are triggers for some type of enhanced functionality and are used to start processes that are defined by an XHTML-FML markup element:

```
<x:button onclick="toggle:page" value="switch the content" />
```

The XHTML-FML elements have special attributes belonging to input validation.

```
<x:textinput validation="strict" ctype="email" />
```

All these changes to the normal XHTML modules enable the average Web author to set up interactive web-based user interfaces or even to create Web-based applications without needing any proprietary plug-in or special programming knowledge.

In this chapter, we have looked at the modularization of XHTML: what it is, why it is important, how you do it, and what it means for the World Wide Web.

Modularization is a sign of the times. It developed out of the realization that there is simply too much incompatible technology spreading on the Web. If there is any sort of chance for us as members of the World Wide Web community redirect this wild energy, reigning the Web back in, we need to take a new approach.

We need to sit back, think things through and see how we can make all these technologies work together. At the same time, we can simplify how we use this technology, so we can concentrate on the business of communicating rather than on learning some complicated code. The easiest way is if everyone used the same type of building blocks. This is what the Modularization of XHTML gives us.

CHAPTER 22

DOCUMENT TYPE DEFINITIONS IN DETAIL

In this chapter   *by Kynn Bartlett*

In previous chapters, you've used the <!DOCTYPE> tag at the beginning of your Web pages to specify which type of XHTML—Strict, Transitional, or Frameset—you want to use. The <!DOCTYPE> tag can almost seem like a magical incantation—a special secret code that looks like gibberish but somehow works after a fashion. This chapter explains exactly what is happening when you use <!DOCTYPE>, teaches you the basics of XML Document Type Definition (DTD) syntax, shows you how to read the XHTML DTDs, and even demonstrates how you can modify the XHTML DTDs to extend the language.

UNDERSTANDING DTDs

An XML DTD is the method by which you define the syntax and structure of an XML language. You'll recall that XML itself is a meta-language that lets you build markup languages that follow certain rules sets. A DTD adds additional rules that state which elements can be used with others, which attributes are allowed in a tag, and what the default values of an attribute should be.

WHAT IS A DTD?

A DTD is a formal specification for a language. It's designed to be machine-readable for automatic parsing, but also understandable and capable of being produced by a human with a text editor—as is the case with XHTML and XML. DTDs are written in a language that will seem familiar to you, as it includes tags, brackets, and values, although a few differences —such as needing no closing tags or even closing "/" marks—might be a little confusing at first.

The concept of DTDs originated with SGML, the predecessor of XML. Until XHTML 1.0, all HTML DTDs have been written in accordance with the SGML rules for DTDs; now, the simplicity and power of XML has been applied to HTML to produce XHTML DTDs.

A DTD for a given language defines the structure of that language and the acceptable syntax that's used in that language. For example, the XHTML DTD specifies that <img> tags must have alt attributes, and that <a> tags cannot be nested. DTDs are limited, however, to only expressing syntax and structure. Actual semantics, such as what is meant by an <h1> or how to display a <b> tag, cannot be expressed in DTDs.

THE DOCTYPE TAG

When you've element> element> used the <!DOCTYPE> tag before, you were referencing a DTD, even if you didn't know it at the time. Here's the <!DOCTYPE> tag that refers to the XHTML 1.0 DTD:

```
<!DOCTYPE html PUBLIC "-//W3C//DTD XHTML 1.0 Strict//EN"
"http://www.w3.org/TR/xhtml1/DTD/xhtml1-strict.dtd">
```

Look at each component of this tag. First is the word !DOCTYPE itself, complete with an exclamation point at the start. This tag is what's called a *declaration*, and it's not an XML element itself—which means that there's no closing tag necessary, not even a slash at the end of the tag. Declarations never have closing tags.

The next item is the word html—note the case, as it's important. This identifies the root element of the document, which is the <html> tag for XHTML. It's important that html is in lowercase, because XML is case sensitive, and XHTML is properly written with lowercase tags.

The word PUBLIC means that the DTD has a public name, referred to as a *Formal Public Identifier* (FPI). Contrasted with public identifiers are system identifiers, which are identified by a URL and tell where the DTD can be found. The example XHTML !DOCTYPE statement provides both an FPI and a system identifier. The first long quoted string is the public identifier, and the second is the system identifier.

Not all DTDs element> element>will have FPIs; usually this is reserved for "well-known" or "famous" DTDs. You can think of an FPI as being like a proper name for a famous building, and a system identifier as being like a street address. For example, you might say "The White House" (a public name) or you might say "1600 Pennsylvania Avenue" (a street address) to indicate the residence of the U.S. President. However, if you wanted to speak of my office, saying "Kynn's Office" wouldn't be understandable to many people, so you would want to include "110 E. Wilshire, Fullerton, CA" as a street address.

Here's what the XHTML FPI looks like:

```
"-//W3C//DTD XHTML 1.0 Strict//EN"
```

An FPI is composed element> element> of four parts, which are separated by double slashes. The first part indicates if the DTD was created by an international standards body, such as the International Standards Organization (ISO); if not, then a hyphen is used. The second part names the organization or company who created the standard. The third part is a name or title for the language. The fourth defines the language that was used—"EN" indicates the English language.

> **Note**
>
> You'll notice that the XHTML FPI starts with a hyphen, which indicates that it was not created by a standards body! This is correct, as the W3C is technically not a standards organization, but rather an industry consortium. It's a fine hair to split, though, and you can usually consider W3C documents to be as standard as you can get. I prefer to use the term *XHTML specification* instead of *XHTML standard* to maintain semantic purity.

The system identifier element> element> is always a URL that identifies a location where the DTD itself can be downloaded. The system identifier is optional for well-known DTDs with FPIs, but it is always prudent to include the system identifier URL anyway, which is why it is included in your <!DOCTYPE> tag.

A <!DOCTYPE> tag without an FPI uses the keyword SYSTEM instead of PUBLIC and skips the FPI entirely, such as this:

```
<!DOCTYPE html SYSTEM
"http://www.w3.org/TR/xhtml1/DTD/xhtml1-strict.dtd">
```

This is a valid <!DOCTYPE> for identifying the XHTML 1.0 Strict DTD, just like 1600 Pennsylvania Avenue is a valid address even if we don't element> element> mention that it is the White House.

DTD SYNTAX

So what does a DTD look like? The simplest way to get you familiar with XML DTDs is probably to show you one, so I've included a rather simple DTD in Listing 22.1. This DTD defines an XML language for describing which cars are in my garage.

LISTING 22.1   A SIMPLE DTD FOR DESCRIBING CARS

```
<!--
  cars.dtd
  By Kynn Bartlett kynn@kynn.com

  A simple DTD for describing cars.
  SYSTEM "http://kynn.com/dtd/cars.dtd"
-->

<!--============= Define some parameter entities ============-->
<!ENTITY % Quality      "(excellent|good|fair|poor|terrible)">
<!ENTITY % Date         "CDATA">  <!-- (DD-)Mon-YYYY -->
<!ENTITY % ModelYear    "CDATA">  <!-- YYYY -->
<!ENTITY % LicPlate     "CDATA">  <!-- 7 letters or digits -->
<!ENTITY % State        "CDATA">  <!-- 2-letter postal code -->

<!ENTITY % CommonAttrs
    "condition      %Quality;       #IMPLIED
     modified       %Date;          #IMPLIED"
    >

<!ENTITY % AppContent "color |  detailing | windows | tires">
<!--============= The root element is "garage" ============-->
<!ELEMENT garage (car)*>

<!ATTLIST garage
    date            %Date;          #IMPLIED
    >

<!--============= Each car is a separate element ============-->
<!ELEMENT car (license, type, appearance)>

<!ATTLIST car
    %CommonAttrs;
    name            CDATA           #IMPLIED
    >

<!ELEMENT license EMPTY>

<!ATTLIST license
    state           %State;         #REQUIRED
    expires         %Date;          #IMPLIED
    plate           %LicPlate;      #REQUIRED
    >
```

LISTING 22.1   CONTINUED

```
<!ELEMENT appearance (%AppContent;)*>

<!ELEMENT color          (#PCDATA)>
<!ELEMENT tires          (#PCDATA)>
<!ELEMENT windows        (#PCDATA)>
<!ELEMENT detailing      (#PCDATA)>

<!ATTLIST color
   %CommonAttrs;
   area            CDATA          "body"
   >

<!ATTLIST tires
   %CommonAttrs;
   brand           CDATA          #IMPLIED
   >

<!ATTLIST windows
   %CommonAttrs;
   >

<!ATTLIST detailing
   %CommonAttrs;
   >

<!ELEMENT type (make, model, style?)>

<!ELEMENT make     (#PCDATA)>
<!ELEMENT model    (#PCDATA)>
<!ELEMENT style    (#PCDATA)>

<!ATTLIST model
   year            %ModelYear;    #REQUIRED
   >
```

Some of this might be obvious and some might be a little harder to understand, so I'll explain each part in order. What does this DTD do? It defines the syntax and the structure of a "language" that can describe cars. A sample listing of an XML file written in this language is included as Listing 22.2.

LISTING 22.2   AN XML FILE WRITTEN ACCORDING TO cars.dtd

```
<?xml version="1.0"?>
<garage date="4-Sep-2000">
  <car name="Beverly">
    <license state="CA" expires="Dec-2000" plate="3BVY900" />
    <appearance>
      <color area="upper body">white</color>
      <color area="lower body">orange</color>
      <color area="interior">black</color>
      <windows>tinted</windows>
    </appearance>
    <type>
```

LISTING 22.2 CONTINUED

```
      <make>Volkswagon</make>
      <model year="1974">bus</model>
    </type>
  </car>
  <car name="Nixby">
    <license state="CA" plate="1NXB337" />
    <appearance>
      <color>metallic green</color>
    </appearance>
    <type>
      <make>Toyota</make>
      <model year="1986">Tercel</model>
      <style>Station Wagon</style>
    </type>
  </car>
</garage>
```

STRUCTURE OF A DTD

As I mentioned before, DTD syntax is similar to the XHTML tags you've been working with before, although it's definitely not well formed. This is because DTDs are composed of declarations—which begin with <! and end with >—and not elements that have to worry about nesting and closing tags. The comment syntax should be familiar to you, as it's the same as in XHTML.

The declarations used in this DTD are listed in Table 22.1.

TABLE 22.1 XML DTD DECLARATIONS

XML DTD Syntax	Function
<!ENTITY>	Declares an entity—parsed, parameter, or other types
<!ELEMENT>	Defines an element in the DTD
<!ATTLIST>	Defines attributes for an element
<!-- Comment -->	A simple comment

PARSED ENTITIES

Entities, in XML DTDs, are a way of substituting one section of a DTD for another. Parsed entities are a specific type of entity that can be used in the document. You're actually familiar with a number of parsed entities, even if you're not aware of it. These are parsed entities of a specific type—character entities. Character entities include <, >, ", Κ, and other such references to characters in XHTML.

The syntax for declaring a parsed entity is

```
<!ENTITY name "value">
```

The value of the entity, in the document, is then referenced by using the following in the markup:

```
&name;
```

A parsed entity can be more than just a single character, although; for example, consider the following:

```
<!ENTITY myname "Kynn Bartlett">
```

If I write a document in an XML language with the previous declaration in the DTD, I can then use the &myname; entity in the document itself, such as

```
<para>The sign on my door reads &myname;.</para>
```

This would expand to

```
<para>The sign on my door reads Kynn Bartlett.</para>
```

In the XHTML 1.0 DTD, the most important uses of parsed entities are to set up the character entities.

PARAMETER ENTITIES

Parameter entities are different from parsed entities—although parsed entities are used in the document, parameter entities are meant for use in the DTD itself. The value of the parameter entity is substituted into the DTD whenever the entity is used, and this allows for a more modular, organized method of constructing DTDs.

The syntax for a simple parameter entity is similar, but not identical, to parsed entities:

```
<!ENTITY % name "value">
```

Notice the % before the name—that's what indicates that it's a parameter entity. To use the value of a parameter entity, you use a slightly different manner as well:

```
%name;
```

Parameter entities also can be "external," which means that the value of the entity is the contents of a file identified by FPI or URL. Declarations of external entities look like one of the following:

```
<!ENTITY % name PUBLIC "FPI" "url">
<!ENTITY % name SYSTEM "url">
```

This allows you to include an external file in a DTD declaration; for example, the XHTML 1.0 Transitional DTD contains the following declaration, which says that the xhtml-lat1.ent file should be included:

```
<!ENTITY % HTMLlat1 PUBLIC
    "-//W3C//ENTITIES Latin 1 for XHTML//EN"
    "xhtml-lat1.ent">
%HTMLlat1;
```

Note that simply declaring the entity doesn't actually import the contents of the file—you must then invoke the entity itself, which explains the presence of `%HTMLlat1;`.

ELEMENT DECLARATIONS

When declaring an element, you declare not only the name, but the content model of the element, using the `<!ELEMENT>` declaration. The attributes are declared separately using `<!ATTLIST>`. The syntax for `<!ELEMENT>` is

```
<!ELEMENT element contentmodel>
```

A content model is a description of which types of content—elements and text—can be appropriately included within the container of the element. Values for the content model are listed in Table 22.2. Parentheses can be used to group elements together, commas to define sequences, and vertical bars to indicate a choice from among several valid options.

TABLE 22.2   CONTENT MODELS IN XML DTDs

Syntax	Description
ANY	Any text and elements can be contained by the element.
EMPTY	The element is not a container, and must always be empty.
(#PCDATA)*	The element can contain textual data.
(tag1, tag2)	The element can only contain the elements tag1 and tag2, in that order.
(tag1 | tag2)	The element can contain either tag1, or tag2 (but only one of them, and just one such element).
(tag1)*	The element can contain zero or more tag1 elements.
(tag1)+	The element must contain at least one tag1 element, and can contain more than one.
(tag1)?	The element might contain one (and only one) tag1 element, but it's optional.
(#PCDATA|tag1)*	The element can contain either text or tag1 elements.

Complex sequences can be built using parentheses, vertical bars, commas, and other indicators. To understand these, you'll just need to break them down into simpler groups. For example, consider the following content model:

```
<!ELEMENT aaa (#PCDATA | (bbb, (ccc | ddd))*>
```

This indicates that the `<aaa>` tag can contain zero or more occurrences of #PCDATA (text) or `<bbb>` tags followed by either `<ccc>` or `<ddd>` tags.

A simple example from the cars DTD is the root element, `<garage>`, which can contain zero or more `<car>` elements:

```
<!ELEMENT garage (car)*>
```

You can use parameter entities in `<!ELEMENT>` declarations, as in the declaration of the `<appearance>` tag in the DTD:

```
<!ELEMENT appearance (%AppContent;)*>
```

To interpret the possible values for the `<appearance>` tag, you'll have to look at the definition for the `%AppContent;` entity:

```
<!ENTITY % AppContent "color | detailing | windows | tires">
```

This tells you that the `<appearance>` tag consists of zero or more tags from `<color>`, `<detailing>`, `<windows>` or `<tires>`.

ATTRIBUTE LIST DECLARATIONS

You declare the valid attributes for an element by using the `<!ATTLIST>` declaration. The syntax for `<!ATTLIST>` is

```
<!ATTLIST element
    attribute    type        default
    attribute    type        default
    >
```

The most common types of attributes you'll encounter are listed in Table 22.3. The type of each attribute determines what kinds of values can legally be assigned to the attribute. The default value indicates whether or not the attribute has a default value assigned, or if a value is required to be set. The options for the default value are listed in Table 22.4.

TABLE 22.3   ATTRIBUTE TYPES USED IN XML DTDs

Syntax	Description
`(value1 | value2 | ...)`	These are literal enumerated values; the attribute can only be one of these values.
`CDATA`	The attribute must be character data, which means any normal text (although special characters such as < or " must be escaped).
`ID`	The value of this attribute must be an ID—XML IDs must be unique with a document, must start with a letter, and can only contain letters, numbers, hyphens, periods, or underscores.
`IDREF`	The attribute must reference an ID elsewhere in the document.

TABLE 22.4   DEFAULT VALUES FOR ATTRIBUTES IN XML DTDS

Syntax	Description
`#IMPLIED`	There is not a default value for this attribute, and setting a value is not mandatory.
`#REQUIRED`	A value *must* be set for this attribute, and there is no default value.
`"value"`	The default value is `"value"`.
`#FIXED "value"`	The value of this attribute is set to `"value"`, and cannot be changed.

You can mix parameter entities with literal values for the attribute type and default values. For example, here is the `<!ATTLIST>` declaration for the `<license>` tag from the sample DTD:

```
<!ATTLIST license
    state         %State;       #REQUIRED
    expires       %Date;        #IMPLIED
    plate         %LicPlate;    #REQUIRED
    >
```

To figure out what values are valid for the state attribute—which is a required attribute for the license tag—you'll need to look up the `%State;` parameter entry, which reads:

```
<!ENTITY % State    "CDATA">  <!-- 2-letter postal code -->
```

This tells you that values for the state attribute can legally be set to any text value (CDATA) but should only be set to two-letter codes (such as "CT" or "MA"), as described by the comment which follows the declaration.

You can even use parameter entities to make whole sets of lists. Here's the declaration for the `%CommonAttrs;` entity:

```
<!ENTITY % CommonAttrs
    "condition      %Quality      #IMPLIED
    modified        %Date         #IMPLIED"
    >
```

This makes it easy to add a whole set of attributes at once, as in the declaration of the `<color>` element:

```
<!ATTLIST color
    %CommonAttrs;
    area             CDATA          "body"
    >
```

The `<color>` tag can take three attributes—condition, modified, and area. Note that if a value is not specified for area, it defaults to `"body"`.

READING THE XHTML DTDS

As an XHTML developer, you might want to become familiar with the XHTML DTDs and what they contain. Although reading XML DTDs can seem intimidating at first, the concepts are actually quite simple and you can learn about the structure of the language by examining the formal syntax definitions. As the authoritative source on XHTML 1.0, the XHTML DTDs can help you understand validation errors and, if you want to extend the language by adding (or removing) elements, you will need to understand how the DTDs are structured.

Downloading the XHTML DTDs

To work with the XHTML DTDs, you'll want to have your own copy of the DTDs. You can read them online, or you can download them to your hard drive. I recommend keeping a local version so that you can read it whenever you like as well as being able to modify it yourself, as you'll do later in this chapter.

> **Note**
>
> You can download the files individually from `www.w3.org/TR/xhtml1/#dtds`, but I recommend that you grab the zip file at `www.w3.org/TR/xhtml1/xhtml1.zip` as it contains the files you need in the DTD subdirectory.

There are three distinct DTDs—one each for the Strict, Transitional, and Frameset versions of XHTML 1.0. In addition, there are three files that contain the parsed entities used in all versions of XHTML. The files you want are shown in Table 22.5.

TABLE 22.5   XHTML 1.0 DTD FILES

Filename	Contents
`xhtml1-strict.dtd`	DTD for Strict XHTML 1.0
`xhtml1-transitional.dtd`	DTD for Transitional XHTML 1.0
`xhtml1-frameset.dtd`	DTD for Frameset XHTML 1.0
`xhtml1-lat1.ent`	Entity definitions for Latin 1 character set
`xhtml1-symbol.ent`	Entity definitions for Mathematical, Greek, and Symbolic characters
`xhtml1-special.ent`	Entity definitions for "Special" (miscellaneous) characters

As the Transitional DTD tends to be the richest in terms of attributes and elements, as well as the one you are most likely to use in practice, we'll focus on that DTD. The principles you'll learn will let you read all three of the XHTML DTDs, however.

Structure of the Transitional XHTML DTD

The Transitional XHTML DTD is arranged in sections, with each section set off by a divider in the form of a long comment. Each section has a specific function and defines different parts of the XHTML specification. These section dividers are listed in Listing 22.4, with the content between them removed so you can more easily see the structure and order of the DTD.

LISTING 22.4   EXCERPTED SECTION DIVIDER COMMENTS FROM XHTML 1.0
TRANSITIONAL DTD

```
<!--========== Character mnemonic entities =========-->
<!--=========== Imported Names ====================-->
<!--============ Generic Attributes ===============-->
<!--============ Text Elements ====================-->
<!--============ Block level elements =============-->
<!--========== Content models for exclusions ======-->
<!--========= Document Structure ==================-->
<!--========= Document Head =======================-->
<!--================= Frames ======================-->
<!--============ Document Body ====================-->
<!--============ Paragraphs =======================-->
<!--============ Headings =========================-->
<!--============ Lists ============================-->
<!--============ Address ==========================-->
<!--============ Horizontal Rule ==================-->
<!--============ Preformatted Text ================-->
<!--============ Block-like Quotes ================-->
<!--============ Text alignment ===================-->
<!--============ Inserted/Deleted Text ============-->
<!--=========== The Anchor Element ================-->
<!--=============== Inline Elements ===============-->
<!--============= Object ==========================-->
<!--============ Java applet ======================-->
<!--============ Images ===========================-->
<!--=========== Client-side image maps ============-->
<!--========= Forms ===============================-->
<!--================= Tables ======================-->
```

You should probably skim through the DTD at this time, and look over the structure. One important thing to notice is the way parameter entities are declared in two general locations: at the start of the document (such as in "Generic Attributes") and in some sections just before they are used.

The first section of the DTD loads the parsed entity lists. These are included in the additional files in the DTD directory of the XHTML 1.0 specification. This is where various character entities are defined, such as γ, ♠, · Á, or >.

Within the DTD there are some groups of attributes and elements that appear repeatedly, and are represented by parameter entities. These allow for grouping and consolidation of these repeated sections, so that they don't need to be listed each time. A short list of some of the more notable parameter entities is shown in Table 22.6.

TABLE 22.6   USEFUL ATTRIBUTE AND ELEMENT GROUPS IN THE XHTML 1.0 TRANSITIONAL DTD

Parameter Entity	Purpose or Function
%coreattrs;	Attributes found on most elements: id, class, style, and title
%i18n;	Attributes for internationalization: lang, xml:lang, and dir
%events;	Intrinsic events such as onClick and onKeyPress
%focus;	Attributes for elements which can hold "focus": accesskey, tabindex, onfocus, onblur
%attrs;	All attributes found in %coreattrs;, %i18n;, and %events;
%special;	"Special" inline text elements, such as , <img>, and <object>
%fontstyle;	Elements that affect the presentation of text, such as: <tt>, <big>, <i>, or <font>
%phrase;	Elements that give semantic meaning to a phrase, including: <strong>, <abbr>, and <q>
%inline.forms;	Form elements that should be rendered inline, instead of on separate lines, such as <input> and <select>
%misc;	A catch-all category for elements that can be inline or "block": <ins>, <del>, <script>, and <noscript>
%inline;	Inline tags: the <a> element, and all of the elements included in %special;, %fontstyle;, %phrase;, %inline.forms;, and %misc;

As you can see, parameter entities can consist of other parameter entities, and are used throughout the DTD to build up the declarations of the elements and their attributes. You might have to backtrack through several layers of parameter entities to decipher the content models or attributes for a specific element.

STRUCTURE VERSUS SEMANTICS

One thing you'll notice as you read the DTDs is that they do not contain all the information one would need to know to write XHTML, or to write a browser to display it. Apart from the comments, nothing describes the *meaning* of the various tags—only the syntax and structure of the markup. For example, the declarations for each of the headers—<h1>, <h2>, to <h6>—are all identical. Data types are assigned to parameter entities, such as %DateTime; or %Number;, but these are all designated as CDATA.

The semantic meaning of each tag is described in the specification, in text, which describes the purpose of each tag, the valid values for each attribute, and how they should be displayed by a browser. As XHTML 1.0 is a direct translation of HTML 4.01, you can find the meaning of each tag by looking it up in the HTML 4.01 specification. HTML 4.01 is described at **www.w3.org/TR/html401/**.

DESIGNING FOR THE REAL WORLD: DEFINING YOUR OWN DTD

Being able to read the XHTML 1.0 DTDs is a very useful skill; however, you don't want to stop there. The "X" in XHTML stands for extensibility, and part of the true power of XHTML is the fact that it can be extended as needed.

In XHTML 1.0, you can extend the language by editing the DTD. This will give you a new DTD you can use in your <!DOCTYPE> statements, and demonstrate some of the flexibility and adaptability inherent in XHTML.

→ The latest version of HTML, XHTML 1.1, is being developed in a modular manner for even greater extensibility. This means that you will be able to add and remove XHTML 1.1 features in an even easier manner. For more on XHTML 1.1 modules, **see** Chapter 21, "XHTML Modularization," **p. 471**.

EXTENDING THE XHTML 1.0 DTD

Apart from the fact that it can be done, why would you *want* to extend the DTD you're using? There are a number of possible reasons, depending on exactly what you're trying to accomplish:

- You might be working on integrating XHTML with another specialized XML-based language.
- Your Web publishing system might require certain tags to be added that are not exposed to the browsers, but are processed on the server side, and you want to use XML tools on those tags.
- Your browser might have additional support for tags that are not defined in the XHTML 1.0 specification, and you want to take advantage of the benefits of writing code to specification, such as validation.

One tag that is very common is <embed>, which is used to embed multimedia objects in web pages. Unfortunately, <embed> is not part of the HTML 4 or XHTML 1.0 specifications—instead, the specification promotes the use of the <object> tag, which is really a more elegant and general solution to adding multimedia objects to Web pages.

However, <embed> remains well-supported by the browsers, while there are several serious problems the implementation of <object> in some of the major browsers. This has left Web designers with difficult choices: use <object> and risk browser support problems, or use <embed> and not be able to code to the specification?

For these reasons, <embed> will make a good example of how the XHTML 1.0 specification can be extended.

→ For more specific information on how you can use <embed> to add multimedia—including movies and background sounds—**see** Chapter 31, "Audio and Video," **p. 641**.

DEFINING THE <embed> TAG

The first thing you will need to do when extending XHTML is decide which attributes of the <embed> tag you want to support. Because each browser implements a different set of attributes for <embed>—and because there is no W3C specification that defines it—you'll have to be selective when you put the tag together.

A good reference for HTML tags is the blooberry.com Web site, which lists every tag supported by the major browsers and the formal specifications. The listing for <embed> is at **www.blooberry.com/indexdot/html/tagpages/e/embed.htm** and lists a number of attributes. I've summarized the most important—and most supported—attributes in Table 22.7.

TABLE 22.7 THE ATTRIBUTES OF THE <embed> TAG

Attribute	Values
src	A URL address
height	Pixels or percentages
width	Pixels or percentages
pluginspage	A URL address
autoplay	"true" or "false"
controller	"true" or "false"
loop	"true," "false," or "palindrome"

→ The use of the <embed> tag's attributes to add multimedia to your site is explained in Chapter 31, "Audio and Video," **p. 641**.

These attributes will give you a good start on defining the <embed> tag. The tag itself will be an EMPTY tag as it has no content. (Actually, this is a matter of debate, as described in the blooberry.com listing for the <noembed> tag, but for this exercise we'll go with the simplest alternative.) Now I'll show you how to modify the DTD and add this element.

1. First, make a copy of the base DTD. You'll want to start with the XHTML 1.0 Transitional DTD, so copy the xhtml1-transitional.dtd file to another name, and edit that file. Call it xhtml1-embed.dtd.

2. Open the new copy in your text editor and go to the very end of the file. We will add our new element there. Add the following at the end of the DTD:

```
<!--===================== Embed =====================-->
<!ELEMENT embed EMPTY>
```

3. This would be a good time to define some parameter entities—both because they might be useful, and also because it will give you practice. On the line below the one where you declared the embed element, add the following lines to define the Boolean and Booloob entities:

```
<!ENTITY % Boolean "(true | false )">
<!ENTITY % Booloob "(true | false | palindrome)">
<!-- Why booloob? It is boolean plus palindrome -->
```

4. Now that you've defined those entities, you can use them and other generic parameter entities from the rest of the XHTML 1.0 DTD to list attributes. First create an attribute list shell for the embed element; leave some spaces between the lines so you can fill them in later. Don't forget the closing angle bracket.

```
<!ATTLIST embed

>
```

5. As you've seen from reading the XHTML specification, many elements use the `attrs` parameter entity, which includes the core attributes, intrinsic events, and internationalization attributes. These are appropriate for the `<embed>` tag, so the `attrs` entity:

```
<!ATTLIST embed
    %attrs;
    >
```

6. Next you need to consider each of the attributes, as listed in Table 22.7. The `src` and `pluginspage` attributes should be URLs, so use the `%URI;` entity. The `height` and `width` attributes will use the `%Length;` entity. Add those to the attribute list:

```
<!ATTLIST embed
    %attrs;
    src            %URI;          #REQUIRED
    height         %Length;       #IMPLIED
    width          %Length;       #IMPLIED
    pluginspage    %URI;          #IMPLIED
  >
```

7. Now we will use the parameter entries we defined before, Boolean and Booloob. The `autoplay` and `controller` attributes take Boolean values and the default should be `"false"`; the default for loop is `"false"` as well, but should use the Booloob entity. Add those attributes and your attribute list is complete:

```
<!ATTLIST embed
    %attrs;
    src            %URI;          #REQUIRED
    height         %Length;       #IMPLIED
    width          %Length;       #IMPLIED
    pluginspage    %URI;          #IMPLIED
    autoplay       %Boolean;      "false"
    controller     %Boolean;      "false"
    loop           %Booloob;      "false"
  >
```

8. With the `<embed>` element and its attributes defined, you are almost done. Locate the part of the DTD marked "Text Elements" and add embed to the "special" entity. Why the special entity? It includes the `<object>` tag, which is the closest in function and syntax to the `<embed>` tag, and is a reasonable place to add the tag. If it is not added, then the tag will exist—but there will be no legal place to use it! Here's what your modified `%special;` declaration should look like:

```
<!--=============== Text Elements ===========================-->
<!ENTITY % special
    "br | span | bdo | object | applet | img | map | iframe | embed">
```

9. Finally, edit the first comment at the beginning of the page to reflect the fact you have changed the DTD. Choose a public identifier and a system identifier URL—here's what I've used:

```
<!--
    Extensible HTML version 1.0 plus Embed DTD
    This is based on the XHTML 1.0 DTD with the addition
    of the embed tag.
    This DTD module is identified by the PUBLIC and SYSTEM identifiers:
    PUBLIC "-//kynn.com//XHTML 1.0 plus Embed//EN"
    SYSTEM "http://kynn.com/dtd/xhtml1-embed.dtd"
    $Revision: 1.0 $
    $Date: 2000/09/03 23:52:20 $
-->
```

You'll notice that I gave this an FPI—the first part indicates that I am not a standards body; the second identifies me as the author by using my domain name. The third part is the name of the DTD, and the last part identifies this as English. The system identifier is a URL on my Web site where I've placed the new DTD. You can use your own values in your DTD, using this as an example.

USING YOUR NEW DTD

Of course, unless you actually use the DTD you just created, this will all be a rather pointless exercise! Now you'll make a Web page that actually uses this DTD, and you can validate the page against the DTD.

1. First, create the framework for the page as you usually would, using the basic template for Web pages:

```
<!DOCTYPE html PUBLIC "-//W3C//DTD XHTML 1.0 Strict//EN"
"http://www.w3.org/TR/xhtml1/DTD/xhtml1-strict.dtd">
<html xmlns="http://www.w3.org/1999/xhtml">
<head>
<title> Document Exercise</title>
</head>
<body>

</body>
</html>
```

2. Change the <!DOCTYPE> tag so that it references your public and system identifiers, instead of the XHTML 1.0 DTD:

```
<!DOCTYPE html PUBLIC "-//kynn.com//XHTML 1.0 plus Embed//EN"
"http://kynn.com/dtd/xhtml1-embed.dtd">
```

3. Add some content which includes the <embed> tag. If you don't have any multimedia handy, that's okay—you're just going to validate this page to see if your DTD works. Use a dummy filename for the src, but be sure to include something as it was declared required:

```
<body>
<h1> This is our test </h1>
<embed src="dummy.mov" height="30" width="30" />
</body>
```

4. Save this file, and if you can, upload it to a Web server so that you can test it using the W3C's HTML and XHTML validator at **validator.w3.org/**. Also make sure that you have saved your new DTD at the location specified by the system identifier, as well as a copy of each of the parsed external entity files included with the XHTML 1.0 DTDs.

5. Validate your file by entering the URL into the W3C's validator. It will validate correctly, even though the <embed> tag isn't normally a valid element for XHTML 1.0! You can play with this a little to confirm that it's working—remove the src attribute and check if it truly is required, or add an extra attribute to <embed> (or make it a container). You'll see that the validator now respects your new DTD as strictly as it matches against the XHTML specification!

XHTML BASIC

In this chapter

WHAT IS XHTML BASIC?

In upcoming chapters, I'm going to delve more deeply into how to design for alternative devices. I'll take a look in great detail as to what they are, why they're important, and the various XML and related technologies that are associated with them.

XHTML 1.0 exists as a means of reformulating HTML as an XHTML document. One of the predominant reasons for doing this is to have the ability to extend XHTML to accommodate alternative devices. Presently, this is seen most clearly in XHTML 1.1, which at the time of this writing is not yet a standard (but it might be at the time you're reading this book—be sure to check with the World Wide Web Consortium for details).

My goal in including XHTML Basic—despite the fact that it's ahead of the standards game at this time—is to show you both how XHTML is moving toward modular constructs, and to provide a clear example of how XHTML is meant to extend to alternative device development.

So, to begin with, it's important to point out that XHTML Basic is *not* part of XHTML 1.0. Instead, it's a subset of XHTML 1.1, which as I've pointed out, isn't currently considered a recommendation. As such, it's more advanced in its concept, yet still basic—as its name implies—in terms of its structure.

XHTML Basic exists as a minimalist method by which to deliver XHTML documents to specialty clients, such as those on mobile phones, PDAs, pagers, and set-top boxes.

As many readers are by now aware, HTML, despite its origins, rapidly became an authoring system for Web-based design. This involves powerful computers, plenty of visual space (at least in comparative terms), and complex methods such as the use of frames. But small devices cannot support these complex issues, so new methods have to evolve. XHTML Basic is one of those methods.

The goal of XHTML Basic is to use certain parts of HTML within the context of XHTML, including only those parts of HTML that can be sensibly applied to an alternative environment.

Some of the appliances XHTML Basic is geared to accommodate are

- Mobile and "smart" phones
- Television sets
- PDAs such as Palm Pilots
- Computerized vending machines
- Pagers
- Navigation systems in automobiles
- Game machines
- Electronic book devices
- "Smart" watches and similar appliances

XHTML Basic is meant to include only those methods in HTML and XHTML that make *sense* to these kinds of appliances. Given that, many elements and methodologies with which authors working with standard Web design, are moved out of XHTML Basic so as to simplify the process by which to deliver consistent information to special appliances.

➔ For details on alternative devices, **see** Chapter 34, "Overview of Alternative Devices, Languages, and Protocols," **p. 683**.

FEATURES IN USE ACROSS APPLIANCES

A number of HTML and XHTML features can be used safely across appliances with little risk of causing problems with rendering. These include the use of text and basic text formatting, such as standard headings, paragraphs, and lists.

A critical feature for all hypermedia is, of course, the link. Basic forms are important to manage input, and basic tables—in this case not for design or layout, but for their original intent: the tabular formatting of data. Images can be used in many instances, although they should be kept very small. Meta information also can be included, and is helpful for document identification, character set encoding, and search engine keywords.

➔ For further information about designing for alternative devices, **see** Chapter 35, "Developing for the Alternative Device," **p. 693.**

XHTML Basic draws from these foundational methods. In some ways, XHTML Basic is much like early HTML. Simple, clean, logical.

OVERVIEW OF WHAT'S SUPPORTED AND WHY

So if XHTML Basic is a pared-down version of HTML and XHTML, what actually makes it tick? Well, there are many things that *can* be included in XHTML Basic, and some things that cannot. Sometimes, a technology is included, but only in part.

Note

> XHTML Basic inherits the HTML 4.0 and XHTML 1.0 concept of separating presentation from formatting. Presentation of an XHTML Basic document beyond the most simplistic is relegated to a style sheet.

Let's take a closer look at what *is* included in XHTML Basic.

- **Text**—Standard text is in fact supported in XHTML Basic. Formatting including paragraphs, headers, breaks, and lists also are supported. Emphasis is supported, but italics are not.

- **Forms**—Very basic forms are allowed. Forms must comply with the XHTML 1.1 Basic Forms Module. This module supports form elements common to HTML 3.2: form, input, select, option, and textarea.

- **Tables**—Tables from the Basic Tables Module in XHTML 1.1 are supported, including the following elements: caption, table, td, th, and tr.

- **Style Sheets**—External style sheets are supported via the link attribute. Elements including div, span, and class are also supported to allow the use of style. It's recommended that developers ensure graceful degradation for those user interfaces that do not support style.

- **Images**—Images are supported using the img element, but it's recommended that images are used very sparingly, and only then when they are extremely small in size.

> **Caution**
>
> Using tables in XHTML Basic in accordance with the XHTML 1.1 Table Module is acceptable, but not necessarily recommended. Tables are difficult for very small devices to display. What's more, no nesting of tables is allowed. Developers also are encouraged to make their tables accessible.

So, with XHTML Basic, I could have body markup that looks like this

```
<p>Welcome to Molly's Wireless Web</p>
```

or like this

```
<h2>Welcome to Molly's Wireless Web</h2>
<p>Here you will find:</p>
<ul>
<li>Book Updates</li>
<li>Speaking Engagements</li>
<li>Contact Information</li>
</ul>
```

or even this:

```
<img src="welcome.gif" /><br /><br />
<p>Select One:</p>
<table border="o" width="100%">
<tr>
<td><a href="updates.html">Book Updates</a></td>
<td><a href="speaking.html">Speaking Engagements</a></td>
<td><a href="contact.html">Contact Information</a></td>
</tr>
</table>
```

For my forms page, I could have a complete (but simple) form, and I also could choose to use an external style sheet to apply style as I saw fit.

> **Note**
>
> Most standard attributes for supported elements, such as border, width, height, and so on, are allowed in Basic XHTML.

OVERVIEW OF WHAT'S NOT SUPPORTED AND WHY

So what's been left out of XHTML basic? Lots! The limitations of alternative appliances at this time make it very difficult for many aspects of Web authoring—things with which we've all become intimately familiar—to make sense in restricted environments.

Here's a look at what you *can't* use in XHTML Basic:

- **Scripting**—The `script` and `noscript` elements are not supported. Scripts demand processing power, which many of the smaller, alternative devices simply do not have.
- **Frames**—Frames are based on the interfaces provided by a Web browser. Because the user agents in alternative devices are very limited, and very small, frames don't make sense (some people feel they've never made sense)! As such, frames are completely unsupported in XHTML Basic.
- **Objects**—The `object` element, which is used for things such as Java applets or Flash files, is prohibited. Once again, the simplicity of alternative devices do not allow for this kind of advanced functionality.
- **Image Maps**—Because mapping requires input from a pointing device, and only a few alternative devices use pointers (for example, PDAs do, but pagers do not), image maps have been left out of XHTML Basic.

PART
V
CH
23

So, any inline script using the `script` element will not be allowed. Conceivably, I could use `[CDATA]` or the `link` attribute to link to an external script. However, the use of scripting for alternative devices is very limited if useful at all, at least at this time. You'll never see a frameset in XHTML Basic, because the user agents don't have the power to support them.

Note

It's important to point out that the W3C expects that XHTML Basic will be expanded upon. This means that as alternative devices become more supportive of various technologies, elements that are currently not allowed will become allowed, or new elements or methodologies will be introduced. It's critical to remember that XHTML and its related technologies are truly in an evolutionary phase.

The same is true of Objects. Imagine trying to deliver a Flash file to a pager? Hardly! And, although small images are supported, the mapping features are not. Consider that original mapping was a server-side process, and later mapping was browser-based. Most user agents for small devices need to be lean and mean, so there simply isn't the support. What's more, the point-and-click options available to us on a computer are not available on most alternative devices.

If all this feels limited, well—it is! But these limitations empower you to deliver content to alternative devices. XHTML Basic doesn't exist for standard browser design. Rather, it is pared down especially because alternative devices are, as a group, limited.

→ To learn how to develop more specific applications for alternative devices, **see** Chapter 35, "Developing for the Alternative Device," **p. 693**, and Chapter 36, "Pagers, Cell Phones, and Other Wireless Devices," **p. 711**.

SPECIFIC MODULES INCLUDED IN XHTML BASIC

With an understanding of the fundamental concepts found in XHTML Basic, it becomes very easy to grasp how XHTML Basic uses XHTML 1.1 modules.

The following modules and associated elements are demonstrated in Table 23.1.

TABLE 23.1 MODULES FOUND IN XHTML BASIC

Module	Elements Included
Structure Module	body, head, html, title
Text Module	abbr, acronym, address, blockquote, br, cite, code, dfn, div, em, h1, h2, h3, h4, h5, h6, kbd, p, pre, q, samp, span, strong, var
Hypertext Module	a
List Module	dl, dt, dd, ol, ul, li
Basic Forms Module	form, input, label, select, option, textarea
Basic Tables Module	caption, table, td, tr, th
Image Module	img
Meta Information Module	meta
Link Module	link
Base Module	base

As you can see, it's modularization that provides the building blocks of any XHTML 1.1 subset. There are other modules available, but only this modules are allowed in XHTML Basic, as it is specifically designed for a precise use.

→ For more information on modularization, **see** Chapter 21, "XHTML Modularization", **p. 471**.

XHTML BASIC DOCUMENT STRUCTURE

An XHTML Basic document follows what should now be very familiar rules. Documents must conform, must validate, and must contain specific syntax to enable this conformance and validation.

An XHTML Basic document must conform to the following guidelines:

- The document validates to the XHTML Basic Document Type Definition (DTD).
- The document must contain a DOCTYPE definition denoting the proper DTD.
- The root element of the document (as in XHTML itself) is html.
- The root element contains the default namespace for XHTML, further defining it as an XHTML-based document.

Conformance is an absolute in XHMTL, and therefore in XHTML Basic. As a result, XHTML Basic documents must validate against the named Basic DTD.

To establish the document as an XHTML Basic document, and to allow for validation, the DOCTYPE definition must be included. The root element is html because HTML is the vocabulary in use within the context of XHTML Basic markup.

Note

If the rules for XHTML Basic sound to you to be exactly like those found in standard XHMTL 1.0, but with a different DTD, you're correct! XHTML Basic is a perfect example of modularization—a primary concept in XHTML 1.1—at work.

Listing 23.1 shows an XHTML Basic document with all the structure elements in place.

LISTING 23.1   THE XHTML BASIC SHELL

```
<?xml version="1.0"?>
<!DOCTYPE html PUBLIC "-//W3C//DTD XHTML Basic 1.0//EN"
"xhtml-basic10.dtd" >

<html xmlns="http://www.w3.org/1999/xhtml" xml:lang="en" >

</html>
```

Note

As with XHTML 1.0, the XML declaration is suggested, but not required.

DESIGNING FOR THE REAL WORLD

CREATING AND DEPLOYING AN XHTML BASIC DOCUMENT

You can put XHTML Basic to work today. To do so, follow these steps:

1. Create an XHTML Basic Document. Begin with the DOCTYPE declaration:
   ```
   <!DOCTYPE html PUBLIC "-//W3C//DTD XHTML Basic 1.0//EN"
   "xhtml-basic10.dtd" >
   ```

2. Add the html root and namespace element:
   ```
   <!DOCTYPE html PUBLIC "-//W3C//DTD XHTML Basic 1.0//EN"
   "xhtml-basic10.dtd" >

   <html xmlns="http://www.w3.org/1999/xhtml" xml:lang="en" >
   </html>
   ```

3. Add the head and title element to the document:
   ```
   <!DOCTYPE html PUBLIC "-//W3C//DTD XHTML Basic 1.0//EN"
   "xhtml-basic10.dtd" >

   <head>
   <title>My First XHTML Basic Page</itle>
   </head>

   <html xmlns="http://www.w3.org/1999/xhtml" xml:lang="en" >
   </html>
   ```

4. Add the body element:

```
<!DOCTYPE html PUBLIC "-//W3C//DTD XHTML Basic 1.0//EN"
"xhtml-basic10.dtd" >

<head>
<title>My First XHTML Basic Page</itle>
</head>

<html xmlns="http://www.w3.org/1999/xhtml" xml:lang="en" >

<body>

</body>
</html>
```

5. Add content (I've kept mine simple):

```
<!DOCTYPE html PUBLIC "-//W3C//DTD XHTML Basic 1.0//EN"
"xhtml-basic10.dtd" >

<head>
<title>My First XHTML Basic Page</itle>
</head>

<html xmlns="http://www.w3.org/1999/xhtml" xml:lang="en" >

<body>

<h2>Welcome to Molly's Wireless Web</h2>
<p>Here you will find:</p>

<ul>
<li>Book Updates</li>
<li>Speaking Engagements</li>
<li>Contact Information</li>
</ul>

<a href="next.html">Follow this link to continue</a>
</body>

</html>
```

6. Save the file as index_basic.html.

7. Upload to your Web server. If you have a PDA or other alternative device, look up the page using that device and test it out.

> **Caution**
>
> You can use the XML declaration in your document if you so desire. However, if certain standard Web browsers comes to this page, it might render improperly. Therefore, I've left it off in this example.

VI

VISUAL DESIGN FOR THE WEB

CHAPTER 24

EFFECTIVE PAGE DESIGN

In this chapter

UNDERSTANDING SITE ARCHITECTURE

Designing a Web page to be effective means understanding a bit about the structure of hypermedia documents, taking the time to plan your page—and how it will interact with other pages on the site—as well as learning at least the basic principles of User Interface Design (UID).

The structure of hypermedia directly relates to the effectiveness of your page because by understanding the underlying, interactive technology available to you, you can make choices for your site and for your audience—eliminating potential problems on either end. Similarly, planning plays a big role in making sure you know what you want and need before you start to work. You spend less time and, in a professional situation, less money by ensuring that your work is well thought out in advance.

A compelling aspect of the Web that stems from the hypermedia environment is that the Web's format can be interpreted as being *non-linear*. I believe that putting the Web in this context will help provide you with a frame of reference for a better understanding about how sites are built.

Books are read page-by-page. This is a linear activity. Another familiar, linear act is how most Westerners perceive time. We see it as a logical order of days, one following another in a line. It's interesting to note that in some cultures, time is perceived as a spiral. Linear activities dominate Western civilization, however, and that the Web is such a curiosity—and challenge to its developers—often relates to the fact that it is essentially unlike most of our familiar constructs.

Web sites, unlike a book, can be constructed to take you from the middle of a sentence or a thought to another, ancillary thought. Or, that link can take you to some data whose relationship to the originating data is not immediately clear.

What happens when a person is interacting with information in this way is that he or she can, and often does, depart from this linear structure into one that allows for a more free-flowing, non-linear event. The popular term, *surfing the Web*, sums up this freedom well—suggesting that moving from Web site to Web site is a fun and fluid journey, rather than a strict, regimented one.

It becomes imperative that the individual designing Web pages understands how this environment offers organizational structures that are both like and unlike those with which we are most familiar—books and flow charts are linear and are perfectly acceptable for certain designs on the Web. But to tap into the non-linear world and make it a relevant experience for the Web site visitor is to enhance his or her experience, and challenge your own capabilities!

LINEAR SITES

Because most readers are accustomed to linear structure, and are most familiar with organizing information into such structures, it's very important to give most functional sites enough linearity to be comfortable and navigable.

A linear Web site is much like a book. Each page is placed to the conceptual "right" of the next, and there's an opportunity to page forward or back. Figure 24.1 is a drawing reflecting the forward/back style of navigation.

Figure 24.1
Linear structures resemble the forward/back layout of a book's pages.

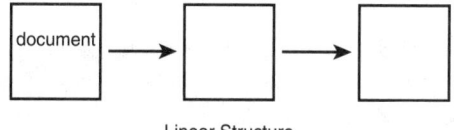

Linear Structure

HIERARCHICAL SITES

Another familiar structure in our linear world is the *hierarchical*, or flow-chart method of mapping a Web site. In a case of this nature, I can offer links that move from level to level as well as from side to side. In Figure 24.2, a hierarchical site is shown. As you begin to add links that take you to multiple areas inside and outside of the site (see Figure 24.3), the linearity becomes less evident.

PART

VI

CH

24

Figure 24.2
Hierarchical structures are more complex linear designs.

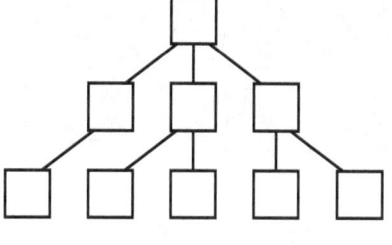

Hierarchical Structure

Figure 24.3
Multiple links to and from different documents inside and outside of the site begin to move the site away from a strict, linear construct.

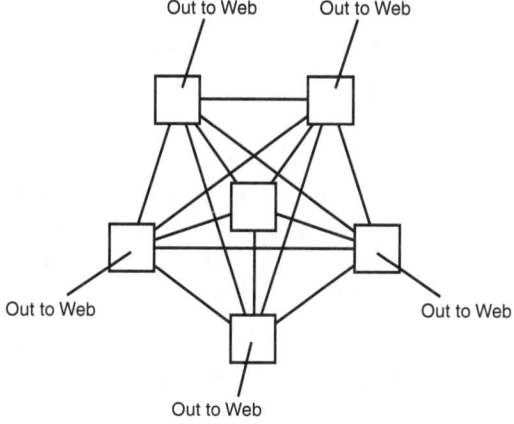

Non-linear Structure

NON-LINEAR SITES

So what of a non-linear site? Well, a true non-linear site would have completely random links. What this means is that no matter where I clicked, I wouldn't know where in the Web world I was going to end up (see Figure 24.4).

Figure 24.4
CoreWave's A Glass Bead Game II uses randomization so that you never know where you'll end up.

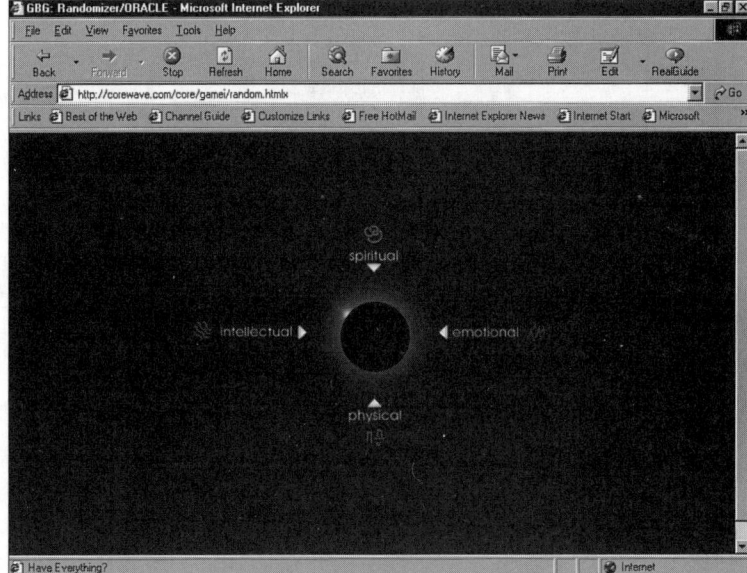

Is there a middle ground? You bet, and it's one that is encouraged because, as I mentioned, in most cases we want to give site visitors enough linearity so they are comfortable within the environment. How do we add some non-linear options to a site?

1. Begin with a linear or hierarchical structure.
2. Add links from any place within that site to another section of that same site.
3. Add links to external sites.

The non-linear experience in the result comes from the allowance for and encouragement of *user choice*. Every person coming to this site can conceivably surf it differently. This, in turn, creates an individual, flowing experience, rather than a highly structured one. However, we've been cautious by beginning with a linear structure to make the site sensible and help people maintain a sense of place.

USER INTERFACE DESIGN

Just as your smile and outward appearance help others identify what is interesting and appealing about you, a user interface is what allows Web visitors to want to stop and enjoy the bounty your site provides.

Interfaces serve to welcome, guide, and provide the functional elements required to assist your visitor in getting to the information or experience he or she is seeking. Considered a critical aspect of multimedia design, a well-built interface is particularly important for the Web. If an individual isn't finding the information required or isn't having a meaningful adventure on your pages, he or she can simply choose to take a sharp turn off the road and visit another site. One, perhaps, that will be more interesting and informative for the visitor and profitable to your competitor.

One step to avoid creating sites that act as pit-stops or U-turns on the Web's highways and by-ways is to be sure that the sites you build make the visitor feel comfortable and provide that visitor with the goods he or she is after. This is done via a number of methods, including intelligent design as well as an attractive and *useful* site interface.

Several time-honored principles of user interface design should be applied to your Web site plans. These concepts are drawn from other media, such as interactive CD-ROMs, kiosks, and even television. The hypermedia environment of the Web—with its links to here, there, and everywhere in the vast and complex Internet world—is often bereft of these foundational principles. The results are ill-designed interfaces that confuse and frustrate rather than inform and assist the people who visit those Web sites.

The reason for the abundance of problems with user interfaces on the Internet has a lot to do with the fact that, very frequently, Web sites are being built by computer engineers, high school students—even fine artists—all of whom have much to contribute content-wise to the Web environment, but little or no experience in what it takes to communicate in the unusual, non-linear structure of the Web.

Tip from
molly

Ever hear the rather rude acronym, KISS? It stands for *Keep It Simple, Stupid!* User interfaces might be complicated technologically, but they should be easy for any user to understand.

The following principles can assist you in avoiding the potholes that inexperienced Web designers can find themselves driving into. Apply these ideas to the sites you build, and you stand a much better chance of a smooth ride toward your Web success.

METAPHOR

In design, *metaphor* refers to the symbolic representation of the structure you're attempting to build. A metaphor acts as a familiar visual aid around which you build the entryway, interiors, windows, doors, and exits of your environment.

In fact, I used metaphor to write the previous paragraph. I defined a Web site as though it was a building—with a selection of the elements you expect to find in a building. Metaphor helps people feel comfortable because they are familiar with the rules of the setting. A simple example of this can be found on Yahoo!, which uses a series of visual metaphors for its navigation, as you can see in Figure 24.5. Users relate the baby chick, which represents "new," to the link that has new information, and so forth. Visitors relate easily to the concept and are able to interact with the interface without having to think too much about how to do so.

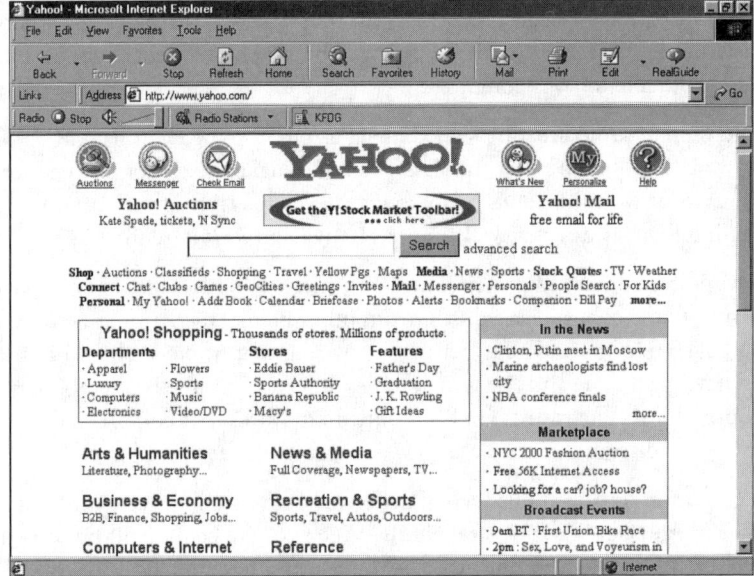

Figure 24.5
Visual metaphor on Yahoo! A baby chicken coming out of an egg represents "What's New," a letter, "Check Email," the word MY for "Personalize," and a question mark for "Help."

One common pitfall of metaphor is the use of overly vague—or overly specific—references. People everywhere can identify with a building metaphor. But the more specific you make your metaphor—relating your site to a milk processing plant rather than a generic building, for example—the greater the chance that at least some of your visitors will become confused.

Tip from

Metaphor should use common, everyday concepts that people from any part of the globe who come upon your site will be able to understand immediately.

Achieve metaphor, and you're one step closer to helping that person make himself or herself comfortable enough to stay and visit with you a while.

CLARITY

To increase a visitor's desire to stay, be sure that he or she understands the elements within your pages. There should be no critical pieces that are abstract or difficult to decipher. This is not to say that abstraction as an art form isn't allowed—a good designer can use abstract art within a very clear Web site. What a good designer cannot do is use abstractions when it comes to those elements necessary to navigate the site, locate information, or return to critical areas within the site.

Elements that fall into this category include any buttons, imagemaps, or links that are necessary for site navigation. A button that leads the visitor to the left shouldn't have an arrow that faces up, and a link that offers a mail option shouldn't pull up your newsreader. It's that simple, and that clear. Clarity is a must for precise communication.

CONSISTENCY

Consistency is not only of utmost importance in interface design, it's one of the skeletal necessities of a Web site. All too often I find myself landing on a Web page and thinking "Wow, this looks great!" Then, as I move to the next page, I find myself wondering what happened to the inviting design and promise that first page offered. If I stay long enough to move through the site, backgrounds change, font styles are inconsistent, headers and navigation are completely irregular—in short, I can't tell from one page to the next where the heck in the Web world I am! Being consistent with design elements allows for a cohesive presentation. This keeps your visitors calm instead of tense, confused, and ready to take a hard right—right off of your site, that is.

PART

VI

CH

24

Tip from

molly

Consistency can be gained by developing a site palette and sticking to the color theme in some regular fashion. Location and order of navigation also is a significant aspect of consistent UID design.

ORIENTATION

Following closely along with each of the prior concepts is the idea that a site visitor must know where he or she is at any given time. This is *orientation*. If I'm deep into a site that has hundreds of pages, it helps to know where in that site I am. It's also really good if I have quick access to other areas of the site and can go back where I came from if I find out I'm somewhere I really don't want, or need, to be.

Orientation is achieved by ensuring that each site has either a header that defines that page's purpose, or another, familiar element that instantly tells me where I am. You have probably seen a variety of methods to ensure orientation.

One example of orientation can be found on the Wilde Rose Coffee Roastery site at `http://desert.net/wilderose/`. Note that an empty coffee cup helps define my location as I move from page to page (see Figure 24.6).

NAVIGATION

Just as you want your visitors to remain oriented as they surf your site, you also want them to be able to figure out how to click from page to page—and back again. This is called *navigation*. Navigation and orientation are closely linked, and your navigational tools—the icons, buttons and menus on each page—can provide some much-needed consistency for your site.

Figure 24.6
The empty coffee cup orients the visitor to the page being visited.

 Navigation goes beyond creating a uniform set of buttons, however. Give careful thought to where those buttons are going to lead your visitors. A menu with too many choices will overwhelm people and detract from the flow of your site. A menu with too few choices will force people to guess at which option will take them to the information they seek.

Tip from

It's one, two, three clicks away! If you make your visitors click more than three times to get to the information he or she is after, you run the risk of disorienting them. Ideally, no piece of data on your site is more than three clicks away from a related piece of data.

Suffice it to say that navigation is an integral part of interface design, and a critical element of any Web site. It's all about getting from way over there to right where you want to be, logically, quickly, and with ease.

PAGE LAYOUT TECHNIQUES

Planning and understanding structure provide a strong foundation for the next step: laying out your pages. There are two good ways of doing this.

COMPOSITING PAGES

This method is always a great way to get your creative juices flowing. It's also a great starting point for individual page designs.

I personally like to use a sketch board and pencils. I'll simply draw a rectangle representing each screen for the individual pages I require. Then I quickly sketch my ideas. This gives me a preliminary starting point, and from here I tend to move on to using Photoshop to jump in and lay out my ideas, adding color and style.

WORKING WITH GRID SYSTEMS

Some people don't bother with the hand-drawn approach, but I find it a great way to begin. Either way, Photoshop is where I, and most professional designers, do their page mockups. If you use another imaging program, you can still work with the concepts presented here.

→ To decide which imaging tool is best for you, **see** Chapter 27, "Web Graphic Tools and Professional Tools," **p. 561**.

One of the reasons I find Photoshop to be superior in this application to other graphic tools is the use of layers and history features. Photoshop allows you to put different elements on different layers, and you can then save that file, enabling you to make adjustments in color and style later. And, should you want to go back and make a change, the history palette keeps all your moves in memory.

Furthermore, Photoshop allows you to control the entire grid of your page, pixel by pixel, as shown in Figure 24.7.

PART

VI

CH

24

Figure 24.7
Laying out a page in Photoshop. Note the rulers and grid.

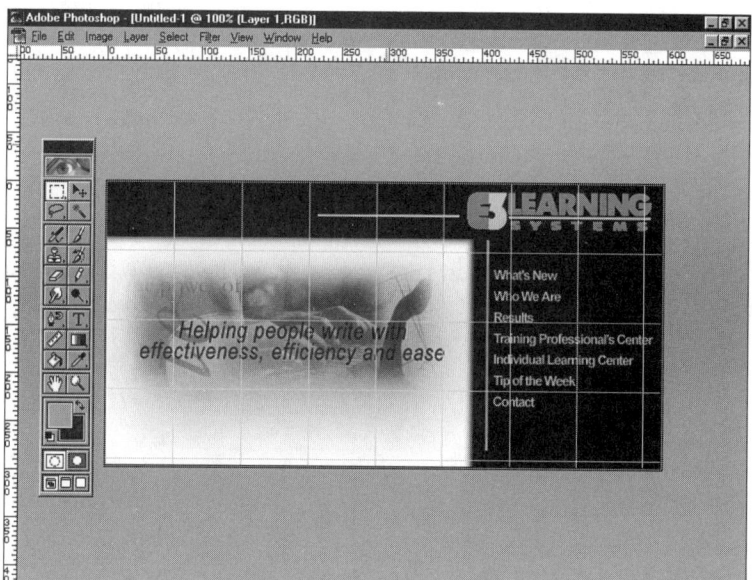

Note

Some designers like to use page layout programs, such as Quark or Adobe InDesign instead of Photoshop. Some WYSIWYG HTML software offers site mapping and management tools, but at the time of this writing, none of them conform to XHTML standards. No matter the tool you choose, the bottom line is to think your plan through and prepare for it visually before beginning to code.

The first step is to create a page. To accommodate the varied resolutions on the Web, many Web designers use the 640×480 pixels per screen rule, with more and more creating for 800×600 resolution. If you add to that the parts of the browser that eat up Web real estate, you're left with a safe 585×295 pixels or 748×415 per screen working area respectively.

→ For more details about working with the computer screen, **see** Chapter 26, "Working with the Computer Screen," **p. 545**.

Designing to this dimension will create a page with no scrolling on either the horizontal or vertical axis. Although your page length can certainly vary, it's wise either to keep to the specific resolution width with which you are working to avoid unstable design or use dynamic layouts.

→ For more details on dynamic layouts, **see** Chapter 14, "Laying Out Tables Within XHTML Documents," **p. 243**.

Note

How long should a Web page be? Most professionals recommend using approximately three screens. That would give you between 295 pixels to 1,000 pixels per low-resolution page. Obviously you will need to be flexible with this measurement, depending upon your audience and particular needs.

The concepts and examples in this chapter should set you well on your way to being able to design effective interfaces using HTML.

Remember that understanding the parts of something is important to relating to it as a whole. This is clearly demonstrated when you study user interface design. By thinking carefully about concepts such as metaphor, clarity, and orientation, you become able to strengthen the parts of interface.

Analyzing audience, intent, and the type of experience you want your site visitors to have gives you perspective as to the bigger picture, leading you to a more cohesive, easier to use, and, ultimately, a more professional Web site.

TROUBLESHOOTING

LINEARITY

I want to create a site that moves from page to page without many links within the pages. I understand that this is a linear site. Is it going to upset visitors if I use strict linearity on the Web?

The answer lies in the intent of the site. If you're creating a portal site, a page-to-page site without many links is simply not going to work. However, if you're creating a guided tour where you want to bring your visitor from one piece in an art exhibit to the next in a precise fashion, the linear site will be absolutely appropriate.

METAPHOR

Is metaphor necessary to create good sites?

Many sites choose not to use metaphorical images to represent navigation elements. Instead, choosing words for the navigable content, such as New, About Us, and Contact, works perfectly well.

DESIGNING FOR THE REAL WORLD

DESIGNING AN EFFECTIVE PAGE

This project teaches you how to use an imaging program to design an effective page. I'll use Photoshop, but you can use the image tool of your choice—the basic instructions will be the same, except where working with layers comes in to play if your software doesn't support layers.

To create a workspace for your page design, follow these steps:

1. Open Photoshop, and choose File, New.
2. In the New dialog box, place your width and height in pixels. Remember that your width should be 585—even if you're going to create a dynamic design. This keeps your page elements to an appropriate size. Your length can vary. In Figure 24.8 I've set up a working area of 585 pixels by 295 pixels for a non-scrolling page.

Figure 24.8
I've set up a work area of 585 pixels by 295 pixels for my non-scrolling splash page.

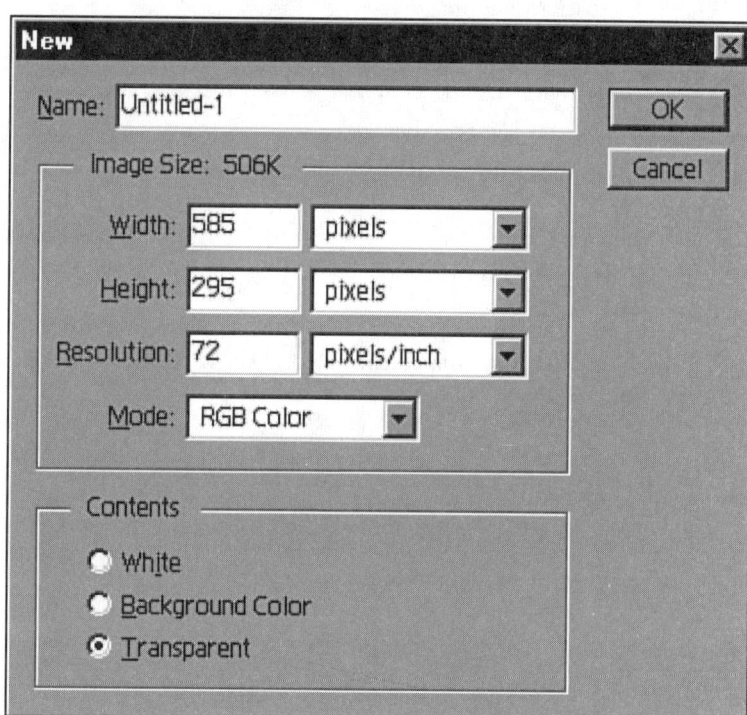

3. Be sure that you're working in RGB (you will optimize individual graphics later), using a transparent page, and that you are set at 72 DPI.

Now you're ready to add color and images.

USING PHOTOSHOP LAYERS

Photoshop layers, as mentioned, are perhaps the most powerful aspect of Photoshop. By using them, you have absolute control over each part of a design.

Remember to create a new layer for each part of your page:

1. With your new image active, choose Layer, New, Layer.
2. Select your background color using the eyedropper tool and color palette. Select Window, Show Color.
3. Fill the layer with the proposed browser-safe color selection you want by choosing Edit, Fill. Make sure you select Foreground and uncheck the Transparency box in the Fill dialog box.
4. Create a new layer, following the directions in step 1.

In this layer, you'll add your background pattern (see Chapter 29, "Creating Professional Web Graphics"). I have mine prepared and saved in native Photoshop format as `background.psd`:

1. Open your background image file.
2. Choose Select, All.
3. Choose Edit, Select Define Pattern.
4. Move to your new layer on the workspace.
5. Choose Edit, Fill, Pattern, and let your image fill the layer.

Now you can add a text header.

1. Click your workspace to bring up the Text dialog box.
2. Now choose your typeface, size, leading, and spacing. In most cases you'll want to be sure you have the Anti-Aliased check box checked. I've chosen a decorative typeface at 14 points (see Figure 24.9).
3. Click OK.
4. Place the text where desired by using the Move tool.

Continue creating layers and adding elements as you want. Remember to create a new layer for each element so that you have optimum control of that element.

Figure 24.9
Here I've added type to a Photoshop layer that will become part of my overall design.

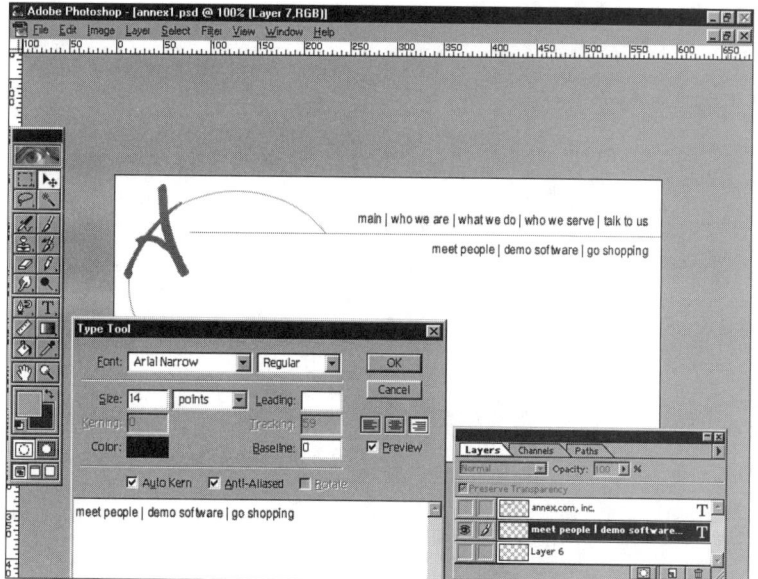

PART
VI
CH
24

Tip from

You can anticipate body text by creating individual layers with the paragraphs you'll want to use, but in most cases you'll be relying on HTML to create that text. Default body text is typically around 12-point Times on the PC, and 12-point Geneva on the Macintosh.

After you have a page with which you are satisfied, save the file as a Photoshop file (choose File, Save, PSD). If you're using a different imaging program that has layers, save to that program's native format. I like to do this so that I can keep the layers intact, enabling me to come back later and make any necessary adjustments to the fonts, colors, and positions of my elements.

Caution

Make sure you save the file with the layers intact. Never flatten a file that you want to use for layout. If you do, you'll lose the ability to go in and manipulate the position, size, color, or other attributes of the element on that layer.

You can now use this layout not only to make adjustments to the design, but to actually generate your graphics.

→ To learn how to generate graphics from a layered file, **see** Chapter 29, "Creating Professional Web Graphics," **p. 595**.

COLOR CONCEPTS

In this chapter

COLOR THEORY

What color blouse or shirt are you wearing today? I'm wearing white. It's a hot day here in the desert, and white seems to make me feel cooler.

If you think about it carefully, you probably were motivated to pick out the clothing you're wearing right now because of a practical or psychological need. Don't laugh! Okay, so maybe you grabbed the last clean shirt in the pile—but undoubtedly that shirt is from a spectrum of colors in which you feel comfortable.

Color, and how it influences the many facets of our world, is a powerful force. Although XHTML is the foundation on which we build our designs, color is a pillar of the design itself—how it affects the site visitor, the emotional message it sends, and how it blends to create an esthetic Web page.

To understand color, it's important to visit the theory that surrounds it. The idea here is to refine your eye and your understanding of how color works so that you can use it in effective ways.

If you have a window nearby, look out. In the natural world, we have a wide range of colors. There's everything from the bright green of a new leaf to the shocking orange of an Arizona sunset. Between these bold extremes, nature shows its subtle hand—a soft-blue sky, a slate-gray rock, the light-tan patches on my cat's fur.

The computer environment is more limited than nature, and when we take a closer look at the Web environment, these limitations become even more stringent. Yet an understanding of the colors that exist and how they work gives you an undeniable edge when it comes to using color in Web design that leaves a lasting impression.

SUBTRACTIVE AND ADDITIVE COLOR

Colors in the natural world are made up of pigments. Pigment is a substance that reacts to light. You might have heard it said that without light, there is no color. This is true, and without pigment, there is no *variation* in color.

Subtractive color is the theoretical premise on which color in the natural world is based. It's called subtractive because it absorbs light first, *before* transmitting or reflecting the results that our eyes perceive as color.

Subtractive color theory exists to help both industrialists and artists understand and try to recreate nature's own design. With this premise as a guide, pigments are recreated chemically in paints, dyes, and inks.

Remember the color wheel? A color wheel is the circular representation of subtractive color, with different colors making up pie slices within the wheel. The color wheel begins with what is known as the *primary* colors: red, green, and yellow. Each of these colors can be mixed together to come up with an entire spectrum of colors.

In *additive synthesis*, color is created by the addition of colors. Computers use three colors to do this: red, green, and blue. It's almost like three individual paint guns are being fired at your screen, combining color and light to create variations.

Red, green, and blue color is referred to as *RGB*. As we look into how to work with digital color, this will be the technical foundation for the decisions we make. However, it's the subtractive world from which we gain our inspiration. It's important to keep this distinction in mind.

So how is it that the natural world can make all colors from red, blue, and yellow, but computers cannot? It goes back to the difference between the ability to absorb versus the ability to transmit light, and how light then interacts with what is absorbed or transmitted. If you mix red and green using paint, you get brown. But guess what happens when a computer mixes those same colors? The resulting color is yellow.

COLOR AND THE COMPUTER SCREEN

Digital information is dealt with differently from the natural world. Computers and computer hardware are quite limited in their capability to deliver color to a screen. You can't compete with nature!

But we do try. And we do this by using a different color method. Because it's not possible for a computer to first absorb light, it must generate light. Therefore, the type of color we see on our computers is backed by additive synthesis.

Computers rely on three primary pieces of hardware to deliver color information to you: a computer's CPU, a video graphics card, and the computer monitor itself.

It stands to reason, then, that the quality of color you see at your computer depends on the quality and capability of these components. If any one of these components is incompatible or unequal in its properties, the end result will not be as true and refined as possible.

Furthermore, computer platforms (OSs) have differing capabilities when it comes to color. In terms of the computers and OSs you might be using, the Macintosh is known for its higher-end color; Windows 3.1 is very limited; Windows 95 and later has very good color control; and, if you're using a standard UNIX machine, you're at a disadvantage with lower color capabilities.

The reason this is important to you is so that you have an understanding of how and why you must learn to work with the color limitations and standards that exist. Knowing your own machine and the capabilities of your viewing audience will help you do just that.

Add to this the fact that any GUI, such as a browser, affects the management of color, and you've got an important issue in color technology: In Web design, it is the browser that limits color significantly.

This is the bane of the Web designer's existence when it comes to color, but I promise you, it's not insurmountable. In this chapter I'll show you some techniques to help you manage color effectively.

If you come from a graphics background or have worked with Photoshop or other professional graphics programs, you're probably familiar with other color-management methods (also referred to as *color spaces*). One of the most familiar is CMYK (cyan, magenta, yellow, black) output. Other management systems include grayscale—which contains black, white, and gradations of gray—and indexed color, which is a limited palette of specific colors defined by the designer. In Web design, indexed color is extremely important because it provides one method by which to intentionally make graphics smaller in weight and therefore easier to download quickly.

→ To learn how to work with indexed color, **see** Chapter 28, "Common Web Graphic Formats," **p. 581**.

COLOR SIGNIFICANCE

To those of you who are familiar with it, the *Wired* look is memorable. Using neon and discordant colors, the magazine as well as the HotWired Web site (`http://www.hotwired.com/`) communicates energy.

My mother hates me in black. She says it makes my skin look lackluster and yellowish. She's right, but I still like to wear black. Why? It soothes me. It neutralizes my sense of my body and calms me.

Ever notice how all-night restaurants are usually very brightly lit? This is thought to help keep people awake.

The more you look for examples of the significance of color, the more you'll find them. Colors are even associated with specific professions, ages, and genders: white and green for doctors and nurses, darker or more neutral colors for older people, pink for girls, and blue for boys.

None of this is accidental. In fact, it's very specific. Color has a strong impact on the human psyche. This has been shown to be true in countless studies.

However, the intriguing issue is that color alone doesn't create this impact. Culture has a profound influence on how we perceive color, too.

Recently, there was a trend in some Western countries to marry in black—the bride and her bridesmaids as well as the men used black material in their formal bridal wear. This upset a lot of people, as Westerners tend to associate black with death and mourning.

But in some cultures, the color that we normally associate with purity and brides—white—is the color of death. In East India, for example, white is the color of the death shroud and mourning costumes.

Tip from molly

Because readers of this book come from different backgrounds, it's a great exercise for each of you to determine what specific emotional and cultural responses given colors represent to you.

It's important for you—a Web designer working in a global medium—to have some sense of what colors signify. Although I can't give you a rundown of cultural color significance in one chapter, I can give you some general meanings of color. I do advise that if you're doing work for a client from a different culture, it is well worth your while to ask a bit about color perception in that individual's culture. This can help you avoid uncomfortable, time-consuming situations.

Table 25.1 shows a bit about color significance in the Western world. Remember, these are generalizations, and other interpretations do exist.

TABLE 25.1   HOW COLORS TEND TO BE PERCEIVED IN THE WEST

Color	Significance
Black	Death, darkness, elegance, sophistication
White	Purity, cleanliness, refinement
Red	Passion, intense energy, anger
Green	Healing, nature, earth
Blue	Dignity, power, stability
Yellow	Happiness, vibrancy, youth
Purple	Royalty, riches, sumptuousness

PART VI

CH 25

Note

Color designer and researcher J.L. Morton offers fascinating information on color at her Web site, Color Matters, at http://www.colormatters.com/. Electronic, "Color Voodoo" books can help inspire and guide you when working with color. You can download these (for a fee) from http://www.colorvoodoo.com/. I've written an article on colors in a global setting, which can be found in *Web Techniques* magazine, September 2000 issue, at http://www.webtechniques.com/.

Color is defined by how colors are combined. Although the method of combination is going to differ when we compare the subtractive, natural world to the digital, additive one, the end results are the same in terms of our perception of color.

Colors categories are defined as follows:

- **Primaries**—All colors are the results of some combination of three colors: red, yellow, and blue. These colors are referred to as primary because they are the first colors to technically exist. Without them, no other color is possible.

- **Secondaries**—The next step is to mix pairs of the primaries together. If I mix red and yellow, I come up with orange. Blue and yellow create green, and mixing red with blue creates purple. Orange, green, and purple are the secondary colors found on the color wheel.

- **Intermediates**—When two primaries are mixed together, the results are referred to as intermediate colors. These colors are gradations that lie between the primary and secondary colors.

Along with these categories, you can achieve additional categories by adding white or black. When you add white to a given color, you achieve *tint*. Black added to a color darkens it. This is referred to as *shade*.

Note

> Colors that are next to one another on the wheel, such as blue and purple, have a distinct relationship and are considered *similar*. Opposing colors, such as orange and blue, are *complementary*. Red and green, which are three colors removed from each other on the wheel, are *contrasting* colors.

PROPERTIES OF COLOR

The past several years have been very exciting in the fashion design world. There's a lot of texture, plenty of style, and a wide host of colorful names for color.

Bordeaux. Banana. Spice. Where do these colors fit into the spectrum? What determines the difference between cobalt and peacock, even if they are both blue?

This differentiation is made is by defining the *properties* of color. The type and amount of color determine color properties as well as how much light is used in that color, as follows:

- **Hue**—This term is used to differentiate one color from another. For example, red is different from green, and purple is different from brown. Whether a color is primary, secondary, intermediate, or tertiary isn't important with regard to hue; that they are different in terms of actual color is.

- **Value**—Chocolate brown is darker than tan, and sky blue is lighter than navy. A color's value is defined by the amount of light or dark in that color.

- **Saturation**—Also referred to as *intensity*, you can think of saturation as being the brightness of a color. Peacock blue is very bright, whereas navy is rather dull. Similarly, those popular neon-lime greens reminiscent of the 1960s are much more intense than a forest green.

- **Warmth**—Hues found in the yellow-to-red range are considered warm. They emit a sense of heat.

- **Coolness**—Cool colors are those ranging from green to blue. Think of ice blue, or the cool sense a forest of deep green can inspire.

If you look at these definitions, you can see that a given hue can contain a value and saturation. When you think of all the variations that are potentially held within each of these properties, you can begin to see that color is much more than meets the eye.

Of course, you might notice that black and white are missing from this list. Black can be described as the absence of light, and white as *being* light. A more technical way to think about black and white is to refer to the properties of hue and saturation. The fact? Neither black nor white possess either hue *or* saturation.

> **Note**
>
> Why then, are there "shades" of gray? The reason is found in value. The amount of light or dark in white or black determines the resulting value of gray.

Colors are emotional, and they have emotional relationships with one another. In a compatible relationship, harmony reigns. In a discordant relationship, clashing occurs.

In design, relationships are very important, because both harmonious as well as discordant color schemes can be effective, depending on the circumstances.

If I'm trying to convey a peaceful environment, I'm going to want to use harmonious colors. An example of this would be creating a palette from soft, subtle pastels. The end result is going to be calm and even feminine.

However, if I want to wake people up and jangle them a bit, I might try a discordant relationship. Bright yellow and red with black is going to create discord, but the visual impact is intense. Depending on the audience and the communication issues at hand, the discordant relationship might be a more appropriate choice than the harmonious one.

Light, and how it interacts with color, creates special color effects. As a designer, you can learn to use these effects to enhance your designs.

Color effects include the following:

- **Luster**—Luster is the term used to describe a shining quality usually seen in fabrics such as satin or silk. Luster results from the way light is absorbed by certain areas of a texture contrasting with black areas of the background color.
- **Iridescence**—The inside of seashells, pearls, and opals are iridescent. Instead of the light splotches contrasting with black, the background color is usually some shade of gray.
- **Luminosity**—Similar to luster and iridescence, the difference here is the *quantity* of contrast. When there is a very delicate contrast between the lighter areas and background areas, luminosity is created.
- **Transparency**—Think of a piece of tape or colored glass. Light passes through, creating a clear, or transparent, effect.

You can create all these effects by mimicking what happens in nature.

To demonstrate what these effects look like, I opened Photoshop and went to work. You can step with me through the process of making examples of special color effects, using any image editor you like that has similar functions.

To create color effects, follow these steps:

1. In Photoshop, select File, New.

2. Create a workspace with the dimensions of 200×200 pixels. Be sure your background is set to Transparent and the mode is RGB. DPI should be 72.

3. On the toolbar, click the color square and fill it with a gray color.

4. Now select Edit, Fill.

5. Fill your workspace with black.

6. Select Layer, Add New Layer from the menu.

7. Select the airbrush from the toolbar.

8. From the brush palette, choose a fairly soft brush (see Figure 25.1).

Figure 25.1
Choosing a soft brush from the Brushes palette in Photoshop.

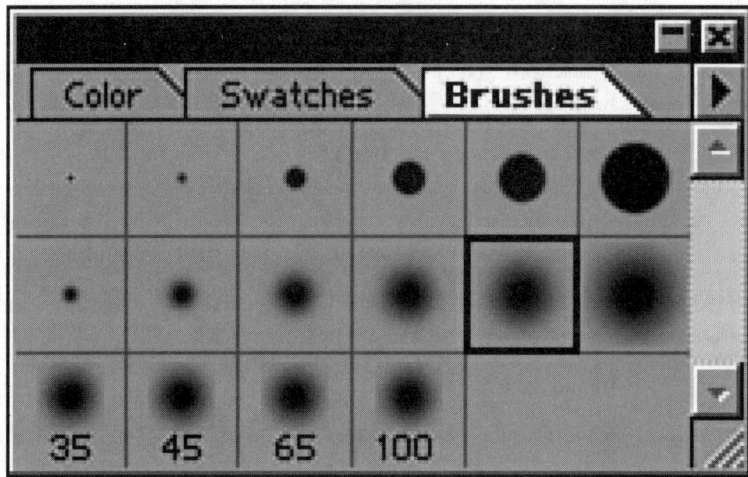

9. Now paint a shape on your second layer, allowing some areas to be gray and others showing the first layer's black, as I have done in Figure 25.2.

The results are a lustrous effect. You can save your file as luster.psd (in Photoshop format) for an example for later reference and use.

To create an iridescent look, follow these steps:

1. In Photoshop, open luster.psd.

2. Fill the background layer with white.

3. Save your results as iridescence.psd, and compare them to Figure 25.3.

Figure 25.2
Luster is achieved by
contrasting color with
black.

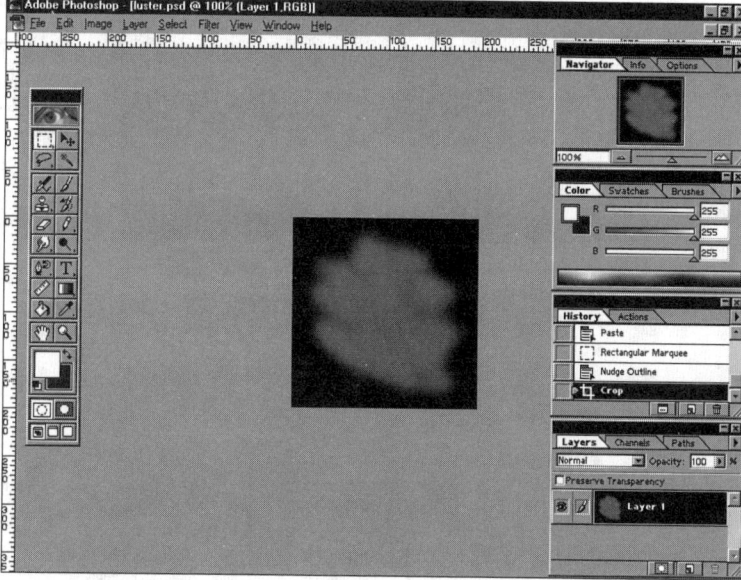

Figure 25.3
Iridescence is the
result of mixing light
and gray.

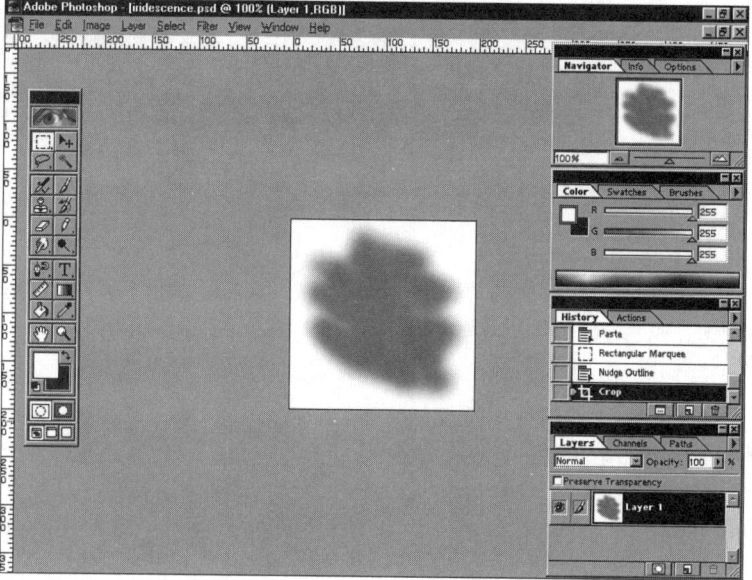

Because luminosity is a more delicate approach, I painted a lighter gray around the edges of the form, and then changed the background in `iridescence.psd` to the same gray as in the original luster example. Figure 25.4 shows my results.

Figure 25.4
Luminescence: delicate, subtle contrast is the name of the luster game.

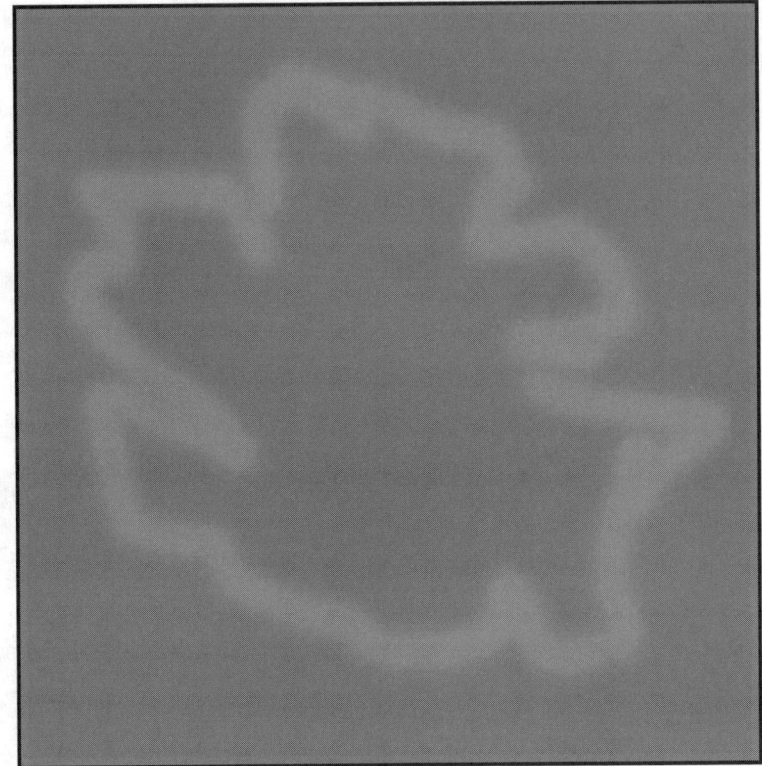

Transparent effects can be created as follows:

1. In Photoshop, create a new 200×200 pixel area workspace.
2. Select any color from the swatches palette (I selected blue).
3. Create a smaller square within your workspace by using the Marquee tool.
4. Fill that square with the blue.
5. From the Layers palette, drag the Opacity slider down to 50%.
6. Your color is now transparent (see Figure 25.5).

You can save this file as transparent.psd for later reference. I went on to add several other sections of transparent color. My results can be seen in Figure 25.6.

Now that you are familiar with the types and meanings of color and have a good foundation in color theory, it's time to apply these ideas to the Web.

Figure 25.5
Transparent color.

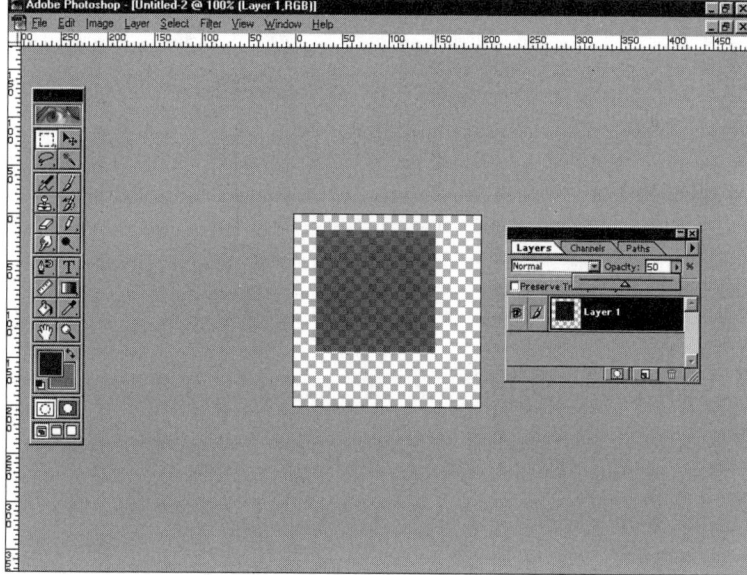

Figure 25.6
In this case, I've layered transparent sections of color on top of one another.

COLOR TECHNOLOGY

You've already become familiar with color-management methods for the computer screen. The one I emphasized as a starting point for Web-based color is RGB, or "red, green, blue" color management.

To effectively work with color on the Web, however, you have to take RGB a step further and convert it into a system of values that XHTML will recognize. This system is known as *hexadecimal*.

Hexadecimal, referred to simply as "hex," is the base-16 number system. Base 16 is an *alphanumeric* system, consisting of both numbers and letters in combinations that, in the context of the Web browser, translate as color. Hexadecimal uses the numbers 0–9 and the letters A–F. All hexadecimal values should contain a total of six characters for XHTML to understand it. The first pair in the series of six equals the amount of red in the color; the second pair equals the amount of green; and the third pair, blue.

Tip from

molly

If at any time you get a single character in hex conversion, such as a single 0 or letter D, simply enter a 0 *before* the hex character so that the resulting binary information will be accurate.

Remember your computer science? A single byte is made up of 8 bits of information. Every two characters within a hex value makes up one byte, or 8 bits. This means that each hex value contains 24 bits of color information.

It's no accident that RGB color is also known as *24-bit color*.

How do you find the hex value of RGB colors? A scientific calculator is one way. Another way is to use one of the many converters available right on the Web.

CONVERTING RGB TO HEX

To convert an RGB value to hexadecimal by using a scientific calculator, follow these steps:

1. Find the RGB value of your color. You can do this in Photoshop by passing your cursor over the color. The information pop-up (see Figure 25.7) displays the red, green, and blue values. In this case, I chose a medium brown.

2. Write down each of these values. From my chosen color in Figure 25.7, I wrote out the following:

   red   86

   green   53

   blue   13

3. Enter the first (red) value into a scientific calculator in standard, decimal mode. I'm using the scientific mode of the resident Windows calculator (see Figure 25.8).

4. Switch to hexadecimal mode.

5. A set of two characters is displayed on the screen. This is the hex equivalent of the specific amount of red within the color you've chosen. For 86, I got a hex value of 56. Write this value down.

6. Now switch back to standard decimal mode and input the green value.

Figure 25.7
RGB color information in Photoshop gives you the information you need to calculate the corresponding hexadecimal value.

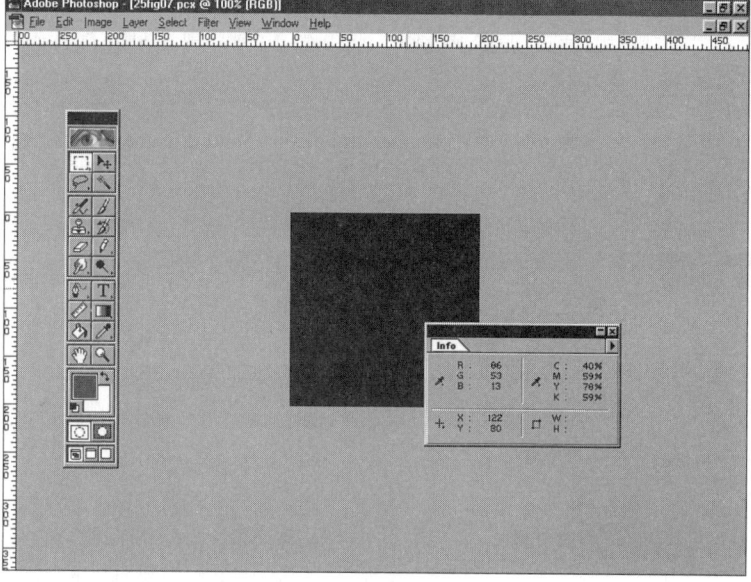

Figure 25.8
Convert RGB values to hexadecimal using any calculator with hexadecimal capability such as the one that is standard with Windows.

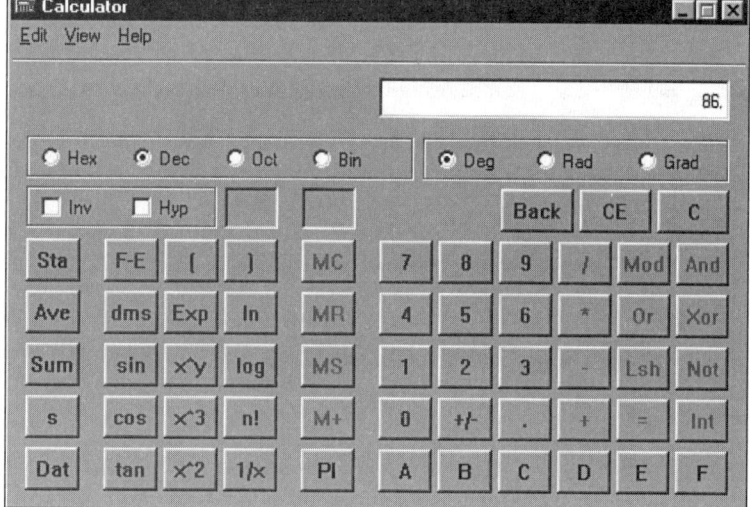

7. Switch again to hexadecimal to get the green alphanumeric set.

8. Repeat this process for the blue (note that you'll end up with a single character here, so enter a **0** before it when writing it down).

For the RGB value of 86, 53, 13 you should have a corresponding hex value of 56350D.

Note

Many imaging programs are now providing hex support. Paint Shop Pro from Jasc, `http://www.jasc.com/` is a perfect example.

→ For more information on Paint Shop Pro, **see** Chapter 27, "Web Graphic Tools and Professional Tools," **p. 561**.

Note

If you want to convert your values over the Internet, visit the following Web sites for RGB-to-hex converters that you can use:

Main Street Earth Hex/Color Converter: `http://www.mainstreetearth.com/features/javascripts/hc-conv.html`

Color Center: `http://www.hidaho.com/colorcenter/cc.html`

BROWSER COLOR

Think of it this way—if you never had to download a graphic, your pages would load really fast. But would you sacrifice speed for visual attraction?

The answer is Probably. But that doesn't mean that you can't use color to create a rich base for the graphics that you will use. What this does is offer the opportunity to have faster loading pages because you're using fewer graphics to achieve visual appeal.

Smoke and mirrors? Hardly! But if you understand how to tap into the colors that are native to your browser, you'll have stable, attractive splashes of color before a graphic is ever downloaded.

THE WEB-SAFE PALETTE

To make this happen, you have to understand the *safe palette*. This is a palette of 216 colors that are reserved by browsers on the Macintosh and Windows platforms for immediate access. Instead of having to download information from a remote server, the browser parses the hexadecimal color codes from the page right away.

A safe palette is the palette made up of 216 colors that remain as stable from one browser to another, between platforms, and at different monitor color capacities and resolutions as possible.

It's important to use the safe palette in most instances because it ensures cross-browser, cross-platform stability. If you use colors outside of the safe palette, you can run into problems with consistency.

→ The Web-safe palette is relevant to CSS, **see** Chapter 18, "Cascading Style Sheets and XHTML," **p. xxx.**

Picture this: You choose a soft, pale blue color for your background, and a very dark blue for your text. There's enough contrast to be readable, and you're happy with the look—proud of your hard design work done on an upper-end machine capable of full 24-bit color.

You put your page up on the Internet, and along comes a pal to check out your work. He gets to the page and sees you've chosen a bright peacock blue for your background, and a similar color for your text. He can't read the content on your page, and he's confused.

How did this happen? Well, you didn't use Web-safe color. Your friend came along with a more limited set of hardware and software, and his color-management system chose to *dither* the colors. This means that his computer grabbed the first blues available because it couldn't identify your unsafe color.

To avoid this, you need to choose from the Web-safe palette. I know that it seems like 216 colors is a limited number, and it's true. My only words of solace are to encourage you to be creative. There are enough colors within the Web-safe palette to create beautiful designs— it's done every day on the Web, and I have no doubts that you can do it, too.

> **Note**
>
> If most color systems can display at least 256 colors, how did the Web-safe palette end up with only 216? It's a complicated story that involves Windows 3.1 having reserved colors for the Operating System. Browsers then went on to use just the available colors to avoid the problem, and the end result was a limited palette. The good news is that the 216-color palette is stable and addresses many problems that occur across platforms—something over which Web designers can breathe a sigh of relief.

Many design programs have created special palettes to accommodate Web-safe colors. Photoshop (versions 4.0 and later for Macintosh and Windows) offers a palette built right in to the program.

> **Note**
>
> Safe-palette information and tools can be found by visiting the following Web sites:
>
> Victor Engel's Color Cube: `http://the-light.com/netcol.html`
>
> Lynda Weinman: `http://www.lynda.com/hex.html`

PART
VI
CH
25

USING UNSAFE COLORS

Once you understand the rules about using a Web-safe palette, you might be tempted to break those rules.

Using unsafe color is risky, and I don't recommend it. However, there are times when unsafe color can be used. Here's a helpful set of guidelines:

- You know your audience. And I *mean* know them! One situation where you might know them well would be a corporate intranet.

- If you're less certain about your audience, but still interested in using unsafe color, test the colors for dithering at lower resolutions

To test colors, drop your monitor down to 256 colors when viewing your page. If the color appears different from what you originally determined, it's probably a good idea to revert to a safe color. You'll also want to be very thorough, testing your pages on a variety of browsers, platforms, and computer systems.

> **Note**
>
> Designing with color is important for visual sites. But what about those Web visitors that have color blindness or vision impairments? The W3C recommends that color should not be used as the sole means of conveying information when developing for broad audiences. For more information on the W3C's work with Web Accessibility, please see `http://www.w3.org/WAI/`.

DESIGNING FOR THE REAL WORLD

WORKING WITH THE SAFE PALETTE

To work effectively with the safe palette, you have to draw from all the information we've covered in this chapter. Beginning with what you know of color, you can think about the look and feel, special effects, and emotion you want to express on your site.

Let's say I want to create a warm and welcoming personal presence that expresses my personal energy. I would begin by selecting colors that are warm as well as vibrant: orange, red, and yellow. Then I would find an appropriate combination of hues—I want the site to be harmonious, not discordant. The harmony of colors helps express the welcoming and personal presence, offering comfort while still conveying energy.

I then turn to my understanding of RGB and hexadecimal values. Add to that the fact that I know I want to choose my colors from a safe palette, and I've narrowed down my choices to a specific set of colors.

What I like to do at this point is create what I call an *individual* palette. This is a selection of five to seven colors that I choose from the safe palette. In this example, I'll create an individual palette in Photoshop.

1. Create a new file by choosing File, New.
2. Anticipating seven colors, create the file as being 50 pixels wide and 350 pixels long. This creates seven 50×50 pixel spaces along the vertical.
3. From a safe color palette, pick out the first two colors. Although Photoshop has a native safe palette, I prefer opening up a file called nhue.gif (see Figure 25.9). This file, created by Lynda Weinman, not only offers the color itself, but the RGB *and* hexadecimal equivalents of that color. Download nhue.gif from `http://www.lynda.com/hexh.html`.
4. With the Marquee tool, mark off the first 50×50 pixel area at the top of the workspace. Fill it with the first color.
5. Continue filling the rest of each space with the colors you've picked from the safe palette. Usually I reserve the sixth and seventh space for black and white respectively.
6. Then switch to the Type tool, and type in the RGB and Hex color values (see Figure 25.10).

Figure 25.9
Nhue.gif is an extremely useful tool created by author and designer Lynda Weinman.

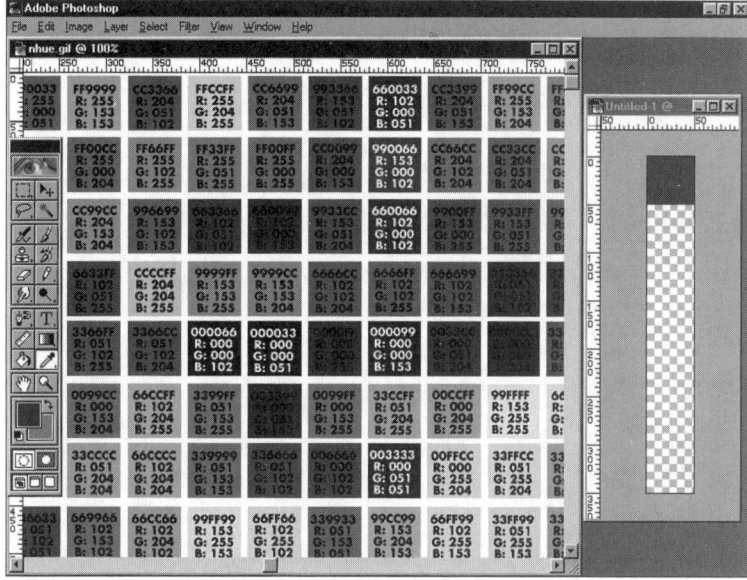

Figure 25.10
Adding the hex and RGB values to the individual palette gives you all the necessary information to begin creating your site using safe colors.

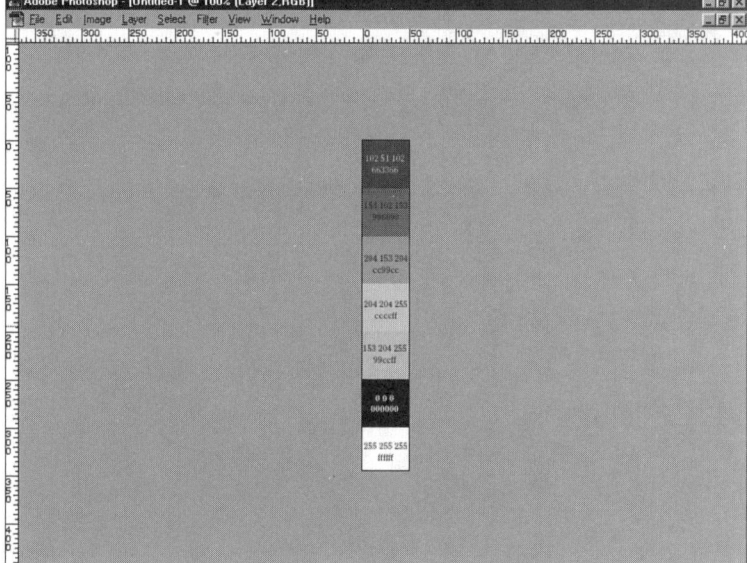

7. Flatten the file by selecting Layer, Flatten Image to combine all the layers into one and save it as a GIF.

You now have a custom palette that you can use while working on your site. It is both a reference for the numeric values of the colors and a palette you can leave open in Photoshop as you create the graphics for your site.

CHAPTER 26

WORKING WITH THE COMPUTER SCREEN

In this chapter

RESOLUTION

I spend a lot of time at my computer. I work on it, use it to retrieve news, to communicate with others, and sometimes just to have fun.

I've always been interested in what makes it tick, how it works, and how I can improve both its performance and my experience with it. In fact, ensuring that I'm comfortable using it for long hours is imperative.

One problem I've encountered is with my eyes—having to look at a screen for many hours at a time can take its toll. There are different issues that directly affect what I end up seeing on my screen—the quality and depth of the images, the colors, the space, the contrast.

As a Web designer, understanding a bit about some of these influences can help you create sites that take the user's experience into consideration—ultimately delivering a higher-quality, more effective site to his or her desktop.

COMMON RESOLUTIONS

What many Web designers are surely familiar with, but many of their site visitors don't know, is how to manage the *resolution* of their computer monitors.

Resolution refers to how many pixels appear on the horizontal and vertical axes of your computer screen. If my resolution is set to the lowest common denominator of 640×480 pixels, that means that 640 pixels are available in width, and 480 pixels in height, total, for the whole screen.

Most computers *used to* ship with 640×480 as a default resolution, and many older computers are only capable of that resolution. For this reason, certain Web site visitors are seeing the Web at 640×480, and either cannot change or do not know *how* to change the resolution of their video monitor screens. At 640×480 resolution, the disadvantage is that there is less space to work with (see Figure 26.1), but for some, the advantage is that everything also appears larger. Similarly, the majority of computers shipping today do so at a default of 800×600 resolution. This is a popular resolution, too—and is common not only to desktop computers, but notebooks as well.

Compare Figure 26.1 to Figure 26.2. In Figure 26.2, you can see what 800×600 looks like. There is much more space to maneuver in, but the objects appear smaller. Of course, you can adjust the size of the objects to make things visible while maintaining the extra work-space on many platforms.

There are higher resolutions, too. 1,024×768 alters the look of one of my desktops considerably (see Figure 26.3), and I can go even higher on that particular computer—to 1,280×1,024 (see Figure 26.4).

Figure 26.1
640×480 screen resolution: the lowest common denominator.

Figure 26.2
800×600: more workspace on my Windows 98 machine.

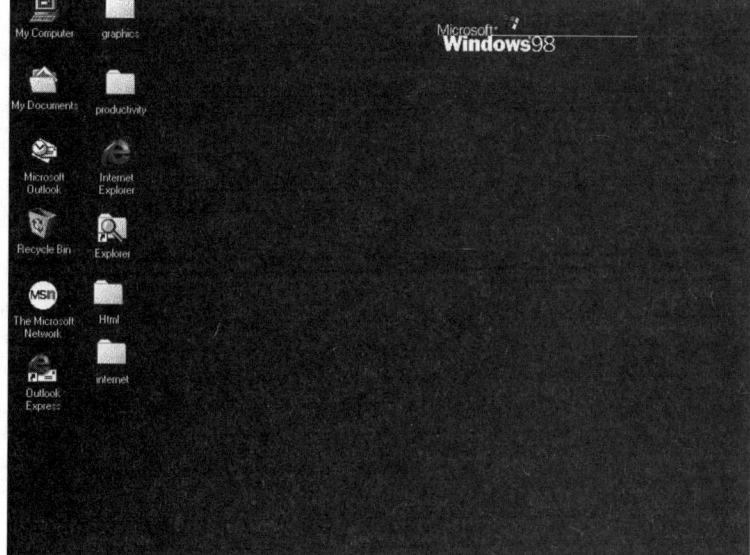

Higher resolutions hav etheir advantage when an individual has alarge screen for specialty reasons—computer-generated design (where detail matters), or large data management.

The bottom line when it comes to screen resolution is this: Web site visitors are seeing your site at a variety of screen resolutions. This directly affects the way your Web sites will be experienced, and it's up to you to do the best you can to design sites that look good no matter the resolution.

Figure 26.3
At 1,024¥768, this desktop is dramatically altered visually.Higher resolutions have their advantage when an individual has a large screen for specialty reasons—computer-generated design (where detail matters), or large data management.

Figure 26.4
A screen resolution of 1,280×1,024 is reserved for high-resolution work.

Tip from

Professional Web developers should have monitors that support a range of resolutions, so they can test their sites at those various resolutions. I have several Windows machines that allow me to test at different resolutions. I also have an iMac, which allows me to test the look of pages from the Mac OS point of view, too. A good range would be 640×480 to 1280×768.

When it comes to Web-site design, one of the worst yet easiest mistakes to make is to not design for the audience. If you're a computer buff, like me, you might enjoy working at higher resolutions and don't immediately think of your audience's limitations.

Knowing the seriousness of some of the mishaps that occur when ignoring audience needs, you're certain to not only know why it's so important to manage screen resolution, but how to do it, too.

One of the first issues you'll need to address is making sure that your pages fit into any screen resolution. This ensures that you'll avoid what Lynch and Horton are referring to: a horizontal scrollbar (see Figure 26.5). To demonstrate the problem, I coded the table in Listing 26.1 to fit a higher rather than lower resolution. I then took the screen shot at a lower resolution and guess what? The horizontal scrollbar appeared.

Figure 26.5
A horizontal scrollbar at 640×480 equals unhappy site visitors.

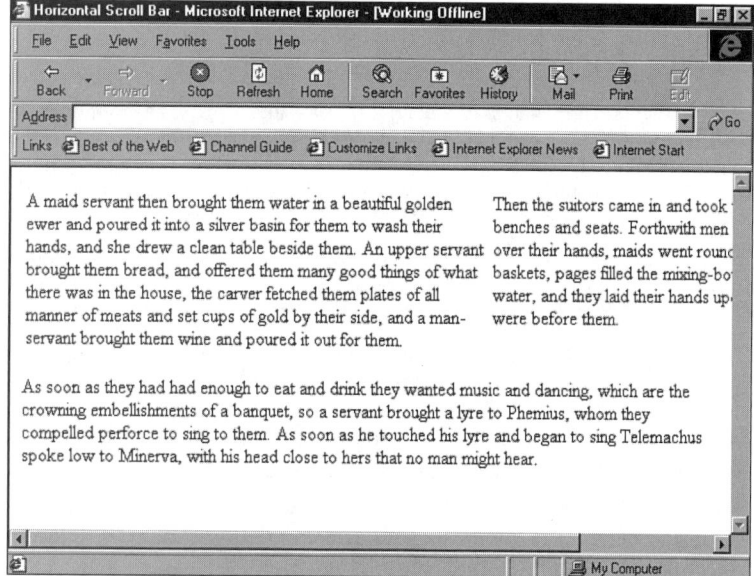

PART

VI

CH

26

LISTING 26.1   DEMONSTRATING A HORIZONTAL SCROLL

```
<!DOCTYPE html PUBLIC "-//W3C//DTD XHTML 1.0 Transitional//EN"
"http://www.w3.org/TR/xhtml1/DTD/xhtml1-transitional.dtd">
<html xmlns="http://www.w3.org/1999/xhtml">

<head>
<title>Horizontal Scroll Sample</title>
</head>

<body>

<table border="0" width="750">
<tr>
```

LISTING 26.1 CONTINUED

```
<td valign="top" width="400">
A maid servant then brought them water in a beautiful golden ewer and poured it
into a silver basin for them to wash their hands, and she drew a clean table
beside them. An upper servant brought them bread, and offered them many good
things of what there was in the house, the carver fetched them plates of all
manner of meats and set cups of gold by their side, and a man-servant brought
them wine and poured it out for them.
</td>

<td valign="top" width="350">
Then the suitors came in and took their places on the benches and seats.
Forthwith men servants poured water over their hands, maids went round with
the bread-baskets, pages filled the mixing-bowls with wine and water, and they
laid their hands upon the good things that were before them.
</td>

</tr>
</table>

<p>As soon as they had had enough to eat and drink they wanted music and
dancing, which are the crowning embellishments of a banquet, so a servant
brought a lyre to Phemius, whom they compelled perforce to sing to them. As
soon as he touched his lyre and began to sing. Telemachus spoke low to Minerva,
with his head close to hers that no man might hear.</p>

</body>
</html>
```

This bar disappears at higher resolutions. But we do know that *at this time* most people are viewing the Web at either 640×480 resolution, or 800×600 resolution.

Theoretically, this means that anything you create must accommodate 640 pixels wide or less to avoid that evil horizontal scroll in *all* situations, even for a person using a higher resolution, but customizing the size of their browser on the desktop. A lot of arguments occur over this issue, with many developers insisting that it's fine to develop for 800×600 resolution, although some designers take a more conservative approach. Whatever you decide, think before you act—and know your audience!

In reality, 640×480 resolution doesn't translate to allowing your fixed designs to measure a full 640 pixels wide; the browser itself eats up significant space. Simply open up your Web browser to see what I mean. In the default view (see Figure 26.6), the browser will have icons and toolbars along the top, a status bar on the bottom, a thin bar to the left, and a thicker scrollbar to the right. All this information eats up precious space.

Note Different browser brands and versions take up different amounts of pixel space.

All told, the viewing area is so significantly reduced by the browser's interface that professional Web designers use a new total screen dimension below the resolution to which they are designing to avoid problems.

Figure 26.6
The Netscape 4.7 interface: Note all the real estate the top and bottom bars eat up.

But wait. Before you scream in frustration, let me first explain where this number comes from, and how you can work to best suit your goals and audience. Lynch and Horton recommend 595 pixels to avoid a horizontal scroll when working within the 640 resolution. However, many Mac screens still have a scroll at this resolution! With the popularity of the iMac, new awareness for Mac users has come into play. Therefore, I recommend 585 pixels for a lowest common denominator, fixed-width design. But, if you decide to design for higher resolutions, do the math and subtract the necessary space from your screen to accommodate the space without causing unwanted scrolling at that resolution.

Let me also reassure you that there are ways to work with this small space to ensure compatibility for higher resolutions, as well as give the illusion that more space exists. What's more, you have dynamic options that allow you to create designs that adjust to the available screen space, and if you're really into covering all your bases, you can use JavaScript to detect and route browsers to the correct resolution for that site visitor.

The following are some screen-resolution guidelines that will help you avoid incompatibility problems:

- Design precision layouts to the lowest common-denominator resolution in your audience. If you want to ensure that all standard desktop computers can see your fixed-with designs without a scroll, design with the 640×480 screen resolution in mind—meaning that you'll need to employ the 585×295 rule.

- For layouts that don't demand precise placement of objects, choose dynamic tables for layout.

PART
VI

CH
26

■ Don't forget that there are people using higher resolutions. Background graphics always tile, so you'll need to control the way those graphics work. Also, when working with tables and frames, be aware that fixed-width tables and frames cause extra space to appear around the fixed design (see Figure 26.7) at higher resolutions (see Figure 26.8).

Figure 26.7
Fixed table design at 640×480 presents the navigation information and content to the site visitor in correct proportions to their viewing area.

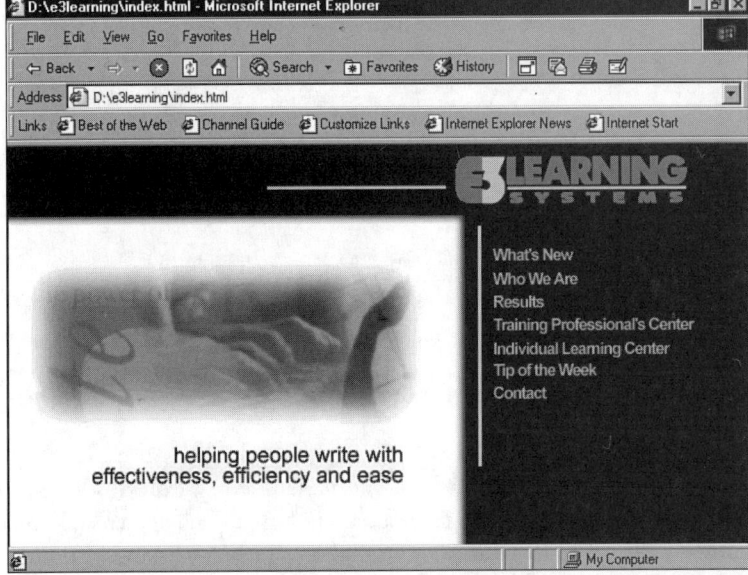

Figure 26.8
The same design at 800×600—more white-space appears to the right and bottom, which looks less appealing to the site visitor.

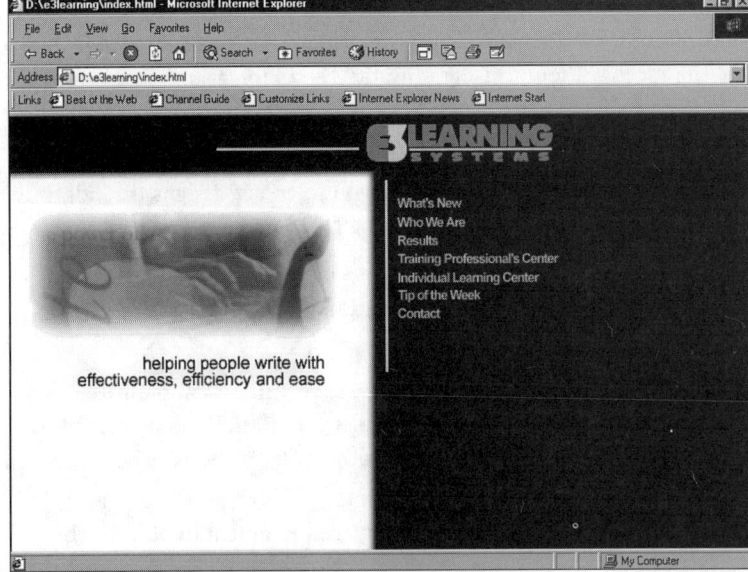

- **Test, test, test!**—This rule should be firm no matter what the circumstances. Test your pages on different systems, different browsers, and at different resolutions. Now—before your site goes live—is the time to troubleshoot horizontal scrolls or any other troublesome areas.

- **Work within the allotted space**—In other words, don't pretend you have more space than you really do. You'll need to focus on proportion, dimension, and whitespace, which I'll show you how to do a bit later in this chapter.

→ For more information on creating dynamic tables, **see** Chapter 14, "Laying Out Tables Within XHTML Documents," **p. 243**.

→ You can detect and route visitors based on screen resolution with JavaScript, **see** Chapter 20, "Adding JavaScript to XHTML Documents," **p. 445**.

These simple guidelines will save you from more trouble than you might imagine. You'll learn how to have greater control over your pages and be able to manage your sites better, providing a much more stable and effective product for your audience.

I can't emphasize how important it is to test your pages—even if you are employing maximum control over your page dimensions. I sometimes teach in a computer lab that uses PowerPCs set to a resolution of 800×600. Due to security concerns on the part of the administration, I can't have my students change their resolution.

We've run into consistent problems with horizontal scrolls despite employing the general guidelines—it's only in testing that you'll find the smaller, seemingly inconsequential problems with your XHTML or graphics.

Tip from molly

If you're just getting started working with resolution issues, set your screen resolution to 640×480 and do all your graphic design and XHTML work at that resolution. This will get you familiar with the way things look at that resolution.

PART VI
CH 26

Some designers actually work only in 640×480 resolution and then test at higher resolutions. Whether you choose to do this, or, like me, work at higher resolutions but *test* those pages, doesn't really matter. The bottom line is that you must check and re-check your work in a variety of circumstances to fully troubleshoot any potential problems.

Note

Download a helpful ruler for measuring your Web page from `http://www.wpdfd.com/wpdtame.htm`.

CONTROLLING PAGE DIMENSION

Here are a few helpful methods to gain maximum control over screen space when designing for the limitations of the Web, beyond those already discussed.

The first place to find control over screen space is to understand that it is a very, very small space that allows little or no opportunity to vary its borders. I call this problem *constraint*. Web space is *constrained space*. When I get home from a long day out and about, the first thing I do is take off my dress shoes. My feet are overjoyed to be free of the constraints. I believe that learning how to manage your sites effectively in constrained space will immediately affect the comfort of your site visitors, making them feel relaxed, at ease, and prepared to enjoy your Web site.

Several design techniques help you create pages that are visually freed from the constraints of the computer and Web environment. They include the following:

- **Use margins**—Add margins wherever you are working with long blocks of text.
- **Think about whitespace**—This is the use of background space (not always white) as a cushion and guide for the eye.
- **Eliminate clutter**—Everything on a page should have a reason for being there.
- **Control dimension and proportion**—Keep the size of your graphic and media elements in balance with not only the size of available space, but with other elements on the page.

USING WHITESPACE APPROPRIATELY

Whitespace is the absence of design, but it is wholly design. What I mean by this axiom is that although we might think of design as being the elements and objects that go into making up a Web page, design is also what *is not* there.

In Figure 26.9 I've blacked out some areas in a layout. I want you to focus only on the white first. If you look carefully, you'll notice that the white area is a shape in and of itself. If I use different shapes, as in Figure 26.10, the whitespace changes, too.

Figure 26.9
Notice the space between the blacked-out elements.

Whitespace adds to design by providing texture and cushioning for page elements. It also can help serve your design by leading and resting the eye.

Figure 26.10
Here I've used different shapes for the elements, and the shape of the whitespace changes, too.

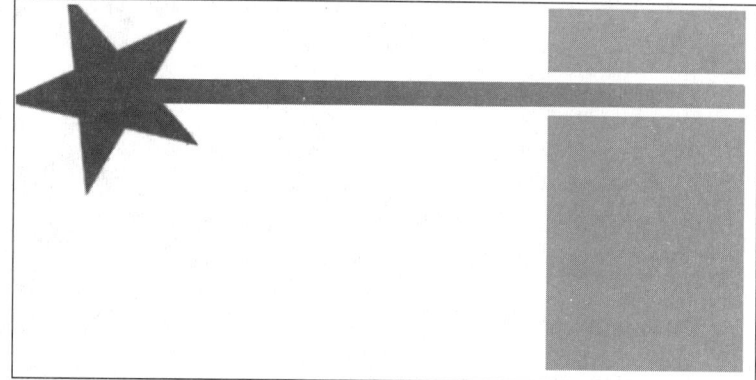

To work with whitespace, you have to gain a feel not only for what you put on a page, but what shapes are created between those elements by the space itself.

READABILITY

Another concern is screen color. Older hardware used on the Web is limited to 256 colors, which in and of itself asks the Web designer to do some pretty fancy tricks.

In general, the "test everything" rule applies with color, because if a visitor is limited to 256 colors and you've been doing your design work in full, 24-bit color, what you see and what your audience sees are going to be different.

→ For more information on working with color, **see** Chpater 25, "Color Concepts," **p. 527**.

CONTRAST

Many of you have undoubtedly visited sites where the background and body text have been difficult to read. In most cases, the problem is due to poor contrast. Contrast on a computer screen can sometimes be very different from contrast in the natural world. A light blue on a slightly darker blue isn't going to have enough contrast to be readable, as you can *try* to see in Figure 26.11. However, black on white is going to be very readable (see Figure 26.12).

Usually, body text should be darker than the background—dark enough so that significant contrast is created, allowing for maximum readability.

Tip from

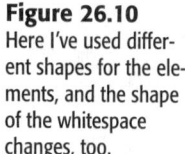

Accessibility experts have found that for visually impaired individuals, severe contrasts such as black and white are the best for readability in low-vision circumstances. If you know that your audience has a lot of older individuals or visually impaired persons, it's wise to plan ahead and ensure that your contrast colors are as solid as possible: black on white for body text is a sure-fire way to go.

Figure 26.11
Not enough contrast creates readability problems.

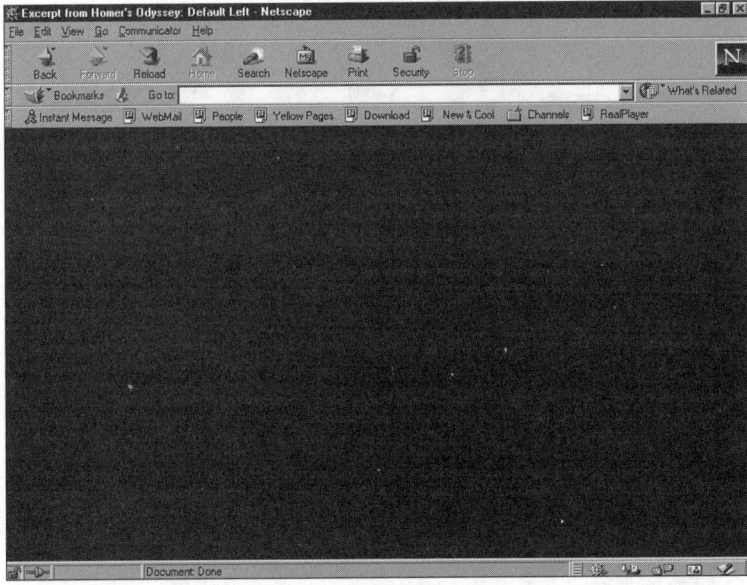

Figure 26.12
Black on white is high contrast, so it's easy to read.

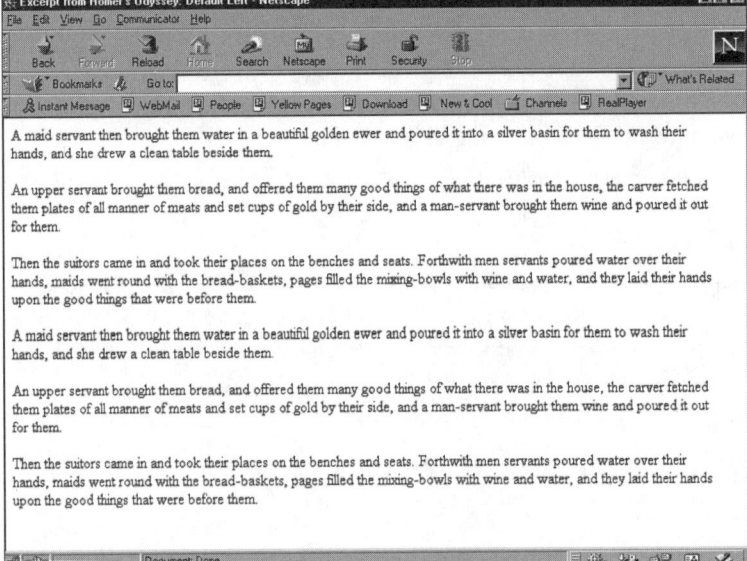

Another approach is to *reverse* this concept, placing light colors on dark colors. This is known as *reverse type* and, if the contrast is good enough, it can be quite effective. Bottom line? Be sure that your content is readable on your background, so people are sure to be able to get to the information you're delivering.

GAMMA

Another important issue related to color that is often overlooked by Web designers is *Gamma*.

Gamma is complex to describe because it involves a lot of math. Put into its most simple terms, Gamma is a system that significantly influences the way that data appears on a computer screen. Gamma must often be manipulated, or *corrected*, to provide the most accurate information to your monitor.

Your hardware determines how Gamma is corrected. One of the reasons Macintoshes have been so popular in the graphic design industry is that a fair amount of Gamma correction is available on the Macintosh. This is especially true with Silicon Graphic machines. It's no wonder that SGIs are the computers of choice for film, animation, and video production.

Because of this correction, Macintoshes and SGIs can display color with greater accuracy. But Windows machines, prevalent on most desktops, are problematic.

Prior to Windows 95 and 98, there was little, if any, Gamma correction available to the Windows platform. Since the release of these more sophisticated GUIs, however, a bit more Gamma correction is available, particularly if you've bought top-of-the line hardware. The better and newer your computer, video card, and video monitor are, the better your chances are of having some inherent Gamma correction.

When Gamma is improperly corrected, the video displays images that are problematic. The dominant problem is that images are displayed very dark, so much of the image is obscured. This is especially true in environments such as the World Wide Web.

What a problem for the Web designer who has worked so hard to get high-quality color for his or her site visitors!

PART
VI
CH
26

Note

To learn more about Gamma, check out the following resources:

"An Explanation of Monitor Gamma," by Robert W. Berger. This excellent article explains monitor problems across platforms, and even provides a visual method of determining your computer's Gamma. See it at `http://www.vtiscan.com/~rwb/gamma.html`.

"Frequently Questioned Answers About Gamma," by Charles Poynton. Facts and fallacies about Gamma are examined in great detail at `http://www.inforamp.net/~poynton/notes/color/GammaFQA.html`.

The Gamma Correction Home Page. A comprehensive article and related Gamma resources at `http://www.cgsd.com/papers/gamma.html`.

Experts claim that working in high-contrast colors is a way around Gamma problems. But of course, this translates into the loss of subtlety in design. Your best defense against Gamma problems is to learn what it is and how it affects your design. As ever, be sure to test your sites with a variety of equipment, gaining a feel for what variations of your design might appear.

TROUBLESHOOTING

RESOLUTION

I've looked at my server statistics, and determined that 80% of my audience is visiting at 800×600 resolution. How can I confidently design my fixed designs for this resolution?

Ultimately, the decision rests with you. However, consider that if you're getting 100 people visiting your site a day, that's 20 people that might see a horizontal scroll. If you have 1,000 people—that's 200 people seeing the unwanted scroll! If you're comfortable with this, go for it. I personally am not comfortable and use the techniques described in Chapter 14, "Laying Out Tables Within XHTML Documents," to improve the user experience of my fixed designs. The other option is to use a JavaScript detect and route.

I've noticed that design trends don't always mesh with sensible approaches to working within the visual space of a design. For example, the trend with portal sites has been top-heavy designs. Is it better to follow a trend to keep sites looking contemporary?

There's no reason you cannot do both. The top-heavy designs that have been so popular in the portal realm seem to me a result of left-margin backlash. For several years, left-margin navigation designs dominated the Net. To give sites a fresh look, developers began to move navigation and primary information to the top of the page; however, clutter ensued in many cases. If you stick to your awareness of space and object relationships, you can combine flavor-of-the-moment designs with design intelligence—providing a contemporary look for your site while keeping it clean and attractive.

DESIGNING FOR THE REAL WORLD

CALIBRATING THE MONITOR TO BALANCE COLORS

Because many readers don't have much experience calibrating their monitors, this exercise will help you do just that. This will improve the way you see color on your screen, work successfully with Gamma, and output colors that are as balanced as possible. This is especially good to do in design shops where people are working on the same projects using different computers, or where people are working on projects remotely. It's important to realize that calibration doesn't affect the output of a design in the context of the Web. Rather, it helps get designers working with greater color consistency.

Mechanical calibration devices are available. Although they are more accurate, they also are fairly cost prohibitive for most people, ranging from $600–$1,200. A number of calibration software packages are on the market which are much less expensive, including Pantone's Personal Color Calibrator. Adobe bundles Gamma software with the Adobe Photoshop software package. For the purposes of this exercise, we'll be walking through the Adobe option. However, your software should be quite similar.

Before calibrating the monitor, you should let it warm up for at least thirty minutes. Set the ambient light in the room to the level that you use under normal working conditions.

Change the background color on your screen to neutral gray for best results.

The Gamma Wizard walks you through calibration step by step. It explains how to control brightness, contrast, Gamma, white point, and black point. To start calibrating your monitor, follow these steps:

1. Start the Gamma Wizard.
2. Click the Load option button.
3. In ICC Profile, select Adobe Monitor. If you already have a previous profile, the name of that profile appears onscreen.
4. Select Next and follow the wizard's instructions.
5. At the final window, you can compare results. After you are satisfied, save the profile.

CHAPTER 27

WEB GRAPHIC TOOLS AND PROFESSIONAL TOOLS

In this chapter

PROFESSIONAL GRAPHICS TOOLS

I've heard many people discuss graphic tools over the years. Some make the argument that only professional graphic design tools will do, others express the well-taken point that it's not the tool but the designer, and ultimately tools don't matter.

For die-hard supporters of tools that are not industry standards, you'll be happy to hear that many of your favorite programs are making a concerted effort to bring you the highest quality output possible. Another exciting issue in the area of Web graphic software is new-and-improved image editing suites from a variety of industry standard vendors.

But the idea that tools don't matter is a very disturbing untruth. Although I hardly mean to imply here that shareware or a variety of professional tools are useless for the casual Web designer, I do have a major concern for those of you who are seeking to be employed in the Web design field.

If you're pursuing professional Web design, you must be willing to purchase and learn the sometimes expensive, higher-end tools to compete.

Furthermore, knowing the skills associated with those tools puts you in the driver's seat when it comes to being able to find employment with design firms. They're going to be using industry standards, and you're not going to be as marketable if you don't have the skills.

In my 10 years' experience as visual designer, design instructor, and in six years as a Web design business owner, I have found that you are infinitely more attractive as a Web graphic designer with Adobe and Macromedia product skills than you are with, say, CorelDRAW skills, PHOTO-PAINT skills, or Paint Shop Pro know-how.

On the other hand, if your design needs are more personal, any one of these and other tools will be helpful to you. It's finding the right fit that counts, particularly if you're not interested in pursuing professional-level jobs where the pro standards are typically Adobe and Macromedia products.

That said, let's turn and take a look at some of the Web graphic design tools out there.

We'll be looking at a variety of tools here, including imaging and illustration programs, optimization tools, multimedia development tools, plug-in and enhancement programs, and stock art and photography resources.

The following section overviews feature programs that enable you to work with photographs, actually create images with color and type, scan images, add enhancements, and optimize graphics.

ADOBE PHOTOSHOP

This is a key player within professional Web graphic production tools (see Figure 27.1). You'll notice throughout this book that I use it almost exclusively to design and optimize my graphics.

Photoshop's features include the following:

■ Photoshop creates raster graphics, which are the suitable type for Web image optimization.

■ Photoshop layers are a powerful way to work with images.

■ GIF89 Export feature allows for the creation of transparency and interlaced GIFs.

■ Versions 4.0 and later contain a Web-safe palette that is useful when optimizing graphics for the Web.

■ Full-feature photographic manipulation and filters allow you to improve the quality of photos, as well as alter and arrange them as you please.

■ Photoshop 5.0 and higher offer powerful typesetting options and other filter features such as bevel, drop shadow, and light sources.

Figure 27.1
The Adobe Photoshop interface. As a design industry standard application, Adobe Photoshop features, support, and third-party solutions are vast.

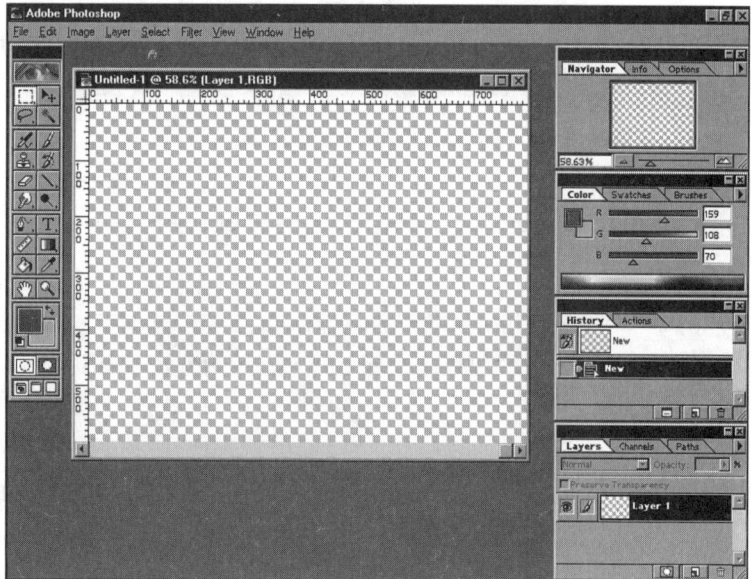

For product information and costs, go to `http://www.adobe.com/`.

ADOBE IMAGEREADY

This exciting product is designed specifically to optimize graphics for Web use. ImageReady is packaged with Photoshop versions 5.5 and later, and has a similar interface (see Figure 27.2), so there is easy adaptability for Photoshop users. ImageReady also is integrated within the Photoshop interface itself, accessible from the Save As Web option on the File menu.

Figure 27.2
The ImageReady interface. ImageReady offers real-time compression and batch processing, as well as tools for animating images.

ADOBE ILLUSTRATOR

An excellent tool for creating vector-based graphics, Adobe Illustrator also offers advanced typesetting options (see Figure 27.3).

Figure 27.3
Setting type in Illustrator. Using Illustrator allows you to move, change, and stylize type with advanced tools.

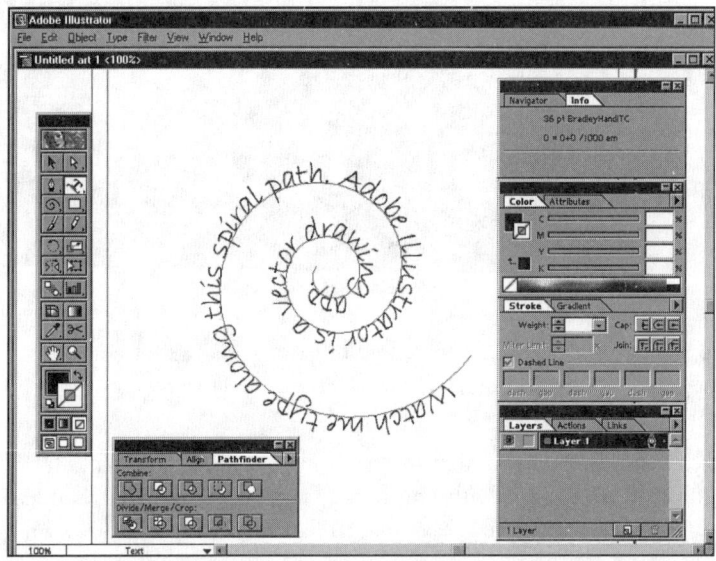

Other features of Illustrator include the ability to link URLs to images. Illustrator is currently in its 9.0 version.

CorelDRAW

CorelDRAW holds an esteemed level as a drawing program among certain computer users—usually those involved in business and industry. However, it's not considered the standard when it comes to professional graphic design. Still, the recent edition of CorelDRAW, version 9.0, includes a number of attractive new features:

- Customizable interface for power users
- Kerning and leading for type
- More sophisticated palette control than in previous versions
- Guidelines for image rotation, nudging, and multiple select
- Interactive tools for Perspective Drop Shadow, Contour, and Mesh Fill

Corel PHOTO-PAINT

Corel's photographic program allows users to scan and manipulate images. Its features include the following:

- Ability to assign hyperlinks to objects for imagemap creation
- Support for animated GIFs
- Ability to preview JPEGs for optimization determination
- Web-safe palette support

Visit the Corel Web site at **http://www.corel.com/** (see Figure 27.4) for more information on Draw and Photo-Paint.

Figure 27.4
Corel's Web site uses graphics created by using Corel software.

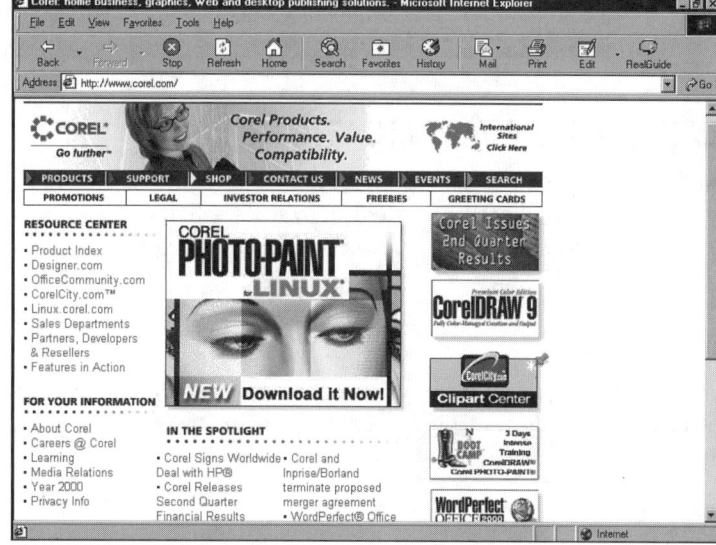

MACROMEDIA FREEHAND

A competitor to Adobe Illustrator, Freehand is a vector graphics design tool with features that make it easier to produce Web-ready image files.

Like Adobe ImageReady, Freehand includes animation capabilities and handy batch processing of graphics.

Macromedia products are available at **http://www.macromedia.com/** (see Figure 27.5). You can download demos, read and join on discussions about Macromedia software, and see Macromedia results in action on their colorful, active Web site.

Figure 27.5
Macromedia's exciting Web site makes use of a wide range of Macromedia software.

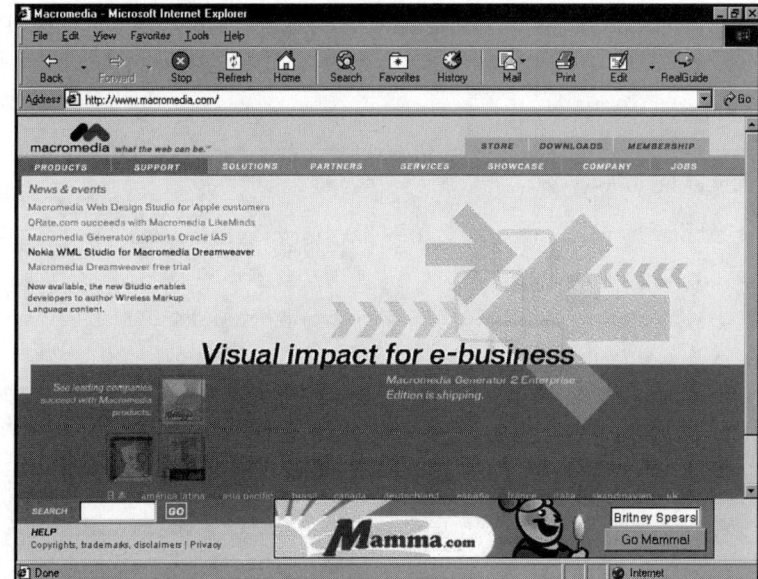

POPULAR DESIGN APPLICATIONS

Although some design applications might not be as highly regarded by professional graphic companies, they should not be overlooked by the small developer. Packages such as Paint Shop Pro are quickly becoming as feature-rich as the high-end design tools, but cost hundreds of dollars less.

JASC PAINT SHOP PRO

A favorite among many Web enthusiasts, Paint Shop Pro is gaining features as we speak. Unfortunately, it's only available for the PC platform, making it a tough sell to professional graphic companies using Macs.

In version 6.0, these features allow users to

- Work in layers, as you can in Photoshop
- Create transparencies

- Interlace GIFs
- Make GIF animations with the built-in Animation Shop

Download a demo of Paint Shop Pro (see figure 27.6) from its parent company, JASC, at **http://www.jasc.com/**. You'll also find support information, extended information about JASC products, and links to related resources.

Figure 27.6
JASC's Paint Shop Pro has numerous enthusiastic fans.

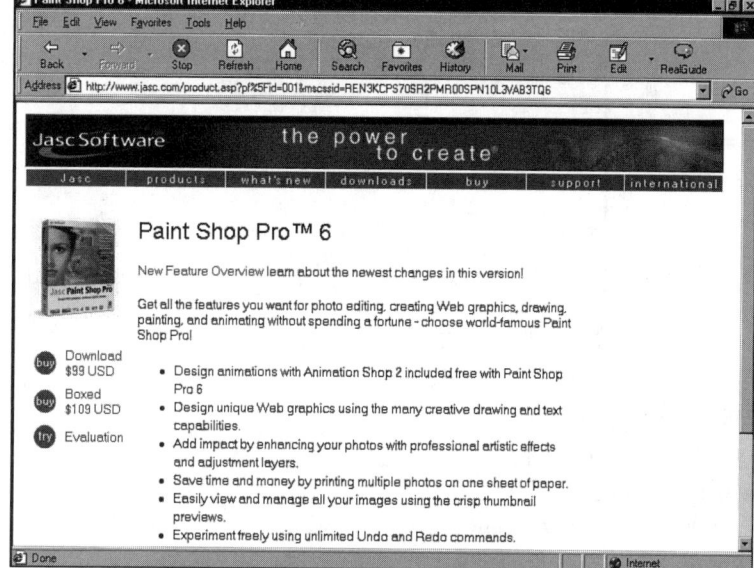

ULEAD PHOTOIMPACT

A very impressive product for a low price: Ulead PhotoImpact and Web Razor Pro are suites designed with the Web in mind. I'm especially impressed with their combined ability to make great specialty graphics, such as background tiles. Note that Web Razor is the effects package that not only works in tangent with PhotoImpact but can be plugged in to both Adobe Photoshop and Paint Shop Pro. Other features include the following:

- Imagemap support
- Button maker
- SmartSaver (a very handy optimization tool)
- Specialty filters

Visit Ulead at **http://www.ulead.com/** for a variety of Web and image-related software applications, clip art, and resources (see Figure 27.7).

PART
VI

CH
27

Figure 27.7
Ulead makes high-quality, flexible software for PCs.

MICROSOFT PHOTODRAW

With its release of Office 2000, Microsoft introduced a new imaging product, PhotoDraw. This interesting program is intended to work as a user-friendly graphics creation tool for people working in any Office program—whether it is Word, PowerPoint, or FrontPage.

PhotoDraw contains some truly fun predesigned objects and built-in effects, which allow non-designers to quickly create graphics for a Web site and easily add shadow effects. That's the positive side—and I certainly recommend taking a look at the product if even just for fun.

However, sometimes PhotoDraw tries to be too many things to too many programs. Despite its fun features, it fails to optimize graphics with the kind of sophistication you can get from other tools mentioned in this chapter. Moreover, it doesn't allow for precise measurement and manipulation of objects within the interface. So, while it's worth taking a look at, I don't recommend it for your professional Web design needs.

MICROSOFT IMAGE COMPOSER

A very nice, compact imaging application (see Figure 27.8), Microsoft Image Composer works in tandem with Microsoft GIF Animator, which gives it maximum impact as a Web imaging program. Image Composer is shipped with FrontPage98 and the standalone version of FrontPage 2000 (Windows versions only). I like this program so much, I'd buy FrontPage just to have Image Composer and its companion animation tool (see *Microsoft GIF Animator* later in this chapter). More information on how it works, how to use it, and new and improved enhancements can be found at `http://www.microsoft.com/` `_imagecomposer/`.

The following are some of Image Composer's features:

- Sprites are similar to layers, allowing you control over your images.
- Text and text styles help you create headers, buttons, and typographic images.
- Patterns, fills, and effects give you a lot of power over your images.

Figure 27.8
In this figure, I'm creating a background graphic using Microsoft's Image Composer.

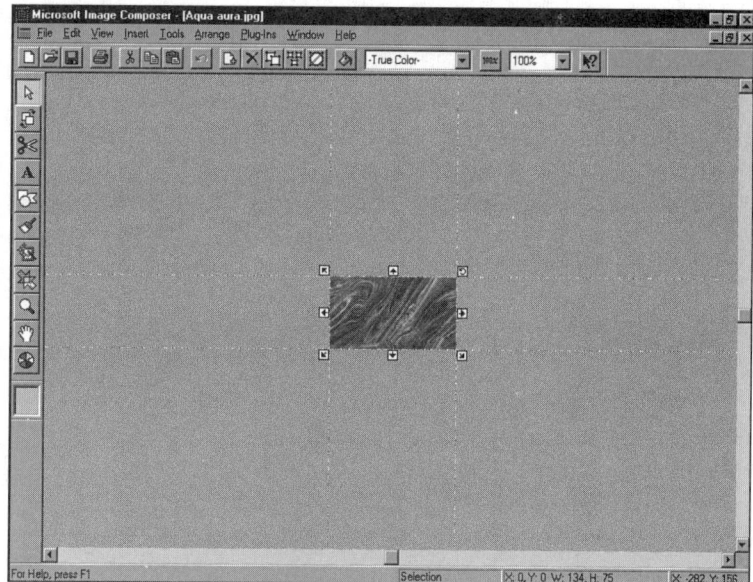

WEB-SPECIFIC APPLICATIONS

The latest entrants into the professional graphics market are Web-specific packages. These packages contain only the tools that allow you to design, animate, slice, and optimize Web graphics. If your interests lie in both traditional print and Web media, you'll want to look elsewhere for your graphics solutions. But consider these tools for your Web-based creations.

ADOBE LIVEMOTION

The newest program in this category, LiveMotion can handle all your Web graphic needs. Not only can you design backgrounds and buttons, but you also can create entire pages that incorporate motion (see Figure 27.9), interactivity, and sound. LiveMotion includes the following features:

- Familiar interface: if you already use Photoshop or Illustrator, the learning curve is minimal
- Styles to create special effects such as cut-outs and bevels, with the ability to add your own styles or download them from the Web

PART
VI
CH
27

- JavaScript rollovers, including remote rollovers
- HTML generation using tables for graphic positioning
- Ability to create animated GIFs and SWF interactive animations

Figure 27.9
Animating a graphic using Adobe LiveMotion.

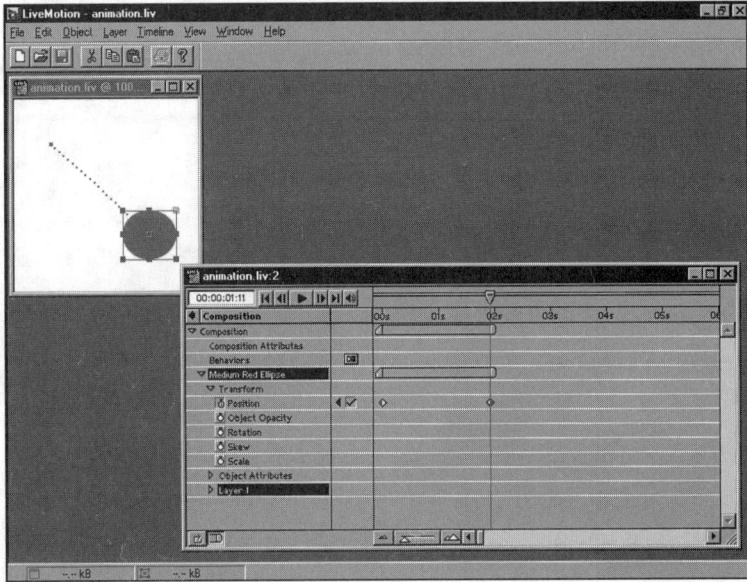

MACROMEDIA FIREWORKS

This exciting program is from Macromedia. Geared specifically to the creation and management of Web graphics, Fireworks includes the following features:

- Advanced support for imagemapping
- Slicing graphics for table positioning
- HTML generation for graphic positioning
- JavaScript rollovers—Fireworks generates the code for you
- Special effects such as bevels and drop shadows
- Live redraw: no need to undo, simply reset the parameters of an effect and it will automatically redraw
- Comparative, same-screen optimization that allows you to choose between a variety of optimization results before exporting the image

Figure 27.10 demonstrates working on a graphic with Macromedia Fireworks.

Figure 27.10
Designing graphics with Macromedia Fireworks.

BEATWARE ePICTURE PRO

A surprisingly powerful program for the Mac, ePicture Pro sports the following features:

- Very easy to use interface
- Live object editing
- Layers
- Animation
- 3D modeling
- Image Slicing and JavaScript Rollovers
- Export to video, vector, and bitmap graphic formats including Windows Media, RealVideo, QuickTime, Flash, SVG, Animated GIF, GIF, JPEG, PNG, TIFF, Targa, Photoshop
- Export to HTML and JavaScript

The fact that ePicture Pro is from a small company and Mac-centric has kept it in the relative dark. Anyone reading this book who uses a Mac should hop on over to the Beatware Web site at **http://www.beatware.com/** and check it out.

PLUG-INS AND SPECIALTY TOOLS

The way you present a graphic is as important as the graphic's quality itself. A well-processed image, although strong on its own, is rendered even more classy when enhanced with drop shadows, feathered edges, and geometric edge designs, just to name a few.

PART
VI
CH
27

These effects, as well as innumerable others, can be achieved through the use of plug-ins to Photoshop or Photoshop-style imaging programs.

ALIEN SKIN SOFTWARE

With 21 filters, Alien Skin's premier plug-in package is Eye Candy. It offers a wide range of powerful standards as well as fun creations such as drop shadows, glows, motion trails, jiggle, weave, and water drop. Find out all about Eye Candy and other Alien Skin products at `http://www.alienskin.com/` (see Figure 27.11).

Figure 27.11
Weird and wacky
stuff can be gotten
from Alien Skin.

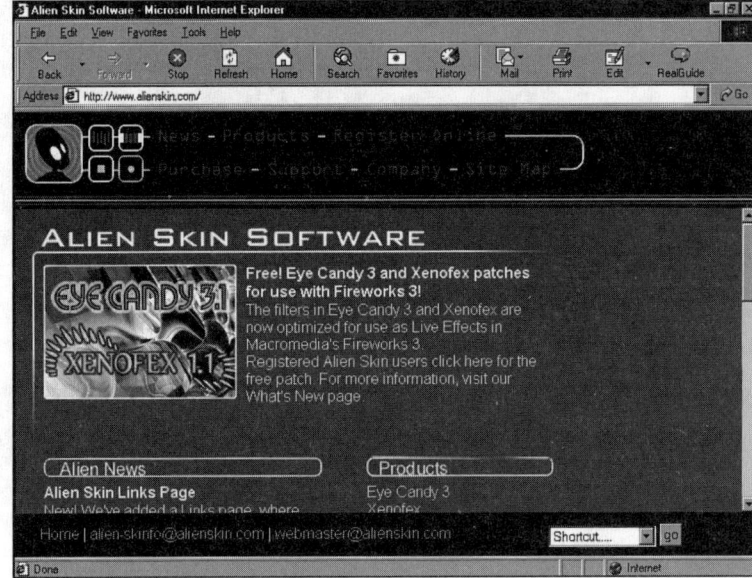

AUTO F/X

With such enhancements as photo edges from Photo/Graphic Edges (see Figure 27.12), type edging with Typo/Graphic Edges, and a powerful image optimizer and color palette controller known as WebVise Totality, Auto F/X makes some mighty plug-ins available on the Macintosh and PC platforms. Photo/Graphic Edges 10,000+ is a standalone package, whereas Typo/Graphic Edges and WebVise Totality come bundled along with nine other graphic tools in a package called Studio Pro 2.0. Visit Auto F/X at `http://www.autofx.com/`.

KAI'S POWER TOOLS

The king of enhancements, Kai's Power Tools can help you create background tiles, Web buttons, and complex color blends. Kai's Power Tools, originally distributed by Metacreations, is now is available for both the Macintosh and Windows platforms from Corel at `http://newgraphics.corel.com/products/kpt6.html` (see Figure 27.13).

Figure 27.12
Working on a graphic in Photoshop using Photo/Graphic Edges. This graphic uses a wavy edge effect and a drop-shadow for a professional edge.

Figure 27.13
Kai's Power Tools

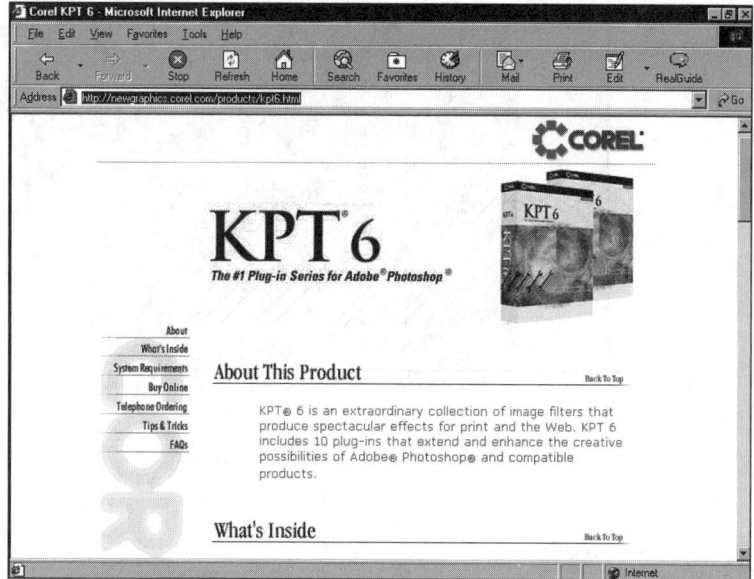

ANIMATED GIF PROGRAMS

One of the easiest ways to add a bit of life to your Web pages is through the use of animated GIF images. The animation is encoded within the image file, meaning that all browsers can read it. Other animation options might cost more money and not be as cross-platform, cross-browser compatible as GIF animations.

Here are some helpful GIF animation programs. As you've already discovered, animation is fast becoming part of the new wave of image production tools, including Photoshop.

GIF CONSTRUCTION SET

A popular shareware tool for constructing animated GIFs on the PC, GIF Construction Set contains a Windows 95-based wizard that walks the creator through the simplified process of creating an animated image. For users more comfortable with the animation process, GIF Construction Set also offers the ability to bypass the wizard and build the images yourself. GIF Construction Set is available at **http://www.mindworkshop.com/**.

GIF MOVIE GEAR

The power of this animation tool lies primarily in its palette control and its ability to optimize each individual graphic, removing unnecessary data. GIF Movie Gear is available from Gamani at **http://www.gamani.com/** (see Figure 27.14). Alas, it's only for the PC.

Figure 27.14
Gamani offers a great animation tool for Windows.

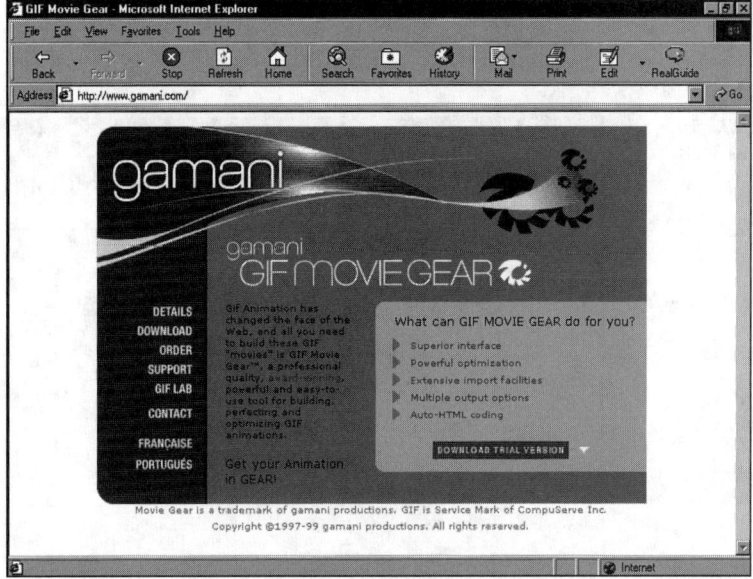

ULEAD GIF ANIMATOR

Another great PC utility, I personally love the way you can add special effects to your graphics by using Ulead GIF Animator. Sweeps, fades, fills, and general fun can be had, all with the click of a mouse.

Ulead products are long on productivity and short on expense. A perfect combination for lower budget projects, they can be found at **http://www.ulead.com/**.

MICROSOFT GIF ANIMATOR

GIF Animator works with Microsoft's Image Composer. Its features include the following:

- Drag-and-drop images directly from Microsoft Image Composer.
- Special effects such as loop, spin, and fade.
- Customize palettes, or let the application optimize the animation for you.

You can find out more about Microsoft GIF Animator at `http://www.microsoft.com/image-composer/gifanimator/gifanin.htm`.

OPTIMIZATION TOOLS

Optimization tools help get your graphics down to Web-ready size. Here's a look at some of the particularly helpful applications.

DEBABELIZER PRO

You can take tedious guesswork out of optimization with this powerful program that processes and optimizes graphics. Although you can do everything that Debabelizer does to a graphic by hand in Photoshop, Debabelizer has the added advantage of batch processing files as well as offering up file type and size comparisons. Debabelizer Pro can be found at `http://www.debabelizer.com/`.

Be wary, however. Debabelizer Pro is a considerable expense. I've only used it when working for design companies requiring large quantities of graphic production. For smaller clients and specific applications, I prefer to use Photoshop and do my optimization by hand or by using one of the other tools listed in this section. You'll need to evaluate your circumstances to come up with the most sensible approach.

ULEAD SMARTSAVER

For the PC user, SmartSaver Pro cannot be beat for a simple interface and great output. What's more, it's a whole lot less expensive than Debabelizer—perfect for smaller Web graphic production facilities and personal use. Ulead SmartSaver can be found at `http://www.ulead.com/`.

STOCK PHOTOGRAPHY AND ART

You'll also want to have sources for icons, patterns, stock photos, and fonts. There are numerous sources of freeware or shareware material on the Internet. Higher-quality material can be acquired on CD-ROM and must be used according to the associated license.

For professional projects, it's definitely worth your while to accumulate a solid library of stock photography, clip art, and fonts.

PART

VI

CH

27

EYEWIRE

Adobe Studios offers an excellent line of quality stock materials. You can get a regular paper catalog delivered via snail mail, or you can browse and purchase stock materials online at `http://www.eyewire.com/`.

PHOTODISC

A visit to Photodisc will provide you with a shopping source for plenty of stock photos, backgrounds, and links to other sites of interest. Free membership entitles you to downloads of comp art and photos at `http://www.photodisc.com/`. You also can order a standard mail catalog.

ARTTODAY

An inexpensive alternative to high-end stock materials such as Adobe Studios and Photodisc, a membership to Art Today (`http://www.arttoday.com/`) gives you unlimited downloads for a very reasonable yearly fee. The quality varies, but you can and will find a variety of useful images and art. I've found this resource to be well worth the price tag of $29.95 per year.

FUN AND FREE SITES

The Web is filled with sites that offer downloadable clip art, photos, backgrounds, and animations galore. It would be impossible to list them all here, but I've got a few favorites.

- **The Internet Baglady**—She's a personal friend, and her site is simply fun! The Baglady has searched for and found a wide number of inexpensive and free ways to get art for and information about building a Web site. The Internet Baglady can be found at `http://www.dumpsterdive.com/`.

- **Pambytes Free Web Graphics**—Hundreds of backgrounds, buttons and fonts, all available at `http://www.pambytes.com/default.html`.

- **Microsoft Images Gallery**—High-end selection of images from Microsoft at `http://www.microsoft.com/gallery/images/default.asp`.

TROUBLESHOOTING

STARTING LIKE A PRO

I want to set myself up as a professional Web graphic designer. What tools are absolutely necessary to purchase?

I would buy Photoshop to start with. Then, I'd think about adding Adobe LiveMotion to my toolbox. If you're concerned about price and are currently a student, you can get student discounts from resellers. These can often be very significant. Educators can also get impressive discounts on software as well. Try before you buy. Download demos and work with them first—it's better to know you're going to use a program than spend good money for it only to find that it never gets used.

PHOTOSHOP A NECESSITY?

I am an ardent admirer of Jasc's Paint Shop Pro. I get excellent results with my Web graphics and am not interested in spending the money and time on Photoshop. Is this a problem?

I've seen some awesome graphics created with Paint Shop Pro, and I'm convinced that any tool that meets your needs and makes you happy is the tool for you if you have no intention of attempting to look for work as a professional Web designer. If you do, the emphasis is very likely going to be on experience with professional tools from Adobe and Macromedia.

TRAINING

I have Photoshop, Illustrator, and Flash and want to learn how to use them well, but don't know where to go for more information?

There are plenty of good books on the market, but I've found that courses and instructional videos can be a tremendous way to jump over the learning curve of some of these products. Try SmartPlanet and eHandsOn for online courses. Lynda Weinman has produced some great videos you can use to learn visual design software, too.

Note
You can find SmartPlanet at `http://www.smartplanet.com/`. eHandsOn is available at `http://www.ehandson.com/`. Lynda Weinman's instructional videos can be ordered from `http://store.lynda.com/`.

DESIGNING FOR THE REAL WORLD

CREATING A BACKGROUND GRAPHIC: COMPARE AND CONTRAST

To give you a feel for graphic design tools and how they work, I'm going to ask you to create a Web background graphic using a compare/contrast process with different tools.

If you don't have the tools in question, download demos from the appropriate Web sites and take it from there. Also, feel free to add any design tool of your choice to the compare and contrast exercise.

Then, you do the activity, write down the time it takes to complete each portion of the activity, and write down your thoughts about what you found to be advantages and disadvantages using these programs.

USING PHOTOSHOP

Begin the exercise by following these steps:

1. Select File, New file. The New dialog box appears.
2. Create a file that is 50 pixels wide by 50 pixels high.
3. Fill the file with a color by selecting a color from the Swatches palette, and then choosing Edit, Fill. Choose Foreground Color from the menu and click OK.

4. Select Filter, Noise, Add Noise. You can achieve a recycled paper look by adding a Noise level of 25, Uniform distribution, Monochromatic. Click OK.

5. Optimize and save the file.

You can create a test HTML page including the image, and load the file into your browser to see how it looks.

USING PHOTOIMPACT

PhotoImpact has a terrific tool called Background Designer which you can use to create backgrounds, as follows:

1. Select Web, Background Designer. The Background Designer dialog box opens.

2. Click the Generate a New Tile option button. Then, put the dimensions of the tile you'd like to create in the Cell-size text boxes. I chose to leave the size at the default 80 pixels by 80 pixels.

3. Choose a Schema from the Schema drop-down menu. I chose Texture 17.

4. Now, select a texture from the texture box. You might like to modify the texture using the Background type choices, the Palette Ramp Editor, and by changing the settings available to you in the dialog box. Each setting you make will be reflected in the preview box at the top right of the Designer's screen (see Figure 27.15).

Figure 27.15
PhotoImpact's
Background
Designer.

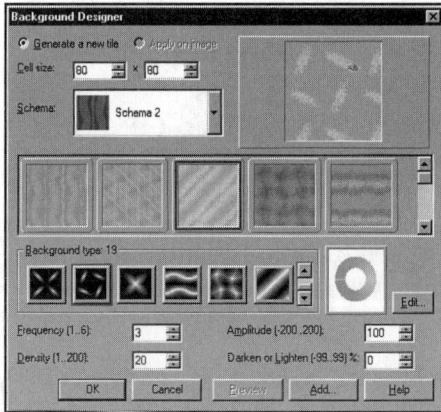

5. Once you're satisfied with the look of your background, click OK. PhotoImpact will generate the tile.

6. Select File, SmartSaver to optimize the graphic.

→ For more information on creating a variety of background graphics, **see** Chapter 29, "Creating Professional Web Graphics," **p. 595.**

USING PAINT SHOP PRO

To create a background tile in Paint Shop Pro:

1. Select File, New. The New Image dialog box appears.

2. Enter the width and height in pixels (I used 50×50). Resolution should be set to 72 pixels per inch (ppi). Select the background color of your choice, and the Image type (I used 24-bit color as I can modify this later). Click OK.

3. Using the paintbrush, gently add some light texture to the tile, or select Image, Add Noise and add noise to the tile.

4. Optimize the file by first selecting Colors, Decrease Color Depth. Select a value that keeps the integrity of the look but allows the lowest number of colors.

5. Select File, Save. Choose GIF format and save your file.

I did the exercises, too. Your results might vary from mine, which is perfectly fine. I just want you to have a chance to actively try the tools and make judgments about how their various features work for you.

Following are some advantages and disadvantages of the process.

PHOTOSHOP

Advantages: I liked the control I had with Photoshop. From being able to choose directly from a color-safe palette to controlling exactly how I would optimize the image, I felt that all decisions were left to me. This enabled me to work quickly and meet my goal with quality results.

Disadvantages: To manage Photoshop quickly, users will need to have some experience working with it. It has so many features that it can be confusing to those who aren't familiar with it.

PHOTOIMPACT

Advantages: Although the control wasn't the same as with Photoshop, what PhotoImpact offers are options. The Background Designer is so much fun that I could spend a lot of time playing around with it. It is a very creative tool. The interface is also quite easy to maneuver, and SmartSaver helped me to see up front what file formats would work best for optimization. Although I already knew what would be the best option in terms of optimization, those designers with less experience are sure to appreciate the features of SmartSaver.

Disadvantages: As with Photoshop, there's a lot of stuff here. Opening up the different applications, which are truly like smaller programs within the parent program, is more time consuming than the pop-up windows in Photoshop and Paint Shop Pro.

PAINT SHOP PRO

Advantages: The easy-to-use interface makes this program especially powerful. There's not a lot you have to think about; you can pretty much jump right in and do what you want to do. And Paint Shop Pro makes the process very simple and straightforward.

Disadvantages: Paint Shop Pro's simplicity is both its power and its problem. I wanted a lot more control over my image production than the program allowed me, and I had to search for workarounds to accommodate my needs.

CHAPTER 28

COMMON WEB GRAPHIC FORMATS

In this chapter

Size matters, so they say. On the Web, you want to keep your sizes small without sacrificing quality. Regardless of the media with which you're working—audio, video, animations, or graphics—ensuring that your files are light and your design still bright is a sure way to successful site design.

Understanding the available file formats used in Web graphic design is essential. One of the most daunting aspects of constructing a new Web site from scratch is the need for high-quality, well-designed graphics. The designer's responsibility isn't just limited to creating visual appeal: This is the Web, not clay or canvas, and working in a digital medium brings with it uniquely digital responsibilities.

Web graphic design is rife with myths about what Web graphics are and how they are created. On one hand, the core ideas are incredibly simple; on the other hand, many try their hands at graphics and just can't seem to get the process right.

Whether you're a well-studied and professional designer or are just learning how to create Web graphics, there is no reason why your Web site should be any less visually strong and technically well optimized than any professional site.

File optimization—the act of working with files to achieve both quality appearance and acceptable download times—begins with an understanding of the file formats that are available. I'll begin by describing file formats available on the Web, and which options are available to you within those formats. After you've gained a strong understanding of file formats, you move on to the tools that will help you work with the format and optimization concepts you've learned.

GRAPHIC INTERCHANGE FORMAT (GIF)

GIF is a file format that uses a type of compression known as *lossless*. Compression, as a general rule, is based on complicated, mathematical algorithms that are best saved for those developers interested in working with compression.

For all individuals developing Web pages, you are best served by learning quickly that GIF compression works by figuring out how much of the image uses the same color information. At that point, the compression algorithm saves those sections by using a numeric pattern.

GIF compression is limited to a total of 256 colors so that a numeric pattern is very specific. This is one of the main reasons it's so important to understand more about color theory and restrictions on the Web.

→ For more information about color theory, **see** Chapter 25, "Color Concepts," **p. 527**.

So, if you have 15 shades of blue within your graphic, that translates to 15 individual patterns. With more than 256 patterns, the algorithm has to decide what to leave out. It does this by limiting those blues to just a few or even just one total blue color.

Because of this process, your neon blue might end up a sky blue, and so forth. This is where experience and a skilled hand comes into play—knowing when and how to deal with color and file types will enable you to gain control over colors within your graphics.

Note

There's a bit of confusion over the pronunciation of GIF. Many people say it with a hard G, because logically, if the "*G*" stands for graphic, it would follow that GIF (as in GIFt) would be the proper pronunciation.

However, many people, including myself, pronounce the *G* like a *J*, or JIF as in JIFFY. Interestingly, when on the phone with Unisys, the owners of the GIF algorithm, they pronounced it just as I do. I figure they're the source, so I've followed suit ever since.

GIFs have been the longest supported graphic file type on the Web, and they are extremely useful for a number of graphic file applications.

There are several important guidelines to determine if you should choose the GIF compression method for a specific graphic:

- **Line-drawn images**—Any graphic that uses few lines, such as a cartoon, is a good choice for GIF compression.

- **Images with few, flat colors**—With only a few colors and no light sources or gradations in that color, there's not going to be a lot of competition for those 256 colors in the compression method.

The image in Figure 28.1 shows a line-drawn cartoon. This image is an excellent choice for GIF compression. Figure 28.2 uses black, white, and two shades of gray—and all the colors are flat, with no light sources or gradations. This makes the image perfect for GIF compression.

Figure 28.1
A line-drawn cartoon image by cartoonist Joe Forkan is a perfect choice for GIF format.

Figure 28.2
This image, using only black, white, and two shades of flat gray, is also a good choice for the GIF format.

PART

VI

CH

28

JOINT PHOTOGRAPHIC EXPERTS GROUP (JPEG)

Frustrated with the limitations of GIFs, a group of photographic experts went to work on compression methods that would allow high quality compression while retaining millions of colors. The results are what we know today as *Joint Photographic Experts Group* (JPEG, also written JPG).

> **Note**
>
> The appropriate file extension, or suffix, for JPEG files is .jpg. There's a lot of confusion around this issue, because of the JPEG name. Always follow standard filenaming conventions and use the .jpg suffix for all JPEG images.

→ For more information on naming conventions, **see** Chapter 8, "Managing XHTML Documents Locally," **p. 119**.

The algorithm that makes up the JPEG is, by nature, more complicated than that using the GIF. JPEGs use a *lossy* compression method. The algorithm focuses on removing data that is felt to be unimportant, instead of first mapping out areas of information that should be saved.

The JPEG method does this by dividing the image data into rectangular sections before applying the algorithm. On the one hand, this method gives you a lot of control in terms of how much information you're going to toss away, but at high compression ratios, you can end up with a blocky, blotchy, blurry result.

These blocky sections are known as *artifacts*. Artifacts occur when you've over-compressed an image. You'll look at this a bit later, when you step through the optimization process. Working with JPEGs, just as with GIFs, requires a bit of skill and a fine hand to achieve the best results.

Because the JPEG format was specifically designed to manage files with a lot of color, there are certain types of images that best lend themselves to JPEG compression. The following list is a helpful guide to use when determining if JPEG is the best format for your image:

- Images with a lot of colors, such as color photographs
- Graphics using gradient fills (see Figure 28.3)
- Graphics using light sources
- Photographs with much gradation, such as skies, sunsets, and oceans (see Figure 28.4)

Figure 28.3
Gradient fills are appropriate for JPEG format. The reason has to due with JPEGs ability to compress files without reducing the number of colors. If you tried this with a GIF, you'd lose the smooth transitions from one hue to the next.

Figure 28.4
Sunset pictures, particularly when in full color, contain a lot of gradation and will normally be processed by using JPEG format.

PORTABLE NETWORK GRAPHICS (PNG)

The PNG graphics format was defined during 1995–1996 to overcome copyright issues surrounding the GIF format at the time. However, aside from the goal of creating a public domain image format, the developers also attempted to improve upon the standard set by GIF. This has resulted in a number of enhanced features:

- indexed color, grayscale, and truecolor image support
- from 1–16 bit depth
- alpha channel for transparency
- better interlacing, resulting in faster display of a usable image

One of the big features in which PNG out-performs GIF is the ability to store images that include an alpha-channel. This enables proper anti-aliasing and eliminates the jagged edges around fonts and images.

Unfortunately, popular support for PNG has not yet been achieved. Although the current versions of the major Web browsers and some of the graphic image packages have added support for this new format, GIF and JPEG are still far more common.

Caution

Despite the fact that 4.0 generation browsers have chosen to support the PNG format, that support is sometimes buggy. The biggest perpetrator of this is Netscape Navigator. As a result, using PNG for Internet-based Web sites is, at this time, risky at best.

PART
VI

CH
28

Like GIF, PNG is a loss-less format. Therefore, it does not supplant JPEGs as the proper format for photographic images. For more information on the PNG format, visit the World Wide Web Consortium's specification for PNG at `http://www.w3.org/TR/REC-png-multi.html`.

GRAPHIC OPTIMIZATION

Optimizing graphics is the technique by which a Web graphic designer reduces the file size of a graphic for acceptable download times, while maintaining the highest quality image he can produce.

The first step in optimization is to determine which file format is appropriate for the file. Using the general guidelines given earlier for GIF and JPEG formats will help you to achieve that crucial first step.

Interestingly, the guidelines discussed within this chapter for GIFs and JPEGs are not always accurate. Take for example a black-and-white photograph, or even a color photo-graph, with very little color information, light source, and gradients. With this example, it's going to take a little experimentation to determine which file type will help you achieve the smallest file size while retaining the most important information.

There's no cut-and-dry answer to this except through trial-and-error or by using one of the many graphic optimization tools available.

→ For more information about optimization tools, **see** Chapter 27, "Web Graphic Tools and Professional Tools," **p. 561**.

After you've determined which file type is most appropriate, work with the available technologies within that graphic file format.

> **Note**
>
> You can optimize graphics with a wide range of tools. I use Photoshop because I'm person-ally most comfortable with its use and find its palette control superior to many of the less professional programs on the market.

Here's a list of helpful terms (see Table 28.1) that you'll find in use in many popular graphic optimization programs.

TABLE 28.1 TERMS AND DEFINITIONS FOR WEB GRAPHIC OPTIMIZATION

Term	Definition
Color palette	There are several types of color palettes. These are numeri-cally determined sets of colors within the graphic program that enable the designer to make specific choices regarding how an image is processed.
Adaptive palette	This palette allows you to make adaptations to a given image, including controlling color, depth, and dithering.

Term	Definition
Indexed color	A software program such as Photoshop will take an image file and count its colors. If there are more than 256 colors in an image, indexing will reduce the image's palette to 256 colors—making it ready for GIF production. At that point, you can use the adaptive palette to further control aspects of the palette.
Exact palette	You'll see this appear when an image already has less than 256 colors—because the colors fit within the indexing limits, the specific number of colors used will appear. You can then determine whether to keep this number, or reduce it further with the adaptive palette.
Bit depth	Also known as *color depth*, this is the amount of total bit data that will be saved with your image. The optimization of images into the GIF format depends upon your ability to control bit depth.
Number of colors	In GIF optimization, there can be as few as 8 colors or as many as 256 colors. Limiting the number of colors is how you reduce the size of a GIF file during the optimization process.
Dithering	This is the process by which the computer and imaging software determine which color to use when reducing a palette. Remember the discussion of the GIF algorithm earlier in this chapter? I mentioned that a neon blue could conceivably show up as a sky blue during reduction. This is *dithering*. Ideally, you don't want your images to dither at all, which speaks to the issue of proper file format selection.
Maximum, High, Medium, Low	These settings are specific to JPEG optimization and refer to how much information is removed during the lossy compression process.

With the terminology defined, you can begin to optimize a graphic.

ADAPTIVE PALETTES

In recent editions of Photoshop, as well as other graphic programs, the inclusion of the Web-safe palette has offered designers a way to save their GIFs specifically to that palette.

→ The Web-safe palette is discussed in detail earlier in this book, **see** Chapter 25, "Color Concepts," **p. 527**.

There's some dissention over this concept. Doesn't it make perfect sense to just use the Web-safe palette when saving GIFs? There are at least two reasons why you might consider not using this method of saving a file:

1. The 216 color palette is just that—it contains 216 colors. Using the Adaptive palette (Figure 28.5), you can reduce that number of colors significantly to have greater control over your file weight.

PART

VI

CH

28

2. Limiting colors by hand gives you much greater control over the palette. The 216-color palette will always dither colors to match that palette, sometimes giving you unacceptable results.

Figure 28.5
Using the Adaptive palette for hand-level control.

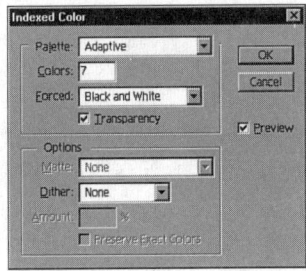

THE WEB (216) PALETTE

How, then, can Web graphic designers ensure that their graphics don't dither when viewed in unsafe circumstances? You can certainly decide to use the Web-safe palette if you prefer. Here are a few other tips:

- If you're creating graphics from scratch, begin with colors selected from the safe palette.

- If you must use unsafe color, try to be sure that the graphics are enhancements rather than necessary to your site if you are concerned about support. An example of a necessary GIF would be anything that contains text pertinent to the page. If this dithers, it could seriously affect readability.

> **Note**
>
> Remember, unless you create a JPEG yourself or replace every color in that JPEG by hand with a Web-safe color, JPEGs will always be unsafe. The JPEG algorithm doesn't limit the palette and, in fact, supports up to 24 bits of color information—that's a lot of color. Users with browser or monitor limitations will see a poorer-quality graphic in these cases.

OPTIMIZING A GIF

With an appropriate file for GIF optimization in hand, you're ready to step through the optimization process. Here's a checklist to be sure you're prepared:

- Your file is obviously ready for GIF optimization if it has flat color, few colors, and is line-drawn.

- You've scanned and sized your file to appropriate Web dimensions.

- The file is in RGB format—either a native Photoshop file, an EPS, or a JPG set to Maximum.

→ For information on scanning and sizing your files, **see** Chapter 29, "Creating Professional Web Graphics," **p. 595**.

→ To read about details on RGB color, **see** Chapter 25, "Color Concepts," **p. 527**.

It's important to point out that the inclusion of ImageReady in Photoshop 5.0 and the addition of the Save for Web feature in Photoshop 5.5 and higher is very powerful and enables you to apply the concepts I'm including here and visually see the results of your choices before saving.

But, because many readers choose to use a range of applications to get the job done, I'm going to keep to the standard step-by-step in Photoshop. This way, whether you're using a current version of Photoshop, an older version, or another program completely, you'll be able to grasp the general production process with ease.

Ready to optimize? Great, here's (in general) how:

1. Select Image, Mode.
2. Choose Indexed Color.
3. When the Indexed Color dialog box pops up, select the Adaptive palette, no Dither, or "none" (see Figure 28.5).
4. Reduce the Colors, Bit, or Color Depth to 7. Click OK.
5. Save the file using the File, Export, GIF89 feature (see Figure 28.6).
6. Name the file `gif_test_7.gif` (be sure to save your original file as you'll be going back to it).
7. View your results. You can compare them to mine in Figure 28.7.

Figure 28.6
Exporting the image with the GIF89 export feature. Using this feature provides you with a dialog box that allows you to control several GIF features including transparency and interlacing.

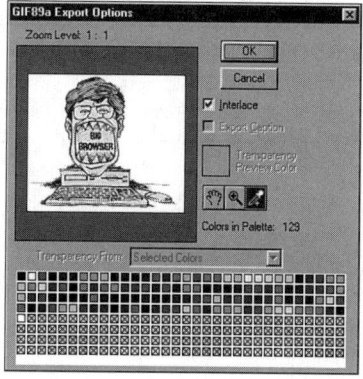

Now, try reducing the bit depth even more.

1. Open the original file. In my case, it's `gif_optimize.psd`.
2. Select Image, Mode.
3. Once again, select Indexed Color.
4. Choose the Adaptive palette, set to no Dither.
5. Reduce the Bit Depth to 3.

Figure 28.7
My GIF, optimized at 7 bits. The image still contains plenty of detail with no obvious loss of critical visual information.

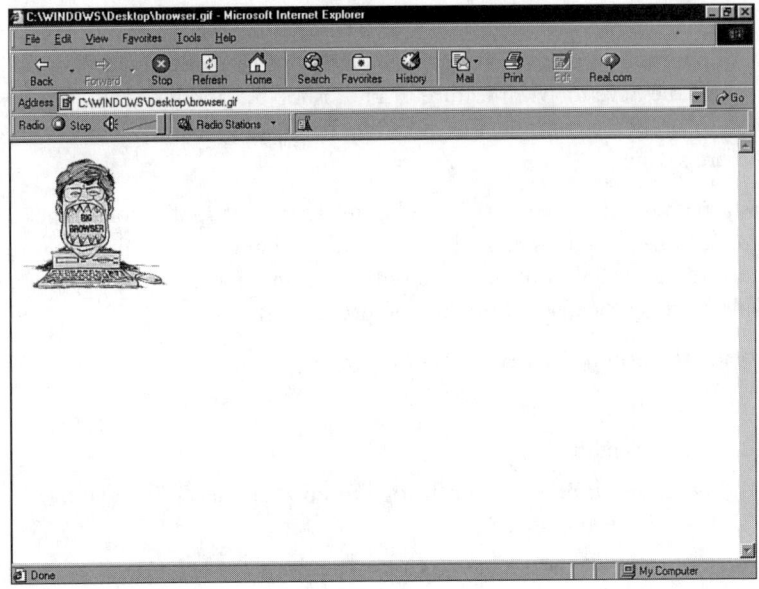

6. Export the file (File, Export, GIF89).

7. Name the file `gif_test_3.gif`.

View your results. Are they acceptable, or did they reduce the colors or line integrity too much? If you liked the first example, but weren't happy with the second at 3 bits, go ahead and try optimizing at a variety of bit depths until you find the right one for your file.

Figure 28.8 shows my results. Note that there's not much visual difference between the two images visually, but the first file, `gif_test_7.gif`, is a total of 9KB, and the second, only 4KB.

OPTIMIZING A JPEG

Begin with a file appropriate for JPEG optimization. Here's a list of helpful guidelines:

- Images appropriate to optimize as JPEG files should have many colors, light sources, or color gradients.

- Your initial file should be in RGB format, either a native Photoshop file, an EPS, or a maximum set JPEG.

- The file to be optimized should be appropriately sized for Web use.

Now you're ready to optimize the file. In Photoshop

1. Select File.

2. Choose Save A Copy from the drop-down menu.

3. Select JPG.

Figure 28.8
My GIF example, this time at a bit depth of 3. This bit depth is quite low, resulting in speckles rather than a smooth look.

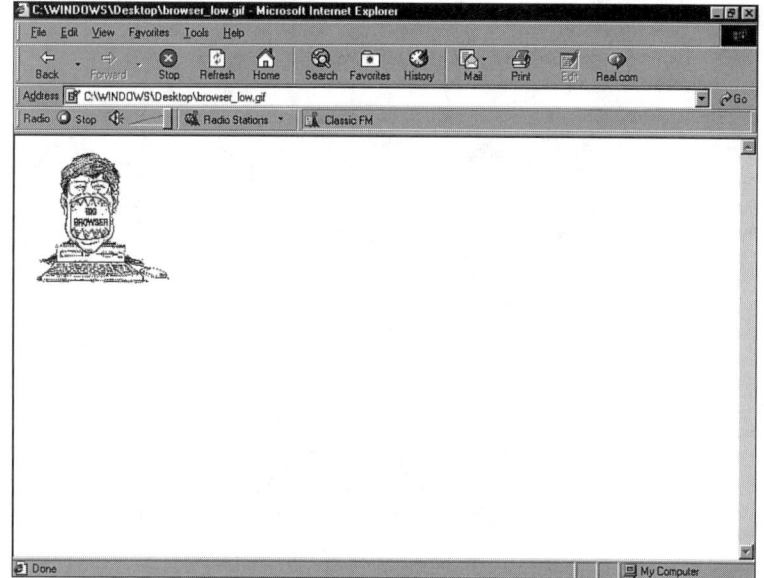

4. You now see a dialog box that allows you to make choices regarding your JPEG algorithm. For this exercise, choose High.

5. Save the file as `jpeg_test_high.jpg`.

View your file. It should be very clear and crisp, with no degradation or appearance of artifacts. However, the file size of my graphic (see Figure 28.9) is weighing in at 18KB. I very likely can get this file weight down without reducing the file so much that artifacts appear.

Figure 28.9
With my JPEG optimized at High setting, the quality of the image is very good, although this file can be optimized more without losing clarity.

1. Re-open the original file (mine is called `jpeg_test.psd`).

2. Choose File.

3. Select Save A Copy.

4. In the dialog box, set the JPEG optimization to Low.

5. Save the file as `jpeg_test_low.jpg`.

Looking at my file, I find that the weight has been reduced to 7KB. However, I see artifacts, as shown in Figure 28.10. This isn't to my taste, so I'm going to start at the beginning and try the Medium setting.

Figure 28.10
At Low setting (image magnified to show detail), my JPEG becomes blocky, blotchy, and blurry—filled with artifacts.

In this case, I'm happy with the Medium setting, which weighs 11KB and doesn't have any noticeable artifacts.

Note

High and Medium are often similar in visual quality, but not always similar in terms of weight. You'll find most of your JPEGs are going to be saved at Medium, with some at High, and—if you truly are looking to keep image integrity—very few will be saved at Low. Maximum is a good setting should you have a reason to want full color with absolutely no degradation. This is helpful when using larger files for specialty viewing.

Usually, I tend to let my JPEGs lean toward the higher setting. Given the choice, I'll sacrifice some page weight for image quality. My eye is particular—I can usually see artifacts appear at the Medium setting. This causes what I call the "Vaseline effect," a blurry, blotchy result that is disturbing to my eye.

I'm always going to opt for quality when the difference in size is 5KB or so. I'd personally much rather have a slightly larger file size at the cost of download time than poor quality, unprofessional images.

Your JPEG mileage might vary. The more you practice optimization techniques, the more skilled you will become at knowing what type of file format to use, how much or how little to optimize a graphic, and when your specific circumstances allow you leeway for variation in file weight.

DESIGNING FOR THE REAL WORLD

CREATING TRANSPARENT GIFs

Transparency is sometimes described as an effect that places your graphic on a clear piece of tape. This means you can place that tape on a background and the background will show through the tape.

This is particularly effective when you're creating graphics that sit on a background, especially graphics that aren't a standard rectangular shape.

The technique takes a little bit of time, patience, and an excellent hand and eye to learn.

I do my transparencies in Photoshop, but your favorite Web graphics program is likely to have a helpful method by which to make an image transparent.

> **Note** Only GIFs can be transparent. JPEG technology does not include a transparency option.

Let's say you want to place a text header image over a background texture. The text selection shown here is ornate, with a lot of circular shapes. Follow these steps to create a transparency:

1. Choose File, New.
2. Because you want your header to be 350 pixels wide by 50 pixels high, enter those values into the New Image dialog box.
3. Set the image type to Transparent (note that this only has to do with Photoshop file management, not the creation of GIF transparency—an entirely different mechanism). Mode is set to RGB.
4. Select Edit, Fill.
5. Fill the image with a color that is sufficiently dissimilar to any color you are using.
6. Now choose Layer, New, Layer.
7. Add your text by using the Type Tool.
8. Flatten the image.
9. Optimize the image as described earlier, by using Indexing and the Adaptive palette.
10. Export as a GIF89, and the GIF89 dialog box will appear.
11. Deselect the background color with the color picker.
12. Save your image as `transparency.gif`.

Place the image into your HTML page and view the results. You can see that the image appears to be seamless with the background in Figure 28.11. This is an effective transparency.

PART

VI

CH

28

Figure 28.11
A transparent GIF appears seamless over textured backgrounds because the background color has been removed from the images

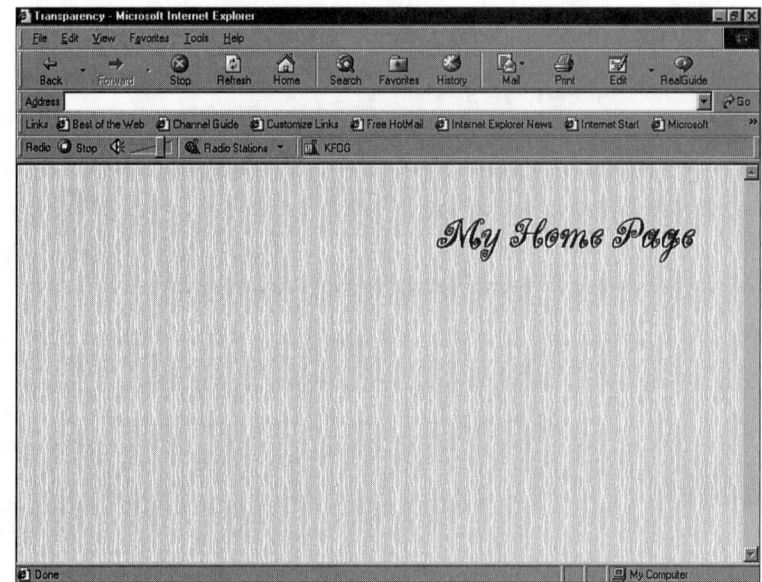

→ To learn about how to add images to an XHTML document, **see** Chapter 13, "Using Images in XHTML Documents," **p. 221**.

Tip from

Don't be disappointed if your image isn't quite correct. You might see white or colored edges or ragged edges around your image. This isn't your fault so much as the limitations of transparency. Keep practicing the technique and selecting from colors that are close enough but far enough from any colors in the image itself. Eventually, you'll master the technique.

CHAPTER 29

CREATING PROFESSIONAL WEB GRAPHICS

In this chapter

WEB GRAPHIC TECHNOLOGY

One of the biggest areas of in-depth study and growth is within Web graphic technology. New graphic formats are on the horizon, and a plethora of new and diverse software tools have come to market. There's an increase in the bandwidth available to the desktop, and more sophisticated methods of technically managing documents so that they are processed and loaded with speed and ease, and all have become available within the past two years.

Knowing how to create professional graphics for the Web is important for any serious developer, and for the hobbyist, learning Web graphics skills will most surely assist your pages in being popular and worthy of regular visits.

This chapter will teach you what kind of graphics to use on a page and how to create those graphics. From backgrounds, headers, navigational buttons, bars and rules, to spot art—you'll learn how to use some of the popular tools, employ professional tricks, and create attractive, appropriate Web graphics. I'll step you through a variety of tasks and demonstrate and describe features, pitfalls, and helpful hints that will make your graphics creations as professional as they get.

USING IMAGES ON YOUR PAGES

A Web site typically uses graphics to design, to identify, and to navigate.

Some of the images you'll want to consider for your pages include background images, headers, navigation buttons, bars and rules, and spot art.

Background images load into the background of the page. Sometimes referred to as wallpaper, background images set the tone of a page. Headers give an individual page its identity by incorporating the site's logo. Headers can also include the parent site's identity, too, as in Molly's Site: What's New. One click of a navigation button and you're on your way to another page within a site. Bars and rules are used to separate text or elements on a page; graphic bars and rules can customize a site's look. Spot art is the term used to describe clip art or photography that will accentuate the textual content on a page.

Within these types of images are a variety of techniques you'll want to employ to ensure professional quality.

SCANNING TECHNIQUES AND STOCK ART

How do you get images? Essentially, three ways exist:

- Scanning and manipulating photographic and organic (real) items
- Working with stock art and photography
- Designing your own graphics from scratch

Sometimes you'll employ all three methods to create a single image. It all depends on the look and feel you've planned for your site.

→ To learn more about effective site planning, **see** Chpater 24, "Effective Page Design," **p. 513**.

I like to refer to a famous acronym, *GIGO*. This means "Garbage In, Garbage Out" and is most appropriate in terms of Web graphics. If you begin with a poor image, whether from scan or stock, you'll end up with a poor image.

To avoid that, I'll teach you some basic scanning tricks and then take a look at how to carefully choose quality stock art and photos. To assist you with designing your own graphics, I've set aside an entire section of this chapter to walk you step-by-step through Web graphic creation.

SCANNING IMAGES

Scanning is in and of itself an art. The good news is that for the Web, we don't need high-resolution scans. This translates into less money spent on hardware, as well as a shorter learning curve for those individuals wishing to get right to the business at hand.

For hardware, a flatbed, color scanner is highly recommended. You can buy very inexpensive scanners that will work well for the Web. The guideline is in resolution—because your final image will be 72dpi (dots per inch), you need a scanner capable of scanning only at this resolution. Just be sure it supports millions of colors and will work with your computer and imaging software.

→ For a list of the best imaging applications on the market today, **see** Chapter 27, "Web Graphic Tools and Professional Tools," **p. 561**.

After your scanner is in place, you'll want to choose the item to be scanned. Typically, this will be a photo, hand drawings or prints, or an organic object, such as a pen or bottle (yes, you can scan "stuff!").

Here are some guidelines to follow as you prepare to scan your work:

- Be sure photos are crisp, clean, and free of dust.
- Drawings and prints should be free of smudges and speckles.
- Organic objects should be wiped down and cleaned before they are placed on the scanner screen.
- The scanner screen itself should be clean and free of dust. Follow your manufacturer's guidelines when cleaning your scanner.

Tip from
molly

To clean photos and other objects to be scanned, buy a can of air! Compressed air, which you can purchase for a reasonable price at any art supply, office, or computer supply store, is very useful to help in the removal of dust and debris from your input materials. Hold the photo or object an arm's length away from you. The canister should be held in your other hand, about a foot away from the object. Aim the nozzle across rather than at the item to be scanned, and clean the item with short shots from the canister. Be careful not to touch any area to be scanned with your fingers after cleaning, as fingerprints can show up on photos and other items.

The next step is to place the item to be scanned on the scanner. Using your favorite software imaging program, you'll import the file from the scanner to the program. I typically use Photoshop to do this, although many popular imaging tools make scanning easy and fast (see Figure 29.1).

Figure 29.1
Using Photoshop, I initiated my scanner's software, DeskScan, and scanned the photo into the imaging program.

After your item is scanned, you'll want to crop it. At this point, you're probably working larger than any recommended Web graphic—both in terms of dpi and dimension. For now, your crop is a preliminary one to remove any whitespace or extra information that you don't want (see Figure 29.2).

Figure 29.2
Cropping the scan will provide you with just the material you want to work with before you start making color and resolution changes.

You'll want to look for any problems with the scan. Is everything smooth and crisp, or are there smudges and speckles? If the scan isn't acceptable, go back and do it right! It can be time consuming, but it's well worth it.

If you're happy with the scanned results, you'll want to set your dpi to 72. If you scanned in at a higher resolution (check your scanning hardware and software for adjusting this), you will see an automatic reduction in the image's dimension.

If you're at 72dpi, you're ready to make any adjustments to the scan. Make alterations to the color, blur or sharpen, and generally sweep, dust, and clean the image to your tastes.

When you're satisfied, resize the image to the size you want. Bear in mind that you might be adding a photographic edge effect, such as a drop shadow or a bevel. For this reason, *save your work* at this point—this is your resource file.

Tip from
molly

Typically, saving the source file in your imaging program's native format is best, as it will retain the most information possible and not compress the image. Because I'm a Photoshop user, I save the file in native Photoshop format. This helps me maintain all the information so that when I reopen this resource, everything is intact.

→ To get up to speed on how color and resolution is to be handled when creating images to be viewed on a monitor screen, **see** Chapter 26, "Working with the Computer Screen," **p. 545**.

Therefore, if you're looking to create a page that is accessible across *all* platforms and browsers, you'll fix your work to a 640×480 screen resolution or you are anticipating a dynamic design (one that will fit to all screen resolutions no matter the layout). I generally recommend that no matter your resolution goals, no graphic should exceed the width of 585 pixels, with the exception of backgrounds, which I'll explain in just a bit. As for height, some occasions exist where you'll be designing longer graphics, but typically, you want to stick to sizes that fit within the screen.

Note

In some instances, you will want to design for higher resolutions. One example is a corporate intranet where hardware and software specifications are tightly controlled.

You're now ready to make additions or changes to your scanned image or to put it aside for later use.

SELECTING STOCK ART

Stock art is clip art and photography that is commercially available and is ready for production. Stock art is widely available, with professional-level art often commanding a considerable price tag for licensing.

→ For a discussion about stock art, **see** Chapter 27, "Web Graphic Tools and Professional Tools," **p. 561**.

Some guidelines for choosing stock art are as follows:

- Photographic images should be crisp and clear, not blurry.
- Line drawings should have no marks or speckles on them.
- You should be able to choose from the file type. Typically, a JPEG file is acceptable, particularly if it's been saved to maximum capacity. What you want to avoid are optimized GIFs, unless you're going to use that file as-is, or make very minimal changes to it.
- Read the licensing agreements *very carefully*. You want to be absolutely certain that you can use the image you're downloading.

In Figure 29.3, I'm browsing through Photodisc. You'll notice that I'm allowed to choose the kind of file I want to purchase—options are available for file type as well as resolution.

Figure 29.3
Browsing through the stock photos at Photodisc allows you to preview the choices and purchase the images that you want.

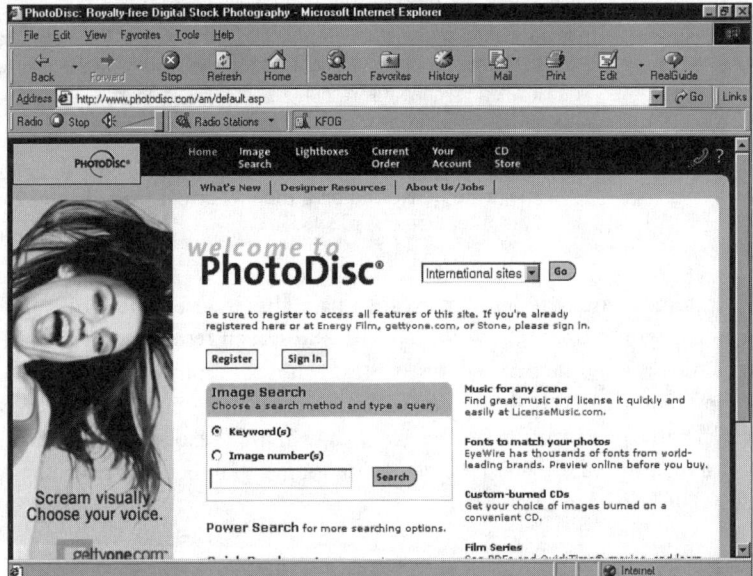

ArtToday is a great resource, too. Be a little more selective when choosing images from this site (see Figure 29.4). Many high-quality images are available, but quality consistency is less than that of the more expensive vendors such as Photodisc.

Free art sites are variable. You can find great stuff, but you need to use the guidelines above to make good decisions when selecting from free clip art and photos.

Note

Visit Photodisc at `http://www.photodisc.com/` and ArtToday at `http://www.arttoday.com/`.

Figure 29.4
Selecting images from ArtToday is a good option; just be careful that you are getting the best-quality image for the price.

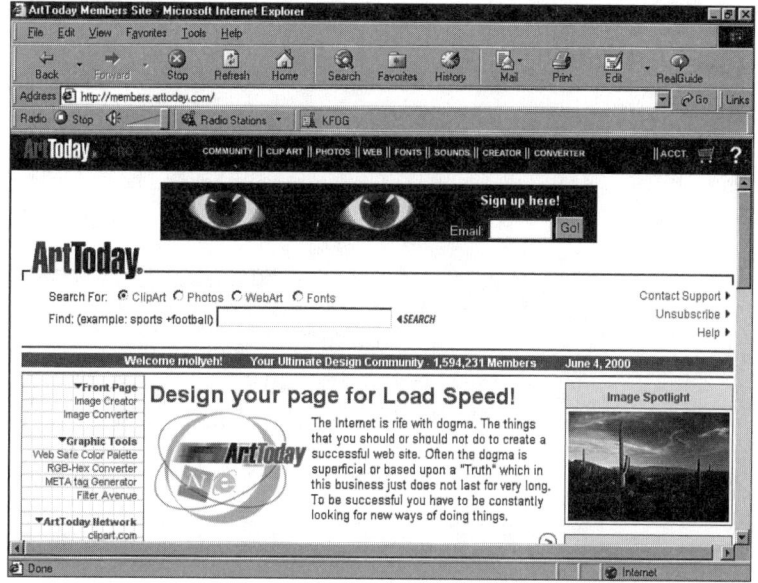

With a good foundation beneath you, you're ready to create some graphics. I'll step you through a variety of tasks and demonstrate and describe features, pitfalls, and helpful hints that will make your graphics creations as professional as they get.

CREATING BACKGROUND IMAGES

Three kinds of background images exist:

- **Wallpaper patterns**—These are small squares that tile to create a smooth, seamless texture that looks like well-installed wallpaper (no bumps, seams, or bungles!).

- **Margin tiles**—Also referred to as *strips* because they are wide and short, margin tiles can be functional or decorative in nature.

- **Watermark style**—This is one large background graphic, usually square, that adds an image, logographic material, or color to the background of a page.

One important issue to remember is that *all backgrounds are tiles*. They might not look like a tile, but they will act like a tile whenever the resolution of a screen changes. Wallpaper patterns, which are squares, will tile into the browser one-by-one until the available space is filled.

Note

Tiling will always occur with conventional coding. If you're using style sheets, you can prevent background tiling from occurring. However, you can fix background tiles only in certain style-sheet compliant browsers, and they will tile in browsers that do not support the style-sheet methods.

→ For information on how to fix backgrounds using style sheets, **see** Chapter 18, "Cascading Style Sheets and XHTML" **p. 377**.

Margin tiles fill the browser in the same way—except it might seem as though they don't because of their size and shape. One way to understand this process is to create a strip that isn't as long as it should be and then view it in your browser. You'll see that it does, in fact, tile along both the horizontal and vertical axes (see Figure 29.5). Finally, watermark tiles, which are very large squares, tile in the same way that wallpaper and margin tiles do (see Figure 29.19, later in this chapter). Therefore, you have to be careful when creating watermarks.

Figure 29.5
I outlined this longer, thin tile so you can see how it flows into the page.

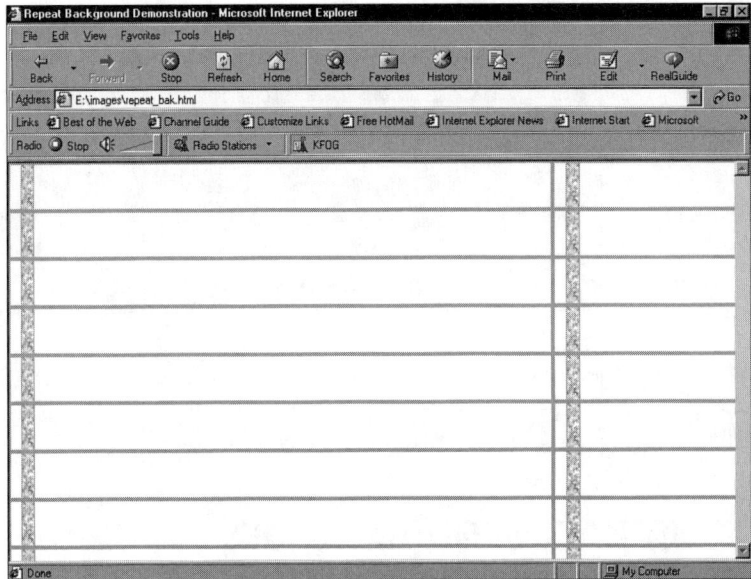

Let's take a closer look at individual types of backgrounds.

WALLPAPER PATTERNS

Wallpaper patterns were the first wave of background graphics. You've probably seen lots of them, in all kinds of styles. They're problematic for a number of reasons, including the fact that if they're too dark or busy, they'll interfere with readability. They're also demanding on the designer—it takes a bit of skill if you're making them completely by hand.

However, if you design them properly, they can create an extremely attractive look for your site.

The following are some general guidelines to use when creating tiles:

- Individual tiles should be at least 50 pixels×50 pixels.
- Work hard to ensure that tiles appear seamless.
- Avoid allowing a small tile with a single image to repeat over and over. Imagine one egg in a single square, tiled repeatedly into the browser.
- Always ensure that you do *not* interlace background graphics.

→ To learn more about interlacing **see** Chapter 28, "Common Web Graphic Formats," **p. 581**.

In this exercise you can create a simple background tile. I'm going to use Paint Shop Pro 6.0, but you can follow along with almost any imaging program:

1. Open the program and create a new file.

2. In the New Image dialog box (see Figure 29.6), place the dimensions of your image (I'm making an image 50×50), the resolution, which should be set to 72, the background color of the graphic (I set mine to white), and the number of colors (set to 256 for GIFs, millions of colors for JPEGs).

PART
VI

CH
29

Figure 29.6
The New Image dialog box in Paint Shop Pro enables you to set the size, resolution, and color for the new image before you create it.

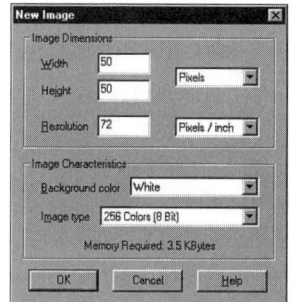

3. Now select any one of the drawing tools. You can choose to use a brush, create geometric shapes—whatever you'd like to try. For this example, I chose the brush with a "chalk" setting and set it to round.

4. I chose a light lavender. My goal is to create a floral wallpaper pattern.

5. In the center of my tile, I painted a flower by simply using three brush strokes.

6. Because I anticipated that this image will tile, I put a partial stroke in each corner of the tile, so when the tiles match up, a small flower will be created by the four corners meeting (see Figure 29.7).

7. From the Colors menu, I chose Decrease Color Depth, and I selected 4-bit color.

8. Now choose File, Save As, and save your file.

Now you can load the image as a background graphic within an HTML document. Figure 29.8 shows my flowery results!

Tip from
molly

To ensure good contrast, keep background tiles very light or very dark, and the body text the opposite. If you have a very light background, black text will help readability because it contrasts well with the background. Similarly, if you have a very dark-green background design, a light color such as cream will provide you with good contrast.

→ To review how images are dealt with in XHTML, **see** Chapter 13, "Using Images in XHTML Documents," **p. 221**.

Figure 29.7
Painting the image takes a little practice, but because you only have to create one square and not an entire background, it's easy to experiment.

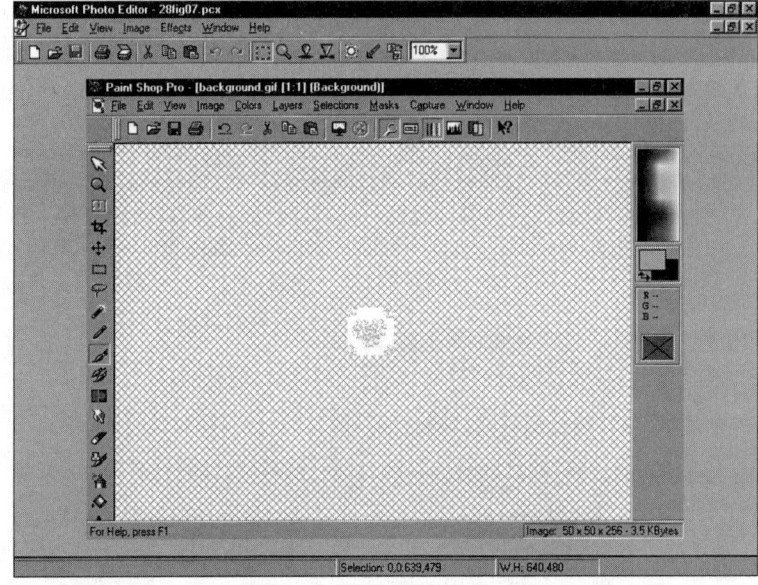

Figure 29.8
Here you can see that, once tiled in the browser, my single flower square has become a flowered, seamless wallpaper.

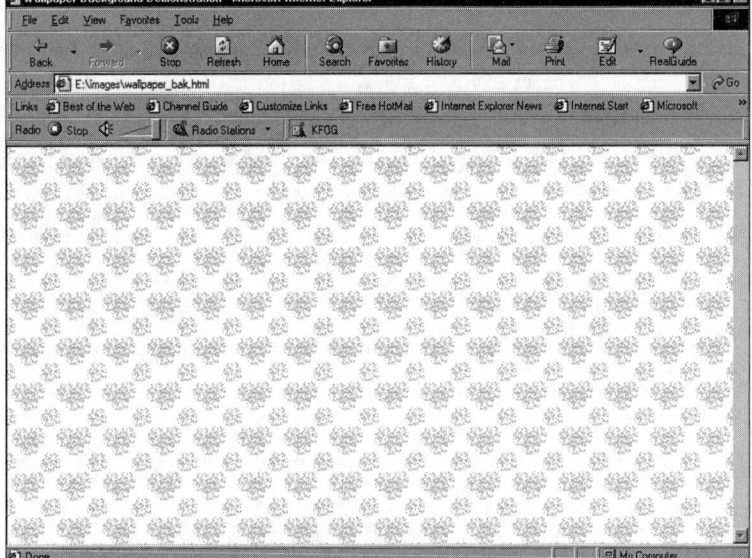

MARGIN TILES

Margin tiles are quite prevalent on the Web. Essentially, two types of margin tiles exist:

- **Functional**—This is a background margin tile that uses the margin space for navigation or other graphic and text information. Because it will be a significant part of your color and design scheme, functional margin design means making sure text, links, and other functional items can be seen and integrated into the margin's space and design (see Figure 29.9).

■ **Decorative**—Decorative margins serve to enhance a design aesthetically. They have no function other than to provide visual interest to a page (see Figure 29.10).

Figure 29.9
This site makes use of a functional margin background by using it to present the navigation for the site.

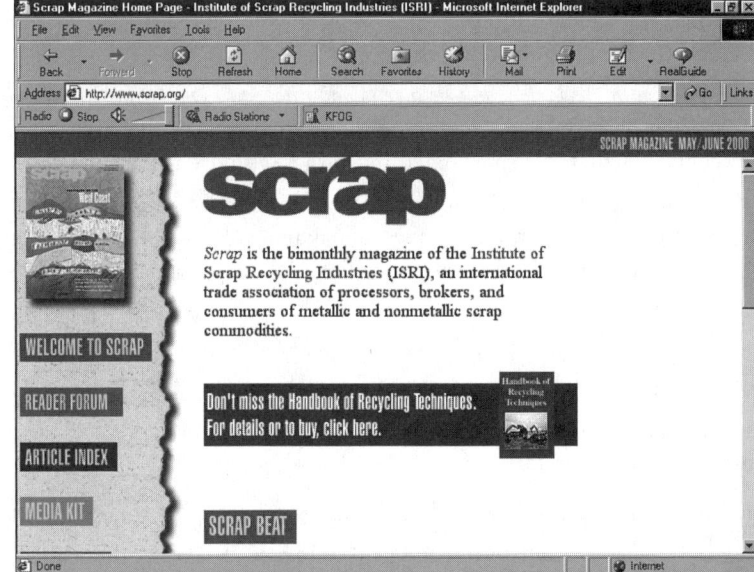

Figure 29.10
This Web site uses a decorative margin background to give an air of sophistication and elegance to the site. The design within the margin portion of the tile can be decorative, as can the body portion. You can use flat areas of color or texture—whatever your imagination and creative influences suggest. However, always lean toward readability!

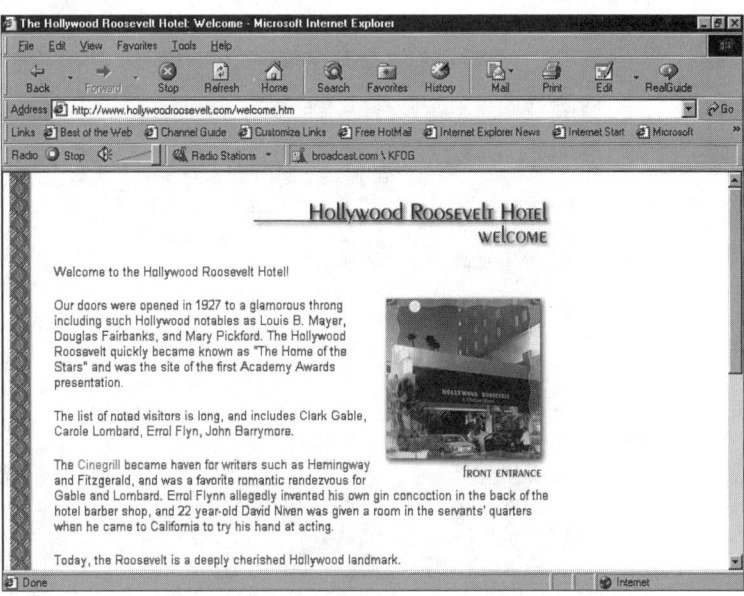

For effective margin tile design, follow these tips:

- *Create long tiles, anticipating various screen resolutions.* You'll want your background margin tiles to be *at least* 1,024 pixels wide. You might even consider making them 1,600 pixels wide, but it's up to you and the awareness of your audience. Choose longer if many of them are using very high resolution monitors; 1,024 is a typical background margin-tile width for standard Internet sites. Height will range from around 50 pixels to 250 pixels or so, depending on your design.

- *Design using few colors, but be sure to add interest by employing shadow, shape, or texture.* Flat margin tiles are very common on the Web. Although they're not unattractive, challenge yourself a bit and create something with a bit more verve.

- *Because you have to anticipate a wide range of resolutions, design your image to size.* If you're creating a right margin, this means making sure that the design begins within the allotted visual space of 595 pixels. Your image should look good no matter the viewing resolution!

FUNCTIONAL

In this case, I'm going to use Macromedia Fireworks 3.0 to create a functional right-margin image with color and texture:

1. Open Fireworks and select File, New.

2. In the New Document dialog box (see Figure 29.11), set the width of your image (I set mine at 1,024) and the height (mine is set for 50). Select your background color; I used a Web-safe lilac.

Figure 29.11
The New Document dialog box in Fireworks enables you to set the size, resolution, and canvas color (or transparency) for the new image.

PART

VI

CH

29

3. Fireworks has some excellent preset texture fills that you can modify. Because I want my margin to be functional, but fun, I'm going to fill it with an interesting texture.

4. Choose the rectangle from the left side of the tools palette.

5. From the Modify menu, select Fill.

6. You can now choose the fill type and intensity you want. My settings are solid, anti-aliased, Fiber (set to 25%).

7. At 450 pixels (remember, we want this to work at 640 resolution), start the rectangle and pull it over to the end of the graphic.

8. Fireworks will fill your graphic with the texture.

9. Go to File, Export.

10. The Export preview will give you a variety of options. I chose to save as a GIF, with the Web Palette, no transparency. I named the file `right_margin.gif`. See Figure 29.12 for the results.

Figure 29.12
A textured, functional margin background.

DECORATIVE

To create a decorative margin graphic, simply place the decorative element as a strip along the left, right, or top margin. Bottom margins might get lost as they won't be immediately seen on longer pages.

Figure 29.13 shows a modification of the functional design I created in the previous exercise, this time designed as a decorative background.

Figure 29.13
A decorative margin helps create a look and feel for a page. Decorative margins are aesthetic rather than functional devices.

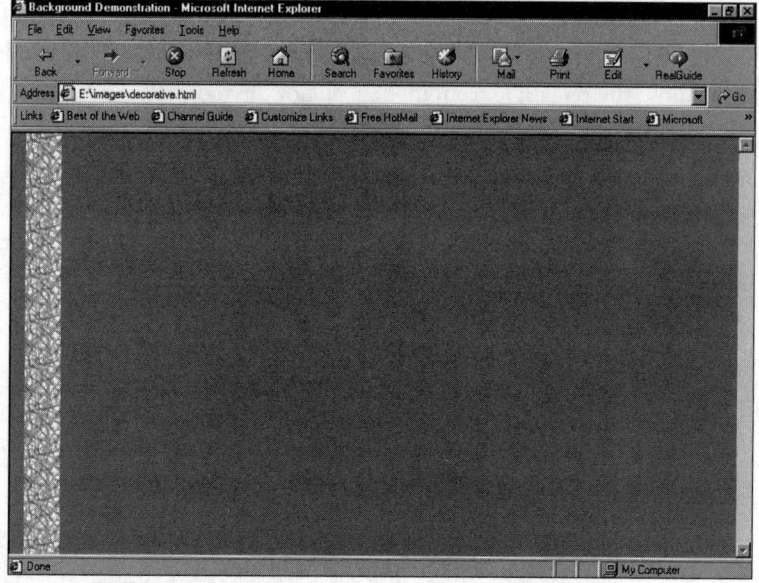

WATERMARK STYLE

Watermarks (Figure 21.14)are especially difficult to create because of the repetitive issue. The idea with watermarks is to keep them simple, with few, flat colors, keeping file sizes low.

I created a watermark using Photoshop. First, I created a very large tile, 1,024×1,200 pixels. This way I know that no matter the resolution, the effect will generally be the same.

I then drew a stylized wave shape onto the tile. I used two colors: white and bright yellow, and optimized the GIF as an 8-bit file. My total file size for this dimensionally large background? 5KB total!

Now when I add XHTML and content to the design, I can use a table to fix the information securely in place. Then, whether the page is viewed at 640×480 resolution or higher, the page is visually attractive.

HEADER GRAPHICS

Headers are used to identify a site and a page within a site. One type of header is the *splash* header. This typically fills a larger piece of real estate on the opening page only. It identifies the site with the company logo or brand and sets the visual tone for the rest of the site.

A *page* header is smaller, but still boldly visible along the top and left, middle, or right of an internal page.

Figure 29.14
A watermark-style background (reduced to show complete design).

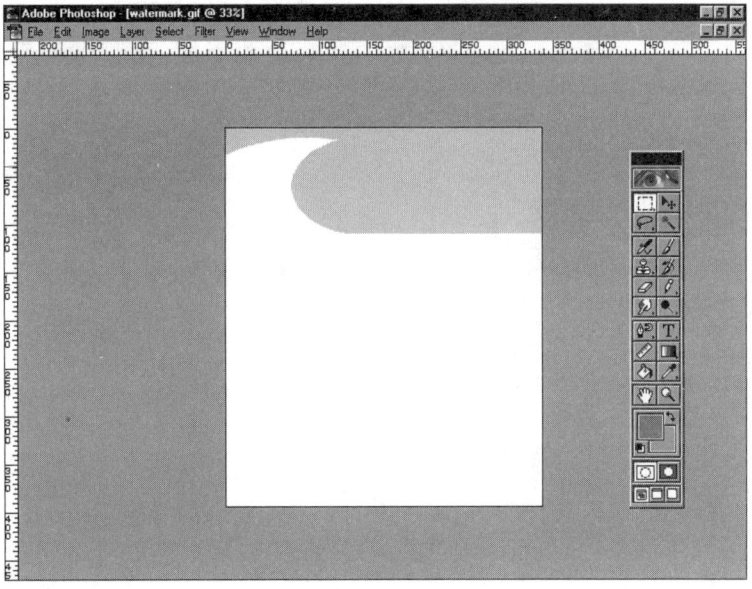

BUILDING A SPLASH DESIGN

In this case, let's create a splash header for the wallpaper background graphic we made in the first exercise.

Because I want to work with interesting type, I'm going to first work in Adobe Illustrator. You can always set type within your favorite imaging program, but Illustrator offers strong typographic options, such as the curving type I'm going to use on this splash:

1. In Illustrator, select File, New.
2. With the Ellipse tool, draw a elliptical path.
3. Select your font, font size, and color, and type along the uppermost curve (see Figure 29.15).
4. Add any other text you'd like.
5. Save the file as an EPS, with font information intact.

Now you'll want to rasterize, crop, and edit the image, which you'll do in Photoshop:

1. Open the EPS file you just created. Be sure to switch from CMYK to RGB color.
2. Crop the file.
3. Add a new layer.
4. Fill the layer with a color suitable for transparency.
5. Send the layer to the back.
6. Flatten the image.
7. From the Image menu, select mode.

Figure 29.15
Drawing along an Illustrator path allows you to create some really spectacular effects with your text.

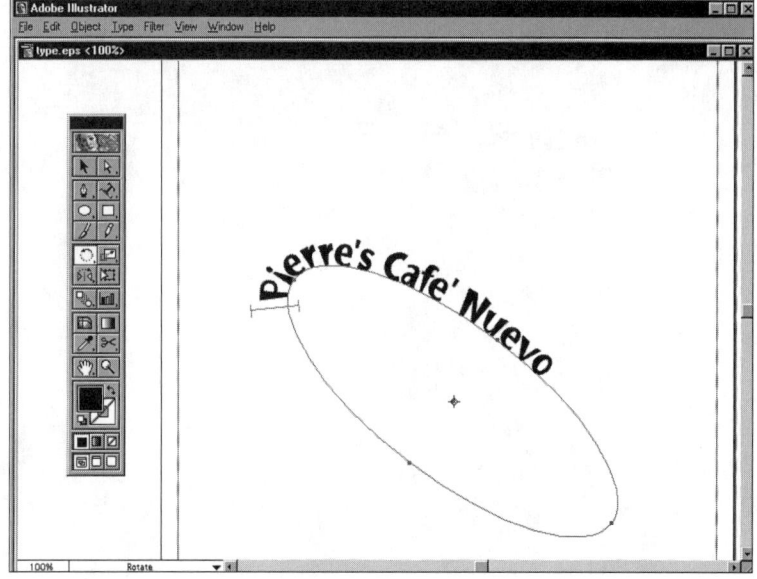

8. Index the colors.

9. Select File, Export.

10. Export the file as a GIF89, processing it as a transparent and interlaced file.

11. Save the file as `splash.gif`.

In Figure 29.16, you can see my splash graphic set over my wallpaper background.

Figure 29.16
The splash graphic in place. The transparency allows the image to flow naturally with the background, creating fluid movement rather than rigid design.

Now, you can create an internal page header using Fireworks (or another imaging software). In this case, I'm going to create a header for the functional background made earlier. My header is a transparent GIF, but depending on your needs, you might choose to use GIF or JPEG format:

1. In Fireworks, select File, New.

2. Set up the graphic to be 400×50 pixels.

3. Fill the image with a color suitable for transparency.

4. From the Window menu, make sure Layers is selected.

5. Create a new layer using the drop down menu.

6. On this layer, set your type, using the Fireworks type tool.

7. When you're satisfied with the look of your graphic, select File, Export.

8. Export as a GIF or JPEG, depending upon your needs.

9. Save the file.

10. Add the file to your HTML and view the results (see Figure 29.17).

Figure 29.17
An internal page header helps keep a visitor oriented within a site, as well as adding visual interest to the page.

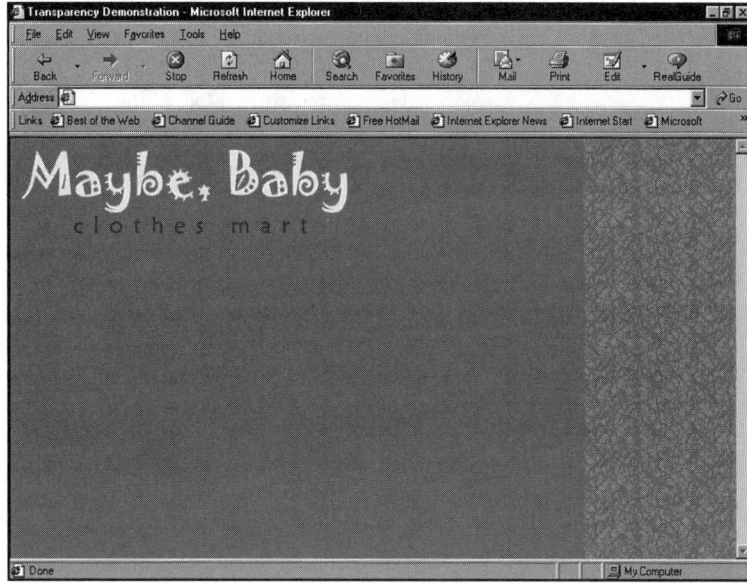

Tip from

Wherever you have the option to anti-alias type, you should do so when the type is 11 points or higher. This will smooth out the lines, preventing jagged type. However, at smaller sizes, type sometimes is more clear with anti-aliasing turned off.

BUTTONS

Button, button, who's got the button?

You will, of course, in just a few minutes!

Navigational buttons can be made up of text, images, or a combination of both. You can go simple by using a static navigation button as a link. Or you might prefer to create visually active buttons, which can be achieved using JavaScript.

→ To learn how to do JavaScript mouseovers, **see** Chapter 20, "Adding JavaScript to XHTML Documents," **p. 445**.

I'm going to show you two kinds of buttons: a beveled button, and a simple method of doing mouseover text buttons.

 Thought your designing was going well until you tested your page in a browser and found that your graphics were ruining your overall design? See "Bevels, Shadows, and Effects" in the "Troubleshooting" section near the end of this chapter for some tips on how to make your graphics work well together without overdoing it.

CREATING A BEVELED BUTTON

For this exercise, I'm going to use Photoshop in combination with the Extensis Photo Bevel plug-in. You can use any imaging program; many have bevel effects built right in (as does Photoshop, but I want to give you an example of plug-in use). But if it does not, many of the beveling plug-ins work with a variety of programs, such as Paint Shop Pro:

1. In Photoshop, create a new file that is 100×50 pixels.
2. Fill with the color of your choice (Select All, Edit, Fill).
3. Using the text tool, choose your typeface and type size.
4. Set your type with the navigational icon or text.
5. Flatten the image (Layer, Flatten Image).

Now it's time to create the bevel.

1. From the Filter menu, select Extensis Photo Bevel.
2. The Extensis interface will pop up with your image inside (see Figure 29.18).
3. Define the bevel settings until you find a setting you like.
4. Click Apply.
5. Optimize the graphic.
6. Save as home_button.gif.

Figure 29.18
The Extensis Photo Bevel plug-in.

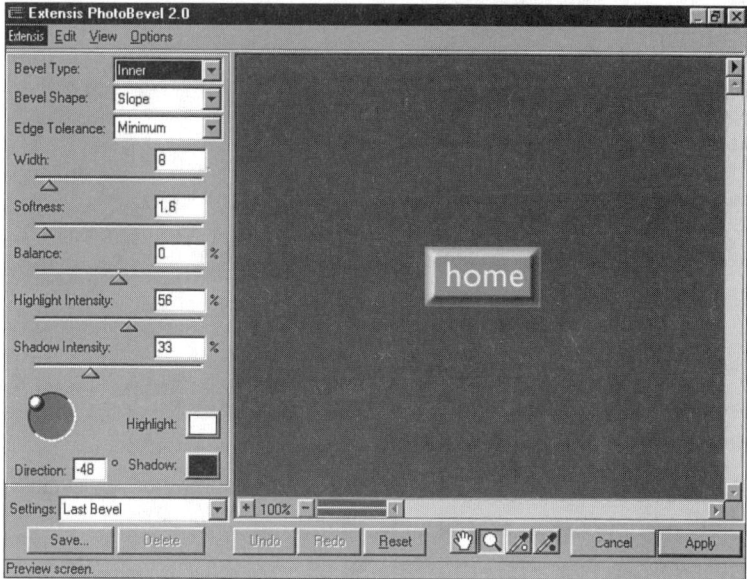

You can now add the button to your page.

CREATING A BUTTON FOR JAVASCRIPT MOUSEOVERS

Use this method with any imaging program that supports layers, including Photoshop, Paint Shop Pro, Adobe LiveMotion, and Fireworks. I'm going to do the exercise in Photoshop:

1. Create a new file to the appropriate size and dimension of your button(s). I'm creating a 100×25 pixel file.
2. Fill the background layer with the color appropriate to your design.
3. Now add a new layer: Layer, New, Layer.
4. Select the Type tool and set the type for your standard button (the button people will see on load, or if they don't support JavaScript) on the new layer.
5. Position the type.
6. Make a copy of the type layer.
7. Fill the copy with the mouseover color.

    You should now have a three-layer graphic: background color, onload type, and mouseover type, as shown in Figure 29.19.

Figure 29.19
The three layers ready for individual export will work together to give the on/off effect on mouseover.

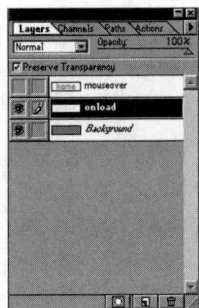

8. Deselect the mouseover layer.

9. Export this combination as a GIF89, File, Export, GIF.

10. Save that file as home_1.gif.

11. Now deselect the onload layer, and reselect the mouseover layer.

12. Repeat the Export process and save this file as home_2.gif.

You now have the makings of an attractive mouseover. The nice thing about this process is that the text remains in the exact position.

Tip from molly

Creating JavaScript mouseovers using Photoshop Layers helps you avoid one of the most common problems—slight shifting due to inexact measuring.

BARS AND RULES

At times you might like an effective, decorative bar or rule to demarcate visual sections of a document.

If you're going to create your own bar, I'd recommend the following:

- Don't stretch the bar from margin to margin. Instead, make a bar that is either centered with some whitespace to either side or aligned to the right or left. Cutting off the margins separates space dramatically and could cause disruption in the cohesiveness of both the design and the experience of the content.

- Use a treatment such as a drop shadow, curved or angled lines, something that's hand drawn, or broken lines—anything to give the rule a fresh look.

In this example, I'm going use type to create my horizontal rule. I selected a typeface and then used the tilde symbol to create a wavy look.

Then I modified the drawing by adding a drop shadow. You can use any number of built-in imaging tools to do this. I did it by creating another layer in Photoshop, filling that duplicate with black, offsetting it 2 pixels to the right, then 2 pixels down, dropping the opacity to 70%, and finally, applying a Guassian blur of 2.5 to the shadow. Figure 29.20 shows how the rule looks.

Figure 29.20
A simple but attractive horizontal rule can perk up any Web page.

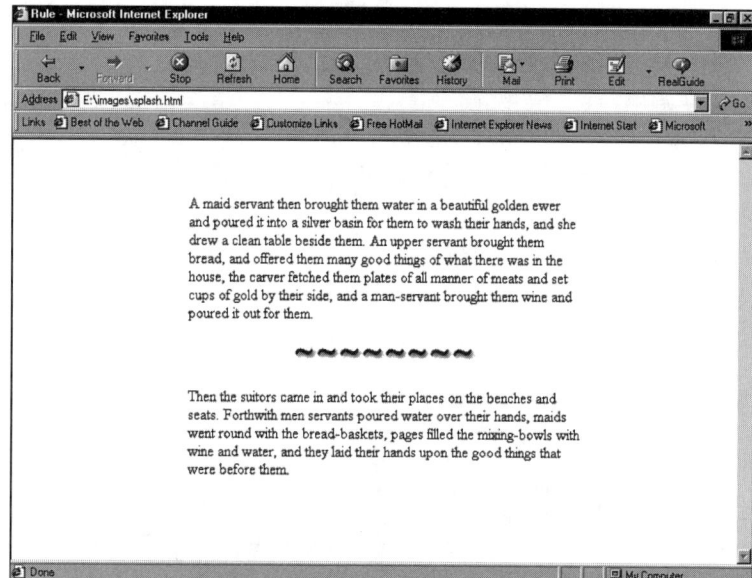

SPOT ART

Spot art serves to enhance and accentuate text. It can be clip art or photographs.

To make spot art stand out from the norm, it's fun to add edges, shadows, or bevels for effect. However, you do have to be careful with the use of effects because of the additional weight they can add to a page.

Tip from

Effects should be planned so that they are consistent and blend well with the overall design.

Hand-drawn art, cartoons, and clip art can add variety and personality to your sites, too.

Whichever you choose, you should be consistent and creative—not conflicting and cliché—throughout a site. It always surprises me to find that people have created a slick graphic only to mix it with a piece of overused, worn clip art!

Another concern is dimension. Spot art is akin to italic or bold on a page—it's about emphasis, not dominance. You want your spot art to blend well into the overall scheme of your design. Pay close attention not only to the dimension in relation to the screen size, but from one photo to another.

PHOTOGRAPHIC TECHNIQUES

I often like to add edge effects to my photos, and to do this I'm especially fond of the Auto/FX photographic edge series. In this example I'm going to take a photo and add an edge to it:

Note Visit `http://www.autofx.com/` for a free trial download of a photographic edge. You can add Auto/FX to Paint Shop Pro or Photoshop.

1. In your imaging program, crop and size the photo to your taste.
2. Choose Filter, Auto F/X, and then your desired filter.
3. The Auto F/X interface will open (see Figure 29.21).

Figure 29.21
The Auto F/X interface is quick and simple to use.

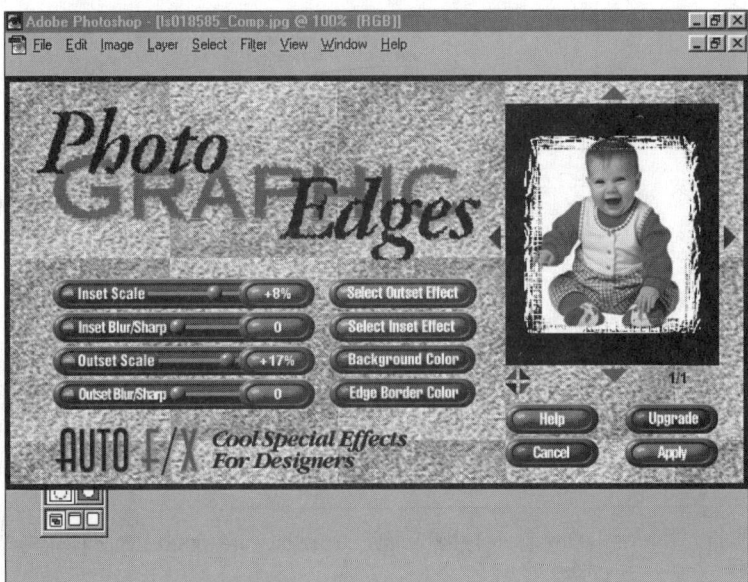

4. Make your modifications using the sliders and preview pane.
5. Apply the effect.
6. Save the file (usually this will be a JPEG). My file is `photo_1.jpg`.

Figure 29.22 shows the edge results.

Figure 29.22
A treated photo on a Web page. The result is interesting as it departs from the hard edges so frequently found on the Web.

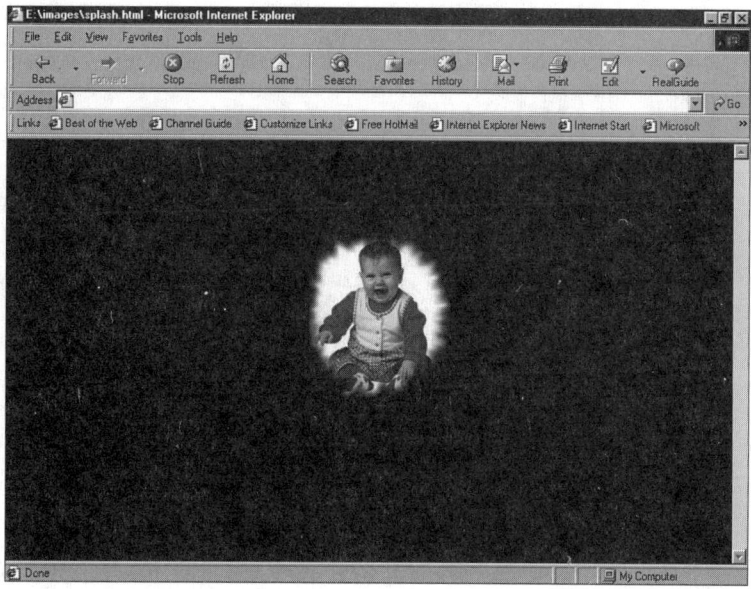

SPLICING GRAPHICS

One of the more interesting uses of graphics is to use a table to create a grid system to place pieces of a whole image. This approach is sensible when you want to animate sections of a larger image or place images in otherwise difficult to reach places on the browser page, such as slightly left of center. Instead of using one really big graphic to accommodate this look, designers splice the graphics, keeping the overall weight down and the load time faster.

In Figure 29.23, I've used Adobe LiveMotion to create a Web-based image that uses numerous pieces. LiveMotion splices the graphics for you, which is very convenient. It even generates the code! The problem is, it generates HTML rather than XHTML, so to be compliant, I went in and refashioned the code into XHTML.

If this image had been created as one graphic, it would have weighed quite a bit. What's more, the navigation has mouseover states, which require JavaScript for the individual graphics, or to be exported to Flash. By splicing the image and placing it within a table, the weight of any standard image is reduced, and so is the page's load time.

More and more tools are becoming available to help with this process. Macromedia Fireworks 3.0 is another example. Many designers also create grid systems in Photoshop and then cut up the separate images.

Figure 29.23
An image that is actually made up of several spliced images.

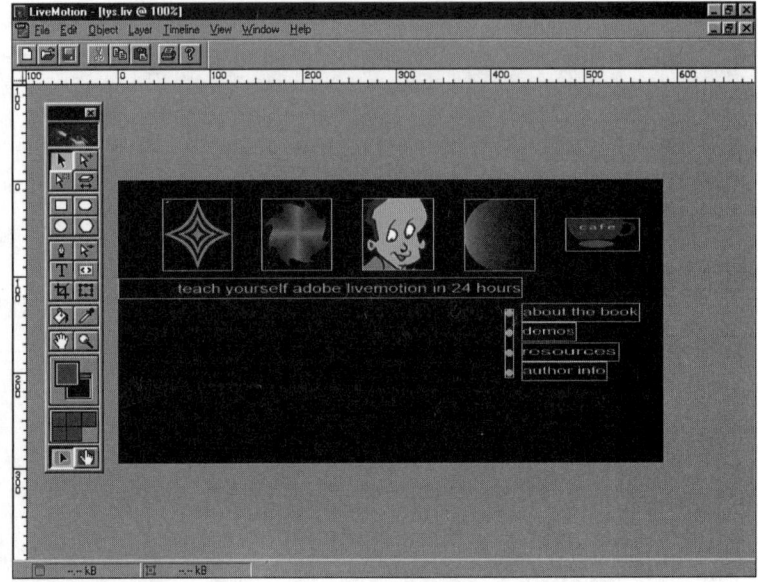

TROUBLESHOOTING

BEVELS, SHADOWS, AND EFFECTS

I wanted to add some panache to my page, so I grabbed up all the cool effects and filters I could find and got to work. The designing is going great, but the results are a bit busy—what happened?

I cannot reiterate that effects must be planned and appropriate to the design. Consistency is a big factor, too. You definitely do not want to do something just because you can.

In fact, bevels and shadow effects have been overused (Figure 29.24). They are sometimes exactly what is needed (Figure 29.25), but think carefully before using any effects. And when you do use them, do so consistently.

Figure 29.24
I've used bevels on every image on this page. It's too much! Cut down on effects for better results.

Figure 29.25
In this case, I've used the bevel only on the spot art, and left the header and navigation buttons consistently plain. This effect is more subtle and less overdone.

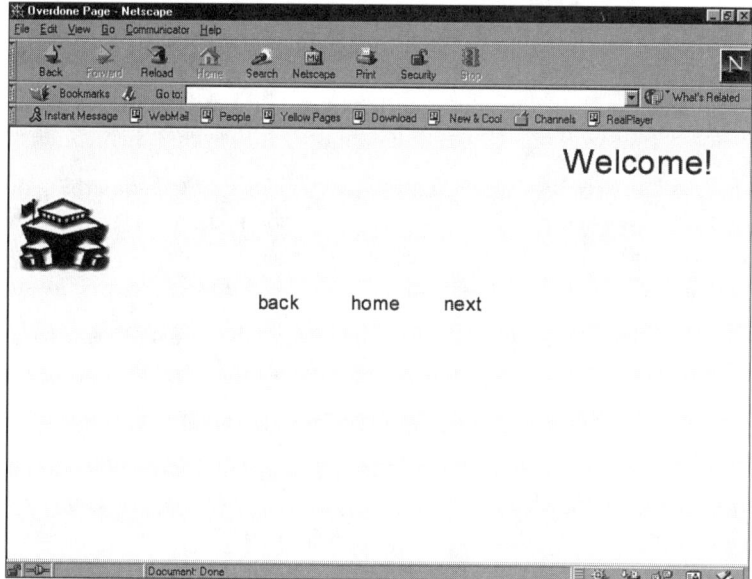

DESIGNING FOR THE REAL WORLD

A PROFESSIONAL'S APPROACH TO DESIGNING THE WEB: INTERVIEW WITH DESIGNER AMY BURNHAM

Amy Burnham is a professional graphic and Web graphic designer who has created the visual identity for sites such as the Weekly Wire, Tucson Weekly, DesertNet, and Buffalo Exchange.

I interviewed Amy about her work as a Web designer.

Amy, what process do you use when you sit down to determine the look and feel of a site?

I always start with brainstorming on paper—identifying the design problem, working out whatever mood or associated imagery would work for the project, just lists of words really to get me thinking in the right vein. I also clarify what the hierarchy of the site will be by working up a site map or flow chart, and then determine what the navigation options will be on each page or level of the site.

From there I thumbnail 20–50 sketches and then work up the best 2 or 3 or 4 in Photoshop. It's funny because sometimes the writing part seems unnecessary, especially if I feel I'm really familiar with a project, but anytime I've tried to shortcut that step it's backfired on me and I've had to go back to it.

I definitely have to think projects out mentally first. Then free-association sketching comes much easier too. I like to work on the thumbnails over a period of days if the timeframe of the job allows, working on it and then putting it away and then coming back to it later.

The best ideas always come when I've had a chance to put something on the back burner and let my subconscious pick at it. That way you make associations with other things around you that might not seem to be related—whether it's whatever books or magazines you're reading, movies, elements in nature, dreams, or things in the grocery store!

I also like to have a couple days at the end when the initial mockups are "done." It's the finessing that comes at this point that really makes a difference in the design.

How do you determine the graphic effects you'll use on a site?

I always base the treatments on whatever the look and feel I'm going for is. That sounds obvious but it's important to think out what you're trying to accomplish before you start thinking about what effects to use—think about what you want to achieve, and then figure out how to do it instead of the other way around.

With that said, I generally try to incorporate mouseovers whenever possible, as long as I can keep the file size down. I like the interactive, tactile feel of it, especially if they're done well. Drop shadows are so overused although there are instances where I'll still use them. But too often they're used as a default, "Oh, its a Web site, it needs to be 3D" kind of thing. Not that depth is a bad thing; often you want to imply some depth somehow, but I'd rather explore other ways like relative size and different planes than using the requisite drop shadow. It's not always the best solution.

What are your favorite, most-used Web design software tools? Anything you specifically do NOT like or use?

Photoshop is where I do close to 90% of my work on computer. The other 10% is probably split between ImageReady, which I use for optimizing images and creating GIF animations, and Quark Xpress to quickly lay out text.

The only software I'd say I'd never use is some of the instant 3-D software and instant filter effects. They're so overused and obviously computer generated that they're just embarrassing to look at. Design is all about coming up with individual solutions to unique problems and those programs aren't the solution to anything.

Where do you get stock art, fonts, and other materials for your work?

I use a lot of found imagery—string, fabric, leaves, jewelry, stamps, knickknacks, rocks, etc.—in conjunction with my scanner to capture textures or objects to use solo or as part of a larger piece. I also use a Polaroid camera, not a digital camera, to capture images, scanning the photos to use themselves or as templates for illustrations.

For stock photos and illustrations, Photodisc and Artville are very useful and immediate. I also love to use illustrators if the budget allows it.

Although all designers will find their own way of working, Amy Burnham's production approaches provide a great example of a professional graphic designer who has moved her method from the print world into that of the Web. The precise method enables her to work faster as well as create better-looking sites as a result of her brainstorming, planning, and professional techniques.

CHAPTER **30**

DESIGNING SPECIALTY GRAPHICS

In this chapter

EXPLORING SPECIALTY GRAPHICS

There are several types of graphics that I consider *specialty* graphics. The reason I separate these from standard Web page graphics is that you won't always want to use them. These graphics are reserved for specific circumstances.

Graphics covered in this chapter are

- **Imagemaps**—Imagemaps are a single graphic image that can be used for multiple links.
- **Animated GIFs**—Use animated GIFs to add movement to a page or for advertising purposes.
- **Advertising banners**—Gain visibility for your Web site through the use of ad banners.

For some, these image types might be familiar. I'm going to walk you through the creation of a variety of images to give newcomers guidelines on how to create specialty images, and for old hats, a refresher course with some tips and techniques that might enable you to work faster and smarter.

IMAGEMAPS

Imagemaps allow a designer to break a single image down into multiple sections of varying shapes. Each of those sections then can be linked to a different Web page.

Although this sounds convenient, and although imagemaps have certainly been a significant part of Web design for some time, the reality is that they are becoming less present on professional sites. Whether this has to do with the fact that more sophisticated and attractive technologies, such as JavaScript mouseovers, are taking precedence over imagemapping, or that mapping is too fixed for today's regularly updated Web sites is difficult to determine.

→ To learn how to create mouseover effects, **see** Chapter 20, "Adding JavaScript to XHTML Documents," **p. 445**.

Despite these changes, the technology and tools related to mapping have remained current, and you will certainly want to add the technique to your repertoire of graphic skills.

IMAGEMAPPING TOOLS

There are several kind of imagemapping tools. They range from those applications packaged with or subsidiary to larger imaging, HTML, or multimedia programs, such as Adobe LiveMotion, Dreamweaver, FrontPage, and even Macromedia Flash.

Standalone mapping tools also are popular. They include the following:

- **MapEdit**—This popular, inexpensive shareware program is available for download from Boutell at **http://www.boutell.com/mapedit/**. Windows and Macintosh platforms are supported.
- **MapMaker**—From TwinMoon, MapMaker makes excellent client- and server-side maps. It's only available for the Macintosh at **http://www.kickinit.net/mapmaker/** (see Figure 30.1).

- **LiveImage**—This is a user-friendly mapping tool. Expanded features include a link checker for your mapped URLs as well as drop-and-drag support. For Windows platforms only at `http://www.mediatec.com/`.

- **Web Hotspots**—Imagemap Editor—Another popular imagemap editor with HTML, client-side and server-side output at `http://www.1automata.com/hotspots/`.

Figure 30.1
MapMaker from TwinMoon for the Macintosh makes imagemapping a breeze.

Another interesting approach is to use an online mapping utility, such as CIMM, the Clickable Image Map Maker. Enter the location of the graphic to be mapped (see Figure 30.2), and follow the online instructions to map your graphic effectively.

Figure 30.2
Mapping an image right online with CIMM!

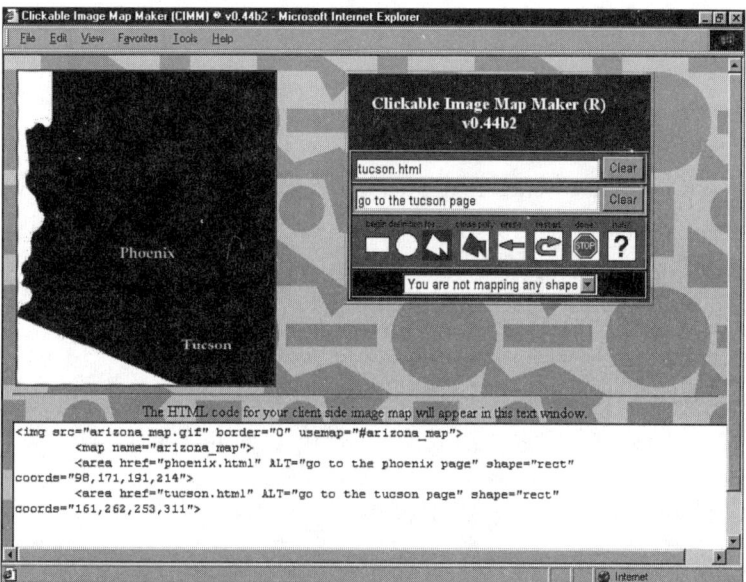

METHODS

There are two methods for imagemapping. The old-fashioned method is server-sided mapping, which requires the browser to work with the server to interpret your imagemap.

The newer, more popular, method is client-side mapping. This means that the browser can interpret the map data without relying on the server to do so.

Both methods originally required understanding the mapping of coordinates. Fortunately, all of the tools mentioned in the imagemap tools section map coordinates for you, no matter the shape of your defined area.

The client-side mapping technique is preferred, but because some older browsers don't support it, many individuals combine the two techniques, ensuring that no matter the browser, the visitor will be able to use the imagemap.

CLIENT-SIDE MAPPING

Client-side maps are fast and stable because they rely on the browser to do the interpretation for them.

Listing 30.1 is an example of a client-side mapping code. Note that the image, mymap.gif, includes the #usemap attribute to work.

LISTING 30.1   CLIENT-SIDE IMAGEMAPPING SYNTAX

```
<!DOCTYPE html PUBLIC "-//W3C//DTD XHTML 1.0 Transitional//EN"
"http://www.w3.org/TR/xhtml1/DTD/xhtml1-transitional.dtd">
<html xmlns="http://www.w3.org/1999/xhtml">
<head>
<title>Contact Our Company</title>
</head>
<body>
<h2>Contact Our Company</h2>
<p>For contact information, please select a city from the map below.</p>
<img src="images/arizona_map.gif" width="278" height="328" border="0"
alt="imagemap of arizona" usemap="#arizona_map" />
<map name="arizona_map">
<area shape="rect" alt="contact info for phoenix office"
coords="86,173,245,294" href="phoenix.html" />
<area shape="rect" alt="click for tucson contact information"
coords="152,245,259,291" href="tucson.html" />
<area shape="default" nohref />
</map>
```

```
</body>

</html>
```

All of the information required to make this map active is now included along with the XHTML. This image is active.

Note

The `nohref` attribute means that if an individual clicks outside the defined areas, no action will occur.

 Having trouble with links in your imagemap not working properly? See "Links Won't Work" in the "Troubleshooting" section near the end of this chapter for some timely tips on how to fix this problem.

SERVER-SIDE MAPPING

To accommodate older browsers, many coders like to use this approach to mapping. To do this, you have to create a map file with the coordinate locations within it, and save it with a `.map` extension.

This type of imagemapping becomes more complicated because of several factors:

- The `.map` file will have to reside on the server. Depending on your ISP, this might be a designated spot. Either way, you'll have to find out where your ISP would like you to store this map—it will affect the way you write the HTML output.
- There are two kinds of map files. One is NCSA style; the other is CERN style. Typically, you'll want to use NCSA, but some servers, such as Microsoft's Information Server, require the CERN style. Once again, you'll have to check with your provider before mapping your image to a server.
- Because server-side mapping relies on CGI, you'll be required to find out from your ISP where the mapping utility is and what its name is.

Here's an example of NCSA map code:

```
#contact info for phoenix office
rect phoenix.html 86,173, 245,294
#click for tucson contact information
rect tucson.html 152,245, 259,291
```

Here's the same map in CERN format:

```
rect (86,173) (245,294) phoenix.html
rect (152,245) (259,291) tucson.html
```

Notice that the information is not only ordered differently, but the CERN map leaves out alternate text information shown in the NCSA code.

If you have the information necessary from your ISP, you are now ready to add the map data to your XHTML. Server-side imagemaps require an attribute added to the IMG tag known as `ismap`:

```
<img src="images/arizona_map.gif" width="278" height="328" border="0"
alt="imagemap of arizona" ismap />
```

This lets the server know that this is a mapped image.

To invoke the script that will interpret the imagemap, you'll need to link your image. Listing 30.2 shows the code for an XHTML page with an NCSA-style server-side imagemap.

LISTING 30.2 SERVER-SIDE IMAGEMAPPING SYNTAX

```
<!DOCTYPE html PUBLIC "-//W3C//DTD XHTML 1.0 Transitional//EN"
"http://www.w3.org/TR/xhtml1/DTD/xhtml1-transitional.dtd">
<html xmlns="http://www.w3.org/1999/xhtml">
<head>
<title>Contact Our Company</title>
</head>
<body>
<h2>Contact Our Company</h2>
<p>For contact information, please select a city from the map below.</p>
<a href="/cgi-bin/contact.map"><img src="images/arizona_map.gif" width="278"
height="328" border="0" alt="imagemap of arizona" ismap /></a>
</body>
</html>
```

If you've uploaded the appropriate .map file to the correct area on your server, and you've linked to the correct area and file on that server within your XHTML, this map will now be active.

COMBINATION MAPPING

If you'd like to embrace the power of the client-side map but use the server-side backup just in case, you can combine server- and client-side syntax. What you do in this case is create all of the information required for the client-side map, and then upload it to your server. Then, you add the XHTML required to the image. Once that's done, include the coordinates and the XHTML server-side within the code that you've just created for the client-side map.

> **Note**
> The browser will always interpret the client-side map first. This way, no trip to the server will be taken if not necessary.

Your final XHTML page should resemble the code in Listing 30.3.

LISTING 30.3 COMBINATION IMAGEMAPPING SYNTAX

```
<!DOCTYPE html PUBLIC "-//W3C//DTD XHTML 1.0 Transitional//EN"
"http://www.w3.org/TR/xhtml1/DTD/xhtml1-transitional.dtd">
```

```
<html xmlns="http://www.w3.org/1999/xhtml">

<head>

<title>Contact Our Company</title>

</head>

<body>

<h2>Contact Our Company</h2>

<p>For contact information, please select a city from the map below.</p>

<p><a href="/cgi-bin/contact.map"><img src="images/arizona_map.gif" width="278"

height="328" border="0" alt="imagemap of arizona"

usemap="#arizona_map" ismap /></a>

<map name="arizona_map">

<area shape="rect" alt="contact info for phoenix office"

coords="86,173,245,294" href="phoenix.html" />

<area shape="rect" alt="click for tucson contact information"s

coords="152,245,259,291" href="tucson.html" />

<area shape="default" nohref />

</map>

</body>

</html>
```

Your client- and server-side bases are now completely covered (see Figure 30.3).

Figure 30.3
An imagemap that is both client- and server-sided ensures that even site visitors with older browsers will be able to use the map.

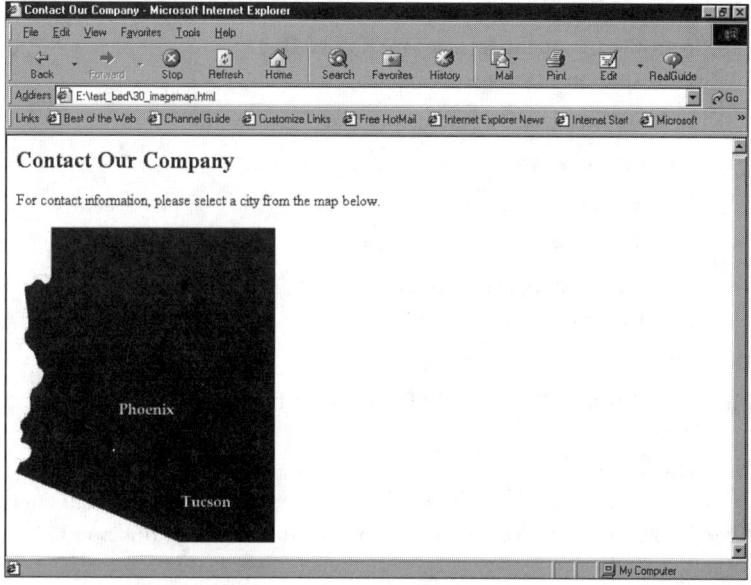

APPLICATION

In this section, you will find an exercise to take you through the creation of an imagemap.

Note

For this example, I use MapEdit, which is available for both Macintosh and Windows platforms. It also will help you create both client- and server-side imagemaps.

The first step in mapping an image is to select an image appropriate for mapping. This means an image with distinct regions or that logically lends itself to mapping, such as the literal map of Arizona I'm using in this sample.

MapEdit prefers that you code your image into XHTML first:

1. Add your image to a standard XHTML page.

   ```
   <!DOCTYPE html PUBLIC "-//W3C//DTD XHTML 1.0 Transitional//EN"
   "http://www.w3.org/TR/xhtml1/DTD/xhtml1-transitional.dtd">
   <html xmlns="http://www.w3.org/1999/xhtml">
   <head>
   <title>Contact Our Company</title>
   </head>
   <body>
   <h2>Contact Our Company</h2>
   <p>For contact information, please select a city from the map below.</p>
   <img src="images/arizona_map.gif" width="278" height="328" border="0"
   alt="image
   map of arizona" />
   </body>
   </html>
   ```

2. Save the file as image_map.html.

3. Open MapEdit.

4. From the File menu, select Open HTML Document. This will cause a dialog box with the images on that page to appear.

5. Highlight the image to be mapped and click OK.

6. MapEdit will now load your image.

7. Now select the shape you'd like to use for the mapped area. I've chosen the rectangle.

8. Hold the mouse down and draw the first area to be mapped.

9. Right-click the mouse, and enter the desired URL and any additional information into the dialog box (see Figure 30.4).

10. Click OK.

11. Repeat steps 7–10 until all of your desired areas are mapped.

Now you'll want to save your file. To save the file as a .map file for server-side mapping, go to the File menu and select Export Old Server Map. Give the map a name, and then select Save. You'll be prompted to save for NCSA or CERN at this point.

Figure 30.4
Entering a URL and comments into MapEdit. Be sure to type your URLs correctly, or you'll end up with a dead link.

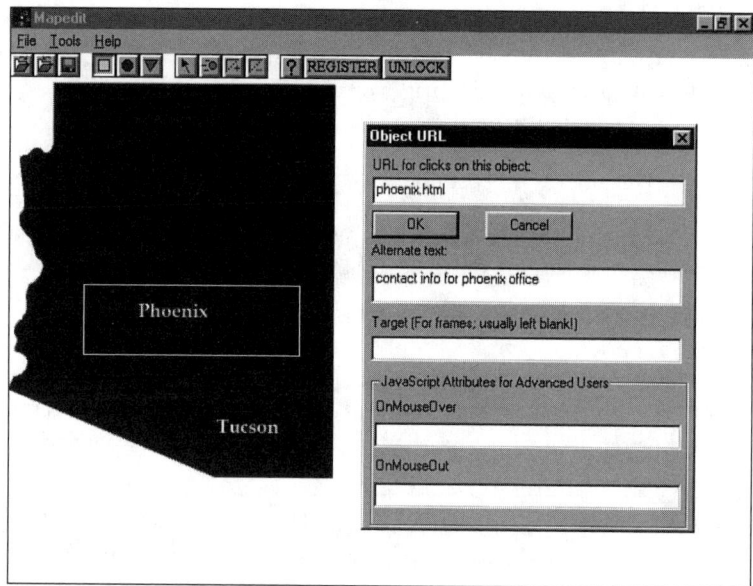

To save the file as a client-side imagemap, select Save As from the File menu. You'll then be prompted to save your information to an HTML file. All of the imagemapping coordinates will be placed directly into that file.

ANIMATED GIFs

Another popular specialty graphic is the Animated GIF. GIF animations exploit a looping process in the GIF89a technology. Compact in size and easy to make, Animated GIFs are a great way to give a page some verve.

→ There are many tools available for making Animated GIFs; **see** Chapter 27, "Web Graphic Tools and Professional Tools," **p. 561**.

> **Caution**
>
> It's important to keep in mind that animations should enhance, but never detract from, a page's design. Many enthusiastic individuals will place more than one animation on a page. Combine this with mouseovers, audio, and other multimedia, and you will lose your message—and your audience—very quickly. Always use a light hand when adding active media to a page.

TOOLS

I'm going to show you how to make an animated GIF using GIF Construction Set and Photoshop. No matter your preferred imaging and animation tools, the methods are very similar, and my example will serve to get you started making GIF animations right away.

You will first need to create the individual images used within the animation. Known as *cells*, imagine each individual image as being a unique action within the animation.

You can use this concept to be as simple or complex as you want. However, I recommend starting out with something quite simple. You should always think about what you're going to need—any specific graphic images or text—in advance. It's also good to know the dimensions of the animation, so you can create or modify your cells to that size.

Tip from 	Try to select images that are going to be lightweight, because you always want to keep your individual file weight down. This will help when you combine all the images into the final format. The smaller the input, the less heavy the output.

METHODS

My plan is to create an animation that reads "I love my cat." However, the words "love" and "cat" will be replaced with a heart and the image of a cat, respectively:

Note	To get the heart and cat, I visited ArtToday at `http://www.arttoday.com/` where I'm a member. I went to the clip art section and did a search for a heart and then a cat.

1. Open an imaging program (in my case, Photoshop).
2. Create the first image in the series. Because the image is 100×100 pixels, select File, New, and then input the file dimensions and type **(RGB)**.
3. Because the first word is "I," select the typeface and set the type by using the Type Tool.
4. Position the type to the center.
5. Flatten the image.
6. Optimize the image as a GIF.
7. Save the file as `image_1.gif`.

To create the next image:

1. Open the existing `image_1.gif` in your imaging program.
2. Size and crop your image to the appropriate dimensions.
3. Index the image and optimize it to the lowest possible number of colors without losing quality
4. Export as a GIF.
5. Save the file as `image_2.gif`.

Now repeat the steps in the first or second sample, depending on whether you are adding text or a graphic. Name each image with its appropriate numeric value in the sequence.

When I was finished, the following is what I had:

`Image_1.gif`—A 100×100–pixel GIF of the word, "I"

`Image_2.gif`—A 100×100–pixel GIF with the image of a heart

`Image_3.gif`—A 100×100–pixel GIF of the word "my"

`Image_4.gif`—A 100×100–pixel GIF with the image of a cat

All of these files are now resident on my hard drive (see Figure 30.5).

Figure 30.5
My four prepared animation cells as seen in Photoshop.

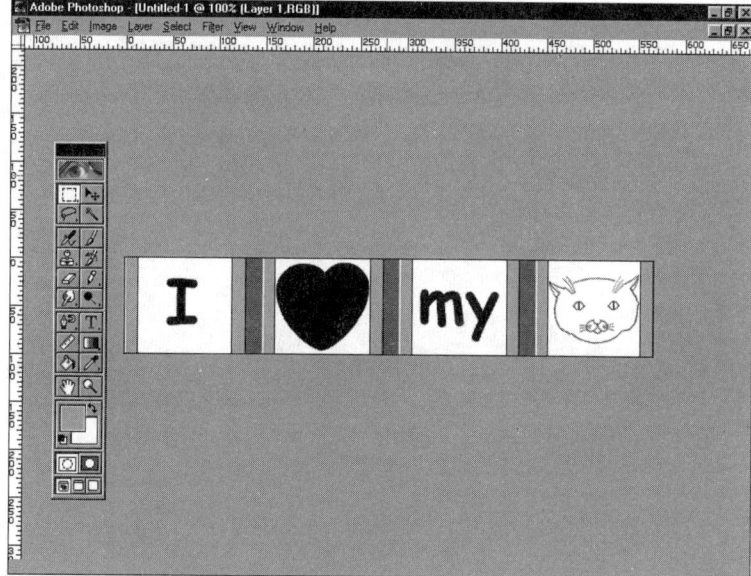

Follow these steps to animate the graphic with GIF Construction Set:

1. Open the GIF Construction set.
2. From File select Animation Wizard.
3. Click Next when asked if you are ready to proceed.
4. Select Yes, for Use with a Web Page.
5. Click Next.
6. Select your looping preference. I recommend only once!
7. The next dialog box will offer preferences for types of graphic. Choose the description that best suits your graphic—mine is Drawn (see Figure 30.6).
8. Now you'll set the delay. For demonstration purposes, stick with the default of 100 hundredths, although you can select any delay you prefer in the future—and you can change this setting later.
9. Click Next.
10. Choose Select.
11. Go to the area where your GIFs are stored.
12. Select each image in order of its appearance to be animated.
13. Click Next, Done.

14. When GIF Construction Set is done animating the image, select Save As and save your file. Mine is saved as `animation_1.gif`.

15. Now view your animation by using the View selection.

Figure 30.6
Selecting the image type in GIF Construction Set. I've chosen the Drawn radio button as my animation is text and line drawn imagery.

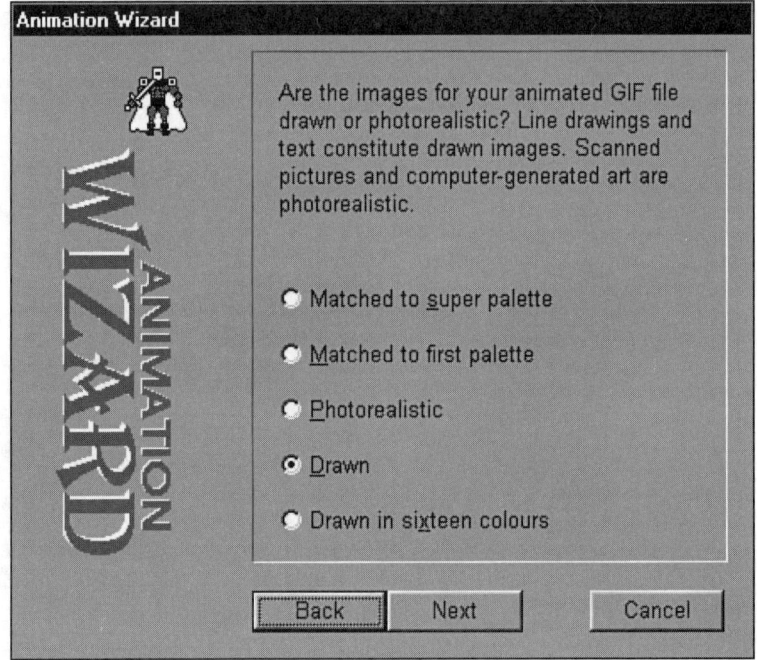

To add your animated image to a Web page, simply use the standard `<img>` tag and attributes (see Listing 30.4). Compliant browsers will understand that this is an animated GIF and play it properly.

LISTING 30.4   ADDING AN ANIMATED GIF TO A WEB PAGE

```
<!DOCTYPE html PUBLIC "-//W3C//DTD XHTML 1.0 Transitional//EN"
"http://www.w3.org/TR/xhtml1/DTD/xhtml1-transitional.dtd">
<html xmlns="http://www.w3.org/1999/xhtml">
<head>
<title>Adding an Animated Image to an XHTML Page</title>
</head>
<body>
<div align="center">
<h2>Tara Made Me Do It!</h2>
<IMG src="images/animation_1.gif" width="100" height="100" border="0"
```

```
alt="I love my cat" />

</div>

</body>

</html>
```

Figure 30.7 shows the animation within my Web browser. Of course, the animation moves through each of the cells before it stops.

Figure 30.7
My animation within a
Web page. When you
open your animation
in a browser, you can
see how the animation
changes frames. If it
goes too fast or slow,
you might want to
open it up again in
your animation pro-
gram and adjust the
timing.

Tip from

You'll notice that I've recommended to loop your animation only once and then stop.
Animations that keep looping tend to be annoying. There are some instances in which
you'll want to loop continuously, such as if you have a slow moving animation or an advertisement. For accent animations, however, be subtle!

Unsure of whether to place multiple animations on your site? See, "Moving Violations" in the
"Troubleshooting" section near the end of this chapter.

Note

For more on GIF animation techniques and technologies, I recommend a visit to Royal E.
Frazier's famous GIF Animation site at `http://members.aol.com/royalef/`
`gifanim.htm`.

ADVERTISING BANNERS

One of the most popular methods of advertising Web sites is getting involved in an advertising banner campaign. Banners improve visibility of a product or Web site and, in some cases, have proven to be a helpful method of gaining product recognition and boosting sales on the Web.

SIZE CONVENTIONS

Typically, advertising groups require specific, standardized sizes and guidelines for banner creation. The average banner size is 468×60 pixels (see Figure 30.8), with a recommended file size of 8KB or less. You do have to check with the methods employed by the group you decide to work with, however, as their guidelines will differ.

Figure 30.8
A standard ad banner image.

GENERAL RECOMMENDATIONS

The following are some general specifications:

- Use GIF or JPG files.
- Use bright colors—This enhances appearance on the page.
- Animated GIFs are considered very effective. Looping is often acceptable with ad banners, but be sure to check with your ad banner partner for more specific guidelines.

> **Note**
> For more information on ad banners, check the popular ad site Doubleclick at
> `http://www.doubleclick.net/`.

TROUBLESHOOTING

MOVING VIOLATIONS

I want to add more than one animation to a page. Should I do it?

The answer lies in audience and context as well as the design of the animation. In most cases, too much movement on a page will distract site visitors and confuse them. This becomes even more true when you've got your own animation *and* an animated banner on the page. I suggest a light hand whenever working with animations and banners.

LINKS WON'T WORK

I created an imagemap but one of my areas isn't linking properly. What could be the problem?

Check your URLs first. You might have mistyped or incorrectly coded a link. If everything is fine with the addressing, you'll need to look more closely at the coordinates to be sure they are working properly.

DESIGNING FOR THE REAL WORLD

DO AD BANNERS WORK?

There's no pat answer to this question. Ad banners are set up to provide an extension of a product's branding via a visual billboard-style effect, and also to provide a method by which interested people will click the banner and go directly to the advertiser's site.

The visual effect is known as *impressions* or *views* and refers to how many times an ad banner gets seen. When a banner is clicked and followed to the next site, this is known as a *click-through*.

In loose polls of adult Web users, very few admit to having ever clicked a banner and followed it. However, people do report noticing them. Stricter polls have taken a look at the Web's most popular sites that use heavy advertising. Let's take a comparison look at the return rate of how much money is spent on a variety of direct marketing ads and how that translates into sales.

Media	Advertising to Sales Ratio
Newspapers	.087
Direct Mail	.096
Magazines	.120
Internet	.143
Radio	.172
Television	.204

Obviously, the Internet is a significant contender, falling happily in the middle (according to this poll) of these most common media. The poll would then suggest that advertising plays a very significant role in improving sales—if you can afford the type of aggressive campaigns the big companies can. If not, the general belief is that you do extend your brand significantly when working with ad banners if only via gaining widespread visibility for your logo, name, product, and service.

Note

The information for this poll was compiled using data found at `http://www.emarketer.com/`.

MULTIMEDIA AND EMBEDDED OBJECTS

CHAPTER 31

AUDIO AND VIDEO

In this chapter

AUDIO AND VIDEO ON THE WEB

Well-managed audio and video can bring your Web pages to life. Poorly managed audio and video can drive your audience away. Who hasn't quickly left a site to escape a droning background sound clip? Who hasn't been excited to see a great video on the Web only to find out that you must commit a good part of an afternoon to downloading it? Audio and video can add a great deal to your site, but it will take some thought and experimentation on your part to make it work for your audience.

If you are interested in venturing into the world of audio and video, there are many factors you must consider. How can you produce high-quality audio and video? How much quality should you sacrifice for efficiency? Should you use downloadable files or streaming technology? Will your audience have the software they need to experience your work? In this chapter, I'll help you make productive decisions and guide you through methodology that will get you up and running with audio and video. First, we'll look at standard audio and video files, and then we'll look more closely at streaming media.

> **Note**
>
> Although downloadable and streaming media are widely used, viable choices in contemporary Web development, professionals are beginning to look toward markup-based technologies such as SMIL and HTML+Time.

→ For more details on SMIL and HTML+Time, **see** Chapter 38, "Synchronized Multimedia Integration Language (SMIL)," **p. 767**.

CREATING AUDIO AND VIDEO FILES

The first step to adding audio and video to your Web site is to create the source files or gather prerecorded source files. It's important to remember that good media content on the Web is the result of good media sampling. If you create a sound clip by taking your tape recorder to a concert and recording your favorite song from the twentieth row, you will have quite a different quality clip from one produced in a studio.

You need a good microphone and good sound editing software if you're recording your own sound sample. For a good video sample, you need a high quality capture device and encoding software.

AUDIO FILES

Most recording devices create analog recordings. To digitize an analog audio source, the signal must be processed through an analog-to-digital (A/D) converter. Most computers now come equipped with the sound cards that have A/D converters. If your computer has a sound input jack, it already has an A/D converter. If your computer has only a sound output jack or an internal speaker, you probably only have digital-to-analog conversion capabilities. Even if you are recording audio from a digital source, such as a digital audio tape (DAT) or compact disc (CD), some kind of A/D conversion is usually involved, because most computers do not come with digital audio inputs yet.

How Audio Is Digitized

An A/D converter uses a "sample and hold" circuit that records the voltage levels of the input signal at a fixed interval. This interval, or rate, at which the signal is sampled is determined by the A/D converter's "sampling rate." The sampling rate also determines the highest frequency that can be recorded or played back. It is important that the recording be played back at the same sampling rate at which it was recorded. For example, 8KHz is a telephony standard that is emerging as a standard for 8-bit *.au mono files. 48.1KHz is the standard audio CD-ROM sampling rate.

After you create your sound file, you need to edit it with a good sound-editing application. There are many shareware packages that will do the trick for simple projects. It wouldn't hurt to first try some shareware options before deciding to invest in professional software.

Tip from

molly

If you decide you need more serious functionality (and you are willing to pay serious money for it), you will want a professional package like Pro Tools by Digidesign (`http://www.digidesign.com/`). A good in-between application, both in terms of price and features, is SoundEdit 16 by Macromedia (`http://www.macromedia.com/`).

PART

VII

CH

31

The following programs will help get you started with audio editing:

- Cool Edit is a digital sound editor for Windows (see Figure 31.1). With this company you have a variety of software choices from a simple shareware package, Cool Edit 96, to a more sophisticated tool, Cool Edit Pro.

Figure 31.1
Cool Edit's Home Page. Begin with a simple shareware package, and if you enjoy using it, upgrade to the more sophisticated Cool Edit Pro.

- Sound Forge by Sonic Foundry is professional sound editing software for Windows (see Figure 31.2) that includes an extensive set of audio processes, tools, and effects for manipulating audio. Sound Forge offers full support for the latest streaming technology, including Microsoft Windows NT Server NetShow Services and RealNetworks' RealAudio/RealVideo. Sonic Foundry also has numerous other sound and multimedia editing software to take a look at.

Figure 31.2
Sonic Foundry offers an extensive set of audio editing tools, including MP3 support and streaming audio.

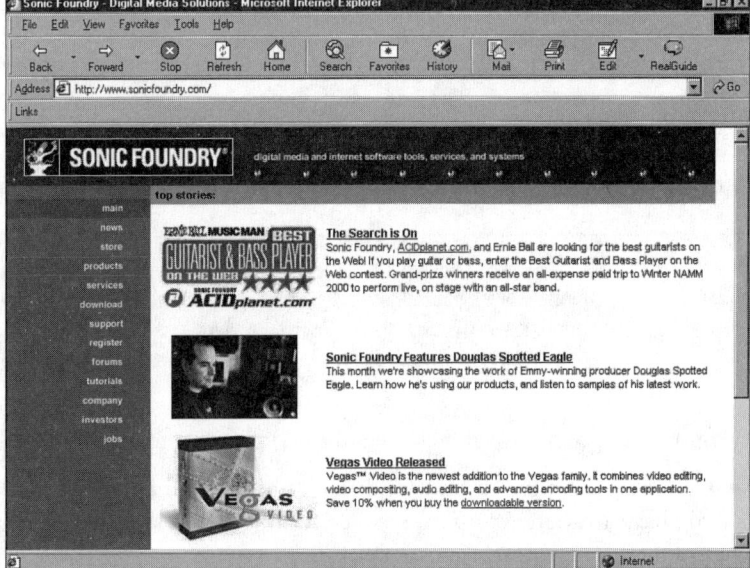

- Waves' AudioTrack is a good audio editor for musicians. It combines audio processors including equalization, compression/expansion, and gating. WaveConvert Pro is a good tool for converting your audio files into another format.

Note

Web sites for the aforementioned products can be found at

Cool Edit by Syntrillium: `http://www.syntrillium.com/`

Sound Forge by Sonic Foundry: `http://www.sonicfoundry.com/`

AudioTrack and WaveConvertPro: `http://www.waves.com/`

VIDEO FILES

When considering the possibility of adding video to your Web site, you must look at a hardware investment as well as purchasing software. It was already mentioned that you must have a very high-quality audio source file before you add it to your Web page. That point is even more important when it comes to producing video content. There are two steps in the processes of creating video when you will sacrifice quality if you do not have good tools.

When you encode video, you capture it to your hard drive. The faster the computer, the faster the video because frames are lost if your computer cannot keep up with the video capture. To produce professional quality video, you need a very fast machine and a high-quality video capture card.

You also will sacrifice quality if during the compression process you do not choose the best video bitrate, bitrate quality, and frame speed to meet your needs.

> **Note**
>
> To make some of these decisions easier for you, RealNetworks has developed video templates you can follow. You can find a list of these templates at
> `http://www.real.com/devzone/library/stream/videohints.html`

DOWNLOADABLE FILE FORMATS

PART
VII
CH
31

There are two methods for delivering audio and video to your audience—downloading and streaming. Downloadable files are ones that are completely loaded on to the user's hard drive before they are played. Streaming files are delivered to the browser in a somewhat steady stream of information.

With streaming media, the user does not need to wait for the entire file to be received before a player begins to playback the source. Both methods have advantages and disadvantages. This chapter section focuses on downloadable formats, with streaming media discussed in Chapter 32, "Streaming Multimedia."

> **Tip from**
> *molly*
>
> Because downloadable media requires a suitable application, you might consider adding a note to your page about the file type, and a link or selection of links where individuals who do not have suitable software can acquire it.

AUDIO FORMATS

All the following formats require a complete download before starting the sound. This can be a great disadvantage if your sound clip is large, because your audience many not be willing to wait for long.

You must always try to make your audio files as small as possible. One important factor that directly impacts file size is quality. The quality of sound clips varies greatly, and different file formats are better suited for different quality clips.

Higher sampling rates and *resolutions* (the number of bits allocated for each "sample") require more storage and throughput. You must decide if you want to sacrifice disk space and bandwidth for high-quality audio files.

A one-minute clip of an 8-bit mono file sampled at 8KHz is approximately 150KB in size. A 16-bit stereo file sampled at 44.1KHz can take up 10MB. Sometimes a lower quality recording will meet the needs of your site's viewers.

The following is a list of the most used audio file formats followed by each one's appropriate MIME type. MIME types allow you to exchange different types of data on the Internet:

- **u-law *.au; audio/basic au snd**—The u-law (pronounced wu-law) format is frequently used on the Internet. Its file size is relatively small, but the quality is considered sub-par because it only supports 8-bit sound. Most people find this format is sufficient for their Web sites, especially because most WWW users are still listening to audio through a monophonic computer speaker.

- **AIFF *.aif; audio/x-aiff aif aiff aifc**—Audio Interchange File Format (AIFF) files can be quite large. AIFF files, used primarily by Macintoshes, are easily converted to other file formats and are often used for high-quality audio applications when storage space is not a concern.

- **AVI *.avi; video/x-msvideo avi**—The Audio/Video Interface is used in Windows operating systems to provide sound and video, with the sound being primary. It might drop frames to keep the sound playing, thereby allowing the format to work on almost any Windows machine, from the least powerful to the most powerful.

- **WAV *.wav; audio/x-wav wav**—A proprietary format sponsored by Microsoft and IBM, it is most commonly used on Windows-based PCs. It is the audio portion of an AVI file.

- **MPEG; *.mp3; audio/x-mpeg mp3**—The International Standard Organization's Moving Picture Expert Group designed this format for both audio and video file compression. The MPEG codecs (compression/decompression methods) have made enormous fans of many Web users. The compression technique yields relatively small files and high quality files.

- **RMF; *.rmf; audio/x-rmf**—Rich Music Format is a relatively new format that is proprietary to the Beatnik music player. It uses JavaScript to add to a page, and its files are extremely small and fast-loading. If an individual does not have the Beatnik player, they simply won't hear the sound (Figure 31.3).

- **MIDI *.mid; audio/x-midi mid midi**—Unlike the other formats discussed here, Musical Instrument Digital Interface (MIDI) is not a specification for sampled digital audio. Rather, it contains a bank of digitized sounds and control information for replaying the file—similar to an electronic synthesizer. MIDI files are much smaller than digitized audio files.

Many people find that they like to provide numerous audio options for download. You can do this, and then provide information about the file, such as size and download times, on the page for the site visitor's convenience.

Note

MPEG 3's (MP3s) have taken the Web world by storm in the past year. You can find innumerable audio resources that use this format. In fact, use of this technology has become so widespread that in some cases, bootlegging of this high-quality audio format has become a significant problem for producers of original audio.

Figure 31.3
The Beatnik home page, `http://www.beatnik.com/`. A worthy way of adding sounds to pages without disrupting load times.

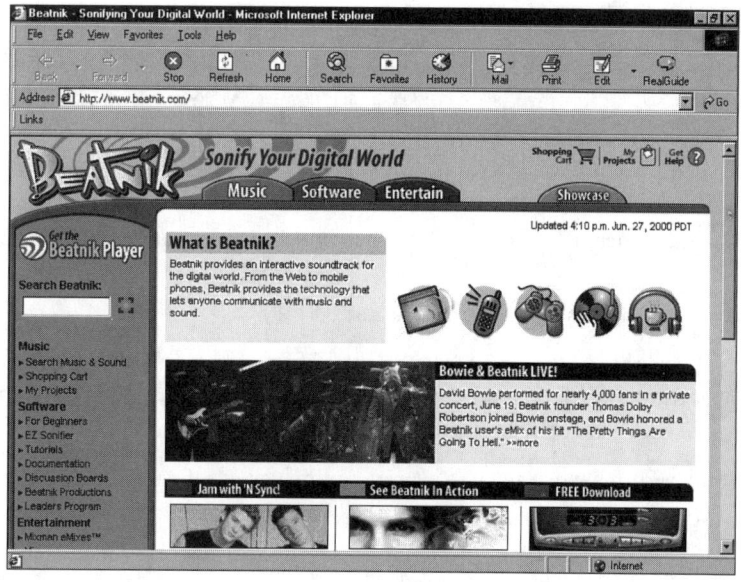

VIDEO FORMATS

The MPEG format is the most standardized video format. It is also a highly efficient format because it has an excellent compression technique. Many developers prefer QuickTime files or AVI files because they are usually smaller and don't require as long to download.

If you want to add video to your Web site, you should experiment with these formats to find what works best for you and your audience. You also must consider that not all video-editing tools support all three formats.

Tip from
molly

Selecting a video format will depend on a variety of factors, including platform availability, which tools you like to use for editing, and personal preference. MPEG and QuickTime tend to be a popular choice over AVIs. MPEG is very widely supported platform-wise, and QuickTime tools and plug-ins are popular. AVI tends to be Microsoft-centric, and although it runs inline in the IE browser, support does vary with other browsers.

ADDING AUDIO AND VIDEO TO A WEB PAGE

There are two ways in which you can place and access most Web-based audio and video that will be read successfully across browsers: by using the anchor tag and the `<embed>` tag.

Note

Beatnik is a proprietary technology that uses HTML and JavaScript to accomplish its audio delivery goals. You can check out the Beatnik Web site, where a range of easy-to-follow tutorials exist.

→ For detailed coverage of the anchor tag, **see** Chapter 12, "Linking Pages with Standard Links," **p. 199**.

> **Caution**
>
> The `embed` tag is *not* included in the HTML 4.0 strict standard and therefore is not available in the XHTML 1.0 standard in deference to the `object` tag. You can choose to use the `object` tag to embed media; however, you won't have the flexibility and interoperability due to cross-browser and platform problems. At this time, it's still recommended that you use `embed` or combine `embed` and `object` when working across platforms and browsers

Using the anchor tag (`<a>. . .</a>`) is the same as placing any link within an XHTML document:

```
<a href ="mydogs.mov">see Bowie and Kelsey</a>
```

If you use this method, your users will either save the file to their desktops, launch a plug-in application, or load a new browser page, depending on which browser they're using and how they have set their preferences.

If you want the video to appear on the same page as the rest of the content, you must embed the clip in the page by using the `<embed>` tag. Use of the `<embed>` tag is similar to the use of the `<img>` tag. However, the `<embed>` tag requires users to have the appropriate plug-in installed, or they will not see your work.

The following sample is for a video clip, but the `<embed>` tag also works for audio files, as well as for streaming video and audio:

```
<embed src="/home/dogs/rope.mov" height="105" width="100" controller="false"
➥autoplay="true" playeveryframe="false" pluginspage="getplug.htm"
➥loop="palindrome" />
```

`<embed>` tag attributes and values are managed as follows:

- **`height="pixel/percent"`**—Unless you need your movie to scale, set this in pixels according to the dimensions of your movie.

- **`width="pixel/percent"`**—Width is best controlled by pixels, but you can use a percentage to describe how much space within the browser frame you want the embedded object to take up.

- **`autoplay="true/false"`**—Answer with `true`, and your movie starts when the page is first accessed. Answer with `false`, and the user must click the play button on the console for the movie to play.

- **`controller="true/false"`**—This adds user controls to the movie. If you set this for `true`, you must find out how many pixels your controller needs for the display and then add that amount to the height of your movie. Otherwise, the movie and the controller will be forced into the space required for the movie.

- **`loop="true/false/palindrome"`**—If you want the movie to play over and over, set this to `true`. If you want to play it once and stop, set it to `false`. Palindrome plays from beginning to end and backwards in a continuous loop.

- **`pluginspage="gohere.htm"`**—This takes users who don't have the right to a page that tells them where to get it.

Tip from

> If you're loading a sound into the background using embed, place the code *at the bottom* of the page, still within the body tag. This allows everything else to load first, with the audio loading last. Your site visitors won't have to wait at a blank page until the audio has loaded.

AUDIO AND VIDEO PLUG-INS

Not too long ago you *had* to download a special program, or "plug-in," to view many audio and video files. Although some file formats still require you to get a special plug-in, many come bundled with operating systems and browsers.

Note

> For a list of audio and video plug-ins supported by Netscape, visit `http://www.netscape.com/plugins/audio-video.html`.

PART

VII

CH

31

Some of the primary and important plug-ins you'll want to have include the following:

- **Apple QuickTime,** `http://www.apple.com/quicktime/`—Apple QuickTime Plug-in allows your audience to view your QuickTime (.mov) video clips as well as many other audio and video formats (see Figure 31.4).

Figure 31.4
Apple's QuickTime Page. QuickTime supports video, audio, and proprietary virtual reality media as well as having many attractive tools and dedicated developer resources.

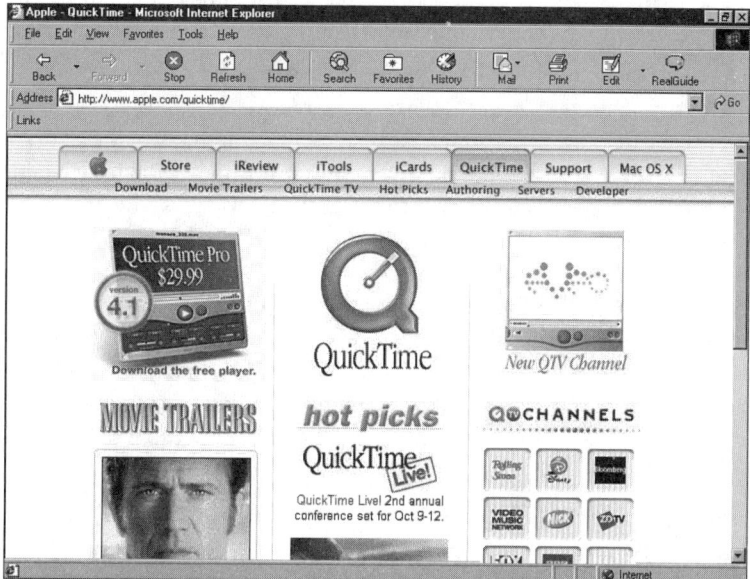

- **Microsoft Media Player,** `http://www.microsoft.com/windows/mediaplayer/`—The new and improved Microsoft Media Player (version 5.2) is being shipped with the later releases of Windows 98 (see Figure 31.5) and is available as a free download for Windows 95 users. This is one-stop shopping for most audio and video formats you will encounter including ASF (a Microsoft format), RealVideo/RealAudio 4.0, MPEG 1, MPEG 2, WAV, AVI, MIDI, MOV, VOD, AU, MP3, and QuickTime files. The Media Player can run as a standalone or can be viewed within Internet Explorer and Netscape.

Figure 31.5
Microsoft's Media Player in Windows 98. The Media Player that shipped with Windows 95 and the early release of Windows 98 only supports WAV, AVI, and MIDI formats.

- **Beatnik Player, http://www.beatnik.com/**—supports Beatnik RMF files. There's also a terrific amount of developer information, tools, and community support.

- **RealPlayer Basic or Plus by RealNetworks,**
  http://www.real.com/products/player/—RealPlayer Basic and Plus support all three Real data types: RealAudio, RealVideo, RealFlash, as well as AVI, WAV, MIDI, MPEG, JPEG, VIVO, VRML, and others. RealNetworks is the leader in delivering audio and video over the Web. Basic is the free player, whereas Plus is the advanced player that is available for $29.99 USD.

When you're deciding on the best format for your audio and video files, you should consider the likelihood that your users will already have the software they need to see your work. Too often, users will not take the time to download a plug-in, so you are better off to provide your files in formats they can already access. Table 31.1 shows an audio file reference, by browser, to assist you when choosing the most applicable sound file for your site.

TABLE 31.1   BROWSER-BASED SUPPORT FOR AUDIO FILES

AIFF	AIF	AIFC	AU	MIDI	SND	WAV
IE 3.0+	x	x	x	x	x	x
NN 4.0+	x			x	x	x

This table demonstrates that if you want to include a downloadable sound file in your site without having to offer a special plug-in, stick with WAV, AIFF, or AU files.

Designing for the Real World

Bandwidth Blues

Bandwidth is a significant concern with any media files, due to the size of those files and the limitations with streaming technologies. Another concern is accessibility—if a site visitor can't see or hear, the message you are sending with your video or audio can be lost without due consideration.

Corporate intranets are especially good candidates for using streaming technology because they most often have high-speed connections and standardized software for viewing the material. Intranets provide an opportunity to develop Web sites for a specific audience.

But, if you are preparing audio and video to be streamed on the Internet to a broad audience, you must remember that not all users have the same hardware and software capabilities. Although the average connection speed today is 56Kbps, some users are still accessing your site at slower speeds and, of course, some connections are much faster. You should consider providing your users with options.

If you are streaming a video, consider offering two speeds for viewing the video, for example, 28.8Kbps and 56Kbps. This will help optimize the video for your user. If you are providing media content that the user might not have the necessary plug-in to view, always offer a link to where the software can be downloaded.

PART

VII

Ch

31

CHAPTER 32

STREAMING MULTIMEDIA

In this chapter

STREAMING MEDIA CONCEPTS

Streaming technology is an attempt to avoid the eternal bandwidth problem. In 1994, RealAudio introduced a way of delivering Internet audio based on the User Datagram Protocol (UDP) rather than the usual Transmission Control Protocol (TCP). UDP technology was later used for transferring video files as well.

UDP technology does not require confirmation of the receipt of all the data; instead, it delivers the file as quickly as possible. This means that a user can begin playing the audio or video file even before the whole file is received. The user's wait time is cut dramatically. Over time, Real has expanded its line of products and services to include a range of enhanced services to bring streaming media to the Web.

The disadvantage of streaming media is that you lose some control over the quality of your data as it travels over the Internet. The quality of the streaming audio and video is dependent on line quality, which varies greatly. However, with the growing proliferation of fast connections, such as T1 and ISDN lines, many of these problems are minimized.

STREAMING AUDIO

Adding streaming audio to your Web site is not a decision to be made lightly. You or a client might agree that streaming audio will greatly enhance the site, but you also must weigh the expense in terms of both time *and* money.

The first steps for creating a streaming audio clip are the same as those for creating a downloadable clip. But the next step is to convert the digital recording into the streaming format.

RealNetworks' RealProducer has long been the most popular software for converting files for streaming. The encoding process compresses the files until they are very small. During the compression, some parts of the sound file are left out.

To have the best quality content after compression, you must start with a good source file. If you're creating sound from scratch, you must use professional quality microphones. If you are using content that has already been recorded, you should use CD-ROM or DAT recordings.

Tip from molly	Some excellent hints for creating a good source file can be found at the RealNetworks electronic library at `http://www.real.com/devzone/library/`.

STREAMING VIDEO

Creating streaming video content is the same process as creating downloadable video content, but you must convert the file to a streaming format. Once again, RealProducer is a popular tool for making videos ready for streaming technology.

Currently RealProducer supports `.AVI` and `.MOV` *input* files. If your input files are of any other type, you must find another tool to convert that type to `.AVI` or `.MOV` files.

Tip from

molly

To convert a wide range of audio file types to `.AVI` or `.MOVF` try CDH's Media Wizard, available for download at `http://www.tiklsoft.com/multimedia/114.html`. Macintosh and Unix/Linux users will want to check out Xing's audio tools for those platforms, `http://www.xing.com/`.

PRODUCING STREAMING MEDIA

In this section, I'll focus on RealNetworks products, because of the availability of free and inexpensive resources for their use. If you are interested in other products or methods mentioned earlier in this chapter, please visit their Web sites for more information.

Note

New methods of delivering streaming multimedia are available. SMIL (pronounced "smile"), the Synchronized Multimedia Integration Language, is an XML application. You can learn more about what SMIL is and how to create a SMIL application in Chapter 38, "Synchronized Multimedia Integration Language (SMIL)."

CREATING A STREAMING AUDIO FILE

To add a streamed audio clip to your page, you will need some special tools and skills.

For my example, I already have an MP3 file that I want to use, which I prepared from a digital sampling by using the techniques discussed earlier in the chapter.

The next step is to convert the MP3 file to a streaming format. To do this, use the RealNetworks product RealProducer. This application allows you to change quickly and easily the MP3 file into the appropriate streaming format.

Note

The RealProducer is free for download from `http://www.real.com/products/tools/index.html`.

Follow these steps to convert an MP3 file to RealMedia format (my specific choices are provided as an example):

1. When RealProducer starts up, it offers a New Session dialog box. In the Input Source section, click the File option button, click Browse, Find, and then select the MP3 file you want to encode. The Output section loads the file location and name under RealMedia file (see Figure 32.1).

2. Then click Save As and type the location and name you want to save the encoded file as (in this case my file is named `outside_inside.rm`).

3. Click Save, and then click OK.

PART
VII

CH
32

Figure 32.1
Select the input and
output files in
RealProducer.

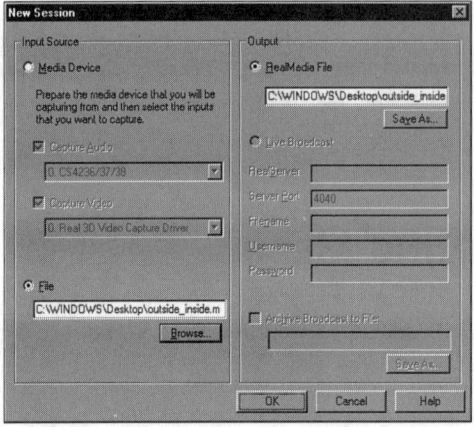

4. In the Clip Information area (Figure 32.2), add the title of the piece (we named it molly_patty, your name, the copyright date, a description, and keywords describing the file.

5. In the Target Audience area there are several check boxes you can use to customize the file to your audience's needs. I chose the 28K Modem check box and also the 56K modem check box, because I want to make sure that I can provide 28.8 access—many of the people coming to the Web site I'm creating are on standard modems.

6. Under Audio Format, choose the type of audio that is most accurate for your music selection from the drop-down menu (I selected Music) as shown in Figure 32.2.

Figure 32.2
Click the appropriate
check boxes to deter-
mine audience format.

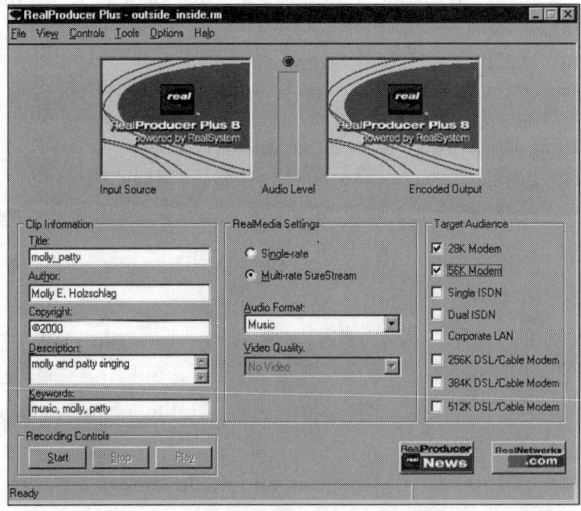

7. In the File Type area, you must choose between Multi-rate and Single-rate. Choose Multi-rate SureStream if you are not using a Web server.

8. Now click Start under Recording Controls.

9. RealProducer encodes the file with an .rm extension, saving it to the location you identified in step 2.

If you want to provide a higher bandwidth access option, follow these steps again, optimizing the file for T1 access, and then save the file under a new name (mine is saved as molly_patty_t1.rm).

Unsure of the bandwidth issues you might be facing? You'll find additional information on the issue in "Bandwidth Blues" in the "Troubleshooting" section near the end of this chapter.

Tip from

You can create as many bandwidth options as you want by simply working through this process and letting RealProducer process the files with the specific bandwidth preferences you set.

WORKING WITH STREAMING VIDEO

Streaming video works similarly to streaming audio. In this case, you begin the process with an .AVI file—I am using one that a friend took while feeding fish on the Great Barrier Reef.

I thought this would be a nice addition to a Web page, so I prepared to encode the file by using the RealProducer, as I did for streaming audio. Here's the process to follow, with my specific choices in parentheses:

1. From RealProducer New Session dialog box, select the .AVI file you want to encode in the Input Source section.

2. Type the name you want to save the encoded file as (in my case, feeding_fish_28.rm).

3. Click Save As and then click OK.

4. In the RealProducer main screen, locate the area called Clip Information, and give the title to the video, name the author, and provide a copyright date, description, and keywords.

5. Choose one of the several check boxes to determine your target audience.

6. Under Audio Format, you can choose to add audio by selecting the audio most appropriate to your .AVI from the drop-down menu (I chose No Audio). Set Video Quality to Normal Motion Video.

7. In the File Type area, choose either Multi-rate or Single-rate; choose Multi-rate SureStream unless you are preparing the file for a Web server.

8. Under Recording Controls, click Start.

9. RealProducer encodes the file with an `.rm` extension and saves it to the location you identified in step 2.

Now you have a streaming version of the video to place into a Web page.

INCORPORATING STREAMING MEDIA INTO YOUR PAGE

There are two ways to add streaming media to a Web page. The first involves the need to set up or have access to streaming hardware. The second is setting up the media to stream via HTTP, the Hypertext Transfer Protocol.

 Want to make your streaming media accessible? There are alternatives! See "Accessibility Alternatives" in the "Troubleshooting" section later in this chapter.

ADDING STREAMING MEDIA USING REALSERVER G2

If you have access to a RealServer G2, you can stream files using the full gamut of RealServer services. This includes working with the RTSP protocol, which is a special protocol designed for streaming media. It streams data with timelines, adjusting the stream with the idea of allowing it to play as smoothly as possible as it transfers. What's more, there's a feature known as Ramgen, which generates a Ram file—a specialized file that will invoke the RealPlayer.

To have your audio or video run from a RealServer, follow these steps:

1. Place your prepared file on the RealServer.

2. Place a link from the referring page to the file as follows:
```
<a
href="http://realserver.yourserver.com:8080/ramgen/molly_patty56.rm">download
molly's audio clip</a>
```

3. Test your file to see if it works properly. The link should automatically invoke the RealPlayer, and the audio or video should begin to stream immediately.

ADDING STREAMING MEDIA TO A PAGE WITH HTTP

If you don't have access to a RealServer, you can stream your audio and video directly via HTTP. There are some services, such as live broadcast, that you will not be able to tap into doing it this way, but even so, this method doesn't have the costs associated with RealServer technology.

You will have to contact your ISP to make sure that the MIME types are entered on the server. The MIME types you'll want to have to support all Real streaming media, including SMIL, are laid out in Table 32.1.

TABLE 32.1   MIME TYPES FOR REALMEDIA FILES

File Type	Extension	MIME Type
Ram	.ram	audio/x-pn-realaudio
Embedded Ram	.rpm	audio/x-pn-realaudioplugin
SMIL	.smil and .smi	application/smil
RealAudio	.ra	audio/x-pn-realaudio
RealVideo	.rm	application/x-pn-realmedia
RealPix	.rp	image/vnd.rn-realpix
RealText	.rt	text/vnd.rn-realtext

To add streaming media to your page, follow these steps:

1. Prepare your file using RealProducer just as you would for use with RealServer.
2. Create a Ram file. To do this, simply open your editor and type in the URL where your clip resides. Save the file with a .ram extension, such as molly_and_patty.ram.
3. Put the Ram file and the audio or video file into the desired directory on your Web server.
4. Link to the Ram file from your Web page, and voila!

Be sure to test your link. The streaming clip should stream when the link is activated.

PART
VII
CH
32

Note

RealProducer generates the HTML for you when you click Create Web Page in the Web Publishing section of the application. A wizard is launched that walks you through the process. However, if you want your code to be XHTML compliant, you will need to edit the generated code.

In Listing 32.1, I've linked from my page to the files, which reside in a directory on my Web server called "audio." You can run files locally, too.

LISTING 32.1   EMBEDDING STREAMING AUDIO

```
<!DOCTYPE html PUBLIC "-//W3C//DTD XHTML 1.0 Transitional//EN"
"http://www.w3.org/TR/xhtml1/DTD/xhtml1-transitional.dtd">
<html xmlns="http://www.w3.org/1999/xhtml">
<head>
<title>Audio Sample</title>
</head>
<body>
<p>My singing partner, Patty Sundberg, and I, are in a duo called Courage
Sisters. We write and perform original acoustic music.</p>
<p>Please enjoy the following RealAudio clip:</p>
<a href="audio/molly_and_patty.ram">Molly and Patty in Concert</a>
</body>
</html>
```

Figure 32.3 shows the RealMedia player with the file playing after the link has been clicked.

Figure 32.3
RealMedia provides a
control panel that
allows the site visitor
to control play of the
audio file.

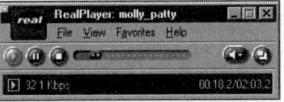

Adding streaming video is essentially the same process. Listing 32.2 is the XHTML code demonstrating how adding a video clip to a Web page was accomplished.

LISTING 32.2 ADDING STREAMING VIDEO

```
<!DOCTYPE html PUBLIC "-//W3C//DTD XHTML 1.0 Transitional//EN"
"http://www.w3.org/TR/xhtml1/DTD/xhtml1-transitional.dtd">
<html xmlns="http://www.w3.org/1999/xhtml">
<head>
<title>Video Sample</title>
</head>
<body>
<p>My friend Kelly, who sadly passed away last year, was a truly inspirational
person. Kelly was a paraplegic. She was paralyzed from the mid-chest area down.
But nothing stopped her from having a very adventurous and active lifestyle.
She was a scuba diver, mountain climber, devoted kayaker, and ski maven, using
adaptive equipment to assist her in achieving her athletic goals.</p>

<p>So if you've been a little concerned about scuba diving, para-sailing—even
extreme sports, Kelly's active life can serve as a great inspiration.</p>
<p>Several years ago, Kelly went scuba diving along the Great Barrier Reef. In
this video, she can be seen feeding beautifully colored fish.  Note: this file is
optimized for 28.8 connections.</p>

<p><a href="video/feeding_fish_28.ram">Kelly Feeding Fish</a><p>

</body>
</html>
```

When a site visitor clicks on the link or "Real" icon, the RealPlayer will launch. In Figure 32.4, you can see the streaming video in the RealPlayer after the link has been activated.

 Link not working? It might be that your MIME type has not been added to the Web server. See "Mime Problems" in the "Troubleshooting" section later in the chapter.

Figure 32.4
Activating the video in
RealPlayer.

TROUBLESHOOTING

BANDWIDTH BLUES

Audio and video options are attractive, but how do you deal with the differences in bandwidth?

Obviously, bandwidth is a significant concern with any media files, due to the size of those files and the limitations with streaming technologies. Another concern is accessibility—if a site visitor can't see or hear, the message you are sending with your video or audio can be lost without due consideration.

Corporate intranets are especially good candidates for using streaming technology because they most often have high-speed connections and standardized software for viewing the material. Intranets provide an opportunity to develop Web sites for a specific audience.

But, if you are preparing audio and video to be streamed on the Internet to a broad audience, you must remember that not all users have the same hardware and software capabilities. Although the average connection speed today is 56Kbps, some users are still accessing your site at slower speeds and, of course, some connections are much faster. You should consider providing your users with options.

If you are streaming a video, consider offering two speeds for viewing the video—for example, 28.8Kbps and 56Kbps. This will help optimize the video for your user. If you are providing media content that the user might not have the necessary plug-in to view, always offer a link to where the software can be downloaded.

MIME PROBLEMS

I've set my page up for HTTP streaming from my Web server, but it isn't working. I've checked all the files and the code looks fine. What's wrong?

It might well be that your ISP has not added the proper MIME types to the Web server. This is not a difficult thing to do, but sometimes ISPs are not able to respond to requests of this nature in a timely fashion. Get back in touch with your contacts there and send them the information found in Table 32.1. Once you've received confirmation that the MIME type is in place, check your work again.

ACCESSIBILITY ALTERNATIVES

How can I incorporate streaming media onto my page and still make that media accessible to people with disabilities?

Alternative page versions or links to text transcripts can (and should!) be provided for content that is otherwise conveyed only through aural or visual media.

DESIGNING FOR THE REAL WORLD

EXPLORING STREAMING OPTIONS

After you decide to add audio and video to a site, you will find that there is no shortage of companies that want to try to make your job easier. It can make your head spin when you realize how many companies are vying for a piece of the growing online multimedia market.

The following is a tour of some of the leading companies in the audio/video industry and their products. Visit the sites and download any tools and players. Become familiar with both using and working with audio and video online.

- **Microsoft Advanced Streaming Media Format (ASF),** `http://www.microsoft.com/windows/windowsmedia/`—Using proprietary streaming technology referred to as *advanced streaming media*, Microsoft has developed a suite of streaming media products and applications. FM stereo sound can be streamed over modem connections, and the ASF format is considered to offer better compression than MP3.

- **VivoActive,** `http://www.vivo.com/`—Vivo Software (now part of RealNetworks) is a leader in the streaming media market. VideoNow and VideoProducer are easy-to-use and affordable tools that allow you to make synchronized streaming video and audio Web pages by using AVI or WAV files. This technology is great for the Web because the content can be played back on any platform by using the VivoActive Player. The Player works on 486/66 or higher systems running Windows 3.1 or later and Power Macintosh systems running Mac OS 7.5 or later.

- **Apple QuickTime,** `http://www.apple.com/quicktime/`—Ensures cross-platform and Internet compatibility for your QuickTime Files. Prior to QuickTime 3, a tool called the Internet Movie Tool was sometimes used to prepare movies for Web delivery. Apple recommends that you no longer use this tool for movie preparation because QuickTime and MoviePlayer now prepare the movie for the Internet automatically (see Figure 32.5).

- **RealNetwork's RealProducer/Real Publisher,** `http://www.real.com/g2/developer/`—RealProducer contains all the tools needed to create RealAudio (WAV, AU, MOV, and SND) and RealVideo (AVI and QuickTime format) content, and it's free! RealPublisher is marketed as an upgrade to RealProducer, but auto coding and uploading them to the Web are the only functions exclusive to RealPublisher. These products are popular because they are made by the leader in the industry—RealNetworks.

- **Adobe Premiere**, `http://www.adobe.com/prodindex/premiere/`—This is an expensive but powerful tool designed for video professionals. Unlike other tools available to you, this one was not designed specifically for making online video and probably has much more capability than you need. One big benefit of this product is that it can smoothly integrate other Adobe products, such as Photoshop and Illustrator.

Figure 32.5
QuickTime home page.

Adding streaming media is not for every Web designer, nor is it appropriate for every audience. It is important to take a close look at it, however, because it is becoming a more popular option as both the streaming technology gets better and connectivity gets faster.

I have rarely used streaming media in standard Web designs. I have had occasion to create streaming media for specific projects, such as an adventure travel site where video and audio of underwater diving or water skiing can really enhance the site visitor's experience. Other instances where streaming media can make a site more powerful include sites for real estate, music, history, art, and education.

In business, streaming media is extremely attractive as a method of communications between distant offices. Of course, the interest in Internet radio and live videocasts has brought a lot of enthusiasm to the medium. Still, as with any media that demands additional software, asks your hardware to work harder, and requires the maximum bandwidth available, careful consideration must be used by the developer before adding it to a given site.

CHAPTER 33

MULTIMEDIA PACKAGES

In this chapter

MULTIMEDIA AND THE WEB

Movement, action, interaction—these are components Web developers strive for to keep Web sites vibrant and interesting, and to keep visitors engaged.

Multimedia has been around for a long time and has been used in multitudes of circumstances, including corporate and information-based presentations, educational activities, and recreation in the form of video games.

It's only natural, then, that businesses, educational institutions, and entertainment-based developers are interested in having multimedia options for their Web sites.

As you by now know, a single graphic must be compressed so that it weighs very, very little to load effectively across browser and platform types, and through a variety of bandwidth situations.

That's just one graphic! Multimedia includes graphics—often many graphics—to create animation and movement, input areas, and responses. And, true to its name, the concept is *multiple*—to have more than one media event occurring in the same environment, meaning the addition of audio and video as well as static graphics and special effects.

How to get all this information compressed and delivered to a Web browser has limited developers to a large degree. Bandwidth is the issue, and although we're certainly seeing more affordable bandwidth options become available in certain parts of the United States, there's an entire world out there with a wide range of special circumstances.

Multimedia specialists such as Macromedia, have made some significant advances addressing this concern with their suite of tools, and as the years pass, integration of those tools with one another increases. That concentration and integration has paid off in the form of some impressive options for multimedia design and delivery over the Web.

Furthermore, changes to hardware and software have been made. The PowerPC and higher-level Macintosh systems have long been graphically oriented, so the addition of multiple media isn't a big step. MMX technology has swept the Windows platform market, with Windows 98 offering full support for the technology.

MMX (Multimedia Extensions) is a set of 57 new instructions that Intel added to certain processors to speed up and enhance multimedia. This new technology means improved performance for image processing, video, audio, videoconferencing, and similar functions.

It also suggests that multimedia presentations over the Internet, and intranets, might become more effective and ultimately an essential part of the Internet industry as time goes on.

MACROMEDIA DIRECTOR, SHOCKWAVE, AND FLASH BASICS

High interactivity, lower bandwidth—that's what these programs strive for, and in some cases, truly achieve.

Macromedia has excelled in the procurement and development of multimedia tools, including Director, which is considered one of the premier multimedia development packages. With applications that far exceed Web interests, Director can create interactive, multimedia presentations for kiosks, CD-ROM computers, games, and other interactive media.

The Director Studio package includes many useful tools—including the Aftershock utility. Aftershock generates the HTML that can deliver Director and Flash Shockwave movies and Java applets to all platforms and browsers.

Director is a big package and a serious commitment. The learning curve is high, and therefore it is recommended for only the very serious multimedia developer.

Shockwave is a technology that was created specifically for the Web. Using Director, the Shockwave technology works by streaming information to the Web browser via a plug-in.

Shockwave hit the Web scene with a serious splash. However, because browser technology is still fickle when it comes to integrating advanced support for such a complex program with plug-in style delivery, it has only caught on in certain situations.

Shockwave does, however, have many advantages over most Web-based media programs. It supports audio, animation, and advanced interactive events. Web pages with Shockwave are considered to be "shocked," and they are popular among certain Web enthusiasts.

Note

For a gallery of Director multimedia presentations and Shockwave sites, visit the following:
Director Gallery: `http://www.macromedia.com/software/director/gallery/_director/`
ShockWave.Com: `http://www.shockwave.com/`

PART VII CH 33

Figure 33.1 shows the Shockwave site. Stay on the page a few moments, and you can enjoy the action. Figure 33.2 shows a different scene with the very weird but popular Joe Cartoon (**http://www.joecartoon.com**). This site is definitely a fun experience, taking the days of static pages to a very different level.

Figure 33.1
The Shockwave site—
enjoyable, colorful,
and full of promise.

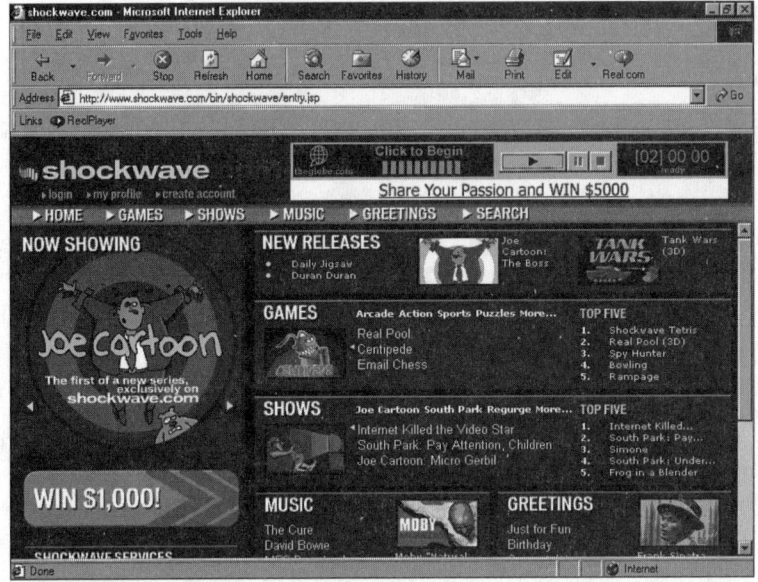

Figure 33.2
Promise fulfilled, espe-
cially for Joe Cartoon
fans.

EXPLORING FLASH IN DETAIL

Flash was originally a compact animation tool called FutureSplash that was later modified to include sound. With intense support from Microsoft, Macromedia Flash was quickly included as a native part of Internet Explorer. At the time of this writing, Flash is in its 4.0 incarnation, with a lot of interface and publishing improvements. Flash will soon be released in its next version, 5.0, but I will focus mostly on 4.0 here. Be sure to visit Macromedia (**www.macromedia.com**) for updates and upgrades.

What's especially interesting about Flash is that it is a vector-based drawing tool, much like Illustrator or Macromedia Freehand, but with the sole purpose of creating Web content.

> **Note**
>
> Adobe's new product, LiveMotion, is in many ways similar to Flash. You can add audio and animation, and it's a vector-based drawing package. However, it also has the added advantage of being very useful as a straight-forward Web graphics tool. For that reason, I've included it in Chapter 27, "Web Graphic Professional Tools," instead of here.

What this means is that the resulting files are very compact, and can include a wide range of high-quality, low-bandwidth design. Add audio to the mix, and you've got a sophisticated and widely accessible tool.

Another cool aspect of Flash 4.0 is its publishing utilities. Flash 4.0 helps you publish your designs to HTML, making your job much easier. Flash 3.0, despite its lack of these advanced publishing tools, does come with a utility known as Aftershock. This utility is a one-step marvel: It takes what you create in Flash and processes it to work across browsers and across platforms, writing the HTML code, the JavaScript, *and* creating an animated or still GIF for those who can't access the Flash file.

One drawback is that Flash still requires a plug-in for pre-4.0 Netscape support. However, Flash is wise, it offers output not only to its native vector-based formats, but to animated GIFs, which can be used in place of the vector movies in those circumstances where Flash is not supported. Flash hasn't been on every Web developer's list of sensible Web site choices because of these difficulties. But, it is a powerful option and enthusiastically used by many.

PART
VII

CH
33

> **Note**
>
> Windows 98 users will be happy to know that Flash and Shockwave players are built directly into the operating systems—no plug-ins required.

 Still unsure as to whether Flash is the way to go? See "Using Flash in the Real World" in the "Troubleshooting" section near the end of this chapter for some additional insight.

Flash is affordable, and the learning curve is not anywhere near as complex as for Director. Although I've always thought the interface (see Figure 33.3) could be a bit more intuitive, Flash still remains an impressive method of creating enhanced visuals.

Figure 33.3
The Flash 4.0 interface complete with menus, timeline, tools, and workspace.

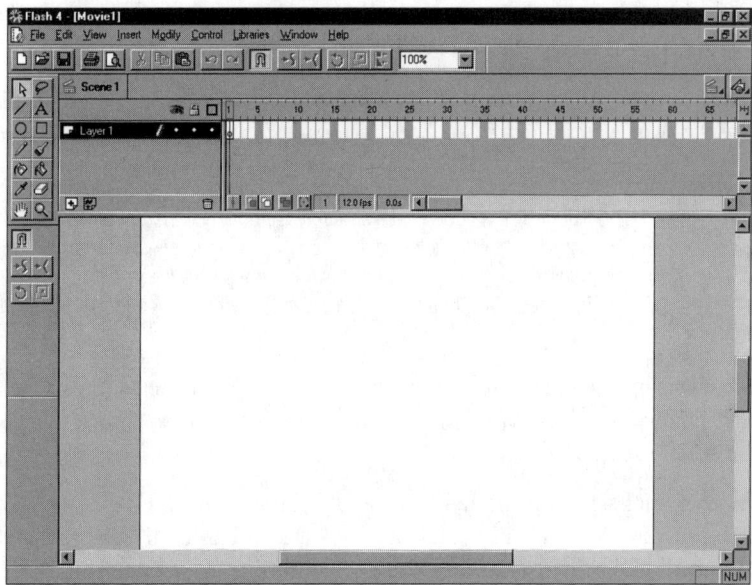

WORKING WITH FLASH

A demo version of Flash is available for download from Macromedia. You can use the demo to walk through all the exercises in this chapter, and if you get hooked, you can purchase the software at your discretion.

Note

You can download the Flash demo from Macromedia at
`http://www.macromedia.com/software/flash/trial/`.

CREATING A FLASH ANIMATION

Before diving into the animation, I want to introduce you to two important terms:

- **Key frame**—This is an animator's term used to describe the point in an animation where the action changes. The action is usually simple—a change in movement or color.

- **Tweening**—This is a concept that makes animation easy. If I put an object on a key frame, move it to another key frame down the timeline, and *tween* the object, Flash paces all the movement necessary to get from the first key frame to the second, the in-be*tween* frames are created for you by the program.

First, you'll need to create a Flash animation. Here's a simple animation exercise using text:

1. Open Flash.
2. Choose File, New.

3. From the Modify menu, choose Movie.

4. You'll get a dialog box where you can set some parameters. Focus for now on image size and background color. For example, choose 400 × 200 pixels, and white as the background color (see Figure 33.4).

Figure 33.4
Setting the animation's dimensions.

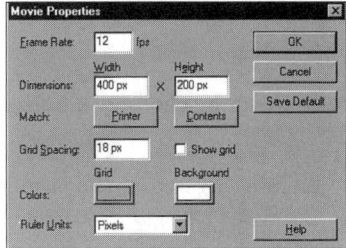

5. Click OK.

6. From the Tools menu, select the Text Tool, represented by an A.

7. Now, select a font, font size, style, and color from the menu that appears and type in a phrase.

8. Click the Text Tool cursor on the Stage—the area where you are creating your Flash animation—to deselect the text.

9. Now, right-click (Win) or hold your mouse down (Mac) on the circle (which represents the key frame) on the Time Line. Choose Insert Blank Keyframe from the drop-down menu that appears (see Figure 33.5).

Figure 33.5
The frame shortcut menu enables you to insert a blank keyframe.

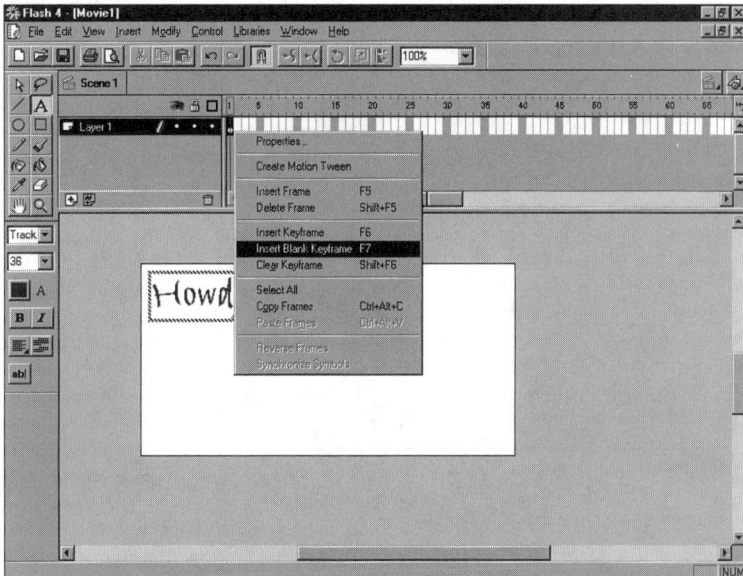

10. Move back down to the stage, select the text by highlighting it and move it to the next spot on the stage in which you want it to appear.

11. Deselect the text.

12. On the timeline, drag the dot over until it reaches 10.

13. Stop and right-click (Win) or hold your mouse down (Mac) on the dot for the shortcut menu shown in Figure 33.5.

14. Once again, choose Insert Blank Keyframe.

15. You can check and see your movie at this point by choosing Control, Play.

16. If you like what you see, right-click the dot.

17. Choose Create Motion Tween from the frame shortcut menu (see Figure 33.6). Flash tweens the frames.

Figure 33.6
Motion tweening automatically creates the in-between frames in the animation.

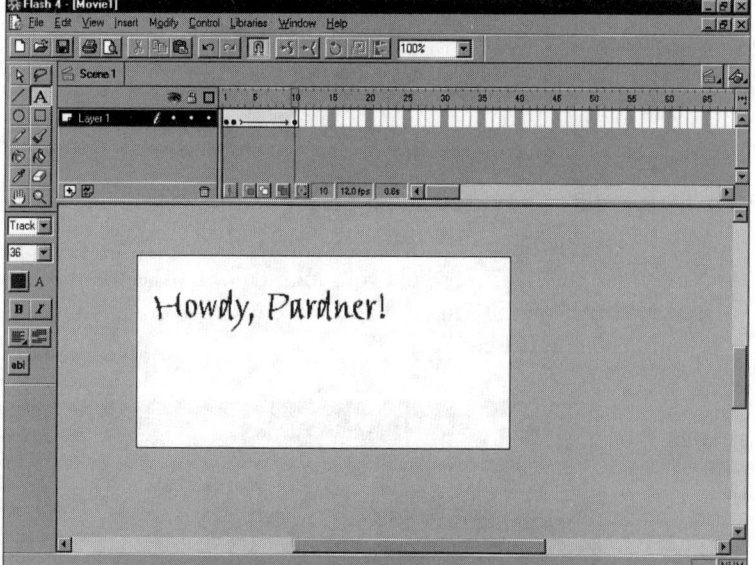

18. Choose File, Export Movie.

19. Save your file with the .swf (Shockwave Flash) extension (I saved my file as molly.swf).

Now you've got your animation. You can either add it to your Web page the old-fashioned way, or use the Publish option to let Flash do it for you.

Note

If you're using Flash 3.0, see the "Publishing with Aftershock" section later in this chapter.

 Concerned about Flash file weights? See "Size Matters" in the Troubleshooting section at the end of this chapter for some additional insight.

PUBLISHING WITH FLASH 4

To tap into Flash 4's publishing power, begin by setting up your publishing preferences:

1. Choose File, Publish Settings. The Publish Settings dialog box appears (see Figure 33.7).

Figure 33.7
The Publish Settings dialog box is Flash's main-brain for the manner in which your Flash designs will be published.

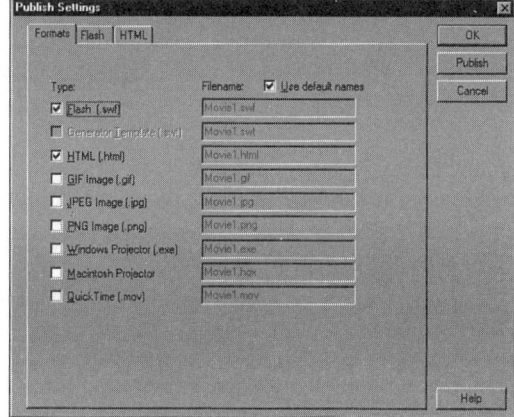

2. The Formats tab is the default view. The two preselected check boxes are Flash and HTML. If you want Flash to generate a wider range of formats, click the corresponding check box.

3. For each check box you click, a new tab appears. You can then make modifications to that format. When you publish, you'll generate all the options you've checked.

To set up the Flash .swf file defaults:

1. Click the Flash tab in the Publish Settings dialog box. The Flash options appear (see Figure 33.8).

Figure 33.8
Setting up the actual Flash movie options. These options help determine the behavior of the movie.

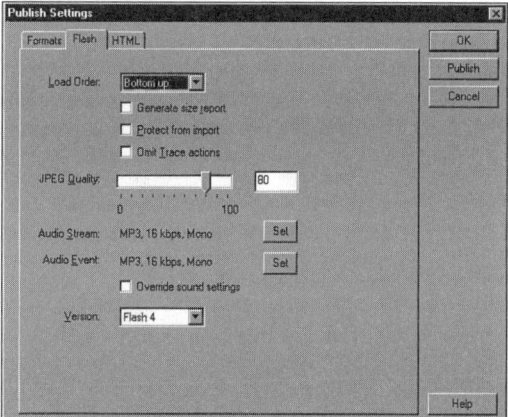

PART

VII

CH

33

2. Select a Load Order from the Load Order drop-down menu. Your choices include Bottom up, which loads the movie onto the page from the bottom horizon line to the top, and Top down, which loads the movie from the Top down.

Tip from
molly

> If you want to satisfy the needs of folks using slower connections, select Top down for the Load Order. This loads the first frame of the Flash animation top-down, allowing the visitor to see the animation appear in logical order.

3. To generate a report that shows the file size of your Flash elements, check the Generate Size Report check box.

4. Your next option is Protect from Import. This handy feature locks your file so that site visitors can't download it and then make their own modifications later on.

Tip from
molly

> Use the Protect from Import option when you want to provide extra copyright protection for your Flash designs.

5. Omit Trace Actions prompts a window open for certain kinds of actions within a Flash movie. To prevent Trace actions, check this box. Usually, the default—which is unchecked—is fine.

6. Select the JPEG Quality. Note that the higher the quality, the better looking the animation, but the higher the weight of your finished design. I recommend choosing High, but you should always test your animation. If you can use a top-quality JPEG output without compromising download time, do so.

7. If you're using audio along with your animation, you can set the MP3 values here, including Override Sound Settings, which allows you to use more than one size of sound file to best meet your site visitor needs. Check this option when you are offering a choice of sound files.

8. The Version drop-down menu allows for compatibility with other Flash versions. Set this to the version with which you want to provide compatibility.

Caution

> Flash 4 contains technology that is not supported in previous versions of Flash. However, without the Flash 4 player, site visitors won't be able to view your Flash 4 designs. Choose the version that best meets the needs of your audience. You can always Publish several different versions and use JavaScript to route browsers to the supported version.

→ For more information about JavaScript, **see** Chapter 20, "Adding JavaScript to XHTML documents," **p. 445**.

You'll want to set up the HTML preferences. Flash offers a variety, all available by clicking the HTML tab in the Publish Settings dialog box (see Figure 33.9).

Figure 33.9
To determine how the
Flash movie appears
in the browser, use
the options found in
the HTML tab.

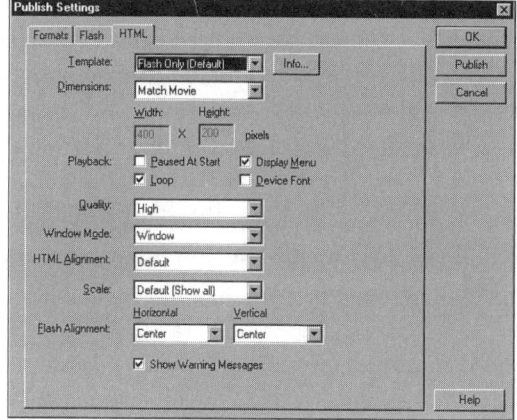

After you're in the dialog box, follow these steps to customize the manner in which your
HTML page is set up:

1. The Template drop-down menu determines the HTML and scripts that will be gener-
   ated. Your options are fairly varied. The default is Flash Only. This option sets your
   Flash file simply into an HTML page using both the embed and object tags. Flash with
   FSCommand adds JavaScript to the fundamentals. Image Map allows you to create an
   Image Map with Flash. The Java Player makes your Flash 4.0 animations readable using
   a Java Applet. QuickTime exports the movie for QuickTime, using the embed tag. User
   Choice generates a JavaScript that sniffs for the Flash 4.0 player. It then routes the
   incoming browser to an appropriate version of the page.

2. Set the dimensions of the output animation here. Typically, you'll want this to match
   your Flash animation dimensions, unless you'll be adding additional components to the
   page.

3. Playback options include Paused At Start, which allows the site visitor to start the animation using a start button. The Loop option allows the animation to repeat continuously. Display Menu ensures that an ancillary Flash menu with shortcuts is available. To
   disable this menu, uncheck the option. Device Font is a Windows-only option for font
   substitution. This is usually left unchecked.

4. Quality refers to the level of anti-aliasing that will occur. You can choose from Auto
   Low (no anti-aliasing), Auto High (adjusts to the frame rate available), High (always
   uses anti-aliasing), and Best (gives the absolute best quality no matter the speed of the
   connection or file size).

5. Set Window Mode to Opaque Windowless or Transparent Windowless when working
   in Internet Explorer-only environments. These modes allow you to tap into positioning
   and transparency movie options within IE.

6. HTML Alignment aligns the movie. The options are standard to the img and object
   tags.

7. Set the Scale to Default (Show all) to show the entire Flash movie. No Border and Exact Fit both are problematic because No Border might result in cropping of the movie, and Exact Fit forces the movie to fit into the area and disregards the original dimensions and aspect ratio of the movie.

8. Flash Alignment is best left to the default Center. Otherwise, unwanted cropping might occur.

9. To show warnings if something goes wrong with the file, leave the Show Warning Messages box checked. If you don't want warnings to show, uncheck the box.

10. Click OK to maintain these settings, or Publish to directly publish the open Flash movie.

→ To better understand the embed and object tags, **see** Chapter 31, "Audio and Video," **p. 641**.

→ For a discussion of image attributes, **see** Chapter 13, "Using Images in XHTML documents," **p. 221**.

PUBLISHING WITH AFTERSHOCK

If you're using Flash 3.0, you'll want to use Aftershock to achieve cross-browser compatibility:

1. Open Aftershock and choose File, Add, Shockwave.

2. Select your recently saved .swf file.

3. On the right side of the Aftershock interface, you'll see that the *scripting* tab is selected. On this page, you can either stick to the preset defaults or use what you think your audience will best benefit from. For my selections, I chose Shockwave Plug-in/ActiveX Control; Static or Animated GIF; and under Installation, I selected all three options.

4. Click the Page Layout tab. Here, you'll want to make any modifications to the layout that you want. I stuck with the defaults.

5. Under the Shockwave tab, you have many options including background color, playback, and quality. I stuck with the defaults on this one, although I sometimes like to pause the playback at start or use a different background color, depending on my needs.

6. For Alternate Image, I chose Animated GIF and selected my preferences. Doing this lets Aftershock not only create an animated GIF that matches the Flash movie, but also create the code that offers it if the visitor's browser can't support Flash.

7. Finally, you can modify the Java selections. I left these at their defaults.

8. Choose File, Save As.

9. Name your HTML file.

10. Aftershock now processes the HTML, the JavaScript, and any alternate image you've chosen.

Listing 33.1 shows the code that Aftershock generated. Note, of course, that this is non-specific, non-standard HTML and *not* XHTML.

LISTING 33.1   CODE GENERATED BY AFTERSHOCK

```
<HTML>
<HEAD>
<TITLE>Shockwave</TITLE>
</HEAD>
<BODY bgcolor="#000000">

<!-- Aftershock molly.swf 3=400 4=50 6=1 38 45 -->
<SCRIPT LANGUAGE="JavaScript" SRC="http://www.macromedia.com/shockwave/download/
smart/getsw.js">
function getShockwave()
{
window.open( "http://www.macromedia.com/shockwave/download/", "" );
}
</script>
<OBJECT classid="clsid:D27CDB6E-AE6D-11cf-96B8-444553540000"
 codebase="http://active.macromedia.com/flash2/cabs/swflash.cab#version=3,0,0,0"
 ID=molly WIDTH=400 HEIGHT=50>
  <PARAM NAME=movie VALUE="molly.swf">
  <PARAM NAME=quality VALUE=autohigh>
  <PARAM NAME=bgcolor VALUE=#000000>
<SCRIPT LANGUAGE=JavaScript>
<!--
var ShockMode = 0;
var OldVersionOfPlugin = 0;
if (navigator.mimeTypes && navigator.mimeTypes["application/x-shockwave-flash"]
&& navigator.mimeTypes["application/x-shockwave-flash"].enabledPlugin) {
      if (navigator.plugins && navigator.plugins["Shockwave Flash"])
             ShockMode = 1;
      else
             OldVersionOfPlugin = 1;
}
function checkForShockwave()
{
      navigator.plugins.refresh();
      if ( navigator.plugins["Shockwave Flash"] ){
             parent.location.reload();
      } else {
             setTimeout( "checkForShockwave()", 1000 );
      }
}
if (!ShockMode && navigator.appName && navigator.appName.indexOf("Netscape")
!= - 1 && navigator.appVersion.indexOf("4.") != - 1
&& navigator.javaEnabled() && netscape.softupdate.Trigger.UpdateEnabled() &&
document.cookie.indexOf("StartedShockwaveInstall") == -1) {
      var jarPath = new String("");
      if (navigator.platform.indexOf("Win33") >= 0 )
             jarPath = "http://download.macromedia.com/pub/shockwave/jars/
english/silentflash33.jar"
      else if (navigator.platform.indexOf("Win16") >= 0 )
             jarPath = "http://download.macromedia.com/pub/shockwave/jars/
english/silentflash16.jar"
      else if (navigator.platform.indexOf("MacPPC") >= 0 )
             jarPath = "http://download.macromedia.com/pub/shockwave/jars/
```

LISTING 33.1   CONTINUED

```
english/silentflashppc.jar"
      if (jarPath.length) {
            netscape.softupdate.Trigger.StartSoftwareUpdate (jarPath,
netscape.softupdate.Trigger.FORCE_MODE);
            document.cookie='StartedShockwaveInstall;path=/;'
            setTimeout("checkForShockwave()", 1000);
      }
}
if ( ShockMode ) {
      document.write('<EMBED SRC="molly.swf"');
      document.write(' swLiveConnect=FALSE WIDTH=400 HEIGHT=50');
      document.write(' QUALITY=autohigh BGCOLOR=#000000');
      document.write(' TYPE="application/x-shockwave-flash"
PLUGINSPAGE="http://www.macromedia.com/shockwave/download/index.cgi?
P1_Prod_Version=ShockwaveFlash">');
      document.write('</EMBED>');
} else if (!(navigator.appName && navigator.appName.indexOf("Netscape")>=0 &&
navigator.appVersion.indexOf("2.")>=0)){
      document.write('<IMG SRC="molly.gif" WIDTH=400 HEIGHT=50 BORDER=0>');
      if (( navigator.appName.indexOf( "Microsoft" ) != -1 ) &&
( navigator.appVersion.indexOf( "Macintosh" ) != -1 ) &&
( navigator.appVersion.indexOf( "3." ) == 0 ))
      {
            document.write( '<P><A HREF="http://www.macromedia.com/shockwave/
download/">' );
            document.write( '<img src="get_shockwave.gif" WIDTH=88 HEIGHT=31
BORDER=0></A>' );
      } else {
            document.write( '<P><A HREF="#" onClick="getShockwave(' );
            document.write( "'Director 0.0','Flash 2.0'" );
            document.write( ')">' );
            document.write( '<img src="get_shockwave.gif" WIDTH=88 HEIGHT=31
BORDER=0></A>' );
      }
      if ( OldVersionOfPlugin )
            document.write( '<P>This page contains a new format movie that the
current
Shockwave plug-in cannot handle. Please update to the new version.</P>' );
}
//-->
</SCRIPT><NOEMBED><IMG SRC="molly.gif" WIDTH=400 HEIGHT=50 BORDER=0></NOEMBED>
<NOSCRIPT>
<IMG SRC="molly.gif" WIDTH=400 HEIGHT=50 BORDER=0><P><A
HREF="http://www.macromedia.com/shockwave/download/"><IMG SRC="get_shockwave.gif"
WIDTH=88
HEIGHT=31 BORDER=0></A></NOSCRIPT></OBJECT><!-- EndAftershock molly.swf -->
</BODY>
</HTML>
```

Tip from

To make your AfterShock code XHTML compliant, open up the code in your favorite editor and revise it. Remember that you'll have to appropriately accommodate the JavaScript code. An excellent tool to help convert non-standard HTML into XHTML is HTML Tidy, which you can download from **www.w3.org/People/Raggett/tidy/**.

Despite the complicated code generated by Aftershock, the compatibility that results is quite desirable. Of course, Flash 4.0 offers more elegant solutions in both the way Flash is displayed and the way the HTML code is written.

TROUBLESHOOTING

USING FLASH IN THE REAL WORLD

I want to use Flash, but I'm concerned about reaching a wide audience. How many people actually have Flash support already?

Internet Explorer supports Flash and ships with the technology. This means no plug-in is required. However, Netscape users require a player. Developers using Flash can encourage site visitors to download the plug-in if they have not yet done so.

Macromedia estimates that about 86% of the Web browsing population has support for Flash. However, this isn't for Flash 4.0 specifically, it's Flash support in general. The upshot is that you'll need to make decisions based on your audience.

SIZE MATTERS!

Flash is great! I've used it to create some attractive animations with sound. But the file sizes are larger than recommended. What do I do?

You have several options here. Flash files can be very small, that's part of their appeal. However, if you're creating a major multimedia presentation with audio, your file sizes can grow large. To accommodate everyone, you can create several versions of your site: a text-only version, a non-Flash version, and the Flash version. You also can combine standard HTML and graphics with portions of Flash within a page. Determine which parts of a page should be in static and which can make use of Flash before designing your page instead of trying to do it all with Flash.

DESIGNING FOR THE REAL WORLD

AUSTIN POWERS IS SHOCKING!

In an effort to add even more enjoyable pastimes to the *Austin Powers: Spy Who Shagged Me* Web site, the developers opted for a Shockwave game.

Called "Move Your Mojo," you begin by choosing your players. I chose Felicity Shagwell to the tune of funky 60s music and twirling flowers (see Figure 33.10). The goal of the game is to dance with Austin using keys on the keyboard.

I went four rounds and lost, alas. But I was really having a great time, demonstrating the absorbing aspect of multimedia on the Web. Even if it's not something you'll be using in the majority of your sites, when it is used, it can be a very useful addition to a site.

Figure 33.10
Shockwave can be used to create a complex game, such as "Move Your Mojo." This game asks the site visitor to use keys on the keyboard that cause the character Felicity Shagwell to perform dance moves. A game of this nature involves the site visitor completely, and can act as a method of bringing people back to the site time and again.

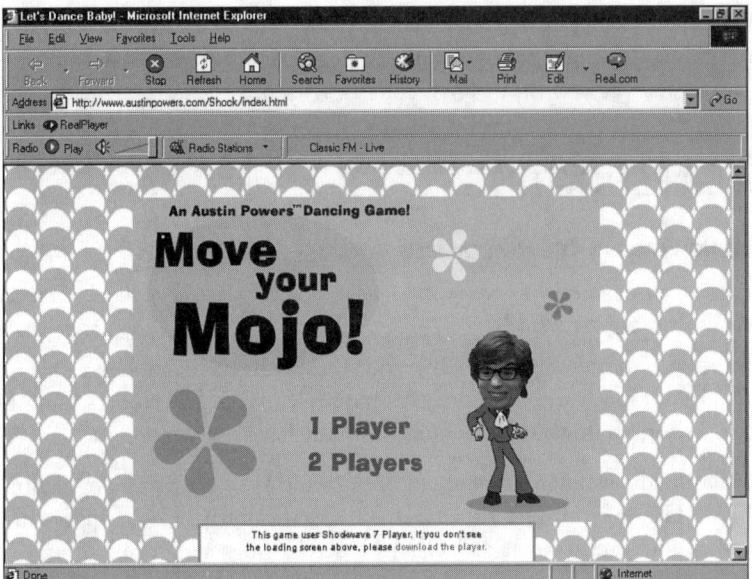

Note

Play "Move Your Mojo" at `http://www.austinpowers.com/Shock/index.html`.

CREATING CONTENT FOR ALTERNATIVE DEVICES

CHAPTER 34

Overview of Alternative Devices, Languages, and Protocols

In this chapter

TYPES OF ALTERNATIVE DEVICES

It's amazing to think that in just under a decade, we've come to a world where the Internet—and the Web—not only have become pervasive at work, in our schools, and in our homes, but that related technologies are advancing beyond the standard computer's scope.

There are numerous devices available that enable us to access and send email and browse the Web without the need to have a heavy desktop or even lightweight notebook computer around! In fact, many of these devices sit in the palm of our hands. Or, they are attached or built in to other devices within our world—our televisions, even some automobiles. Eventually, it's felt that we'll be able to access online services using home appliances. Need a recipe? Simply look it up from a built-in browser on your refrigerator.

I know it sounds a little odd, and perhaps these technological advances don't suit everyone's tastes. But it's really happening, and developers who are aware of new and even experimental applications and methods will be better enabled to make choices about their career goals. Instead of being an XHTML author, you might find yourself writing WML, or other, proprietary languages for special devices. The opportunities are only as endless as the new ideas coming to light.

OPERATING SYSTEMS FOR ALTERNATIVE DEVICES

Alternative devices require operating systems to, well, operate! As most readers are aware, an operating system (referred to as an OS for short) is the meta-management software found on your computer or related device. Its job is to manage memory, allocating systems input and output, communicate with and between applications on your computer, and so forth.

Operating systems for alternative devices are essentially no different from the OSes with which we are already familiar: Windows, MacOS, Unix, Linux, and the like. However, their job is modified due to the hardware and software that exist in the alternative environment. In most cases, the alternative devices I discuss in this chapter are pretty small—some smaller than your hand. This means that processing speed and memory are relatively limited, at least as compared to the desktops and notebook computers.

Note

It's interesting to point out that where Java was once considered to be a contender for the delivery of Web-based content, the language has in fact found one unforeseen use: the development of mobile operating systems and applications. Many small devices use Java as the underlying language driving their systems. Another popular language for this is C++.

The primary OSs in use by mobile devices are

- **Windows CE**—Developed by Microsoft, Windows CE is a pared-down version of Windows. It draws from the same iconography and interface design as Windows, making the products that support it very user-friendly to individuals familiar with Windows.

- **EPOC**—Designed for wireless phones and related devices, EPOC has its origins in an operating system that Psion (see the PDA section below) introduced. Originally an open source OS, EPOC has been further developed by Symbian, EPOC is now a license-based OS.

- **PalmOS**—Totally proprietary to the Palm computing platform, PalmOS was developed by 3Com and is used in Palm and some related products.

- **Linux**—This popular open-source computer OS is starting to be used in mobile devices, to the delight of Linux and open-source fans.

> **Note**
>
> For developer information about Windows CE, see `www.microsoft.com/windows/embedded/`. Information on EPOC can be found at `www.symbian.com/technology/platform.html`. PalmOS resources and developer sites are available from `www.palmos.com/`. A great overview by Derrick Story (a contributor to this book and Managing Editor of O'Reilly Networks) on the state of Linux on Palm devices is available at `www.oreillynet.com/pub/a/network/2000/09/01/maga-zine/linux_pda.html`.

PDAs

Do you have a PDA? PDAs are *Personal Digital Assistants.* These devices are small, mobile computers that help us manage our schedules and keep our personal and business contacts organized. Some PDAs have built-in or add-on modems, enabling us to send and receive email and surf the Web wirelessly.

New developments in PDA technology are occurring at a rapid-fire pace. Color support and even sound and video are starting to show up in some PDAs. Some of the most popular PDAs include

- **PocketPC**—PocketPCs are a group of PDAs by various manufacturers that run on the Windows CE OS. PocketPCs are a powerful contender in the PDA game. It offers all the standard calendar and contacts available in most common PDAs, but certain models sport games, audio support, full color support, and even the ability to view and edit Microsoft Word and Excel documents.

- **Palm**—Palm has been in the handheld device game since 1996, when it came out with its very popular PalmPilot product. Today, Palm has several PDA versions that can be used for wireless computing applications, including the Palm III, the Palm V, and the Palm M100. The Palm VII has wireless built directly into the device. All a user need do is flip up the antenna and go surfing. You can send and retrieve email, surf the Web, and use a special, proprietary technology known as *Web Clippings*. Palm devices integrate with desktop software to make the management of calendar, contact, financial, and other data very easy.

- **Visor**—The Visor handheld, from Handspring, is an affordable alternative to some of its more expensive cousins. Interestingly, Visor uses the Palm Computing Platform. An interesting aspect to the Visor is its Springboard Module Expansion slot, which enables a variety of hardware and software to be modularly added to the Visor, turning it into a pager, a digital music player, and even a phone.

- **Psion**—Psion uses the EPOC OS, and offers a number of handheld devices with wireless technology available as part of, or as a modular attachable portion of, the given device. Psion is noted as being the first manufacturer of widespread, commercially distributed handhelds.

Note

For information on the PocketPC, see www.pocketpc.com/. Palm PDAs are showcased at www.palm.com, Visor's at www.handspring.com, and Psion is at www.psion.com/. There's information for developers wanting to develop for a given platform at each of these sites.

Developers interested in extending their Web site information to PDA environments need to be aware of the limitations of PDAs. They include

- **Very small screen size**—Most PDAs are the size of your hand. Screens tend to be limited in their ability to display complex visual or lengthy text-based data.

- **Limited color support**—Many PDAs don't offer color at all, and those that do offer limited color. So, special care regarding how color is used for PDA device development must be taken.

- **Limitations on technology**—Although some PDAs support multimedia such as audio, video, and Flash animation, JavaScript, and Java Applets, many do not. When developing for specific PDAs, I advise researching what technologies are supported by a given PDA, and when developing for broad-spectrum audiences, avoid the use of these technologies.

→ For further information about designing for alternative environments and Web Clippings, **see** Chapter 35, "Developing for the Alternative Device", **p. 693**.

MOBILE COMPUTERS

Mobile computers are typically the same size or bigger than a PDA, but smaller than an ultra-light notebook. These computers pack more power than a PDA, but typically have less resources available than a desktop or notebook computer. Handheld computers run on scaled-down OSs such as Windows CE. Several popular tablet computers are

- **Cassiopeia**—Casio's popular entry into the mobile computing market. Has an 80MHz processor and 8MB of RAM, and a screen resolution of 640×240. Also, it has color support!

- **Clio**—By Mainstreet Networks, with an 80MHz processor, up to 32MB RAM, and a screen resolution of 640×480.

- **IBM Workpad**—With more power than most handhelds, this computer offers 131MHz processing, up to 48MB of RAM, and a screen resolution of 640×480.

For developers, the often low processing power and limited screen resolution of mobile computers means pared-down pages that use very straight-forward markup, or table-based layouts specifically designed to fit the available screen resolution. Avoidance of multimedia and processor-intensive technologies is advised.

> **Note**
>
> You can check out Casio's personal PCs at `www.casio.com/personalpcs/`. Clio can be found at `www.clio.com/`, and IBM Workpad at `www.ibm.com/workpad/`.

SMART PAGERS AND PHONES

A smart pager or phone is one that has features beyond the basics of paging or voice communications. Many smart pagers and phones offer PDA-style software, including contact lists, calendars, and email and of course—Web browsers. They use a variety of OSs, including proprietary technology.

Of course, the limitations of screen space and color support on these very small displays also limits the developer. Information has to be tightly organized for display. Screen space is especially variegated in these devices.

Some popular smart phones and pagers include

- **Nokia Communicator**—This is a hybrid digital cellular phone and PDA. It has a keyboard, 8MB of RAM, and a screen resolution of 640×200 pixels.
- **Qualcomm pdQ Phone**—This smart phone uses the PalmOS, has 2MB of RAM, and a display of 160×240 pixels.
- **Motorola PageWriter**—With 1.25MB of memory, this pager isn't very powerful, but it's surprisingly versatile. Screen display is 240×160 pixels.

> **Note**
>
> Phone developers should drop by Phone.Com's developer site, `www.phone.com/developers/index.html`.

SET-TOP BOXES

The convergence of television and the Web has been discussed for some years. Set-top boxes are appliances that enable televisions to connect to the Internet. Some current technologies include WebTV, the most familiar application of the merging of television and the Web. PersonalJava from Sun Microsystems is a technology being used to enable Web connectivity devices, including set-top boxes.

PART

VIII

CH

34

> **Note**
>
> Set-top boxes also are being used to enable analog TVs to decode digital broadcasts. For more information on WebTV, see `www.webtv.com/`. PersonalJava information can be found at `www.sun.com/software/personaljava/index.html`.

→ For complete details about designing for WebTV, **see** Chapter 35, "Developing for the Alternative Device", **p. 693**.

EBOOKS

At an author's conference a few years ago, I was introduced to the concept of the eBook. These devices enable users to download digital books and other related material from the Web. Although the idea of getting cozy with a digital device and a hot cup of tea seems remote for most people who were raised with paper books, the eBook is a concept that bears consideration.

This is especially true when we think about technical documentation, search features, and wireless Internet connectivity. Conceivably, an individual working in the field and requiring a remote update to a troubleshooting document could use an eBook to retrieve the necessary information immediately, and then read it on a screen display that's more comfortable than a mobile computer.

Whether the eBook concept will take off is yet to be seen. Introduced in 1998, eBooks are of mild interest but do not seem to be as popular as other mobile technologies.

> **Note**
>
> See www.nuvomedia.com/ for more information on eBooks.

ALTERNATIVE DEVICE LANGUAGES

Here are a few of the languages you'll need to familiarize yourself with if you want to design sites that can be handled by tomorrow's handheld devices.

XHTML AND XML

As a meta-language, XML allows the development of applications for a very wide range of data types, and therefore is attractive to developers working with alternative languages and protocols, including WAP. WML and XHTML are both examples of this.

XHTML allows Web pages to be backward compatible but positions them to integrate with XML and other related technologies. Part of the rationale for XHTML is to position Web content for easy modification and access by alternative devices. This is most clearly seen in the work being done with XHTML Basic.

→ To read more about XHTML Basic, **see** Chapter 23, "XHTML Basic," **p. 503**.

XSL/XSLT

Extensible Style Language/Extensible Style Language Transformations embody a write once, display anywhere concept. Developers using transformations will create a stylesheet that basically says, "If this device requests the page, deliver it using this style." These technologies are in the Working Draft stage.

The advantage to transformations is that multiple options for display can be offered. So, let's say you want a page to display using specific design parameters on a standard computer screen, but also be available to display on a PDA. Ideologically, XSLT allows developers to do this.

→ To learn about XSL/XSLT, **see** Chapter 19, "Extensible Stylesheet Language (XSL)," **p. 419**.

WML

The Wireless Markup Language is to WAP (Wireless Application Protocol, see "WAP" section later in this chapter) as HTML is to TCP/IP. WML works in tandem with WAP to help deliver content to wireless applications.

WML is an application of XML. In other words, XML is the meta-language from which WML is derived. As a result, its syntax and structure will be familiar to those readers who've spent time working with XHTML, which also derives from XML. WML uses a "card" concept, organizing content for wireless pages to be delivered in a stacked rather than distributed fashion.

→ For a more detailed look at WML authoring, **see** Chapter 36, "Pagers, Cell Phones, and Other Wireless Devices," **p. 711**.

HDML

HDML is the *Handheld Device Markup Language*. It was submitted for discussion to the W3C in 1997 by Unwired Planet. HDML proposed the concept of cards and decks, as well as providing a DTD and syntactical structure for the management of wireless content.

HDML has been set aside for WML, but the early concepts of HDML have contributed significantly to the development of wireless markup.

> **Note**
>
> You can find the HDML submission to the W3C at `www.w3.org/TR/NOTE-Submission-HDML-spec.html`.

WEB CLIPPINGS

Web Clippings is a proprietary methodology of developing miniature Web applications for use with the Palm VII. Web Clippings draws from simple HTML, using a pared-down version of HTML and a restricted technologies menu to achieve delivery of specialized Web content to this wireless PDA.

→ Develop your own Web Clipping! **See** Chapter 35, "Developing for the Alternative Device," **p. 693**.

PART
VIII

CH
34

WIRELESS PROTOCOLS

A protocol is a method of managing conversation points between connections. The Internet uses a number of familiar protocols, including TCP/IP (two protocols, the Transmission Control Protocol and the Internet Protocol, which work together to transmit packets and messages over the Internet); HTTP, the Hypertext Transfer Protocol, which supports the exchange of Web-based content via HTML and related pages; and FTP, which manages the transfer of binary and ASCII files over the Internet. There are additional protocols for electronic mail and other Internet functions.

Wireless requires similar methods to establish and maintain connectivity between points of connection and transfer. A number of protocols exist to manage this. By far the most significant at this time is WAP. Another protocol extension that should be of great interest to Web developers is CC/PP.

WAP

Now in use, the Wireless Application Protocol delivers content to wireless devices like pagers and cell phones. WAP is felt to be the most widely supported protocol method of delivering wireless content to alternative devices.

Some highlights about WAP include

- WAP is an open-industry standard
- Uses existing markup and protocol standards including XML (mostly in the form of WML) and IP
- WAP is working with the W3C to ensure the appropriate adherence to and development of current and future standards

→ For more information on WAP, **see** Chapter 36, "Pagers, Cell Phones, and Other Wireless Devices," **p. 693**.

> **Note**
>
> For more information on WAP, visit the WAP Forum, `www.wapforum.org/`.

CC/PP

Web developers are all too-well aware of how difficult it is to develop across browsers, browser versions, and platforms. Some developers create dynamic designs, opt to design for a specific browser, test their work extensively, and/or use JavaScript detection and routing to ensure that a given browser displays the correct layout.

These challenges in and of themselves are time consuming. But what happens when all these new, cool devices are added to the soup? Imagine developing a site that must not only be cross-browser, cross-platform compatible in terms of standard OSs and resolutions, but it now also must be deliverable to PDAs, smart phones and pagers, Set-top boxes, and other, alternative devices.

Currently a work in progress, the Composite Capability/Preference Profile (CC/PP) is a framework by which user preferences and device profiles can be delivered by a user agent to a server. The server then returns custom content based on the information received.

Ideologically, CC/PP will enable the definition of a device for the proper page delivery to the that device occurs. This will happen on the server rather than client side, as is currently possible with JavaScript detection-and-routing. The advantage to a protocol such as CC/PP is that it is device-independent. JavaScript is useless if the client or device doesn't support

JavaScript, or the client has scripting disabled. Server-based definition methods remove that concern. The software and hardware will be profiled, as well as any preferences that are set by the user. The Web server can then deliver the code that is best optimized for that browser.

Note

For more information on CC/PP, visit the W3C's CC/PP working group at `www.w3.org/Mobile/CCPP/`.

CHAPTER 35

DEVELOPING FOR THE ALTERNATIVE DEVICE

In this chapter

ALTERNATIVE DEVICE DESIGN

Web designers and developers are traveling at warp speed toward an unknown future. Unusual acronyms whiz past our heads, looking much like alien creatures with three- or four-letter bodies, speaking unfamiliar languages and negotiating obscure protocols.

While working long hours creating Web sites, developers might be aware that there's an alternative device revolution taking place. The culture kings are telling us so—Steve Case recently made a public commitment to creating devices for the wireless Web. "This is the second Internet revolution," Case said in his keynote speech at Spring Internet World 2000. "You should have simple devices that make connecting to the Internet simple and easy."

What's more, forecasters such as Jesse Berst of ZDNet say that by 2002, most people will be accessing Web content using handheld devices instead of PCs.

Disconcerting? You bet. Only a handful of developers are actually working to deliver content to alternative devices, and the rest of us are wondering how to negotiate these alien lands.

DEMYSTIFYING FUTURE DELIVERY SYSTEMS

The overview of these new technologies found in Chapter 34 will help you get comfortable with the devices you need to know about. That chapter introduced a number of devices and technologies that might seem alien to many readers. Some readers will be familiar with one or two of these, and a few of you might already be working with them. Take a moment to view or review some of the languages and protocols that you could be working with in the coming years.

→ Know your alternative devices! **See** Chapter 34, "Overview of Alternative Devices, Languages, and Protocols," **p. 683**.

You're probably asking, "Do I really need to know this stuff?" You might very well need to expand your language and protocol horizons beyond XHTML and HTTP, depending upon your personal and professional goals.

However, many designers work in teams and can leave the weighty technology to others. While those of you in this group might not need to know how to work with these technologies, you'll need to know how to design for them. Moreover, being aware of what the technologies are, what they do, and how they influence the way you design will put you in better control of your work and make you infinitely more attractive to recruiters in years to come.

UNDERSTANDING ALTERNATIVE ENVIRONMENTS

So how do designers actually plan and design for alternative applications? Simplest is best in the alternative world. This is because displays on most of these devices are very small and almost wholly text based. Were you getting excited over the growing room available to you on PCs? Using fixed table designs at 800 × 600 or larger? That's great for the Web as it's delivered to the desktop, but you're going to have to reorient yourself entirely if you also want to design for teeny, tiny alternative devices.

Those of you who designed for the Web back in the days of the line-based browser Lynx (see Figure 35.1) appreciate these limitations. You might remember that a page had limited display features, basically allowing for a bit of text, some links, and some minimal text formatting. The text-based Web forced designers to plan intelligent content that displayed logically.

Figure 35.1
Browsing the Web with Lynx. A reminder of days past, and alternative device days to come!

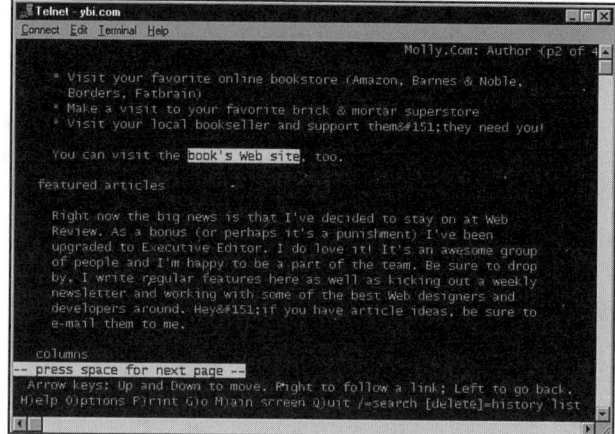

Designing for alternative devices means studying the device, looking at its limitations and features, and thinking about how your information will be structured. Set aside beautiful visual designs—at least for now. Think instead of content and structure. Later, as certain handheld interfaces become more advanced, we can return to more complex visual presentations. For now, simplicity reigns supreme.

First of all, let's examine why people are attracted to appliances for accessing Web content. Aside from the "toy" factor that drives many to purchase the latest and greatest technology just because it's cool, many people are looking to their Palms, pagers, and cell phones as methods of gathering personal and professional information. They want that information quickly. They also want it on the run—whether checking a stock quote while catching a plane, or checking baseball scores at the opera, the alternative-device user needs the requested information to be fast, accurate, and easy to access.

Data must be very streamlined for these devices. You won't be able to have three screens of options and information, or multiple areas that users click through to get to the data they want and need.

If you examine your cell phone or pager, you'll immediately notice that not only is the display quite small, but there are few buttons to press. This means that people will navigate your content and make choices in limited and awkward ways. Simplifying navigation for these devices is not just a guideline, it's an imperative.

If these limitations haven't injured your design-oriented soul, wait until you hear this: At least for now, wireless networks are very, very slow. Add to that the fact that alternative devices have very limited processing speed and memory, and those of you who had been pouring a cold one to celebrate the growing distribution of broadband access had better grab a quick breath and hold it. If you're planning to deliver alternative device content, everything you create will have to weigh less, be more precise, and somehow still be intelligent.

ALTERNATIVE DEVICE DESIGN TIPS

Speaking of intelligence, I'm sure you want more details about the concepts that you'll need to design effective alternative device information. I'll provide some general tips and advice here, but bear in mind that many of these technologies aren't nearly mature.

- **Sensible architecture**—A good place to begin is by understanding the architecture of device design. When beginning a site map, most designers use some sort of hierarchical structure to build pages. This structure might have a home page, and branch from there into subgroups of pages. Designing for an alternative device doesn't allow you this much leverage. Instead, you have to bring as much information to the top as possible. Instead of the page metaphor, wireless development uses a card deck metaphor. In this methodology, information is stacked rather than distributed over pages. The first card in your stack might have the identity of the site and a few links to the information, such as stock quotes, sports scores, or weather. One click, and the users are at the data they seek.

- **Clean code**—As you know by now, XHTML exists largely due to the need for syntactical rigor in HTML. Whether you're working with XML, XHTML, WML, or proprietary methods such as Palm's Web Clippings, you'll be at a significant disadvantage from both design and technological standpoints without good coding practices. Technologically speaking, keeping code clean and accurate makes it readily portable. Good code helps deliver content that's clean and fast. From a design perspective, the integrity of a document's structure is imperative to the way it appears onscreen. Using logical structure, including properly labeled headings, text formatting, and text emphasis makes these limited playing cards of information more sensible both logically and visually.

- **Meaningful navigation cues**—When developing for the visual Web, designers can choose from a variety of navigation metaphors. You can opt to use concrete visual cues or abstract cues, or mix text and abstract visual design to make a composition that's compelling and unique.

- **In the text environment**—abstractions are dangerous. Every navigation element must be clearly denoted. If you want someone to scroll down, an arrow pointing down with the words "scroll down" might be your best bet to ensuring people know how to navigate your information. Every navigation cue, whether symbolic, textual, or some combination thereof, should be very clear in its intent.

- **Images and Color**—Not every alternative device is limited to text content. When you use images, keep in mind that they must be extremely light, weighing in at less than 1.5KB. Also, never use images to replace text. Rather, use images to enhance or extend the meaning of text. In addition, if the language with which you're developing allows an image to contain an alternative text `alt` attribute, use it! Because of the limited memory, processing, and access speeds of wireless devices, many people with image support turn it off.

It's interesting to point out that color is starting to appear on more Palm-style devices. Color support can be very limited or more mature, such as on devices using thin film transistor (TFT) active matrix displays. This is good news for the designer interested in adding some visual interest to his or her alternative device design. However, if it doesn't degrade gracefully to traditional text displays, it's unwise to rely on color until the market offers more devices that support color numbers and values.

BACK TO THE FUTURE

Does this mean that the days of expanded design opportunities via traditional Web browsers are limited? Not in the least! Take comfort that some of you will never have to design for alternative devices. Others among you will jump at the opportunity, knowing that a limited design environment can encourage innovation. Still others will want the flexibility and options born of expanded knowledge and technique.

If XSLT and profiling through the proposed CC/PP framework take off—and many say they will—ideally you'll be designing information that will be written once and played anywhere. Although designers will certainly have to prepare their content for a wide array of devices, the desktop will still be a popular choice on the Web browsing menu.

→ For more information about XSLT **see** Chapter 19, "Extensible Stylesheet Language (XSL)," **p. 419**.

The grand irony is that designers, especially those who once designed for a kinder, simpler Web, have little to fear. Aside from learning some new concepts that should not be as daunting as they might first appear, it looks as though our jobs will be very much like creating pages for the Web in 1993. But this time, you'll be using different languages and protocols to achieve your designs.

DESIGNING FOR WEBTV

I personally don't have a burning passion for WebTV, but as a developer I do recognize that it's an important format. Despite the fact that WebTV users are still a very small part of the browsing population—not quite totaling a million—knowing how to properly accommodate those users can only serve to broaden the scope of our Web sites. What's more, the Web and TV will become more closely entwined over time—and the savvy developer will do well to learn what's up and coming in our convergent future.

PART

VIII

CH

35

WHY WEBTV?

The demographic of the Web is changing. What used to be the domain of skilled computer users and motivated curiosity seekers has become a public utility. Technically interested but less-adept audiences want—and deserve—an easy way to get online. We see this clearly within the senior audience, which happens to be one of the largest growing Web populations. WebTV makes the Web approachable by putting it in the context of a familiar medium.

From a more technical standpoint, convergence is something developers have foreseen for some time now. Convergence (a late '90s word describing the integration of the Web and other media, such as TV and handheld devices) is realistically a critical concern for developers. The familiar (albeit already frustrating) domain of the Web browser isn't the only focus of our future. We need to become aware that we'll soon be dealing with user agents running on devices as small as pagers and at least as large as big-screen TVs. That means negotiating changes in the languages we use, and the way we do design.

WebTV is a perfect place for developers to start, because although there are concerns unique to working with WebTV, these concerns aren't too far outside the ones we already deal with today. We stay in the realm of the familiar—a browser, conventional HTML methods—but make a move into the realm of a user agent that's not running on a standard computer.

DESIGNING FOR WEBTV

How is designing for WebTV different from designing for standard browsers? For starters, the WebTV browser is a proprietary technology that's significantly different from the more familiar browsers such as Microsoft Internet Explorer and Netscape Navigator. But there are some unusual concerns common to both WebTV and conventional TV. I've broken the major concerns for developers into four groups: resolution, code rendering, design, and technology. Within each category there are specific considerations for Web developers when working with WebTV. Here's a closer look.

RESOLUTION

The resolution of a television screen in the United States is akin to a 640 × 480 computer screen. European TVs use a PAL standard, equivalent to an 800 × 600 computer environment. Upcoming HDTV standards will be considerably different by virtue of the technology they encompass. I say "akin" and "equivalent" because there are factors affecting TV—such as technical concepts including scan lines, blanking intervals, and interlacing—that make TV resolution different from that of a computer monitor.

However, knowing that you have some familiar equivalents is a good starting point. As mentioned earlier, just as most designers recognize a lowest common denominator of around 585 pixels for fixed-design Web sites, WebTV browsers come in a bit smaller, due to the capabilities of North-American and Japanese displays. The width for a WebTV screen is 544 pixels, and height per screen is 372.

I can hear the screams of agony now. Please don't despair! If you're designing with tables, you have several options. You can design fixed-width tables to accommodate WebTV at 544 pixels. You can use dynamic table layouts. You also can use a browser detect and route for WebTV along with other resolutions.

→ To learn more about tables, **see** Chapter 14, "Laying Out Tables Within XHTML Document," **p. 243**, and Chapter 26, "Working with the Computer Screen," **p. 545**.

Of course, you can ignore resolution issues altogether. But beware: WebTV will restrict fixed tables by wrapping or compressing them to the size it can accommodate, squishing (that's a technical term) your graphics to fit. In some cases, this can result in spliced graphics being rendered in bizarre ways, as shown in Figure 35.2.

Figure 35.2
Tables in WebTV are often compressed, potentially rendering your spliced designs in strange, ineffective ways.

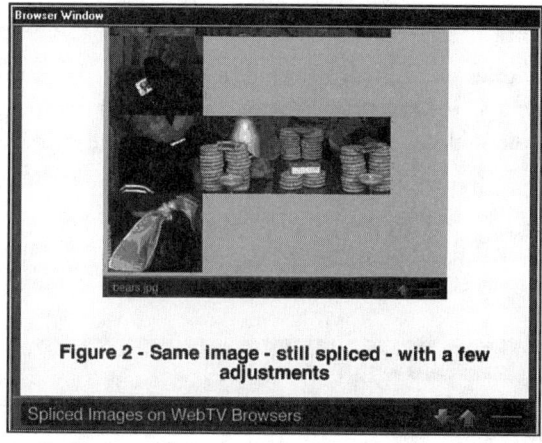

Figure 2 - Same image - still spliced - with a few adjustments

Spliced Images on WebTV Browsers

To ensure that fixed tables (and the images within them) that are wider than 544 pixels behave, use the guide shown in Table 35.1 to accomplish the results you'd like. If any of these options are not present, and your table is wider than 544 pixels, the WebTV browser will wrap any information that can't fit within this maximum width.

TABLE 35.1   WEBTV TABLE DESIGN OPTIONS AND RESULTS

Code Option	WebTV Result	Code Sample

Store all images within separate table cells.	All images will be compressed in a given row to fit the screen.	`<tr>`
		`<td><img></td>`
		`<td><img></td>`
		`</tr>`

Keep images in the same cell but use the `<nobr>` element around the images.	Images will first be compressed in an attempt to have all images fit on the same line. Any images that still don't fit will wrap to the next line.	`<td> <nobr>`
		`<img><img><img>`
		`</nobr> </td>`

PART

VIII

CH

35

TABLE 35.1	CONTINUED	
Fix the width of the table cell containing the images.	Images will first be compressed, then wrapped if necessary.	`<td width="600">` `<img><img><img> </td>`

CODE RENDERING

WebTV renders HTML differently in some cases from what you might expect. We've already seen this in the resolution example described, where compression and wrapping of tables by the browser can occur.

Page titles, frames, forms, and image maps have specific issues to contend with, as follows:

- **Page titles**—Page titles for the title bar tend to be truncated to 35 total characters or less. Therefore, it's wise to keep titles concise. "Molly.Com: Home" will work just fine, but "Welcome to the Web Site of Molly E. Holzschlag" will truncate.

- **Frames**—In terms of frames, it's interesting to note that the WebTV browser converts frames into tables. This means that any static portion of a frame viewed in a browser will not remain static if there's a scrollbar. Figure 35.3 shows a framed page with the top static navigation in place. Figure 35.4 shows the same page in the context of WebTV.

Figure 35.3
A standard framed page.

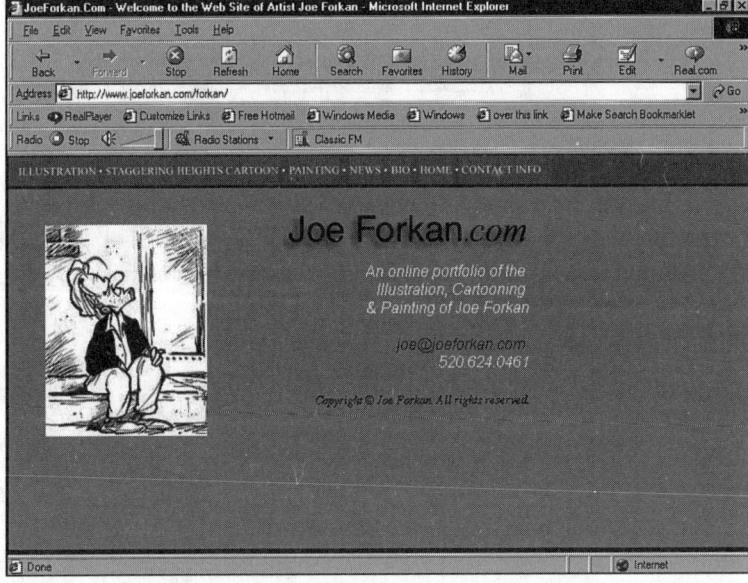

Figure 35.4
WebTV turns the framed page into a table.

- **Forms**—Forms will work just fine if they're kept simple, with very clean HTML code. Complex forms and incorrectly coded attributes can cause the WebTV browser to choke. Interestingly, there are some fun attributes specific to WebTV browsers, enabling the addition of background color, cursor color, text color, and even having selections automatically activated. Forms using JavaScript might not work properly (see JavaScript, below).

- **Image maps**—It's important to know that WebTV doesn't support server-side image mapping. It does, however, support client-side image mapping. The one caveat is that any shape other than a rectangle might prove problematic, since WebTV users aren't using a mouse to navigate. Rather, links are surrounded by a selection box (see Figure 35.5). If you're using image maps when designing for WebTV, be sure to include client-side mapping information and keep your map areas rectangular.

Note

For more information on WebTV support and information, visit the WebTV `developer.webtv.net/`. You can also download the WebTV viewer, which simulates the way your work will look on WebTV right from your computer. It's an excellent way to test your pages for WebTV compatibility.

DESIGN

There are several visual concerns of which to be aware. In general, because TV uses different technology from computer monitors to generate images, things are just going to look somewhat different in the TV environment.

The good news is that TV supports many more colors than browsers—and, what's more, no colors will dither, ever. The bad news is that there are certain colors, especially red and (gasp) white, that can appear very bright and disconcerting when displayed on a TV. Television backgrounds are generally better dark, with light text. The Web is more flexible in this regard.

PART
VIII

CH
35

So you'll need to think carefully about who you're designing for and why. Obviously, white backgrounds are simply too important in Web design to restrict them just to accommodate the smaller population of WebTV users. Furthermore, the use of colors that are not Web-safe when designing for diverse audiences is a consideration that developers always need to think carefully about. However, if you're developing content specifically for WebTV, you'll want to keep these issues in mind.

Another critical difference in terms of visual design is the way fonts are rendered. WebTV ignores most HTML and CSS fonts unless you stick to the two fonts that the WebTV browser uses—Helvetica for proportional text and Monaco for fixed-width text. WebTV also has its own sizing system for fonts. Users control the size by setting up their preferences to read fonts as small, medium, or large. Therefore, designers will always be at the mercy of having their information display to the user preference. This will especially affect any floating images within text, and wrap headers or display text that you've so carefully designed.

At this point, the only thing you can do about these concerns is to test your pages to see just how they render at different sizes.

TECHNOLOGY

WebTV browsers are limited in the technology they support. Because audio, video, and multimedia such as Flash are a natural for the TV environment, you won't encounter technological problems there, although file formats and Flash versions are still limited because of restrictions within the WebTV browser. Flash 1 is supported by both WebTV Classic and WebTV Plus (two WebTV browsers), whereas Flash 2 is only available in WebTV Plus, and Flash 3 isn't supported at all.

Technologies that rely on browser intelligence such as JavaScript and DHTML, Java applets, and style sheets all have limitations in WebTV or aren't supported whatsoever. Table 35.2 provides some general information about common technologies and how the WebTV browser deals or doesn't deal with them.

TABLE 35.2 TECHNOLOGIES AND WEBTV

Technology	WebTV Support
JavaScript	Limited to 1.1, with no support for multiple browser windows.
Java	Not supported in any way.
CSS	Pared-down version of CSS1. No font faces are supported, and font sizing is relative to WebTV's browser interpretation of the font's size.
DHTML	Limited to DOM level 0 technology. If it works in NN 3.0 or IE 3.0, it *might* work in WebTV.
Emerging Technologies (XML, XSL, SMIL)	Not supported in any way.

There's also significant contention as to how seamlessly server-side technologies work. There's not a lot of information out on this, but I found no problems with ColdFusion. Conceptually, nothing happening on the server side should affect the end results within a browser. However, if you take a peek into the Web Design for WebTV Forum, you'll see numerous problems encountered by designers using CCI, SSL, ASP, and other server-based technologies.

Note

For the WebTV Forum, point your browser to `developer.webtv.net/wwwboard/webd/`.

As with all Web development, testing plays a critical role in the way design decisions are made or revised. If you're seriously committed to developing for WebTV, owning a WebTV unit might be desirable. Alternatively you can simulate WebTV by using the helpful WebTV Viewer, which you saw earlier in Figure 35.4.

As more and more media becomes intertwined, developers are finding that instead of technologies scaling down into some semblance of routine, the daily code demands are getting more complex. Fortunately, extensible markup languages such as XML and XHTML are gaining more attention and support, as their native customization features allow for ways in which to better integrate the diverse platforms and agents available.

WEB CLIPPINGS

Not long ago I bought a Palm VII. I really love this little device, because not only does it have all the features of a standard PDA—contact list, scheduler, organization features, and so on, it also allows me to connect to the Web in a completely wireless way. The technology is built right in, no need for an additional modem, which previous Palm devices and other PDAs have required.

But another interesting feature found in the Palm VII is the Web Clipping. A Web Clipping is a little application that allows users to access Web content that is specialized for the Palm VII. Examples of such content include stock quotes, sports scores, news headlines, email, POP email, there's even personal messaging available. It's pretty cool stuff for the wireless fan.

And, for the developer, creating a Web Clipping is as easy as using HTML 3.2, or a simplified version of XHTML, such as XHTML Basic (see Chapter 23). Which, in fact, is what is used to mark up Web Clippings. So combine a little knowledge—knowledge readers of this book already have, with a few tools from Palm, and you'll be making your own Web Clipping in no time.

PART
VIII

CH
35

WHAT YOU NEED

To begin developing a Web Clipping, you need a few tools. They are

- A text editor. Notepad or SimpleText will do just fine.

- The Web Clipping Application Builder. This is a free tool available for download from Palm. It is available for Mac and PC platforms.

- If you want to work with images, you might want to download the Palm Image Checker, a specialized graphics viewer that verifies if your images are displaying properly. This tool comes with the Web Clippings Application Builder.

- If you do not have a Palm VII, you will need to test your applications on the Palm OS (POSE) emulator. You can download the emulator, but be forewarned: you must apply for membership to the Developer area if you want to get all the necessary files to run POSE.

- If you have a Palm VII, you won't need the emulator and can build and test your application using your Palm VII and the Palm Desktop software with the HotSync manager.

> **Note**
>
> Download the Web Clipping Application Builder from www.palm.com/devzone/palmvii/, and the Palm OS emulator from www.palm.com/devzone/pose/.

It's also helpful to know the steps involved in creating a Web Clipping application. They are

1. **Authoring**—In this step, you'll author the components of your application using a pared-down version of HTML 3.2. You'll also develop your graphics according to Palm's guidelines at this time.

2. **Converting**—Using the tools available from Palm, you'll convert all pages and images to create the PQA file—this is the Web Clipping Application file.

3. **Testing**—Test your work using either your Palm VII or POSE.

4. **Distributing**—Once your Web Clipping is a happening thing, you'll distribute the .pqa file for others to download and use. This can be done via your Web site, or via Palm's site as well.

With this information in hand, you can study the basic design guidelines for Web Clippings.

WEB CLIPPINGS GENERAL DESIGN GUIDELINES

Web Clippings follow the same general principles as laid out in the beginning of this chapter. The idea is to keep things as simple as possible, using limited text and graphics. It's especially important to keep the card-stack rather than distributed concept in mind.

Here are some specific guidelines when planning your Clipping application:

- Page length should be limited to one screen.

- The total weight of your `.pqa` file should be 15KB or less, including *all* pages and graphics.
- Graphics must be very small, and cannot exceed 153 pixels in length, or they won't fit on the PDA screen.
- The only colors supported in Web Clippings are black, white, silver, and gray.
- GIF and JPEG formats are supported. BMPs also are supported for application icons (these are the icons that denote your individual Web Clipping). You cannot use animated GIFs.
- Use the `alt` attribute when using images. This is always a smart thing to do, but especially helpful in PDA development.

Note For complete design details and tutorials on creating Web Clippings, download the Web Clipping Developer's Guide, **www.palmos.com/dev/tech/docs/**.

SUPPORTED MARKUP

While Palm Web Clippings don't use XHTML, it's interesting to note that they do use HTML 3.2, in a pared-down version. In a way, this is a lot like XHTML Basic, which I discussed in Chapter 23.

The following elements and tags are supported:

- Document formatting elements such as `html`, `head`, `title`, and `body`.
- Most common tags for formatting such as `p`, `br`, and lists.
- Links via the a element.
- Simple tables. No nesting, no widths beyond 153 pixels, no dynamic (percentage-based) tables (although you can use percentages within cells.
- Form elements (limited).
- Font sizes (restricted).
- Hex colors for black, gray, silver, and white as follows: #000000; #808080; #C0C0C0; #FFFFFF.

Caution The silver and gray used for Palm Web Clippings do not conform to Web safe browser colors. This is important if you are creating pages for Web viewing on a palm that also will be accessible to a standard Web browser.

PART
VIII

CH
35

Elements and technologies that are decidedly *not* supported:

- Type faces
- Stylesheets of any kind

- Image maps
- Frames
- Nested tables
- Scripts
- Java applets
- Flash
- Cookies

In addition to these general guidelines, there are some meta elements and values that can be included in a Web Clippings Application. They are

- Meta information for platform identity. The PalmComputingPlatform helps the incoming user agent understand that the page is designed for or applicable to a Palm device.

- History. To store the clipping name in the history list, you'll want to include the HistoryListText information in a meta tag.

- Version of application. The palmlaunchrevision value sets the version of the application.

- The names and locations of your icons.

Listing 35.1 shows a basic shell for a Web Clipping Application.

LISTING 35.1   A BASIC MARKUP OUTLINE FOR A WEB CLIPPING

```
<html>
<head>
<title>Web Clipping Application Sample</title>
<meta name="palmcomputingplatform" content="true">
<meta name="historylisttext" content="Molly.Com Update">
<meta name="palmlauncherrevision" content="1.0">
<meta name="localicon" content="molly_logo.gif">
<body>


</body>
</html>
```

With this information, and the tools from Palm, you are ready to create your first Web Clipping Application.

DESIGNING FOR THE REAL WORLD

CREATING A WEB CLIPPING

Because I'm so taken with the Palm VII, I thought it would be fun to create a Web Clipping for my Web site. It would provide information about upcoming books, allow for contests, and offer an email option for people to get in touch.

I decided I'd keep things very simple so as to get the hang of the process. I created three separate documents. The first is my intro page (Listing 35.2), the second, my books page (Listing 35.3), and the third, my contest page (Listing 35.4).

LISTING 35.2   MY WELCOME PAGE MARKUP

```
<html>
<head>
<title>Web Clipping Application Sample</title>
<meta name="palmcomputingplatform" content="true">
<meta name="historylisttext" content="Molly.Com Update">
<meta name="palmlauncherrevision" content="1.0">
<meta name="localicon" content="molly_logo.gif">
<body>

<h2>Molly.Com: Welcome!</h2>

<p>Welcome to Molly.Com on the Wireless Web. Here, you'll find the latest book
➥available, contest news, and means of getting in touch.</p>

<p><a href="book.html">Next</a></p>

</body>
</html>
```

Note

You'll see that this code is decidedly *not* XHTML 1.0. It is HTML 3.2 because Web Clippings have yet to embrace XHTML as the language of choice.

LISTING 35.3   MY BOOKS PAGE MARKUP

```
<html>
<head>
<title>Web Clipping Application Sample</title>
<meta name="palmcomputingplatform" content="true">
<meta name="historylisttext" content="Molly.Com Update">
<meta name="palmlauncherrevision" content="1.0">
<meta name="localicon" content="molly_logo.gif">
<body>

<h2>Molly.Com: Recent Book</h2>
<p>My latest book is Special Edition Using XHTML 1.0 from Que. Please visit
➥your favorite online or local bookstore for more information.</p>

<p>I give away books on a regular basis. Follow the "next" link
➥below to enter.</p>

<p><a href="contest.html">Next</a></p>

</body>
</html>
```

PART
VIII

CH

35

LISTING 35.4   MY CONTEST PAGE MARKUP

```html
<html>
<head>
<title>Web Clipping Application Sample</title>
<meta name="palmcomputingplatform" content="true">
<meta name="historylisttext" content="Molly.Com Update">
<meta name="palmlauncherrevision" content="1.0">
<meta name="localicon" content="molly_logo.gif">
<body>


<h2>Molly.Com: Contest</h2>
<p>This week's contest is about Web Clippings.</p>

<p>The first three people who can name three things that are not included in
➥the HTML markup used for making Web Clippings win a copy of
➥my XHTML 1.0 book.</p>

<p>Please <a href="mailto:molly@molly.com">email me</a> your answers.</p>

<p>Thanks for visiting Molly.Com on the Web!</p>

</body>
</html>
```

Next, I built my application icons. You need two versions for display. The first is for the Application icon view. This icon is a GIF, JPEG, or BMP and is sized at 32 × 22 pixels. There's a list view, too, which uses a smaller icon at 15 × 9 pixels (Figure 35.5).

Figure 35.5
Creating the application icons for Web Clippings.

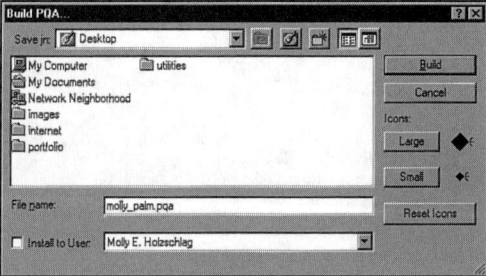

With my files and icons in place, I was able to open up the Web Clipping Application Builder and put it to work. Here are the steps you'll follow, as I did:

1. **Select File, Open Index**—Browse for the index and when the file is found, highlight it and click OK. The application will automatically load it, and any linked files, to the builder (Figure 35.5).

2. **Select File, Build PQA**—From the Build PQA dialog, choose Large icon, and select the large icon file. Repeat for the small icon.

3. **Click Build**—The builder will now build your PQA file.

To test your file, go ahead and load the PQA file on your Palm VII, which is what I did, using HotSync. Or, if you don't have a Palm VII, you can use the emulator to check out your work.

When you're happy with the clipping, and I was very excited to create one and find it to be *so* easy, you'll want to distribute it. To do so, simply upload it to your site and provide a link, or contact Palm and submit it there.

Note

You can download my modest Web Clipping sample from `http://www.molly.com/molly/designer.html`.

CHAPTER 36

PAGERS, CELL PHONES, AND OTHER WIRELESS DEVICES

In this chapter

THE WIRELESS WORLD

The past two chapters have given you an overview for alternative devices, among them wireless devices, and methodology used to design for these devices.

In this chapter, I'll examine in greater detail what's going on in terms of developing for wireless applications such as smart pagers, phones, and the like, and provide helpful resources so you can get more information should you be interested in working more with wireless development.

Note

Although WAP and WML aren't the only methods of delivering wireless information, they are the most widespread and of educational interest to developers. Therefore, I will focus on WAP and WML in this chapter.

WIRELESS APPLICATION PROTOCOL (WAP) OVERVIEW

Every few years, a new acronym appears in technology news and creates quite a stir. It happened with HTML, it happened with XML. And in the last couple of years, it's happening with WAP.

And, although WAP has, at least for the early years, been left to the domain of the wireless industry, WAP is becoming of greater interest to the standard Web developer. This is particularly true for those Web designers interested in developing for wireless devices. Inevitably, those individuals will come across WAP information and want to know what WAP is. This becomes even more important as the demand for get-it-anywhere Web and Internet access increases.

Note

Forecasters such as Jesse Berst, from Ziff Davis' AnchorDesk, believe that by the year 2002, there will be more people accessing Internet information via wireless, mobile devices than via the desktop.

The protocols that manage Internet data, especially TCP/IP and HTTP, were built for land-based connections. They are not particularly well suited to managing wireless transmissions. Two of the major problems with current protocols are that:

- They demand high processing power.
- The speed of current methods of sending wireless data via current Internet protocol is very slow, resulting in long transmission delays, referred to as *latency*.

So a couple of things could have occurred here. A completely new network could have evolved, leaving the Internet to itself. Or, a network using the available intelligence and enormous content base of the Internet and Web could have emerged. As it happens, WAP grew out of the latter.

Instead of a completely new network structure, WAP uses the client-server concept of the Internet. The client, in the case of a wireless transmission, is the WAP enabled phone, pager, or other wireless device. The server is usually a pre-existing Web server that also is configured to serve WAP content as well.

However, for this relationship to work, there are two additional components: the wireless network, which is a network employing radio or satellite transmission; and a WAP gateway, which interprets Web content from the server and makes it suitable for transmission and interpretation on a WAP client.

WAP has its historical origins in Unwired Planet, the company that introduced HDML (Unwired Planet is now Phone.Com). In an effort to encourage a wireless future, Phone.Com teamed up with Ericsson, Nokia, and Motorola (three top manufacturers of mobile devices).

→ For more information on Phone.Com, HDML, and WAP **see** Chapter 34, "Overview of Alternative Devices, Languages, and Protocols," **p. 683**.

Out of this meeting of businesses came the WAP Forum, an organization dedicated to the development and promotion of wireless devices, protocols, and languages.

EXPLORING WML

WML, The *Wireless Markup Language*, is an application of XML. It is used to build content for the wireless world via WAP. Because XML is the meta-language from which WML comes, WML is more rigorous than, say, HTML. You must write syntactically correct documents for WML content to be displayed within a WAP device. As with XHTML, WML demands lowercase, the proper nesting of tags, the closing of non-empty elements and termination of empty elements with a slash, and the inclusion of the appropriate XML declaration and DOCTYPE definition information.

WML structure, as you will soon see, is pretty easy to follow. Anyone who has been developing for the Web using HTML and now, XHTML, should find he or she has no trouble. Of course, developers who have used XML for some time will find WML quite easy too.

ALL HANDS ON DECK

In Chapter 34 and 35, I introduced the concept of perceiving alternative device design as a deck of cards rather than a distributed group of pages (which is more akin to the Web as we know it). HDML is the origin of that concept, and WML has embraced it thoroughly.

Think about holding a deck of cards in your hand. The deck is small, compact, and only a certain amount of information can be present on a given card. But, you can always remove a card to reveal another card, where more information is displayed. This concept is the foundational structure of WML.

And, although a WAP enabled mobile device will only display one card at a time, it can download numerous related cards—a deck. This is one way that browsing the Internet via

WAP is streamlined. Grabbing a deck, or parts of a deck, all at once reduces the lag (latency) when browsing using the mobile device.

WML DOCUMENT STRUCTURE

Just as XML, HTML, and XHTML documents have a set structure, so does a WML document. Here are the basics of a WML document's structure:

- **An XML declaration**—Because WML is an XML application, you'll begin your WML document by declaring it to be so.
- **A DOCTYPE definition**—WML documents refer to the WML DTD, which is found on the WAP forum.
- **A root element of WML**—WML's root element is wml. An opening and closing tag are used to contain the WML code.
- **The head element**—This element, just as with XHTML, is used for meta-data. You can include the character set of the document, for example, in a meta tag within the head.
- **The card element**—Akin to the body element in HTML and XHTML, card is used to define individual cards within a deck. Card tags support attributes, including title, which is used to define the title of the card. Another attribute used frequently is the id attribute, which identifies the card.

Caution

Note that there is no title tag placed in the head of a WML document. There is, however, a title attribute for each card within the document markup. But, using the title attribute in a WML document doesn't ensure it will be displayed in the requesting client. Some WAP devices support it, others do not. Use it, but don't rely on its being viewable.

Listing 36.1 shows a WML shell.

LISTING 36.1 A WML DOCUMENT SHELL

```
<?xml version="1.0"?>
<!DOCTYPE wml PUBLIC "-//WAPFORUM//DTD WML 1.1//EN"
"http://www.wapforum.org/DTD/wml_1.1.xml">
<wml>
<head>
<meta content="charset" name="character-set=ISO-10646-UCS-2" />
</head>
<card id="top" title="My First WML Card">

</card>
</wml>
```

Because multiple cards can exist in a given document, I've included Listing 36.2 to show a shell for a deck of three cards.

LISTING 36.2   A WML DOCUMENT SHELL WITH THREE CARDS

```
<?xml version="1.0"?>
<!DOCTYPE wml PUBLIC "-//WAPFORUM//DTD WML 1.1//EN"
"http://www.wapforum.org/DTD/wml_1.1.xml">
<wml>
<head>
<meta content="charset" name="character-set=ISO-10646-UCS-2" />
</head>
<card id="top" title="My First WML Card">

</card>

<card id="middle" title="Card Two">

</card>

<card id="final" title="Card Three">

</card>

</wml>
```

So now you've got the basic document structure down. What about adding content? It's pretty straightforward in WML.

CONTENT AND NAVIGATION

To add content to and navigate content within your WML document, you'll need some basic tags. Content in WML is formatted very similarly to that in XHTML.

Tags include

- **Paragraphs**—Text in WML documents must be presented inside of an opening `<p>` and closing `</p>` paragraph tag pair. Otherwise, the text will not display. Paragraphs can be aligned using the `align` attribute, with `left`, `right`, or `center` for the attribute values.

- **Line breaks**—Use the standard line break in XML format `<br/>` (no space is required to manage browser bugs as in XHTML) to indicate a specific break in a line. The text in question must still be within a paragraph, however. It can't stand alone.

- **Links**—You'll use a combination of tags to move between cards, including `anchor`, `go`, and the familiar a.

- **Text style**—All of the standard text styles are available in WML: Bold, italic, underline, emphasis, strong, big, and small. These use the familiar XHTML tags to format the text style.

- **Images**—As you already realize, the limitations of mobile devices make images a questionable choice. However, you can use them. Interestingly, a new image format, known as WBMP is available for use in these devices. The `img` tag is used to insert images into a WML document.

- **Tables**—Tables can be used for mobile access. However, the smaller the screen, the more difficult it is to ensure that table-based layouts are going to display consistently or well.

- **Special characters**—WML has set aside characters for special symbols. The same encoding as used in XHTML is used in WML. For example, a copyright symbol can be displayed using © and a non-breaking space is .

I'll step you through a few simple WML examples so you can get the hang of creating some basic WML markup.

ADDING PARAGRAPHS

To add paragraph content to your cards, follow these steps:

1. Open your favorite text editor and copy in the markup for the WML document shell:

```
<?xml version="1.0"?>
<!DOCTYPE wml PUBLIC "-//WAPFORUM//DTD WML 1.1//EN"
"http://www.wapforum.org/DTD/wml_1.1.xml">
<wml>
<head>
<meta content="charset" name="character-set=ISO-10646-UCS-2" />
</head>
<card id="top" title="Welcome!">

</card>
</wml>
```

2. Add the opening and closing paragraph tags within the first card:

```
<?xml version="1.0"?>
<!DOCTYPE wml PUBLIC "-//WAPFORUM//DTD WML 1.1//EN"
"http://www.wapforum.org/DTD/wml_1.1.xml">
<wml>
<head>
<meta content="charset" name="character-set=ISO-10646-UCS-2" />
</head>
<card id="top" title="Welcome!">

<p>

</p>

</card>
</wml>
```

3. Add your content:

```
<?xml version="1.0"?>
<!DOCTYPE wml PUBLIC "-//WAPFORUM//DTD WML 1.1//EN"
"http://www.wapforum.org/DTD/wml_1.1.xml">
<wml>
<head>
<meta content="charset" name="character-set=ISO-10646-UCS-2" />
</head>
<card id="top" title="Welcomme!">
```

```
<p>

Welcome to my first WML document!

</p>


</card>
</wml>
```

4. Save your document as my_first.wml.

5. View your document in a phone or emulator. I used the Deck-It WML Previewer (see Figure 36.1)

Figure 36.1
Using the Deck-It WML emulator to view the WML document.

> **Tip from**
> **molly**
>
> Conceivably, you can create as many paragraphs in a card as you want. However, designers will bear in mind that the displays of mobile devices are very small, and the methods used to scroll down pages are often cumbersome. Therefore, less is more in card design!

ADDING PARAGRAPHS AND LINE BREAKS

To break lines where you'd like them to break, you'll want to use both the paragraph (necessary to display the text) *and* the line break. A good example of this would be an address, where line breaks are desirable.

To create a line break, follow these steps:

1. Begin in your text editor with a WML shell. I've identified my card and added a title:

```
<?xml version="1.0"?>
<!DOCTYPE wml PUBLIC "-//WAPFORUM//DTD WML 1.1//EN"
"http://www.wapforum.org/DTD/wml_1.1.xml">
<wml>
<head>
<meta content="charset" name="character-set=ISO-10646-UCS-2" />
</head>
<card id="contact" title="Get in Touch">

</card>
</wml>
```

2. Add the paragraph tags:

```
<?xml version="1.0"?>
<!DOCTYPE wml PUBLIC "-//WAPFORUM//DTD WML 1.1//EN"
"http://www.wapforum.org/DTD/wml_1.1.xml">
<wml>
<head>
<meta content="charset" name="character-set=ISO-10646-UCS-2" />
</head>
<card id="contact" title="Get in Touch">

<p>

</p>

</card>
</wml>
```

3. Add your content:

```
<?xml version="1.0"?>
<!DOCTYPE wml PUBLIC "-//WAPFORUM//DTD WML 1.1//EN"
"http://www.wapforum.org/DTD/wml_1.1.xml">
<wml>
<head>
<meta content="charset" name="character-set=ISO-10646-UCS-2" />
</head>
<card id="contact" title="Get in Touch">

<p>
Please get in touch with us!
We are located at:
2001 Sunrise Drive
Wilmotshire, USA
</p>

</card>
</wml>
```

4. Add the break tags where desired:

```
<?xml version="1.0"?>
<!DOCTYPE wml PUBLIC "-//WAPFORUM//DTD WML 1.1//EN"
"http://www.wapforum.org/DTD/wml_1.1.xml">
<wml>
<head>
```

```
<meta content="charset" name="character-set=ISO-10646-UCS-2" />
</head>
<card id="contact" title="Get in Touch">

<p>
Please get in touch with us!
We are located at:
2001 Sunrise Drive<br/>
Wilmotshire, USA<br/>
</p>

</card>
</wml>
```

5. Save the file as break_test.wml. You can now upload and test your files with your smart pager, phone, or wireless device, or with an emulator, as I have.

Caution

Despite the correct markup, a given cell phone or pager might not be able to properly display that markup. Much of this is due to the fact that display screens are very small (see Figure 36.2).

Figure 36.2
Paragraphs and breaks are in the code, but the breaks don't work in this particular environment.

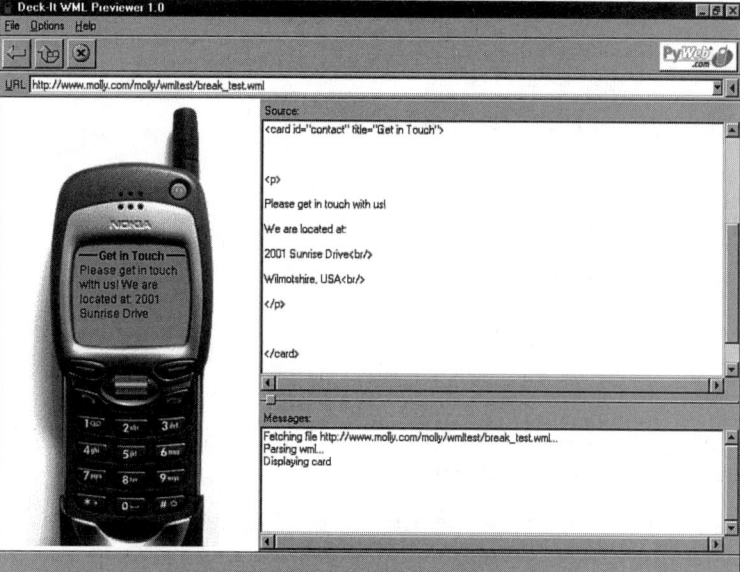

Tip from

molly

You can add text styles to your content wherever you see fit. Go ahead and try adding a bold or italic to the example in this section.

ADDING LINKS

To add a link from one card to another you can use the combination of the anchor and go tags as shown in Listing 36.3.

LISTING 36.3   LINKING BETWEEN CARDS

```
<?xml version="1.0"?>
<!DOCTYPE wml PUBLIC "-//WAPFORUM//DTD WML 1.1//EN"
"http://www.wapforum.org/DTD/wml_1.1.xml">
<wml>
<head>
<meta content="charset" name="character-set=ISO-10646-UCS-2" />
</head>

<card id="welcome" title="Welcome">

<p>
Welcome to Wilmotshire. We are pleased to have you here visiting.
<anchor>
<go href="#contact"/>Next
</anchor>
</p>


</card>


<card id="contact" title="Get in Touch">

<p>
Please get in touch with us!
We are located at:
2001 Sunrise Drive<br/>
Wilmotshire, USA<br/>
</p>

</card>
</wml>
```

Figure 36.3 shows the first card with the highlighted link. Figure 36.4 shows the card that appears when I follow the link.

If you'd like to link to an external page, you can use the anchor and go method as shown in Listing 36.4, or use a standard link, as shown in Listing 36.5.

Figure 36.3
The first card in the deck, displayed in an emulator.

PART

VIII

CH

36

Figure 36.4
I follow the link and the second card loads. Notice the URL with the addition of the identifier, #contact.

LISTING 36.4 LINKING EXTERNALLY

```
<?xml version="1.0"?>
<!DOCTYPE wml PUBLIC "-//WAPFORUM//DTD WML 1.1//EN"
"http://www.wapforum.org/DTD/wml_1.1.xml">
```

LISTING 36.4 CONTINUED

```
<wml>
<head>
<meta content="charset" name="character-set=ISO-10646-UCS-2" />
</head>

<card id="anchor_method" title="Welcome">

<p>
Welcome to the wireless web.
<anchor>
<go href="http://www.molly.com/ "/>Next
</anchor>
</p>

</card>
</wml>
```

Figure 36.5 shows the anchor external link example in the emulator.

Figure 36.5
An anchor example of external linking.

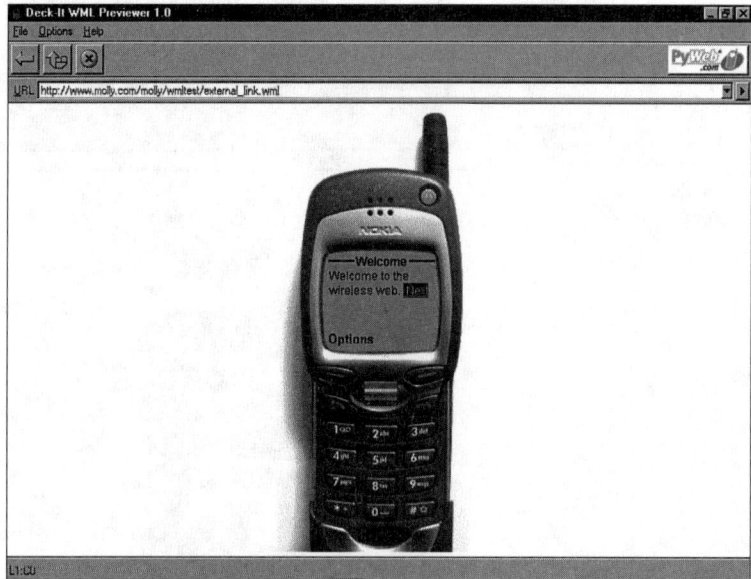

LISTING 36.5 LINKING EXTERNALLY

```
<?xml version="1.0"?>
<!DOCTYPE wml PUBLIC "-//WAPFORUM//DTD WML 1.1//EN"
"http://www.wapforum.org/DTD/wml_1.1.xml">
<wml>
<head>
<meta content="charset" name="character-set=ISO-10646-UCS-2" />
</head>
```

```
<card id="standard_method" title="Get in Touch">

<p>
<a href="http://www.molly.com/">Next</a>

</p>

</card>
</wml>
```

Figure 36.6 shows the standard link document in the emulator, and Figure 36.7 shows the XHTML document that is displayed after the link is followed.

Figure 36.6
A standard link document.

At this point, you should have the basic hang of how to create WML documents. For additional resources, I'm including a note with links that you'll find helpful if you choose to explore WAP and WML more extensively.

Note

For detailed information on WAP and WML, visit the WAP Forum, www.wapforum.org.

Of course, Phone.Com is a central point of information for developers, www.phone.com/.

Rich and detailed information on wireless development is available at the Wireless Developer's Network, www.wirelessdevnet.com/.

A variety of WAP emulators can be downloaded from www.anywhereyougo.com/ayg/ayg/Content.po?name=waptools/Emulators.

Figure 36.7
An XHTML document
displayed after the link
is followed.

XML AND RELATED TECHNOLOGIES OVERVIEW

TOWARD XML

MAKING ALL THINGS POSSIBLE WITH XML

The Internet community is pouring an enormous amount of energy, money, and effort into developing an extensive suite of related standards centered around XML, Extensible Markup Language, the next generation of document delivery methods on the Web. In 1999 alone, more standards and drafts, almost all XML-related, had been delivered or proposed than in the history of the World Wide Web Consortium (W3C) , the body responsible for Web standards. In 2000, several dozen more XML-related standards have be delivered, doubling the number of W3C standards and extending the cohesive power of XML into all corners of the Worldwide Web.

XML and its related standards allow you to replace or extend proprietary tagging systems, such as Allaire's Cold Fusion and Microsoft's Active Server Pages (ASP), with platform-independent languages that fit the problem space of your page precisely. Instead of (or in addition to) inserting special tags or comments explaining what a particular field means, the field itself can be made meaningful to both applications and human readers. So an annotated price list in HTML that might look like this:

```
<!--Price list for individual fruits -->
<dl>
  <!-- Fruit -->
  <dt>Apples</dt>
    <!-- Price -->
    <dd>$1</dd>
  <!-- Fruit -->
  <dt>Oranges</dt>
    <!-- Price -->
    <dd>$2</dd>
</dl>
```

can be made to look like this:

```
<FruitPriceList>
  <Fruit>Apples</Fruit>
    <Price>$1</Price>
  <Fruit>Oranges</Fruit>
    <Price>$2</Price>
</FruitPriceList>
```

The previous shows a tiny example of what can be accomplished in making data easier to access using XML. Not only is the information less cluttered and more clearly presented, but also the fields are identifiable by a search engine. So, apples to eat can be readily distinguished from the Big Apple (New York City) and the apple of one's eye (a person or thing one is fond of). Whereas we had to fit our HTML data into the Procrustean bed of an HTML definition list to lay out the list in the manner we wanted, in XML we can let the data structure flow from the data itself, and use XML-related standards like Cascading Style Sheets (CSS) or Extensible Stylesheet Language (XSL) to format the page.

→ For more information on CSS, **see** Chapter 18, "Cascading Style Sheets and XHTML," **p. 377**. To learn about XSL, try Chapter 22, "Document Type Definitions in Detail," **p. 485**.

Also, the XML version allows us to retain information about the type of data entered in every field. HTML allows us to identify only a half-dozen or so datatypes: abbreviations, acronyms, addresses, block quotes, citations, and variables. And even these are most often (mis)used to affect formatting rather than to identify a logical field.

XML enables you to describe your document exactly in a way that can be "understood" by a machine. Although humans have no trouble looking at a page and deducing what certain layouts mean, such as an invoice, for example, computers aren't quite that smart. They need help. Descriptive XML tags such as `<seller>` and `<price>`, make far more sense to machines than the anonymous layout tags that HTML currently provides. XML provides a mechanism, the Document Type Definition (DTD), which lets you share knowledge about the structure of your data with anyone you choose.

This chapter will introduce you to XML, help you understand the relationship between HTML, XML, XHTML, and their parent   SGML. It will also get you started with basic principles and syntax for XML.

> **Note**
>
> This chapter was excerpted from Lee Anne Phillips' *Special Edition Using XML*, from Que. It's an excellent next step for Web authors looking from HTML and XHTML toward XML.

PART

II

CH

37

UNDERSTANDING THE RELATIONSHIP BETWEEN SGML, XML, AND XHTML

XML is a *meta-language*, a special language that allows you to completely describe a class of other languages, which in turn describe documents. It's like an island in the sea of SGML, another and more powerful meta-language. XML is defined as a "proper subset" of SGML, which means no pieces are added to SGML to make XML, but pieces are taken away to make the language easier to parse, understand, and use. XHTML is a production of XML, as HTML is a production of SGML.

Because XML is designed to be extensible, the languages created with XML are extensible as well. As in SGML, the language descriptions created by XML are called DTDs, Document Type Definitions. You'll find out much more about them later. But first, take a look at SGML, the mother of XML and its related standards.

SGML

SGML, the Standard Generalized Markup Language, is a more powerful ancestor of XML and also a meta-language used to describe application languages. Although it has many useful features, the complexity of the language makes it extremely hard to use and learn. It's also not quite true that nothing was added to SGML to make XML. For example, when multiple ATTLIST declarations defining the same ELEMENT were needed in XML, they were added to SGML and then worked back into XML so that you could still call XML a proper subset. Language designers are devious sometimes.

Although used by many major corporations and government organizations, the expense and difficulty of learning and using SGML, HyTime, Text Encoding Initiative (TEI), and other complex document description languages made it difficult for laypersons and smaller organizations to access the tremendous power of these languages to format structured data. XML is an attempt to make most of the power of SGML and the rest accessible to non-specialists. Another goal is to make stable implementations of a structured document language easy to create so that the cost of editors, validators, and other tools comes within reach of ordinary people.

Tip from

If your XML project relates to a major industry, asking major firms and associations questions that address the needs of that industry might reveal existing SGML DTDs. If so, these might be able to be used as a basis for XML DTDs and enable your project to address a larger audience than if you just started from scratch. It pays to investigate your target market thoroughly.

IBM, one of the largest publishers in the world, with hundreds of millions of pages of documentation required for its computers and other systems, has used SGML from the earliest days as a data repository and prepress layout engine.

The Federal government uses SGML for parts procurement, manuals, automating bids on government contracts, inventory control, and many more sophisticated database systems. The armed services, the space program, and the U.S. Government Printing Office all use SGML to ensure interoperability and data accessibility.

Because XML is a subset of SGML, many applications originally coded in SGML are being ported to XML. For the most part, the changes required are more-or-less mechanical in nature, although some difficulties exist. For technical reasons, many of these problems will be resolved by simplifying the descriptions and making them more exact. As an XML designer, you might find yourself working with SGML DTDs, so gaining an understanding SGML DTDs will help you successfully modify and use them.

Remember that SGML has been around for a long time, at least in computer lifetimes. Many problems have already been solved and have huge installed user bases. Being able to communicate with these existing systems and users might mean the difference between success and failure for startups looking for a market. Although XML can be used to access SGML databases, it takes some DTD design work.

Tip from

If your target market includes government agencies or contractors, there are probably existing SGML DTDs exactly suited to at least part of their problem space. If so, there are probably industry groups already translating those DTDs to XML. So it pays to do your homework before undertaking XML DTD development. An appropriate DTD might already be available.

Although you don't have to know SGML to learn and use XML, it is fairly common to modify existing or legacy SGML DTDs into XML DTDs in the course of daily life as an XML expert. You will learn enough about this process to be able to do it with some confidence.

Caution

A caution is in order here. Many SGML DTDs are huge because the problems they address are large. You can't expect to waltz up to a 900-page SGML DTD that took a team of 20 experts five years to develop and convert it to XML in an afternoon. It might take a wee bit longer than that. It might take a year or more.

XHTML

XHTML redefines—as you already know—HTML as an XML application. This makes it more useful in an XML world. In particular, this means that the XHTML language is extensible, allowing users and groups of users to extend the language in powerful ways. Implications of this extensibility include:

- Single-edit-cycle documents that encapsulate databases, printed user manuals, and Web display functionalities in one file.

- Tremendous opportunities for extended e-commerce transactions and information exchange automation using standardized XML vocabularies.

- An easy way to reuse or convert many of the millions of HTML Web pages in existence today, retaining compatibility with existing browsers while enabling new features for those using XML-enabled agents.

- Allowing XML Web pages to be automatically validated, completely eliminating many common coding errors while retaining compatibility with legacy browsers.

- Providing simple mechanisms that enable the Web to evolve to meet the needs of the diverse communities it encompasses without requiring proprietary or non-standard additions that make life difficult.

XML IN THEORY AND PRACTICE

XML is so logical you might wonder why it took so long to be invented. Part of the answer is that the basic concepts have been around for a long time but were only recently applied to computer data files. A component-based parts list, for example, is a trivial requirement for putting together any complex mechanical device. But the idea of extending this paper tool to the electronic one, and generalizing the concept so it could be used for anything made up of component parts, including non-physical objects, was a flash of insight very typical of human progress over the centuries.

People organize almost everything into hierarchies. It's the only way to handle truly complex tasks, from buying supplies for the Department of Defense to building space shuttles. Any hierarchical structure can be described with XML, from the parts list that makes up an airliner to the corporate structure of IBM. But XML has limitations. It's not truly object-oriented, for example, so users with problem sets requiring a fully object-oriented (O-O) approach will have some trouble applying XML to their tasks. Initiatives are underway, however, to extend the domain of XML in object-oriented ways, so this limitation might be resolved eventually.

As an example of their non-object-orientedness, XML documents can't really inherit from their ancestors and are not truly encapsulated because their internals are fully exposed. They do exhibit polymorphism and other object-oriented behaviors, so they're a step in the right direction as far as the O-O world is concerned.

In the meantime, there's much that can be done with XML. Look at a few simple ones to start.

Note

Markup tags aren't the only mechanisms that can affect the context and representation of text. There are various pointer mechanisms used to create a database of characteristics and then point to each instance of it in your document. Microsoft Word uses this technique, as do Tagged Image Format Files (TIFF). The weakness of these schemes is that they are not robust. If any part of the header that contains the pointers becomes corrupt, the entire document is destroyed. One of the reasons for the rapid growth and success of the Web is the robust behavior of text-based markup.

PRACTICAL EXAMPLES OF XML

So, applying your existing knowledge of HTML and XHTML is one good way to start learning about XML. It's a language of tags and attributes, just like XHTML, and uses many of the same conventions. In XHTML, matching pairs of tags surround most content, an opening tag and a closing tag, like this:

```
XHTML: <h1>Headline</h1>
```

XML works the same way. XML encourages, but doesn't enforce, slightly more verbosity than HTML does, so the preceding code in a real XML application might look like this:

```
XML: <headline1>Headline</headline1>
```

Now might be the time to point out that, unlike HTML, all XML languages (including XHTML) are case sensitive. How the tag is defined, case-wise, is the way you have to use it. So, many XML applications use all lowercase and none can accept different capitalizations of their keywords or attributes.

Attributes, as with XHTML, must be quoted every time. So although you can get away with this in HTML

```
<IMG height=20 width=20 src="myimage.gif">
```

in any XML-based language you would use this:

```
<image height="20" width="20" source="myimage.gif />
```

And of course, you notice the now-familiar slash at the right end of the <image> tag. Although HTML allowed certain tags to be used without closing tags, XML and XHTML do not. Every tag has to be closed, even when it's an empty tag such as the HTML <IMG> tag or the XHTML <img> tag. The best way to do this is to put a slash at the end of the tag, separated by a space from the rest of the attributes and content. This doesn't seem to break any HTML browsers and tells XML that the tag is closed.

```
XML/HTML-compliant examples: <br />   <img src=" ... />
```

This syntax might appear odd at first, but it makes perfect sense when you think about it. HTML DTD information, or what passes for it in most browsers, is contained internally in the browser itself. XML allows a parser to be validating or non-validating, in which case it can't access the DTD to be able to tell the difference between tags with content and empty tags. So, you have to tell the parser directly using this simple format.

XML TAG ORDER

XML isn't as loose about the order of tags either. Tags must be closed in the context in which they were opened. Always. So putting tags in the wrong order, allowed by most HTML browsers in spite of the fact that it's officially disallowed, is forbidden in XML. The first tag opened is always the last one closed:

```
Wrong: <i><b>Italics Bold Text<i><b>
Right: <i><b>Italics Bold Text<b><i>
```

Tip from

Tag order is important! *Context* is another term for scope, so if you think of tags like plates in the push down stack of plates in a cafeteria you can't go wrong. If you open an <i> tag within the scope or context of a <b> tag, it has to be closed within the same scope or context. You can't do it after you close the <b> tag. It has to be closed before.

It doesn't matter how far away the tags are from each other. The tag context acts like a pushdown stack of plates in a serve-yourself restaurant. The tags have to come off the stack in the exact reverse order as when they were pushed down. Alternatively, you can't traverse the document structure tree by swinging from limb to limb like an ape. You have to walk it like an ant.

Tip from

First in, last out. This simple rule is easy to follow and, if your source is pretty printed, easy to see. Every nesting level has to close all its tags before exiting. And, all these metaphors are implied by the tree structure of XML documents.

Speaking of trees, most of the things you use every day have component parts that are more or less invariant and can be organized into a tree-like hierarchy. A bottle of aspirin, for example, has component bits, a body, a lid or top of some sort, one or more labels that describe the contents, and the contents themselves. If you were given the job of assembling aspirin bottles from their components, you would find that there is an order you have to do things in to avoid spilling the pills. Labels go on first, then tablets, then top. Top, label, tablets won't work at all. Tablets, label, top *might* work but you do risk spilling tablets if the bottle goes on its side. So an XML description might go as shown in Listing 37.1.

LISTING 37.1   AN ASPIRIN BOTTLE BROKEN DOWN TO COMPONENTS

```
<bottle>
  <top>
    type 3 childsafe
  </top>
  <body>
    <body-type>
      100 count plastic
    </body-type>
    <contents>
      <count>
        100
      </count>
      <content-type>
        aspirin
      </content-type>
    </contents>
  </body>
  <labeling>
    <frontlabel>
      XYZ brand generic
    </frontlabel>
    <rearlabel>
      XYZ directions and warning
    </rearlabel>
  </labeling>
</bottle>
```

Every sub-element is properly nested inside its container element and there is exactly one root element, the bottle. This is most of what's truly necessary for an XML file to be considered well formed. Of course there are many ways of describing an aspirin bottle and every description is more-or-less arbitrary. A particular bottle might come in a box, for example, and have a printed package insert. Or it might be blister-packed for a different market. Or it might have many different labels for different languages.

The possibilities are as endless as the world of goods and services. However, the bottle as a whole is made up of a container body, the labeling, the top, and the aspirin contained within it. One can easily understand that aspirin tablets are nested within the bottle. It might be slightly less obvious that the bottle itself is made up of parts that are logically nested within the concept of "bottle" used here. But overall, because it's a container, an aspirin bottle is about the most intuitive and accessible example of nesting commonly available.

PART

II

CH

37

> **Tip from**
> *molly*
>
> If aspirin bottles aren't clear, try thinking of any other object or idea with a hierarchy. People do this kind of classification all the time, from the organization chart for your firm (absent dotted lines) to the scientific classifications of plants and animals. Anything with a parts list is a hierarchy. Those little nested Russian Easter dolls are also a good example, or a set of nested mixing bowls.

Taxonomy is the difficult science of dividing up the analog world into digital classifications. Various trade groups have come together to decide how to create standard names and structures for their products and component pieces. That way a bottle manufacturer can tell an aspirin maker what sorts of bottles are available in the catalog and how much they cost. Or an aspirin maker can tell a pharmacy what sorts of packaging are available. User-friendly tools will make it easy to author documents described in this way.

UNDERSTANDING XML STRUCTURE

XML is actually two languages, or meta-languages really, both described in the same document. The first is a set of rules for producing well-formed XML documents whereas the second is a set of rules for producing an XML Document Type Definition, or DTD, which allows the structure of the XML document to be constrained and validated against those constraints. The distinction between these two languages is often blurred, because a complete XML document includes at least the optional presence of a DTD, whether it's actually present or not. To complicate things further, the DTD might consist of two parts, an *internal subset* and an *external subset*.

This chapter looks at the XML document without dwelling too much on the DTD, because it's possible to create an XML document without reference to a DTD. For performance reasons, many XML documents will be used without ever validating against the DTD, even if the DTD is available. Over slow connections, reading in a DTD located external to your local machine might be tediously slow, and because DTDs might contain references to other documents, resolving all the external references might take an inordinate amount of time even with a high speed connection. Users are accustomed to seeing HTML documents load incrementally, so they can be read before the document finishes loading, but validating XML parsers aren't allowed to display the document unless it's valid, so the document won't appear on the user's screen until everything is loaded. This can be disconcerting.

However, every document is created with a DTD in mind, whether the DTD is explicit or not. Even when creating documents without a DTD, a tentative sort of DTD has to be floating around in your mind as you create the document, because a DTD describes a data structure.

GETTING TECHNICAL WITH XML

The W3C XML 1.0 standard uses the Extended Backus-Naur Form (EBNF) to define it. Selected EBNF production rules are supplemented by terse descriptions of the explicit validity and/or well-formedness constraints with which W3C has modified or extended particular EBNF rules. Although EBNF is wonderfully compact, allowing legal productions in a programming language to be succinctly defined as a series of grammatical transformation rules, W3C has left quite a bit out of the EBNF description of the language for simplicity. Most of the missing bits are in the form of constraints, verbal descriptions of additional criteria that a given production must obey, but some are actually found in the text of the standard.

EBNF is just a shorthand way of saying things about programming languages, and you could just as easily describe XML in a slightly more accessible way using words, although the EBNF is concise by comparison with the plain English equivalent. However, some things are difficult (or tedious) to express in EBNF, and EBNF itself is terse to the point of obscurity for most people, so W3C has chosen to mix the two styles of language description in its recommendation. Some production rules are described fully in the EBNF notation and the accompanying text is only an explanation of what the EBNF actually says. Some production rules are described fully only by a combination of the EBNF rule and its accompanying commentary in the text, so the EBNF rule serves as a sort of overall framework to which the textual comments must be added to characterize the actual rule.

In practice, the EBNF in the XML 1.0 Recommendation from W3C is and must be supplemented by various textual constraint additions contained in the body of the document to really understand it. But after you understand how it all fits together, the EBNF rules are useful as a quick crib sheet to jog your memory of how the language works.

> **Note**
>
> Although there is an EBNF syntax for XML, that description is not complete. Without taking into account the various constraints listed in the Recommendation and carefully reading the text, an incorrect understanding and implementation is almost inevitable.

That's why the EBNF listing is available for you in the appendix, not to learn how to use XML, but to remind you of how it's used when you don't want to search through the entire specification looking for a particular construction. Because the XML 1.0 Recommendation is fairly concise, you might also want to keep a bookmark pointing to Tim Bray's Annotated XML 1.0 Recommendation at http://www.xml.com/axml/testaxml.htm because it more plainly explains some of the thinking that went into the specification. Note also that you have to read the errata section of the specification carefully. Many substantive changes have been made and, although these changes are reflected in this book, more changes might be made in future.

Now this might all sound complicated but it's really not. You are probably familiar with following rules that might change in context. For example, the rule that says you have to stop at a red light when driving a car is a simple rule and universally applicable, so when you learned to drive, you learned that rule quickly. But in some states, a special modification of the red light rule allows you to turn right after stopping unless otherwise posted. That sounds like a simple rule as well, but that rule would have to have a validity constraint attached to it because not all states allow this. A footnote would suffice for most purposes.

The alternative would be to make lots of similar rules about red lights with special conditions built in to handle exceptions. This sort of thing is tedious to do in EBNF, so W3C stuck with a simple rule and added constraints, which are more or less like footnotes, to the rules that needed them.

DESCRIBING NEW VOCABULARIES WITH XML

XML is dual-natured—a meta-language which allows you to describe new document structures and vocabularies as well as the language used to express that structure and vocabulary in a document instance. There is a clear difference between an XML document, which might or might not be associated with a DTD expressed in the XML meta-language, and an XML DTD. They use completely different syntaxes to describe an XML document, the one by example and the other prescriptive.

XML Document Type Definitions (DTDs) describe instances of XML languages, which are sometimes called XML vocabularies. XML documents are created using those languages. Unfortunately, that distinction is sometimes lost in casual speech, and particular XML vocabularies and associated DTDs are described loosely as "XML."

Although you need to know both to fully master XML, it's actually not necessary to define a DTD to create and use an XML vocabulary as long as you obey the rules. A user of an XML language or vocabulary might never see nor care about the DTD used to describe her particular application anymore than the thousands of individuals working in Web design using HTML might know or care about the W3C HTML 4.0 SGML DTD used to describe HTML. In fact, a DTD might not even exist. It just doesn't matter all that much at the application level. Because you're reading this book, however, it's assumed that you will be called upon to design or work with DTDs in some way, and a truly deep knowledge of XML requires that you understand how and why a DTD is constructed and used.

→ Want to know more about DTDs? **See** Chapter 22, "Document Type Definitions in Detail," **p. 485**.

UNDERSTANDING DOCUMENT TYPE DEFINITION ADVANTAGES

Although DTDs are optional because an XML processor can infer a reasonable DTD from an instance of XML, having a DTD available offers many advantages:

- A DTD describes the organization of a document in a way that can be easily shared.

- A DTD allows a designer to create a *robust* transformation between a given type of XML document and another format for display or transfer. Because you know everything possible about documents with a DTD, you'll know how to handle structures that might not exist in a particular sample but are allowed by the document type, even if you've never seen them.

- A DTD allows a *validating* parser to determine whether a particular document is constructed according to the rules set up by the originators of the specification. This is extremely important for EDI and other applications in which documents will be shared and used by other processes.

- Without a DTD, an XML authoring environment cannot give hints about which elements are required or optional at a given point and which attributes the current element can take. Context-sensitive menus or hints are an enormous help in speeding document development and preventing errors.

- Without a DTD, the creator of an authoring manual or style document has no way of knowing how the defined document should be constructed. An authoring manual is an embodiment of the knowledge expressed in a DTD, although not a DTD in itself.

- Specifying the DTD used in a document identifies the revision level of the standard used to create it. When documents evolve in functionality and syntax, this can be an important clue about how to display or transform a document in new situations.

Having a DTD available conveys significant information and benefits, *if* you need those benefits. But like everything else in life, there's a cost involved.

COPING WITH DOCUMENT TYPE DEFINITION DISADVANTAGES

For all their advantages, DTDs are not without problems. They use a different syntax than the rest of XML, so it requires a slightly different skill set to construct one. In addition, like any technical description, getting involved in the DTD design before thinking about the way you want your data structures to look in the document itself can bog you down in detail when you should be looking at the overall structure. Many people design the XML document using the intended XML vocabulary and then use an automatic DTD extraction tool to generate a DTD from the document itself. After this is done, the DTD can be fine-tuned by adding to or tweaking the source code.

The following disadvantages of DTDs exist as well:

- With a DTD, a validating XML user agent requires at *least* one extra read operation to access the location where the DTD is available. Although caching might lessen the performance hit for some network users, many foreseeable uses of XML documents will preclude the use of cache storage.

- A DTD greatly increases the complexity of the parser required to determine whether a document should be displayed. For some devices, this might not be feasible.

- Some *validating* authoring environments that use a DTD make it difficult to save your workspace at the end of the day or restore it the next day unless the document is in a valid state. This can be annoying if you have a lot of work left to do and need to leave it for a while.

- A DTD is theoretically capable of continuing external reads without limit because a DTD can incorporate other DTDs and entity sets. It's possible that some complex documents might take unacceptable amounts of time before they render on the display device when using a validating parser.

The basic tradeoff in deciding whether to use a DTD is between the free-wheeling ability you're used to with HTML—being able to do pretty much whatever you want and patch things up on-the-fly—and a much more structured environment in which every "i" must be dotted and every "t" crossed. In many situations, such as when you are creating documents meant for general availability and distributed creation, you need that strict enforcement of rules and will want a DTD. In others, such as when you are developing a new XML document type, you won't need or want strict enforcement and can do without a DTD, at least during initial design.

But after development has led to a stable product, you'll want to formalize your design so it can be easily distributed. Although you might also want to create a user's manual, a DTD is a simple way of letting users test their document to be sure that they truly follow the guidelines they read in the manual. At that point, you might even regret that DTDs allow so much flexibility. If you intend a field to contain a phone number, defining the field as CDATA leaves a lot to be desired.

In fact, XML Schema allows even stricter rule-making capabilities, which can be useful in situations that demand very strict control over field content.

PART

II

CH

37

IS XML JUST HTML ALL OVER AGAIN?

XML is a language of tags and attributes much like HTML, but an HTML mutated almost beyond recognition. XML is HTML on steroids.

XML is far more structured than HTML. Where HTML processors routinely accept wildly inaccurate and mal-formed code and attempt to make sense of it on the screen, XML is *required* to abort when it encounters a fatal error, which is almost any error at all. This is a throwback to the early days of data processing in some ways, when any error in code was punished with a core dump that you could spend hours deciphering. Expect to spend a bit more time debugging XML than you have previously spent on HTML.

Along with this unforgiving behavior, however, XML is far more powerful. Where HTML contented itself with 77 tags or so, depending on who was counting, XML has a potentially infinite number of tags, structured in almost any way you choose.

The basics are still the same, however, and your experience with HTML will make it easy to accept the evolutionary step that XML and its associated standards represent. Using XML is not quite as easy as rolling off a log but it's not like climbing Mount Everest either. With a little discipline and knowledge, which this book will help you gain, you'll be coding XML before you know it.

In fact, in a way you've been coding XML all along with your previous use of HTML. Not only is well-made HTML awfully close to XHTML—the XML-compliant replacement for HTML—but *clean* HTML 4.0 code is quite readable as XHTML 1.0. Because HTML 4.0 was structured as an SGML application and XML is a subset of SGML, this makes a lot of sense. The minor syntactic differences between XHTML, an XML vocabulary, and HTML, an SGML vocabulary, can be automatically adjusted if desired.

An XML document author is usually issued an authoring or coding manual (or sheet, for small DTDs) describing the tags used in the XML application, their attributes and possible values, and how they nest within each other. Following such a coding manual is no more difficult than remembering that a table row <tr> has to nest inside a table <table> and has, orshould have, no meaning outside that context.

For most purposes, this is enough. XML authors are no more likely to be technical gurus who can instantly extrapolate the structure and use of an application from a glance at the DTD than are freeway commuters likely to be expert automobile mechanics. XML is able to give authors quite a bit of help in learning how to use a particular application, because they're encouraged to give tags meaningful names that are easy to remember. The creator of an application *should* provide an authoring manual that explains how to use it in simple terms. The theory is that any future data analyst could look at your XML code and figure out what it is and how it's structured without recourse to the original design documentation (presumably lost in the dust of history) based on structure and element names alone.

Tip from
molly

Although any XML processor can tell you whether your code is well-formed and a manual can help you construct a valid document, the DTD lets you check your work unambiguously. This can be a separate step from the writing process, however, depending on the type of authoring tool used.

Whether your code fulfills that ideal is largely up to your use of tag names within some tiny limits:

- Tag names starting with the string "xml" in any case combination are reserved; that is, you're not permitted to create them no matter what the provocation. Don't invent them on your own. If you feel you *must* have one, submit it to W3C as part of a Member Submission (assuming, of course, that you are a member) and see what happens.

- Tag names containing a colon are apt to be interpreted as identifiers with an associated namespace, so using colons in tag names is strongly discouraged and might eventually be forbidden. Why take a chance? Avoid them.

- A tag name has to start with a "letter," which in this context is any Unicode/ISO/IEC 10646 letter or ideograph, or an underscore (or a colon, which you already know to avoid to prevent confusion with namespaces).

After that, a tag name can include any Unicode/ISO/IEC 10646 "letter," ideograph, or digit, plus the combining characters, extenders, periods, hyphens, spaces, or colons. A few human languages have otherwise legal characters that cannot begin a legal name in that language. These characters are excluded from the list of characters if they're in a position that could be viewed as "first" after a hyphen or other logical word break. But if you know the language, that will be obvious.

The Thai character *mai yamok (looks like a backward f without a crossbar)*, for example, looks like a letter but can't be used to begin a word because it signifies repetition of the previous letter.

The combining characters are special characters used to add an accent to another character, many of which normalize to a single accented character. This is a convenience for keyboard entry, because many languages that include accented characters allow you to enter them using special "zero-width" accent characters, which can attach themselves to any other character.

The extenders are various special punctuation marks such as (in European languages) middle dot, triangular colon, and half-triangular colon. The extended characters are similar in other world scripts, not alphabetic exactly, but fitting in there somehow. If you need to use one in a language other than English, you'll probably know what they are so they're easy to find. But if you don't speak or write Arabic, using an Arabic "tatweel" in your tag name is probably an affectation, although strictly allowed.

PART

II

CH

37

STARTING WITH XML

In a sense you already know how to code in XML if you have become used to writing clean, well-made HTML 4 code. You might need only to eliminate some bad habits to become a competent XML coder, so here you will concentrate on the differences between XML and HTML. This focus highlights the skill sets required for XML and makes clear the many similarities between XML and HTML:

- **XML is case sensitive because capital letters are not a universal concept**—If you were to accommodate capital letters as equivalents, you would have to do the same for thousands of other letter variations in other languages, an onerous task. Some languages don't even have cases. There's no such thing as lowercase Hebrew, for instance, and Arabic distinguishes between initial, medial, and final forms of letters. For those who like to put their tags in uppercase and attributes in lowercase to make them stand out, this is terrible news. But modern coding editors make this less of an issue than it might have been previously. It's common to define special colors to mark tags, for example, so using uppercase is somewhat of an historical anachronism, like line numbers in COBOL.

- **XML is very sensitive to the proper nesting of tags**—Tags cannot end in a different context from which they started. So if you want `<bold><italics>`, you have to close your emphasized phrase with `</italics></bold>` to avoid a fatal error. Because XML can reference and include XML documents and document fragments anywhere on the Web that you have no control over, every XML document has to obey the same rules so you don't break one another's documents.

- **XML is not well protected against recursion**—Although it's possible to set up explicit exclusions at a given level, with a complex document structure it's difficult to maintain those exclusions at lower levels, especially when using tags that might apply at any level. So, the HTML prohibition of including an anchor `<a>` tag within another anchor tag is there in XHTML, but not enforced beyond direct inclusion.

- **XML requires you to close every tag, even empty tags**—Because it's possible to create an XML document that doesn't use a DTD, an XML processor has no way of knowing whether a tag is empty. Because all XML documents have to be *well-formed*, you have to mark empty tags with a special syntax that tells an XML processor the tag is empty and closed. You do that by placing a space and a slash mark at the end of the tag like this:

    ```
    <break />
    ```

    There's an alternate syntax that works just as well for real XML processors but often breaks HTML Web browsers when used with XHTML, which is to close an empty tag such as `<br>` with `</br>` like this:

    ```
    <br></br>
    ```

    Unfortunately it's too dangerous to use safely. Many current and most legacy browsers don't recognize the non-HTML closing tag and do odd things with it. Navigator 4.7, for example, might trash the display when it stumbles across a closing break tag. The exact behavior might vary by position in the code and the exact empty tag being closed. In short, it's error prone and should be avoided.

- **XML requires the use of either single or double quotes around attribute values**—Where HTML is lax about numbers especially and almost anything without included spaces, XML treats everything as character strings and lets the application figure everything out.

- **XML supports multiple languages**—It doesn't really support the extended character sets used in many European languages by default, as does HTML. There's an easy mechanism for including these, as well as the entire Unicode (also known as ISO/IEC 10646) character set of more than a million characters, so support for Chinese, Arabic, and many of the more exotic languages of the world is a piece of cake.

Other than the differences noted in this list, XML is very similar to HTML in the way tags are marked, attributes are argued, and content is placed between tag pairs. If you write *clean* HTML, the conversion of your HTML to XML-based XHTML is so trivial that it's possible to let a machine do it for you. Of course, XML is not limited to languages that look like HTML, so your document structure is limited only by the necessary tree structure and by your own imagination.

Tip from
molly

For Windows machines, it's hard to beat the power and functionality of the HTML-Kit program from Chami.com (`http://www.chami.com/`), which uses Dave Raggett's excellent Tidy program to clean up and optionally convert your code to clean XML. It inserts all those pesky closing tags and the special EMPTY closing tag syntax, tweaks tags that don't nest properly, and much more. Tidy is available on the Mac with a port from Terry Teague at `http://www.geocities.com/SiliconValley/1057/tidy.html` and there are several UNIX flavors hanging around the Web. There's also a Java port for O-O enthusiasts. See Dave Raggett's Web page at W3C for up-to-date details on these and other versions at `http://www.w3.org/People/Raggett/tidy/`.

Using skills you probably have today, you could start producing simple XML documents within a few hours of practice. The language was designed to be transparent in use, so it could be easily understood and used. The terse or obscure descriptions of XML in most documents are hard to understand in an effort to be precise in a way that programmers can translate easily into applications that work. There's a bit more to learn before real mastery is obtained, but it's not all that difficult.

Before you begin dismembering the language, you should look at the XML document as a whole.

DEFINING THE XML DOCUMENT AS A WHOLE

An XML document is a collection of entities, which can be either parsed or unparsed. *Unparsed data* is anything that the XML processor can't understand, binary data or data that is only meaningful to other applications. *Parsed data* is anything that XML can understand, either as characters or markup.

An XML document must be well-formed. In the W3C XML 1.0 Recommendation, quoted here precisely, this status is laconically described as meeting these requirements:

- Taken as a whole, it matches the production labeled *document*.
- It meets all the well-formedness constraints given in this specification (the XML 1.0 Recommendation).
- Each of the parsed entities referenced directly or indirectly within the document is well-formed.

The first constraint says that to be well-formed, an XML document has to obey all the rules that describe a document in the XML 1.0 Recommendation. Those rules essentially say that an XML document has to contain a prolog and a single element that forms the root element of the document together with optional comments and processing instructions. They also say that you can tack on comments and processing instructions to the end of the document but, unfortunately, the XML parser has no way of telling whether these tacked on comments and processing instructions are associated with the document. Because they can follow the closing tag, an XML parser can't even tell whether all tacked on processing instructions and comments were received. This violates the general rule in XML that the parser must be able to tell whether a document is complete. If you use processing instructions or comments, put them in the prolog where they are far safer and can't get lost.

The second constraint says that the document follows the well-formedness constraints described in the document. These constraints are examined in the following "Understanding the Well-Formedness Constraints" section. One of the well-formedness constraints is that recursive parsed entities are forbidden. Recursion in this prohibition refers to the formation of an entity loop, in which one entity incorporates itself or another entity that incorporates itself to whatever level of indirection. This also means that a document cannot refer to itself, even indirectly through an external entity. It can't refer to an external entity unless that too doesn't refer to itself, even indirectly. Non-validating parsers might not catch this error, but it's still an error. Logically, it's apparent that if document A includes document B, defining B as containing A leads to an endless loop. It's the endless loop that's forbidden.

> **Note**
>
> In XML terms, being well-formed is another way of saying that an XML document forms a tree, or a branch of a tree, that is complete in and of itself. This is necessary because XML allows you to build larger documents from smaller ones and is a key to being able to use XML over the Web. You'll discover more formal rules later in this chapter.

Although being well-formed might be considered enough because a well-formed document has a DTD that describes it, an infinitely large number of DTDs can be constructed that also describe it. So for full validity, an associated DTD is required.

The document production is defined in only two statements, again quoting from the XML 1.0 Recommendation:

- It contains one or more elements.
- There is exactly one element, called the *root* or *document element*, no part of which appears in the content of any other element. For all other elements, if the start-tag is in the content of another element, the end-tag is in the content of the same element. More simply stated, the elements, delimited by start and end tags, nest properly within each other.

The first statement says that there has to be at least one element in a document or, alternatively, that a well-formed document can't be empty.

The second statement says that the document has to be a tree in the narrow sense. It can't be an arbitrary connected network or have any other topology that doesn't reduce to a simple tree. It has to be complete so you can tell the difference between a successful download and a partial one.

> **Note**
>
> Technically, a *tree* is a connected graph that contains no circuits. In other words, a tree branches from its root without connecting back to itself and therefore doesn't contain multiple edges or loops. Anything that contains loops or multiple edges isn't a tree but something else and you can't do that in XML. An interesting side effect of this is that you can pick any arbitrary point on a tree, shake it a bit, and convert a node into a root, rearranging the tree into another with a different order of traversal. This illustrates the whimsical nature of classification schemes.

A partial download is possible in HTML, because HTML doesn't require a closing `</html>` tag, or indeed almost any closing tags. Sometimes the browser can detect the interruption but it's not guaranteed. This means that a partial document can masquerade as complete and the user has no way of knowing unless there's some obvious fault in the text. XML prevents these problems, which might be important if a user later claims that a license agreement, for example, wasn't displayed in total. Insisting on a complete tree, an example of which is shown in Figure 37.1, eliminates these potential problems.

Figure 37.1
This depicts a well-formed tree. You could make an XML document out of the structure represented by this tree.

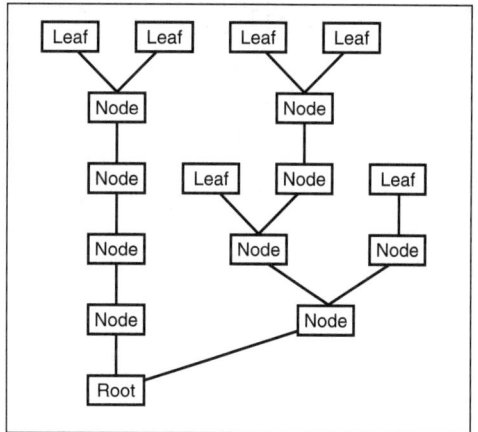

A graph that doesn't form a tree, on the other hand, cannot be made into an XML document unless the graph can be pruned to eliminate any non-tree features. In Figure 37.2, for example, the graph on the left could be pruned by eliminating one path from the topmost leaf to either node. In the same figure, the graph on the upper right would have to have one root eliminated, because an XML document can have only one root.

Figure 37.2
This illustration depicts two graphs that are not trees. They are not capable of being turned into XML documents.

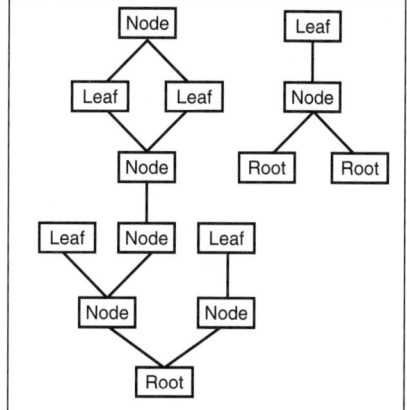

You should also be aware that trees are often depicted growing upside down, with the root at the top and the branches growing downward. This is done to accommodate our habit of reading pages from top to bottom, so the first thing we encounter on this upside down tree is the root, just as an XML parser would, and scanning down the page brings us deeper into the foliage of the tree.

UNDERSTANDING THE WELL-FORMEDNESS CONSTRAINTS

Besides the basic properties required in an XML document as listed in the previous "Defining the XML Document as a Whole," section, an XML document must meet certain extra criteria called constraints. The following list describes the well-formedness constraints:

- Parameter entities in the internal subset can only occur where markup can occur. They can't occur inside markup. This is a completely arbitrary rule and was done to simplify the task of parsing internal DTDs.

- The name in an element's end-tag must match the name in the start-tag. This is almost trivial. Few of us would expect to be able to close a `<cite>` tag with a `</citation>` tag.

- An attribute name cannot appear more than once in the same start-tag or empty-element tag. Again, this is fairly obvious. What are you supposed to do with a mal-formed line of code like this?

  ```
  <image src="one.gif" src="two.gif" />
  ```

- Attribute values cannot contain direct or indirect references to external entities. This is more subtle and was done to simplify life for XML processors. In an environment in which arbitrary character encodings are possible in external entities, it would be hard to handle them all correctly in an attribute.

- The replacement text of an entity referred to directly or indirectly in an attribute value (other than `"&lt;"`) must not contain a <. This is for simplicity and error handling. If you allowed an un-escaped < inside an attribute, it would be hard to catch a missing final quote mark. Also, because you have to escape < in running text anyway, treating it differently inside an attribute value would be inconsistent.

- Characters referred to using character references must be legal characters. In other words, you can't hide characters that would otherwise be illegal by indirection or by defining them as numeric equivalents. So, for example, `&#x0000;` is not a legal character no matter how you refer to it.

- In a document without a DTD, a document with only an internal DTD subset containing no parameter entity references or a document with a value of `"standalone='yes'"` on the XML declaration, the name given in the entity reference must match that in an entity declaration. One exception is that well-formed documents need not declare any of the following entities: `&amp;`, `&lt;`, `&gt;`, `&apos;`, or `&quot;`.

  Basically, the declaration of a parameter entity must precede any reference to it, but there are some situations in which a non-validating XML processor stops processing entity declarations. So if the non-validating processor is confident that all declarations have been read and processed, then it can declare a well-formedness error and abort processing if it finds an undeclared entity. On the other hand, if any of the ways in which the non-validating XML processor stops processing entities have occurred, then it's not an error to encounter an undeclared entity. This is a complicated way of saying that non-validating XML processors might or might not catch undeclared entities, depending on the situation.

- An entity reference must not contain the name of an unparsed entity. In short, you can't plunk binary data into the middle of text without some sort of handling mechanism declared. So, the following code is permitted and the value passed on to the user agent or browser if and only if it represented an external unparsed entity that had already been declared as a notation:

```
<image &myimage; />
```

- A parsed entity must not contain a recursive reference to itself, either directly or indirectly. Although dictionary makers might like to declare that a hat is a chapeau and a chapeau is a hat as if this means something, XML won't let you get away with it.

- Parameter-entity references might only appear in the DTD. In other words, you can't carry over processing data into the final document and expect it to mean anything. You might as well expect that you could insert a C statement, say `printf("Hello, world"\n);`, onto your typewritten page and expect it to be replaced with some value and have the carriage returned for you. On the other hand, although it's a logical error if you *expect* it to happen, such text wouldn't actually break anything either, any more than printing the above line of C code in your text generates an error. Because `%` is only a character and doesn't have to be escaped inside your document, it's hard to see how such an "error" would be found out. Although factually interesting, this is a null statement as far as error processing goes.

THE PROLOG: THE XML DECLARATION

Every XML document should begin with an XML declaration that identifies the file as an XML file and also identifies the version of XML being used in this particular document. The fact that this is not mandatory is due only to the fact that there are many HTML and SGML files lying about on the Web that were perfectly well-formed XML as well. Why break what's already working? The XML declaration is also the place you declare your encoding and whether the document is standalone. The order shown in the following snippet is mandatory, although the `encoding` and `standalone` attributes are both optional:

```
<?xml version="1.0" encoding=" ISO-8859-1" standalone="yes">
```

Encodings let you identify which of many character sets you plan to use in the document. This is important because, unlike HTML, which presupposes ASCII and forces you to use ASCII names, XML allows speakers of Hindi, for example, to use a Devanagari encoding and make their text and editing environment readable to ordinary citizens who happen to be XML authors. Or a Chinese author might prefer Chinese characters in tags and content. With few limitations based on the rules for the languages themselves, you can use scripts and ideographs in element names as well as content.

As a simple example of the sorts of limitations that exist based on language rules, consider the superscript letters "st" in the quasi-abbreviation "1st." The letters really modify the "1" so that you know it's supposed to be pronounced "first." There is no legal situation in English (or any European language) in which you are free to use this construction at the beginning of a "word." So "stwhile" doesn't legally expand into the word "erstwhile."

Similarly, "St Ives" should be pronounced "Saint Ives." In XML, you could define an element named `<s`^{t}`>` according to the rules, but because the superscript letters aren't legal at the beginning of words in any European language, you can't define an element named `<`^{t}`misbehaving>` (to be pronounced "ain't misbehaving") because it would violate the rules of our language. Interestingly, although you can't use ordinary numeric digits at the beginning of a name, you can use Roman numerals, even though the Roman numeral "3" is defined as a single character, "III." This handles relatively uncommon constructions like "XIVth Century."

The `standalone` attribute allows you to turn off an external DTD if you want to. It might have other effects as well but it's difficult to say exactly what in a few words. You'll learn more about this attribute in the "Standalone Documents" section later in this chapter.

CHARACTER ENCODINGS

The most likely character encoding for American English (and any other language) is probably UTF-8, which is the default. This is the Unicode extended character set often used on UNIX systems. It's a variable-length encoding, using anywhere from 1 to 5 bytes of data for each character, which might cause problems in Java and other environments. If your system demands a fixed byte length, UTF-16, which uses two bytes per character like Java, is a good choice because XML processors must be able to detect either encoding without any declaration at all. UTF-8 and UTF-16 are the only encodings that XML parsers are *required* to recognize and are sufficient to handle any world language in common use.

On the other hand, most Windows systems don't produce UTF-8 but rather ISO-8859-1, which is the ISO-Latin-1 character set used for British and American English and most other Western European languages. This is not a default value, so it should be specified in your encoding declaration like this:

```
<?xml version="1.0" encoding="ISO-8859-1">
```

Otherwise, certain characters might not map to UTF-8 correctly and might cause readability problems in your document. In general, if you plan to produce primarily English text with an occasional word or phrase in another European language, that's all you need to know about character encodings.

The following information is of primary interest to those whose primary language is something other than English and who will probably recognize the encodings their word processing applications produce or infer it from context. If you don't plan to produce documents using these encodings, you can skip the "Other Encodings" section entirely.

OTHER ENCODINGS

Other common encodings are ISO-10646-UCS-2 and ISO-10646-UCS-4, which should be used for two of the various encodings of Unicode/ISO/IEC 10646 used most often for some European languages.

The values ISO-8859-1, ISO-8859-2, and so on through ISO-8859-10 should be used for the various parts of ISO 8859 (8-bit fonts) used for Latin-1 (West European), Latin-2 (East European), Latin-3 (South European), Latin-4 (North European), Cyrillic, Arabic, Greek, Hebrew, Latin-5 (Turkish), and Latin-6 (Nordic), in that order. The values ISO-2022-JP, Shift_JIS, and EUC-JP should be used for the Japanese language encoding forms of JIS X-0208-1997. Every XML processor should, but might not, recognize at least these encodings. XML processors might recognize other encoding names as well, such as ASCII, US-ASCII, or EBCDIC-US. It's suggested by the W3C XML 1.0 Recommendation that character encodings registered with the Internet Assigned Numbers Authority (IANA), other than those just listed, should be referred to using their registered names.

PART
II

CH

37

Tip from
molly

These registered names are defined to be case insensitive, so processors wanting to match against them should do so in a case-insensitive way.

If you choose a particular character encoding, other than the defaults, UTF-8 or UTF-16, which potentially address the entire Unicode/ISO character space of more than a million characters, you should also ensure that the relevant entity sets are imported into your document for clarity and ease of use (if you're using an English word processor or authoring environment). You would do this most commonly for ISO-8859-1 and the special characters defined for HTML and XHTML. For most MS-Windows machines in Western Europe and the Americas, you should choose a character encoding of ISO-8859-1, the Latin-1 character set that Windows uses, mostly. You'll use ENTITY declarations that look like this:

```
<!-- Latin-1 characters for XHTML -->
<!ENTITY % HTMLlat1 PUBLIC "-//W3C//ENTITIES Latin1//EN//HTML"
      "http://www.w3.org/TR/xhtml1/DTD/HTMLlat1x.ent">
    %HTMLlat1;
<!-- Special characters for XHTML -->
<!ENTITY % HTMLspecial PUBLIC "-//W3C//ENTITIES Special//EN//HTML"
       "http://www.w3.org/TR/xhtml1/DTD/HTMLspecialx.ent">
    %HTMLspecial;
<!-- Mathematical, Greek and Symbolic characters for XHTML -->
<!ENTITY % HTMLsymbol PUBLIC
      "-//W3C//ENTITIES Symbols//EN//HTML"
       "http://www.w3.org/TR/xhtml1/DTD/HTMLsymbolx.ent">
    %HTMLsymbol;
```

You'll learn more about character declarations later in this chapter, but you should take away from this discussion that for ordinary documents in English using Windows-based authoring software, you'll probably want to explicitly declare the ISO-8859-1 character set to ensure that the ISO-Latin-1 character set is properly interpreted. Although the ordinary English typewriter keyboard letters are equivalent in UTF-8 and ISO-8859-1, certain accented and special characters are different and the ISO-8859-1 character set is much smaller.

If you're using non-English word processing or authoring software, especially if you're using a non-European operating system, you should ascertain which encodings are being generated so you call upon the appropriate encoding in your declaration.

There's probably more information here than most people want to know about character encodings, but when you need the information to produce a readable document in, say, Russian, you need it badly. The Roman Czyborra Web site has links to a lot more information, including images of some common character sets: http://czyborra.com/charsets/iso8859.html.

STANDALONE DOCUMENTS

According to the W3C XML 1.0 Recommendation, "Standalone documents have no external markup declarations which affect XML information passed from the XML processor to an application."

This is a stunningly terse and obscure way of saying that standalone="yes" means that

- There are no default attribute values declared in an external DTD which aren't explicitly set in the document.
- There are no entities other than &, <, >, ', and " used which have not been declared locally or possibly read in from a file by reference.
- There are no elements with only element content containing whitespace in any form.
- There are no external attributes subject to normalization, which means that the contents of attributes cannot have whitespace in them, or character or entity references.

It *doesn't* mean there is nothing external to the document. There might be. It mainly means that at whatever point the non-validating XML processor stops reading external documents, the processing of *all* declarations stops.

You can do all these things if and only if you put them into the internal DTD subset.

External data that are not markup are not within the scope of this statement. So, you can still have graphics files, included text files, and anything else as long as they aren't markup and as long as you declare them in the internal DTD subset.

After all that, the XML processor isn't required to notify the application as to whether the document is standalone. In fact, the processor isn't required to do much of anything with this information or behave in any particular way when it encounters this information.

Basically, the designer of the DTD has to figure out whether documents authored using that DTD can be standalone and tell people, including authors. Authors who know that the DTD has been designed to be standalone or who have converted a document not designed to be standalone into the alternative format, can insert standalone="yes" into their XML declaration as documentation of that fact:

```
<?xml version="1.0" standalone="yes" ?>
```

Documents that are not standalone can be automatically converted, assuming that a facility to do this is available, or manually if otherwise, into standalone documents algorithmically.

CONSTRUCTING THE XML DOCUMENT PROLOG: THE DOCUMENT TYPE DECLARATION

The prolog of an XML document contains several statements. The first, the XML declaration, declares that the following document is XML. The second, the Document Type Declaration, is the method you use to identify the Document Type Definition (DTD) used by a particular document. The fact that the acronym DTD might apply to the Document Type Declaration is an unfortunate coincidence. DTD refers only to the latter, not the former. There can be only one Document Type Declaration in an XML document, so it's entered on the document instance itself. Because multiple DTDs can be combined to make a single document, this allows control of DTD loading to reside in each individual document.

The Document Type Declaration (DOCTYPE) has two parts, both optional. The first references an external DTD and uses the keywords PUBLIC or SYSTEM to identify a catalog entry or a URI, respectively. If catalogs aren't implemented in your XML processor, you can specify both parts at once without the second keyword:

```
<!DOCTYPE your-doc-name PUBLIC "{catalog id}">
<!DOCTYPE your-doc-name PUBLIC "{catalog id}" "{uri}">
<!DOCTYPE your-doc-name SYSTEM "{uri}"
```

The second optional part of the DOCTYPE declaration allows you to enter an internal DTD subset directly into your document. There are severe restrictions on the sort of information that you can put into the internal DTD, but you can do quite a lot anyway. The internal DTD subset is surrounded by square brackets like this:

```
<!DOCTYPE your-doc-name [ {internal DTD declarations} ]>
```

You can also combine the two, allowing you to add certain types of declarations and entities almost at will:

```
<!DOCTYPE your-doc-name PUBLIC "{catalog id}" "{uri}" [ {internal DTD
➡declarations} ]>
```

For clarity, the internal subset is usually set off with carriage returns like this:

```
<!DOCTYPE your-doc-name PUBLIC "{catalog id}" "{uri}" [
 {internal DTD declarations}
]>
```

The DOCTYPE declaration must use the name of the root ELEMENT of the DTD, whether internal or external, as the field labeled your-doc-name in the previous examples. So if the name of the root element of your DTD is Dave, your DOCTYPE declaration should start like this:

```
<!DOCTYPE Dave ... >
```

Your coding manual or sheet tells you what to say on the DOCTYPE if you are an author. If you are a DTD designer, you should supply such a coding manual or sheet to every author.

You might also create one master DTD that calls in the DTD parts you need, much like ordering from a menu. When you have a mix of functionality that allows you to create the document structure you need, you can publish the resulting DTD and save the trouble of doing it again and again for each new document.

CONSTRUCTING THE DOCUMENT BODY

An XML document consists of text, which usually consists of mingled markup and character data. The prolog contains markup only, but that isn't the interesting part, because you need data to go with your markup before it's anything other than empty boxes to put things in. The body of your document contains almost everything that counts from an application (and human) perspective, sprinkled liberally within your markup.

CHARACTER DATA

A DTD can declare many types of data that might be used in your document, but the default data type is always CDATA, for ordinary character data. The coding sheet or manual tells you what sort of data can be entered into each attribute or element content field.

Assuming that the type is CDATA, you can put pretty much anything you want into the field as long as it doesn't contain unescaped markup.

It's entirely possible to construct a DTD that contains no text within elements. Instead, one can put the significant data inside attributes associated with each element, which can all be declared as empty or containing element content only. This is sometimes done to convert a document using an encoding standard such as MARC, which is basically a binary format, to XML.

MARKUP

Markup consists of the entirety of the non-character data content of an XML file. The various forms that markup can take are shown in Table 37.1.

TABLE 37.1   XML MARKUP SYNTAX

Markup Type	Markup Syntax
Start tags	`<elementName [attributes] > ...`
End tags	`... </elementName>`
empty-element tags	`<elementName [attributes] />`
entity references	`&entityName; or %parameterEntityName;`
character references	`&#decimalNumber; or &#xhexNumber;`
comments	`<!-- comment -->`

TABLE 37.1   CONTINUED

Markup Type	Markup Syntax
CDATA section delimiters	`<![CDATA[ cdata stuff ]]>`
document type declarations	`<!DOCTYPE name externalID? [DTDstuff]>`
processing instructions	`<?processorID data ?>`
XML declaration	`<?xml version encoding standalone ?>`

Everything else is character data.

Markup always starts with either the < character, in which case it always ends with the > character, or with the & character, in which case it always ends with the ; character. The rest of this chapter explores different kinds of markup.

UNDERSTANDING HOW XML FORMS LOGICAL STRUCTURES

The nesting of elements is the only mechanism used to indicate logical structure in an XML document. The start and end tags in the text stream tell the XML processor that a node has been encountered.

If the XML processor encounters another start tag before the matching end tag, the processor knows that it's either on a new node in the tree or a leaf. If no new start tag is encountered and the end tag is found, the processor knows that this is a leaf and can proceed iteratively at that level of the tree until another start or end tag is encountered. Processing proceeds stepwise based on this simple rule. If the processor is validating the document, each node can be associated with a rule governing what sorts of content can appear within it. An empty tag is, by definition, a leaf because it can contain no further content.

Note

Most of the data structure contained in an XML document can be accessed sequentially and without building the structure in memory. A start tag starts a node or leaf and the matching end tag ends it. Any tags encountered between a start tag and its matching end tag start a new node or leaf. This principle is the basis of SAX and other event-driven XML processors.

The rest of the logicalstructure of the document is defined by the attributes associated with each element. In addition, the logical structure can vary based on the contents of conditional sections contained within the document or its subparts.

HOW XML FORMS PHYSICAL STRUCTURES

The nesting of entities is the only mechanism used to indicate physical structure in an XML document. The entity definitions encountered in the text stream tell the XML processor that a separate entity has been encountered.

There are many types of entities, from the tiny entities that form individual characters like this: (space) or &sp; (space), to the external entities that allow you to incorporate portions of other XML documents into your own or include references to unparsed data, such as multimedia files in a document for later rendering by a user agent.

An XML document is a collection of such entities. Each of those subentities must be complete in and of itself. This means that because the structure of the document as a whole must be a simple tree, each subentity must be a single node or must also be a simple tree. You build larger structures by grafting on subentity nodes or trees as portions of your larger tree.

If you look at Figure 37.1, shown previously, you could partition that diagram into sub-trees only as long as you could take a pencil and circle all the elements of your proposed tree and only cross one line, the branch that joins your group of elements to the main tree. If you cross more than one line, you can't form a legal sub-tree. This means that you have to include a single lowest node that will form the root of your new sub-tree.

If your documents contain multiple sub-trees in different files, every sub-tree file must be a complete XML document tree in and of itself.

Look at the two connected graphs shown previously in Figure 37.2. You see that either there are two roots, which you'll remember is forbidden in XML, or a simple circuit (a loop) in the graph, which prevents it from being an XML structure in the first place. There are, in fact, substructures of that tree that seem to be simple trees; however, the one loop is a fatal flaw. As a whole, these structures cannot be made into XML documents. In the first case, by rearranging the structure, you could probably turn it into a simple tree, but one root would become a leaf in the new structure.

In the second case, you could isolate a large portion of the structure as a simple tree and make that part into an XML structure. But you would have to find some other way of representing that part that is not a tree unless you cut one of the circular paths and transform it into a simple tree.

Tip from

molly

A connected graph with a circuit can be trimmed by cutting any part of the circuit that leaves a complete tree.

As one possible solution, the looping structure could be declared as a notation and passed on to some other application to handle.

Alternatively, as a primitive and almost trivial idea, a hyperlink might solve your problem, depending on what you're trying to say with this structure. At a hyperlink, you jump from the document to somewhere else, metaphorically above the plane of the paper your document is printed on. You can land anywhere, including the document itself, thereby performing the otherwise impossible feat of leaping from leaf to leaf or even to another tree entirely.

A hyperlink thus represents meta-information about the structure of the tree, or about the structure of other trees, that stands to some extent outside the tree itself.

START TAGS AND END TAGS

There are two types of tags used in XML, tags with content and empty tags. Tags with content must have a start tag and an end tag. The start tag contains the name of the element inside angle brackets with optional attribute arguments. The end tag contains the name of the element preceded by a slash and all within angle brackets. You can't argue attributes in an end tag. The following code represents a tag with content:

```
<title subtitle="A Journey Home">There and Back Again</title>
```

They look very much like standard HTML tags and shouldn't cause any problems other than that of well-formedness, which demands that they truly nest within each other. You can't have tags that alternate with each other like this malformed example:

```
<bold><italic>EMPHASIZED TEXT</bold></italic>
```

Although it's a common error in HTML, XML is far more finicky and won't permit this construct. You have to nest the tags properly as shown here:

```
<bold><italic>EMPHASIZED TEXT</italic></bold>
```

Notice that the tags now nest properly within each other.

> **Caution**
>
> You *must* close every tag that starts in the context of a given tag (or tags) before the context of that tag is closed.

Empty tags have a special format available, although the same start tag/end tag scheme can be used for them as long as you remember not to put content of any sort between the start tag of the empty element and its immediately following end tag. Also, you might be concerned if it's possible that your XML document will be seen by an ordinary Web browser because end tags for elements that look like empty HTML tags might cause the browser to crash or behave in strange ways. For general use, however, the special format is mnemonic in itself, an advantage because you can *see* that the tag is empty, and it doesn't break most browsers.

Ordinarily, you start and end empty tags within the same angle brackets by following the name of the element and all its potential attributes with a space, a forward slash, and then the closing angle bracket:

```
<image source="myphoto.jpeg" type="JPEG" />
```

Of course the type must be declared as a notation, but that will be discussed in the "Unparsed Entities" section.

NORMALIZATION

Normalization is a fancy word for bringing things down to the lowest common denominator and putting them into a sort of canonical form. In the context of XML, it refers to the process of resolving entity references in locations in which such references can occur, regularizing linefeeds to account for the several different ways of treating them in different operating systems, and tidying up a few more things that need doing in certain cases.

> **Note**
>
> The designer rarely has to worry about normalization except in a negative way. The XML parser should perform all needed normalizations, so the only thing the document architect need think about is whether normalization will affect his data when making a round trip from un-normalized form to normalized and back again.

It turns out that there are two places where whitespace might be encountered: in character data within the document and in character data argued in element attributes.

In the first case, it's difficult to distinguish "significant" whitespace from insignificant whitespace in parsed entities. It seemed best to the designers to pass on all whitespace to the application along with the processor's best guess, based on the DTD, about which data is definitely insignificant and which might or might not be. This passing of the buck makes sense because the application is in the best position to know what to do with extra whitespace.

> **Caution**
>
> The XML processor can only make a guess about what's significant whitespace and what's not based on whatever has been defined in the DTD or any other schema language used. Your application must be prepared to handle erroneous guesses.

With end-of-line handling, also a form of whitespace, there's another problem. Newlines are treated differently on different systems. The common alternatives are a linefeed (UNIX), a carriage return (MacOS), and both carriage return and linefeed characters (MS Windows). It's also common for applications to insert anomalous sequences of any of these in any order when they encounter a file from a foreign system. W3C decided they couldn't do everything and chose a set of reasonable rules. If the parser sees either ;#x0D;
 (carriage return, linefeed) or  (carriage return) it replaces it with
 (linefeed), the UNIX newline character. A few Microsoft Windows programmers were somewhat less than pleased.

> **Note**
>
> Microsoft and Apple chose differing mechanisms to separate lines, with Microsoft choosing the "belt and suspenders" technique common with teletypes and using a carriage return and then a line feed character to indicate a newline. Apple decided that the line feed was redundant and felt that a solitary carriage return would do, modeled presumably after the way an ordinary typewriter behaves. UNIX had been using a solitary line feed character to accomplish the same thing all along, and that was the standard agreed upon for XML. So both Microsoft and Apple have to use special logic to handle carriage returns in XML and HTML documents.

In attributes, there is a standard transformation sequence and then special added processing for everything except CDATA:

- Character references are processed by appending the referenced character to the output attribute value.

- Entity references are processed by recursively processing the replacement text of the entity.

- Whitespace characters, #x20 (space), #x0D (carriage return), #x0A (linefeed), #x09 (horizontal tab), are processed by appending #x20 (space) to the normalized output value, except that only a single #x20 (space) is appended for a "#x0D#x0A" (carriage return, linefeed) sequence that is part of an external parsed entity or the literal entity value of an internal parsed entity.

- Other characters are processed by appending them to the normalized output value.

- Yet another transformation is applied if the attribute datatype is *not* CDATA, the default. Leading and trailing spaces are stripped and multiple spaces are collapsed into one space.

The distinction between the two types of normalization lies in that you can conveniently pass long strings in an attribute, folding lines to fit the page, although element content remains relatively pristine.

ELEMENT TYPES

Surprisingly, if you're validating, it's not an error to use an element type that hasn't been declared although the parser might issue a warning. In fact, allowing undeclared element types within other elements, no matter what their content model says, is the basis of being able to supplement a document's DTD with elements from other namespaces. So all you have to do is use the undeclared element in a correct, well-formed manner while possibly identifying the namespace it comes from. Because you've already explored what well-formed means, take a look at the more interesting case, a valid document.

Note

In XML terms, being well-formed is another way of saying that it forms a tree, or a branch of a tree, that is complete in and of itself. This is necessary because XML allows you to build larger documents from smaller ones and is a key to being able to use XML over the Web. Other more formal rules are discussed elsewhere in this chapter.

Every element in a valid XML document has been defined in the DTD associated with that document by the DOCTYPE declaration. The DTD declares the following:

- Actual names of the elements

- Rules used to determine which elements can nest within other elements and in what order

- Possible attributes and their default or constant values
- Character values of enumeration types
- Unparsed entities used in the document and how they are referenced by name
- Language encodings used in the document
- Character entities used in the document
- Other information important for the processing and rendering of the document

Following those rules, you're able to create documents according to the template the document designer had in mind when she created the DTD. In a non-validating environment, you can just make up tags and attributes as you go along.

The coding sheet or manual lays all this out in an easy-to-read and understand format, *if* your DTD author has done her job. When authoring an XML document or correcting an error, you might not have the luxury of a full authoring environment. You might be using vi over telnet from a thousand miles away. It's always important to keep the coding documentation handy in case you're called up in the middle of the night and asked if you wouldn't mind fixing your million-dollar database access system, please?

Figure 37.3, later in this chapter, shows a validating authoring environment that can save a lot of time and make life easier for you by automatically encapsulating the DTD informa-tion that might otherwise have to be presented in a coding document in programmatic form. However, such tools are neither infallible nor available on every platform. Although they might generate "helpful" error messages when they stop processing your file, the actual message might have little or nothing to do with the error you actually made. You'll have to use your head, not a tool, in many cases.

ENTITY NAMING RULES

Entity names must start with a character, which is any character glyph within a given writing system that corresponds to our usual idea of a Latin character plus the ASCII characters underscore and colon. The first character can be followed by characters, digits, and a selec-tion of accents and extenders representing glyph combinations of one sort or another. Processing instructions must not start with the ASCII letters XML, xml, or any mixed-case variations of those three characters. It's a very bad idea to use the ASCII colon character except when using namespaces, although it's possible to do so legally, because the presence of a string followed by a colon in a name *looks* like it refers to a namespace even when it doesn't.

Note

Surprisingly, many explanations of XML get this part wrong. Although everyone agrees that you can use encodings in content, the fact that this freedom extends to markup as well is harder to grasp. Everyone is so used to the limitations of HTML that it's difficult to remem-ber to embrace this freedom.

The only place that *some* ASCII is mandatory is in a DTD, which is a behind-the-scenes document that ordinary authors might never actually see. Literals that name public identifiers—the characters that fill the literal parts of a `<!DOCTYPE PUBLIC "-//public identifier" "uri">` declaration—must be ASCII characters because that's an Internet standard. Numeric character references such as `&#x0D;` must be entered using a very limited ASCII number set. The ISO 639 language codes and the ISO 3166 country codes used in the `XML:lang` amd XHTML `lang` attributes must also be in ASCII, again because these are Internet standards. There are a few other places such as quote marks, which must be ASCII quotes, special markup characters like `&gt;`, keywords, like `<!ELEMENT ... >` and `IDREF`, and so on, where ASCII is required, but in general you don't have to worry about using equivalent characters from the national language character sets defined in the Unicode/ISO/IEC 10646 standards.

The rest of XML is friendly to speakers of languages other than English. Even what Unicode and ISO call "combining characters" and "extenders" are allowed in tags as well as content. These are essentially the accent marks that can be placed in names to signal to display engines that an accent should be combined with the previous character, however that might be performed. So the French, Germans, and many others who use a Latin alphabet can see tags that are spelled correctly in their own language with proper accents and umlauts, as can speakers of Hindi, Hebrew, Arabic, and the many other languages that use such characters.

Caution

Although it's great that XML allows Chinese characters in markup and content, that doesn't mean your system actually supports the display and entry of Chinese characters, or any other of the many ideographic, syllabic, and alphabetic writing systems in use around the world. You'll need a character set as well as a keyboard and operating system support for full functionality.

After years of Eurocentric, even Anglocentric, dependence on ASCII and extended ASCII on the Web, XML has evened the playing field somewhat for all players at the Web level, including the myriad of users who will be able to access information in their native languages and scripts. Having a single standard means of communicating in, say, Chinese, in which there are three main "standards" and a number of variations, is sure to improve the availability of rendering engines as well as reduce their cost.

ATTRIBUTE LISTS AND TYPES

In your XML coding sheet, you'll find a list of attributes for each element. If you're using a validating editor such as XML Pro 2.0, you'll probably have a menu of available attributes whenever you place the working cursor on an element in the document tree view. There is also a menu of elements that can be inserted at this point in the file.

Such an editor can be a tremendous timesaver because it takes away some of the burden of learning a coding sheet or manual. However, a good coding sheet can give a far more accessible general overview and explain the rationale behind the document structure, something even a validating editor cannot do.

Figure 37.3 shows some of the strengths of this sort of editor. The tree structure of the document is clearly displayed although a large or complex document can quickly overwhelm the limits of readability on a small screen. The highlighted cursor shows where you are in the document at any given time. A list of available attributes for the element you've highlighted is visible on the screen as well. You can scroll down through them and pick the ones you want to employ for this particular element.

Figure 37.3
XML Pro 2.0 is being used to edit an XHTML file. Note the list of available attributes for an anchor element based on the position of the element cursor.

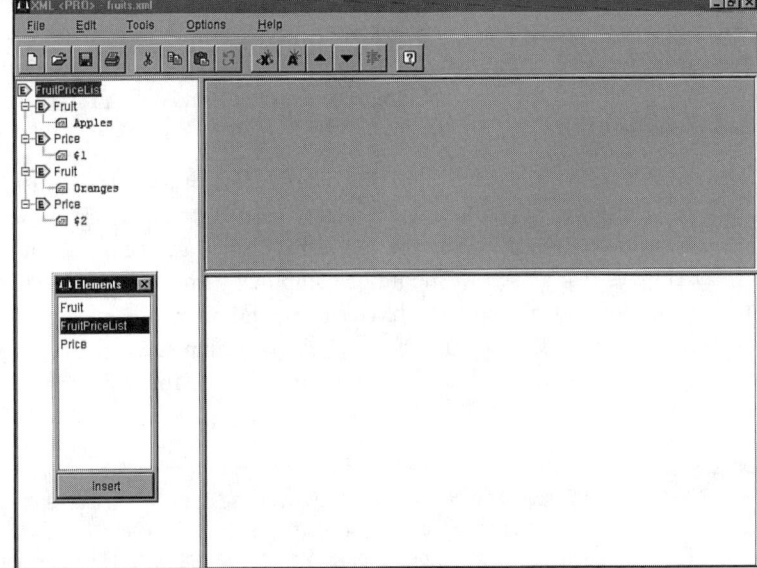

There is very little checking of your attribute values that can be done at the processor level. XML by itself doesn't offer facilities to validate attributes and element content in detail beyond checking that enumerated choices have been entered correctly, which a validating editor does automatically, and a few other minor details. XML Pro and other authoring environments might offer you a pull-down list of enumerated values so you can't make a mistake, but that's about it. The solution to this dilemma is XML schemas.

Even the little field checking provided might not be reasonable in actual use. If you think telephone numbers have to be numeric, for example, you're flying in the face of various language-dependent conventions that might use periods, hyphens, commas, slashes, parentheses, or even spelled-out words on the telephone keypad to represent numbers. For some purposes, the U.S. military uses a hexadecimal telephone keypad that adds the "digits" A, B, C, and D to the usual 0–9 plus * and #. Telephone TouchTone™ standards, officially called DTMF (Dual Tone Multi-Frequency) tones, allow for this, so you should too. Postal (ZIP) codes in many countries include letters as well as digits. And large numbers and decimal fractions might have punctuation marks inside them that vary from country to country, often a comma and period respectively but quite often period and comma in an exact reversal of meaning. In general, everything is more complicated than you think, and adding silly restrictions on input is almost guaranteed to cause problems and make you look bad.

Caution

In a global environment, it pays to be really careful about what is allowed and what is not in any data field. Although many schemes are on their way to allowing fine detail in field constraints, the examples given should give you pause. Telephone numbers might look like this: 011 41 09 23 44 23 in France or like this on a small island in the Pacific: 011 8524 99 99 22 33. You have to come to some happy compromise between what the user demands and what you're prepared to accept. In many cases, the capability to override range checking at user demand can help alleviate frustration. You could remind U.S. customers about the "correct" number of digits in a phone number while allowing anyone to type in whatever they want if they insist.

Although an XML application might only be enforcing constraints in an underlying database, before finalizing your analysis, consider the fact that the database might be designed in an insular or shortsighted manner that doesn't meet the real demands of a global marketplace. Some data is inherently regional in nature, and a mature individual is cognizant of that fact. Whether one eats with the fork in the right hand or the left is a matter of taste, not error checking. In the case of cosmetic differences, consider normalizing the data before error checking or storage. There's no earthly reason a British user has to guess that we often surround area codes with parentheses in the United States and Canada before her input is accepted.

UNPARSED ENTITIES

An unparsed entity is anything the XML processor can't recognize, whether it be binary data such as an image or audio file, or text that should be passed to an application without being processed in any way. HTML uses comments to hide such text from the HTML browser, but XML has several mechanisms that work more reliably. In fact, XML is not required to pass comments onto the application at all, so they can't be used as freely as they are in HTML. This was, I think, a bit of pique on the part of some of the designers, who hated the idea of using comments for real data. In HTML, the contents of a <SCRIPT> tag are defined to be PCDATA, which can contain anything at all.

Be that as it might, you should follow the new rules with XML.

An unparsed entity must first be declared as a NOTATION, a special declaration that names a helper application that knows how to deal with entities of a particular type. You give the notation a name, an optional public identifier, and then the less optional name of the helper application, like one of these options:

```
<!NOTATION mnemonic-name PUBLIC "public-identifier">
<!NOTATION mnemonic-name PUBLIC "public-identifier" "application-name.exe ">
<!NOTATION mnemonic-name SYSTEM "application-name.exe ">
```

The first option works only if you have a catalog. The second and third work whether you have a catalog or not. You can't count on a catalog because it's an SGML tool that many current XML processors have tacitly inherited from their SGML predecessors. Catalog lookup isn't specified in the W3C recommendation and it can never be counted on. Use the last two versions if you possibly can. On the other hand, hard-coding knowledge of the location and identity of a helper application into each and every DTD is an error-prone anachronism on the Web.

> **Caution**
>
> By redefining the way scripts behave in the presence of comments, the designers of XML have introduced an incompatibility problem between XML and HTML. In all likelihood, XML processors will continue to pass on comments to the application because many pages will break without that behavior. Also, the processors are *permitted* to pass on the commented information by the same language by which they're *permitted* not to.

After you've defined an unparsed entity notation, it has to be declared as an entity like this

```
<!ENTITY mnemonic-name NDATA mnemonic-name>
```

and then listed as an attribute in an element so you can actually use it:

```
<!ELEMENT name EMPTY>
<!ATTLIST name type NOTATION "mnemonicname"
          ... >
```

The mnemonic names don't share the same namespace so it doesn't matter whether they duplicate each other, which I encourage if only for the sake of keeping things clear.

At this point, you're back on the coding sheet and can use the datatype so defined. The datatype can only be used as an attribute of an element declared to be of that type or have that type available to it in an enumeration. Other attributes collect the information that the external helper application needs to be able to process the data.

A typical application might be an image file that could be argued like this:

```
<image source="uri" alt="graphic description" type="gif89a">
```

This element would require the following declarations in the DTD:

```
<!NOTATION gif89a     PUBLIC "-//CompuServe//NOTATION Graphics Interchange Format
89a//EN" "explorer.exe ">
<!ENTITY gif89a NDATA gif89a>
<!ELEMENT image EMPTY>
<!ATTLIST image source CDATA #REQUIRED
               alt    CDATA #IMPLIED
               type   NDATA gif89a >
```

With most tools, it won't matter whether you specify the format as gif87a or gif89a, because the same tools handle both formats. It's unreasonable to expect the person coding the file to know the difference between the two anyway.

Notations will be much improved with the addition of the facilities of XLink/XPointer to help keep track of helper locations. With the overall instability of the Web at its present level and the wide variety of facilities and architectures on user machines, any help the poor user can get will make configuring XML tools easier. The DTD as it exists now requires far too much UNIX-style tweaking of files for ordinary users to have much fun with it.

PART

II

CH

37

Note

XLink and XPointer are trying to overcome the limitations of current pointer technology. They allow all sorts of relationships, including reverse pointers to be generated on-the-fly in documents without write access, performing their magic on the display copy itself rather than crude physical insertion of tags in content.

XML requirements for notations as they now exist are exacting in the extreme. Being able to point out the location of a helper application might be handy for notations that are uncommon or highly specialized. However, the user agent can be expected to know how to display many of the more common types such as GIFs, JPEGs, PNGs, WAVs and other more or less standard binary file types used on the Web. Here's a list of common notations:

```
<!NOTATION eps       PUBLIC "+//ISBN 0-201-18127-4::Adobe//NOTATION
➥    Postscript Language Reference Manual//EN" >
<!NOTATION tex       PUBLIC "+//ISBN 0-201-13448-9::Knuth//NOTATION The
➥    TeXbook//EN" >
<!NOTATION cgmchar   PUBLIC "ISO 8632/2//NOTATION Character encoding//EN" >
<!NOTATION cgmbinary PUBLIC "ISO 8632/3//NOTATION Binary encoding//EN" >
<!NOTATION cgmclear  PUBLIC "ISO 8632/4//NOTATION Clear text encoding//EN" >
<!NOTATION tiff      PUBLIC "ISO 12083:1994//NOTATION TIFF-1//EN" >
<!NOTATION jpeg      PUBLIC "ISO/IEC 10918:1983//NOTATION Digital
➥    Compression and Encoding of Continuous-tone Still Images (JPEG)//EN" >
<!NOTATION gif87a    PUBLIC "-//CompuServe//NOTATION Graphics Interchange
➥    Format 87a//EN" >
<!NOTATION gif89a    PUBLIC "-//CompuServe//NOTATION Graphics Interchange
➥    Format 89a//EN" >
<!NOTATION fax       PUBLIC "-//USA-DOD//NOTATION CCITT Group 4 Facsimile
➥    Type 1 Untiled Raster//EN" >
```

Of course, you'll have to add a system ID to actually use these, either as a pointer to a local helper application or in the catalog file, if available for your tools, that centralizes the locations of these helpers.

REAL-WORLD APPLICATIONS

You've already seen some of the tools you might use to author an XML document above but where do you find DTDs to author against? Well, you can read further in this book and write your own or you can use one already in existence.

Many DTDs are in the public domain or are available as standards from ISO, ANSI, or other standards body. Here are a few of the more important applications of XML that are making waves in the world today:

■ Health Level-7 (HL7), the Health Informatics Standard was founded in 1987 to develop standards for the electronic interchange of clinical, financial, and administrative information among health care computer systems. The HL7 focus is on using SGML and XML as a transport mechanism between differing health care information systems.

■ Real Estate Transaction Standard (RETS) is an XML-based method of exchanging real estate transaction information. A competing standard is Real Estate Markup Language (RELML) that uses XML DTDs to describe residential, commercial, and open land listings for posting on the Web.

- RosettaNet, the Lingua Franca for Business, is an EDI/E-Commerce initiative aimed at procurement for the computer industry.

- MathML and ChemML are two scientific XML standards that allow mathematicians to publish equations and chemists to present chemical formulae.

- SMIL, the Synchronized Multimedia Markup Language, is HyTime for Everyman, a multimedia markup language that lets content providers produce sophisticated visual and audio presentations.

- ICE, Information and Content Exchange, although not strictly an XML application being a transport mechanism, allows the exchange of online assets and personal information over the Web.

- SAE J2008 is an XML-based ordering and inventory system for the automotive industry; MISTI, the Missile Industry Supply-chain Transaction Infrastructures, does the same for the space industry.

- Chinese DTDs provide the specialized structure needed for Chinese language publishing. Similar DTDs exist for Japanese, Korean, Vietnamese, and many other human languages.

- GedML, a genealogy XML standard, encourages the free flow of genealogical data over the Web. Software already exists to convert standard GEnealogical Data COMmunication (GEDCOM) files to GedML.

The list goes on and on. As you can see, the range of applications is immense, touching almost every field of human endeavor. Few businesses can safely ignore XML, although there are so many existing and proposed standards in many fields that there's bound to be some sort of shakeout as major contenders jockey for pole position in a fracas of dueling proposals.

Tip from

molly

With so many proprietary proposals on the table, you might wonder what the differences are between them. For the most part, you'll have to ask potential vendors to disclose their DTD as there are comparatively few DTDs available on the Web. There are two repositories that might give you a start. On Microsoft platforms, the BizTalk consortium at `http://www.biztalk.org/` has a searchable list, although it's not easy to use and requires you to guess what the appropriate keywords might be that describe the sort of DTD you're looking for. The Organization for the Advancement of Structured Information Standards (OASIS), at `http://www.oasis-open.org/` plans another but only has the DocBook DTD and a subset of the CALS table model DTD called Exchange Table Model up for public view right now. Many vendors are treating their DTDs as if they were state secrets.

Each browser maker has proposed standards that the others cry are slanted toward themselves. Just as the browser wars led to the development of proprietary "extensions" to HTML, which tended (or tried) to lock out other browsers creating a Babel of incompatible methods that still plague us today, XML is going to be in flux for some time to come.

The basics are already there, however, and a user community increasingly demanding of open standards is driving the various proposals toward convergence. Many of the major successes have been with standards from ISO and ANSII, which sell documentation to support their standards-making efforts but provide neutral ground for all partners. For the price of the documentation, usually a few hundred dollars, anyone can play on the same level ground.

GETTING DOWN TO CASES

Now that you know something about the basics of XML, you need to decide how to use it. You've already learned that DTDs are a way of precisely describing the format and layout conventions of an XML document and why they should be used in some situations but not in others. You've also learned some of the differences between XML and XHTML, and how they make a world of difference for the Web as a whole through the internationalization of character sets and tagging languages.

Some of these security facilities have already been implemented in hardware implementing transaction dispatching, digital signature, and Secure Sockets Layer (SSL) in silicon, the XML equivalent of a graphics accelerator chip. This means the infrastructure required to support high-volume XML transaction processing is becoming readily available.

Defining a B2B transaction processing system requires the ability to communicate very clearly what the records to be passed between systems look like, because those systems might be on different platforms and implemented in different programming languages. An XML DTD is ideal for communicating this information, because it can be guaranteed to be unambiguous and platform independent. After the transaction is implemented in an application, neither system involved in a transaction will need access to the DTD, because all knowledge about the DTD required for any particular processing requirement will be captured in the program code that handles the transaction on either end.

This scenario is common for any interprocess communications application using XML; the initial stages require a mutually agreed upon DTD that serves as part of the system documentation and testing facilities, but the need for a DTD goes away after the system is up and running. This is in contrast to documents that might be served to anyone without a prearranged and transaction-aware process on the other end. When a document is viewed in a general-purpose browser, the information contained in the DTD might be required for proper presentation and handling of the information contained therein. So DTDs are potentially more important for casual users than they are for communications between prearranged partners in an ongoing relationship.

CHAPTER 38

SYNCHRONIZED MULTIMEDIA INTEGRATION LANGUAGE (SMIL)

In this chapter

by Derrick Story

SMIL, the *Synchronized Multimedia Integration Language*, can be considered the masterful conductor leading an orchestra of musicians. Or maybe it's the traffic cop who tells you when to go and when to stop. And in the right hands, it can be the loom that allows the artist to weave a tapestry of sight and sound.

You don't create music with SMIL, but you can use it to start the first note at precisely the right moment. You can't create a compelling picture with SMIL, but you can bring an image to life by adding music and text to it. If you learn nothing else in this chapter, remember this: SMIL is the synchronization of sight and sound.

This prodigy of the W3C allows you to easily position various multimedia elements within a player window, synchronize them, and allow users to play back those elements according to their bandwidth, language choice, and other individual preferences.

Even though we don't currently have browsers that can play SMIL presentations directly without some sort of plug-in, RealNetworks, Apple QuickTime, and a handful of others have begun to integrate aspects of the SMIL initiative into their players and plug-ins. RealNetworks in particular, has embraced SMIL as the tool of choice for synchronizing its various streaming formats such as RealAudio and RealPix to produce compelling multimedia presentations on the Web (see Figure 38.1).

Figure 38.1
RealPlayer G2 supports SMIL. It's easy to synchronize imagery, text, and music for playback on a G2 player.

At the moment, SMIL's potential still remains largely untapped. But the language shows the promise of a gifted child musician. And even though we enjoy the music now, we can't help but wonder what the future might bring.

SMIL IS AN XML-BASED LANGUAGE

SMIL is an XML-based language that incorporates the precision and versatility of extensible code. If you're already adhering to the rules of XHTML, then learning how to code in SMIL (pronounced "smile") is really quite easy—at least in the beginning stages. You can see a snippet of SMIL code in Listing 38.1. You probably recognize many of the tags.

LISTING 38.1   SMIL SAMPLE

```
<smil>
   <head>
<layout>
<root-layout width="320" height="240"
   background-color="white" />
<region id="ed_button" left="0" top="20"
   width="125" height="22" />
</layout>
     </head>
     <body>
<img src="ed_button.gif" alt="button"
   region="ed_button" dur="2s" begin="2s" />
     </body>
</smil>
```

BASIC SMIL CODE GUIDELINES

Because SMIL is an application of XML—just like XHTML—you'll notice a lot of syntactical rules that are familiar. SMIL rules include the following:

- Tags must be written in lowercase only.
- Each opening tag must have a corresponding closing tag.
- Self-closing tags are allowed, such as `<meta name = "copyright" contents = "name" />`.
- Smile files must have the SMIL extension at the end:
  `.smi` or `.smil`.
- Spaces are not allowed in the file name, use an underscore instead.
- Comment tags are allowed.

One of the first things you probably notice is that all the tags are closed and in lowercase. The document has two parts: the head and the body. Both parts are wrapped within `smil` tags. The `layout` tag is located in the head and contains the layout information including the window dimensions. For example, the window for the code shown in Listing 38.1 is 320 pixels wide by 240 pixels high.

Tip from

molly

SMIL code can be written using a basic text or HTML editor such as NotePad, SimpleText, HomeSite, or BBEdit.

In the body of the document there's information about the image source, how long into the presentation before it appears, and the duration it stays on screen.

I'll delve more into the components of a SMIL document later in this chapter. Before I get to that though, I want to take a look at the roots of this markup language, and the direction that it appears to be headed.

SMIL HISTORY

The first public release of the SMIL specification was available in late 1997, and by mid-1998, the World Wide Web consortium published SMIL 1.0. This initial version generated a great deal of excitement in the online multimedia world because multimedia developers could now use a simple text editor to choreograph sounds, images, and text for presentation on the Web.

In August of 1999, the W3C released a new version referred to as *SMIL Boston*. This draft took SMIL functionality and divided it into nine modules (although not all the modules were detailed in the draft). The advantage of modularity is that the specification could be implemented and improved in parts instead of having to rewrite the entire spec every time a change was desired.

The following are the nine modules of SMIL Boston:

- Animation
- Content Control
- Layout
- Linking
- Media Object
- Metainformation
- Structure
- Timing and Synchronization
- Transition Effects

Soft sync, as outlined in the Timing and Synchronization Module, is an example of the many SMIL Boston improvements. In version 1.0, only *hard sync* was possible. That means that the streaming relationships of the components within presentations were fixed to specific time synchronizations.

This is fine for presentations played off local hard drives. But hard sync doesn't allow for disruptions due to network congestion. Soft sync, on the other hand, allows for network fluctuations allowing SMIL presentations to work much better on the Web. Authors working within the SMIL Boston draft can specify hard or soft sync to various elements within the presentation.

The SMIL Boston draft has yet to be accepted across the industry. A competing specification, HTML+TIME, is currently favored by Microsoft, Macromedia, and Compaq. Although HTML+TIME seemed to have advantages over SMIL 1.0, the modularity aspect of SMIL Boston might allow for an agreement upon a single spec across the industry.

What Is HTML+Time?

HTML+Time builds upon the existing HTML tag set by adding time-based attributes in the form of DHTML extensions. It was introduced after SMIL 1.0 by Microsoft (along with Compaq and Macromedia) and has been integrated into the Windows version of Internet Explorer 5.0.

HTML+Time allows developers to add time attributes to HTML elements, and it also allows for integration of multiple multimedia elements right there in the browser. It uses CSS for positioning and for applying styles.

At this point, the future of HTML+Time is as unclear, as is that of SMIL.

Optimists point out that it's possible that the best of both worlds will someday be combined into one standard.

Currently, SMIL attributes are supported heavily by RealNetworks authoring tools and players (see Figure 38.2). Apple has jumped on board with SMIL support within specific areas of QuickTime 4.1. SMIL's potential and fertile development environment also has attracted new names to the multimedia arena such as GriNS (Graphical iNterface to SMIL) that have created a host of tools and players that run on many platforms. We've yet to see integrated big-name browser support for SMIL, but if the W3C can push through industry-wide agreement on a spec, implementation by the popular browsers might quickly follow.

PART
IX
CH
38

Figure 38.2
RealSlideshow Plus uses SMIL's synchronization capabilities to build streaming slide shows that you can share with others online.

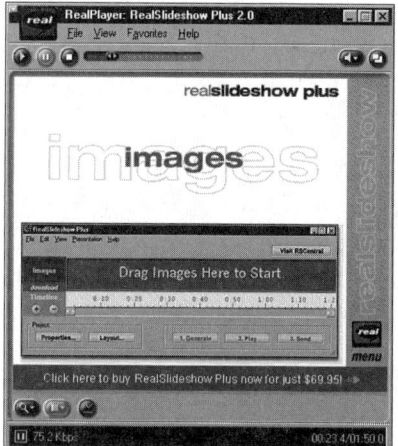

BUILDING A SMIL DOCUMENT

All SMIL documents contain certain elements. I'm going to build a basic SMIL presentation and explain the basic elements used along the way.

SMIL DOCUMENT TAGS

A SMIL document begins and ends with `<smil>` tags, and the familiar head and body elements are contained within them. The head element is where you include the meta and layout information, and the body element contains the media content and the synchronization specifications (see Listing 38.2).

LISTING 38.2   A SMIL DOCUMENT WITH SMIL, HEAD, AND BODY COMPONENTS

```
<smil>
   <head>
<meta name="copyright" content="author name or title" />
<layout>
<! -- Set the basic frame dimensions here.
         For example ... -- >
<root-layout width="320" height="240"
         background-color="white" />
</layout>
   </head>
   <body>
      <! -- Put media and synch tags here.
           For example ... -- >
<img src="ed_button.gif" alt="button" />
   </body>
</smil>
```

In this example, you also can see information for layout, color, and an image. Nothing here should be unfamiliar to the HTML or XHTML author.

USING THE Region TAG WITH ABSOLUTE AND RELATIVE POSITIONING

I want to place my first graphic within the 320×240 pixel window. There are two ways to position the media: *absolute* and *relative*. I'll first use the region tag to place my graphic using absolute positioning (see Listing 38.3).

LISTING 38.3   ABSOLUTE POSITIONING

```
<smil>
   <head>
<meta name="copyright" content="creator name" />
<layout>
<root-layout width="320" height="240"
   background-color="white" />
<region id="ed_button" left="20" top="30"
         width="125" height="22" />
</layout>
   </head>
</smil>
```

Figure 38.3 shows the results.

In absolute positioning, the layout window is viewed as a grid with the "zero" position in the upper left corner. To precisely position a graphic, I specify the position in pixels from the upper left corner. In this example, the graphic, ed_button, is placed 20 pixels to the left and 30 pixels down from the top. The width and height of the graphic area is 22 pixels high by 125 pixels wide.

Figure 38.3
Graphic placed within a 320 × 240 pixel window using absolute positioning.

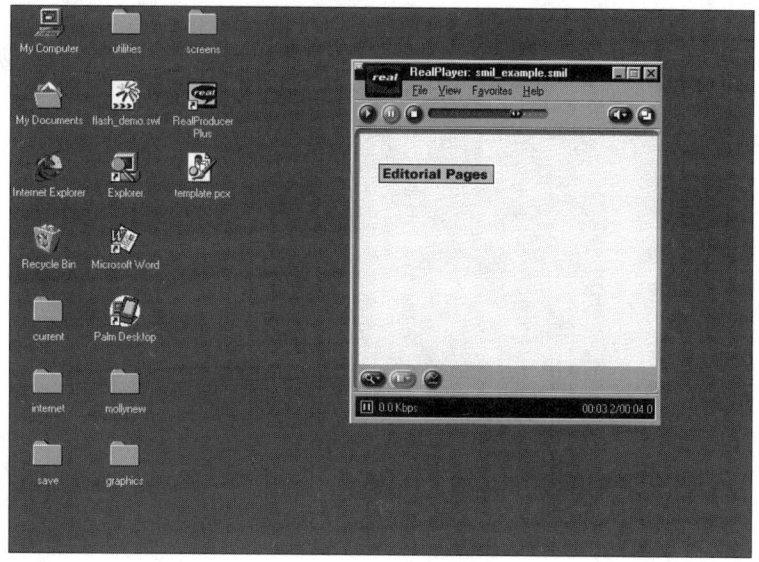

I also can place this graphic in the window by using relative positioning, which uses percentages from the top and left frame instead of fixed pixel locations. In other words, this graphic will be positioned 30 percent from the left border and 20 percent from the top (see Listing 38.4).

LISTING 38.4   RELATIVE POSITIONING

```
<smil>
   <head>
<meta name="copyright" content="creator name" />
<layout>
      <root-layout width="320" height="240"
   background-color="white" />
      <region id="ed_button" left="30%" top="20%"
         width="125" height="32" />
</layout>
   </head>
</smil>
```

You can see the relative positioning results in Figure 38.4.

Relative positioning is sometimes preferred in instances where window size varies based on user preferences.

Figure 38.4
Graphic positioned 30 percent from the left border and 20 percent from the top using relative positioning. Note the difference between the position of this graphic as opposed to that in Figure 38.3.

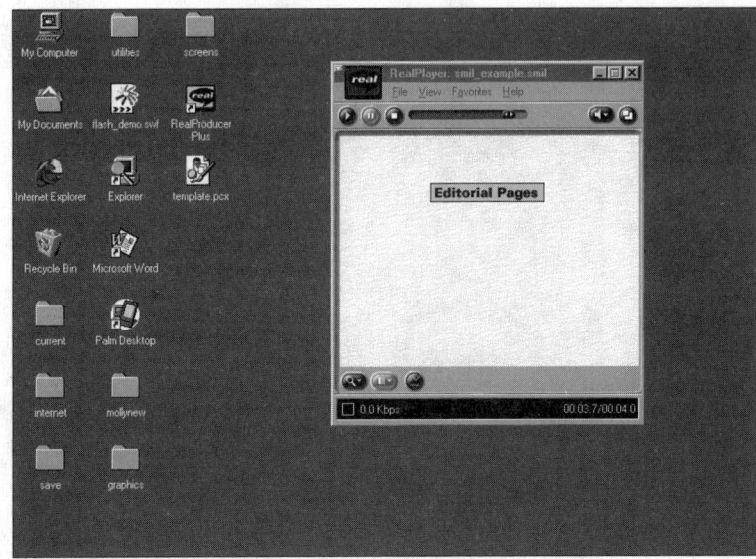

USING THE REGION TAG WITH THE fit ATTRIBUTE

There are a few mechanisms that allow you to make your image fit a specific area within a window, even if the image's original size is smaller than that area you've called out in the header. Appropriately, this function is called the fit attribute, and I'm going to take a look at a few of its variations.

First, I'll set up a logo in a RealPlayer window. As you can see from the code in the next example, the window dimensions are 320 × 240 pixels, and the graphic will be located 10 pixels down from the top and 10 over from the left (see Figure 38.5).

```
<smil>
  <head>
    <layout>
    <root-layout width="320" height="240"
        background-color="white" />
    <region id="logo.jpg" left="10" top="10" width="180" height="50" />
    </layout>
  </head>

  <body>
    <img src="http://www.storyphoto.com/logo.jpg" alt="button"
        region="logo.jpg" />
  </body>
</smil>
```

Figure 38.5
The graphic positioned inside the player window without using the `fit` attribute.

Now I'll apply a specific `fit` attribute called `"fill"` to the `region id` tag. This attribute enlarges an image to meet the dimensions called out in the `region id` tag. You'll notice the image degradation that's displayed as it's stretched to fill the area I've specified (see Figure 38.6), as follows:

```
<smil>

  <head>
    <layout>
    <root-layout width="320" height="240"
        background-color="white" />
<region id="logo.jpg" left="10" top="10" width="300" height="220"
         fit="fill" />
    </layout>
  </head>
  <body>
    <img src="http://www.storyphoto.com/logo.jpg" alt="button"
        region="logo.jpg" />
  </body>
</smil>
```

PART

IX

CH

38

Figure 38.6
The graphic positioned inside the player window using the `fit` attribute set to `"fill"`.

You also can call out "meet" to have the image meet the closest border of the area specified in the region tag (see Figure 38.7):

```
<smil>
   <head>
    <layout>
    <root-layout width="320" height="240"
        background-color="white" />
<region id="logo.jpg" left="10" top="10" width="300" height="220"
        background-color="white" fit="meet" />
    </layout>
    </head>

    <body>
     <img src="http://www.storyphoto.com/logo.jpg" alt="button"
        region="logo.jpg" />
    </body>
</smil>
```

Figure 38.7
Here's our graphic positioned inside the player window using the fit attribute set to "meet".

The "Slice" setting causes a non-distortion enlargement of the graphic, but will extend parts of it outside of the window area if it's not proportionally equal to your window dimensions (see Figure 38.8).

```
<smil>
   <head>
    <layout>
    <root-layout width="320" height="240"
        background-color="white" />
<region id="logo.jpg" left="10" top="10" width="300" height="100"
        background-color="white" fit="slice" />
    </layout>
    </head>
    <body>
     <img src="http://www.storyphoto.com/logo.jpg" alt="button"
        region="logo.jpg" />
    </body>
</smil>
```

Figure 38.8
Here's the graphic positioned inside the player window using the `fit` attribute set to `"slice"`.

THE `img` TAG WITH THE REGION ATTRIBUTE

The `img` tag resides in the body of the document and corresponds to the `region` tag in the header area. The `img` tag contains the source information for the graphic, the `alt` text, and of course the region name established in the header.

Each graphic in your presentation needs a `region` and a `img` tag set. So if you have 10 images in your slide show, you'll need 10 `region` tags in the header with 10 corresponding `img` tags in the body:

```
<smil>
   <head>
<meta name="copyright" content="creator name" />
<layout>
     <root-layout width="300" height="200"
  background-color="white" />
      <region id="ed_button" left="20%" top="25%"
       width="30" height="20" />
    </layout>
   </head>
    <body>
<img src="ed_button.gif" alt="button_graphic"
   region="ed_button" />
   </body>
</smil>
```

By giving the `region` ids logical names in the header information, you can easily keep track of your "image sources" in the body area.

When you're specifying the "source" for an image, you usually only need to list the image's filename if it is located in the same directory as the `.smi` file. Keep in mind however, that if the media is located on another server, you need to include to complete file path or URL.

CONTROLLING WHEN THE IMAGE APPEARS

Synchronization is at the core of SMIL functionality, and I'm going to show you a few of the timing controls that are available.

By adding the `begin` attribute to the `img` tag, I can precisely control when our graphic makes its appearance:

```
<body>
<img src="ed_button.gif" alt="button_graphic"
   region="ed_button" begin="4s" />
</body>
```

As you can see from the code, the graphic will show up on screen four seconds after the presentation has begun.

IMAGE DURATION AND ORDER

So, now that I have the image positioned within the frame, and I know when it will appear, I'm going to specify how long it appears. By adding the `dur` attribute to the `img` tag, I can precisely control its length of stay:

```
<body>
<img src="ed_button.gif" alt="button_graphic"
   region="ed_button" begin="4s" dur="5s" />
</body>
```

Obviously any multimedia presentation is going to consist of more than one image. By nesting my `img` tags within `seq` tags, I can control the sequence in which they appear (see Figures 38.9 and 38.10):

```
<smil>
   <head>
<meta name="copyright" content="creator name" />
<layout>
      <root-layout width="300" height="200"
   background-color="white" />
        <region id="ed_button" left="20%" top="25%"
   width="30" height="20" />
        <region id="pic_button" left="20%" top="25%"
   width="30" height="20" />
</layout>
   </head>
   <body>
<seq>
        <img src="ed_button.gif" alt="button_graphic"
region="ed_button" dur="5s" />
        <img src="pic_button.gif" alt="button_graphic"
region="pic_button" begin="2s" dur="5s" />

</seq>
   </body>
</smil>
```

In this presentation the ed_button is on screen at the beginning and remains for five seconds. Then the pic_button appears two seconds after the ed_button disappears, and the pic_button also remains for five seconds.

Remember to include a region tag in the header for each image specified in the body.

Figure 38.9
The first graphic appears and stays on the screen for 5 seconds.

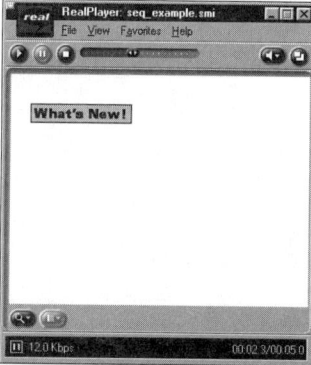

Figure 38.10
Now the second graphic replaces the first one using the sequence command.

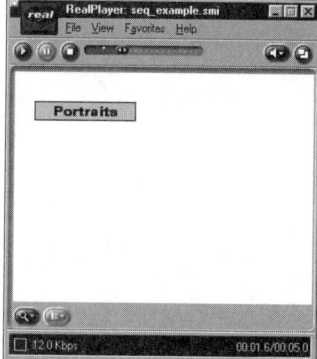

PRESENTING TWO IMAGES AT THE SAME TIME

Now I want two or more graphics to appear on the screen at the same time, so I'm going to use the par tag to display them in parallel. The img tags in the body are now nested within the par tags instead of the seq tags.

Notice that I've also changed their position within the window by changing the information in the region tags in the header. Before, when one image was replacing another, I positioned them in the same area within the window. Now that the graphics are displayed at the same time, I've repositioned them so they don't overlap (see Figure 38.11):

```
<smil>
   <head>
<meta name="copyright" content="creator name" />
<layout>
<root-layout width="300" height="200"
   background-color="white" />
<region id="ed_button" left="20%" top="25%"
   width="30" height="20" />
      <region id="pic_button" left="20%" top="60%"
   width="30" height="20" />
</layout>
   </head>
```

```
    <body>
<par>
        <img src="ed_button.gif" alt="button_graphic"
region="ed_button" dur="5s" />
        <img src="pic_button.gif" alt="button_graphic"
region="pic_button" dur="5s" />
</par>
    </body>
    </smil>
```

Figure 38.11
Using the parallel command I can have both graphics appearing at the same time in the player window.

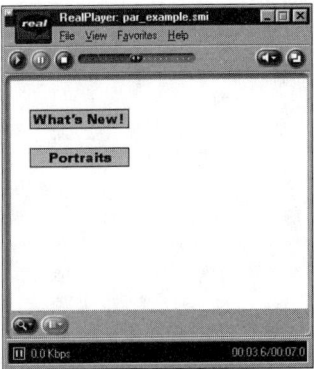

Even though the images are appearing in parallel, I can still play with the timing of their display. For example, by adding the begin attribute to the second image, I can specify how long after the first image appears before the second is displayed.

```
<par>
    <img src="ed_button.gif" alt="button_graphic"
region="ed_button" dur="5s" />
    <img src="pic_button.gif" alt="button_graphic"
region="pic_button" begin="2s" dur="5s" />
</par>
```

Now the pic_button appears below the ed_button two seconds later.

USING THE switch TAG TO MEET USER NEEDS

By incorporating the switch tag in the body of my SMIL document, my presentation can be customized on the fly to meet to the viewer's language and computer preferences.

For example, if my viewer prefers to read German captions, has a 800 × 600 monitor resolution, and has a 28.8 modem connection, I can accommodate his preferences through use of the switch tag. Let's incorporate the switch tag into the body of a slide show to give the viewer a German/English caption option.

First there are the language qualifiers themselves. English is represented by en and German by de. The user's SMIL-compatible player will read the language options in the mark-up text and choose the appropriate one based on the user's chosen preferences. The code would look like this:

```
<body>
  <switch>
  <! -- This is the English version -- >
<par system-language="en">
<text src="i_am_english.txt" />
  <! -- This is the German version -- >
<par system-language="dr">
<text src="ich_bin_deutsch.txt" />
  </switch>
</body>
```

By using the switch tag, my presentation will read the preferences established by the user's player, and then provide the appropriate language text file to accompany the images in your presentation.

Basic switch Tag Attributes

Bitrate: provides options to accommodate the connection speed of the user's computer. `<system-bitrate="14400, 28800, etc">`

Captions: turns captions on or off depending on user preferences. `<system-captions="on or off">`

Language: provides text in the appropriate language. `<system-language="de, en, fr, it, etc">`

Screen depth: reads the number of bits per pixel. `<system-screen-depth="4, 8, 16, etc">`

Screen dimension: reads the screen dimension of the user's monitor. `<system-screen-size="640x480, 800x600, etc">`

PART

IX

CH

38

Note

If you include more than one attribute in a `<switch>` tag, then list a series of `<switch>` tags with different attribute combinations, the first `<switch>` tag encountered by the player where all attributes prove true will be the one implemented.

Tools for Creating and Playing SMIL Documents

Even though we currently don't have full, integrated browser implementation of SMIL documents, there are a number of environments available right now that use SMIL to assist in synchronizing multimedia. In this section I'm going to look at two of the most popular providers of multimedia content for the Web: RealNetworks and Apple QuickTime.

RealNetworks Embraces SMIL

The RealNetworks family of authoring tools and players are widespread in the online universe. RealNetworks pioneered the online streaming format when it introduced RealAudio in 1997. Since that initial offering, Real has added streaming text and video capabilities and currently boasts more than 100 million downloads of its popular player. Real also was one of SMIL's earliest proponents, and fully incorporated SMIL capability in its G2 Player technology.

With G2 and subsequent RealPlayers, there are two fundamental methods for using SMIL. First, a SMIL document can function as an organizing document for other Real streaming formats such as RealPix (.rp, for images), RealAudio (.ra, for sound), and RealText (.rt, for text). These files reside on a RealServer and can be synchronized for playback via the SMIL document.

The advantage of this approach is that changes can be made to the presentation by simply editing the code in the SMIL document with a text editor instead of having to generate an entirely new presentation using one of Real's authoring tools such as RealProducer. SMIL brings tremendous flexibility to organizing Real presentations.

But the flexibility doesn't end there. You don't have to use RealPix, RealAudio, and RealText elements to play media via the RealPlayer. If you wish, you can callout and synchronize the elements themselves within the SMIL document for RealPlayer playback.

Note Keep in mind that this route is best suited for playback from a hard drive rather than streamed over the Internet–unless, that is, you are an advanced SMIL programmer and understand how to implement soft sync from the SMIL Boston "Timing and Synchronization" module.

You can use AIFF, AU, and WAV files for your audio; JPEG, GIF, and PNG for your images; and TXT files for your streaming text. You can even stream these presentations over a network and play them on the RealPlayer G2. Remember though, you need to have a steady stream of data in order for your presentation to flow smoothly because basic SMIL 1.0 documents are what is referred to as hard sync and don't provide the cushion to deal with data stream interruptions.

→ For more information on audio file types, **see** Chapter 31, "Audio and Video," **p. 641**.

If you want to stream over a busy network, especially the busiest network of them all, the Internet, then I recommend you use a RealServer and use SMIL functionality to synchronizing the various elements.

That being said, it's really a lot of fun to write presentations from scratch in a text editor and play them back on a RealPlayer. I've even served these documents to others on a LAN with decent success.

CREATING A SIMPLE SLIDESHOW FOR PLAYBACK IN REALPLAYER

I'm going to build a slideshow from scratch that synchronizes music, text captions, and images. All I need to create this is a text editor, a hand full of jpegs sized to 320 × 240 pixels, and a .wav audio track. I'm going to use a current version of RealPlayer to watch my presentation (see Figure 38.12).

First I create a directory on my hard drive and place all the jpegs inside of it. In my text editor, I write a one-line caption for each jpeg, and save it as a .txt file. Then I create a 20-second audio file and save it to the .wav format. Now I'm ready to build my slideshow. The code is shown in Listing 38.5.

Figure 38.12
This slideshow will
have captions beneath
the images. I will also
have background
music to set the mood.

LISTING 38.5   A SIMPLE SLIDESHOW

```
<smil>
   <head>
<meta name="© 2000 Derrick Story" content="JavaOne
   SlideShow" />
        <layout>
             <! -- Here are the dimensions for the player window.
Notice that we've added an extra 40 pixels to the height
for the captions. -- >

             <root-layout width="320" height="280" background-
   color="black"/>

<! -- Here's where we callout the four images. -- >

             <region id="entrance.jpg" left="0" top="0" width="320"
                 height="240" />
             <region id="attendees.jpg" left="0" top="0" width="320"
                 height="240" />
               <region id="computers.jpg" left="0" top="0" width="320"
                 height="240" />
               <region id="foosball.jpg" left="0" top="0" width="320"
                 height="240" />

         <! -- Here's where we callout our four captions. -- >

             <region id="caption1" left="0" top="240"
                 width="320" height="40" />
             <region id="caption2" left="0" top="240"
                 width="320" height="40" />
             <region id="caption3" left="0" top="240"
                 width="320" height="40" />
             <region id="caption4" left="0" top="240"
                 width="320" height="40" />

         <! -- Here's the callout for our closing title. -- >
```

LISTING 38.5 CONTINUED

```
            <region id="title_region" left="0" top="0" width="320"
                height="240" />
        </layout>
    </head>
    <body>

        <! -- We're going to create image and caption sequences and
synch them together with each other and the audio using the
parallel tag. -- >

        <par>
        <seq>
            <img src="entrance.jpg" alt="entrance"
                    region="entrance.jpg"  dur="4s" />
                <img src="attendees.jpg" alt="attendees"
                    region="attendees.jpg" dur="4s" />
                <img src="computers.jpg" alt="computers"
                    region="computers.jpg" dur="4s" />
                <img src="foosball.jpg" alt="foosball"
                    region="foosball.jpg" dur="4s" />

                <text src="javaone_title.txt" region="title_region"
    dur="4s"/>
        </seq>
        <seq>
            <text src="javaone_caption1.txt"
                region="caption1" dur="4s" />
            <text src="javaone_caption2.txt"
                region="caption2" dur="4s" />
            <text src="javaone_caption3.txt"
                region="caption3" dur="4s" />
            <text src="javaone_caption4.txt"
                region="caption4" dur="4s" />
        </seq>
            <audio src="music.wav" />
        </par>
    </body>
</smil>
```

This slideshow only has four images. You can add as many as you need using this code as a template, but remember to keep the presentation to 3 minutes or less (for the sake of the viewer).

Once you've added the desired number of images, create a new audio file the appropriate length.

You'll notice that the URLs for all the media are "relative" because all the files are contained in the same directory. This is fine for playback off a local hard drive, but RealPlayer will demand "absolute" URLs if you serve this presentation over any kind of network.

You don't need to use a RealServer for this show even though it's designed to be played on RealPlayer, but as I mentioned before, there's no accommodation for data stream interruptions with this presentation. If you want to create a slideshow for serving over the Internet for playback on RealPlayer, then you'll want to take advantage of "SureStream" technology. An easy way to do that is use the authoring tool, RealSlideshow Plus, which is also SMIL compliant.

CREATING A SMIL PRESENTATION WITH REALSLIDESHOW PLUS

An easy way to create a functional SMIL document that can be dependably served over the Internet is by using RealSlideshow Plus. Based on the current implementation of SMIL, this environment also is probably one the most effective uses of SMIL's synchronization capabilities (Figure 38.13).

Figure 38.13
The RealSlideshow Plus authoring environment is clean and intuitive. Images can be added to the timeline by using "drag and drop" from their directory home.

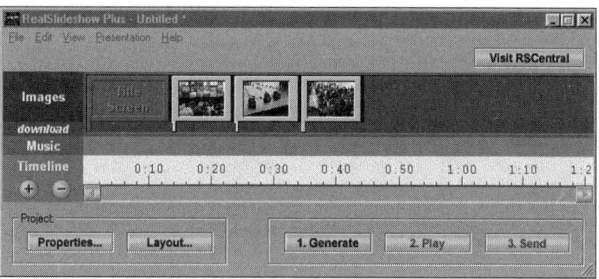

The advantages of RealSlideshow Plus are that you have an easy-to-use authoring environment to create your SMIL documents, you can easily edit the SMIL text files it creates with a text editor, and it automatically creates RealText, RealPix, and RealAudio files from your media that take advantage of SureStream technology.

The disadvantage of RealSlideshow Plus is that you need access to a RealServer to stream your SMIL presentations. However, RealNetworks offers access to RealServers for registered RealSlideshow Plus users.

Note   RealSlideshow Plus can be downloaded from Real's Web site at www.real.com.

A SMIL DOCUMENT CREATED WITH REAL SLIDESHOW PLUS

Here's the code from a SMIL presentation created with RealSlideshow Plus. This show has still images, a single audio track, and text captions (see Listing 38.6 38

LISTING 38.6   REAL SLIDESHOW PLUS PRESENTATION

```
<smil>
    <head>
        <meta name="title" content="JavaOne Scenes from SF" />
        <meta name="author" content="Derrick Story" />
        <meta name="copyright" content="© 2000 Derrick Story" />
```

Listing 38.6   Continued

```
        <meta name="keywords" content="JavaOne, Derrick Story" />
        <meta name="description" content="Scenes from the JavaOne
Conference held June 2000 at Moscone Center in SF, CA." />
        <meta name="robots" content="all" />
        <meta name="pics-label" content='(PICS-1.1
"http://www.classify.org/safesurf" labels comment
"RealSlideshow Plus 6.0.0.550 Windows" ratings
(SS-~000 1))'/>
        <meta name="file_id" content="3f6d8ada-daf1-0ede-ff35-
bd0c39f7c915" />
        <layout type="text/smil-basic-layout">
            <root-layout width="320" height="280" background-
color="black"/>
            <region id="title_region" left="0" top="0" width="320"
height="240" z-index="2" />
            <region id="pix_region" left="0" top="0" width="320"
height="240" z-index="1" />
            <region id="caption_region" left="0" top="240"
width="320" height="40" z-index="1" />
        </layout>
    </head>
    <body>
        <par>
            <seq>
                <text src="javaone_show.rt" region="title_region"/>
                <par>
                    <img src="javaone_show.rp"
region="pix_region" fill="freeze"/>
                    <text src="javaone_show-captions.rt"
region="caption_region" fill="freeze"/>
                </par>
            </seq>
            <audio src="javaone_show.rm"/>
        </par>
    </body>
</smil>
```

You'll notice that there's quite a bit of meta information in the header area. Real uses this data to display author and copyright information in the player, and for the opening title. There is also information contained here required by the RealServer.

By now, the data in the layout tag should look very familiar. Note the third region tag that positions the text captions so that they will appear in the 40 pixel area at the bottom of the player window.

In the body of the document are the source references for the RealText, RealPix, and RealAudio files on the RealServer. This is an excellent example of how to use par and seq tags together.

Notice that the audio file is placed within the top level par tag. It will start playing immediately as the show is streamed. Next, within a seq tag, there's the source that displays the show title. After that, you'll see a nested <par> tag that streams the RealPix images in concert with the RealText captions.

Quickly you can see how easy it is to organize and synchronize various multimedia elements with SMIL. And because of SMIL's flexibility, you can either callout the various pieces of media individually as we did in our hand-coded slideshow, or you can synchronize streaming containers as we did with RealSlideshow Plus.

But RealNetworks isn't the only SMIL-show in town. Apple has recently added this capability to its QuickTime Player, and I'm going to take a look at how they use SMIL to organize and synchronize QuickTime movies.

APPLE QUICKTIME 4.1 ADDS SMIL

Apple recently incorporated SMIL support in QuickTime 4.1. As you dig in to the white paper that outlines Apple's SMIL integration, you'll see that Apple has realized that QuickTime movies are well-suited to function as the core of sophisticated multimedia presentations, but that developers needed a way to orchestrate the various elements. By adding SMIL support to QuickTime, content creators now have the ability to easily synchronize a variety of multimedia elements for playback on current QuickTime players.

Two of the best integrations also are the easiest to implement: creating media sequences and wrapping content around a QuickTime movie.

CREATING A QUICKTIME PLAY LIST

Now, to create a sequence of QuickTime audio, video, and images, all you have to do is create a simple SMIL document, but instead of giving it a .smil extension, you give it a .mov extension. By doing so, you can double-click the file and the SMIL document will launch the QuickTime Player 4.1 or later and begin playing the first source file in the sequence. Listing 38.8 shows what the code looks like.

LISTING 38.8   A QUICKTIME PLAY LIST

```
SMILtext
<smil xmlns:qt="http://www.apple.com/quicktime/resources/smilextensions"
qt:autoplay="true" qt:time-slider="true">
   <head>
        <layout>
<root-layout width="640" height="480"
         background color="black" />
<region id="region_1" left="0" top="0" width="640"
         height="480" fit="meet" />
    </layout>

        <meta name="full-name" content="SMIL Movie Sequence" />
        <meta name="copyright" content="d_story©2000" />
        <meta name="information" content="www.storyphoto.com" />
    </head>
    <body>
```

LISTING 38.8   CONTINUED

```
<seq>
<video src="../Multimedia%20%C4/darn_cats.mov" alt="movie"
            region="region_1" begin="0s" />
        <video src="../Multimedia%20%C4/jobs_celebrates_wr.mov"
            alt="movie" region="region_1" begin="2s" />
</seq>
    </body>
</smil>
```

Notice that the XML namespace is defined at the top of the document. Much of the information in the `head` looks familiar by now, except that the meta data is coded so as to appear in the traditional locations on the QuickTime Player: `"full-name"` is the title that appears on the face at the top of the player; and `"copyright"` and `"information"` data appears at the bottom of the player when you hit the information button.

In the body of the document you list the sources for the multimedia components in the order you want them automatically played, one after another, using the `seq` tag. Just like any SMIL document, you can list as many sources as you want, or change them just by altering the code in any text editor.

One note for Macintosh users: because SimpleText can actually play QuickTime movies, it isn't the best application for editing this particular type of SMIL document. When you try to open the movie sequence for editing, SimpleText wants to play the video instead of displaying editable text. For editing, it's best to use a "regular" text editor such as BBEdit that isn't going to try to play the movie (Figure 38.15).

Figure 38.15
Here's a QuickTime movie playing in a SimpleText window. For this reason, SimpleText isn't the best choice for editing QuickTime SMIL code because it wants to play the sequence instead of editing it.

Also, you'll notice in the previous example, I used relative URLs for the media sources, which SMIL allows. But remember that relative URLs sometimes create problems when reading SMIL documents off remote servers. If you are having such problems, then list the entire URL (absolute) as the source.

WRAPPING IMAGES AROUND A QUICKTIME MOVIE

Another handy QuickTime trick is to create a SMIL template to wrap content around a .mov file for adding boilerplate information to your presentations without having to edit the presentations themselves.

For example, if you want to have the company logo at the beginning and the ending of all your QuickTime training videos, you simply create the SMIL template and drop your video source files into it. If a few days later you receive a request to use a different version of the logo at the end of the movie, you simply change a few lines of code using a text editor instead of having to reproduce the entire QuickTime movie (Figure 38.16).

Figure 38.16
This company logo isn't really a part of the QuickTime movie. I created a "wrapper" in SMIL. Now if I want to change the logo, I simply edit a few lines of code.

This functionality is particularly useful in closed networks such as intranets where you can make sure all the clients have the latest version of the player that supports SMIL functionality. The QuickTime movies could be corporate training videos, company reports, footage from the recent company picnic, or anything else useful to employees.

LISTING 38.9   A WRAPPER TEMPLATE

```
SMILtext<smil xmlns:qt="http://www.apple.com/quicktime/"
   qt:autoplay="true" qt:time-slider="true">

   <head>
      <layout>
<root-layout width="240" height="160" background-
         color="gray" />
<region id="logo" left="0" top="0" width="240" height="160"
         fit="fill" />
<region id="wedding" left="0" top="0" width="240"
         height="160" />
      </layout>
<meta name="full-name" content="Andy & Victoria" />
        <meta name="copyright" content="© 2000 Story Photo" />
        <meta name="information" content="www.storyphoto.com" />
   </head>
```

LISTING 38.9   CONTINUED

```
    <body>
        <seq>
<img src="static_logo_med.gif" region="logo" dur="3s" />
<video src="web_wed.mov" region="wedding" />
<img src="static_logo_med.gif" region="logo" dur="5s" />
        </seq>
    </body>
</smil>
```

In the header area you call out the regions for the logo image and the movie. Notice that I've also included the meta information to display on the player.

In the body you simply list the sources in the order you want them to play. Notice that I have the logo onscreen for three seconds at the beginning of the movie and five seconds at the end. In this example, all the source files are in the same directory as the SMIL document.

Save the document with a movie extension (.mov), instead of with a SMIL extension (.smil). By saving it as a movie file, it will behave as a regular QuickTime movie, and the sequencing of images and video will play seamlessly as if it were a regular QuickTime movie.

I incorporated these SMIL/QuickTime presentations into my XHTML pages using the embed tag with varied results. On the Macintosh platform using QuickTime 4.1, this technique worked very well when played off the hard drive or http served to Netscape 4.7 with the QuickTime 4.1 plug-in.

But I had difficulties getting this technique to work via http server using Netscape for Windows. I also used the param tag to embed the SMIL presentation in an XHTML page for playback with Internet Explorer. The tests went well on both platforms. If you want to play with this technique, make sure you include tags for both Netscape and IE in your code.

As I've mentioned before, please test your SMIL implementations in as many different environments as needed before depending on them to synchronize important content. Or, if you're lucky enough, serve these documents to a controlled environment so you can use the best client software for the job.

DESIGNING FOR THE REAL WORLD

BECOME A BETTER ARTIST WITH SMIL

Multimedia tools such as Macromedia's Flash and SMIL help us bring our pictures, music, and words together to create presentations that exceed the sum of their parts. Through the process of learning how to put together a SMIL presentation, we begin to realize the importance of well-placed, well-timed elements. As a result, our presentations become more engaging.

In this chapter you've learned only the basic elements of a SMIL document. But even at this early stage, you might have already noticed yourself asking these types of questions out loud:

- In what order should I organize my pictures?
- How can I write the captions so that they flow from one to another telling the story in the best way possible?
- What's the best music for the opening scene?
- Now that I know how to orchestrate various music clips, should I use something more somber for the middle of the show? How about an upbeat ending?
- Wouldn't a video clip be a nice addition to the middle of this show?
- Maybe I can add a few drawings to better make my point?

Suddenly you'll find yourself pushing your multimedia presentations to a new, compelling level. The bottom line is that you now have an enhanced ability to edit and reorganize your presentations.

This is why SMIL, and tools like it, excite me. Because now, an average developer such as myself has the ability to move audiences in ways that were previously beyond my reach. Take an evening and put together a SMIL presentation with your pictures and words. You'll see what I mean.

PART
IX
CH
38

CHAPTER **39**

SCALABLE VECTOR GRAPHICS (SVG)

In this chapter

SCALABLE VECTOR GRAPHICS (SVG)

The "pipe" is getting faster. Many people—especially in the United States—are now accessing the Internet at speeds no one could have imagined commercially possible just eight years ago. And, it's affordable! Access in the form of ISDN, cable, and DSL are common in many households, and a T1 line in the workplace is frequently encountered.

In the homesteading days of the Web, there was a great deal of emphasis on keeping pages lightweight. The goal was to ensure that they loaded quickly. Of course, this is *still* a goal for many sites, although many designers and developers pay a lot less attention than perhaps they should to this concern. After all, we've gotten spoiled.

But that doesn't mean that large numbers of people—in fact, the majority of Web site visitors worldwide—are accessing at the speeds those with access to broader and broadband connectivity that some of us enjoy. The realities of needing to create fast graphics that look good and load quickly still remains. In fact, in the context of alternative device design, it has once again become imperative that graphics—if used at all—are extremely lightweight.

Scalable Vector Graphics (SVG) is an application of XML. Via markup, graphic images, animations, and interactive graphic designs can be designed and implemented for Web viewing. Of course, browsers must support the technology, which is one reason that many developers haven't looked into it too seriously, or perhaps haven't heard of it at all.

SVG is being developed under the auspices of the W3C. As a result, much work has been done to make it compatible with other standards including XML, XSLT, CSS2, DOM (Document Object Model), SMIL, HTML 4.0, XHTML 1.0, and sufficient accessibility options via the WAI (Web Accessibility Initiative).

→ For more information on XML, **see** Chapter 37, "Toward XML," **p. 727.**
→ For an overview of XSL and XSLT, **see** Chapter 19, "Extensible Stylesheet Langauge (XSL)," **p. 419.**
→ For more on CSS2, **see** Chapter 18, "Cascading Style Sheets and XHTML," **p. 377.**
→ SMIL is described in Chapter 38, "Synchronized Multimedia Integration Language (SMIL)," **p. 767.**

The status of SVG at this writing is *Candidate Recommendation*. The working group responsible for SVG has declared it stable, and if it passes several more tests, it moves into the Recommendation phase.

> **Note**
>
> To check on the current status of SVG, please see the SVG news page at the W3C, `www.w3.org/Graphics/SVG/`.

SVG CONCEPTS

Perhaps the most important concept to grab first when studying SVG is that it is *scalable*. This means that any graphic is not limited by a fixed pixel. Like vector graphics, a scalable graphic can be made larger or smaller, without distortion of the graphic. This is especially important for designing across resolutions. Scalable graphics adjust to the available screen resolution. This alone makes SVG very attractive to designers, as it solves one of the most frustrating issues we face: creating designs that are as interoperable yet visually rich as possible.

SVG elements are based on standard graphic design elements. They are as follows:

- **Geometric shapes**—A geometric shape is a line, combination of lines, a curve, or combination of curves, or a combination of curves and lines.

- **Text**—Text elements are represented as characters and combination of characters.

- **Raster (also referred to as *bitmapped*) images**—Raster graphics are those that are mapped to bits. This means that they do not contain scalable methods. Raster graphics are typically used in combination with scalable graphics, and are comprised of photographs and specialty filters.

SVG follows other methodologies familiar to graphic designers. The rendering of SVG is based on a paint model. Color, gradients, and patterns are painted onto the screen to gain the end results. Shapes and text can be filled or stroked. Other graphic techniques, such as masking and opacity, can all be applied.

WebCGM: Another Scalable Option

Another method of delivering scalable graphics to the Web is WebCGM. WebCGM works on a metafile concept. CGM, *Computer Graphics Metafile*, is a technology that has been around since 1987, and an ISO standard for graphics since 1995. WebCGM takes the basic concepts of CGM and orients them to the Web.

However, work on WebCGM seems to be very slow, despite the fact that WebCGM has actually been a Recommendation since 1999! SVG, with its XML basis, has encouraged a great deal more interest.

More information on WebCGM can be found at `www.w3.org/Graphics/WebCGM/` and `www.cgmopen.org/`.

SVG allows access to scripting and to the DOM (Document Object Model), which is how SVG supports animations and interactive graphics.

The interesting aspect to SVG is that the scalable methodology is rendered via ASCII language, which is interpreted, rather than the formulation of a binary graphic file (see Listing 39.1). The exception to this is whenever a bitmapped graphic is used within an SVG environment, the image is included using the SVG `image` element.

LISTING 39.1   THE XML SHELL USED IN SVG

```
<?xml version="1.0" standalone="no"?>

<!DOCTYPE svg PUBLIC "-//W3C//DTD SVG 20000802//EN"
  http://www.w3.org/TR/2000/CR-SVG-20000802/DTD/svg-20000802.dtd>

<svg width="100%" height="100%">


</svg>
```

Note

To learn the detailed syntax of SVG, please see the current draft, available at `www.w3.org/TR/2000/CR-SVG-20000802/`.

SVG SOFTWARE AND BROWSERS

SVG is, as one can imagine, quite complex in its syntax. And the more complex a design becomes, the more complex the markup becomes. As a result, the development of graphical user interface (GUI) tools for SVG began early. There are several of these tools available that offer a standard drawing environment but export to SVG for use in supported browsers. Also, many familiar graphic companies and graphic design products are adding SVG export support to their product lines.

Current tools and support include

- Adobe SVG support. Adobe has an aggressive interest in SVG and provides a developer site for SVG enthusiasts. There's built-in support for SVG in Illustrator 9, and an SVG plug-in that enables Web browsers to view SVG graphics (see Figure 39.1). Adobe is promising SVG export in a number of programs including LiveMotion.

- Jasc Software, makers of Paint Shop Pro, offer a product for Windows called Trajectory Pro, which at the time of this writing was in preview release. Trajectory Pro allows you to create graphics in a standard drawing environment. The results are saved as SVG files (see Figure 39.2). The SVG markup can be seen in Listing 39.2.

- ePicture Pro from Beatware is a very cool product for Mac platform only. It offers a wide range of vector graphic and animation options, with SVG export.

- ImageMagick, which runs on Unix and Linux as well Windows, Mac, VMS, and even OS2, provides some support for SVG.

- Corel offers an SVG export file-filter plug in for CorelDRAW 9.

- IBM has a prototype SVG viewer for Windows. It has some interesting features, including the ability to save what's being viewed as a JPEG file.

- Jackaroo is an SVG viewer created for the purpose of evaluating W3C technologies. It is distributed open-source.

Figure 39.1
Testing the SVG plug-in at Adobe's Web site.

Figure 39.2
Drawing in Jasc's Trajectory Pro.

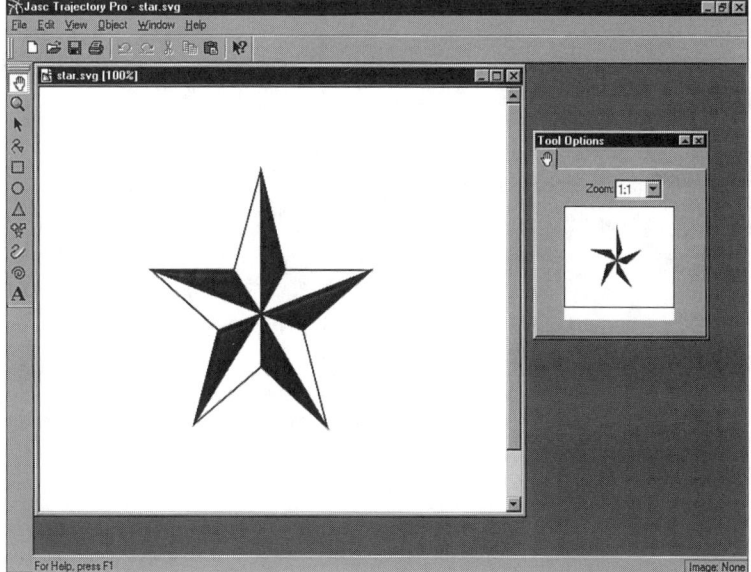

LISTING 39.2   SCALABLE VECTOR GRAPHICS MARKUP FOR THE IMAGE IN FIGURE 39.2

```
<?xml version="1.0" standalone="no"?>
<!DOCTYPE svg SYSTEM "svg-20000303-stylable.dtd" >
<svg width="500" height="500">
    <defs>
```

LISTING 39.2 CONTINUED

```
        <filter id="Bevel">
            <feGaussianBlur result="blur" in="SourceAlpha" stdDeviation="3"/>
            <feSpecularLighting result="specOut" in="blur" surfaceScale="5"
           ➥specularConstant="1" specularExponent="10" lightColor="#c00000">
                <fePointLight x="-5000" y="-10000" z="20000"/>
            </feSpecularLighting>
            <feComposite result="specOut" in="specOut" operator="in"
           ➥in2="SourceAlpha"/>
            <feComposite result="litPaint" in="SourceGraphic"
           ➥operator="arithmetic" k1="0" k2="1" k3="1" k4="0"
           ➥in2="specOut"/>
        </filter>
    </defs>
    <text style="stroke:#000000; stroke-width:1; stroke-opacity:1;
   ➥font-size:24; font-family:Arial; font-weight:400; fill:#000000;
   ➥fill-opacity:1" x="99" y="227"></text>
    <g style="filter:url(#Bevel); stroke:#000000; stroke-width:1;
   ➥stroke-opacity:1; stroke-miterlimit:10; fill:#000000; fill-opacity:1" >
        <polygon id="inside" points="238,86,238,236,283,253,355,190,238,236,238,
       ➥291,309,354,238,236,192,253,166,351,238,236,209,190,120,190,
       ➥238,236,264,190" />
        <polygon id="outside" style="fill:none" points="238,86,264,190,355,190,
       ➥283,253,309,354,238,291,166,351,192,253,120,190,209,190" />
    </g>
</svg>

<!-- Generated by Jasc Trajectory Pro on 09/03/00 07:30:56 -->
```

> **Note**
>
> Adobe's SVG plug-in for Mac and Windows is downloadable from `www.adobe.com/svg/viewer/install/`.
>
> Jasc's Trajectory Pro for Windows can be found at `www.jasc.com/trj.asp`.
>
> For ePicture Pro from Beatware, check out `www.beatware.com/`.
>
> ImageMagick, a drawing and conversion tool that supports numerous platforms is available at `www.imagemagick.org/`.
>
> To download the Corel SVG filter for CorelDRAW 9, point your browser `venus.corel.com/nasapps/DrawSVGDownload/index.html`.
>
> IBM's prototype viewer can be downloaded from `www.alphaworks.ibm.com/tech/svgview`.
>
> Jackaroo's home page is at `www-sop.inria.fr/koala/jackaroo/`.

Browser support is currently sketchy in terms of inline support without a plug-in. Support information for SVG can be found in Table 39.1.

TABLE 39.1 GENERAL BROWSER SUPPORT INFORMATION FOR SVG

Browser	SVG Support
Microsoft Internet Explorer	With a plug-in only
Netscape Navigator	Plug-in only
Mozilla	Some support in certain Mozilla builds
Opera	With a plug-in

The browser limitations are certainly an issue with SVG. As time goes on—and especially if SVG becomes a Recommendation—there will be more support for SVG, both from browser manufacturers and from makers of popular software.

DESIGNING FOR THE REAL WORLD

CREATING A GRAPHIC USING SVG

In this section, you'll create a simple SVG banner, just to get a taste of working with SVG. I'm using Jasc's Trajectory Pro. If you're on a Mac, try ePicture Pro. The steps are fairly similar in both programs.

To create a background graphic:

1. Select File, New.
2. The New Image dialog box appears. Enter the width and height. To create a banner, I entered 400 pixels as my width, and 50 pixels as my height.
3. Select the Rectangle tool to draw a thin line along the bottom of the banner (Figure 39.3).
4. Black is the default color. To change the color, select the line using the Select tool. Then, choose Object, Apply Effect from the drop-down menu. The Effects palette appears. Click once in the Color box and the Color dialog box appears. Choose a color with the color picker. Click OK to close the Color dialog box, and then click OK again to close the Effects dialog box (ePicture Pro users simply can select color from the color palette).
5. Click the canvas to deselect the line. To create text, choose the Text tool. In the Tool Options palette, click the Font tab and select your font. I chose Arial, 24 pt (Figure 39.4).
6. Click the Text tab in the Tool Options palette, and type your header text into the box. Then, click on the canvas. Your text will appear. To move it, select it using the Select tool. You can nudge it using the arrow keys on your keyboard.
7. To save the file, select File, Save. Name the file (note the .svg extension) and save it to the location of your choice. I named mine banner.svg.

PART
IX
CH
39

Figure 39.3
Drawing a rectangle in
Trajectory Pro.

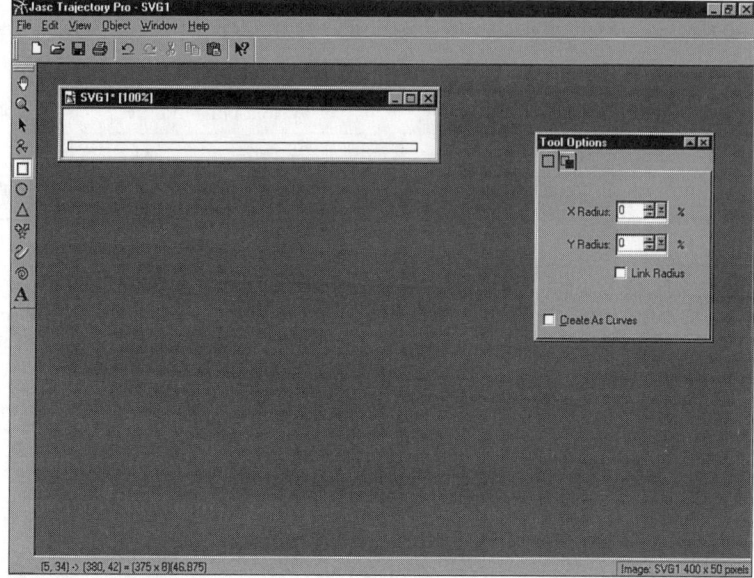

Figure 39.4
Choosing a font.

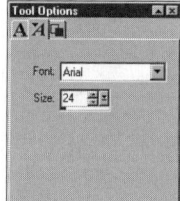

Figure 39.5 shows my results.

Caution

Go ahead and try viewing your SVG document in a browser. As long as you have a plug-in
installed, you should see the results. However, be advised that not all plug-ins support all
aspects of SVG, so your results will vary at this time.

Listing 39.3 shows the markup generated by Trajectory Pro to create this banner.

Figure 39.5
The final figure.

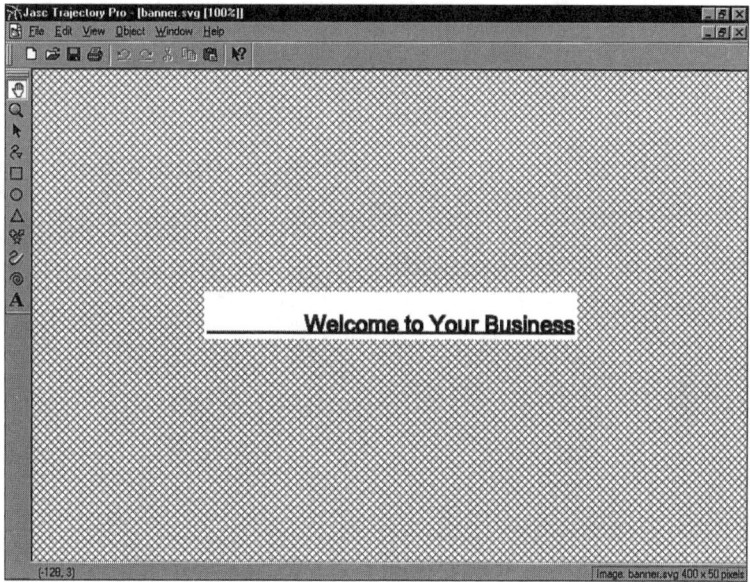

LISTING 39.3   THE MARKUP GENERATED FOR THE BANNER IN FIGURE 39.5

```xml
<?xml version="1.0" standalone="no"?>
<!DOCTYPE svg SYSTEM "svg-20000303-stylable.dtd" >
<svg width="400" height="50">
    <defs>
        <filter id="Bevel">
            <feGaussianBlur result="blur" in="SourceAlpha" stdDeviation="3"/>
            <feSpecularLighting result="specOut" in="blur" surfaceScale="5"
            ➥specularConstant="1" specularExponent="10"
            ➥lightColor="#800000">
                <fePointLight x="-5000" y="-10000" z="20000"/>
            </feSpecularLighting>
            <feComposite result="specOut" in="specOut" operator="in"
            ➥in2="SourceAlpha"/>
            <feComposite result="litPaint" in="SourceGraphic"
            ➥operator="arithmetic" k1="0" k2="1" k3="1" k4="0"
            ➥in2="specOut"/>
        </filter>
        <filter id="Bevel1">
            <feGaussianBlur result="blur" in="SourceAlpha" stdDeviation="3"/>
            <feSpecularLighting result="specOut" in="blur" surfaceScale="5"
            ➥specularConstant="1" specularExponent="10"
            ➥lightColor="#800000">
                <fePointLight x="-5000" y="-10000" z="20000"/>
            </feSpecularLighting>
            <feComposite result="specOut" in="specOut" operator="in"
            ➥in2="SourceAlpha"/>
            <feComposite result="litPaint" in="SourceGraphic"
            ➥operator="arithmetic" k1="0" k2="1" k3="1" k4="0"
            ➥in2="specOut"/>
```

LISTING 39.3   CONTINUED

```
      </filter>
  </defs>
  <rect style="filter:url(#Bevel); stroke:#000000; stroke-width:1;
  ➥stroke-opacity:1; fill:#000000; fill-opacity:1" x="4" y="36"
  ➥width="392" height="6" transform="matrix(1 0 0 0.333333 0 30)" />
  <text style="filter:url(#Bevel1); stroke:#000000; stroke-width:1;
  ➥stroke-opacity:1; font-size:24; font-family:Arial; font-weight:400;
  ➥fill:#000000; fill-opacity:1"  transform="matrix(1 0 0 1 107 42)">
  ➥Welcome to Your Business</text>
</svg>

<!-- Generated by Jasc Trajectory Pro on 09/03/00 09:08:26 -->
```

XHTML Reference

In this appendix

DATA TYPES: XHTML 1.0 VERSIONS AND SPECIFICATIONS

This appendix is based primarily on the information provided in the *XHTML 1.0 Specification W3C Recommendation*, dated January 26, 2000. The latest version of this document can be found at **www.w3.org/tr/xhtml1/**.

ALPHABETICAL XHTML 1.0 ELEMENT LISTING

All the elements in the XTML 1.0 Recommendation are listed alphabetically in this appendix, and the following information is presented:

- **Element**—The heading shows at a glance:

  The general notation of the element. For example, `<table>...</table>`.

- **Usage**—A general description of the element.

- **Syntax**—The syntax of the element is given, showing where the attributes and content are placed. *Italicized* information (such as *attributes*) is not part of the element but indicates you should replace that with the values described further in the element reference.

- **Attributes**—Lists the attributes of the element, the actual values allowed or a value data type, and a short description of their effect. Some attributes have the actual values given, such as `shape="rect | circle | poly | default"`, with the default value in **bold**. Others have *italicized* data types, such as `charset="character-set"`. You should refer to the "Data Types" section at the end of this appendix for an explanation of the different data types allowed. Deprecated and Transitional DTD attributes are annotated with an icon. Strict DTD attributes have no icon and are present in the Transitional and Frameset DTDs. No attempt has been made in this reference to identify browser support for a given attribute.

- **Content**—Shows the possible content allowed inside an element, ranging from document data to a variety of other elements.

- **Browsers**—Shows if the element is supported in the top two current browsers (Microsoft Internet Explorer and Netscape Navigator) and the earliest version of the browser supporting the element.

- **Notes**—Relates any special considerations when using the element.

`<!--... -->` COMMENTS

Usage:	An SGML construct used to insert information that is not to be displayed by the browser.

Syntax:	`<!-- content -->`
Attributes:	None
Content:	User text
Notes:	Comments are not restricted to one line and can be any length. The comment close delimiter (`"--"`) and the markup declaration close delimiter (`">"`) are not required to be on the same line as the markup declaration open delimiter (`"<!"`) and the comment open delimiter (`"--"`).
	Placing double hyphens inside a comment technically ends the comment and any text after this might not be treated as a comment.
Browser:	MSIE 1; NNav 1

`<!DOCTYPE...>`

Usage:	Version information appears on the first line of an XHTML document in the form of a Standard Generalized Markup Language (SGML) declaration.
Syntax:	`<!doctype top-element availability "registra-tion//organization//type label//language" "uri">`
Identifiers:	`top element`—Top-level element type declared in the DTD. For XHTML documents, this value is `xhtml`.
	`Availability`—Notes the availability. XHTML documents are publicly accessible objects; therefore this value is `public`.
	`Registration`—Indicates whether (+) or not (-) the following organization is registered by the ISO. The W3C is not a registered ISO organization.
	`Organization`—The organization responsible for the creation and maintenance of the DTD. The `W3c` is responsible element> element>for all official XHTML DTDs.
	`Type`—The type of object being referenced. In the case of XHTML, this is the XHTML `dtd`.
	`Label`—Describes or names the item being referenced. For XHTML 1.0 this refers to the XHTML DTD (Strict, Transitional, or Frameset) being called upon, `xhtml 1.0`, `xhtml 1.0 transitional`, or `xhtml 1.0 frameset` respectively.

APP

A

Language—The language of the object. For XHTML, this is en, meaning English.

Uri—Provides the location of the DTD and any entity sets for user agents to download.

Notes: Mandatory for document to be valid.

Browser: None element> element> appear to process this information.

\<a\>...\</a\>

Usage: Defines anchors that might be the source of one link and/or the destination of multiple links.

Syntax: `<a attributes>content</a>`

Attributes: core—See "Common Attributes" section.

i18n—See "Common Attributes" section.

Events—See "Intrinsic Events" section.

charset="character-set"—Specifies the character encoding of the linked resource. Values (such as iso-8859-1 or us-ascii) must be strings approved and registered by IANA, The Internet Assigned Numbers Authority.

type="content-type"—Specifies the content or media (MIME) type (such as text/xhtml) of the linked resource.

name="data"—Names the current anchor so that it can be the destination of other links.

href="uri"—Specifies the location of the linked resource or anchor. Anchor URIs are identified by a pound sign # before the name value.

hreflang="language-code"—Identifies the language of _the linked resource. This attribute might only be used in conjunction with the href attribute.

target="user-defined | _blank | _self | _parent | _top"—Identifies the frame in which the linked resource will be opened:

user-defined—Document opens in the frame designated by the user-defined name that is set by the name attribute of the frame. The name must begin with an alphabetic character.

_blank—Document opens in a new, unnamed window.

`_self`—Document opens in same frame as the originating link.

`_parent`—Document opens in the immediate `frame-set` parent of the current frame, or itself if the current frame has no _parent.

`_top`—Document opens in the full, original window, or itself if the frame has no parent.

`rel="link-type"`—Defines the relationship between the document and that specified by the `href` attribute.

`rev="link-type"`—Defines the relationship between the resource specified by the `href` attribute and the current document.

`accesskey="character"`—Assigns an access key (or shortcut key) to the element. When the key is pressed, the element receives focus and is activated.

`shape="rect | circle | poly | default"`—Defines a region by its shape:

`rect`—Defines a rectangular region.

`Circle`—Defines a circular region.

`Poly`—Defines a polygonal region.

`Default`—Specifies the entire region.

`coords="coordinates"`—Defines the position of a shape displayed on screen. All values are of the length data type and separated by commas. The number and order of the coordinates depends on the value of the `shape` attribute:

`rect`—left-x, top-y, right-x, bottom-y

`circle`—center-x, center-y, radius

`poly`—x1, y1, x2, y2, ..., xn, yn

`tabindex="number"`—Defines the tabbing order between elements. This is the order (from lowest first to highest last) in which they receive focus when the user navigates through them using the Tab key.

`onfocus="script"`—Triggered when the element receives focus by either a pointing device (such as a mouse) or tabbed navigation.

`onblur="script"`—Triggered when the element loses focus by either a pointing device (such as a mouse) or tabbed navigation.

APP

A

Content:	Zero or more inline elements, to include the following:

       Document text and entities

       Fontstyle elements (`tt | i | b | u | s | strike | big | small`)

       phrase elements (`em | strong | dfn | code | samp | kbd | var | cite | abbr | acronym`)

       special elements (`img | applet | object | font | basefont | br | script | map | q | sub | sup | span | bdo | iframe`)

       Form Control elements (`input | select | textarea | label | button`)

Notes:	Cannot be nested. Anchor names must be unique.
Browser:	MSIE 1; NNav 1

`<abbr>...</abbr>`

Usage:	Indicates an abbreviated form.
Syntax:	`<abbr attributes>content</abbr>`
Attributes:	`core`—See "Common Attributes" section.
	`i18n`—See "Common Attributes" section.
	`events`—See "Intrinsic Events" section.
Content:	Zero or more inline elements, to include the following:

       Document text and entities

       Fontstyle elements (`tt | i | b | u | s | strike | big | small`)

       Phrase elements (`em | strong | dfn | code | samp | kbd | var | cite | abbr | acronym`)

       Special elements (`a | img | applet | object | font | basefont | br | script | map | q | sub | sup | span | bdo | iframe`)

       Form Control elements (`input | select | textarea | label | button`)

Notes:	The content of the element contains the abbreviated form, which is expanded by using the `title` attribute.
Browser:	In IE 5.0 for the Mac, this will appear as a tooltip.

`<acronym>...</acronym>`

Usage:	Indicates an acronym.
Syntax:	`<acronym attributes>content</acronym>`
Attributes:	`core`—See "Common Attributes" section.
	`i18n`—See "Common Attributes" section.
	`events`—See "Intrinsic Events" section.
Content:	Zero or more inline elements, to include the following:

> Document text and entities
>
> Fontstyle elements (`tt | i | b | u | s | strike | big | small`)
>
> Phrase elements (`em | strong | dfn | code | samp | kbd | var | cite | abbr | acronym`)
>
> Special elements (`a | img | applet | object | font | basefont | br | script | map | q | sub | sup | span | bdo | iframe`)
>
> Form Control elements (`input | select | textarea | label | button`)

Notes:	The content of the element contains the acronym, which is expanded by using the `title` attribute.
Browser:	MSIE 5 will display `title` in a tool tip.

`<address>...</address>`

Usage:	Provides a special format for author or contact information.
Syntax:	`<address attributes>content</address>`
Attributes:	`core`—See "Common Attributes" section.
	`i18n`—See "Common Attributes" section.
	`events`—See "Intrinsic Events" section.
Content:	Zero or more inline elements, to include the following:

> Document text and entities
>
> Fontstyle elements (`tt | i | b | u | s | strike | big | small`)
>
> Phrase elements (`em | strong | dfn | code | samp | kbd | var | cite | abbr | acronym`)

APP

A

Special elements (a | img | applet | object | font | basefont | br | script | map | q | sub | sup | span | bdo | iframe)

Form Control elements (input | select | textarea | label | button)

| Browser: | MSIE 1; NNav 1 |

`<applet>...</applet>`

Usage:

Includes a Java applet.

Syntax:

`<applet attributes>content</applet>`

Attributes:

core—See "Common Attributes" section.

codebase="uri"—Sets the base URI for the applet. If not specified, the default value is the base URI of the current document.

archive="uri-list"—List URIs (separated by commas) for archives containing classes and other resources that will be preloaded. This can significantly speed up applet performance.

code="data"—Identifies the compiled .class file of the applet, to include the path if necessary.

object="data"—Names a resource containing a serialized representation of an applet's state.

alt="text"—Alternate text to be displayed if the user agent cannot render the element.

name="data"—Specifies a name for the applet's instance.

width="length"—Sets the initial width of the applet's display area.

height="length"—Sets the initial height of the applet's display area.

align="top | middle | bottom | left | right"—Aligns the object with respect to context.

top—Vertically align the top of the object with the top of the current text line.

middle—Vertically align the center of the object with the current baseline.

bottom—Vertically align the bottom of the object with the current baseline.

`left`—Float object to the left margin.

`right`—Float object to the right margin.

`hspace="pixels"`—Sets the amount of space to be inserted to the left and right of the element.

`vspace="pixels"`—Sets the amount of space to be inserted to the top and bottom of the element.

Content:

One or more `param` elements.

Zero or more block elements, to include the following:

> `-p | dl | div | center | noscript | noframes | blockquote | form | isindex | hr | table | fieldset | address`
>
> Heading elements (`h1 | h2 | h3 | h4 | h5 | h6`)
>
> List elements (`ul | ol | dir | menu`)
>
> Preformatted elements (`pre`)

Zero or more inline elements, to include the following:

> Document text and entities
>
> Fontstyle elements (`tt | i | b | u | s | strike | big | small`)
>
> Phrase elements (`em | strong | dfn | code | samp | kbd | var | cite | abbr | acronym`)
>
> Special elements (`a | img | applet | object | font | basefont | br | script | map | q | sub | sup | span | bdo | iframe`)
>
> Form Control elements (`input | select | textarea | label | button`)

Notes:

Either `code` or `codebase` attributes must be identified. If both are used, the class files must match.

The content of the element is normally given to provide alternate content for user agents not configured to support Java Applets.

The `param` element (which resides in the `applet` element content) should come before any other content.

Deprecated in favor of the `object` element.

Browser:

MSIE 3; NNav 2

APP

A

`<area />`

Usage: Specifies the geometric regions of a client-side imagemap and the associated link.

Syntax: `<area attributes />`

Attributes: `core`—See "Common Attributes" section.

`i18n`—See "Common Attributes" section.

`events`—See "Intrinsic Events" section.

`shape="rect | circle | poly | default"`—Defines a region by its shape:

`rect`—Defines a rectangular region.

`circle`—Defines a circular region.

`poly`—Defines a polygonal region.

`default`—Specifies the entire region.

`coords="coordinates"`—Defines the position of a shape displayed onscreen. All values are of the length data type and separated by commas. The number and order of the coordinates depends on the value of the `shape` attribute:

`rect`—left-x, top-y, right-x, bottom-y

`circle`—center-x, center-y, radius

`poly`—x1, y1, x2, y2, ..., xn, yn

`href="uri"`—Specifies the location of the linked resource or anchor.

`target="user-defined | _blank | _self | _parent | _top"`—Identifies the frame in which the linked resource will be opened:

`user-defined`—Document opens in the frame designated by the `user-defined` name, which is set by the `name` attribute of the frame. The `name` must begin with an alphabetic character.

`_blank`—Document opens in a new, unnamed window.

`_self`—Document opens in same frame as the originating link.

`_parent`—Document opens in the immediate `frameset` parent of the current frame, or itself if the current frame has no parent.

`_top`—Document opens in the full, original window, or itself if the frame has no parent.

`nohref`—Specifies that the region has no associated link.

`alt="text"`—Alternate text to be displayed if the user agent cannot render the element. This attribute is required in XHTML 1.0.

`tabindex="number"`—Defines the tabbing order between elements. This is the order (from lowest first to highest last) in which they receive focus when the user navigates through them using the Tab key.

`accesskey="character"`—Assigns an access key (or shortcut key) to the element. When the key is pressed, the element receives focus and is activated.

`onfocus="script"`—Triggered when the element receives focus either by pointing device (such as a mouse) or by tabbed navigation.

`onblur="script"`—riggered when the element loses focus either by pointing device (such as a mouse) or by tabbed navigation.

Notes:

Because the `area` element has no content to be displayed, an imagemap consisting of one or more `area` must have alternate text for each `area`.

Browser:

MSIE 1; NNav 2

`<b>...</b>`

APP

A

Usage:

Displays text with a boldface font style.

Syntax:

`<b attributes>content</b>`

Attributes:

`core`—See "Common Attributes" section.

`i18n`—See "Common Attributes" section.

`events`—See "Intrinsic Events" section.

Content:

Zero or more inline elements, to include the following:

Document text and entities

Fontstyle elements (`tt` | `i` | `b` | `u` | `s` | `strike` | `big` | `small`)

Phrase elements (`em` | `strong` | `dfn` | `code` | `samp` | `kbd` | `var` | `cite` | `abbr` | `acronym`)

Special elements (a | img | applet | object | font | basefont | br | script | map | q | sub | sup | span | bdo | iframe)

Form Control elements (input | select | textarea | label | button)

Notes:	Although not deprecated, the W3C recommends using style sheets in place of this element.
Browser:	MSIE 1; NNav 1

`<base />`

Usage:	Sets the base URI for the document.
Syntax:	`<base attributes />`
Attributes:	`href="uri"`—Sets the absolute URI against which all other URIs are resolved.
	`target="user-defined	_blank	_self	_parent	_top"`—Identifies the frame in which the linked resource will be opened:
	`user-defined`—Document opens in the frame designated by the `user-defined` name that is set by the `name` attribute of the frame. The `name` must begin with an alphabetic character.
	`_blank`—Document opens in a new, unnamed window.
	`_self`—Document opens in same frame as the originating link.
	`_parent`—Document opens in the immediate `frameset` parent of the current frame, or itself if the current frame has no parent.
	`_top`—Document opens in the full, original window, or itself if the frame has no parent.
Notes:	The base element must appear in the `head` element of the document, before any references to an external source.
Browser:	MSIE 1; NNav 1

`<basefont />`

Usage:	Sets the base font size.
Syntax:	`<basefont attributes />`
Attributes:	`id="id"`—A global identifier.

`size="data"`—Sets the font size in absolute terms (1 through 7) or as a relative increase or decrease along that scale (for example +3).

`color="color"`—Sets the font color. Colors identified by standard RGB in hexadecimal format (`#rrggbb`) or by predefined color name.

`face="data"`—Identifies the font face for display (if possible). Multiple entries are listed in order of search preference and separated by commas.

Notes:

Deprecated in favor of style sheets.

Changes to fonts through the `font` element are resolved against the values specified in the `basefont` element when present.

There are conflicting implementations across browsers, and contents of tables appear not to be effected by `basefont` values.

Browser:

MSIE 1; NNav 1

`<bdo>...</bdo>`

Usage:

The bidirectional algorithm override element selectively turns off the default text direction.

Syntax:

`<bdo attributes>content</bdo>`

Attributes:

`core`—See "Common Attributes" section.

`lang="language-code"`—Identifies the human (not computer) language of the text content or an element's attribute values.

`dir="ltr | rtl"`—Specifies the text direction (left-to-right, right-to-left) of element content, overriding inherent directionality. This is a mandatory attribute of the `bdo` element.

Content:

Zero or more inline elements, to include the following:

Document text and entities

Fontstyle elements (`tt | i | b | u | s | strike | big | small`)

Phrase elements (`em | strong | dfn | code | samp | kbd | var | cite | abbr | acronym`)

APP

A

Special elements (`a` | `img` | `applet` | `object` | `font` | `basefont` | `br` | `script` | `map` | `q` | `sub` | `sup` | `span` | `bdo` | `iframe`)

Form Control elements (`input` | `select` | `textarea` | `label` | `button`)

Notes:	Care should be taken when using the `bdo` element in conjunction with special Unicode characters that also override the bidirectional algorithm.
	The `bdo` element should only be used when absolute control over character sequencing is required.
Browser:	MSIE 5

`<big>...</big>`

Usage:	Displays text in a larger font size.
Syntax:	`<big attributes>content</big>`
Attributes:	`core`—See "Common Attributes" section.
	`i18n`—See "Common Attributes" section.
	`events`—See "Intrinsic Events" section.
Content:	Zero or more inline elements, to include the following:

Document text and entities

Fontstyle elements (`tt` | `i` | `b` | `u` | `s` | `strike` | `big` | `small`)

Phrase elements (`em` | `strong` | `dfn` | `code` | `samp` | `kbd` | `var` | `cite` | `abbr` | `acronym`)

Special elements (`a` | `img` | `applet` | `object` | `font` | `basefont` | `br` | `script` | `map` | `q` | `sub` | `sup` | `span` | `bdo` | `iframe`)

Form Control elements (`input` | `select` | `textarea` | `label` | `button`)

Notes:	Although not deprecated, the W3C recommends using style sheets in place of this element.
Browser:	MSIE 3; NNav 1.1

`<blockquote>...</blockquote>`

Usage:	Designates text as a quotation.
Syntax:	`<blockquote attributes>content</blockquote>`
Attributes:	`core`—See "Common Attributes" section.

i18n—See "Common Attributes" section.

events—See "Intrinsic Events" section.

cite="uri"—The URI designating the source document or message.

Content:
Zero or more inline elements, to include the following:

Document text and entities

Fontstyle elements (tt | i | b | u | s | strike | big | small)

Phrase elements (em | strong | dfn | code | samp | kbd | var | cite | abbr | acronym)

Special elements (a | img | applet | object | font | basefont | br | script | map | a | sub | sup | span | bdo | iframe)

Form Control elements (input | select | textarea | label | button)

Notes:
When compared with the a element, the blockquote element is used for longer quotations and is treated as block-level content.

Quotation marks, if desired, should be added with style sheets.

Normally rendered as an indented block of text.

Browser:
MSIE 1; NNav 1

`<body>...</body>`

Usage:
Contains the content of the document.

Syntax:
content or

`<body attributes>content</body>`

Attributes:
core—See "Common Attributes" section.

i18n—See "Common Attributes" section.

events—See "Intrinsic Events" section.

onload="script"—Intrinsic event triggered when the document loads.

onunload="script"—Intrinsic event triggered when document unloads.

background="uri"—Location of a background image to be displayed.

`bgcolor="color"`—Sets the document background color. Colors identified by standard RGB in hexadecimal format (#rrggbb) or by predefined color name.

`text="color"`—Sets the document text color. Colors identified by standard RGB in hexadecimal format (#rrggbb) or by predefined color name.

`link="color"`—Sets the link color. Colors identified by standard RGB in hexadecimal format (#rrggbb) or by predefined color name.

`vlink="color"`—Sets the visited link color. Colors identified by standard RGB in hexadecimal format (#rrggbb) or by predefined color name.

`alink="color"`—Sets the active link color. Colors identified by standard RGB in hexadecimal format (#rrggbb) or by predefined color name.

Content:

Zero or more block elements, to include the following:

> p | dl | div | center | noscript | noframes | blockquote | form | isindex | hr | table | fieldset | address

> Heading elements (h1 | h2 | h3 | h4 | h5 | h6)

> List elements (ul | ol | dir | menu)

> Preformatted elements (pre)

Zero or more inline elements, to include the following:

> Document text and entities

> Fontstyle elements (tt | i | b | u | s | strike | big | small)

> Phrase elements (em | strong | dfn | code | samp | kbd | var | cite | abbr | acronym)

> Special elements (a | img | applet | object | font | basefont | br | script | map | a | sub | sup | span | bdo | iframe)

> Form Control elements (input | select | textarea | label | button)

Zero or more block/inline elements to include (ins | del)

Notes:	Style sheets are the preferred method of controlling the presentational aspects of the body.
Browser:	MSIE 1; NNav 1

`<br />`

Usage:	Forces a line break.
Syntax:	`<br attributes />`
Attributes:	`core`—See "Common Attributes" section.

`clear="left | all | right | none"`—Sets the location where next line begins after the line break. This attribute is deprecated in favor of style sheets:

`left`—The next line begins at the nearest line on the left margin following any floating objects.

`all`—The next line begins at the nearest line at either margin following any floating objects.

`right`—The next line begins at the nearest line on the right margin following any floating objects.

`none`—Next line begins normally.

Notes:	The `clear` attribute is deprecated in favor of style sheets.
Browser:	MSIE 1; NNav 1

`<button>...</button>`

Usage:	Creates a button.
Syntax:	`<button attributes>content</button>`
Attributes:	`core`—See "Common Attributes" section.

`i18n`—See "Common Attributes" section.

`events`—See "Intrinsic Events" section.

`name="data"`—Defines a control name.

`value="data"`—Assigns an initial value to the button.

`type="button | submit | reset"`—Defines the type of button to be created:

`button`—Creates a push button.

`submit`—Creates a submit button.

`reset`—Creates a reset button.

`disabled`—Identifies that the button is unavailable in the current context.

`tabindex="number"`—Defines the tabbing order between elements. This is the order (from lowest first to highest last) in which they receive focus when the user navigates through them using the Tab key.

`accesskey="character"`—Assigns an access key (or shortcut key) to the element. When the key is pressed, the element receives focus and is activated.

`onfocus="script"`—Triggered when the element receives focus by either a pointing device (such as a mouse) or tabbed navigation.

`onblur="script"`—Triggered when the element loses focus by either a pointing device (such as a mouse) or tabbed navigation.

Content:

Zero or more block elements, to include the following:

> p | dl | div | center | noscript | noframes | blockquote | hr | table | address

> Heading elements (h1 | h2 | h3 | h4 | h5 | h6)

> List elements (ul | ol | dir | menu)

> Preformatted elements (pre)

Zero or more inline elements, to include the following:

> Document text and entities

> Fontstyle elements (tt | i | b | u | s | strike | big | small)

> Phrase elements (em | strong | dfn | code | samp | kbd | var | cite | abbr | acronym)

> Special elements (img | applet | object | font | basefont | br | script | map | a | sub | sup | span | bdo)

Notes:

An important distinction between buttons created with the `button` element and those created by the `input` element is that the former allows content to be associated with the control.

Browser:

MSIE 4

`<caption>...</caption>`

Usage:

Displays a table caption.

Syntax:

`<caption attributes>content</caption>`

Attributes:	core—See "Common Attributes" section.
	i18n—See "Common Attributes" section.
	events—See "Intrinsic Events" section.
	align="top | bottom | left | right"—Positions the caption relative to the table:
	top—Places the caption at the top of the table.
	bottom—Places the caption at the bottom of the table.
	left—Places the caption at the left side of the table.
	right—Places the caption at the right side of the table.
Content:	Zero or more inline elements, to include the following:

> Document text and entities
>
> Fontstyle elements (tt \| i \| b \| u \| s \| strike \| big \| small)
>
> Phrase elements (em \| strong \| dfn \| code \| samp \| kbd \| var \| cite \| abbr \| acronym)
>
> Special elements (a \| img \| applet \| object \| font \| _basefont \| br \| script \| map \| a \| sub \| sup \| span \|_bdo \| iframe)
>
> Form Control elements (input \| select \| textarea \| label \| button)

Notes:	The caption might only be placed immediately following the opening table tag, and only one caption per table is allowed.
Browser:	MSIE 2; NNav 1.1

APP

A

`<center>...</center>`

Usage:	Centers content on the page.
Syntax:	`<center attributes>content</center>`
Attributes:	core—See "Common Attributes" section.
	i18n—See "Common Attributes" section.
	events—See "Intrinsic Events" section.
Content:	Zero or more block elements, to include the following:

> p \| dl \| div \| center \| noscript \| noframes \| blockquote \| form \| isindex \| hr \| table \| fieldset \| address

Heading elements (h1 | h2 | h3 | h4 | h5 | h6)

List elements (ul | ol | dir | menu)

Preformatted elements (pre)

Zero or more inline elements, to include the following:

Document text and entities

Fontstyle elements (tt | i | b | u | s | strike | big | small)

Phrase elements (em | strong | dfn | code | samp | kbd | var | cite | abbr | acronym)

Special elements (a | img | applet | object | font | basefont | br | script | map | a | sub | sup | span | bdo | iframe)

Form Control elements (input | select | textarea | label | button)

Notes:

Deprecated in favor of style sheets.

Using the center element is the equivalent of <div align="center">, although this method also is deprecated in favor of style sheets.

Browser:

MSIE 1; NNav 1

<cite>...</cite>

Usage:

Identifies a citation or a reference.

Syntax:

<cite attributes>content</cite>

Attributes:

core—See "Common Attributes" section.

i18n—See "Common Attributes" section.

events—See "Intrinsic Events" section.

Content:

Zero or more inline elements, to include the following:

Document text and entities

Fontstyle elements (tt | i | b | u | s | strike | big | small)

Phrase elements (em | strong | dfn | code | samp | kbd | var | cite | abbr | acronym)

Special elements (a | img | applet | object | font | basefont | br | script | map | a | sub | sup | span | bdo | iframe)

Form Control elements (input | select | textarea | label | button)

Notes:	Usually rendered as italicized text.
Browser:	MSIE 1; NNav 1

`<code>...</code>`

Usage:	Identifies a fragment of computer code.
Syntax:	`<code attributes>content</code>`
Attributes:	`core`—See "Common Attributes" section.
	`i18n`—See "Common Attributes" section.
	`events`—See "Intrinsic Events" section.
Content:	Zero or more inline elements, to include the following:

> Document text and entities
>
> Fontstyle elements (`tt | i | b | u | s | strike | big | small`)
>
> Phrase elements (`em | strong | dfn | code | samp | kbd | var | cite | abbr | acronym`)
>
> Special elements (`a | img | applet | object | font | basefont | br | script | map | a | sub | sup | span | bdo | iframe`)
>
> Form Control elements (`input | select | textarea | label | button`)

Notes:	Usually rendered in monospaced font.
Browser:	MSIE 1; NNav 1

`<col>`

Usage:	Groups columns within column groups to share attribute _values.
Syntax:	`<col attributes />`
Attributes:	`core`—See "Common Attributes" section.
	`i18n`—See "Common Attributes" section.
	`events`—See "Intrinsic Events" section.
	`span="number"`—Sets the number of columns the `col` element spans (1 is the default). Each column spanned in this manner inherits its attributes from that `col` element.
	`width="multi-length"`—Sets the default width of each column spanned by the `col` element.
	`align="left	center	right	justify	char"`—Horizontally aligns the contents of cells:

APP

A

left—Data and text aligned left. This is the default for table data.

center—Data and text centered. This is the default for table headers.

right—Data and text aligned right.

justify—Data and text aligned flush with left and right margins.

char—Aligns text around a specific character.

char="character"—Sets a character on which the column aligns (such as ":"). The default value is the decimal point of the current language.

charoff="length"—Offset to the first alignment character on a line. Specified in number of pixels or a percentage of available length.

valign="top | middle | bottom | baseline"—Vertically aligns the contents of a cell:

top—Cell data flush with top of cell.

middle—Cell data centered in cell.

bottom—Cell data flush with bottom of cell.

baseline—Aligns all cells in a row with this attribute set. Textual data aligned along a common baseline.

Notes:

The col element groups columns only to share attribute values, not group them structurally, which is the role of the colgroup element.

Browser:

MSIE 3

`<colgroup>...</colgroup>`

Usage:

Defines a column group.

Syntax:

`<colgroup attributes />content`

or

`<colgroup attributes>content</colgroup>`

Attributes:

core—See "Common Attributes" section.

i18n—See "Common Attributes" section.

events—See "Intrinsic Events" section.

span="number"—Sets the number of columns in a colgroup (1 is the default). Each column spanned in this manner inherits its attributes from that colgroup element.

width="multi-length"—Sets the default width of each column spanned by the colgroup element. An additional value is "0*" (zero asterisk), which means that the width of the each column in the group should be the minimum width necessary to hold the column's contents.

align="left | center | right | justify | char"—Horizontally aligns the contents of cells:

left—Data and text aligned left. This is the default for table data.

center—Data and text centered. This is the default for table headers.

right—Data and text aligned right.

justify—Data and text aligned flush with left and right margins.

char—Aligns text around a specific character.

char="character"—Sets a character on which the column aligns (such as ":"). The default value is the decimal point of the current language.

charoff="length"—Offset to the first alignment character on a line. Specified in number of pixels or a percentage of available length.

valign="top | middle | bottom | baseline"— Vertically aligns the contents of a cell:

top—Cell data flush with top of cell.

middle—Cell data centered in cell.

bottom—Cell data flush with bottom of cell.

baseline—Aligns all cells in a row with this attribute set. Textual data aligned along a common baseline.

Notes:	The purpose of the colgroup element is to provide structure to table columns.
Browser:	MSIE 3

<dd>...</dd>

Usage:	Contains the definition description used in a dl (definition list) element.
Syntax:	<dd attributes>content</dd>
Attributes:	core—See "Common Attributes" section.
	i18n—See "Common Attributes" section.

events—See "Intrinsic Events" section.

compact—Tells the browser to attempt to display the list more compactly.

Content:

Zero or more block elements, to include the following:

> p | dl | div | center | noscript | noframes | blockquote | form | isindex | hr | table | fieldset | address
>
> Heading elements (h1 | h2 | h3 | h4 | h5 | h6)
>
> List elements (ul | ol | dir | menu)
>
> Preformatted elements (pre)

Zero or more inline elements, to include the following:

> Document text and entities
>
> Fontstyle elements (tt | i | b | u | s | strike | big | small)
>
> Phrase elements (em | strong | dfn | code | samp | kbd | var | cite | abbr | acronym)
>
> Special elements (a | img | applet | object | font | basefont | br | script | map | a | sub | sup | span | bdo | iframe)
>
> Form Control elements (input | select | textarea | label | button)

Notes:

The dd element might contain block-level or inline content.

Browser:

MSIE 1; NNav 1

`<del>...</del>`

Usage:

Identifies and displays text as having been deleted from the document in relation to a previous version.

Syntax:

`<del attributes>content</del>`

Attributes:

core—See "Common Attributes" section.

i18n—See "Common Attributes" section.

events—See "Intrinsic Events" section.

`cite="uri"`—A URI pointing to a document that should give reason for the change.

`datetime="datetime"`—Sets the date and time of the change.

Content:	Zero or more block elements, to include the following:

p | dl | div | center | noscript | noframes | blockquote | form | isindex | hr | table | fieldset | address

Heading elements (h1 | h2 | h3 | h4 | h5 | h6)

List elements (ul | ol | dir | menu)

Preformatted elements (pre)

Zero or more inline elements, to include the following:

Document text and entities

Fontstyle elements (tt | i | b | u | s | strike | big | small)

Phrase elements (em | strong | dfn | code | samp | kbd | var | cite | abbr | acronym)

Special elements (a | img | applet | object | font | basefont | br | script | map | a | sub | sup | span | bdo | iframe)

Form Control elements (input | select | textarea | label | button)

Notes:	Might serve as a block-level or inline element, but not both at the same time. Changes to nested block-level content should be made at the lowest level.
Browser:	MSIE 4

APP
A

`<dfn>...</dfn>`

Usage:	The defining instance of an enclosed term.
Syntax:	`<dfn attributes>content</dfn>`
Attributes:	core—See "Common Attributes" section.
	i18n—See "Common Attributes" section.
	events—See "Intrinsic Events" section.
Content:	Zero or more inline elements, to include the following:

Document text and entities

Fontstyle elements (tt | i | b | u | s | strike | big | small)

Phrase elements (em | strong | dfn | code | samp | kbd | var | cite | abbr | acronym)

Special elements (a | img | applet | object |
font | basefont | br | script | map | a | sub
| sup | span | bdo | iframe)

Form Control elements (input | select |
textarea | label | button)

Notes:	Usually rendered in italics.
Browser:	MSIE 1

`<dir>...</dir>`

Usage:	Creates a multicolumn directory list.
Syntax:	`<dir attributes>content</dir>`
Attributes:	core—See "Common Attributes" section.
	i18n—See "Common Attributes" section.
	events—See "Intrinsic Events" section.
	compact—Tells the browser to attempt to display the list more compactly.
Content:	One or more li element, which might contain the following:

List elements (ul | ol | dir | menu)

Zero or more inline elements, to include the
following:

Document text and entities

Fontstyle elements (tt | i | b | u | s |
strike | big | small)

Phrase elements (em | strong | dfn | code |
samp | kbd | var | cite | abbr | acronym)

Special elements (a | img | applet | object |
font | basefont | br | script | map | a |
sub | sup | span | bdo | iframe)

Form Control elements (input | select |
textarea | label | button)

Notes:	Deprecated in favor of unordered lists (UL).
Browser:	MSIE 1; NNav 1

`<div>...</div>`

Usage:	Creates author-defined block-level structure to the document.
Syntax:	`<div attributes>content</div>`

Attributes:	core—See "Common Attributes" section.
	i18n—See "Common Attributes" section.
	events—See "Intrinsic Events" section.
	align="left | center | right | justify"—Horizontal alignment with respect to context. The default depends on the directionality of the text. For left-to-right it is left and for right-to-left it is right:
	left—Text aligned left.
	center—Text centered.
	right—Text aligned right.
	justify—Text aligned flush with left and right margins.
Content:	Zero or more block elements, to include the following:

> p | dl | div | center | noscript | noframes | blockquote | form | isindex | hr | table | fieldset | address
>
> Heading elements (h1 | h2 | h3 | h4 | h5 | h6)
>
> List elements (ul | ol | dir | menu)
>
> Preformatted elements (pre)

Zero or more inline elements, to include the following:

> Document text and entities
>
> Fontstyle elements (tt | i | b | u | s | strike | big | small)
>
> Phrase elements (em | strong | dfn | code | samp | kbd | var | cite | abbr | acronym)
>
> Special elements (a | img | applet | object | font | basefont | br | script | map | a | sub | sup | span | bdo | iframe)
>
> Form Control elements (input | select | textarea | label | button)

Notes:	Used in conjunction with style sheets this is a powerful device for adding custom block-level structure.
	Might be nested.
Browser:	MSIE 3; NNav 2

APP

A

`<dl>...</dl>`

Usage:	Creates a definition list.
Syntax:	`<dl attributes>content</dl>`
Attributes:	`core`—See "Common Attributes" section.
	`i18n`—See "Common Attributes" section.
	`events`—See "Intrinsic Events" section.
	`compact`—Tells the browser to attempt to display the list more compactly.
Content:	One or more `dt` or `dd` elements.
Notes:	This element provides the structure necessary to group definition terms and descriptions into a list. Aside from those elements (`dt` and `dl`), no other content is allowed.
Browser:	MSIE 1; NNav 1

`<dt>...</dt>`

Usage:	The definition term (or label) used within a `dl` (definition list) element.
Syntax:	`<dt attributes>content</dt>`
Attributes:	`core`—See "Common Attributes" section.
	`i18n`—See "Common Attributes" section.
	`events`—See "Intrinsic Events" section.
	`compact`—Tells the browser to attempt to display the list more compactly.
Content:	Zero or more inline elements, to include the following:

> Document text and entities
>
> Fontstyle elements (`tt` | `i` | `b` | `u` | `s` | `strike` | `big` | `small`)
>
> Phrase elements (`em` | `strong` | `dfn` | `code` | `samp` | `kbd` | `var` | `cite` | `abbr` | `acronym`)
>
> Special elements (`a` | `img` | `applet` | `object` | `font` | `_basefont` | `br` | `script` | `map` | `a` | `sub` | `sup` | `span` | `_bdo` | `iframe`)
>
> Form Control elements (`input` | `select` | `textarea` | `label` | `button`)

Notes:	The `dt` element might only contain inline content.
Browser:	MSIE 1; NNav 1

`<em>...</em>`

Usage:	Displays text with emphasis in relation to normal text.
Syntax:	`<em attributes>content</em>`
Attributes:	`core`—See "Common Attributes" section.
	`i18n`—See "Common Attributes" section.
	`events`—See "Intrinsic Events" section.
Content:	Zero or more inline elements, to include the following:

> Document text and entities
>
> Fontstyle elements (`tt` | `i` | `b` | `u` | `s` | `strike` | `big` | `small`)
>
> Phrase elements (`em` | `strong` | `dfn` | `code` | `samp` | `kbd` | `var` | `cite` | `abbr` | `acronym`)
>
> Special elements (`a` | `img` | `applet` | `object` | `font` | `_basefont` | `br` | `script` | `map` | `a` | `sub` | `sup` | `span` | `_bdo` | `iframe`)
>
> Form Control elements (`input` | `select` | `textarea` | `label` | `button`)

Notes:	Usually rendered in italics.
Browser:	MSIE 1; NNav 1

APP

A

`<fieldset>...</fieldset>`

Usage:	Groups related controls and labels of a form.
Syntax:	`<fieldset attributes>content</fieldset>`
Attributes:	`core`—See "Common Attributes" section.
	`i18n`—See "Common Attributes" section.
	`events`—See "Intrinsic Events" section.
Content:	One `legend` element.
	Zero or more block elements, to include the following:

> `p` | `dl` | `div` | `center` | `noscript` | `noframes` | `blockquote` | `form` | `isindex` | `hr` | `table` | `fieldset` | `address`

Heading elements (h1 | h2 | h3 | h4 | h5 | h6)

List elements (ul | ol | dir | menu)

Preformatted elements (pre)

Zero or more inline elements, to include the following:

Document text and entities

Fontstyle elements (tt | i | b | u | s | strike | big | small)

Phrase elements (em | strong | dfn | code | samp | kbd | var | cite | abbr | acronym)

Special elements (a | img | applet | object | font | _basefont | br | script | map | a | sub | sup | span | _bdo | iframe)

Form Control elements (input | select | textarea | label | button)

| Notes: | Proper use of the fieldset element facilitates user understanding of the form and eases navigation. |
| Browser: | MSIE 4 |

`<font>...</font>`

Usage:	Changes the font size and color.
Syntax:	`<font attributes>content</font>`
Attributes:	core—See "Common Attributes" section.
	i18n—See "Common Attributes" section.
	size="data"—Sets the font size in absolute terms (1 through 7) or as a relative increase or decrease along that scale (for example, +3). If a base font is not specified, the default is 3.
	color="color"—Sets the font color. Colors are identified by standard RGB in hexadecimal format (#rrggbb) or by predefined color name.
	face="data"—Identifies the font face for display (if possible). Multiple entries are listed in order of search preference and separated by commas.
Content:	Zero or more inline elements, to include the following:

Document text and entities

Fontstyle elements (tt | i | b | u | s | strike | big | small)

Phrase elements (em | strong | dfn | code | samp | kbd | var | cite | abbr | acronym)

Special elements (a | img | applet | object | font | _basefont | br | script | map | a | sub | sup | span | _bdo | iframe)

Form Control elements (input | select | textarea | label | button)

Notes:

Deprecated in favor of style sheets.

Changes to fonts through the font element are resolved against the values specified in the basefont element when present.

Browser:

MSIE 1; NNav 1

`<form>...</form>`

Usage:

Creates a form that holds controls for user input.

Syntax:

`<form attributes>content</form>`

Attributes:

core—See "Common Attributes" section.

i18n—See "Common Attributes" section.

events—See "Intrinsic Events" section.

action="uri"—Specifies the form processing agent that will process the submitted form.

method="get | post"—Specifies the HTTP method used to submit the form data:

get—The form data set is appended to the URI specified by the action attribute (with a question mark ("?") as separator), and this new URI is sent to the processing agent.

post—The form data set is included in the body of the form and sent to the processing agent.

enctype="content-type"—Specifies the content or media (MIME) type used to transmit the form to the server. The default is "application/x-www-form-urlencoded".

onsubmit="script"—Triggered when the form is submitted.

onreset="script"—Triggered when the form is reset.

target="user-defined | _blank | _self | _parent | _top"—Identifies the frame in which the linked resource will be opened:

APP

A

user-defined—Document opens in the frame designated by the user-defined name, which is set by the name attribute of the frame. The name must begin with an alphabetic character.

_blank—Document opens in a new, unnamed window.

self—Document opens in the same frame as the originating link.

parent—Document opens in the immediate frameset parent of the current frame, or itself if the current frame has no parent.

_top—Document opens in the full, original window, or itself if the frame has no parent.

accept-charset="character-set"—Specifies the list of character encodings for input data that must be accepted by the server processing this form.

accept="content-types"—List of content types.

Content: Zero or more block elements, to include the following:

> p | dl | div | center | noscript | noframes | blockquote | isindex | hr | table | field-set | address
>
> Heading elements (h1 | h2 | h3 | h4 | h5 | h6)
>
> List elements (ul | ol | dir | menu)
>
> Preformatted elements (pre)

Zero or more inline elements, to include the following:

> Document text and entities
>
> Fontstyle elements (tt | i | b | u | s | strike | big | small)
>
> Phrase elements (em | strong | dfn | code | samp | kbd | var | cite | abbr | acronym)
>
> Special elements (a | img | applet | object | font | _basefont | br | script | map | a | sub | sup | span | _bdo | iframe)
>
> Form Control elements (input | select | textarea | label | button)

| | Browser: | MSIE 1; NNav 1 |

`<frame />`

| | Usage: | Defines the contents and appearance of a single frame or subwindow. |

Syntax:

`<frame attributes />`

Attributes:

`core`—See "Common Attributes" section.

`longdesc="uri"`—Links to a resource containing a long description of the frame.

`name="data"`—Names the current frame.

`src="uri"`—Specifies the URI containing the initial contents of the frame.

`frameborder="1 | 0"`—Toggles borders to be drawn around the frame.

`1`—A border is drawn.

`0`—A border is not drawn.

`marginwidth="pixels"`—Sets the margin between the contents of the frame and its left and right borders.

`marginheight="pixels"`—Sets the margin between the contents of the frame and its top and bottom borders.

`noresize`—Prohibits resizing of the frame by the user agent.

`scrolling="auto | yes | no"`—Determines whether the user agent provides scrolling devices for the frame:

`auto`—The user agent provides scrolling devices if necessary.

`yes`—Scrolling devices are provided even if not necessary.

`no`—Scrolling devices are not provided even if necessary.

Notes:

The contents of a frame must not be in the same document as the frame's definition.

Browser:

MSIE 3; NNav 2

APP

A

`<frameset>...</frameset>`

Usage:

Defines the layout of `frames` within the main window.

Syntax:

`<frameset attributes>content</frameset>`

Attributes:	core—See "Common Attributes" section.
	rows="multi-length"—Defines the horizontal layout, or number of rows, of the frameset.
	cols="multi-length"—Defines the vertical layout, or number of columns, of the frameset.
	onload="script"—Intrinsic event triggered when the document loads.
	onunload="script"—Intrinsic event triggered when the document unloads.
Content:	One or more frameset or frame elements.
	Zero or one noframes element
Notes:	A frameset document contains the head element, which is followed immediately by a frameset. Content between the head and frameset will void the frameset. The only place the body element is allowed within a frameset document is within the noframes tags.
Browser:	MSIE 3; NNav 2

`<h1>...</h1>` Through `<h6>...</h6>`

Usage:	The six headings (h1 is the uppermost, or most important) structure information in a hierarchical fashion.
Syntax:	`<hx attributes>content</hx>`
Attributes:	core—See "Common Attributes" section.
	i18n—See "Common Attributes" section.
	events—See "Intrinsic Events" section.
	align="left | center | right | justify"—Horizontal alignment with respect to context. The default depends on the directionality of the text. For left-to-right it is left, and for right-to-left it is right:
	left—Text aligned left.
	center—Text centered.
	right—Text aligned right.
	justify—Text aligned flush with left and right margins.

Content:	Zero or more inline elements, to include the following:
	Document text and entities
	Fontstyle elements (tt | i | b | u | s | strike | big | small)
	Phrase elements (em | strong | dfn | code | samp | kbd | var | cite | abbr | acronym)
	Special elements (a | img | applet | object | font | _basefont | br | script | map | a | sub | sup | span | _bdo | iframe)
	Form Control elements (input | select | textarea | label | button)
Notes:	The headings are rendered from large to small in order of importance (1 to 6).
Browser:	MSIE 1; NNav 1

\<head\>...\</head\>

Usage:	Contains elements that provide information to users and search engines as well as containing other data that is not considered to be document content (for example, style and script information).
Syntax:	content
	or
	\<head attributes\>content\</head\>
Attributes:	i18n—See "Common Attributes" section.
	profile="uri"—Specifies the location of one or more meta data profiles.
Content:	One title element, zero or one isindex, and zero or one base elements.
	Zero or more script, style, meta, link, object elements.
Notes:	Information in the head is not displayed (with the exception of the title, which is displayed in the title bar of the browser).
	The title element is required.
Browser:	MSIE 1; NNav 1

APP

A

`<hr />`

Usage:	Horizontal rules displayed to separate sections of a document.
Syntax:	`<hr attributes />`
Attributes:	`core`—See "Common Attributes" section.
	`i18n`—See "Common Attributes" section (as per the XHTML 1.0 Specification Errata, 14 April 1998).
	`events`—See "Intrinsic Events" section.
	`align="left	center	right"`—Alignment of the hr with respect to the surrounding context:
	`left`—Rule aligned left.
	`center`—Rule centered.
	`right`—Rule aligned right.
	`noshade`—Renders the hr as a solid color rather than a shaded bump.
	`size="length"`—Sets the length of the hr.
	`width="length"`—Sets the height of the hr.
Browser:	MSIE 1; NNav 1

`<html>...</html>`

Usage:	The root container of an HTML or XHTML document.
Syntax:	`content`
	`<html attributes>content</html>`
Attributes:	`i18n`—See "Common Attributes" section.
	`version="data"`—Specifies the XHTML DTD that governs the current document.
Content:	One head element and one body element if using the Strict or Transitional DTD.
	One head element and one frameset element if using the Frameset DTD.
Notes:	version has been deprecated because of its redundancy with the `<!doctype>` declaration.
Browser:	MSIE 1; NNav 1

`<i>...</i>`

Usage:	Displays italicized text.
Syntax:	`<i attributes>content</i>`
Attributes:	`core`—See "Common Attributes" section.
	`i18n`—See "Common Attributes" section.
	`events`—See "Intrinsic Events" section.
Content:	Zero or more inline elements, to include the following:

> Document text and entities
>
> Fontstyle elements (`tt | i | b | u | s | strike | big | small`)
>
> Phrase elements (`em | strong | dfn | code | samp | kbd | var | cite | abbr | acronym`)
>
> Special elements (`a | img | applet | object | font | _basefont | br | script | map | a | sub | sup | span | _bdo | iframe`)
>
> Form Control elements (`input | select | textarea | label | button`)

Notes:	Although not deprecated, the W3C recommends using style sheets in place of this element.
Browser:	MSIE 1; NNav 1

`<iframe>...</iframe>`

Usage:	Creates an inline frame, or window subdivision, within a document.
Syntax:	`<iframe attributes>content</iframe>`
Attributes:	`core`—See "Common Attributes" section.
	`longdesc="uri"`—Links to a resource containing a long description of the frame.
	`name="data"`—Names the current frame.
	`src="uri"`—Specifies the URI containing the initial contents of the frame.
	`frameborder="1	0"`—Toggles borders to be drawn around the frame:
	`1`—A border is drawn.
	`0`—A border is not drawn.
	`marginwidth="pixels"`—Sets the margin between the contents of the frame and its left and right borders.

APP

A

`marginheight="pixels"`—Sets the margin between the contents of the frame and its top and bottom borders.

`noresize`—Prohibits the user agent from resizing the frame.

`scrolling="auto | yes | no"`—Determines whether the user agent provides scrolling devices for the frame:

`auto`—The user agent provides scrolling devices if necessary.

`yes`—Scrolling devices are provided even if not necessary.

`no`—Scrolling devices are not provided even if necessary.

`align="top | middle | bottom | left | right"`—Aligns the object with respect to context:

`top`—Vertically aligns the top of the object with the top of the current text line.

`middle`—Vertically aligns the center of the object with the current baseline.

`bottom`—Vertically aligns the bottom of the object with the current baseline.

`left`—Floats object to the left margin.

`right`—Floats object to the right margin.

`height="length"`—Sets the frame height.

`width="length"`—Sets the frame width.

Content:

Zero or more block elements, to include the following:

> `p | dl | div | center | noscript | noframes | blockquote | form | isindex | hr | table | fieldset | address`

> Heading elements (`h1 | h2 | h3 | h4 | h5 | h6`)

> List elements (`ul | ol | dir | menu`)

> Preformatted elements (`pre`)

> Zero or more inline elements, to include the following:

> Document text and entities

Fontstyle elements (tt | i | b | u | s | strike | big | small)

Phrase elements (em | strong | dfn | code | samp | kbd | var | cite | abbr | acronym)

Special elements (a | img | applet | object | font | _basefont | br | script | map | a | sub | sup | span | _bdo | iframe)

Form Control elements (input | select | textarea | label | button)

Notes: The content to be displayed is specified by the src attribute. The content of the element will only be displayed in user agents that do not support frames.

Browser: MSIE 3

`<img />`

Usage: Includes an image in the document.

Syntax: `<img attributes />`

Attributes: core—See "Common Attributes" section.

i18n—See "Common Attributes" section.

events—See "Intrinsic Events" section.

src="uri"—Specifies the location of the image to load into the document.

alt="text"—Alternate text to be displayed if the user agent cannot render the element.

longdesc="uri"—Links to a resource containing a long description of the resource.

height="length"—Sets the display height of the image.

width="length"—Sets the display width of the image.

usemap="uri"—Associates an imagemap as defined by the map element with this image.

ismap—Used to define a server-side imagemap. The img element must be included in an a element and the ismap attribute set.

align="top | middle | bottom | left | right"—Aligns the object with respect to context:

top—Vertically aligns the top of the object with the top of the current text line.

middle—Vertically aligns the center of the object with the _current baseline.

bottom—Vertically aligns the bottom of the object with the current baseline.

left—Floats object to the left margin.

right—Floats object to the right margin.

border="length"—Sets the border width of the image.

hspace="pixels"—Sets the amount of space to be inserted to the left and right of the element.

vspace="pixels"—Sets the amount of space to be inserted to the top and bottom of the element.

Notes: Has no content.

Browser: MSIE 1; NNav 1

`<input />`

Usage: Defines controls used in forms.

Syntax: `<input attributes />`

Attributes: core—See "Common Attributes" section.

i18n—See "Common Attributes" section.

events—See "Intrinsic Events" section.

type="text | password | checkbox | radio | submit | reset | file | hidden | image | button"—Defines the type of control to create.

text—Creates a single-line text input control.

password—Creates a single-line text input control that hides the characters from the user.

checkbox—Creates a check box.

radio—Creates a radio button.

submit—Creates a submit button.

reset—Creates a reset button.

file—Creates a file select control.

hidden—Creates a hidden control.

image—Creates a graphical submit button that uses the src attribute to locate the image used to decorate the button.

button—Creates a pushbutton.

name="data"—Assigns a control name.

`value="data"`—Sets the initial value of the control.

`checked`—Sets radio buttons and check boxes to a checked state.

`disabled`—Disables the control in this context.

`readonly`—Changes to the control (text and password) are prohibited.

`size="data"`—Sets the initial size of the control.

`maxlength="number"`—Sets the maximum number of characters a user might enter into a text or password control.

`src="uri"`—Identifies the location of the image when the _control type has been set to `image`.

`alt="data"`—Provides a short description of the control.

`usemap="uri"`—Associates an imagemap as defined by the `map` element with this control.

`tabindex="number"`—Defines the tabbing order between elements. This is the order (from lowest first to highest last) in which they receive focus when the user navigates through them using the Tab key.

`accesskey="character"`—Assigns an access key (or shortcut key) to the element. When the key is pressed, the element receives focus and is activated.

`onfocus="script"`—Triggered when the element receives focus by either a pointing device (such as a mouse) or tabbed navigation.

`onblur="script"`—Triggered when the element loses focus by either a pointing device (such as a mouse) or tabbed navigation.

`onselect="script"`—The event that occurs when text is selected in a text field.

`onchange="script"`—The event that occurs when a control loses the input focus and its value has been modified since gaining focus.

`accept="content-type"`—A list of content (MIME) types the server will accept for file upload.

`align="top | middle | bottom | left | right"`—Aligns the object with respect to context:

`top`—Vertically aligns the top of the object with the top of the current text line.

APP

A

`middle`—Vertically aligns the center of the object with the current baseline.

`bottom`—Vertically aligns the bottom of the object with the current baseline.

`left`—Floats object to the left margin.

`right`—Floats object to the right margin.

Notes: Has no content.

Browser: MSIE 1; NNav 1

`<ins>...</ins>`

Usage: Identifies and displays text as having been inserted in the document in relation to a previous version.

Syntax: `<ins attributes>content</ins>`

Attributes: `core`—See "Common Attributes" section.

`i18n`—See "Common Attributes" section.

`events`—See "Intrinsic Events" section.

`cite="uri"`—A URI pointing to a document that should give reason for the change.

`datetime="datetime"`—Sets the date and time of the change.

Content: Zero or more block elements, to include the following:

> `p | dl | div | center | noscript | noframes | blockquote | form | isindex | hr | table | fieldset | address`
>
> Heading elements (`h1 | h2 | h3 | h4 | h5 | h6`)
>
> List elements (`ul | ol | dir | menu`)
>
> Preformatted elements (`pre`)

Zero or more inline elements, to include the following:

Document text and entities

Fontstyle elements (`tt | i | b | u | s | strike | big | small`)

Phrase elements (`em | strong | dfn | code | samp | kbd | var | cite | abbr | acronym`)

Special elements (`a | img | applet | object | font | basefont | br | script | map | a | sub | sup | span | bdo | iframe`)

	Form Control elements (input | select | textarea | label | button)
Notes:	Might serve as a block-level or inline element, but not both at the same time. Changes to nested block-level content should be made at the lowest level.
Browser:	MSIE 4

`<isindex />`

Usage:	Creates a single-line text input control.
Syntax:	`<isindex attributes />`
Attributes:	core—See "Common Attributes" section.
	i18n—See "Common Attributes" section.
	`prompt="text"`—Displays a prompt for user input.
Notes:	Deprecated in favor of using input to create text-input controls.
Browser:	MSIE 1; NNav 1

`<kbd>...</kbd>`

Usage:	Identifies and displays text a user would enter from a keyboard.
Syntax:	`<kbd attributes>content</kbd>`
Attributes:	core—See "Common Attributes" section.
	i18n—See "Common Attributes" section.
	events—See "Intrinsic Events" section.
Content:	Zero or more inline elements, to include the following:

> Document text and entities
>
> Fontstyle elements (tt \| i \| b \| u \| s \| strike \| big \| small)
>
> Phrase elements (em \| strong \| dfn \| code \| samp \| kbd \| var \| cite \| abbr \| acronym)
>
> Special elements (a \| img \| applet \| object \| font \| _basefont \| br \| script \| map \| a \| sub \| sup \| span \| _bdo \| iframe)
>
> Form Control elements (input \| select \| textarea \| label \| button)

Notes:	Usually displayed with monospaced font.
Browser:	MSIE 1; NNav 1

APP

A

`<label>...</label>`

Usage:	Labels a form control.
Syntax:	`<label attributes>content</label>`
Attributes:	`core`—See "Common Attributes" section.
	`i18n`—See "Common Attributes" section.
	`events`—See "Intrinsic Events" section.
	`for="idref"`—Associates the `label` with a previously identified control.
	`accesskey="character"`—Assigns an access key (or shortcut key) to the element. When the key is pressed, the element receives focus and is activated.
	`onfocus="script"`—Triggered when the element receives focus by either a pointing device (such as a mouse) or tabbed navigation.
	`onblur="script"`—Triggered when the element loses focus by either a pointing device (such as a mouse) or tabbed navigation.
Content:	Zero or more inline elements, to include the following:
	Document text and entities
	Fontstyle elements (`tt` | `i` | `b` | `u` | `s` | `strike` | `big` | `small`)
	Phrase elements (`em` | `strong` | `dfn` | `code` | `samp` | `kbd` | `var` | `cite` | `abbr` | `acronym`)
	Special elements (`a` | `img` | `applet` | `object` | `font` | `_basefont` | `br` | `script` | `map` | `a` | `sub` | `sup` | `span` | `_bdo` | `iframe`)
	Form Control elements (`input` | `select` | `textarea` | `_button`)
Notes:	More than one `label` might be associated with a control; however, each `label` is only associated with one control.
Browser:	MSIE 4

`<legend>...</legend>`

Usage:	Assigns a caption to a `fieldset` element.
Syntax:	`<legend attributes>content</legend>`
Attributes:	`core`—See "Common Attributes" section.

i18n—See "Common Attributes" section.

events—See "Intrinsic Events" section.

accesskey="character"—Assigns an access key (or shortcut key) to the element. When the key is pressed, the element receives focus and is activated.

align="top | bottom | left | right"—Specifies the position of the legend with respect to the `fieldset`:

top—Places the legend at the top of the fieldset.

bottom—Places the legend at the bottom of the fieldset.

left—Places the legend at the left side of the fieldset.

right—Places the legend at the right side of the fieldset.

Content:

Zero or more inline elements, to include the following:

> Document text and entities
>
> Fontstyle elements (tt | i | b | u | s | strike | big | small)
>
> Phrase elements (em | strong | dfn | code | samp | kbd | var | cite | abbr | acronym)
>
> Special elements (a | img | applet | object | font | _basefont | br | script | map | a | sub | sup | span | _bdo | iframe)
>
> Form Control elements (input | select | textarea | label | button)

Notes:

The use of legend improves accessibility for nonvisual user agents as well as aids general understanding of the form layout.

Browser:

MSIE 4

`<li>...</li>`

Usage:

Defines a list item within a list.

Syntax:

`<li attributes>content</li>`

Attributes:

core—See "Common Attributes" section.

i18n—See "Common Attributes" section.

events—See "Intrinsic Events" section.

type="1 | a | a | i | i | disc | square | _circle":

APP

A

	1—Arabic numbers.
	a—Lowercase alphabet.
	a—Uppercase alphabet.
	i—Lowercase Roman numerals.
	i—Uppercase Roman numerals.
	disc—A solid circle.
	square—A square outline.
	circle—A circle outline.
	value="number"—Sets the value of the current list item.

Content:	Zero or more block elements, to include the following:
	p | dl | div | center | noscript | noframes | blockquote | form | isindex | hr | table | fieldset | address
	Heading elements (h1 | h2 | h3 | h4 | h5 | h6)
	List elements (ul | ol | dir | menu)
	Preformatted elements (pre)

	Zero or more inline elements, to include the following:
	Document text and entities
	Fontstyle elements (tt | i | b | u | s | strike | big | small)
	Phrase elements (em | strong | dfn | code | samp | kbd | var | cite | abbr | acronym)
	Special elements (a | img | applet | object | font | _basefont | br | script | map | a | sub | sup | span | _bdo | iframe)
	Form Control elements (input | select | textarea | label | button)

Notes:	Used in ordered (ol), unordered (ul), directory (dir), and menu (menu) lists.
Browser:	MSIE 1; NNav 1

`<link />`

Usage:	Defines a relationship with another document.
Syntax:	`<link attributes />`

Attributes:

core—See "Common Attributes" section.

i18n—See "Common Attributes" section.

events—See "Intrinsic Events" section.

charset="character-set"—Specifies the character encoding of the linked resource. Values (such as iso-8859-1 or us-ascii) must be strings approved and registered by IANA, The Internet Assigned Numbers Authority.

href="uri"—Specifies the location of the linked resource or anchor.

hreflang="language-code"—Identifies the language of the linked resource. This attribute might only be used in conjunction with the href attribute.

type="content-type"—Specifies the content or media (MIME) type (such as text/xhtml) of the linked resource.

rel="link-type"—Defines the relationship between the document and that specified by the href attribute.

rev="link-type"—Defines the relationship between the resource specified by the href attribute and the current document.

media="media-descriptor"—Identifies the intended destination medium for style information. The default is screen.

target="user-defined | _blank | _self | _parent | _top"—Identifies the frame in which the linked resource will be opened:

user-defined—Document opens in the frame designated by the author-defined name, which is set by the name attribute of the frame. The name must begin with an alphabetic character.

_blank—Document opens in a new, unnamed window.

_self—Document opens in same frame as the originating link.

_parent—Document opens in the immediate frame-set parent of the current frame, or itself if the current frame has no parent.

_top—Document opens in the full, original window, or itself if the frame has no parent.

APP

A

Notes:	Might only be used in the head of a document, but any number of link elements can be used.
	Common uses are linking to external style sheets, scripts, and search engines.
Browser:	MSIE 2; NNav 4

`<map>...</map>`

Usage:	Specifies a client-side imagemap.
Syntax:	`<map attributes>content</map>`
Attributes:	core—See "Common Attributes" section.
	i18n—See "Common Attributes" section.
	events—See "Intrinsic Events" section.
	name="data"—Assigns a name to the imagemap.
Content:	Zero or more block elements, to include the following:

> p | dl | div | center | noscript | noframes | blockquote | form | isindex | hr | table | fieldset | address
>
> Heading elements (h1 | h2 | h3 | h4 | h5 | h6)
>
> List elements (ul | ol | dir | menu)
>
> Preformatted elements (pre)
>
> *or*
>
> One or more area elements

Notes:	Can be associated with img, object, or input elements via each element's usemap attribute.
Browser:	MSIE 1; NNav 2

`<menu>...</menu>`

Usage:	Creates a single-column menu list.
Syntax:	`<menu attributes>content</menu>`
Attributes:	core—See "Common Attributes" section.
	i18n—See "Common Attributes" section.
	events—See "Intrinsic Events" section.
	compact—Tells the browser to attempt to _display the list more compactly.

Content:	One or more `li` elements, which might contain the following:

> List elements (`ul` \| `ol` \| `dir` \| `menu`)
>
> Zero or more inline elements, to include the following:
>
> Document text and entities
>
> Fontstyle elements (`tt` \| `i` \| `b` \| `u` \| `s` \| `strike` \| `big` \| `small`)
>
> Phrase elements (`em` \| `strong` \| `dfn` \| `code` \| `samp` \| `kbd` \| `var` \| `cite` \| `abbr` \| `acronym`)
>
> Special elements (`a` \| `img` \| `applet` \| `object` \| `font` \| `_basefont` \| `br` \| `script` \| `map` \| `a` \| `sub` \| `sup` \| `span` \| `_bdo` \| `iframe`)
>
> Form Control elements (`input` \| `select` \| `textarea` \| `label` \| `button`)

Notes:	Deprecated in favor of unordered lists (`ul`).
Browser:	MSIE 1; NNav 1

`<meta />`

Usage:	Provides information about the document.
Syntax:	`<meta attributes />`
Attributes:	`i18n`—See "Common Attributes" section.
	`http-equiv="name"`—Identifies a name with the meta-information, which might be used by HTTP servers gathering information.
	`name="name"`—Identifies a name with the meta-information.
	`content="data"`—The content of the meta-information.
	`scheme="data"`—Gives user agents more context for interpreting the information in the `content` attribute.
Content:	Empty
Notes:	Each `meta` element specifies a property/value pair. The `name` attribute identifies the property, and the `content` attribute specifies the property's value.
	There can be any number of `meta` elements within the `head` element.
Browser:	MSIE 2; NNav 1.1

APP

A

`<noframes>...</noframes>`

Usage:	Specifies alternative content when frames are not supported.
Syntax:	`<noframes attributes>content</noframes>`
Attributes:	`core`—See "Common Attributes" section.
	`i18n`—See "Common Attributes" section.
	`events`—See "Intrinsic Events" section.
Content:	User agents will treat content as in the body element (excluding `noframes`) if configured to support the `noframe` element.

Otherwise:

Zero or more block elements, to include the following:

> `p | dl | div | center | noscript | noframes | blockquote | form | isindex | hr | table | fieldset | address`
>
> Heading elements (`h1 | h2 | h3 | h4 | h5 | h6`)
>
> List elements (`ul | ol | dir | menu`)
>
> Preformatted elements (`pre`)

Zero or more inline elements, to include the following:

> Document text and entities
>
> Fontstyle elements (`tt | i | b | u | s | strike | big | small`)
>
> Phrase elements (`em | strong | dfn | code | samp | kbd | var | cite | abbr | acronym`)
>
> Special elements (`a | img | applet | object | font | _basefont | br | script | map | a | sub | sup | span | _bdo | iframe`)
>
> Form Control elements (`input | select | textarea | label | button`)

Notes:	The `noframes` element can be used within the `frameset` element.
Browser:	MSIE 3; NNav 2

`<noscript>...</noscript>`

Usage:

Provides alternative content for browsers unable to execute a script.

Syntax:

`<noscript attributes>content</noscript>`

Attributes:

`core`—See "Common Attributes" section.

`i18n`—See "Common Attributes" section.

`events`—See "Intrinsic Events" section.

Content:

Zero or more block elements, to include the following:

`p | dl | div | center | noscript | noframes | blockquote | form | isindex | hr | table | fieldset | address`

Heading elements (`h1 | h2 | h3 | h4 | h5 | h6`)

List elements (`ul | ol | dir | menu`)

Preformatted elements (`pre`)

Zero or more inline elements, to include the following:

Document text and entities

Fontstyle elements (`tt | i | b | u | s | strike | big | small`)

Phrase elements (`em | strong | dfn | code | samp | kbd | var | cite | abbr | acronym`)

Special elements (`a | img | applet | object | font | _basefont | br | script | map | a | sub | sup | span | _bdo | iframe`)

Form Control elements (`input | select | textarea | label | button`)

Notes:

The content of the element should only be rendered if the user agent does not support scripting.

Browser:

MSIE 3; NNav 3

`<object>...</object>`

Usage:

Includes an external object in the document such as an image, a Java applet, or other external application.

Syntax:

`<object attributes>content</object>`

Attributes:

`core`—See "Common Attributes" section.

`i18n`—See "Common Attributes" section.

APP

A

events—See "Intrinsic Events" section.

declare—Indicates the object will be declared only and not instantiated.

classid="uri"—Used to locate an object's implementation.

codebase="uri"—Sets the base URI for the object. If not _specified, the default value is the base URI of the current document.

data="uri"—Identifies the location of the object's data.

type="content-type"—Specifies the content or media (MIME) type (such as application/mpeg) of the object identified by the data attribute.

codetype="content-type"—Identifies the content type (MIME) of the data to be downloaded.

archive="uri"—List URIs (separated by spaces) for archives containing classes and other resources that will be preloaded. This could significantly speed up object performance.

standby="text"—Provides a message to be displayed while the object loads.

height="length"—Sets the display height of the object.

width="length"—Sets the display width of the object.

usemap="uri"—Associates an imagemap as defined by the map element with this object.

name="data"—Assigns a control name to the object for use as part of a form.

tabindex="number"—Defines the tabbing order between elements. This is the order (from lowest first to highest last) in which they receive focus when the user navigates through them using the Tab key.

align="top | middle | bottom | left | right"—Aligns the object with respect to context:

top—Vertically aligns the top of the object with the top of the current text line.

middle—Vertically aligns the center of the object with the current baseline.

bottom—Vertically aligns the bottom of the object with the current baseline.

`left`—Floats object to the left margin.

`right`—Floats object to the right margin.

`border="pixels"`—Sets the width of the border drawn around the object.

`hspace="pixels"`—Sets the amount of space to be inserted to the left and right of the element.

`vspace="pixels"`—Sets the amount of space to be inserted to the top and bottom of the element.

Content:	One or more `param` elements.

Zero or more block elements, to include the following:

> `p | dl | div | center | noscript | noframes | blockquote | form | isindex | hr | table | fieldset | address`
>
> Heading elements (`h1 | h2 | h3 | h4 | h5 | h6`)
>
> List elements (`ul | ol | dir | menu`)
>
> Preformatted elements (`pre`)

Zero or more inline elements, to include the following:

> Document text and entities
>
> Fontstyle elements (`tt | i | b | u | s | strike | big | small`)
>
> Phrase elements (`em | strong | dfn | code | samp | kbd | var | cite | abbr | acronym`)
>
> Special elements (`a | img | applet | object | font | _basefont | br | script | map | a | sub | sup | span | _bdo | iframe`)
>
> Form Control elements (`input | select | textarea | label | button`)

Notes:	Might appear in the `head`, although it will generally not be rendered. In such cases it is wise to limit `object` elements in the `head` to those with content not requiring visual rendering.

The `object` content is meant to be rendered by user agents that do not support the specified type of `object`.

APP

A

object elements can be nested, allowing the author to provide the same object in various forms in a preferred order.

Browser: MSIE 3

`<ol>...</ol>`

Usage: Creates an ordered, or numbered, list.

Syntax: `<ol attributes>content</ol>`

Attributes: core—See "Common Attributes" section.

i18n—See "Common Attributes" section.

events—See "Intrinsic Events" section.

`type="1 | a | a | i | i"`:

1—Arabic numbers.

a—Lowercase alphabet.

a—Uppercase alphabet.

i—Lowercase Roman numerals.

i—Uppercase Roman numerals.

compact—Tells the browser to attempt to display the list more compactly.

`start="number"`—Sets the starting number of the ordered list.

Content: One or more `li` element

Notes: When the `start` attribute is a number and the list type is non-numeric, the `start` value refers to that number in the sequence of non-numeric values.

Nested lists are allowed.

Browser: MSIE 1; NNav 1

`<optgroup>...</optgroup>`

Usage: Used to group `option` elements within a `select` element.

Syntax: `<optgroup attributes>content</optgroup>`

Attributes: core—See "Common Attributes" section.

i18n—See "Common Attributes" section.

events—See "Intrinsic Events" section.

disabled—Disables these controls for user input.

`label="text"`—Labels the option group.

Content:	One or more `option` elements.
Notes:	All `optgroup` elements must be specified in the `select` element and cannot be nested.
Browser:	None at this time.

`<option>...</option>`

Usage:	Specifies choices in a `select` element.
Syntax:	`<option attributes>content</option>`
Attributes:	`core`—See "Common Attributes" section.
	`i18n`—See "Common Attributes" section.
	`events`—See "Intrinsic Events" section.
	`selected`—Sets the option as being preselected.
	`disabled`—Disables these controls for user input.
	`label="text"`—Provides a shorter label for the option than that specified in its content.
	`value="data"`—Sets the initial value of the control.
Content:	Document text.
Notes:	If the `label` attribute is not set, user agents will use the contents of the element as the option.
	`option` elements might be grouped in an `optgroup` element.
Browser:	MSIE 1; NNav 1

`<p>...</p>`

Usage:	Defines a paragraph.
Syntax:	`<p attributes>content</p>`
Attributes:	`core`—See "Common Attributes" section.
	`i18n`—See "Common Attributes" section.
	`events`—See "Intrinsic Events" section.
	`align="left	center	right	justify"`—Horizontal alignment with respect to context. The default depends on the directionality of the text. For left-to-right it is `left`, and for right-to-left it is `right`:
	`left`—Text aligned left.
	`center`—Text centered.
	`right`—Text aligned right.
	`justify`—Text aligned flush with left and right margins.

APP

A

Content:	Zero or more inline elements, to include the following:

        Document text and entities

        Fontstyle elements (tt | i | b | u | s | strike | big | small)

        Phrase elements (em | strong | dfn | code | samp | kbd | var | cite | abbr | acronym)

        Special elements (a | img | applet | object | font | _basefont | br | script | map | a | sub | sup | span | _bdo | iframe)

        Form Control elements (input | select | textarea | label | button)

Notes:	Cannot contain block-level elements.
Browser:	MSIE 1; NNav 1

`<param />`

Usage:	Specifies a set of values that might be required by an object at runtime.
Syntax:	`<param attributes />`
Attributes:	`id="id"`—A unique identification of the element.

`name="data"`—Defines the name of a runtime parameter required by an object (such as `width`).

`value="data"`—Sets the value required by the runtime parameter previously identified and named.

`valuetype="data | ref | object"`—Identifies the type of runtime parameter being used in the `value` attribute:

`data`—Indicates the `value` will be passed to the `object` implementation as a string.

`ref`—Indicates the `value` is a reference to a URI where runtime values are stored.

`object`—Indicates that the `value` identifies an `object` in the same document. The identifier must be the value of the `id` attribute set for the declared `object`.

`type="content-type"`—Specifies the content or media (MIME) type (such as `application/mpeg`) of the object when the `valuetype` attribute is set to `ref` (but not `date` or `object`).

Content:	Empty

Notes:	Multiple `param` elements are allowed in either the `object` or `applet` elements but must immediately follow the opening tag.
Browser:	MSIE 3; NNav 2

`<pre>...</pre>`

Usage:	Displays preformatted text, which normally includes extra whitespace and line breaks.
Syntax:	`<pre attributes>content</pre>`
Attributes:	`core`—See "Common Attributes" section.
	`i18n`—See "Common Attributes" section.
	`events`—See "Intrinsic Events" section.
	`width="number"`—Identifies the desired width of the preformatted content block.
Content:	Zero or more inline elements, to include the following:

> Document text and entities
>
> Fontstyle elements (`tt` \| `i` \| `b` \| `u` \| `s` \| `strike`)
>
> Phrase elements (`em` \| `strong` \| `dfn` \| `code` \| `samp` \| `kbd` \| `var` \| `cite` \| `abbr` \| `acronym`)
>
> Special elements (`a` \| `br` \| `script` \| `map` \| `a` \| `span` \| `bdo` \| `iframe`)
>
> Form Control elements (`input` \| `select` \| `textarea` \| `label` \| `button`)

Notes:	The use of tabs in preformatted text is strongly discouraged because of the possibility of misaligned content.
Browser:	MSIE 1; NNav 1

`<q>...</q>`

Usage:	Designates text as a short quotation.
Syntax:	`<q attributes>content</q>`
Attributes:	`core`—See "Common Attributes" section.
	`i18n`—See "Common Attributes" section.
	`events`—See "Intrinsic Events" section.
	`cite="uri"`—The URI designating the source document or message.

APP

A

Content:	Zero or more inline elements, to include the following:
	Document text and entities
	Fontstyle elements (`tt` | `i` | `b` | `u` | `s` | `strike` | `big` | `small`)
	Phrase elements (`em` | `strong` | `dfn` | `code` | `samp` | `kbd` | `var` | `cite` | `abbr` | `acronym`)
	Special elements (`a` | `img` | `applet` | `object` | `font` | `_basefont` | `br` | `script` | `map` | `a` | `sub` | `sup` | `span` | `_bdo` | `iframe`)
	Form Control elements (`input` | `select` | `textarea` | `label` | `button`)
Notes:	When compared with the `blockquote` element, the `q` element is used for shorter quotations not normally requiring a line break and is treated as inline content.
	The browser should automatically insert quotation marks around the content of a `q` element.
Browser:	MSIE 4

`<s>...</s>`

Usage:	Displays text as strikethrough.
Syntax:	`<s attributes>content</s>`
Attributes:	`core`—See "Common Attributes" section.
	`i18n`—See "Common Attributes" section.
	`events`—See "Intrinsic Events" section.
Content:	Zero or more inline elements, to include the following:
	Document text and entities
	Fontstyle elements (`tt` | `i` | `b` | `u` | `s` | `strike` | `big` | `small`)
	Phrase elements (`em` | `strong` | `dfn` | `code` | `samp` | `kbd` | `var` | `cite` | `abbr` | `acronym`)
	Special elements (`a` | `img` | `applet` | `object` | `font` | `_basefont` | `br` | `script` | `map` | `a` | `sub` | `sup` | `span` | `_bdo` | `iframe`)
	Form Control elements (`input` | `select` | `textarea` | `label` | `button`)

Notes: Although not deprecated, the W3C recommends using style sheets in place of this element.

Browser: MSIE 1; NNav 3

`<samp>...</samp>`

Usage: Identifies and displays sample output from a computer program, script, and so on.

Syntax: `<samp attributes>content</samp>`

Start/End Tag: Required/Required

Attributes: `core`—See "Common Attributes" section.

`i18n`—See "Common Attributes" section.

`events`—See "Intrinsic Events" section.

Content: Zero or more inline elements, to include the following:

Document text and entities

Fontstyle elements (`tt | i | b | u | s | strike | big | small`)

Phrase elements (`em | strong | dfn | code | samp | kbd | var | cite | abbr | acronym`)

Special elements (`a | img | applet | object | font | _basefont | br | script | map | a | sub | sup | span | _bdo | iframe`)

Form Control elements (`input | select | textarea | label | button`)

Notes: Usually displayed with monospaced font.

Browser: MSIE 1; NNav 1

APP
A

`<script>...</script>`

Usage: Inserts a script into the document.

Syntax: `<script attributes>content</script>`

Attributes: `charset="character-set"`—Specifies the character encoding of the linked resource. Values (such as `iso-8859-1` or `us-ascii`) must be strings approved and registered by IANA, The Internet Assigned Numbers Authority.

`type="content-type"`—Specifies the content or media (MIME) type (such as `text/javascript`) of the script language.

language="data"—Specifies the scripting language through a predefined name.

src="uri"—Identifies the location of an external script.

defer—Indicates to the user agent that no document content will be output by the script and it might continue rendering the page.

Content:
Script expression

Notes:
Might appear any number of times in the head or body of the document.

If the src attribute is present, the user agent loads an external script. Otherwise, the content of the element is treated as the script.

Browser:
MSIE 3; NNav 2

<select>...</select>

Usage:
Creates a menu whose choices are represented by option _elements, either separately or grouped into optgroup elements.

Syntax:
<select attributes>content</select>

Attributes:
core—See "Common Attributes" section.

i18n—See "Common Attributes" section.

events—See "Intrinsic Events" section.

name="data"—Assigns a name to the control.

size="number"—If represented by a scrolling list box, this sets the number of choices to be displayed at one time.

multiple—Allows multiple selections.

disabled—Disables these controls for user input.

tabindex="number"—Defines the tabbing order between elements. This is the order (from lowest first to highest last) in which they receive focus when the user navigates through them using the Tab key.

onfocus="script"—Triggered when the element receives focus by either a pointing device (such as a mouse) or tabbed navigation.

onblur="script"—Triggered when the element loses focus by either a pointing device (such as a mouse) or tabbed navigation.

onchange="script"—The event that occurs when a
control loses the input focus and its value has been
modified since gaining focus.

Content:	One or more optgroup or option elements.
Notes:	Must contain at least one option or optgroup element.
	All optgroup elements must be specified in the select element and cannot be nested.
Browser:	MSIE 1; NNav 1

`<small>...</small>`

Usage:	Displays reduced-size or smaller text.
Syntax:	`<small attributes>content</small>`
Attributes:	core—See "Common Attributes" section.
	i18n—See "Common Attributes" section.
	events—See "Intrinsic Events" section.
Content:	Zero or more inline elements, to include the following:

> Document text and entities
>
> Fontstyle elements (tt | i | b | u | s | strike | big | small)
>
> Phrase elements (em | strong | dfn | code | samp | kbd | var | cite | abbr | acronym)
>
> Special elements (a | img | applet | object | font | _basefont | br | script | map | a | sub | sup | span | _bdo | iframe)
>
> Form Control elements (input | select | textarea | label | button)

Notes:	Although not deprecated, the W3C recommends using style sheets in place of this element.
Browser:	MSIE 3; NNav 1.1

`<span>...</span>`

Usage:	Creates author-defined inline structure to the document.
Syntax:	`<span attributes>content</span>`
Attributes:	core—See "Common Attributes" section.
	i18n—See "Common Attributes" section.
	events—See "Intrinsic Events" section.

APP

A

Content:	Zero or more inline elements, to include the following:
	Document text and entities
	Fontstyle elements (tt | i | b | u | s | strike | big | small)
	Phrase elements (em | strong | dfn | code | samp | kbd | var | cite | abbr | acronym)
	Special elements (a | img | applet | object | font | _basefont | br | script | map | a | sub | sup | span | _bdo | iframe)
	Form Control elements (input | select | textarea | label | button)
Notes:	Used in conjunction with style sheets, this is a powerful device for adding custom inline structure.
Browser:	MSIE 3; NNav 4

`<strike>...</strike>`

Usage:	Text displayed as strikethrough.
Syntax:	`<strike attributes>content</strike>`
Attributes:	core—See "Common Attributes" section.
	i18n—See "Common Attributes" section.
	events—See "Intrinsic Events" section.
Content:	Zero or more inline elements, to include the following:
	Document text and entities
	Fontstyle elements (tt | i | b | u | s | strike | big | small)
	Phrase elements (em | strong | dfn | code | samp | kbd | var | cite | abbr | acronym)
	Special elements (a | img | applet | object | font | _basefont | br | script | map | a | sub | sup | span | _bdo | iframe)
	Form Control elements (input | select | textarea | label | button)
Notes:	Deprecated in favor of style sheets.
Browser:	MSIE 1; NNav 1.1

`<strong>...</strong>`

Usage:	Displays text with a stronger emphasis in relation to normal text than that of the `em` element.
Syntax:	`<strong attributes>content</strong>`
Attributes:	`core`—See "Common Attributes" section.
	`i18n`—See "Common Attributes" section.
	`events`—See "Intrinsic Events" section.
Content:	Zero or more inline elements, to include the following:

> Document text and entities
>
> Fontstyle elements (`tt | i | b | u | s | strike | big | small`)
>
> Phrase elements (`em | strong | dfn | code | samp | kbd | var | cite | abbr | acronym`)
>
> Special elements (`a | img | applet | object | font | _basefont | br | script | map | a | sub | sup | span | _bdo | iframe`)
>
> Form Control elements (`input | select | textarea | label | button`)

Notes:	Usually rendered in boldface font.
Browser:	MSIE 1; NNav 1

`<style>...</style>`

Usage:	Creates stylesheet rules for use in the document.
Syntax:	`<style attributes>content</style>`
Attributes:	`i18n`—See "Common Attributes" section.
	`type="content-type"`—Specifies the content or media (MIME) type (such as `text/css`) of the style language.
	`media="media-descriptor"`—Identifies the intended medium (such as `screen`) of the style information.
	`title="text"`—Offers advisory information about the element.
Content:	Stylesheet rules
Notes:	Any number of `style` elements might be present, but they must be in the `head` element only.
	Browsers that do not support the element should not render its contents. Style sheet rules may be enclosed in comments to hide styles from older browsers.

APP

A

Browser:	MSIE 3; NNav 4

`<sub>...</sub>`

Usage:	Displays text as subscript (lower in vertical alignment) inrelation to surrounding text.
Syntax:	`<sub attributes>content</sub>`
Attributes:	`core`—See "Common Attributes" section.
	`i18n`—See "Common Attributes" section.
	`events`—See "Intrinsic Events" section.
Content:	Zero or more inline elements, to include the following:

> Document text and entities
>
> Fontstyle elements (`tt | i | b | u | s | strike | big | small`)
>
> Phrase elements (`em | strong | dfn | code | samp | kbd | var | cite | abbr | acronym`)
>
> Special elements (`a | img | applet | object | font | _basefont | br | script | map | a | sub | sup | span | _bdo | iframe`)
>
> Form Control elements (`input | select | textarea | label | button`)

Browser:	MSIE 3; NNav 1.1

`<sup>...</sup>`

Usage:	Displays text as superscript (higher in vertical alignment) in relation to surrounding text.
Syntax:	`<sup attributes>content</sup>`
Attributes:	`core`—See "Common Attributes" section.
	`i18n`—See "Common Attributes" section.
	`events`—See "Intrinsic Events" section.
Content:	Zero or more inline elements, to include the following:

> Document text and entities
>
> Fontstyle elements (`tt | i | b | u | s | strike | big | small`)
>
> Phrase elements (`em | strong | dfn | code | samp | kbd | var | cite | abbr | acronym`)

Special elements (a | img | applet | object | font | _basefont | br | script | map | a | sub | sup | span | _bdo | iframe)

Form Control elements (input | select | textarea | label | button)

Browser:	MSIE 3; NNav 1.1

`<table>...</table>`

Usage:	Creates a table.
Syntax:	`<table attributes>content</table>`
Attributes:	core—See "Common Attributes" section.

i18n—See "Common Attributes" section.

events—See "Intrinsic Events" section.

summary="text"—Text explanation of table structure and purpose for nonvisual user agents.

width="length"—Sets width of entire table.

border="pixels"—Sets the width of a border drawn around the table.

frame="void | above | below | hsides | lhs | rhs | vsides | box | border"—Specifies which borders around the table are visible:

void—No sides visible.

above—Top side only.

below—Bottom side only.

hsides—Top and bottom only.

lhs—Left side only.

rhs—Right side only.

vsides—Left and right sides only.

box—Top, bottom, left, and right sides.

border—Top, bottom, left, and right sides.

rules="none | groups | rows | cols | all"—Specifies which interior lines of the table are visible:

none—No rules visible.

groups—Rules appear between row groups and column groups only.

rows—Rules between rows only.

cols—Rules between columns only.

APP

A

all—Rules visible between rows and columns.

`cellspacing="length"`—Determines the spacing between cells.

`cellpadding="length"`—Determines the space between cell content and its borders.

`align="left | center | right"`—Aligns the `table` with respect to the page. Left-to-right is the default inherited directionality, but this can be overridden using the `dir` attribute:

`left`—Table aligned left.

`center`—Table centered.

`right`—Table aligned right.

`bgcolor="color"`—Sets the background color for cells in the table. Colors identified by standard RGB in hexadecimal format (`#rrggbb`) or by predefined color name.

Content:

Zero or one `caption` element

Zero or more `col` or `colgroup` elements

Zero or one `thead` element

Zero or one `tfoot` element

One or more `tbody` or `tr` elements

Notes:

The `table` element has no content by itself but relies on other elements to specify content and other formatting attributes.

Browser:

MSIE 2; NNav 1.1

`<tbody>...</tbody>`

Usage:

Groups table rows into a table body.

Syntax:

`<tbody attributes>content</tbody>`

Attributes:

`core`—See "Common Attributes" section.

`i18n`—See "Common Attributes" section.

`events`—See "Intrinsic Events" section.

`align="left | center | right | justify | char"`—Horizontally aligns the contents of cells:

`left`—Data and text aligned left. This is the default for table data.

`center`—Data and text centered. This is the default for table headers.

`right`—Data and text aligned right.

`justify`—Data and text aligned flush with left and right _margins.

`char`—Aligns text around a specific character.

`char="character"`—Sets a character on which the column aligns (such as `":"`). The default value is the decimal point of the current language.

`charoff="length"`—Offset to the first alignment character _on a line. Specified in number of pixels or a percentage of available length.

`valign="top | middle | bottom | baseline"`— Vertically aligns the contents of a cell:

`top`—Cell data flush with top of cell.

`middle`—Cell data centered in cell.

`bottom`—Cell data flush with bottom of cell.

`baseline`—Aligns all cells in a row with this attribute set. Textual data aligned along a common baseline.

Content:	One or more `tr` elements.
Notes:	Must contain at least one table row.
	The `tfoot` and `thead` elements should appear before the `tbody` element.
Browser:	MSIE 4

`<td>...</td>`

Usage:	Specifies a table cell's data or contents.
Syntax:	`<td attributes>content</td>`
Attributes:	`core`—See "Common Attributes" section.

`i18n`—See "Common Attributes" section.

`events`—See "Intrinsic Events" section.

`abbr="text"`—An abbreviated form of the cell's content.

`axis="data"`—Organizes cells into conceptual categories.

`headers="idrefs"`—Associates the content of a cell with a previously identified header.

`scope="row | col | rowgroup | colgroup"`— Defines the set of data cells for which the header provides header information:

APP

A

row—Header information provided for the rest of the row.

col—Header information provided for the rest of the column.

rowgroup—Header information provided for the rest of the row group (as defined by a thead, tbody, or tfoot element) that contains it.

colgroup—Header information provided for the rest of the column group (as defined by a col or colgroup element) that contains it.

rowspan="number"—Sets the number of rows spanned by the current cell. The default is 1.

colspan="number"—Sets the number of columns spanned by the current cell. The default is 1.

align="left | center | right | justify | char"—Horizontally aligns the contents of cells:

left—Data and text aligned left. This is the default for table data.

center—Data and text centered. This is the default for table headers.

right—Data and text aligned right.

justify—Data and text aligned flush with left and right margins.

char—Aligns text around a specific character.

char="character"—Sets a character on which the column aligns (such as ":"). The default value is the decimal point of the current language.

charoff="length"—Offset to the first alignment character on a line. Specified in number of pixels or a percentage of available length.

valign="top | middle | bottom | baseline"—Vertically aligns the contents of a cell:

top—Cell data flush with top of cell.

middle—Cell data centered in cell.

bottom—Cell data flush with bottom of cell.

baseline—Aligns all cells in a row with this attribute set. Textual data aligned along a common baseline.

nowrap—Disables automatic text-wrapping for the cell.

`bgcolor="color"`—Sets the background color for cell. Colors identified by standard RGB in hexadecimal format (`#rrggbb`) or by predefined color name.

`width="pixels"`—Recommended cell width.

`height="pixels"`—Recommended cell height.

Content:

Zero or more block elements, to include the following:

p | dl | div | center | noscript | noframes | blockquote | form | isindex | hr | table | fieldset | address

Heading elements (h1 | h2 | h3 | h4 | h5 | h6)

List elements (ul | ol | dir | menu)

Preformatted elements (pre)

Zero or more inline elements, to include the following:

Document text and entities

Fontstyle elements (tt | i | b | u | s | strike | big | small)

Phrase elements (em | strong | dfn | code | samp | kbd | var | cite | abbr | acronym)

Special elements (a | img | applet | object | font | _basefont | br | script | map | a | sub | sup | span | _bdo | iframe)

Form Control elements (input | select | textarea | label | button)

Notes:

Cells defined by `td` might be empty.

Browser:

MSIE 2; NNav 1.1

`<textarea>...</textarea>`

Usage:

Creates an area for user input with multiple lines.

Syntax:

`<textarea attributes>content</textarea>`

Attributes:

`core`—See "Common Attributes" section.

`i18n`—See "Common Attributes" section.

`events`—See "Intrinsic Events" section.

`name="data"`—Assigns a name to the control.

`rows="number"`—Sets the number of visible rows or text lines.

cols="number"—Sets the number of visible columns measured in average character width.

disabled—Disables this control for user input.

readonly—Prohibits the user from making changes to the control.

tabindex="number"—Defines the tabbing order between _elements. This is the order (from lowest first to highest last) in which they receive focus when the user navigates through them using the Tab key.

accesskey="character"—Assigns an access key (or shortcut key) to the element. When the key is pressed, the element receives focus and is activated.

onfocus="script"—Triggered when the element receives focus by either a pointing device (such as a mouse) or tabbed navigation.

onblur="script"—Triggered when the element loses focus by either a pointing device (such as a mouse) or tabbed navigation.

onselect="script"—The event that occurs when text is selected in a text field.

onchange="script"—The event that occurs when a control loses the input focus and its value has been modified since gaining focus.

Content:	Document text.
Notes:	The content of the element serves as the initial value of the control and is displayed by the user agent.
Browser:	MSIE 1; NNav 1

<tfoot>...</tfoot>

Usage:	Groups a table row or rows into a table footer.
Syntax:	<tfoot attributes>content</tfoot>
Attributes:	core—See "Common Attributes" section.
	i18n—See "Common Attributes" section.
	events—See "Intrinsic Events" section.
	align="left | center | right | justify | char"—Horizontally aligns the contents of cells:
	left—Data and text aligned left. This is the default for table data.

`center`—Data and text centered. This is the default for table headers.

`right`—Data and text aligned right.

`justify`—Data and text aligned flush with left and right margins.

`char`—Aligns text around a specific character.

`char="character"`—Sets a character on which the column aligns (such as `":"`). The default value is the decimal point of the current language.

`charoff="length"`—Offset to the first alignment character on a line. Specified in number of pixels or a percentage of available length.

`valign="top | middle | bottom | baseline"`—Vertically aligns the contents of a cell:

`top`—Cell data flush with top of cell.

`middle`—Cell data centered in cell.

`bottom`—Cell data flush with bottom of cell.

`baseline`—Aligns all cells in a row with this attribute set. Textual data aligned along a common baseline.

Content:	One or more `tr` elements.
Notes:	The table footer contains table data cells that describe the content of the columns above it.
	Must contain at least one `tr`.
Browser:	MSIE 3

`<th>...</th>`

Usage:	Specifies a table cell as being an information, or header, cell.
Syntax:	`<th attributes>content</th>`
Attributes:	`core`—See "Common Attributes" section.
	`i18n`—See "Common Attributes" section.
	`events`—See "Intrinsic Events" section.
	`abbr="text"`—An abbreviated form of the cell's content.
	`axis="data"`—Organizes cells into conceptual categories.
	`headers="idrefs"`—Associates the content of a cell with a previously identified header.

APP

A

`scope="row | col | rowgroup | colgroup"`—Defines the set of data cells for which the header provides header information:

`row`—Header information provided for the rest of the row.

`col`—Header information provided for the rest of the column.

`rowgroup`—Header information provided for the rest of the row group (as defined by a `thead`, `tbody`, or `tfoot` element) that contains it.

`colgroup`—Header information provided for the rest of the column group (as defined by a `col` or `colgroup` element) that contains it.

`rowspan="number"`—Sets the number of rows spanned by the current cell. The default is 1.

`colspan="number"`—Sets the number of columns spanned by the current cell. The default is 1.

`align="left | center | right | justify | char"`—Horizontally aligns the contents of cells:

`left`—Data and text aligned left. This is the default for table data.

`center`—Data and text centered. This is the default for table headers.

`right`—Data and text aligned right.

`justify`—Data and text aligned flush with left and right margins.

`char`—Aligns text around a specific character.

`char="character"`—Sets a character on which the column aligns (such as `":"`). The default value is the decimal point of the current language.

`charoff="length"`—Offset to the first alignment character on a line. Specified in number of pixels or a percentage of available length.

`valign="top | middle | bottom | baseline"`—Vertically aligns the contents of a cell:

`top`—Cell data flush with top of cell.

`middle`—Cell data centered in cell.

`bottom`—Cell data flush with bottom of cell.

`baseline`—Aligns all cells in a row with this attribute set. Textual data aligned along a common baseline.

`nowrap`—Disables automatic text-wrapping for the cell.

`bgcolor="color"`—Sets the background color for the cell. Colors identified by standard RGB in hexadecimal format (#rrggbb) or by predefined color name.

`width="pixels"`—Recommended cell width.

`height="pixels"`—Recommended cell height.

Content: Zero or more block elements, to include the following:

> p | dl | div | center | noscript | noframes | blockquote | form | isindex | hr | table | fieldset | address

> Heading elements (h1 | h2 | h3 | h4 | h5 | h6)

> List elements (ul | ol | dir | menu)

> Preformatted elements (pre)

Zero or more inline elements, to include the following:

> Document text and entities

> Fontstyle elements (tt | i | b | u | s | strike | big | small)

> Phrase elements (em | strong | dfn | code | samp | kbd | var | cite | abbr | acronym)

> Special elements (a | img | applet | object | font | _basefont | br | script | map | a | sub | sup | span | _bdo | iframe)

> Form Control elements (input | select | textarea | label | button)

Notes: Header cell usually rendered in boldface font.

Browser: MSIE 2; NNav 1.1

`<thead>...</thead>`

Usage: Groups a table row or rows into a table header.

Syntax:

`<thead attributes>content`

or

`<thead attributes>content</thead>`

Attributes:	core—See "Common Attributes" section.
	i18n—See "Common Attributes" section.
	events—See "Intrinsic Events" section.
	align="left | center | right | justify | char"—Horizontally aligns the contents of cells:
	left—Data and text aligned left. This is the default for table data.
	center—Data and text centered. This is the default for table headers.
	right—Data and text aligned right.
	justify—Data and text aligned flush with left and right _margins.
	char—Aligns text around a specific character.
	char="character"—Sets a character on which the column aligns (such as ":"). The default value is the decimal point of the current language.
	charoff="length"—Offset to the first alignment character on a line. Specified in number of pixels or a percentage of available length.
	valign="top | middle | bottom | baseline"—Vertically aligns the contents of a cell:
	top—Cell data flush with top of cell.
	middle—Cell data centered in cell.
	bottom—Cell data flush with bottom of cell.
	baseline—Aligns all cells in a row with this attribute set. Textual data aligned along a common baseline.
Content:	One or more tr elements.
Notes:	The table header contains table data cells that describe the content of the columns below it.
	Must contain at least one tr.
Browser:	MSIE 3

`<title>...</title>`

Usage:	Identifies the contents of the document.
Syntax:	`<title attributes>content</title>`
Attributes:	i18n—See "Common Attributes" section.
Content:	Document text

Notes:	The `title` element is required and is located within the `head` element. The title is displayed in the browser window title bar.
Browser:	MSIE 1; NNav 1

`<tr>...</tr>`

Usage:	Defines a row of table cells.
Syntax:	`<tr attributes>content</tr>`
Attributes:	`core`—See "Common Attributes" section.

`i18n`—See "Common Attributes" section.

`events`—See "Intrinsic Events" section.

`align="left | center | right | justify | char"`—Horizontally aligns the contents of cells:

`left`—Data and text aligned left. This is the default for table data.

`center`—Data and text centered. This is the default for table headers.

`right`—Data and text aligned right.

`justify`—Data and text aligned flush with left and right margins.

`char`—Aligns text around a specific character.

`char="character"`—Sets a character on which the column aligns (such as `":"`). The default value is the decimal point of the current language.

`charoff="length"`—Offset to the first alignment character on a line. Specified in number of pixels or a percentage of available length.

`valign="top | middle | bottom | baseline"`—Vertically aligns the contents of a cell:

`top`—Cell data flush with top of cell.

`middle`—Cell data centered in cell.

`bottom`—Cell data flush with bottom of cell.

`baseline`—Aligns all cells in a row with this attribute set. Textual data aligned along a common baseline.

`bgcolor="color"`—Sets the background color for a table row. Colors identified by standard RGB in hexadecimal format (`#rrggbb`) or by predefined color name.

Content:	One or more th or td elements.
Notes:	No table data is supplied by this element; its sole purpose is to define structural rows of table cells.
Browser:	MSIE 2; NNav 1.1

`<tt>...</tt>`

Usage:	Displays text as Teletype or monospaced font.
Syntax:	`<tt attributes>content</tt>`
Attributes:	`core`—See "Common Attributes" section.
	`i18n`—See "Common Attributes" section.
	`events`—See "Intrinsic Events" section.
Content:	Zero or more inline elements, to include the following:

> Document text and entities
>
> Fontstyle elements (`tt` | `i` | `b` | `u` | `s` | `strike` | `big` | `small`)
>
> Phrase elements (`em` | `strong` | `dfn` | `code` | `samp` | `kbd` | `var` | `cite` | `abbr` | `acronym`)
>
> Special elements (`a` | `img` | `applet` | `object` | `font` | `_basefont` | `br` | `script` | `map` | `a` | `sub` | `sup` | `span` | `_bdo` | `iframe`)
>
> Form Control elements (`input` | `select` | `textarea` | `label` | `button`)

Notes:	Although not deprecated, the W3C recommends using style sheets in place of this element.
Browser:	MSIE 1; NNav 1

`<u>...</u>`

Usage:	Displays underlined text.
Syntax:	`<u attributes>content</u>`
Attributes:	`core`—See "Common Attributes" section.
	`i18n`—See "Common Attributes" section.
	`events`—See "Intrinsic Events" section.
Content:	Zero or more inline elements, to include the following:

> Document text and entities
>
> Fontstyle elements (`tt` | `i` | `b` | `u` | `s` | `strike` | `big` | `small`)

Phrase elements (`em` | `strong` | `dfn` | `code` | `samp` | `kbd` | `var` | `cite` | `abbr` | `acronym`)

Special elements (`a` | `img` | `applet` | `object` | `font` | `_basefont` | `br` | `script` | `map` | `a` | `sub` | `sup` | `span` | `_bdo` | `iframe`)

Form Control elements (`input` | `select` | `textarea` | `label` | `button`)

Notes:	Deprecated in favor of style sheets.
Browser:	MSIE 1; NNav 3

`<ul>...</ul>`

Usage:	Creates an unordered (unnumbered) list.
Syntax:	`<ul attributes>content</ul>`
Attributes:	`core`—See "Common Attributes" section.
	`i18n`—See "Common Attributes" section.
	`events`—See "Intrinsic Events" section.
	`type="disc	square	circle"`—Sets the style of bullets in an unordered list:
	`disc`—A solid circle.
	`square`—A square outline.
	`circle`—A circle outline.
	`compact`—Tells the browser to attempt to _display the list more compactly.
Notes:	Nested lists are allowed.
Content:	One or more `li` elements
Browser:	MSIE 1; NNav 1

APP

A

`<var>...</var>`

Usage:	Identifies and displays a variable or program argument.
Syntax:	`<var attributes>content</var>`
Attributes:	`core`—See "Common Attributes" section.
	`i18n`—See "Common Attributes" section.
	`events`—See "Intrinsic Events" section.

Content:	Zero or more inline elements, to include the following:
	Document text and entities
	Fontstyle elements (tt | i | b | u | s | strike | big | small)
	Phrase elements (em | strong | dfn | code | samp | kbd | var | cite | abbr | acronym)
	Special elements (a | img | applet | object | font | _basefont | br | script | map | a | sub | sup | span | _bdo | iframe)
	Form Control elements (input | select | textarea | label | button)
Notes:	Usually displayed in italics.
Browser:	MSIE 1; NNav 1

COMMON ATTRIBUTES

Four attributes are abbreviated as core in the preceding sections:

- id="id"—A global identifier.
- class="data"—A list of classes separated by spaces.
- style="style"—Style rules information.
- title="text"—Provides more information for a specific element, as opposed to the title element, which entitles the entire Web page.

Two attributes for internationalization (i18n) are abbreviated as i18n:

- lang="language-code"—Identifies the human (not computer) language of the text content or an element's attribute values.
- dir="ltr | rtl"—Specifies the text direction (left-to-right, right-to-left) of element content, overriding inherent directionality.

INTRINSIC EVENTS

The following intrinsic events are abbreviated events:

Support for intrinsic events in Netscape Navigator is limited to the 1.0 and above versions, and is only applicable to form elements, links, and images.

- onclick="script"—A pointing device (such as a mouse) was single-clicked.
- ondblclick="script"—A pointing device (such as a mouse) was double-clicked.
- onmousedown="script"—A mouse button was clicked and held down.

- `onmouseup="script"`—A mouse button that was clicked and held down was released.
- `onmouseover="script"`—A mouse moved the cursor over an object.
- `onmousemove="script"`—A mouse was moved within an object.
- `onmouseout="script"`—A mouse moved the cursor off an object.
- `onkeypress="script"`—A key was pressed and released.
- `onkeydown="script"`—A key was pressed and held down.
- `onkeyup="script"`—A key that was pressed has been released. intrin

DATA TYPES

Table A.1 summarizes and explains the data types used in the information in this appendix.

TABLE A.1 DATA TYPES

Name	Description
character	A single character or character reference from the document character set.
character-set	Specifies the character encoding. Values (such as `iso-8859-1` or `us-ascii`) must be strings approved and registered by IANA, The Internet Assigned Numbers Authority.
color	Colors are identified by standard RGB in hexadecimal format (`#rrggbb`) or by predefined color name (with corresponding hex value) shown here:
	`black = "#000000"`
	`silver = "#c0c0c0"`
	`gray = "#808080"`
	`White = "#ffffff"`
	`maroon = "#800000"`
	`red = "#ff0000"`
	`purple = "#800080"`
	`fuchsia = "#ff00ff"`
	`green = "#008000"`
	`lime = "#00ff00"`
	`olive = "#808000"`
	`yellow = "#ffff00"`
	`navy = "#000080"`
	`blue = "#0000ff"`

APP

A

TABLE A.1   CONTINUED

	`teal = "#008080"`
	`aqua = "#00ffff"`
content-type	Content types, also known as MIME types, specify the nature of the resource (such as "`text/xhtml`" or "`image/gif`").
data	A sequence of characters or character entities from the document character set.
datetime	Legal datetime strings follow the following format:
	`yyyy-mm-ddthh:mm:sstZd`.
	`yyyy` = four-digit year.
	`mm` = two-digit month (`01` = January, and so on).
	`dd` = two-digit day of month (`01` through `31`).
	`t` = beginning of time element. The "`t`" must appear in uppercase.
	`hh` = two digits of hour (`00` through `23`) (am/pm *not* allowed).
	`mm` = two digits of minute (`00` through `59`).
	`ss` = two digits of second (`00` through `59`).
	`tZd` = time zone designator. The time zone designator is one of the following:
	`Z`—indicates UTC (Coordinated Universal Time). The "`Z`" must be uppercase.
	`+hh:mm`—indicates that the time is a local time that is `hh` hours and `mm` minutes ahead of UTC.
	`hh:mm`—indicates that the time is a local time that is `hh` hours and `mm` minutes behind UTC.
	A valid datetime is
	`1998-06-13t19:30:02-05:00`
id	An identifier token that must begin with a letter (`A`ñ`Z` or `a`ñ`z`) and might be followed by any number of letters, digits (`0`ñ`9`), hyphens (`-`), underscores (`_`), colons (`:`), and periods (`.`).
idref	A reference to an ID token defined by other attributes.
idrefs	A space-separated reference list to ID tokens defined by other attributes.

TABLE A.1 CONTINUED

language-code	A language code that identifies a natural language spoken, written, or otherwise used for the communication of information among people. Computer languages are explicitly excluded from language codes. Language codes are identified by a primary code (such as `en`) followed by a hyphen and a two-letter subcode (such as `-us`) that identifies the country if necessary. The complete language code is: `en-us` for the U.S. version of English.
length	A value representing either a number of pixels (such as `100`) or a percentage of available space (such as `%50`).
link-type	A space-separated list of link types:
	`alternate`—Designates substitute versions for the document in which the link occurs. When used together with the `lang` attribute, it implies a translated version of the document. When used together with the `media` attribute, it implies a version designed for a different medium (or media).
	`-appendix`—Refers to a document serving as an appendix in a collection of documents.
	`bookmark`—Refers to a bookmark. A bookmark is a link to a key entry point within an extended document.
	`chapter`—Refers to a document serving as a chapter in a collection of _documents.
	`contents`—Refers to a document serving as a table of contents.
	`copyright`—Refers to a copyright statement for the current document.
	`glossary`—Refers to a document providing a glossary of terms that pertain to the current document.
	`help`—Refers to a document offering help.
	`index`—Refers to a document providing an index for the current document.
	`next`—Refers to the next document in a linear sequence of documents.
	`prev`—Refers to the previous document in an ordered series of documents.
	`section`—Refers to a document serving as a section in a collection of documents.
	`start`—Refers to the first document in a collection of documents.

APP

A

TABLE A.1	CONTINUED
	stylesheet—Refers to an external stylesheet. This is used together with the link type alternate for user-selectable alternate style sheets.
	subsection—Refers to a document serving as a subsection in a collection of documents.
	user-defined—Relationship defined by the content author. If used, the profile attribute of the head element should provide explanatory information.
media-descriptor	A comma-separated list of recognized media descriptors:
	all—Suitable for all devices.
	aural—Intended for speech synthesizers.
	braille—Intended for Braille tactile feedback devices.
	handheld—Intended for handheld devices (small screen, monochrome, bitmapped graphics, limited bandwidth).
	print—Intended for paged, opaque material and for documents viewed onscreen in Print Preview mode.
	projection—Intended for projectors.
	screen—Intended for nonpaged computer screens.
	tty—Intended for media using a fixed-pitch character grid, such as Teletypes, terminals, or portable devices with limited display capabilities.
	tv—Intended for television-type devices (low resolution, color, limited scrollability).
multi-length	A value representing either a number of pixels (such as 100), a percentage of available space (such as %50), or a relative length designated by an integer followed by an asterisk: "i*". The "i" is a proportional modifier of any remaining space that will be divided among relative length elements. For example, if there are 120 pixels remaining and competing relative lengths of 1*, 2*, and 3*, the space would be allocated as 20, 40, and 60 pixels respectively.
name	An identifier token that must begin with a letter (AñZ or añz) and might be _followed by any number of letters, digits (0ñ9), hyphens (-), underscores (_), colons (:), and periods (.).
number	A number composed of at least one digit (0ñ9).
pixels	An integer representing a number of pixels.

TABLE A.1   CONTINUED

script	Script data. This is not evaluated as XHTML markup but passed as data to the script engine. Value is determined by scripting language.
style	Stylesheet rules. This is not evaluated as XHTML markup. Value is _determined by style language.
text	Text that is meant to be read and understood by the user.
URI	A Uniform Resource Identifier, which includes Uniform Resource Locators.

APP

A

CSS2 REFERENCE

In this appendix

STYLE SHEETS PROPERTIES

If you've looked into the details of cascading style sheets-Level 1, much of this appendix will look familiar. However, there are a large number of properties that you won't recognize. CSS22 has taken style sheets to a new level, and this appendix details all the new additions.

Currently, CSS1 is implemented in Netscape Navigator 4+, Opera 3.0+, and Microsoft's Internet Explorer 4+. CSS2 implementation is available to a certain degree in the Internet Explorer 5.0 and Opera 4.0+ browsers, and expected in Netscape's 6.0 browser as it becomes available. CSS2 is a W3C recommendation and can be found at **www.w3.org/TR/REC-CSS2/**.

Note
> Neither Internet Explorer or Netscape have fully implemented CSS in either the first or second level. For a regularly updated, comprehensive look at style sheet properties and browser support, see Eric Meyer's Safe CSS Properties table in **style.webreview.com/**.

The properties in this appendix are grouped into areas according to their function. In many cases, one property affects another and I've tried to present them in a logical order. The property groups include the following:

- Text
- Colors and backgrounds
- Fonts
- Box model
- Visual formatting and positioning
- Generated content and lists
- Tables
- Paged media
- Aural style sheets

Note
> All properties that are new to the CSS2 specification are marked with an asterisk right after the property name.

SELECTORS

Selectors are the tag elements defined at the beginning of a style sheet definition that tell the browser where to apply the style. After the selector, the style definition is included within curly brackets. In this example, BODY is the selector.

```
BODY {color: blue)
```

Several selectors can be grouped together if they are separated with commas.

```
H1, H2, H3 {font-family: san-serif}
```

In place of selectors, you can use the * wildcard. This example applies a font size style to all tags on the page:

```
* {font-size: 14pt}
```

Another wildcard character is the > sign. This tells the browser to search for child selectors within a certain parent. This example applies the style only to LI elements with OL lists:

```
OL > LI {list-style-type: decimal}
```

Using class selectors, you can apply different styles to the same tag. A period and a name follow a general selector and the style is applied to the tag whose class attribute matches the class name. The following example applies the style to any H2 tags that have the class attribute equal to "myBlue".

```
H2.myBlue {background-color: blue}
<H2 class="myBlue">This header has a blue background.</H2>
```

Selectors also can be identified by the id attribute using the # character. The following example matches the style to any tags whose ID attribute is "duckie".

```
#duckie {border-color: yellow}
```

PSEUDO CLASSES

To access the control of elements that aren't referred to by normal tags, CSS2 defines several pseudo classes. An example is the first line of a paragraph. HTML and XHTML have no way of identifying this element, so a pseudo class called :first-line is used. All pseudo classes have colons in front of them. They are located after a selector like the following:

```
P:first-line {color: red}
```

The following are identified pseudo classes in CSS2:

- :first-child—This is the first child element of another element.
- :link—These are links that have not yet been visited.
- :visited—These are visited links.
- :hover—This is an element that the cursor is currently over.
- :active—This is the currently activated link element.
- :focus—This is the element that has the focus.
- :lang—This defines the current language.
- :first-line—This is the first formatted line of a paragraph.
- :first-letter—This is the first letter of a paragraph.
- :before—This positions content to come before an element.
- :after—This positions content to come after an element.

APP

B

RULES

Rules are used to access files and documents located outside of the current document. There are five rules defined in CSS2, and all of them begin with the @ character: `@charset`, `@font-face`, `@import`, `@media`, and `@page`.

PROPERTIES

Properties are the main descriptors of the style sheet language. They appear within brackets and include the property name and a value separated by a colon. Some properties can include more than one value. These values are typically separated by a single space.

TEXT

The text properties include aligning properties such as `text-align` and `word-spacing`, as well as style-altering properties such as `text-decoration` and the new `text-shadow` properties.

`text-indent`

Description:	Defines the length of the indent applied to the first line of text in a block.
Values:	Any valid length—Can include negative values. Default is 0.
	Any valid percentage.
	`inherit`—Takes the same value as its parent.
Example:	`P {text-indent: 40px}`

`text-align`

Description:	Defines how an inline box of text is aligned.
Values:	`left`—Aligns text to the left.
	`center`—Aligns text to the center.
	`right`—Aligns text to the right.
	`justify`—Justifies the text.
	Any valid string—Defines a string on which table cells will align.
	`inherit`—Takes the same value as its parent.
Example:	`P {text-align: right}`

`text-decoration`

Description:	Defines decorations added to the text of an element.
Values:	`none`—(default) Applies no text decoration.
	`underline`—Underlines the text.
	`overline`—Puts a line over the text.
	`line-through`—Strikes out the text.

blink—Causes the text to blink.

inherit—Takes the same value as its parent.

Example: `P {text-decoration: underline}`

text-transform

Description: Defines capitalization effects to the text of an element.

Values: none—(default) Applies no capitalization.

capitalize—Capitalizes the first letter of each word.

uppercase—Capitalizes all letters.

lowercase—Converts all letters to lowercase.

inherit—Takes the same value as its parent.

Example: `H3 {text-transform: uppercase}`

text-shadow*

Description: Describes values to create a text shadow effect. Several lists of shadow values can be included and must be separated by commas. Each separate shadow effect value list must include offset values and can include a blur radius and color.

Values: none—(default) Applies no shadow effect.

color—Color of text shadow.

First valid length—Horizontal distance to the right of the text. Negative values are to the left of the text.

Second valid length—Vertical distance below the text. Negative values are above the text.

Third valid length—Text shadow blur radius.

inherit—Takes the same value as its parent.

Example: `H1 {text-shadow: blue 5px 5px 3px, yellow -2px -2px 3px}`

letter-spacing

Description: Defines the space between text characters.

Values: normal—(default) Applies normal text spacing for the used font.

Any valid length—The length of the space between letters.

inherit—Takes the same value as its parent.

Example: `P {letter-spacing: 0.3em}`

`word-spacing`

    Description: Defines the space between words.

    Values: `normal`—(default) Applies normal text spacing for the font being used.

                Any valid length—The length of the space between letters.

                `inherit`—Takes the same value as its parent.

    Example: `P {word-spacing—1.3em}`

`white-space`

    Description: Defines how to handle whitespace in an element.

    Values: `normal`—(default) Collapses whitespace if necessary to fit boxes. This is the same as how HTML handles whitespace.

                `pre`—Treats all whitespace literally as it appears in code.

                `nowrap`—Collapses all whitespace.

                `inherit`—Takes the same value as its parent.

    Example: `P {white-space: pre}`

COLORS AND BACKGROUNDS

Adding colors and backgrounds to elements creates a visually stimulating Web page. Style sheets include many properties that give your page the zing it needs.

`color`

    Description: Defines the text color.

    Values: Any valid color—Colors the text.

                `inherit`—Takes the same value as its parent.

    Example: `P {color: green}`

                `P {color: rgb(0, 255, 0)}`

`background-color`

    Description: Defines the background color of an element.

    Values: Any valid color—Colors the background.

                `transparent`—(default) Makes the element's background transparent.

                `inherit`—Takes the same value as its parent.

    Example: `DIV {color: blue}`

                `DIV {color: rgb(0, 0, 255)}`

CSS2 provides access to all the colors used by a viewer's system. All properties that use color can reference the system colors using the following keywords: `ActiveBorder`, `ActiveCaption`, `AppWorkspace`, `Background`, `ButtonFace`, `ButtonHighlight`, `ButtonShadow`, `ButtonText`, `CaptionText`, `GrayText`, `Highlight`, `HighlightText`, `InactiveBorder`, `InactiveCaption`, `InactiveCaptionText`, `InfoBackground`, `InfoText`, `Menu`, `MenuText`, `Scrollbar`, `ThreeDDarkShadow`, `ThreeDFace`, `ThreeDHighlight`, `ThreeDLightShadow`, `ThreeDShadow`, `Window`, `WindowFrame`, and `WindowText`. For example, the `color` property set to `MenuText` would use the same color as the menu text your system uses.

`background-image`

Description: Defines the background image of an element.

Values: none—(default) Sets no background image.

Any valid URL—URL of the background image.

inherit—Takes the same value as its parent.

Example: `H1 {background-image: url("texture3.gif")}`

`background-repeat`

Description: Defines the direction that the background image is tiled.

Values: repeat—(default) Background image repeats both horizontally and vertically.

repeat-x—Background image repeats only horizontally.

repeat-y—Background image repeats only vertically.

no-repeat—Background image doesn't repeat.

inherit—Takes the same value as its parent.

Example: `BLOCKQUOTE {background-repeat: repeat-x}`

`background-position`

Description: Defines the upper-left corner position of the background image. Single values set the horizontal distance and default the vertical offset to 50%. Several keywords can be combined.

Values: First valid length—Horizontal distance the background image is placed from the left edge. Accepts negative values.

Second valid length—Vertical distance the background image is placed from the top edge. Accepts negative values.

First valid percentage—Percent of the element box the background image is offset from the left edge. Default is 0% or upper-left corner.

Second valid percentage—Percent of the element box the background image is offset from the top edge.

top—Positions the background image along the top edge.

center—Positions the background image in the center of the element box.

bottom—Positions the background image along the bottom edge.

left—Positions the background image along the left edge.

right—Positions the background image along the right edge.

inherit—Takes the same value as its parent.

Example: BLOCKQUOTE {background-position: top center}

background-attachment

Description: Defines whether the background image is fixed to the window or scrolls with the document.

Values: scroll—(default) Background image scrolls along with the window.

fixed—Background image is permanently fixed to its location. Background image repeats only horizontally.

inherit—Takes the same value as its parent.

Example: body {background-attachment: fixed}

background

Description: Shorthand property for defining all background properties at once. If not included, a property is set to its default value.

Values: background-color—Background color value.

background-image—Background image value.

background-repeat—Background repeat value.

background-attachment—Background attachment value.

background-position—Background position value.

inherit—Takes the same value as its parent.

Example:

```
P {background: blue url("texture3.gif") repeat
fixed top right}
```

FONTS

Font control adds style and flair to your Web pages whether you change the family, size, or weight.

font-family

Description:

Defines a font to use for the element's text. It can include several font families separated by commas. The list order defines the priority.

Values:

Font name—Font to use to render the text. Fonts with more than one word need to be in quotes.

Generic font name—Generic font class to use to render the text. Generic fonts include the following: serif, sans-serif, cursive, fantasy, and monospace.

inherit—Takes the same value as its parent.

Example:

```
BODY {font-family: "Times Roman", courier,
serif}
```

font-style

Description: Defines a font style, such as italic or oblique.

Values: normal—(default) Uses the normal font style.

italic—Uses an italic font style.

oblique—Uses an oblique or slanted font style.

inherit—Takes the same value as its parent.

Example: SPAN {font-style: italic}

font-variant

Description: Defines whether a font is rendered using small caps.

Values: normal—(default) Uses the normal font style.

small-caps—Renders the font in small caps.

inherit—Takes the same value as its parent.

Example: H4 {font-variant: small-caps}

APP

B

font-weight

    Description: Defines how thick text appears.

    Values: normal—(default) Uses the normal font thickness.

bold—Uses a bold font weight.

bolder—Uses a bolder font weight.

lighter—Uses a lighter font weight.

100-900—Number indicates the font thickness. 100 is the lightest (same as lighter), 400 is normal, 700 is bold, and 900 is bolder.

inherit—Takes the same value as its parent.

    Example: H1 {font-weight: bolder}

font-stretch*

    Description: Defines the font's width.

    Values: normal—(default) Uses the normal font width.

wider—Increases the width by one over current setting.

narrower—Decreases the width by one over current setting.

ultra-condensed—Defines the tightest width setting.

extra-condensed—Looser than the preceding value.

condensed—Looser than the preceding value.

semi-condensed—Looser than the preceding value.

semi-expanded—Wider than normal.

expanded—Wider than the preceding value.

extra-expanded—Wider than the preceding value.

ultra-expanded—Defines the widest setting.

inherit—Takes the same value as its parent.

    Example: BODY {font-stretch: condensed}

font-size

    Description: Defines the size of the font.

    Values: Absolute size—Uses keywords to express font size. Values include xx-small, small, medium (default), large, x-large, and xx-large.

Relative size—Uses relative keywords to express font size. Values include larger and smaller.

Any valid length—Defines the absolute font size. Negative values are not accepted.

Valid percentage—Defines the percent increase or decrease from the parent font size.

inherit—Takes the same value as its parent.

Example: BODY {font-size: 16pt}

font-size-adjust*

Description: Defines an aspect ratio to maintain when sizing fonts. This enables users to adjust for the text height when resizing.

Values: none—(default) Font's aspect ratio ignored.

Any valid number—Number representing the aspect value for the font.

inherit—Takes the same value as its parent.

Example: P {font-size-adjust: 0.45}

font

Description: Shorthand property for defining all font properties at once. If not included, a property is set to its default value.

Values: font-style—Font style value.

font-variant—Font variant value.

font-weight—Font weight value.

font-size—Font size value.

line-height—Line height value.

font-family—Font family value.

inherit—Takes the same value as its parent.

Example: BODY {font: italic bold 16pt 110% impact Garmond san-serif}

Tip from

molly

The font property can also use system fonts defined by the system. Valid values include caption, icon, menu, message-box, small-caption, and status-bar. For example, a font property set to menu would use the same font properties that the menus on your system use.

BOX MODEL

All elements are enveloped in a box made from the actual content, padding, border, and margins. Learning how to control these properties helps as you lay out your pages.

`margin-top, margin-right, margin-bottom, margin-left`

Description:	Defines the margin width for the designated side.
Values:	Any valid length—Number representing the width of the margin. Default is 0.
	Any valid percentage—Percentage of window to use for the width of the padding.
	inherit—Takes the same value as its parent.
Example:	`P {margin-top: 20px}`

`margin`

Description:	Shorthand property for defining margins for all sides of an element at once. This property can include one to four values. One value sets only all margins to that value. Two sets the top and bottom to the first and the left and right to the second. Three values set the top to the first, left and right to the second, and the bottom to the third.
Values:	`margin-top`—Width of the top margin.
	`margin-right`—Width of the right margin.
	`margin-bottom`—Width of the bottom margin.
	`margin-left`—Width of the left margin.
	inherit—Takes the same value as its parent.
Example:	`BODY {margin: 20px 30px 5px}`

`padding-top, padding-right, padding-bottom, padding-left`

Description:	Defines the padding width for the designated side. Padding separates the text from the border.
Values:	Any valid length—Number representing the width of the padding. Default is 0.
	Any valid percentage—Percentage of window to use for the width of the padding.
	inherit—Takes the same value as its parent.
Example:	`P {padding-top: 20px}`

padding

Description: Shorthand property for defining padding widths for all sides of an element at once. This property can include one to four values. One value sets all padding widths to that value. Two sets the top and bottom to the first and the left and right to the second. Three values set the top to the first, left and right to the second, and the bottom to the third.

Values: padding-top—Width of the top padding.

padding-right—Width of the right padding.

padding-bottom—Width of the bottom padding.

padding-left—Width of the left padding.

inherit—Takes the same value as its parent.

Example: `BODY {padding: 20px 30px 5px}`

border-top-width, border-right-width, border-bottom-width, border-left-width

Description: Defines the border width for the designated side. The border comes between the padding and margin.

Values: thin—Creates a thin weight border.

medium—(default) Creates a medium weight border.

thick—Creates a thick weight border.

inherit—Takes the same value as its parent.

Example: `P {border-top-width: 10px}`

border-width

Description: Shorthand property for defining border widths for all sides of an element at once. This property can include one to four values. One value sets all border widths to that value. Two sets the top and bottom to the first and the left and right to the second. Three values set the top to the first, left and right to the second, and the bottom to the third.

Values: border-top-width—Width of the top border.

border-right-width—Width of the right border.

border-bottom-width—Width of the bottom border.

border-left-width—Width of the left border.

inherit—Takes the same value as its parent.

Example: `BODY {border-width: 20px 30px 5px}`

APP

B

`border-top-color, border-right-color, border-bottom-color, border-left-color`

Description:	Defines the border color for the designated side. The border comes between the padding and margin.
Values:	Any valid color—Specifies the border color.
	`inherit`—Takes the same value as its parent.
Example:	`P {border-top-color: rgb(255, 0, 255)}`

`border-color`

Description:	Shorthand property for defining border colors for all sides of an element at once. This property can include one to four values. One value sets all border colors to that value. Two sets the top and bottom to the first and the left and right to the second. Three values set the top to the first, left and right to the second, and the bottom to the third.
Values:	`border-top-color`—Color of the top border.
	`border-right-color`—Color of the right border.
	`border-bottom-color`—Color of the bottom border.
	`border-left-color`—Color of the left border.
	`transparent`—Makes the borders transparent.
	`inherit`—Takes the same value as its parent.
Example:	`BODY {border-color: blue red pink}`

`border-top-style, border-right-style, border-bottom-style, border-left-style`

Description:	Defines the border style for the designated side. The border comes between the padding and margin.
Values:	`none`—Specifies no border style.
	`hidden`—Also specifies no border style, but acts differently for tables.
	`dotted`—Creates a series of dots.
	`dashed`—Creates a series of dashed lines.
	`solid`—Creates a solid, non-breaking line.
	`double`—Creates two parallel, solid, non-breaking lines.
	`groove`—Creates a 3D carved-style border.
	`ridge`—Creates a 3D raised-style border.
	`inset`—Creates a 3D inset-style border.

`outset`—Creates a 3D outset-style border.

`inherit`—Takes the same value as its parent.

Example: `P {border-top-style: double}`

`border-style`

Description: Shorthand property for defining border styles for all sides of an element at once. This property can include one to four values. One value sets all border styles to that value. Two values set the top and bottom to the first and the left and right to the second. Three values set the top to the first, left and right to the second, and the bottom to the third.

Values: `border-top-style`—Style of the top border.

`border-right-style`—Style of the right border.

`border-bottom-style`—Style of the bottom border.

`border-left-style`—Style of the left border.

`inherit`—Takes the same value as its parent.

Example: `BODY {border-style: double solid}`

`border-top, border-right, border-bottom, border-left`

Description: Shorthand properties for defining several border properties at once for the designated side. Each separate property applies to its named side. The following definitions use the top.

Values: `border-top-width`—Width of the top border.

`border-top-style`—Style of the top border.

`border-top-color`—Color of the top border.

`inherit`—Takes the same value as its parent.

Example: `P {border-top: thin double blue}`

`border`

Description: Shorthand property for defining borders for all sides of an element at once. The values are applied equally to all sides of the element.

Values: `border-width`—Width of the border.

`border-style`—Style of the border.

`border-color`—Color of the border.

`inherit`—Takes the same value as its parent.

Example: `BODY {border: 4px solid red}`

`outline-width*`

Description:

Shorthand property for defining outline widths for all sides of an element at once. This property can include one to four values. One value sets all outline widths to that value. Two values set the top and bottom to the first and the left and right to the second. Three values set the top to the first, left and right to the second, and the bottom to the third.

Values:

`thin`—Creates a thin weight border.

`medium`—(default) Creates a medium weight border.

`thick`—Creates a thick weight border.

`inherit`—Takes the same value as its parent.

Example:

`BODY {outline-width: 20px 30px 5px}`

`outline-style*`

Description:

Shorthand property for defining outline styles for all sides of an element at once. This property can include one to four values. One value sets all outline styles to that value. Two values set the top and bottom to the first and the left and right to the second. Three values set the top to the first, left and right to the second, and the bottom to the third.

Values:

`none`—Specifies no border style.

`dotted`—Creates a series of dots.

`dashed`—Creates a series of dashed lines.

`solid`—Creates a solid, non-breaking line.

`double`—Creates two parallel, solid, non-breaking lines.

`groove`—Creates a 3D carved-style border.

`ridge`—Creates a 3D raised-style border.

`inset`—Creates a 3D inset-style border.

`outset`—Creates a 3D outset-style border.

`inherit`—Takes the same value as its parent.

Example:

`BODY {outline-style: double solid}`

outline-color*

Description:
Property for defining outline colors. This property can include one to four values. One value sets all outline colors to that value. Two values set the top and bottom to the first and the left and right to the second. Three values set the top to the first, left and right to the second, and the bottom to the third.

Values:
Any valid color—Specifies the border color.

invert—(default) Inverts the colors of the outline.

inherit—Takes the same value as its parent.

Example:
BODY {outline-color: blue red pink}

outline*

Description:
Shorthand property for defining outlines. The values are applied equally to all sides of the element.

Values:
outline-width—Width of the outline.

outline-style—Style of the outline.

outline-color—Color of the outline.

inherit—Takes the same value as its parent.

Example:
BODY {outline: 4px solid red}

VISUAL FORMATTING AND POSITIONING

The display property provides a way to define elements for the style sheet. Once defined, the position properties can place the elements exactly where you want them to go.

display

Description:
Defines the type of display box the element creates. These different types of boxes interact differently with each other as they are laid out on a page.

Values:
inline—(default) Creates an inline display box.

block—Creates a block display box.

list-item—Creates a list-item inline display box.

marker—Creates generated content to appear before or after a display box. Only used with the :before and :after pseudo elements.

none—Creates no display box. The element has no effect on the overall layout.

run-in—Creates a box like a block display box depending on its location.

APP

B

compact—Creates a box like an inline display box depending on its location.

`table, inline-table, table-row-group, table-column, table-column-group, table-header-group, table-footer-group, table-row, table-cell, table-caption`—Creates a table display box matching the property name.

`inherit`—Takes the same value as its parent.

Example: `P {display: block}`

position

Description: Defines the positioning method to use.

Values: `static`—(default) Defines a normal box using default HTML layout.

`relative`—Positioned box is offset from its normal layout position.

`absolute`—Positioned box is offset from its containing box's position and they don't effect the layout.

`fixed`—Positioned box is offset like the absolute model, but is fixed in the browser window and doesn't move when the window is scrolled.

`inherit`—Takes the same value as its parent.

Example: `IMG {position: absolute}`

top, right, bottom, left

Description: Defines the offset width from the designated edge.

Values: `auto`—(default) Enables the browser to select an offset width to position all elements.

Any valid length—Number representing the width from the edge.

Any valid percentage—Percentage of window to offset from the edge.

`inherit`—Takes the same value as its parent.

Example: `UL {top: 20px; right: 40px}`

width

Description: Defines the width of a display box.

Values: `auto`—(default) Enables the browser to select a width for the display box.

Any valid length—Number representing the width of the display box.

Any valid percentage—Percentage of window to use for the display box width.

`inherit`—Takes the same value as its parent.

Example: `BLOCKQUOTE {width: 260px}`

`min-width*, max-width*`

Description: Defines the minimum or maximum widths of a display box.

Values: Any valid length—Number representing the minimum or maximum widths of the display box.

Any valid percentage—Percentage of window to use for the minimum or maximum widths.

`none`—No width limit, applies only to the `max-width` property.

`inherit`—Takes the same value as its parent.

Example: `BLOCKQUOTE {min-width: 100px; max-width: 400px}`

`height`

Description: Defines the height of a display box.

Values: `auto`—(default) Enables the browser to select a height for the display box.

Any valid length—Number representing the height of the display box.

Any valid percentage—Percentage of window to use for the display box height.

`inherit`—Takes the same value as its parent.

Example: `BLOCKQUOTE {height: 260px}`

`min-height*, max-height*`

Description: Defines the minimum or maximum heights of a display box.

Values: Any valid length—Number representing the minimum or maximum heights of the display box.

Any valid percentage—Percentage of window to use for the minimum or maximum heights.

none—No height limit, applies only to the max-height property.

inherit—Takes the same value as its parent.

Example: BLOCKQUOTE {min-height: 100px; max-height: 400px}

line-height

Description: Defines the line spacing for an element box.

Values: normal—(default) Enables the browser to set the value to fit all elements on the page.

Any valid length—Number representing the height of the display box.

Any valid percentage—Percentage of window to use for the box height.

Any valid number—Number times the font size height.

inherit—Takes the same value as its parent.

Example: BLOCKQUOTE {line-height: 2.2}

vertical-align

Description: Defines the vertical positioning inside a line box.

Values: baseline—(default) Aligns the box's baseline to its parent baseline.

middle—Aligns the box's middle to its parent's baseline.

top—Aligns the box's top with the top of the line box.

bottom—Aligns the box's bottom to its parent's baseline.

sub—Aligns the box's text to be at subscript level to its parent's baseline.

super—Aligns the box's text to be at superscript level of its parent's baseline.

text-top—Aligns the box's top to the top of the parent's text.

text-bottom—Aligns the box's bottom to the bottom of the parent's baseline.

Any valid length—Defines the distance to raise the box's level. Negative values lower its level.

Any valid percentage—Percentage to raise the box's level. Negative values lower its level.

inherit—Takes the same value as its parent.

Example:

BLOCKQUOTE {vertical-align: super}

float

Description:

Defines whether the display box should float to the left or right.

Values:

none—(default) The display box doesn't float.

left—Causes the display box to float to the left and content flows to the right.

right—Causes the display box to float to the right and content flows to the left.

inherit—Takes the same value as its parent.

Example:

IMG {float: right}

clear

Description:

Defines whether content appears adjacent to the side of float box or not.

Values:

none—(default) Content not constrained next to float boxes.

left—Content doesn't appear to the left of a float box.

right—Content doesn't appear to the right of a float box.

both—Content doesn't appear to the left or right of a float box.

inherit—Takes the same value as its parent.

Example:

IMG {clear: both}

overflow*

Description:

Defines whether a display box is displayed when it overflows the element's box.

Values:

visible—(default) The overflowed box is visible and not clipped.

hidden—The overflowed portion is clipped.

scroll—The overflowed portion is clipped and any scrollbars are made visible.

App

B

auto—Enables the browser to determine whether overflowed areas are clipped.

inherit—Takes the same value as its parent.

Example: PRE {overflow: visible}

clip*

Description: Defines the clipping area for overflowed sections.

Values: auto—(default) Causes the clipping region to have the same size and location as the element's box.

rect(top, right, bottom, left)—The clipping area is defined by the offsets from the top, right, bottom, and left length values.

inherit—Takes the same value as its parent.

Example: BLOCKQUOTE {clip: rect(5px, 4px, 2px, 4px)}

visibility

Description: Defines whether an element is visible.

Values: visible—Makes the element visible.

hidden—Makes the element hidden, but it still effects the layout.

collapse—Same as hidden, except when used on tables.

inherit—(default) Takes the same value as its parent.

Example: IMG {visibility: visible}

z-index

Description: Defines the stacking order for elements.

Values: auto—(default) Causes the element box to accept the same stacking order as its parent's box.

Any valid integer—An integer value representing the stacking order. Lower values have a lower stacking order.

inherit—Takes the same value as its parent.

Example: IMG {z-index: 3}

cursor*

Description: Defines how the cursor looks when moved over an element.

Values:

auto—(default) Cursor determined by the browser.

crosshair—Cursor resembles a crosshair.

default—Cursor is the default cursor for the user's system.

pointer—Cursor resembles a pointer indicating a link.

move—Cursor indicates that something is to be moved.

e-resize, ne-resize, nw-resize, n-resize, se-resize, sw-resize, _s-resize, w-resize—Cursor indicates a corner position.

text—Cursor text.

wait—Cursor indicates the system is busy.

help—Cursor indicates a help location.

Any valid URL—URL of a cursor file.

inherit—Takes the same value as its parent.

Example:

IMG {cursor: pointer}

direction*

Description:

Defines the writing direction for text blocks.

Values:

ltr—(default) Sets writing direction from left to right.

rtl—Sets writing direction from right to left.

inherit—Takes the same value as its parent.

Example:

BODY { direction: ltr; unicode-bidi: embed}

unicode-bidi*

Description:

Enables the text writing direction to be changed.

Values:

normal—(default) Doesn't enable other writing directions.

embed—Enables writing direction to be set using the direction property.

bidi-override—Enables writing direction to be set using the _direction property. Applies to additional blocks.

inherit—Takes the same value as its parent.

Example:

IMG {unicode-bidi: embed}

APP

B

GENERATED CONTENT AND LISTS

With these properties, you have control over the style of your list boxes and how the numbers or bullets are presented. They make it easy to have your list count by twos starting from seven.

content*

Description:	Used with the :before and :after pseudo elements to generate content.
Values:	Any valid string—String to appear before or after the element.
	Any valid URL—URL to an external file to appear before or after an element.
	counter()—Defines a counter with a name to insert the value controlled by the counter-increment and counter-reset properties.
	open-quote, close-quote—Enables quote marks to be included. Used with the quotes property.
	no-open-quote, no-close-quote—Inserts no quote marks.
	attr()—Inserts the value of an attribute for the element.
	inherit—Takes the same value as its parent.
Example:	PRE:after {content: "thank you and good-night."}

quotes*

Description:	Defines the pairs of quotation marks to use for each level of embedded quote marks.
Values:	First valid string—Pair of characters to use for the outmost _quotation marks.
	Second valid string—Pair of characters to use for inner quotation marks.
	none—No quote marks are created.
	inherit—Takes the same value as its parent.
Example:	Q {quotes: `"` `"` `<' `>'}

`counter-increment*`

Description: Increases the value of the specified counter.

Values: none—(default) Counter is not incremented.

Counter name and valid number—Identifies the counter and accepts an integer value that counter is incremented. Negative values are valid.

inherit—Takes the same value as its parent.

Example: `H1 {counter-increment: MyCounter 2}`

`counter-reset*`

Description: Resets the value of a specified counter.

Values: none—(default) Counter is not reset.

Counter name and valid number—Identifies the counter and accepts an integer value that the counter is reset. Negative values are valid.

inherit—Takes the same value as its parent.

Example: `H1 {counter-reset: MyCounter 2}`

`marker-offset*`

Description: Defines the distance between a list marker (such as a bullet) and the text.

Values: auto—(default) Enables the browser to determine the spacing.

Any valid length—The space between a marker and the text.

inherit—Takes the same value as its parent.

Example: `H1 {marker-offset: 12px}`

`list-style-type`

Description: Defines the list style to be applied to the list markers.

Values: disc—(default) Creates a disc-shaped bullet.

circle—Creates a circular-shaped bullet.

square—Creates a square-shaped bullet.

decimal—Numbers lists using decimal numbers, beginning with 1.

decimal-leading-zero—Numbers lists using decimal numbers padded with a zero, such as 01, 02, 03, and so on.

`lower-roman`—Numbers lists using lowercase Roman numerals.

`upper-roman`—Numbers lists using uppercase Roman numerals.

`hebrew`—Numbers lists using Hebrew numerals.

`georgian`—Numbers lists using Georgian numerals.

`armenian`—Numbers lists using Armenian numerals.

`cjk-ideographic`—Numbers lists using ideographic numerals.

`lower-latin`, `lower-alpha`—Uses lowercase ASCII characters.

`upper-latin`, `upper-alpha`—Uses uppercase ASCII characters.

`lower-greek`—Uses lowercase Greek characters.

`hiragana`—Uses Japanese hiragana characters.

`hiragana-iroha`—Uses Japanese hiragana iroha characters.

`katakana-iroha`—Uses Japanese katakana iroha characters.

Values: `none`—No marker is used.

`inherit`—Takes the same value as its parent.

Example: `OL {list-style: upper-alpha}`

`list-style-image`

Description: Defines the image of a list marker.

Values: `none`—(default) Sets no marker image.

Any valid URL—URL of the marker image.

`inherit`—Takes the same value as its parent.

Example: `UL {list-style-image: url("bullet3.gif")}`

`list-style-position`

Description: Defines the location of the list box markers.

Values: `inside`—Markers appear within the element box.

`outside`—(default) Markers appear outside the element box.

`inherit`—Takes the same value as its parent.

Example: `H1 {list-style-position: inside}`

`list-style`

Description:	Shorthand property for defining all list style properties at once. If not included, a property is set to its default value.
Values:	`list-style-type`—Marker type.
	`list-style-position`—Marker position.
	`list-style-image`—Marker image.
	`inherit`—Takes the same value as its parent.
Example:	`UL {list-style: circle inside url("bullet4.gif")}`

TABLES

Table control is new to CSS2. These properties enable you to define the style, spacing, and layout of your tables.

`caption-side*`

Description:	Defines the position of a table caption relative to the table.
Values:	`top`—(default) Positions the caption at the top of the table.
	`right`—Positions the caption to the right of the table.
	`bottom`—Positions the caption at the bottom of the table.
	`left`—Positions the caption to the left of the table.
	`inherit`—Takes the same value as its parent.
Example:	`TABLE {caption-side: top}`

`table-layout*`

Description:	Defines how the table is laid out.
Values:	`auto`—(default) Enables the browser to decide how to lay out the table.
	`fixed`—Tables are laid out using a fixed method.
	`inherit`—Takes the same value as its parent.
Example:	`TABLE {table-layout: fixed}`

`border-collapse*`

Description:	Defines how the table borders are displayed.
Values:	`collapse`—(default) Collapses the table cell borders into a common border.

APP

B

separate—Keeps each table cell's border separated.

inherit—Takes the same value as its parent.

Example: TD {border-collapse: separate}

border-spacing*

Description: Defines the spacing between table borders. Only one length value applies equally to both horizontal and vertical directions.

Values: First valid length—Defines the horizontal width separating table cell borders.

Second valid length—Defines the vertical width separating table cell borders.

inherit—Takes the same value as its parent.

Example: TABLE {border-spacing: 4px}

empty-cells*

Description: Defines how to render the border of empty cells.

Values: show—(default) Enables the borders of empty cells to be seen.

hide—Hides the borders of empty cells.

inherit—Takes the same value as its parent.

Example: TABLE {empty-cells: show}

speak-header*

Description: Enables a screen reader to speak table headers.

Values: once—(default) Causes the header to be spoken only once for each column of cells.

always—Causes the header to be spoken each time for a column of cells.

inherit—Takes the same value as its parent.

Example: TABLE {speak-header: once}

column-span*

Description: Defines the number of columns to span.

Values: Any valid number—The number of columns to span. Default is 1.

inherit—Takes the same value as its parent.

Example: TD {column-span: 3}

row-span*

Description: Defines the number of rows to span.

Values: Any valid number—The number of rows to span. Default is 1.

inherit—Takes the same value as its parent.

Example: TD {row-span: 3}

PAGED MEDIA

These properties enable you to split your page content into predefined pages that output correctly to a printer or external device.

size*

Description: Defines the size and orientation of a page.

Values: auto—(default) Enables the browser to determine the page size.

First valid length—Sets the page width.

Second valid length—Sets the page height.

landscape—Sets the page orientation to landscape.

portrait—Sets the page orientation to portrait.

inherit—Takes the same value as its parent.

Example: P {size: 8.5in 11in portrait}

marks*

Description: Enables printed pages to have crop and cross marks.

Values: none—(default) No printing marks are included.

crop—Displays crop marks.

cross—Displays registration marks.

inherit—Takes the same value as its parent.

Example: P {marks: crop cross}

page-break-before*

Description: Defines the page breaks for a page.

Values: auto—(default) Enables the browser to determine the page breaks.

always—Always forces a page break before a box.

avoid—Avoids placing a page break before a box.

left—Always forces a page break before a box so that the next page is on the left.

APP

B

right—Always forces a page break before a box so that the next page is on the right.

inherit—Takes the same value as its parent.

Example: P {page-break-before: avoid}

page-break-after*

Description: Defines the page breaks for a page.

Values: auto—(default) Enables the browser to determine the page breaks.

always—Always forces a page break after a box.

avoid—Avoids placing a page break after a box.

left—Always forces a page break after a box so that the next page is on the left.

right—Always forces a page break after a box so that the next page is on the right.

inherit—Takes the same value as its parent.

Example: P {page-break-after: avoid}

page-break-inside*

Description: Defines the page breaks for a page.

Values: auto—(default) Enables the browser to determine the page breaks.

avoid—Avoids placing a page break within a box.

inherit—Takes the same value as its parent.

Example: P {page-break-inside: avoid}

page*

Description: Identifies a page with a name.

Values: auto—(default) Enables the browser to identify pages.

Any valid name—Gives a page a name. The name can be any string.

Example: P {page: Mypage}

orphans*

Description: Defines how many sentences can be left at the bottom of a page before starting a new one.

Values:	Any valid number—An integer defining the number of sentences that must be left on the bottom of a page. Default is 2.
	inherit—Takes the same value as its parent.
Example:	P {orphans: 4}

`widows*`

Description:	Defines how many sentences can be left at the top of a new page.
Values:	Any valid number—An integer defining the number of sentences that must be left on the top of a page. Default is 2.
	inherit—Takes the same value as its parent.
Example:	P {widows: 4}

AURAL STYLE SHEETS

As a way to define Web pages for individuals with visual handicaps, or provide audio information for hands-free environments such as automobiles, aural style sheets enable designers to specify how screen readers interpret Web pages.

> **Note**
>
> Aural style sheets are not well supported. As such, there are very few examples of them in use.

`volume*`

Description:	Defines the loudness of text read by a screen reader.
Values:	Any valid number, 0–100—An integer ranged between 0 and 100 with 0 being minimum and 100 being maximum.
	Any valid percentage, 0–100—A percentage increase or decrease from the current value.
	silent—No sound emitted.
	x-soft—Quietest level of sound, same as 0.
	soft—Quiet level of sound, same as 25.
	medium—(default) Normal level of sound, same as 50.
	loud—Loud level of sound, same as 75.
	x-loud—Loudest level of sound, same as 100.
	inherit—Takes the same value as its parent.
Example:	BODY {volume: soft}

APP

B

`speak*`

Description: Defines how the words are spoken.

Values: `normal`—(default) Words are spoken normally.

`none`—Words are not spoken.

`spell-out`—Words are spelled letter by letter.

`inherit`—Takes the same value as its parent.

Example: `ACRONYM {speak: spell-out}`

`pause-before*`

Description: Causes a pause before the element is read.

Values: Any valid time—The amount of time to pause before reading the element.

Any valid percentage—The percent to pause before reading the element.

`inherit`—Takes the same value as its parent.

Example: `SPAN {pause-before: 500ms}`

`pause-after*`

Description: Causes a pause after the element is read.

Values: Any valid time—The amount of time to pause after reading the element.

Any valid percentage—The percent to pause after reading the element.

`inherit`—Takes the same value as its parent.

Example: `SPAN {pause-after: 500ms}`

`pause*`

Description: Shorthand property for setting the `pause-before` and `pause-after` the element is read. If only one time or percent value is given, it applies to both before and after.

Values: First valid time—The amount of time to pause before reading the element.

Second valid time—The amount of time to pause after reading the element.

Any valid percentage—The percent to pause before reading the element.

Any valid percentage—The percent to pause after reading the element.

inherit—Takes the same value as its parent.

Example: `SPAN {pause: 500ms 300ms}`

cue-before*

Description: Causes a cue before the element is read.

Values: Any valid URL—URL of an audio file to play before reading the element.

none—No audio is played before the element is read.

inherit—Takes the same value as its parent.

Example: `SPAN {cue-before: url("bell.wav")}`

cue-after*

Description: Causes a cue after the element is read.

Values: Any valid URL—URL of an audio file to play after reading the element.

none—No audio is played after the element is read.

inherit—Takes the same value as its parent.

Example: `SPAN {cue-after: url("bell2.wav")}`

cue*

Description: Shorthand property that causes a cue before and after the element is read. If only one URL is given, it applies to both before and after.

Values: First valid URL—URL of an audio file to play before reading the element.

Second valid URL—URL of an audio file to play after reading the element.

none—No audio is played before the element is read.

inherit—Takes the same value as its parent.

Example: `SPAN {cue: url("ding.wav") url("dong.wav")}`

play-during*

Description: Defines an audio file to be played in the background while text is being read.

Values: Any valid URL—URL of an audio file to play in the background while reading the element.

APP

B

mix—Mix the current audio with the parent audio file and play both together.

repeat—Repeat the audio until all the text has been read.

auto—(default) Enable the parent element's audio to continue to play.

none—No background audio is played.

inherit—Takes the same value as its parent.

Example: BODY {play-during: url("chatter.wav") mix}

azimuth*

Description: Defines the spatial location of an audio file horizontally around the listener's head.

Values: Any valid angle—An angle value between 0 and 360 degrees. Negative values are not allowed.

left-side—Sound from the left side of the head, or 270 degrees.

far-left—Sound from the distant left of the head, or 300 degrees.

left—Sound from the left of the head, or 320 degrees.

center-left—Sound from the center left of the head, or 340 degrees.

center—Sound from the center of the head, or 0 degrees.

center-right—Sound from the center right of the head, or 20 degrees.

right—Sound from the right of the head, or 40 degrees.

far-right—Sound from the distant right of the head, or 60 degrees.

left-side—Sound from the right side of the head, or 270 degrees.

leftwards—Sound moved to the left of the current location.

rightwards—Sound moved to the right of the current location.

behind—Sound moved to behind the head at that location.

inherit—Takes the same value as its parent.

Example: `H1 {azimuth: left-side}`

elevation*

Description: Defines the spatial location of an audio file vertically around the listener's head.

Values: Any valid angle—An angle value between 90 and -90 degrees. Negative values are allowed.

below—Sound from below the head, or -90 degrees.

level—Sound from the front of the head, or 0 degrees.

above—Sound from above the head, or 90 degrees.

higher—Sound moved up form the current location.

inherit—Takes the same value as its parent.

Example: `H1 {elevation: above}`

speech-rate*

Description: Defines how quickly the element text is read.

Values: Any valid number—The speaking rate in words per minute.

x-slow—80 words per minute.

slow—120 words per minute.

medium—(default) 180–200 words per minute.

fast—300 words per minute.

x-fast—500 words per minute.

faster—Causes the words to be read faster than the current speed, adds 40 words per minute.

slower—Causes the words to be read slower than the current speed, subtracts 40 words per minute.

inherit—Takes the same value as its parent.

Example: `BODY {speech-rate: fast}`

voice-family*

Description: Defines the voice type to use to read the element's text. It can include several voice families separated by commas. The list order defines the priority.

APP

B

Values: Voice name—Voice to use to read the text.

Generic voice name—Generic voice class to use to read the text. Generic voices include: male, female, and child.

inherit—Takes the same value as its parent.

Example: `BODY {voice-family: Bob, male}`

pitch*

Description: Defines the pitch of the element text.

Values: Any valid frequency—The pitch in Hertz (Hz).

x-low—Lowest pitch.

low—Low pitch.

medium—(default) Average pitch.

high—Higher than normal pitch.

x-high—Highest pitch.

inherit—Takes the same value as its parent.

Example: `BODY {pitch: high}`

pitch-range*

Description: Defines the pitch range of the element text as its read.

Values: -Any valid number—A value between 0 and 100 that defines the pitch range. The default, 50, is normal inflection.

inherit—Takes the same value as its parent.

Example: `BODY {pitch-range: 50}`

stress*

Description: Defines the stress of the element text as its read.

Values: Any valid number—A value between 0 and 100 that defines the pitch range. The default, 50, is normal.

inherit—Takes the same value as its parent.

Example: `BODY {stress: 50}`

richness*

Description: Defines the richness of the element text as its read.

Values: Any valid number—A value between 0 and 100 that defines the pitch range. The default, 50, is normal.

inherit—Takes the same value as its parent.

Example: `BODY {richness: 50}`

`speak-punctuation*`

Description: Defines how punctuation is spoken.

Values: `code`—Punctuation is spoken literally.

`none`—Punctuation is not spoken.

inherit—Takes the same value as its parent.

Example: `BODY {speak-puncuation: code}`

`speak-numeral*`

Description: Defines how numbers are spoken.

Values: `digits`—Numbers are spoken as individual digits.

`continuous`—Numbers are spoken as a full number.

inherit—Takes the same value as its parent.

Example: `SPAN.phone {speak-numeral: digits}`

APP

B

INDEX